Law and Anthropology

The International Library of Essays in Law and Legal Theory
Series Editor: Tom D. Campbell

Schools

Natural Law, Vols I & II *John Finnis*
Justice *Thomas Morawetz*
Law and Economics, Vols I & II *Jules Coleman and Jeffrey Lange*
Critical Legal Studies *James Boyle*
Marxian Legal Theory *Csaba Varga*
Legal Reasoning, Vols I & II *Aulis Aarnio and Neil MacCormick*
Legal Positivism *Mario Jori*
American Legal Theory *Robert Summers*
Law and Language *Fred Schauer*
Sociological Theories of Law *Kahei Rokumoto*
Rights *Carlos Nino*
Law and Psychology *Martin Levine*
Feminist Legal Theory *Frances Olsen*
Law and Society *Werner Krawietz*

Areas

Criminal Law *Thomas Morawetz*
Tort Law *Ernest Weinrib*
Contract Law, Vols I & II *Larry Alexander*
Anti-Discrimination Law *Christopher McCrudden*
Consumer Law *Iain Ramsay*
International Law *Martti Koskenniemi*
Property Law, Vols I & II *Elizabeth Mensch and Alan Freeman*
Constitutional Law *Mark Tushnet*
Procedure *Denis Galligan*
Evidence and Proof *William Twining and Alex Stein*
Administrative Law *Denis Galligan*
Child Law *Harry Krause*
Family Law, Vols I & II *Harry Krause*
Welfare Law *Peter Robson*
Medicine and the Law *Bernard Dickens*
Commercial Law *Ross Cranston*
Communications Law *David Goldberg*
Environmental Law *Michael Blumm*
Conflict of Laws *Richard Fentiman*
Law and Religion *Wojciech Sadurski*
Human Rights Law *Philip Alston*
European Community Law, Vols I & II *Francis Snyder*

Legal Cultures

Comparative Legal Cultures *Csaba Varga*
Law and Anthropology *Peter Sack*
Hindu Law and Legal Theory *Ved Nanda*
Islamic Law and Legal Theory *Ian Edge*
Chinese Law and Legal Theory *Michael Palmer*
Socialist Law and Legal Theory *W. Butler*
Japanese Law and Legal Theory *Koichiro Fujikura*
Law and Development *Anthony Carty*
Jewish Law and Legal Theory *Martin Golding*
Legal Education *Martin Levine*

Future Volumes

Labour Law, Common Law and Legal Theory, Civil Law and Legal Theory, African Law and Legal Theory, Legal Ethics and Cumulative index.

Law and Anthropology

Edited by

Peter Sack

Senior Fellow, The Australian National University, Canberra

and

Jonathan Aleck

The Australian National University, Canberra

NEW YORK UNIVERSITY PRESS
REFERENCE COLLECTION

Manufactured in Great Britain

First published in the U.S.A. in 1992 by
NEW YORK UNIVERSITY PRESS
Washington Square
New York NY 10003

Library of Congress Cataloging-in-Publication Data
Law and anthropology / edited by Peter Sack.
p. cm. – (The International library of essays in law and legal theory. Legal cultures)
"New York University Press reference collection."
Includes bibliographical references and index.
ISBN 0-8147-7954-9
1. Law and anthropology. I. Sack, Peter G. II. Series.
K487.A57L38 1992
340'115–dc20 92-4207
CIP

Contents

Acknowledgements vii
Series Preface xi
Introduction xiii

PART I STATES OF THE ART

1 Laura Nader (1965), 'The Anthropological Study of Law', *American Anthropologist*, **67**, No.6, pp. 3–32. 3
2 Jean Poirier (1970), 'The Current State of Legal Ethnology and its Future Tasks', *International Social Science Journal*, **XXII**, No.3, pp. 476–94. 33
3 Daisy Hilse Dwyer (1979), 'Substance and Process: Reappraising the Premises of the Anthropology of Law', *Dialectical Anthropology*, **4**, pp. 309–20. 53
4 Francis G. Snyder (1981), 'Anthropology, Dispute Processes and Law: A Critical Introduction', *British Journal of Law & Society*, **8**, No.2, pp. 141–80. 65
5 June Starr and Jane F. Collier (1987), 'Historical Studies of Legal Change', *Current Anthropology*, **28**, No.3, pp. 367–72. 105

PART II LEGAL THEORY, ANTHROPOLOGY, ANTHROPOLOGICAL THEORY AND LAW

6 G. MacCormack (1978), 'Anthropology and Legal Theory', *Juridical Review*, pp. 216–32. 113
7 Sally Engle Merry (1988), 'Legal Pluralism', *Law & Society Review*, **22**, No.5, pp. 869–96. 131
8 Sherry B. Ortner (1984), 'Theory in Anthropology since the Sixties', *Comparative Studies in Society and History*, **26**, pp. 126–66. 159
9 Colin M. Turnbull (1984), 'The Individual, Community and Society: Rights and Responsibilities from an Anthropological Perspective', *Washington and Lee Law Review*, **41**, pp. 77–132. 201

PART III THE 'NEW' ETHNOGRAPHY

10 Fitz John Porter Poole (1986), 'Personal Control, Social Responsibility, and Image of Person and Self Among the Bimin-Kuskusmin of Papua New Guinea', *International Journal of Law and Psychiatry*, **9**, pp. 295–319. 259

11 Marilyn Strathern, (1985), 'Discovering "Social Control"', *Journal of Law and Society*, **12**, No.2, pp. 111–34. 285
12 Peter Sack (1985), '*Bobotoi* and *Pulu* – Melanesian Law: Normative Order or Way of Life?', *Journal de la Société des Océanistes*, **41**, pp. 15–23. 309
13 Carol J. Greenhouse (1989), 'Just in Time: Temporality and the Cultural Legitimation of Law', *The Yale Law Journal*, **98**, No.3, pp. 1631–51. 319
14 Boaventura De Sousa Santos (1987), 'Law: A Map of Misreading. Toward a Postmodern Conception of Law', *Journal of Law and Society*, **14**, No.3, pp. 279–302. 341

PART IV NON-WESTERN PERSPECTIVES

15 Na'im Akbar (1984), 'Africentric Social Sciences for Human Liberation', *Journal of Black Studies*, **14**, No.4, pp. 395–414. 367
16 R. Panikkar (1982), 'Is the Notion of Human Rights a Western Concept?', *Diogenes*, **120**, pp. 75–102. 387
17 Masaji Chiba (1989), 'Three Dichotomies of Law in Pluralism', in *Legal Pluralism: Toward a General Theory Through Japanese Legal Culture*, Tokyo: Tokai University Press, Chapter 12, pp. 171–80. 415
18 Bernard Narokobi (1989), 'Law and Custom in Melanesia', *Pacific Perspectives*, **14**, No.1, pp. 17–26. 425
19 Chief Justice Tom Tso (1989), 'The Process of Decision Making in Tribal Courts', *Arizona Law Review*, **31**, No.2, pp. 225–35. 435

PART V COURTS, CUSTOM AND ANTHROPOLOGISTS

20 Campbell MacLachlan (1988), 'The Recognition of Aboriginal Customary Law: Pluralism Beyond the Colonial Paradigm – A Review Article', *International and Comparative Law Quarterly*, **37**, Part 2, pp. 368–86. 449
21 Mari J. Matsuda (1988), 'Native Custom and Official Law in Hawaii', *Internationales Jahrbuch für Rechtsanthropologie*, **3**, pp. 135–46. 469
22 La'auli A. Filoiali'i and Lyle Knowles (1983), 'The Ifoga: the Samoan Practice of Seeking Forgiveness for Criminal Behaviour', *Oceania*, **53**, No.4, pp. 384–8. 481
23 Alison Dundes Renteln (1989), 'Culture and Culpability: A Study of Contrasts', *Beverly Hills Bar Journal*, No.XVI, pp. 17–27. 487
24 Lawrence Rosen (1977), 'The Anthropologist as Expert Witness', *American Anthropologist*, **79**, No.3, pp. 555–78. 499

Name Index 523

Acknowledgements

The editor and publishers wish to thank the following for permission to use copyright material.

American Anthropological Association for essays: Laura Nader (1965), 'The Anthropological Study of Law', *American Anthropologist*, **67**, No.6, pp. 3–32, and Lawrence Rosen (1977), 'The Anthropologist as Expert Witness', *American Anthropologist*, **79**, No.3, pp. 555–78. Reproduced by permission of the American Anthropological Association from American Anthropologist, **67**:6, pt.2, December 1965, and **79**:3, September 1977. Not for further reproduction.

Basil Blackwell for the essays: Boaventura De Sousa Santos (1987), 'Law: A Map of Misreading. Toward a Postmodern Conception of Law', *Journal of Law and Society*, **14**, No.3, pp. 279–302, and Marilyn Strathern (1985), 'Discovering "Social Control"', *Journal of Law and Society*, **12**, No.2, pp. 111–34.

Beverly Hills Bar Association for essay: Alison Dundes Renteln (1989), 'Culture and Culpability: A Study of Contrasts', Newsletter of the Commission on Folk Law and Legal Pluralism, *Beverly Hills Bar Journal*, No.XVI, pp. 17–27.

Cambridge University Press for the essay: Sherry B. Ortner (1984), 'Theory in Anthropology since the Sixties', *Comparative Studies in Society and History*, **26**, pp. 126–66.

W. Green & Son Ltd for the essay: G. MacCormack (1978), 'Anthropology and Legal Theory', *Juridical Review*, pp. 216–32. Copyright © W. Green & Son Ltd.

The International and Comparative Law Quarterly for the essay: Campbell MacLachlan (1988), 'The Recognition of Aboriginal Customary Law: Pluralism Beyond the Colonial Paradigm – A Review Article', *International and Comparative Law Quarterly*, **37**, Part 2, pp. 368–86. This article is reproduced from (1988) Vol.**37**, No.2 *I.C.L.Q.* 368–86 with permission from the publishers The British Institute of International and Comparative Law.

Kluwer Academic Publishers for the essay: Daisy Hilse Dwyer (1979), 'Substance and Process: Reappraising the Premises of the Anthropology of Law', *Dialectical Anthropology*, **4**, pp. 309–20. Reprinted by permission of Kluwer Academic Publishers.

Law & Society Association for the essay: Sally Engle Merry (1988), 'Legal Pluralism', *Law & Society Review*, **22**, No.5, pp. 869–96. Reprinted by permission of the Law and Society Association.

Oceania Publications for the essay: La'auli A. Filoiali'i and Lyle Knowles (1983), 'The Ifoga: the Samoan Practice of Seeking Forgiveness for Criminal Behaviour', *Oceania*, **53**, No.4, pp. 384–8.

Pergamon Press for the essay: Fitz John Porter Poole (1986), 'Personal Control, Social Responsibility, and Image of Person and Self Among the Bimin–Kuskusmin of Papua New Guinea', *International Journal of Law and Psychiatry*, **9**, pp. 295–319.

Revue Diogenes for the essay: R. Panikkar (1982), 'Is the Notion of Human Rights a Western Concept?', *Diogenes*, **120**, pp. 75–102.

Sage Publications, Inc. for the essay: Na'im Akbar (1984), 'Africentric Social Sciences for Human Liberation', *Journal of Black Studies*, **14**, No.4, pp. 395–414. Copyright © 1991 by Sage Publications, Inc. Reprinted by permission of Sage Publications, Inc.

Francis G. Snyder (1981), 'Anthropology, Dispute Processes and Law: A Critical Introduction', *British Journal of Law & Society*, **8**, No.2, pp. 141–80. Copyright © Francis G. Snyder.

Société des Océanistes for the essay: Peter Sack (1985), '*Bobotoi* and *Pulu* – Melanesian Law: Normative Order or Way of Life?', *Journal de la Société des Océanistes*, **41**, pp. 15–23.

Tokai University Press for the essay: Masaji Chiba (1989), 'Three Dichotomies of Law in Pluralism', in *Legal Pluralism: Toward A General Theory Through Japanese Legal Culture*, Tokyo: Tokai University Press, Chapter 12, pp. 171–80.

The University of Arizona for the essay: Chief Justice Tom Tso (1989), 'The Process of Decision Making in Tribal Courts', *Arizona Law Review*, **31**, No.2, pp. 225–35. Copyright © 1989 by the Arizona Board of Regents. Reprinted by permission.

The University of Chicago Press for the essay: June Starr and Jane F. Collier (1987), 'Historical Studies of Legal Change', *Current Anthropology*, **28**, No.3, pp. 367–72. Copyright © The University of Chicago Press.

United Nations Educational Scientific and Cultural Organization for the essay: Jean Poirier (1970), 'The Current State of Legal Ethnology and Its Future Tasks', *International Social Science Journal*, **XXII**, No.3, pp. 476–94. Article from the International Social Science Journal, Vol.**XXII**, No.3 © Unesco 1970. Reproduced with the authorization of Unesco.

Washington and Lee University for the essay: Colin M. Turnbull (1984), 'The Individual, Community and Society: Rights and Responsibilities from an Anthropological Perspective', *Washington and Lee Law Review*, **41**, pp. 77–132.

The Working Group on Legal Anthropology for the essay: Mari J. Matsuda (1988), 'Native Custom and Official Law in Hawaii', *Internationales Jahrbuch für Rechtsanthropologie*, **3**, pp. 135–46.

The Yale Law Journal and Fred B. Rothman & Co. for the essay: Carol J. Greenhouse (1989), 'Just in Time: Temporality and the Cultural Legitimation of Law', *The Yale Law Journal*, **98**, No.3, pp. 1631–51. Reprinted by permission of The Yale Law Journal Company and Fred B. Rothman & Co. from The Yale Law Journal, Vol.**98**, pp. 1631–51.

Every effort has been made to trace all the copyright holders, but if any have been inadvertently overlooked the publishers will be pleased to make the necessary arrangement at the first opportunity.

Series Preface

The International Library of Law and Legal Theory is designed to provide important research materials in an accessible form. Each volume contains essays of central theoretical importance in its subject area. The series as a whole makes available an extensive range of valuable material which will be of considerable interest to those involved in the research, teaching and study of law.

The series has been divided into three sections. The Schools section is intended to represent the main distinctive approaches and topics of special concern to groups of scholars. The Areas section takes in the main branches of law with an emphasis on essays which present analytical and theoretical insights of broad application. The section on Legal Cultures makes available the distinctive legal theories of different legal traditions and takes up topics of general comparative and developmental concern.

I have been delighted and impressed by the way in which the editors of the individual volumes have set about the difficult task of selecting, ordering and presenting essays from the immense quantity of academic legal writing published in journals throughout the world. Editors were asked to pick out those essays from law, philosophy and social science journals which they consider to be fundamental for the understanding of law, as seen from the perspective of a particular approach or sphere of legal interest. This is not an easy task and many difficult decisions have had to be made in order to ensure that a representative sample of the best journal essays available takes account of the scope of each topic or school.

I should like to express my thanks to all the volume editors for their willing participation and scholarly judgement. The interest and enthusiasm which the project has generated is well illustrated by the fact that an original projection of 12 volumes drawn up in 1989 has now become a list of some 60 volumes. I must also acknowledge the vision, persistence and constant cheerfulness of John Irwin and the marvellous work done by Mrs Margaret O'Reilly and Mrs Sonia Bridgman.

TOM D. CAMPBELL
Series Editor
The Faculty of Law
The Australian National University

Introduction

Lawyers know that it pays to take words seriously, no matter what they are talking about and no matter whether they want to clarify or to manipulate the facts. The need to take words seriously is especially important in fields (such as the one to be covered by this volume) where everything is in flux and none of the old assumptions remain unchallenged. Despite their ambiguity, words may thus offer us the most reliable map of the terrain we want to traverse; and words are surprisingly informative, provided we are prepared to listen to them, instead of treating them as if they were audiotapes which are either prerecorded or blank and which we must therefore either take as gospel or which are ready to carry whatever message we choose for them.

What then do we, can we, or should we mean when we say, with the title of this volume: 'law and anthropology'? Are we free to define these words or to refuse defining them? Do we have some discretion in this regard? Or do they each have one, and only one, correct meaning? These are not idle questions as the continuing debate about 'What is law?' demonstrates. Instead of leading us once more along this particular path, however, I would like to begin by reminding us of the obvious, namely that we are initially confronted by mere words which belong (in contrast to the sounds of which they are composed) to the world of ideas where not even the sky is the limit. Yet, most words are, most of the time, not used to represent ideas but phenomena which are supposed actually to exist 'out there'.

This would appear to apply, in our case, to the words 'law' as well as 'anthropology' – but what about the word 'and'? It is different in that it does not refer to any kind of object but to a relationship between other objects. Nevertheless, even such relationships are perceived as actual and not just in our thoughts: the rabbit is meant to hide in the magician's hat, before it is pulled out of it, not only in our imagination. Still, such relationships have more to do with logic than with observation. They begin as mental constructs, which may or may not exist 'out there', and which do not become false if they have no real counterpart.

By contrast, we would rightly feel cheated if someone used the word 'law' in a meaning which did not correspond to any actually existing phenomena – unless it was made clear to us that this is what 'law' (for one reason or another) *ought* to (or could?) look like, not how it was actually shaped, unless, that is, we were told beforehand that the word 'law' was used as a normative and not as an analytical concept.

On the other hand, we seem to have a great deal more elbow-room when defining the range of phenomena to be represented by a certain verbal label than when defining relationships between them. It makes sense (although it may not be constructive) to ask 'What is law?' whereas it is difficult to have similar arguments about what is meant by an 'and' ('in', 'or', etc.) relationship.

The word 'law', it should be stressed, is by no means unusual in this respect. A 'steam engine' also does not exist as such 'out there' but is primarily an idea (which turns an arrangement of metal into something else). Even 'natural' (as opposed to artificial, manmade, cultural) phenomena are largely what we perceive them to be when we talk about them. To say that 'a rose is a rose, is a rose' is indeed a statement of fact, while to say 'the law is the law, is the law' is an incantation. Yet, even a 'rose' means significantly different 'things' to different people. The borderlines between ideas and facts, between the real and the imagined, between description and prescription, are everywhere blurred and always problematic. Whether we like it or not, we are taking part in word battles whenever we think, talk, write or read. These battles are unavoidable but not necessarily silly, as some lawyers have claimed.[1] They are silly only if their vital importance is not appreciated. Once this is done, those who refuse to take part consciously in them are revealed as the fools instead of being the sober realists which they like to see themselves to be.

It is therefore sensible to approach the writings collected in this volume, however descriptive or analytical they claim to be, as contributions to an ongoing word battle, in which not only sides and weapons are changing and which serves the (legitimate) purpose of altering the shape of what is being talked about. The 'law' as well as the 'anthropology', with which this volume is concerned, are cultural and, more precisely, modern western cultural constructs. They are neither universal nor eternal and both in a deep crisis, so much so that it may well become absurd in ten years or so to compile a volume entitled 'law and anthropology'. But this makes the enterprise today all the more interesting.[2]

What then does the title of this volume stand for? We shall make a cautious start by looking at the harmless word 'and'.

Although it appears to be non-committal, it sets the scene we are invited to inspect. It tells us that 'law' and 'anthropology' are to be treated as different entities of potentially equal weight which are to be seen in relation to each other – the word order indicating that the main focus will be on 'law' and not on 'anthropology'. It asks us to consider what, if any, relevance they have for each other. Moreover, we are expected to approach these actual and possible relations with an open mind. We are not meant to test a particular thesis – as we would be told to do by a title like 'law *or* anthropology' or 'law *as* anthropology'. On the contrary, we are encouraged to understand 'law' and 'anthropology' – provided we do have a choice in this regard – in a manner which maximizes the significance of the relations between them, instead of minimizing them.[3]

Since we are all familiar with the difficulty in arriving at a generally acceptable definition of 'law', I suggest that we turn our attention to the meaning of 'anthropology' – in the hope that we will profit from this detour in the long run.

The *Concise Oxford Dictionary* (7th ed.) gives two alternative definitions of 'anthropology': the 'study of structure and evolution of man as an animal'; 'the study of mankind, esp. of its societies and customs'.[4]

The first of these definitions is closer to the 'literal' meaning of 'anthropology' (as the study of man), but, apart from being overly specific,[5] it is unhelpful for our purposes because most of the recent contributions to the English 'law and anthropology' literature – with which this volume is concerned – do not understand the term in that sense. This is different in continental Europe where a volume with this title might well deal exclusively with the relevance of man's biological nature for 'law' and thus with the relations between 'law' and 'human' or 'social' biology rather than those with 'anthropology' as conventionally understood in (English) English, where only the increasingly exotic branch of '*physical* anthropology' retains this pronounced biological flavour.

On the other hand, what is conventionally called 'anthropology' in (English) English – a meaning which the *Concise Oxford Dictionary* tries to capture in its second definition – is on the European Continent (and even in the United States) still more commonly called 'ethnology'. This has good reasons because the 'literal' meaning of 'ethnology' (as the study of human beings as members of 'ethnic' groups rather than of a biological species) has indeed a strong *sociological* bias.[6]

In its second definition, the *Concise Oxford Dictionary* has little choice but to accept *anthropos* (=man) as a biological starting point, but it moves rapidly towards the social by proclaiming the object of 'anthropology' to be the study of 'mankind' – as a kind of species-wide, quasi-social body – before expressly referring to 'its societies and customs' as the core of 'anthropology'.

Although one should not read too much into general-purpose definitions of this kind, it is fair to draw attention to their key characteristics. The overall impression is that this social (rather than biological) type of 'anthropology' is a decidedly holistic and generalistic (and therefore a somewhat unscientific) enterprise. The singling out of 'customs' – as opposed to 'laws' – could even suggest that 'anthropology' is a bag of leftovers which remains after the specialists, including the lawyers, have finished with mankind. Not only, it seems, is law not the business of anthropologists, but the same applies to politics, psychology, medicine and so on, so that 'anthropology' is eventually reduced to the study of *folklore*, of quaint and obsolete customs.[7] Conversely, and more importantly, the emphasis on the *social* aspect of man makes it impossible to distinguish 'anthropology' – so defined – from 'sociology' as the study of (human) society.

I am not pointing this out in order to criticize the '*Oxford*' definition. On the contrary, that definition properly reflects a growing unease about the justification of this distinction. Its roots become visible if we move to the less controversial subject of 'sociology'. Here the mask slips and the definition in the *Concise Oxford Dictionary* reveals the full ethnocentric arrogance which permeates not only English but many other western and non-western languages; for 'sociology' is defined as 'the science of the development and nature and laws of human (esp. civilized) society'.

I refrain from commenting on the differences between 'study' and 'science', between 'evolution' and 'development', between 'societies' (as a reflection of cultural diversity) and 'society' (as a human universal) – and will only note in passing that the term 'law' in the definition of 'sociology' refers, of course, to *scientific* laws rather than to the 'advanced' (legal) laws as opposed to 'primitive' (social) custom – since all these differences follow from the crucial distinction between 'civilized' and 'uncivilized' societies.

This is the criterion which marks the conventional dividing line between 'anthropology' and 'sociology' – the latter dealing with civilized society, the former with uncivilized (or pre-industrial, or savage, or stateless) society (the specific term chosen does not matter). It ties the distinction between 'anthropology' and 'sociology' to an evolutionary model of human history which moves the objects of anthropological study in the vicinity of apes and civilized society near the throne of deified rationality.

Although this conventional dividing line has become offensive, it remains convenient because it is defined by reference to two distinct subject matters, whereas the often advocated alternative approach, which tries to distinguish 'anthropology' from 'sociology' by reference to the different *methods* employed, fails to provide us with any convincing boundaries[8] – quite apart from encouraging the dangerous belief that scholarship was concerned with means rather than ends.

Fortunately the distinction between 'anthropology' and 'sociology' is not our problem. We neither have to justify its existence nor to fight for its abolition. Indeed, we not only can but must acknowledge that such a distinction exists and that public opinion is quite clear as to the location of the dividing line. But we can remove the sting which it contains by replacing the loaded contrast between 'civilized' and 'uncivilized' with a neutral contrast between 'western' and 'non-western' societies – understood in a geographical (not cultural) sense, to avoid, if we can, subsidiary complications arising from the (cultural) 'westernization' of (geographically) non-western societies.[9]

Let us disregard this first warning sign that our operation may turn out to be cosmetic and proceed, on the basis that 'anthropology' means 'the study of non-western societies'.

As a first step we can begin to rephrase the title of this volume. It now reads: 'law and the study of non-western societies' or, more pointedly: 'the relevance for law of the results of the study of non-western societies by anthropologists'.

What are these results? Since 'anthropology' is primarily an academic discipline, one would expect them to consist of theories – and since 'law' is also an established subject of academic studies, it would seem that this volume is concerned with the question as to whether and how anthropological theory can help lawyers in gaining a better theoretical understanding of 'law'. Brief reflection, however, shows that we are, in fact, confronted by a more complex configuration.

To start with, 'law' is not only legal theory but, first and foremost – and in sharp contrast to 'anthropology' – the *subject matter* of legal theory. Hence we must not only consider the relevance of 'anthropology' for legal theory but also for legal practice, in particular for all aspects of law *reform*. What can 'anthropology' teach us about making better laws, about making the administration of justice more just?

Secondly, it is by no means clear that only anthropological *theory* is relevant for 'law'. Hence we need to make a parallel distinction on the side of 'anthropology' as well. That is to say, we must also consider 'anthropological' *facts* – the ethnographic descriptions of non-western societies and, especially, of their 'law' – and now the fun really starts.

If non-western societies also have 'law', and if it is this 'law', rather than the theories of anthropologists about it, which matters, then this volume would amount to an enquiry into the relevance of 'law' for itself. If, on the other hand, non-western societies do not have 'law', we would be enquiring into the relevance of 'non-law' for 'law', and we would have to ask, first, who decides (and on what basis) what 'law' is, and, second, why it is important to compare one kind of 'non-law' with 'law' – namely the kind of 'non-law' which is the domain of 'anthropology' – rather than another (which is the domain of, say, 'zoology' or 'theology')? If we avoid these awkward questions by saying instead that non-western societies do have 'law' but that their 'law' is different from that of western societies, and that our title only means 'western law' when it speaks of 'law', we only tie ourselves into a larger number of smaller knots. Moreover, these definition games prevent us from recognizing that a crucial factor is still missing in our equation. If anthropologists study the 'law' of non-western societies as *social scientists* they do not and cannot provide us with the *legal* theory of that 'law' which would be the equivalent of what is conventionally understood to be legal theory in western societies, since this theory is perceived as being the self-understanding of the 'law' in question, as representing an internal point of view. In other words, in addition to 'law' and 'legal theory', to 'anthropology' and the 'ethnography of law', we need to consider the relevance of the *indigenous* theories of non-western societies concerning their own 'law' – or, for that matter, any other form of 'law'.

Finally, what do we do about cases where non-western societies have adopted (or had imposed upon them) western forms of 'law'? Or if we discover that western societies practise forms of 'law' which are similar to non-western forms of 'law' but which are not recognized as 'law' by their own legal system? Or if we find that western societies include non-western minorities whose legal problems occupy western legal institutions, which may or may not draw on the expertise of western anthropologists or non-western lawyers? And what do we do about alegal or even anti-legal theories about western forms of 'law'? In a nutshell, what do we do if we open our eyes and see the position in the field of 'law' in every human society of which mankind is currently composed as it actually presents itself?

How do we deal with this 'chaos'? The 'classical' western approach is to sort it out by pressing it into some kind of rational order. Although this exercise is essentially prescriptive, it is ideologically vital that its normativity not be disclosed. Hence it is assumed that the entire universe is in fact a given rational system, so that this order is merely discovered, instead of being invented; that it is therefore necessary instead of representing a choice which would require justification; and that it can and should be treated 'scientifically'.

What happened in the field of 'law' is instructive in this regard. Our legal Hercules attacked his Augean stables not with a broom (or a diverted river) but with a definitional hatchet. 'What is [and, more importantly, what is not] law?', he asked – knowing that it would simplify his job dramatically if he could persuade his taskmaster that henceforth only structures housing one-eyed legal boars would count as 'stables' he had to clean. This means to say that Hercules was no longer interested in the possible meaning of words but in practical results. It was meant to make an actual difference whether a phenomenon was classified as 'law' or as 'non-law'. What was at issue was not concepts but power (and not merely the power of words). And the powers that be just happened to favour 'law' to the detriment of 'non-law' (which was no longer Hercules's responsibility). 'Law', as defined, became institutionalized, professionalized and privileged, politically as well as ideologically. Legal rights did, in fact, grow stronger than moral claims or social responsibilities. 'Law' became capable of declaring 'custom' to be illegal, to reserve the practice of 'law' to lawyers, and so on.[10]

It is crucial under these circumstances that the definition of 'law' itself is claimed to be necessary rather than good (let alone merely 'better than'). Jurisprudence must be dressed up as a descriptive sociology of law, since this 'positivistic' jurisprudence maintains that it is only telling us about the way 'law' actually is and that its shape has nothing to do with the personal preferences of positivistic theorists (who have no more choice in the matter than anybody else).[11]

But then we all know that things do change. To cope with change, history also needs to be incorporated into the assumed, universal, rational order. This is where 'evolutionism' comes in, this ideological linchpin of modern western civilization which figures so prominently in the *Oxford* definitions of 'anthropology' and 'sociology' discussed above.

History, too, is pronounced to be orderly. Time as well as space are assumed to be governed by natural laws which provide a proper place for everything, since the clockwork of evolution can conveniently tick over at different speeds in different places. There is nothing anyone can do – apart from avoiding unnecessary hiccoughs and from softening the pains of those crushed by the cog-wheels of progress – nothing but watch and adjust one's behaviour to the grand design. We can afford to be positivists, legal and otherwise, if history is evolution (indeed, we cannot afford to be anything else), but when the feet of clay crumble, everything comes tumbling down and no one can put Humpty-Dumpty together again.

This is precisely what we can see happening in the field of 'law and anthropology' today. But we can only appreciate the magnitude of the shock – which lawyers are still trying to ignore (in the vain hope that it will bypass their domain) – if we first understand the integrative force which 'evolutionism' provided for a positivistic perception of law, by making 'natural law' superfluous and a 'law' which was neither positive nor natural, unthinkable.

To describe the state of affairs which exists today in the field of 'law and anthropology' as chaotic, as I have done above, is a negative way of putting it. To describe it as a reflection of the *plurality* of 'law' is a neutral alternative.

How do we respond to such a plurality? It calls for a negative or positive but *active* reaction, whereas a detached 'so what?' approach is psychologically unlikely, at least in the western cultural context. Westerners are culturally conditioned to take sides and, in this case, their conditioning weighs heavily in favour of the negative rather than the affirmative.

Plurality, if it means diversity rather than mere duplication (the co-existence of a multitude of clones of the same thing), implies that this 'thing' does not exist at all, that there is, in our case, no such thing as 'law' which could be defined. To ask, 'What is law?' becomes pointless if there is a plurality of 'law'. We can only ask: 'What *can* law be?' – and we must admit the possibility that it can take shapes which we cannot even imagine. Put more strongly, if 'law' is a plural phenomenon it can no longer be positive or natural.

Hence the need for a 'normative' definition which prescribes what 'law' is supposed to be and which declares all phenomena within the field of 'law' which do not fit this description as 'non-law'. This is what the 'What is law?' game is about. It defines away the plurality of 'law' and provides the basis for a prescriptive conceptual order: this is not 'law' but 'custom', this is not a 'legal' norm but a 'moral' norm, this is not a 'legal' way of handling disputes but something else. Yet this is only the first step. We still have to deal with the actual plurality in the field of law – and we need to justify our normative definition of 'law'. In other words, our task has a practical as well as a theoretical and ideological dimension, and it goes without saying that these dimensions overlap. Let us focus on the ideological aspect since it provides, so to speak, the marching orders.

The general direction of this march is plain to see: towards greater centralization, unification and uniformity in the field of 'law'. But why? The answer to this question is provided by 'evolutionism' – and it is most convincing, as long as 'evolutionism' is not itself questioned.[12]

The 'natural' laws of history, whose existence is demonstrated by history itself, demand that 'law' becomes increasingly centralized, unified and uniform because this is progress, because it makes 'law' better and better and better.[13] The actual plurality in the field of 'law' merely shows that we are not as yet living in the best of all possible worlds and that some societies are progressing faster than others – the stragglers (those who try to resist the laws of history instead of letting themselves be carried along by them towards a glorious future) representing the earlier stages of the development through which the leaders have long passed. Hence the latter are not merely entitled but duty-bound to assist the stragglers in the acceleration of their own advancement. They do not only have the general forces of history behind them in doing so, but they make their less fortunate brothers and sisters (or contemporary forebears) a generous present of the fruits of their own painful historical experience.[14]

Once the road has been mapped out in this manner, the actual march of history becomes a triumphant self-fulfilling prophecy, as long as the forces of history play the game according to the rules. But if they start doing their own thing (whatever that may be), the lights suddenly go out – and not only in the field of 'law'.

Strange as this may sound, the preceding comments contain an outline of the history of the relations between 'law' and 'anthropology' during the last 200 years or so.

'Anthropology', or, rather, the 'ethnography' of the 'law' of non-western societies, became interesting from a western legal perspective as a geographical extension of an evolutionary model of western legal history.[15] The data it yielded were used to explain the history of 'law' in western societies by providing illustrations of the stages through which it too had passed. At the same time, the history of western 'law' was universalized. Henceforth, there was only one law with one history, transformed from an (interpretive) art into a science, because this universal history of 'law' was assumed to be governed by natural laws which could be studied as if 'law' (as well as 'society') was a physical phenomenon.

This approach dominated the field from the days of the 'founding fathers' of legal anthropology, like, Morgan, Maine or Bachofen – capturing the grand theorists, such as Marx, Durkheim or Weber – until quite recently. Even 'functionalists', including Malinowski, with their polemics against historical speculations about 'primitive' 'law', are unthinkable outside a broad 'evolutionist' framework, since it was this framework which permitted them to disregard history because it could be expected to look after itself in a most satisfactory manner.

'Evolutionism' permeates theorizing about all aspects of human affairs, since it is an essential part of the 'positivistic' package deal. The assumption of an orderly, rational universe cannot possibly exclude its time dimension. If there is to be order, it must be temporal as well as spatial, historical as well as physical; the two aspects stand and fall together.[16]

Moreover, once history is assumed to be orderly, the borderline between comparative typologies and schematic history evaporates. Legal history and comparative law become extensions of each other. At the same time, they become predictable and hence superfluous. We no longer need either of them (apart from confirming our ideological position); we are entitled to adopt a positivist, instrumentalist and isolationist perspective of 'law'. 'Law' becomes, in principle, a positive, self-contained and self-explanatory system.

The only remaining purpose of studying positive 'law' comparatively or historically is to assist in making 'law' actually more centralized, unified and uniform. Law reform ceases to be the reform of 'law' and turns into reform through 'law'. 'Law' becomes social engineering in the service of universal 'development', the instrument by which 'evolutionism' fulfils itself.

This was how things were supposed to turn out. Instead 'evolutionism' itself is disintegrating because people begin to see that the results its implementation produces are neither good nor necessary – and because even the physical universe, as understood by 'post-modern' natural science, is not a strict, predictable rational order but a mixture of certainty, probability and chance, which requires a holistic approach and precludes blinkered and self-assured specialization.

As far as 'anthropology' is concerned, this 'post-modern' scenario may still lead to its demise. Although the changed intellectual and ideological environment should be in its favour, and although the fate of non-western societies is no longer doomed by 'evolution', the ship 'Anthropology' drifts along, manned by a multiplying but demoralized crew which tries to move it at the same time into every conceivable direction. At any rate, anthropologists are preoccupied with saving themselves and their discipline and are unlikely to play the prince who will deliver the princess of western legal theory from a hundred years of positivistic coma.

This would give cause for sadness to few people, if the castle of western 'law' had not in the meantime been covered by a luxuriant growth of 'positive' brambles and if faithful replicas of this structure had not by now been constructed in all corners of the globe.

This is a consequence of the fact that the relationship between 'law' and legal theory differs from that between 'anthropology' and the shape of non-western societies. While few anthropologists believe that it was ever possible or desirable to treat anthropology as a positivistic science, and although non-western societies have changed much more dramatically under the impact of 'evolutionism' than has western 'law', it was not 'anthropology' which brought those changes about, although it was itself shaped by the forces which did.

Within western 'law', on the other hand, theory and practice have become intimately and perhaps inextricably linked. Modern western legal theory *is* 'the law' – or, rather, modern western law is legal theory in the sense that it makes no difference to its structure that a legal argument is put forward in a court of law or in a piece of academic writing. Modern western 'law' is neither theory nor practice, or theory as well as practice. Modern western 'law' uses legal theory to cause legal effects – but legal effects are as such purely theoretical: nobody dies by being *sentenced* to death. Modern western 'law' – and perhaps many other forms of 'law' – are no more and no less than talk.

This peculiar nature of modern western 'law' gives modern western legal theory a strong immunity against changes which occur around it. It can afford to ignore the winds of change in a way 'anthropology' cannot. To do so may even protect 'law' from dangerous infections – but it may also endanger its survival by preventing it from adjusting to an altered environment. Modern western legal theory can remain unaltered – and theoretically valid – as long as 'law' itself remains unaltered. Indeed, as 'doctrinal' legal theory (that is to say *legal* theory as opposed to theories *about* 'law') it is even forced to remain positivistic to the extent 'the law' itself remains positivistic. It can refuse to listen to better judgement instead of being swept away by it. It can resolve, like a sea captain, to go down with its sinking ship.

Put differently, modern western legal theory not only combines descriptive and prescriptive elements, it is *constitutive*. The American legal realists were right in claiming that 'law', in the United States, is (primarily) what the courts in fact do. But, apart from not explaining *what* the courts do (beyond talking), and how they do it, this leaves the question as to whether there are other ways of 'doing' 'law' and whether this particular way of 'doing' 'law' is good for modern American or any other society.

Although modern western legal theory may be an extreme case, it is not unique in this respect. All theories, including anthropological theories, have ideological consequences, and all ideologies are, more or less successfully, 'constitutive'. Human beings are not just capable of changing their environment (and themselves) by their thoughts and words, as well as by their actions, they cannot help doing so, however hard they may try. There is no impenetrable wall between what is and what we perceive it to be. We cannot step outside the universe to observe it with scientific detachment – as (post?) modern physics has conclusively demonstrated even for the realm of nature. We are bound to be participants and contribute, consciously or otherwise, to what is going on around us.

What makes the field of 'law' special is that it is the *purpose* of 'law', certainly of modern western 'law', to change nature, to supplement and modify the instinctive reactions of human beings, and that 'law' tries to achieve this aim by talk rather than by action. This does not mean that 'law' is primarily concerned with social *change*; indeed social stability is one of its central and legitimate goals. Rather, it means that 'law' wants to change the biological nature of man ('as an animal') by placing it into an artificial, cultural 'framework' which is essentially created and maintained by words and battles about words.

It is for this reason that the combination of 'positivism' and 'evolutionism', the two aspects of a legalistic perception of space and time, constitutes a powerful weapon in the field of 'law'. In the western cultural context this combination comes about quite naturally because it merely requires an extension of the time-honoured normative approach not only to 'law' but to nature, society and history. On the other hand, it dramatically reduces the ability of 'law' to change itself in response to changes in its environment it cannot control. 'Positive' 'law', it appears, can *only* 'evolve'; it can only perfect the normative techniques of which it is composed.

Legal positivism, then, is not just a theoretically unsatisfactory way of looking at what is actually happening in the field of 'law', it is a particular technology. It aims at perfecting 'law' through a process of specialization, rationalization and professionalization, but it does so at the expense of 'outlawing' alternative 'legal' techniques and theories, of putting all 'legal' eggs into a single basket. It is an orchestrated gamble; and what is at stake is not the future of 'positive' 'law' but the future of society.

In short, while it can safely be left to anthropologists to work out whether or not they are willing and able to transcend 'positivism' and 'evolutionism' in their field, it is vital that this task in the field of 'law' is *not* left to lawyers – which brings us back to the relations between 'law' and 'anthropology'.

'Anthropology' can be safely left to anthropologists because it makes no direct difference to the actual shape of non-western societies – their subject matter – what theoretical position they take.[17] 'Law' cannot be safely left to lawyers because they are 'doing' 'law' and because the 'law' they are 'doing' may be harmful (or, at least, not as helpful as it could be) to the societies within which they and their 'law' are operating. Since lawyers can only 'do' the 'law' they know, it is of utmost practical importance that lawyers not only learn what 'their' 'law' is but also what 'law' can be – and not merely in the sense of the range of substantive rules which can be enacted in relation to a particular subject matter, but also in the sense of the range of legal technology which can be employed: What are the alternatives to norms, to legislation (as norm creation), to courts, to law enforcement and so on? Lawyers and non-lawyers must accept the plurality of 'law' and learn to handle it constructively – in theory as well as practice – instead of trying to define it away to the detriment of all of us.

This implies, of course, a switch from legal positivism and its bias in favour of an increasing centralization, unification and uniformization of 'law' to legal pluralism. However, the justification of legal pluralism as a superior legal ideology is no more our problem than the justification of an abolition of 'anthropology'[18] – although it should be noted in passing that legal pluralism does not require us to take a 'the more, the merrier' attitude to 'law' and that it has ample room for positivistic as well as non-positivistic forms of legal technology. The question we need to address is whether 'anthropology', or, rather, the 'law' of non-western societies, instead of being used to construct an imaginary (but ideologically useful) universal history of 'law' can also be used in working out constructive approaches to the plurality of 'law', keeping firmly in mind that this plurality is as much an intra-cultural and intra-societal as an inter-cultural and inter-societal problem.

What concerns us is not merely that English 'law' is different from Chinese 'law', Bantu 'law' or German 'law' – that there is a global plurality of 'law' – but that the 'law' of each society is itself plural and that it must remain plural in the interests of that society's well-being. Moreover, it is not simply a matter of there being different ways of 'regulating' marriages or of 'settling' disputes – all with their own, limited strengths and weaknesses – but that there are different ways of organizing all aspects of human affairs and different ways of seeing ourselves and the world around us, which all have a direct bearing on 'law'.

It is neither necessary nor necessarily desirable (and only of limited usefulness) to see nature as being governed by a rational system of laws. The same applies to our view of 'law' – and society. 'Law' can be normative and rational and systematic but it cannot be and must not even try to be totally normative or rational or systematic.[19] And so it goes all the way up and down the line, from the most general and central to the most specific or peripheral, wherever we choose to locate the centre (or centres) in the field of 'law'.

The resulting 'chaos' in the field of 'law' is only chaotic if we want to see it as such, just as 'anarchy' becomes 'disorder' and 'confusion' only if we let ourselves be bamboozled into believing that (governmental) 'rule' is synonymous with 'order' and that 'order' is per se 'good' – instead of (also) being a questionable limitation of 'freedom' (compare the relevant definitions in the *Concise Oxford Dictionary*).

The plurality of 'law' is a challenge, not a disaster; it is hope and responsibility, now that the illusion that the history of 'law' will take care of itself is shattered. The 'rule of law' is no less an illusion than total 'anarchy'. They are both part of the same word battle which will continue to shape the future of mankind – unless we manage to decide it, once and for all, by our own annihilation.

What can 'anthropology', or, rather, an understanding of other cultures, of other ways of seeing and shaping 'law', life, the universe and everything, contribute to what is going on on this battlefield? It can help us, first and foremost, to appreciate the range of technological and ideological alternatives in the field of 'law' which are not only possible but which have been tried and found to work. And we must not forget that non-western societies do not represent a single type (as modern western society supposedly does) but a variety of cases whose diversity suggests that any form of social *typology* (an important weapon in our word battle) may be harmful, especially if societies are henceforth type-cast and expected to perform in accordance with their type.

On the other hand, 'anthropology' can demonstrate that while all societies (and all forms of 'law') are peculiar, none is unique in the sense that it has nothing in common with any other. There is probably not a single feature of any human society (past, present or future) which is not repeated elsewhere. Cultural specificity is not a matter of raw materials but a matter of mix and emphasis which add up to an overall pattern which can never be repeated.

Thirdly, 'anthropology' shows the need for a holistic approach, since these patterns cannot otherwise be discerned. But it also shows the danger of jumping from there to the conclusion that societies are in fact wholes which do, can or should operate as 'systems' – or, worse still, as subsystems of a single universal system. Like the physical universe, the social universe is both limited and endless; and just as in the case of the former it makes no sense to assume either that it has or that it has not a beginning or an end. All these *explanations* – again an essential part of the word battle – are more or less persuasive imagery which tries to express what is inexplicable, although it can be experienced and used to alter our experiences.

Finally, 'anthropology' teaches us that all problems are universal and eternal but that all solutions are temporal and of limited usefulness, so that we can and should take nothing for granted – and, in particular, never can or should trust any kind of expert, although we cannot avoid taking their advice.

This, you may say, is all very well (although there is no reason to take this non-expert's word for it) but what does it mean as far as 'law' is concerned? What follows from it, specifically and concretely? Let us get down to brass tacks!

This, I would answer, is precisely the problem. The proverbial brass tacks only make sense if we can take for granted the structure to which we want to tack something and the material which we want to tack on to it – that, in our case, the throne of 'law' as well as the brocade with which we want to reupholster it actually exists 'out there' in a given shape so that we merely need expert advice as to where we best place the optimal number of brass tacks of optimal length to hold the new material firmly in place. But this is, fortunately or unfortunately, simply not the position.

True, there are plenty of physical objects in the field of 'law' – books, buildings, people, wigs and batons – but it is doubtful whether anything which is 'legal' is real in the physical sense. What makes a house a 'court'-house (an inscription above the door?), a 'judgment' more than a string of words, a 'statute' more than a piece of paper?

The same applies, *mutatis mutandis*, to the whole social realm: What makes a 'marriage', or a 'university'? Is a judge a 'judge' when he/she is asleep? A medical doctor a 'medical doctor' when he/she has been deregistered? What happens if someone is 'elected' or 'appointed', 'sacked', 'promoted' or 'retired'?

We are surrounded by mysteries, not only in the field of 'law'. We all know (intuitively?) that these familiar non-objects are somehow 'real'. We know that their non-physical, social reality has to do with perception, with conventions, with relationships of power. We know that they come and go, and change in between, but that their meaning and their existence is more than purely subjective. Intellectual reductionism can peel the onion until nothing is left of it but we continue to consume these onions (or throw them at each other) in everyday life as if nothing had happened because they are the essence of social life. We do not have to find a rational explanation for the 'realness' of 'legal' (or social) reality, we just have to live with it, as best as we can – and that means to accept that 'law' is mysterious as well as real, but that its mysteriousness is perfectly natural; and that we improve our survival skills by facing instead of denying it.

To consider how other cultures handle the mystery of 'law' may be the easiest way of understanding what we ourselves are doing, more or less mechanically, in the field of 'law'; of appreciating that our 'law' represents, objectively, a choice, of which we may not be aware and from which we may be unable or unwilling to free ourselves, but which we can learn to see more clearly for what it is in terms of its limitations and its potential.

This is where 'anthropology' comes in – but where does 'law' fit into the picture?

Science, art, religion, philosophy, magic, and mythology are all means of dealing with the mystery of human existence and, at the same time, part of it. Is 'law' yet another possibility?

Is 'law' a distinct way of acting out the social drama? A magical ritual? A science of balancing interests? A form of social medicine, or social engineering? A spectator sport? An unending struggle to uphold justice? An instrument of oppression? A cunning way of making a living out of talking about other people's problems?

'Law' can be all of these things and much else besides. It will, in most cases, be a mixture of many of these ingredients. To try to go further than this may well be counterproductive since, to repeat this point for the last time, 'law' as such does not exist. 'Law' is part of social life, just as politics or the economy, love or hate, aggressiveness or compassion are part of social life, and just as social life is part of life in general, and life part of 'everything'.

'Law' is part of social life in the sense of being encompassed by it, but it is neither a discrete component nor a discrete aspect of social life, which is similarly undefinable. Where does the social, the political, the economic, the religious, the rational begin and end? What is the point of asking these questions? What is the point of insisting that 'law' should have a limit, that it should be distinguishable from other phenomena? Is lack of definability a negative property of 'law'? Does it make 'law' more difficult to understand theoretically if it cannot be defined? Does it make 'law' less capable of functioning effectively in practice? Do we want to achieve analytical clarity by defining concepts or do we define concepts because we want to manipulate reality? Does the statement that the Nuer have no 'law' help us to understand Nuer society?[20] Or does it make it easier to do things to Nuer society which we would otherwise be more reluctant to do?

Whatever the answer to any of these questions, it is tempting under these circumstances to abandon 'law' altogether as a focal point and settle instead for some easier alternative, for example 'dispute management' or 'social control'.

But trying to run away from the problem does not help us, since these notions are also complex cultural constructs which are neither easily definable nor representations of universal social phenomena. We cannot take for granted that all societies are concerned with 'social control' or that 'disputes' everywhere are essentially the same. Besides, modern western 'law' for one is plainly a great deal more than a particular – legal – form of 'dispute management' or 'social control' – quite apart from the fact that there would be no need for moving away from 'law' as a focal point, if we knew what makes anything distinctively 'legal'.

On the contrary, despite its culture-boundness, 'law' has become more 'globalized' (as opposed to 'universalized') than any other alternative focal point we could choose. Even societies whose 'indigenous' cultures are not preoccupied with the maintenance of 'order' do now have a western form of 'law' as an important, if not dominant, part of their social environment, whether they are situated in Europe, Asia, Africa, Australia, America or Oceania. Whether we like it or not, 'law' is at the centre of a now worldwide word battle, and it would, for this very reason, be as foolish of mankind to leave 'law' to lawyers as it would be to leave 'health-care' to medical doctors, 'education' to educators, 'nature' to natural scientists, 'politics' to politicians or 'religion' to the priests of one particular denomination.

We are stuck not only with 'law' but with lawyers and the particular brand of 'law' they are taught and administer and we must learn to make the best of the position in the field of 'law' as we actually find it – which brings us back to 'anthropology' and to what it can do to help us in this task.

Let us imagine 'law' not as a thing but as a battlefield where the actual shape 'law' takes in a particular society at a particular point in time is determined. There may be cannons firing in all directions, or there may be a total cease-fire, but the target of all activity (or inactivity) is power and, to be more precise, power over other human beings. Whatever 'law' is, it is concerned with human behaviour, concerned with influencing what people do or do not do, do or do not say, think and feel. 'Law' wants to achieve practical results. Nonetheless, its primary weapon is talk rather than action, and its own shape is also moulded by talk rather than by action. This is true at least to the extent that 'law' can only be what is said to be 'legally' possible, or, put negatively, that which is regarded as 'legally' impossible can never become part of 'law', so that, for example, the identification of 'law' with a particular legal technology prevents alternative techniques from ever becoming 'law', irrespective of their potential usefulness.

This does not mean that 'law' is altogether talked in and out of existence, but it comes close to saying it – and with good reason. Theoretical considerations apart, it is prudent, if we want to help 'law' to perform as best as it can, to proceed on the assumption that everything in the field of 'law' is possible, and that nothing should be ruled out as being 'non-legal' – which does not mean that everything which is 'legally' possible is also desirable or likely to work.

Once we accept that the plurality of 'law' has no theoretical limits, it also becomes unproductive to consider the practical limitations of 'law' in any given society. Instead we should be looking at the range of 'legal' possibilities human beings have actually realized in the course of their history.

It is in this regard that 'anthropology', or, rather, legal ethnography, can make its most important contribution, not merely by enlarging the overall size of our 'legal' inventory (and potential armoury), but also by showing the different ways in which the various components of the 'law' of different human societies do, or do not, 'hang together'.

Our global legal inventory may, for example, show that there are not only many different ways of 'regulating' the 'inheritance' of property (some favouring spouses, others siblings or children, or male relatives; some favouring the keeping together of the 'inheritance', others its wide distribution, and still others the free choice of the deceased, in disposing of his or her property) but that in some societies *any* form of 'inheritance', and 'property', is minimalized: because members 'customarily' give away their property during their lifetime; because there is no *personal* property or because property is so personal that it is destroyed when its owner dies, or because alternative, non-property-oriented forms of resource management have been adopted.

Our inventory may or may not demonstrate that 'customs' are linked with particular forms of economic activity, or of social organization, with the shape of the physical environment – or the ways the world is viewed by different cultures – so that, for instance, the 'law' of fishermen, desert dwellers, matrilineal societies or monotheists has important elements in common which distinguishes it from the 'law' of pastoralists, agriculturalists, mercantilists, industrialists, atheists, individualists and so on.

It may show that some legal techniques are readily 'transplantable' to different physical or cultural environments, whereas others rarely take root outside their home ground; that diverse legal techniques operate side by side in some societies and not in others; that almost everything in the field of 'law' makes sense in retrospect but that almost nothing can be predicted; that some societies are more concerned with intellectual order than others; that some societies are more normative than others; that some societies encourage their members to live in harmony and others to fight for their rights. One result, however, is certain: that in all human societies, alternative 'legal' techniques and ideologies co-exist. It is therefore not merely impossible to devise a *universal* theory of 'law' but also to devise a single theory of, say, the 'law' which operated in England in 1950.

'Law' can be more or less centralized and systematic, but it can never be a single, unified and uniform, operating system, even if large parts of the field of 'law' are defined away. 'Law' cannot be wholly concerned, for example, with the enforcement of legislated rights. There always were and always will be alternatives to legislation, rights and law-enforcement at every level of society. Social change will always occur, whether it is legislated for or not. There will always be persuasive claims which are not based on 'legally'-recognized rights. It is impractical to adjudicate *all* disputes (or to turn every infringement of rights into a dispute, or every dispute into an alleged infringement of rights). A legal profession can never establish an *exclusive* monopoly in the field of 'law', however hard it tries.

This does not imply that all theorizing about 'law' is futile or that, for instance, greater centralization (or decentralization) of 'law' is unachievable. It requires us, however, to learn to live with the fact that 'law' is like a multidimensional net which stretches beyond the horizon in all directions, wherever we stand. We can only lift it at a particular point and inspect its mesh as far as we can see, knowing that it is changing even while we are observing it in response to a multitude of forces of which we ourselves are part – and that even its most permanent configurations are the product of conventionalized and institutionalized human imagination and perception.

It is in helping us to understand the different ways in which 'law' has been perceived that 'anthropology' can make its most valuable contribution to 'law'. Of course, by showing that there is more than one possibility of perceiving 'law', and by showing that these possibilities are not variations on a single theme but different tunes, 'anthropology' makes the life of 'law' more complicated. But these complications are also a reflection of an increased 'legal' freedom, which a 'positivistic' theory of 'law' persistently denies.

'Anthropology' can liberate 'law', not by offering a vast arsenal of 'legal' weapons ready to be used in any society at any time, but by demonstrating what has proved to be 'legally' possible, and under what circumstances it has been found to work. 'Anthropology' can place a wide range of 'ethnic' 'legal' cuisines at our disposal. Although those who cater for the 'legal' appetites of English society may still find some Burmese 'legal' speciality revolting or that some Ovambo 'legal' ingredients are frustratingly unavailable, they can at least no longer claim that only 'legal' roast beef is fit for human consumption.

The liberation of 'law' which 'anthropology' can help to bring about is theoretical, just as the complication it will create for 'law' is, at least initially, theoretical. Yet, we must not lose sight of the peculiar relationship between theory and practice in the field of 'law' – and, more generally, in the construction of social reality.

This peculiarity comes again to the fore when we consider that 'anthropology' can only play the role as a midwife in the birth of a 'post-positivist' 'law' after it has itself been liberated from its own cultural blinkers.

As already pointed out, the collapse of 'positivism' affects 'anthropology', not in the same way as it affects 'law'. While it makes 'anthropology' as a positivist theoretical enterprise untenable, it has this effect in the field of 'law' only in so far as positivist theories *about* 'law' are concerned. But legal positivism has altered the actual shape of 'law', whereas anthropological positivism did not, by itself, alter the actual shape of non-western societies. 'Law' has, to some extent, itself become positivistic so that a positive theory *of* 'law' remains to that extent not only legitimate but necessary. Legal positivism has not merely erected a theoretical wall between 'law' and morality – which has now collapsed – it has institutionalized 'law' in such a way that morality has, in fact, been shut out of the halls of justice, so that 'law' (rather than merely the theorizing about 'law') needs to be changed in order to accomplish its readmission.

'Law' is the social reality with which legal theory is dealing whereas the subject matter of anthropological theory is non-western societies rather than 'anthropology'. At least this is what positivist anthropological theory used to claim. But was this indeed the position? Certainly not, since positivistic 'anthropology' constructed a fictitious 'human society', as a counterpart of 'positive' 'law', which it then proceeded to study scientifically. It is this fiction which collapses with 'positivism', since it has not been institutionalized in the manner of 'positive' 'law', so that 'post-positivist' 'anthropology' has no choice but to face the diversity of actual human societies, so to speak, in the flesh (although the latter, of course, also do not exist as physical entities 'out there').

So far so good, but the parallels between 'law' and 'anthropology' are even closer than this picture suggests. While individual anthropologists engaged in fieldwork always had to face non-western societies in the flesh, 'anthropology', even 'post-positivist' 'anthropology', as an academic discipline, cannot deal directly with non-western societies but only with what has been reported about them. The subject matter of 'anthropology' is, unavoidably, the anthropological literature rather than the social reality of non-western societies – just as 'positive' 'law' forms a layer of distinctly 'legal' reality which separates lawyers from the social problems of their clients.

The point I am driving at is this: although 'positivism' in the field of 'anthropology' did not directly alter the social reality of non-western societies it has – together with a variety of other personal, professional and cultural prejudices – shaped the anthropological literature about those societies. It has shaped the ethnographic record; and this record remains permanently disfigured, even after the collapse of 'positivism' – in the same way as 'positive' 'law' remains 'positivistic'.

Hence we cannot treat the ethnography of 'law' presented by the anthropological literature as a complete or objective account of the 'law' of non-western societies. Instead we are confronted by a collection of more or less explicit and conventionalized 'tribal' mythologies (and I mean 'tribes' of anthropologists and other observers rather than the 'tribes' which they have observed).

There is nothing wrong with mythology, especially in the field of 'law' where it plays a vital role. But we must recognize it as such and come to grips with the various forms it can take, instead of letting ourselves be taken in by one particular version. And we must come to grips with mythology as mythology, instead of trying to demythologize it, since this leads only to another, singularly dull and unproductive, delusion.

Mythology, ideology, call it what you like, is an integral part of 'law' and social reality in general. 'Law' is mysterious. It is comprehensible only if it is seen not as a unique universal but as a humble variable. Thus it can only be comprehended through a comparison of its manifest variations. But this comparison must be multi-directional. That is to say, while it is legitimate to use one form of 'law' as a yardstick and ask: Where are courts, codes and constables in non-western societies, we must also ask (to name but one possibility) where are *karma* and *dharma* in modern western societies – or traditional African societies? It is only through multi-directional, cross-cultural comparisons that 'law' can be understood. Without 'anthropology', 'law' cannot even see itself, let alone where it is going.

'Anthropology' can help to liberate 'law' by showing that a great deal more is 'legally' possible than the now globalized western legal positivism would have us believe. On the other hand, 'anthropology' cannot tell us what we should be doing with this increased 'legal' freedom. Like any other process of liberation, this one is painful and dangerous. It destroys a false but comforting sense of security. It opens the door, but without teaching us how to deal with what may be waiting for us on the other side.

To use 'anthropology' as a big stick with which to beat 'legal positivism' is not the purpose of the exercise. The main lesson to be learned from 'anthropology' is not to be too sure about what we think we know about 'law' and what we think is right or wrong in human affairs. The challenge 'anthropology' poses for 'law' is to learn to handle constructively the plurality of 'law', which 'anthropology' demonstrates. To replace the misguided 'positivist' clear-felling exercise in the field of 'law' with another such exercise is not the answer. 'Law' is not a fight between good and evil. Simple dichotomies like these are counter-productive illusions. There will never be ideal legal arrangements in any society. The art is to keep an open mind and to learn to combine tolerance and commitment. This does not require us to suspend our beliefs or to abandon our convictions, but it requires more than a passive respect of other people's right to disagree with us. We must be prepared to learn from them – however alien their views may appear to be – and to accept that we ourselves have, at best, only part of a possible answer which is not the final word, even as far as it goes.

This applies, of course, to everything I have said in this introduction. I have presented a particular case, seen from an unashamedly idiosyncratic perspective. Yet, I have done so, instead of surveying the vast literature relevant for the field of 'law and anthropology' with as much detachment as I am able to muster, not merely because I prefer to develop my own argument but also because there are already too many surveys of this kind – a safe indication of an unhappy state of affairs which cries out to everybody to raise their hand and be counted.

Some of these surveys comprise the first part of this collection of readings. The second part contrasts lawyers' views about the relevance of 'anthropology' for legal theory with the theoretical concerns of anthropologists (among which neither 'law' nor legal theory rate even a mention) and presents anthropological approaches to 'law' and legal theory. The third part brings together attempts by western scholars to understand non-western forms of 'jurisprudence' in their own terms, whereas the fourth part illustrates diverse non-western approaches to 'law', western as well as non-western. By contrast, the fifth and final part is more practical and specific in that it concentrates on the role of 'custom' and anthropologists in courts of law.

The main difficulty in selecting and arranging the articles included in this collection has been the immense variety of issues and approaches in this inter-disciplinary area. 'Legal anthropology' has not become a distinct academic discipline which produces its own specialist literature. Instead we are entering a twilight zone which is peripheral to both legal and anthropological theory. It has attracted adventurous individuals from both camps who occasionally form networks but are reluctant to form schools, let alone a feeling of shared professional identity.

The position will change if the plurality of 'law' becomes accepted as a central – intra-societal as well as inter-cultural – issue. But we have a long way to go until this happens and, if it does, the scenario will have changed dramatically. The plurality of 'law' will have become a major concern of mainstream legal theory, and 'anthropology' might have been absorbed into 'sociology'. At any rate the twilight zone will have disappeared; its occupants will have migrated; and a messy but colourful volume such as this will no longer be necessary or justified.

In the meantime we must live with a paradox. The sands are shifting. Dichotomies like those between 'law' and 'custom', 'sociology' and 'anthropology', 'western' and 'non-western' are dissolving. The plurality of 'law' is acquiring greater social reality. But, at the same time, 'legal positivism' continues to conquer new terrain. 'Non-western' lawyers are often among its staunchest adherents. Non-western countries may 'out-centralize' and 'out-bureaucratize' the rest of the world. 'Post-colonial' governments may engage in forms of 'colonial' exploitation which are just as blatant, brutal and arrogant as those employed by their former colonial masters.

It is a complex and fluid world in which the most illuminating contributions to the 'new' legal ethnography may be concerned with western societies, in which legal revolutions may take the form of a return to ancient religious orthodoxies and which we can only capture in a collection of readings which is itself mildly anarchical.

A constructive form of non-systematic cohesion in the field of 'law' can only emerge if we expose ourselves to the risk of confusion inherent in intellectual fermentation. Those who believe in legal systems should stay away from 'law and anthropology', this volume is not for them. If it has a purpose, it is not reassurance but disconcertment.

Notes

1 See: Williams, G. (1956), 'The Controversy Concerning the Word "Law"', in P. Laslett (ed.), *Philosophy, Politics and Society*, pp. 134–56, Oxford: Basil Blackwell.

2 On 'crises' in legal theory see: Unger, R.M. (1983), *The Critical Legal Studies Movement*, Cambridge, MA: Harvard University Press; Sibley, S.S. and Sarat, A. (1987), 'Critical Traditions in Law and Society Research', *Law and Society Review*, **21**, (1), 165–74.

On 'crises' in anthropological theory see: Clifford, J. (1988), *The Predicament of Culture: Twentieth-Century Ethnography, Literature and Art*, Cambridge, MA: Harvard University Press; Zamora, M.D. (1987), 'Crises and Concerns in Anthropology and the Validity of the Anthropological Enterprise', *Eastern Anthropologist*, **40**, (4), 293–305.

3 For some discussion of the relationships between 'law', 'culture' and 'society', see: Nader, L. (1969), 'Introduction', in L. Nader (ed.), *Law in Culture and Society*, Chicago: Aldine Publishing Co. (especially pp. 8–10); Starr, J. and Collier, J.F. (1989), 'Introduction: Dialogues in Legal Anthropology', in J. Starr and J.F. Collier (eds), *History and Power in the Study of Law: New Directions in Legal Anthropology*, Ithaca and London: Cornell University Press.

4 For some discussion of definitions of 'anthropology' see: Keesing, R.M. (1981), *Cultural Anthropology: A Contemporary Perspective*, pp. 1–2, New York: Holt, Rinehart and Winston.

5 Why only 'evolution'? Are non-evolutionary changes ruled out, or to be disregarded? And why man as an *animal* and not, for example, as a 'living being'?

6 This is not the place to investigate the reasons for these different terminologies. But it is worth mentioning that the *Concise Oxford Dictionary* – which translates '*ethnos*' anachronistically as 'nation' – identifies 'ethnology' with the (ideologically suspect?) study of human *races*. When it comes to defining 'ethnicity' it takes a different position – letting the cat of its own residual

racism unwittingly out of the bag by suggesting that ethnicity was 'usually' a characteristic of *minority* groups (which can be distinguished by reference to race, language or other factors) – as if majorities have no ethnicity, as if ethnicity was a regrettable Fourth World peculiarity.

7 On the polemics of distinguishing between 'law' and 'custom', see: Moore, S.F. (1978), *Law as Process: An Anthropological Approach*, London: Routledge and Kegan Paul. For a more 'legalistic' approach to the distinction, see: Lloyd, D. (1981), *The Idea of Law*, Harmondsworth: Penguin Books Ltd. (especially Chapter 10).

8 Does an 'anthropologist' who employs 'sociological' methods cease to be an anthropologist – or does he/she do so by developing a new method? Is a new form of madness, for the same reason, sanity – or vice versa?

9 On the western/non-western distinction, in geographic terms, compare Mair, L. (1965), *An Introduction to Social Anthropology*, p.2, New York: Oxford University Press.

10 Refer, here, to Starr and Collier (this volume), Chapter 5, pp. 105–10.

11 See Hart, H.L.A. (1961), *The Concept of Law*, Oxford: Clarendon Press.

12 Refer, here, to Griffiths, J. (1986), 'What is Legal Pluralism?', *Journal of Legal Pluralism*, (24), 24–55.

13 On law/modernity/progress, see: Nisbet, R.A. (1969), *Social Change and History: Aspects of the Western Theory of Development*, New York: Oxford University Press.

14 On 'law and development' issues, see: Burg, E.M. (1977), 'Law and Development: A Review of the Literature and a Critique of "Scholars in Self-Estrangement"', *American Journal of Comparative Law*, **25**, (3), summer, 492–530; Fitzpatrick, P. (1983), 'Law, Plurality and Underdevelopment', in D. Sugarman (ed.), *Legality, Ideology and the State*, pp. 159–83, London: Academic Press.

15 Refer here to the bibliographic entries in Nader (this volume), Chapter 1 and, with particular respect to the 'evolutionary models' issue, to: Chanock, M. (1983), 'Signposts or Tombstones? Reflections on Recent Works on the Anthropology of Law', *Law in Context*, **1**, 107–25.

16 Refer, here, to Greenhouse (this volume), Chapter 13, pp. 319–39.

17 But compare: Keesing, R.M. (1989), 'Creating the Past: Custom and Identity in the Contemporary Pacific', *The Contemporary Pacific*, **1**, (1) and (2), spring and autumn, 19–42.

18 The question of the abolition of 'law' – or, for that matter, of alternatives to 'law' – becomes a non-issue once the plurality of 'law' is accepted. Since 'law', seen in this light, is potentially anything we want it to be, it *has* no alternatives: we are stuck with it. But since it does not exist as such it has, as such, no specificity. The question of legal specificity only arises in connection with actual forms of 'law', and at this level it indeed makes sense to argue whether one form of 'law' should be replaced by another.

19 Refer, here, to: Saltman, M. (1985), '"The Law is an Ass": An Anthropological Appraisal', in J. Overing (ed.), *Reason and Morality*, pp. 226–39, London: Tavistock Publications.

20 Refer, here, to Evans-Pritchard, E.E. (1940), *The Nuer*, Oxford: Clarendon Press.

References

Law and Anthropology

Bentley, G.C. and Westermark, G.D. (1983), 'Law, Anthropology and Mediation' in *Windsor Yearbook of Access to Justice*, pp. 171–2 (Introduction to seven related articles), Ontario Canada: Windsor University.

Black, D. (1981), 'The Relevance of Legal Anthropology', *Contemporary Sociology*, **10**, (1), January, 43–6.

Bohannan P. (ed.) (1967), *Law and Warfare: Studies in the Anthropology of Conflict*, Garden City, NY: The Natural History Press.

Chamblis, W.J. and Seidman, R.B. (1982), *Law, Order and Power*, 2nd ed., Reading, MA: Addison-Wesley Publishing Co.

Diamond, S. (1971), 'The Rule of Law versus the Order of Custom', in R.P. Wolf (ed.), *The Rule of Law*, pp. 115–44, New York: Simon and Schuster.
Epstein, A.L. (1973), 'The Reasonable Man Revisited: Some Problems in the Anthropology of Law', *Law & Society Review*, (7) 4, summer, 643–66.
Fitzpatrick, P. (1985), 'Is it Simple to be a Marxist in Legal Anthropology?', *Modern Law Review*, **48**, (4), July, 472–85.
Gadacz, R. (1987), 'Folk Law and Legal Pluralism: Issues and Directions in the Anthropology of Law in Modernizing Societies', *Legal Studies Journal*, **11**, (2), 125–44.
Hamnett, I. (ed.), (1977), *Social Anthropology and Law*, ASA monograph no. 14, London: Academic Press.
Hoebel, E.A. (1954), *The Law of Primitive Man: A Study in Comparative Legal Dynamics*, Cambridge, MA: Harvard University Press.
Hogbin, H.I. (ed.) (1972), *Law and Order in Polynesia: A Study of Primitive Legal Institutions*, 1934 Report, New York: Cooper Square Publishers, Inc.
Krygier, M. (1980), 'Anthropological Approaches' in E. Kamenka and A.E. Tay (eds), *Law and Social Control*, pp. 27–39, London: Edward Arnold.
Malinowski, B. (1926), *Crime and Custom in Savage Society*, London: Routledge and Kegan Paul.
Merry, S.E. (1984), 'Anthropology and the Study of Alternative Dispute Resolution', *Journal of Legal Education*, **34**, 277–83.
Moore, S.F. (1978), *Law as Process: An Anthropological Approach*, London: Routledge and Kegan Paul.
Nader, L. (ed.) (1969), *Law in Culture and Society*, Chicago: Aldine Publishing Co.
Newman, K.S. (1983), *Law and Economic Organization: A Comparative Study of Preindustrial Societies*, Cambridge: Cambridge University Press.
Pospisil, L. (1971), *Anthropology of Law: A Comparative Theory*, New York: Harper and Row.
Roberts, S. (1979), *Order and Dispute: An Introduction to Legal Anthropology*, New York: St Martin's Press.
Roberts, S. (1981), 'Where Two Worlds Meet: A Time for Reassessment in the Anthropology of Law', *Michigan Law Review*, **79**, March, 737–47.
Rosen, L. (1989), *The Anthropology of Justice: Law as Culture in Islamic Society*, Cambridge: Cambridge University Press.
Starr, J. and Collier, J.F. (eds) (1989), *History and Power in the Study of Law: New Directions in Legal Anthropology*, Ithaca and London: Cornell University Press.

Legal Pluralism

Allott, A. and Woodman, G.R. (eds) (1985), *People's Law and State Law: The Bellagio Papers*, Dordrecht: Foris Publications.
Galanter, M. (1981), 'Justice in Many Rooms: Courts, Private Ordering and Indigenous Law', *Journal of Legal Pluralism*, **19**, 1–47.
Griffiths, J. (1986), 'What is Legal Pluralism?', *Journal of Legal Pluralism*, **24**, 24–55.
Hooker, M.B. (1975), *Legal Pluralism: An Introduction to Colonial and Neo-Colonial Laws*, Oxford: Clarendon Press.
Moore, S.F. (1986), 'Legal Systems of the World: An Introductory Guide to Classifications, Typological Interpretations and Bibliographical Resources', in L. Lipson and S. Wheeler (eds), *Law and the Social Sciences*, pp. 11–62, New York: Russel Sage Foundation.
Morse, B.W. and Woodman, G.R. (eds) (1988), *Indigenous Law and the State*, Dordrecht: Foris Publications.
Sack, P. and Minchin, E. (eds) (1986), *Legal Pluralism*, proceedings of the Canberra Law Workshop VII, Law Department, Research School of Social Sciences, Australian National University, Canberra.

Part I
States of the Art

[1]

Reprinted from AMERICAN ANTHROPOLOGIST, Vol. 67, No. 6, Part 2
December, 1965

The Anthropological Study of Law[1]

LAURA NADER
University of California, Berkeley

INTRODUCTION

IT IS my belief that we are just now on the growing edge of an anthropological understanding of law in its various manifestations. Despite the fact that many of our pioneering ancestors were lawyers by training (Morgan, Maine, Bachofen, McLennen, and more lately Redfield), interest in the anthropology of law has, until recently, had a gradual growth. Between the classic monographs of the nineteenth century (Maine 1861, 1871; and Fustel de Coulanges 1864) and the next milestones in the anthropological study of law (Barton 1919; Gutmann 1926; Malinowski 1926; Hogbin 1934; Schapera 1938) several decades elapsed during which the majority of works on law in preliterate societies were written by colonial administrators, missionaries, and the like rather than by anthropologists (see Nader, Koch, and Cox 1964). Studies of primitive law developed from collections of normative rules ('laws') to observations on the actual application of such rules; in the 1940's, Richardson (1940), Hoebel (1940), and Llewellyn and Hoebel (1941) (whose work provides the only examples of substantial results from joint research by a law professor and an anthropologist to date) began to publish on the 'trouble case.' Since 1954 a series of monographs have been published (Howell 1954, Smith and Roberts 1954, Hoebel 1954, Gluckman 1955a, Bohannan 1957, Pospisil 1958a, Berndt 1962, Gulliver 1963. It was this intellectual productivity which led Bohannan to say: "The literature in legal anthropology is small and almost all good—neither claim can be made for very many other branches of the subject" (1964:199).

For the most part, the studies mentioned above utilized the case method and were essentially descriptive. Furthermore, it must be confessed that the anthropological study of law has not to date affected, in any grand way at least, the theory and methodology of the anthropological discipline, in the way that studies of kinship and language have, for example. Witness in this connection the scant mention of law studies in the volumes of *Anthropology Today*, *Current Anthropology*, and the biennial reviews of Anthropology. Although why this should be so is not the subject matter of this essay, Riesman's analysis (1954) of the anthropological study of law is relevant for those interested in the broader picture of intellectual developments in anthropology.

What follows is, first, a thumbnail sketch of the main themes and questions about law that have concerned anthropologists;[2] second, a description of relevant studies in two related fields—the sociology of law and anthropological conflict studies; and finally, a discussion of present trends and new directions in anthropological studies of law.

MAIN THEMES AND QUESTIONS

Some of the main topics that have characterized anthropological work for well over a century may be noticed in terms of the following questions: Is law universally present in all societies? What are the universal characteristics of law wherever it is found? How is the law related to other aspects of culture and social organization? Is the range of variation limited and patterned so that typologies of law can be constructed and are such typologies of use in understanding the relation of law to other aspects of culture and social organization? How and why does law change through time? What happens when the legal systems of different cultural groups come into contact? What is the effect of a multiplicity of legal systems within one society? How can we describe legal systems? And under what conditions and how is the comparison of legal systems possible?

We may begin our sketch by noting that it was a common belief among eighteenth-century intellectuals interested in the study of man that certain general principles of law (*the* law as Frenchmen or Englishmen knew it) were universal, although differentially reflected in any particular legal system. By the twentieth century a raging debate was under way as to whether all societies had law. This was largely a definitional debate hinging on the question: What is law? If law is defined in terms of procedure as Radcliffe-Brown and his adherents define it, "social control through the systematic application of the (physical) force of politically organized society" (1933:202), then not all societies could be said to have law: for example, the Adamanese, the Yurok, and the Ifugao. If, however, law is defined in the broadest sense as "most processes of social control," as Malinowski is alleged to define it, then all societies may be said to have law. However, at this point one would have to take into account the charge that this use of the term "law" renders it meaningless, or identical with social control. Nor was this debate of theory concerned solely with the domain of "law." The attempt to distinguish between law and custom revealed a further confusion as to what custom was as well (Nadel 1956:161–164; Kantorowicz 1958). Whether law and custom were considered one and the same depended upon whether custom meant culture (in Tylor's sense), customary behavior, or social norms—the "ought" or ideal aspects of culture.

The conflict of opinion on the meaning of law is an old one in sister disciplines. In political theory, for example, one tradition identifies the laws of a society as the minimal rules of conduct acknowledged by the members of that society, whereas the opposing tradition identifies the laws of a society as the formal commands of the governing authority of that society. Thus a theorist of the first tradition, such as Locke, would agree that there is law in primitive societies, and a theorist of the second, such as Hobbes, would argue that there is no law without a state political organization. Interestingly enough, Marxian theory takes a divided stand on this question. Lenin denies that law exists in societies without developed government, and Marx and Engels, having been influenced by the American anthropologist Morgan, admit that law does exist in primitive communities (cf. Moore 1960).

Hart (1961:1–14), a legal scholar, makes the following clarifying statements:

> Few questions concerning human society have been asked with such persistence and answered by serious thinkers in so many diverse, strange, and even paradoxical ways as the question "What is Law?" . . . No vast literature is dedicated to answering the questions "What is chemistry?" or "What is medicine?", as it is to the question "What is law?" . . . No one has thought it illuminating or important to insist that medicine is "what doctors do about illnesses," or "a prediction of what doctors will do," or to declare that what is ordinarily recognized as a characteristic, central part of chemistry, say the study of acids, is not really part of chemistry at all. . . .
>
> "What officials do about disputes is . . . the law itself"; "The prophecies of what the courts will do . . . are what I mean by the law"; "Statutes are sources of Law . . . not parts of the Law itself"; "Constitutional law is positive morality merely"; "One shall not steal; if somebody steals he shall be punished. . . . If at all existent, the first norm is contained in the second norm which is the only genuine norm. . . . Law is the primary norm which stipulates the sanction." These are only a few of many assertions and denials concerning the nature of law. . . .

Hart goes on to say that any educated man might be expected to identify the salient features of a legal system as follows:

> They comprise (i) rules forbidding or enjoining certain types of behaviour under penalty; (ii) rules requiring people to compensate those whom they injure in certain ways; (iii) rules specifying what must be done to make wills, contracts, or other arrangements which confer rights and create obligations; (iv) courts to determine what the rules are and when they have been broken, and to fix the punishment or compensation to be paid; (v) a legislature to make new rules and abolish old ones.

If this is common knowledge says Hart, how is it that the question "What is law?" has persisted?

> Is it because, besides the clear standard cases constituted by the legal systems of modern states, which no one in his senses doubts are legal systems, there exist also doubtful cases, and about their "legal quality" not only educated men but even lawyers hesitate? Primitive law and international law are the foremost of such doubtful cases . . . it is quite obvious why hesitation is felt in these cases. International law lacks a legislature, states cannot be brought before international courts without their prior consent, and there is no centrally organized effective system of sanctions. Certain types of primitive law, including those out of which some contemporary legal systems may have gradually evolved, similarly lack these features, and it is perfectly clear to everyone that it is their deviation in these respects from the standard case which makes their classification appear questionable.

These exceptions or questionable cases cannot, says Hart, account for the "prolonged and somewhat sterile controversy . . . about the general nature of law expressed in the question 'What is law?'," and he goes on to outline the three recurrent issues that have formed a constant focus of argument about the nature of law: "How does law differ from and how is it related to orders backed by threats? How does legal obligation differ from, and how is it related to, moral obligation? What are rules and to what extent is law an affair of rules?" (see also Gluckman 1962).

Anthropologists have contributed indirectly to the definition of law by extending our knowledge of human variation in law ways. Direct attempts to define law, however, have not borne much fruit. Presently our interest has shifted from this philosophical and theoretical question to empirical questions as to universal attributes of law and the multiple legal levels within a society. In each society there may be a multiplicity of legal frameworks corresponding to the multiplicity of groups within that society which may be independent from the other, interdependent, interpenetrating, or all three. This idea was iterated by Durkheim first in 1893 in *The Division of Labor* (1960), and recently elaborated upon by a number of anthropologists (Schneider 1957, Pospisil 1958a, Gulliver 1963, Nader and Metzger 1963, Winans and Edgerton 1964). Anthropologists are no longer attempting to prove the absence or presence of law in primitive societies by reference to any single definition of law. Rather the question has become: How is the law best conceived of for research purposes?

Certainly for cross-cultural purposes, for example, we would have to agree upon an operational definition of law in order to agree upon what is to be compared. Such a working definition might read as follows: All societies have rules governing behavior; some are preferential and others are prescribed by society. In some situations, when a prescribed rule is violated society will have delegated and agreed upon ways of punishing the violator(s). This latter situation falls squarely within the domain of interest of the anthropologist of law. However, the anthropologist could conceivably begin with one of the acts that in our society are handled by legal apparatus, for example homicide or theft. Bohannan (1960) poses the question, Do Africans kill one another for the same reasons and in the same situations as Europeans and Americans? A cross-cultural investigation of homicide or theft might lead us, as it did Bohannan, to an investigation of phenomena that Westerners call law or it might lead us to investigate phenomena that from the point of view of Western society are only peripherally relevant to law.

Although it is not easy to separate the question "what is law" from "what are the universal attributes of law," I would like to mention some research that has been done on the subject of universal characteristics. This subject has been discussed for a long time, and from disparate points of view, by philosophers before there were anthropologists, and more recently by jurists and anthropologists. Certainly Blackstone in his *Commentaries on the Laws of England* (1765) was an example of a legal historian and philosopher in search of the more general aspects of law. Boorstin (1958:12–43) quotes the following statements from Blackstone: "Certain uniformities are inevitable from the nature of society," and

> the universal law of almost every nation . . . has either given the dying person a power of continuing his property, by disposing of his possession by will; or, in case he neglects to dispose of it . . . the municipal law of the country then steps in. . . . The general structure of the courts is nearly everywhere the same—from Mexico to Peru, to that established in the Jewish republic by Moses.

The manner in which Blackstone goes about finding universals is different from the anthropological approach primarily because his basic assumption is that every institution of English law has an analogue in some other legal system. This is principally because he concentrates solely on similarities rather than differences, on development and independent invention rather than on diffusion and the ways in which legal systems affect one another. The results are interesting observations; the attempt admirable in that he touched on some aspects of law, such as inheritance, which may possibly be universal.

I mention Blackstone because he was attempting to ask and answer questions that some present-day anthropologists interested in making empirical generalizations are attempting to ask and answer. Strangely enough, however, little empirical work in the anthropology of law has touched on the question of universals. Some nineteenth-century evolutionists postulated theories of stages of legal development, such as Maine's three stages (law by themistes, customary law, and the code of law) 1861, which are still assumed to express universals by a number of scholars in related disciplines. But since Maine, the treatment of universals in the law remained in the background until Malinowski (1926) and more recently Hoebel (1954), Gluckman (1955a, 1965), and Pospisil (1958a). Their treatments of universals are, however, quite different one from the other, and all differ from Maine. Malinowski, in his introduction to Hogbin's *Law and Order in Polynesia*, refers to law as one of the "derived or instrumental needs" that in all societies "have to be satisfied as urgently as biological requirements if man is to survive" (1934:xxxii). Or, as Malinowski states in *Crime and Custom* "there must be in all societies a class of rules too practical to be backed up by religious sanctions, too burdensome to be left to mere goodwill, too personally vital to individuals to be enforced by any abstract agency. This is the domain of legal rules" (1926:67f). Pospisil (1958 :257–272), by means of cross-cultural research, derived four universal attributes of law: authority, obligation, intention of universal application, and sanction. Hoebel, taking a different route, gets into the question of universals by means of an assumption: that certain legal relations are present universally and thus may be used as categories in cross-cultural comparisons. "The essential and fundamental legal concepts have been reduced to simplicity, precision and universality in the system advanced by . . . Hohfield." He was referring to four reciprocal relationships that Hohfield claimed for all legal relations, i.e., demand-right-duty, privilege-right-no-demand-right, power-liability, immunity-no-power (Hoebel 1954:46–63).

Gluckman (1955a) addresses himself to the question, to what extent are the features of the judicial process and legal reasoning invariant throughout the cultures of the world? He attacks the question by an analysis of the "reasonable man" concept, and the certainty-uncertainty attribute of legal concepts. Nadel, only one of many reviewers (March 1956, Hoebel 1961, Ayoub 1961, and others) of the "reasonable man" concept, thinks that such a principle as reasonableness is so basic as to be taken for granted: " . . . inasmuch as reasonable conduct equals customary conduct it seems clear that any legal system, being after all meant to maintain the existing mores, must of necessity imply the criterion of reasonableness . . . " (1956a:166). But then again Nadel qualifies his statement by pointing to the possibility that the principle of reason may be applied only in certain contexts:

> Since the courts whose activities he [Gluckman] describes do not deal with grave crimes and accusations, e.g. of homicide, assault, or witchcraft, we learn nothing about the judicial process appropriate to problems in the case of which reasonableness must prove a very inadequate if not altogether meaningless standard. If I am right, the Lozi would, in these situations, discard their guiding fiction of "reasonable man" for the sharper dichotomy of things simply lawful and unlawful, permitted and forbidden (1956a:167).

Hoebel has mentioned a few general or universal characteristics of substantive law, some of which are deserving of cross-cultural testing.

> Homicide within the society is, under one set of conditions or another, legally prohibited everywhere. . . . Virtually every society assumes the relative social inferiority of women. . . . Thus it appears to be universal on the primitive level (and general on the civilized level) that the husband may kill the adulterous wife caught in flagrante delicto. For the wife to enjoy such a privilege-right is most rare. . . . Law universally supports the principle of relative exclusiveness of marital rights.
>
> Adultery seems always to be punishable under the law, although just what constitutes adultery will be variable as marriage and kinship forms vary. . . . All legal systems, primitive and civilized, assume the importance of the kinship group, and all support it as a medium of inheritance of property rights. . . . All legal systems give cognizance to the existence of rights to private property in some goods; but among primitives land is legally treated as belonging directly or ultimately to the tribe or the kinship group; it is rarely sustained legally as an object of private property (1954:286–287).

The universality of Sir Henry Maine's generalization, "The movement of the progressive societies has hitherto been a movement from status to contract —gradual dissolution of family dependency and growth of individual obligation in its place" (1861:165), which was so quickly accepted in the nineteenth century, has not been directly challenged by anthropologists. Maine's work has been evaluated by Redfield (1950) and has been expanded upon by Gluckman (1959, 1965). Apropos of Maine, V. C. Uchendu has sought to investigate the universal elements in contracts made in nonliterate societies in order to "gain methodological emancipation from the overworked idea that all institutions of nonliterate societies are subsumed in the nest of kinship" (1964:93).

Other generalizations about the universal evolution of legal systems, such as Durkheim's postulate of the progressive substitution of restitutive law for repressive law from primitive to civilized societies, given today's body of ethnographic information, would not stand the cross-cultural test. This postulate might prove useful in other than an evolutionary context, as Metzger illustrated when he noted an interesting pattern in a Mexican village: property cases end in restitutive sanctions whereas in personas cases there is a choice of restitution or penalty sanctions. He concludes: "These findings suggest a basic difference between people and goods in this culture: goods are replaceable, and their values can be assessed and repaid in money or in kind; people are unique" (1960:43). Mead (1961) suggested that the discovery of a set of universals in law might effectively streamline the creation of new legal systems. Most of the universal characteristics referred to above could be described as empirical generalizations. Apart from Malinowski's contribution there has been little work directed towards explaining these generalizations.

The idea that there are as many frameworks of law as there are types of groups has a long history. It was Aristotle who spoke of monarchic, aristocratic, tyrannic, oligarchic, and democratic law. He also discussed the law of the conjugal and domestic family, the laws of villages or associations of families, of cities, of fraternal organizations, the law of the political group—the State. And there were other European scholars who, in the seventeenth and eighteenth centuries, continued to construct jural typologies, adding groups important to their time: insurance societies, guilds, convents, and so forth, and observing the conflict of these laws. As I have already mentioned, Durkheim (1893) was also interested in typology based on the kind of sanction (repressive or restitutive) that prevailed in a particular type of society (organic or mechanical), whereas Maine in his discussion of tort and crime, for example, described the law in kin organized versus territorially organized society in the context of the progression from status to contract. The only anthropologist in recent times to attempt anything like a typology in law is E. A. Hoebel (1954) and although his aim is to work out the jural postulates of societies from substantive cases, a typology of procedures used in law settlement is also achieved.

Functionalism as a descriptive approach characterized many of the nineteenth-century works, as did the comparative historical approach. Maine's central interest in comparing Roman and modern Western law with the law of India and Eastern Europe was to link changes in social affiliation with changes in the law (1861). Fustel de Coulange's *La Citê Antique* (1864) is a classic functionalist study of the interrelations between religion and Greek and Roman law. Bachofen in *Das Mutterecht* (1861) investigated the legal status of women in various societies, and McLennen in *Primitive Marriage* (1865) showed that rules of exogamy were widely prevalent in human societies. Frazer in *The Golden Bough* (1890) explored the relations between magic, religion, and the origins of the law. Durkheim, in the French intellectual tradition influenced by Montesquieu's *The Spirit of Laws* (1748), was inspired to speculate on questions involving the relation between density of population and the forms of legal systems available to a group; in *The Division of Labor* (1893) he postulated that densely populated societies correlate with restitutive law, and less densely populated ones with repressive law. Mauss and Beuchat (1906) conclude that among the Eskimos winter law was connected with concentrated settlements and collectivist tendencies, whereas summer law, regulating the life of small, scattered families, had a more secular character favorable to individualism. Jane Richardson (1940) in her study of the Kiowa Apache also makes note of the seasonal variations affecting the law.

There are a few works on the interrelation of law and economics, among them Marx's works (1906, 1948) describing the determining effects of economics on the law, Weber's (1954) emphasis on the reciprocal influence between law and economics, and Hobhouse, Wheeler, and Ginsburg's (1915) cross-cultural attempt to find correlations between the level of economy and the types of law. Hoebel (1954) attempts to relate the degree of complexity in procedural law with different levels of subsistence. Nader (1965a) contrasts two societies on the same level of peasant subsistence and finds that social organization is more determining than economy. Rothenberger, concerned with but two aspects of a legal system, the substantive and the procedural, states that: "The procedure, including the judicial process, was seen to be correlated with and indeed a part of the political or governmental organization of a society. The substantive law, on the other hand, is determined by and correlated with the social and economic aspects of the society" (1963:28).

The most obvious interdependence between law and other aspects of society is that between law and politics. Indeed many students of politics assume that judicial behavior is a part of political behavior. It is not surprising then that most studies of political organization include a mention or a description of judicial organization and vice versa. One of the most elegant field studies on the interrelation between law and politics is that of Nadel (1947); for other contributions on this subject see Hoebel (1940), Kaberry (1941, 1942), Busia (1951), Schneider (1957), Burridge (1957), S. F. Moore (1958), Barnes (1961), Gluckman (1965:27–74), and Nicholas and Mukhopadhyay (n.d.).

The degree to which modern anthropological studies of law insist that "the law cannot be understood apart from its social and cultural context" depends upon our descriptive methodologies. I stated at the outset that recent contributions in the anthropological study of law were primarily descriptive. Now I raise the question, To what extent have we been consciously concerned with the methodology of description? Two major contributors to the methodology of describing particular legal systems are Llewellyn and Hoebel (1941), and Bohannan (1957). I view the contributions of Llewellyn and Hoebel and of Bohannan as being constructive in the following ways: Llewellyn and Hoebel's formulation of the law jobs and in particular their use and explication of the trouble-case method came as a fresh approach. Their very use of the term law jobs, rather than the law or legal systems, precluded endless fruitless criticism about what indeed a definition of law or the domain of law should include. The use of cases was not unique to Llewellyn and Hoebel (Barton in 1919 and Richardson in 1940 had used case materials extensively), but they served to remind anthropologists why, in fact, cases are collected and to illustrate clearly one extensive use that can be made of case materials. In their own words:

> The case of trouble, again, is the case of doubt, or is that in which discipline has failed, or is that in which unruly personality is breaking through into new paths of action or of leadership, or is that in which an ancient institution is being tried against emergent forces. It is the case of trouble which makes, breaks, twists, or flatly establishes a rule, an institution, an authority. Not all such cases do so. There are also petty rows, the routine of law-stuff which exists among primitives as well as among moderns. For all that, if there be a portion of a society's life in which tensions of the culture come to expression, in which the play of variant urges can be felt and seen, in which emergent power—patterns, ancient security-drives, religion, politics, personality, and cross-purposed views of justice tangle in the open, that portion of the life will concentrate in the case of trouble or disturbance. Not only the making of new law and the effect of old, but the hold and the thrust of all other vital aspects of the culture, shine clear in the crucible of conflict.
>
> The trouble-cases, sought out and examined with care, are thus the safest main road into the discovery of law. Their data are most certain. Their yield is richest. They are the most revealing (Llewellyn and Hoebel 1941:21).

Llewellyn and Hoebel, then, see society and culture in the law; they discover the law in trouble cases, but they are not seeking to relate patterns of law with any other aspect of society.

Bohannan's contribution to methodology of description lies in his formulation of the folk versus the analytical system—while not "new," an argument that strikes at the very core of the translation and meaning problem in anthropology. He raises for inspection statements made by Hoebel (1954:46) and more recently by Gluckman (1962) that encourage anthropologists to discuss tribal law using the principal concepts of Western jurisprudence. Gluckman states, "The very refinement of English jurisprudence makes it a better instrument for analysis . . . than are the languages of tribal law" (1962:14). Bohannan (1957), on the contrary, contends that to describe and analyze the system of justice and judgment of one culture through the interpretation of a system indigenous to a second society can only lead to confusion and distortion. He implicitly charges Gluckman with having converted the Western legal folk system into an analytical sytem and with having forced the Lozi folk concepts into a Western model. He presents a variety of instances illustrating for example how the Tiv concept of "correction" when translated to "sanction" may misconstrue what final action does actually involve for the Tiv. Ayoub (1961), Gluckman (1962), and Hoebel (1961) discuss the problems inherent in Bohannan's approach. Nadel (1956) and Ayoub (1961) discuss the perplexing questions inherent in Gluckman's assumptions, as does the whole body of literature in ethnoscience. See in this volume the paper by Black and Metzger. The answer probably lies solely neither with Gluckman nor Bohannan, for how an ethnographer goes about laying bare or describing his society is intimately related to what use he believes can be made of such a description. This brings us to the question of comparison. Bohannan's intention is to discover and portray the Tiv view of justice and judgment. He shirks the problems that such a relativistic approach implies for comparison, but then he was not interested in comparison at the time. Gluckman's work has been characterized as analogous to that of a linguist who attempts comparison by jamming Barotse grammar into Roman Dutch categories.

Gluckman's (1962) is the only major attempt of late to discuss the obstacles deterring comparison in the anthropology of law, and in the process he makes a number of very basic suggestions.

> . . . when the anthropologist has set out as clearly as he can the classifications of the tribe he is studying, he has merely taken the first step. We have thereafter to relate these classifications to the types of social relations which characterize this tribe, and this inevitably involves comparative analysis, with translation of concepts from one culture to another (p. 9).

In his paper, he explores three areas of inquiry which are specifically relevant here:

> 1) why a particular people have the ideas about law, government, enforcement, debt, contract and agreement, injury and wrong, which they do have; 2) the study of judicial process and the enforcement of law; and 3) the problems involved in the study of social control, and the nature of obligatory rules, in particular domains of relationship (p. 11).

His intentions may be made quite clear by his own statements:

> This [the process of adjudication] is the process by which, in African tribes with courts, judges take and assess the evidence, examine what they regard as the facts, and come to a decision in favour of one party rather than another. Epstein and I have tried to analyze this situation by comparing it with the models of the judicial process erected by jurists in Europe and America. We considered that this comparison enabled us to relate similarities and differences in the processes of trial in these varied societies *so as to bring out how judicial aims and reasoning were related to other elements in social life* (p. 3). (Emphasis supplied.)

Gluckman is interested in testing the implications of certain observations; e.g.,

> . . . most African cases involve disputes between closely related persons, involved in a close-knit network of relations, whereas most English cases involve persons who are strangers to one another outside of a single linking relationship (pp. 5–6),

and of certain hypotheses:

> . . . how does the existence of enforcing mechanisms influence the process of judicial reasoning? A priori, we should expect that where a judge is backed by powers of enforcement, he may feel that he can shorten the process of listening to the evidence and coming to a decision, while the judge who is not thus supported, may be more patient (p. 6).

Or:

> But procedures of enforcement where there are no courts differ radically from enforcement through courts, even if both types of process are associated with what may be called the political organization (p. 7).

Furthermore he specifies the kind of data and the specializing words that we need:

> . . . I suggest here that if we distinguish the champion-at-law, the intermediary, the negotiator, the mediator, the conciliator, and the arbitrator, in augmenting authoritativeness. we would clarify our problems by focusing attention on the ranges of social pressure which back their actions. Secondly, we would make clear how far they call for evidence and cross-examine. . . . Thirdly, and most importantly, we would examine in which several ranges of relationships between parties the different procedures are effective, or ineffective, both within single societies and comparatively (p. 6).

Comparison through time and space is at least implicit and some times explicit in the works mentioned thus far. But as has been noted by Leach (1961:1) and others, most recent anthropological works are descriptive rather than comparative. This certainly applies to the law monographs of the 1950's which have been heavily slanted towards studies of individual societies. There are comparative data buried in chapters of monographs such as those by Nadel (1947), Colson (1958), and Nader (1964b). There are, furthermore, several relevant articles that are comparative: Schneider (1957), Harper (1957), Gluckman (1962), Hazard (1962), Nader and Metzger (1963), Schwartz and Miller (1964), Nader (1965a), Nicholas and Mukhopadhyay (n.d.). Curiously, the only recent cross-cultural law studies are not written by anthropologists but rather by scholars in other disciplines—a political scientist (Nagel 1962), sociologists (Schwartz and Miller 1964), and psychologists (Bacon, Child, and Barry 1963). The papers in this volume by Whiting and Roberts are firsts in this respect. (It is interesting in this context to note Nagel's comment: "Comparative law, like comparative government in general, has largely confined itself to unintegrated descriptions of European legal principles" [1962:147].) The outstanding work in twentieth-century comparison, resembling in its manner of parallel presentation *African Political Systems*, is, of course, E. A. Hoebel's *The Law of Primitive Man* (1954).

There is only one outstanding within-society comparison. Gulliver's work (1963) is an extraordinary contribution to the study of law in the total context of adult social control systems because little attention has been paid to comparisons of the structure and functions of various social control patterns within a society. Indeed, this was one of Malinowski's most vehement criticisms of jurisprudential studies. " . . . If anthropology can influence jurisprudence to the extent of making it recognize the positive side of law and also acknowledge that law is only part and parcel of a wider system of norms, this will be of some benefit to all social science" (1934:xvii). Needless to say, Schapera is quite correct in chastising Malinowski for this statement since many prominent jurists such as Ehrlich, Pound, and Vinogradoff are quite aware that laws take their place among other rules of conduct. To be aware, however, is not necessarily to be influenced, and the work of men such as the aforementioned does not *concentrate* on an ethnographic description of law in the context of these other systems of social control. But neither perhaps should we expect this of a scholar in jurisprudence. It is interesting to note that legal scholars interested in experimental jurisprudence have found it wise to consider the law in the broader context. When anthropologists have concerned themselves with such questions (Whiting 1950; Colson 1953; Gulliver 1963), they are usually dealing with societies where there are "no obvious political institutions concerned in the maintenance or order" (Colson 1953:199).

The study of change and the law has been pursued in terms of the evolution or development of a particular system, in terms of the differences in growth between the ideal and real aspects of law and their relative rates of change, and, more recently, in terms of the contact between legal systems; such a study may also examine the change of law due to internal rather than external or acculturative influences; and such change may be directional, cyclical, or repetitive. The evolutionary approach is best illustrated by Maine's works (1861, 1871), although Barton (1919, 1930, 1949) attempted to analyze Ifugao and Kalinga materials in terms of an evolutionary system such as postulated by Maine. Hoebel (1954) implies an evolutionary development in his societies that illustrates varying levels of economic complexity.

At present, most legal anthropologists are working in societies with little or no written history. The interest in change over long periods of time has been largely replaced by studies of short-time change and by a study of change resulting from culture contact situations. Since the turn of the century, studies of the change resulting from culture contact have been carried out principally by administrators or legal specialists. Two modern examples are Allott (1960, 1961) and Howell (1954). Keuning (1963) presents an interesting view of the problems faced by administrative legal specialists. Some of the noteworthy anthropological studies in this field were made by Nadel (1942, 1947), Stirling (1957), Cohn (1959), Barnes (1961), Fallers (1962).

There is a striking difference between the goals of anthropologists and nonanthropologists in this area. Anthropologists are interested in what is happening, in describing a changing situation in order to understand the implications that follow from change. They are not (with the exception of Fallers 1956 and Kaplan 1965) directly concerned with the practical problems confronting new nations; that is, they are not seeking "to arrive at one truly national law" (Keuning, 1963:3). The administrative legal specialist is principally concerned with policy questions, which *ipso facto* seems to mean that they do not carry out depth studies. Allott succinctly distinguishes the concerns of anthropologists from administrators as follows:

> The anthropologist seeks to show the social purpose of customary rules, and how they fit into the structure of behaviour. The aim of legal research is narrow, to record those rules of custom or usage which are either enforced in the courts, or are of a kind which the courts would enforce. Appreciation of the part which these rules play in the social structure is therefore irrelevant, or at most only needed as background-knowledge, or for the better elucidation of the meaning of these rules (1953:172).

The above-quoted opinion is extremely narrow in its conception of the study of law and certainly does not reflect the opinion of some of the great legal researchers of our time such as Pound and Frank. Certainly the anthropologist has not developed his methodology to the point where nonanthropologists could acquire depth materials in a relatively short time.

Apart from the acculturation studies that we have mentioned above, short-term studies of change within a society are few. One such study of legislation in preliterate societies is that by Pospisil (1958b), in which he records how a marriage "rule" was deliberately altered by a single individual. Pospisil's interpretation of where change begins, however, is challenged by Leach (1959) who suggests that Pospisil was merely describing the phenomenon of fission in a segmentary society. In an earlier work Schapera (1943) notes examples of legislation by chiefs in council but as Gluckman (1965b) has noted, such materials are rare. Rheinstein (1963:241–243) comments on the order of change in Africa in the light of similar occurrences in the history of European law:

> With respect to both institutions of customary law, status of women and land tenure, changes of the law are needed, but in the former field the task will be primarily that of following social change, in the latter that of rendering the social change possible [e.g. through legislation]. . . . The courts of customary law have more and more to deal with problems for which certainty and predictability of judicial decisions become important. Such predictability is essential to all those topics that belong to the modern market and credit economy, that is, especially, the fields of contract and property.

Anderson (1957) describes the mechanisms used for changing Moslem law—"a divine law which as such is essentially immutable." Change has been achieved in part by putting Islamic law to one side, such as in reference to penal and commercial law, or by means of a series of ingenious expedients with reference to the law of personal status and family relations. One example of such ingenuity is described in this volume by Hoebel. Nader (n.d.) attempts to correlate change in Zapotec legal procedure with concomitant change in the forms of social grouping, the style of architecture, and a system of intervillage competition patterns. Nicholas and Mukhopadhyay (n.d.) describe change in village politics as affecting the character of traditional judicial decision making.

THE SOCIOLOGY OF LAW AND ANTHROPOLOGICAL CONFLICT STUDIES

The list of authorities I have thus far alluded to in this paper is parochial in the omission of great minds that have surely influenced, and in turn have been influenced by, anthropologists. Such are the pitfalls of a thumbnail sketch. Among these omissions are Pound, to be remembered for his contributions to the analysis of the legal *system;* Brandeis, to be recalled in connection with his analysis of legal change arising in response to modern technology; and Oliver Wendell Holmes, a comparative ethnographer of law par excellence. Although these men influenced anthropologists, there has never developed a tradition of joint research between law professors and anthropologists in this country.

There is also little joint research (and few spheres of mutual influence) between sociologists and anthropologists. Some of what is being done and what has been done by sociologists should be of central interest to anthropologists, especially those working in societies where social stratification is a factor to be considered. For as Skolnick (1965)[3] has noted, stratification is a theme which runs through much of the sociological studies—for example, the jury studies (Strodtbeck 1962), investigations of the legal profession (Carlin 1963), patterns of selective administration of justice (Carlin 1963, O'Gorman 1963, Smiegl 1964, Carlin and Howard 1965), and the general question of justice in mass society. (For an intelligent analysis of arbitration in mass society see Jones 1964.) Furthermore, in their studies of jurimetrics, sociologists, political scientists, and lawyers have again raised the question of the judge's role in society, the question being, What is the basis of judicial decision making? Certainly this is an area of interest to anthropologists and most would do well to examine Schubert's *Quantitative Analysis of Judicial Behavior* (1959) (especially sections on how the political process of recruitment affects judicial decision making) as well as his excellent review of the literature (Schubert 1963). But it still remains true that anthropologists for the most part have had little to do with sociological studies of law.

Riesman (1954:444) comments on some possible reasons:

> Sociologists . . . have until quite recently been as much concerned with immediate social reform as their brethren of the bar; thus, they have looked at the law only where it impinged on the disadvantaged groups in society—on the criminal, the juvenile delinquent, the poverty-stricken seeker of divorce, etc. . . . they view the law as unjust as well as irrational; their aim is to show up, perhaps to change, the law and the legal mentality rather than to understand it sympathetically. Furthermore, the sociologists who are theoretically inclined have concerned themselves with formal definitions of law . . . and with the problem of the origins of law—both perfectly valid enterprises but not good ways to bring the sociologist into actual contact with the legal profession as a going concern.

One need only scan the table of contents of a text such as Evan (1962) to realize that there are differences in approach and interest. Most obvious is the fact that we deal with different units. The sociologist deals with the prison, the court, the D.A.'s office, the administrative agency; the anthropologist's unit is usually a settlement, that is, the village, ward, town, city, and the like. Furthermore, Skolnick (1965) states, "Virtually all empirical studies directly in the sociology of law in America—that is, work by professional sociologists that is not mainly criminological—began later than 1950."

Sociologists, then, do not have a long tradition of empirical field work; they are policy oriented. Anthropologists, on the contrary, have thus far not shared the applied and policy orientation of the sociologists; they have been oriented, implicitly at least, by a cross-cultural or comparative perspective. Such works as Tappan (1947) on the juvenile court is aimed at suggesting reforms in juvenile legislation and administration, or in delinquency rehabilitation; Carlin and Howard (1965) are interested in revealing selective enforcement patterns of a court system supposed to be egalitarian; others are interested in the social consequences of various types of criminal law labels. Regardless of whether he is interested in applied aims (or law for that matter), the anthropologist will nevertheless be interested in some of the sociologists' findings, such as the general suggestion, for example, that an accusation is virtually as stigmatic as an acquittal on a criminal charge of assault, revealed by the observation that various types of criminal law labels (accused, acquitted, certified innocent) all affect a job applicant's ability to get menial work.

If the anthropologist turns his attention to the American law scene there will be many more meeting grounds in the future. Apropos of this as yet unexplored possibility is an article by a practicing lawyer John Simonett (1963) "The Common Law of Morrison County." His introductory paragraphs should encourage anthropologists.

> "There are three great branches of the law," the Senior member of the Bar told me when I just arrived at the county seat. . . . "First, there is the statutory law, the law enacted by the legislature, found in the codes and statute books; second, there is the common law, the law handed down in court decisions since before the days of Coke and found in the reported court cases; and finally, and most important, there is the common law of Morrison County."
>
> . . . Never a day passes but new volumes appear off the presses, but all of them deal with the first two great branches of the law, never the third.

Anthropologists interested in law would also do well to scan the conflict literature, for much in the coverage of such studies is relevant: Beals (1964), Colson (1953), Gluckman (1955b), Jayawardena (1963), Lewis (1958), Siegel and Beals (1960), Simmel (1956), Turner (1957), to mention only a few. Especially relevant are the descriptions of trouble cases before they are found in a recognized court or tribunal (cf. Turner 1957 and Beals 1964). Such descriptions are important if we are to enhance our understanding of the origin of breaches of norms and the reaction of society to breaches of its rules; such "social dramas" are important as well for an understanding of the function of conflict as a product of culture change, a source of culture change, or as an aspect of a stable social system. Such data would help us to evaluate the role and function of formal agencies such as the courts; they would help us to know what the range of conflict-indicating patterns are—for undoubtedly it would be a much broader range than is ever found adjudicated by formal institutional arrangements. Finally the literature on conflict resolution should be of obvious interest to scholars concerned with processes of adjudication. I merely draw attention to the mutual lack of interest of those who study something called "conflict resolution" and those who study "legal procedure" or "judicial process." Indeed in the presentation of Cohn's paper (in this volume) it was interesting to note that when the author spoke of village councils he spoke of law and legal procedure; where he spoke of the absence of village panchayats he talked of conflict and conflict resolution. The similarity of interests of 'conflicts people' and 'law people' is often unappreciated by both.

PRESENT TRENDS AND NEW DIRECTIONS

During the past two decades the major contributions to the ethnography of law have been descriptive, functional analyses of systems both isolated and in contact situations. The tendency has been to treat the legal system as an institution virtually independent and isolated from other institutions in society, except insofar as 'society' is gleaned from the law materials. This last tendency is especially evident where courts are present, less so where the lack of court institutions virtually forces the anthropologist to elicit the whole life history of the case. Furthermore, we have not been interested in historical developments although the history of our civilization is rich in data (cf. Rheinstein 1963 and H. Kay in this volume). Nor have we pursued to any great extent the examination of hypotheses—either in the manner which Evans-Pritchard (1963) refers to as illustrative (the citing of examples in support of a thesis arrived at deductively), or by cross-cultural statistical studies, or by means of intensive controlled comparison. Our work for the most part has not been comparative.

If we are to develop a true ethnography of law the angle of vision of the ethnographer needs to be broadened in order to include descriptions that would explicate law as part of a many-threaded fabric. Furthermore we should look at both the latent and the manifest functions of the law. We need to understand what the generally agreed upon functions of the law are, as well as to note its other functions which may or may not be recognized in a society. Malinowski observed years ago, "An ethnographer who sets out to study only religion, or only technology, or only social organization cuts out an artificial field for inquiry, and he will be seriously handicapped in his work" (1922:11). A legal system reflects many facets of a society; because of this an ethnographic study of law is more than a study of judicial institutions. Law and politics are sometimes discussed together in anthropology—what about other aspects of social life that may be relevant to the "law," such an economics, language, ecology, or stratification and rank systems?

As a working frame I would like to reiterate what others have said before—namely that (1) empirical studies of law should be set in the general context of social control (although of course not equated with social control); (2) we should consider the possibility that the range of functions of a legal system may vary cross-culturally; and (3) we should aim at both empirical and explanatory generalizations.

It has often been stated that legal systems constitute only a part of a larger system of social control, and that sometimes the social control functions of law can be understood only when viewed as part of the larger system. Schneider (1957) provides us with one example of the way in which the legal and supernatural systems complement each other in the differential handling of fratricide and patricide on Yap. Nader and Metzger (1963) describe the procedures for handling husband-wife conflict in the court and family systems of two Mexican villages where an important variable is the amount of authority allocated to the court and kinship groups. However, in most of the recent monographs, Gulliver (1963) being a major exception, the law has been treated as isolated from other social control systems, and indeed in some monographs it has been left for the reader to place the law in its socio-cultural context. This is a criticism that Malinowski (1942:1253) leveled at Llewellyn and Hoebel as authors of *The Cheyenne Way*. It is also a criticism that can legitimately be made of most of the law monographs produced since *The Cheyenne Way*.

Furthermore it is not always clear whether the social control functions of law are to "clean up social messes" (Llewellyn and Hoebel 1941), or to maintain order (Malinowski 1942), although how the law handles the breach is usually clearer than how in fact it serves to maintain order. Law may settle conflicts by a variety of means (adjudication, mediation, arbitration, etc.); it may perform solely a punitive function; it may prevent or deter breaches of the law; it may maintain order in the fields of law, politics, and economics—or it may accomplish *all* these tasks. It is not always clear which of these functions the law in a particular society is intent upon performing. Our elaboration of these tasks is not always as precise as we would wish if we are to use ethnographic data for comparative ends, or even if we are to explore the relations between means and ends. In this context I would like to call attention to Aubert's example (1963:19) of the function of legislative formulations. In his discussion of the Norwegian housemaid law he noted that "the language of the law is shaped more profoundly by the function of solving conflicts than by the function of influencing the legally naive"; that is, it was directed at the legal professional rather than at informing the lay citizen of what the law was.

While we have assumed that there was a probable cross-cultural difference in the content and form of a legal system, we have at the same time ignored the variety of different functions a legal system may have. This is in spite of the fact that Riesman (1954:445) credits anthropologists with thinking otherwise:

> The anthropologist is not likely to harbor the naive assumption that the law, or any other institution, serves only a single function—say, that of social control—and that any other functions which in fact it serves are excrescences or "contradictions." The concept of ambivalence is part of his equipment; he tends to search for latent functions, transcending the ostensible.

The truth of the matter is, however, that (anecdotal exceptions to one side) the functions of law have generally been assumed to be universally the same,[4] and this is as true of anthropologists as of other social scientists. Aubert (1963:17) states the essence of these functions: "Law seems to have two distinct although interrelated functions: to create conformity with norms, and to settle conflicts."

The oral tradition of the practicing American bar is full of examples which lead us to believe that the law performs many other functions. Every lawyer and perhaps most citizens could cite examples: A businessman may bring a competitor to court with the express purpose of ruining his credit rating. During political campaigns opposing candidates have accused one another of innumerable legal wrongs, usually ending with the filing of a lawsuit for libel, with the object of winning elections. Wives may demand or even initiate divorce actions with little intention of actually obtaining a divorce but rather to frighten the husbands into behavior more acceptable to them. Or an ex-husband may request a change of child custody to harass an ex-wife. Similarly arbitrary enforcement of vagrancy laws or Sunday "blue laws" provides an avenue by which "the law" may harass a less than ideal citizen. Selective application of obscenity laws may perform the function of witchcraft hunts in other societies.

Riesman (1954:448–449) brings two interesting novels to our attention: James West's *Plainville U.S.A.* and James Gould Cozzens' *The Just and the Unjust.* These novels provide examples of the trial as both a cohesive and devisive force in small towns, as in West's case of the garagekeeper and the undertaker—a trial that caused a factional split in town. Or, Riesman states, the trial may serve as a divisive point "in terms of a moral turning point, such as . . . the Western world experienced in the trial of Sacco and Vanzetti." A familiar example of the political function of judgeships is also quoted by Riesman (1954:442): "In the big cities . . . judgeships become part of the system of ethnic brokerage by which the party machines keep the urban peace—the rise of the Italian judge is a recent illustration." Riesman also comments on the entertainment value of the law as well as its socialization functions.

Thurmond Arnold (1935) adumbrates some of the latent functions of the law. He comments on the drama of the court as partly a socialization or enculturation agency—a place where values are tested, changed, or consolidated, and further notes that these may be "legal" values or other such as religious values. (Cf. Hoebel's paper in this volume as an example.) His observations on the ritual value of the trial should be of interest to anthropologists.

Ethnographic examples from other societies are not easy to locate in the literature although they are probably well known to most fieldworkers. In this volume Cohn states:

> The use of the courts for settlement of local disputes seems in most villages to be almost a minor one. In Senapur, courts were, and are, used as an arena in the competition for social status, political and economic dominance in the village. Cases are brought to court to harass one's opponents, as a punishment, as a form of land speculation and profit making, to satisfy insulted pride, and to maintain local political dominance over one's followers. The litigants do not expect a settlement that will end the dispute to eventuate from recourse to the state courts.

And as Cohn notes these were 'functions' of the court that the British failed to understand; the British system was in many ways at odds with traditional Indian procedures.

Beals (1955:91) reports: "After 1920, a number of individuals in Namhali used the [urban] law courts to acquire land or to bring about the economic ruin of their enemies." The law may function to bring about a more equitable distribution of resources or alternatively it may function to maintain an unequal distribution of power. Berreman (1963:270) gives an example of a typically false legal charge.

> A villager's prosperity was envied by his caste-fellows. They had once tried unsuccessfully to get some of his land by bribing the government records officer to testify that he had acquired the land illegally. Failing in this, they obtained revenge by hiding liquor in his house and calling the police to say that he was dealing in illicit liquor.

Along these same lines Bailey (1958:106) mentions various measures taken by the village (i.e. the high castes) to insure that the village servants (i.e. the low castes) do not become too rich:

> This particularly applies to the washerman since his eldest son has been working. He has been fined 2 or 3 times for letting his buffaloes stray into other men's gardens, and the fine has been demanded in cash while other offenders are penalized only by admonition or a demand for a small amount of paddy in compensation.
>
> When a village servant shows signs of getting a lot of money, the village seems to resent this and penalizes him. In the dispute that follows, the victory goes always to the village, since the specialist castes are not organized to protect their members against these attacks.

Different sorts of models are brought to our attention by others. In discussing the therapeutic function of Kpelle moots, Gibbs (1963:6) notes: "Moot procedures are therapeutic in that, like psychotherapy, they re-educate the parties through a type of social learning brought about in a specifically structured interpersonal setting." Gluckman (1955a) illustrates the potential socializing effects of the judicial process. Armstrong (1954) considers the case of a Nigerian inquest into the death of a prominent politician. The inquest is shown to serve various functions in Senne Province: it enforces respect for the elders forming the council of the conclave, allows leaders to enhance their social position, serves to place the blame for the death, repair relationships among the living, excite public spectacle, and so on.

Nader (n.d.) illustrates the use of Zapotec courts to increase the revenue of the town treasury.

> The court sees itself as an institution which protects community interests at all times and places. Therefore they reason, the court may readily look for redress in situations where a party has not complained. . . . There are also practical considerations which have modeled this court initiative, for in Talea laws governing personal behavior are being redefined with economic gain in mind. During one of my field stays when the Talean treasury needed replenishing for the big fiesta of the year, the president ruled that any individual *echando un grito* would be fined five pesos for each grito. Earlier in this century when the new municipio was still being built the presidente would send a *regidor* out on market day with money especially destined to get visiting Rinconeros drunk. The court would then jail them for drunkenness and the following day would fine them a day or two labor on the municipal building. Although Talean citizens easily discuss the economic motives of the court, the court officials insist that new laws are being created to impress the neighboring towns, as well as the citizens of Talea, with peace and orderliness.

That law courts should be used for purposes other than the maintenance of peace and order is not unique with the Talean Zapotec. Throughout the development of the British common law, the King's court was well known for defining property laws with economic gain in mind.

Colson's materials however, illustrate another way in which the law may be used for economic gain:

> They [court councillors] claim that if a man brings his wife to court a third time on an adultery charge they will refuse to grant damages and will instead inform the husband that his only recourse is to divorce his wife and get back his bridewealth, that the woman is now making a business of adultery and is a professional woman of the road [1958:170].
>
> Fathers refuse to listen to a suitor until after an elopement, for they realize that they can then collect both elopement damages and bride-wealth. They also disregard the legal limitations on elopement damages, and their demands for damages have steadily increased. The lover, if he wishes, can take the matter to court and refuse to pay more than the legal amount. If he does this, the girl's father will refuse to listen to his suit. He will then have to elope with another girl, and again pay elopement damages before he can hope to pay bridewealth and receive his bride [1960:112].

In terms of conflict theory the function of the breach varies. Disputes may serve to solidify groups or individuals in a society (Beidelman 1959:66, Nader 1965b); they may prevent the formation of political factions (Glasse 1959), or serve to intensify disharmony and cause the development of new factions (Lewis 1958:148, Beidelman 1959:66).

And finally Frake (1963:221) reports on a Philippine group:

> Litigation in Lipay, however, cannot be fully understood if we regard it only as a means of maintaining social control. A large share, if not the majority, of legal cases deal with offenses so minor that only the fertile imagination of a Subanum legal authority can magnify them into a serious threat to some person or to society in general. . . . A festivity without litigation is almost as unthinkable as one without drink. If no subject for prosecution immediately presents itself, sooner or later, as the brew relaxes the tongues and actions, someone will make a slip.
>
> In some respects a Lipay trial is more comparable to an American poker game than to our legal proceedings. It is a contest of skill, in this case of verbal skill, accompanied by social merry-making, in which the loser pays a forfeit. He pays for much the same reason we pay a poker debt: so he can play the game again. Even if he does not have the legal authority's ability to deal a verbalized "hand," he can participate as a defendant, plaintiff, kibitzer, singer, and drinker. No one is left out of the range of activities associated with litigation.
>
> Litigation nevertheless has far greater significance in Lipay than this poker-game analogy implies. For it is more than recreation. Litigation, together with the rights and duties it generates, so pervades Lipay life that one could not consistently refuse to pay fines and remain a functioning member of society. Along with drinking, feasting, and ceremonializing, litigation provides patterned means of interaction linking the independent nuclear families of Lipay into a social unit, even though there are no formal group ties of comparable extent. The importance of litigation as a social activity makes understandable its prevalence among the peaceful and, by our standards, "law-abiding" residents of Lipay.

More examples can be found. However, for the most part the inclusion of such extralegal functions in the anthropological literature has been anecdotal. The previous series of examples are not meant to illustrate *the law*; rather they are examples of what should be included in any truly *ethnographic* study of the law.

And finally a word about comparison and generalization. One function of comparative study is to identify uniformities and differences and to explain them. Although it is true that we have a healthy handful of excellent monographs on certain aspects of law, are they indeed comparable? In some respects they are. For example, the mechanisms for dispute settlement (the procedural aspects of law ways) could profitably be compared to isolate answers to questions such as those proposed by Kluckhohn (1960:136): first, "What is apparently incompatible with what else?" Endogamous dual organization villages are found to be incompatible with the development of a court system of judge-made decisions (Nader 1965a); second, "What is extremely likely to be found with what else?" The use of a go-between as an important mechanism of nonfamily dispute settlement will be characteristic of societies which are politically decentralized and bilateral in kin form; finally, "Are some concantenations of cultural features or elements indifferent as far as minimal necessary coherence of the system is concerned and hence found associated or not associated merely as a result of the accidents of the historical process?" Here, we may note that crime rates may or may not be related to any procedural characteristic of law, and some evidence for this is presented by Beatrice Whiting in this volume. Whiting compares the frequencies of assault and homicide in six societies and considers the differences in the light of the concept of "protest masculinity" and the status envy hypothesis of identification.

But there are problems inherent in comparison, even leaving to one side the difficulties of comparing total legal systems, which we believe to be a task not likely to yield much fruit. A major problem, common to all cross-cultural comparative studies, relates to the formulation of concepts or categories which will permit cross-cultural analysis without distortion of the "folk-system" of a particular society. Or phrased in another way, how do we reconcile "the new ethnography" and the importance of generalization in anthropology. Bohannan (1957) is correct in viewing the description of the folk and the analysis of the system as two separate tasks, but his threefold social action model (action, counteraction, correction) is much too general for comparative usefulness. So is Gluckman's (1955a) conceptual model used to describe the judicial process of the Barotse. Yet a comparison of the formal institutions used for settling disputes raises certain problems inherent in Hoebel's volume *The Law of Primitive Man* (1954), that is, the problems of comparing a court system, with a go-between system, with an Eskimo song duel, or even the problems in comparing a grade D court among the Tiv with the *presidente's* and/or the *alcalde's* courts among the Zapotec. We get into further complications by comparing the functions of these formal systems. These problems are similar to those faced in kinship research. For example, we compare a kinship system based on lineage and clan principles with one based on the nuclear family. In kinship we never 'solved' the problem of comparable units and yet comparison was not ignored. Rather we started with certain assumptions about the regularity of kinship forms and with certain questions the answers to which were sought through comparison: Why is it that "marriage" is more brittle in some societies than in others? What aspects of social organization are intimately connected to the marriage pattern? The comparative papers in this volume on law ask such questions. Whiting asks: Why is there more physical aggression resulting in legal wrongs in some societies than in others? Roberts queries: Why do only some societies have oaths and ordeals? Cohn pursues yet another question: What relation is there between coalition formation in villages and frequency of dispute? But if we are going to ask and answer such questions we need good descriptive data, which leads us back to questions of description.

If field studies of law are to result in comparable data what essential materials should be covered by the ethnographer?[5] First, several assumptions should be made clear: 1) there is a limited range of dispute for any particular society; that is, all societies do not fight about all the possible things human beings could fight about; 2) a limited number of formal procedures are used by human societies in the prevention of and/or settlement of grievances (e.g. courts, contests, ordeals, go-betweens, etc.); 3) there will be a choice in the number and modes of settlement (e.g. arbitration, mediation, compromise, adjudication, and so on). How people resolve conflicting interests and how they remedy strife situations is a problem with which all societies have to deal; and usually they find not one but many ways to handle grievances. In any society also there are various remedy agents which may be referred to when a grievance reaches a boiling point, and an understanding of all such agencies is necessary for a comprehensive analysis of social control and for a sophisticated contextual analysis of the court system, should one exist.

Having in mind the range of remedy agents (or agencies) in a society certain empirical questions come to mind: 1) What do people fight and argue about publicly, and how, when, and where do conflicts come about? 2) How do societies handle disputes and what is the outcome for the individual(s) involved as well as for the society? 3) Within what groups are disputes concentrated? 4) How do disputes at one group level (family, kindred, lineage, etc.) affect that at another (village, region, nation, etc.)?

Information on these four areas should enable us to provide answers to such developmental questions as: At what ages (speaking of biological and sociological age) in the life cycle, in what roles, at what rank, and under what conditions do citizens fit into the picture as parties to specific disputes? What is the relation between the composition of the family, the frequency of crime, and the use of the courts? The Gluecks (1950) and B. Whiting in this volume suggest a relation between the composition of the family and delinquent acts. A relation between family structure and the use of the courts is illustrated by the Zapotec situation where the absence of a father and/or brother often forced women to take recourse to formal law agencies as plaintiffs. Why should this be? What are the social and cultural correlates of sex and age-linked offenses? Among the Zapotec for example, women are rarely defendants in dispute cases involving assault and battery, while men on the other hand are rarely defendants in slander cases. These informations should also enable us to answer the question: 5) What are the manifest and latent jobs of the law and how are they related to the social structure?

A quantitative and qualitative sampling of dispute cases from each society could provide key material around which comparison would be made—provided that sampling problems are resolved or indeed that one could guarantee witnessing more than a handful of cases in some populations. The dispute case, unlike any particular form of adjudication or class of disputes or functions, is present in every society. Universally such cases share most of the following components depending on what stage the dispute is in: the dispute or grievance (property, custody, theft, homicide, marital obligations, or however the society may class such disputes); the parties to a grievance (sex, age, rank, status, relation between parties); presentation of the grievance (before a remedy agent such as a judge, go-between, lineage head); procedure or manner of handling a grievance; the outcome; the termination of the grievance; and the enforcement of a decision. Mapping the component parts of a case so that the sociological aspects of conflict can be systematically discerned has been attempted for the Zapotec material (Nader 1964a). The results are mainly descriptive generalizations which have proved useful as a springboard for comparative work (Nader and Metzger 1963).

In examining monographs that included case materials, certain neglected areas were noted: frequency estimates, sociological data on the parties such as age and status, detailed descriptions of the legal and extralegal factors determining the outcome. The decision-making process is often ignored or barely mentioned. Typically, for example, there might be a statement of a case, then a sentence declaring that "after much wrangling" the case was settled in such and such a manner. We need to know more about the "wrangling." If we are dealing with a society with courts we need to investigate the dispute case in the context of the range of social institutions which adults use in the resolution or prevention of trouble situations, that is, we should sample out-of-court cases as well as court cases. In this way we may reveal the intricate balance between the use patterns of various authority systems. See Schneider 1957, Nader and Metzger 1963, and Gulliver 1963.

But how do we arrive at an understanding of our last question: 6) What jurisprudential ideas are expressed in legal reasoning? If prior to field work we attempt to make a category listing of substantive areas of the law such as family law, tort law, property law, we run into difficulties. Who could say, at this stage of knowledge, what the major categories of family law would be when viewed cross-culturally? The range of possibilities in terms of substantive law are too great to be handled in the same way as procedure, given our present knowledge. Is inheritance, for example, a universal category of law? (Cf. Hoebel 1948 for an example of a comparative treatment of inheritance.) Llewellyn and Hoebel might suggest that we "find" substantive law by noting cases of breach, and this one can do in the field only. But there is another possibility, one which admittedly has its drawbacks. Field workers, both implicitly and explicitly, have described the law ways of preliterate and nonliterate groups usually against a backdrop of Western European law. Hence the familiar chapters of family, property, contract, torts, etc. This has been the subject of much criticism. While I do not believe that we can adopt wholesale Western jurisprudential categories of law for use in non-Western cultures, it is possible that we could explicitly state that we are using an outline of Anglo-American common law, for example, against which or from which we view exotic legal systems. At least we would be clear about what our biases were. Such straightforward comparisons might serve field workers at least as one system against which to contrast their materials. It would also enable us to provide answers to the question, What jurisprudential ideas are expressed in legal reasoning? We could thereby *test* a suggestion made most recently by Gluckman (1965a) that certain jurisprudential ideas found in English and Roman law are universal ideas.

For example, Gluckman (1965a:113) states as a universal legal distinction that

> Both developed and underdeveloped legal systems distinguish sharply between immovable and movable property. Basically the distinction is between rights and duties of persons in relation to land, and rights and duties in relation to others with respect to goods, animals and people.

He continues his discussion by accepting a more generalized version of this distinction:

> As Maine pointed out, the difference between the two types of property is not absolutely between land and chattels—between immovables and movables. The Roman *res mancipi* included slaves, horses, and oxen besides land. Maine cites Scottish law as ranking a certain class of securities with land, and Hindu law as grouping slaves with land.

And he proposes an interesting hypothesis to explain what contributes to this dichotomy in classifying property:

> Immovable property and chattels have different functions in the maintenance, through time. of a social system as an organized pattern of relations. Immovable property provides fixed positions which endure through the passing of generations, through quarrels, and even through invasions and revolutions, and many social relationships are stabilized about these positions (p. 116). . . . Chattels . . . break up the exclusiveness of corporations aggregate by drawing their individual members into other relationships [cross-linkages] (p. 133).

Even disagreement with the universality of the dichotomy that Gluckman poses does not detract from the fact that Gluckman in these recent essays makes a distinctive contribution to an anthropological understanding of both Western and Barotse jurisprudence. His essays also clearly illustrate the stimulus value of Western jurisprudential ideas. However, another approach in the exploration of cognitive categories is illustrated in this volume by Black and Metzger. Their approach is a contribution to the methodology of description while Gluckman's essays provide an example of anthropological legal interpretation of given descriptive categories. At any rate it remains clear that aspects of law assumed to be universal by eighteenth-century intellectuals remain a matter of search for twentieth-century scholars.

NOTES

[1] In conceiving the original outline of this paper I have profited immensely from the papers and discussions at the Winner-Gren Conference on law, April 1964. I am especially indebted to Paul Bohannan, Herma Kay, and Julius Stone for many stimulating interchanges at the Center

for Advanced Study in the Behavioral Sciences. For their critical comments and readings of earlier drafts I wish to thank Eugene Hammel, Mel Perlman, Penny Addiss, Carl McCarthy, John Rothenberger, and most of all Norman Milleron. Penny Addiss served as research assistant during the writing of this paper. Anne Brower kindly edited several drafts. My colleagues at Berkeley, especially Elizabeth Colson and C. Lancaster were helpful in directing me to African and Indian materials. The responsibility for the paper in its present form, alas, is solely mine.

[2] This paper is *not a survey* of the literature past and present. Such would be the subject for a book. The examples quoted are primarily in English; a few French references are included. There is a long German tradition totally ignored here. We have elsewhere (Nader, Koch, and Cox 1964) annotated the German literature but for the most part the German literature is not utilized here. It would be important to consider such obvious scholars as Kohler and Trimborn in any historical treatment of the subject. Most relevant work can be found in *Zeitschrift für Vergleichende Rechtswissenschaft*, but see especially Leonhard Adam (1937) "Ethnologische Rechtsforschung," still the best review article on the development of German legal ethnology.

[3] For a broad review of trends in American sociology of law see Skolnick 1965.

[4] Anthropologists have more commonly analyzed other institutions as having legal functions rather than legal institutions as having other than legal functions. See Kaberry 1941 and 1942 for example.

[5] The Berkeley project on comparative village law has been concerned with the problem of conducting comparable ethnographic field studies of law. This group met during 1963–64 to work on the formulation of a field guide. In its broadest scope the field guide was intended to cover the social relations and contexts in which breaches of the law tend to develop, the institutions and mechanisms which serve to prevent social conflict, and the systematic collection of dispute cases.

REFERENCES CITED

ADAM, LEONHARD

1937 Quellennachweis. *In* Lehrbuch der Völkerkunde. Konrad Theodor Preuss, ed., Stuttgart, F. Enke, pp. 302–306.

ALLOTT, A. N.

1953 Methods of legal research into customary law. Journal of African Administration 5(4):172–177.

1960 Essays in African law with special reference to the law of Ghana. London, Butterworths.

1961 The changing law in a changing Africa. Sociologus, Vol. II, pp. 115–131.

ANDERSON, J. N. D.

1957 Law as a social force is Islamic culture and history. Bulletin of the School of Oriental and African Studies 20:13–40.

ARMSTRONG, R. G.

1954 West African inquest. American Anthropologist 56:1051–1069.

ARNOLD, T.

1935 The symbols of government. New Haven, Yale University Press.

AUBERT, V.

1963 Researches in the sociology of law. The American Behavioral Scientist 7(4):16–20.

AYOUB, V.

1961 Review: the judicial process in two African tribes. *In* Community Political Systems, Morris Janowitz, ed., Glencoe, The Free Press.

BACHOFEN, J. J.

1861 Das Mutterrecht. Stuttgart, Krais and Hoffmann.

BACON, M. K., I. L. CHILD and H. BARRY, III

1963 A cross-cultural study of correlates of crime. Journal of Abnormal and Social Psychology 66(4):291–300.

BAILEY, F. G.

1958 Caste and the economic frontier. Bombay and Oxford, Oxford University Press.

BARNES, J. A.

1961 Law as politically active: an anthropological view. *In* Studies in the Sociology of

Law, G. Sawer, ed., Canberra, Australian National University, pp. 167–196.

BARTON, R. F.

1919 Ifugao law. University of California Publications in American Archaeology and Ethnology 15(1):1–186.

1930 The half way sun: life among the headhunters of the Philippines. New York, Brewer and Warren.

1949 The Kalingas: their institutions and custom law. Introduction by E. Adamson Hoebel. Chicago, the University of Chicago Press.

BEALS, A. R.

1955 Interplay among factors of change in a Mysore village. *In* Village India: Studies in the Little Community, McKim Marriott, ed., Chicago, University of Chicago Press.

1964 Gopalpur: a South Indian village. New York, Holt, Rinehart and Winston.

BEIDELMAN, T. O.

1959 A comparative analysis of the Jajman system. Locust Valley, New York, Published for the Association for Asian Studies by J. J. Augustin.

BERREMAN, G. D.

1963 Hindus of the Himalayas. Berkeley and Los Angeles, University of California Press.

BLACKSTONE, SIR WILLIAM

1765 Commentaries on the laws of England. Oxford, Clarendon Press.

BOHANNAN, P. J.

1957 Justice and judgment among the Tiv. London, Oxford University Press for the International African Institute.

1960 African homicide and suicide. Princeton, New Jersey, Princeton University Press.

1964 Anthropology and the law. *In* Horizons of Anthropology, S. Tax, ed., Chicago, Aldine Publishing Co., pp. 191–199.

BOORSTIN, D. J.

1958 The mysterious science of the law. Boston, Beacon Press. First published 1941.

BERNDT, R. M.

1962 Excess and restraint. Social Control Among a New Guinea Mountain People. Chicago and London, The University of Chicago Press.

BURRIDGE, K. O. L.

1957 Disputing in Tangu. American Anthropologist 59(5):763–780.

BUSIA, K. A.

1951 The position of the chief in the modern political system of Ashanti: a study of the influence of contemporary social changes on Ashanti political institutions. London and New York, Oxford University Press for the International African Institute.

CARLIN, J. E.

1963 Lawyers on their own. New Brunswick, Rutgers University Press.

CARLIN, J. E. and J. HOWARD

1965 Legal representation and class justice. UCLA Law Review 12(2):381–437.

COHN, B. S.

1959 Some notes on law and change in North China. Economic Development and Cultural Change, Vol. 8, pp. 79–93.

COLSON, E.

1953 Social control and vengeance in plateau Tonga society. Africa 23:199–212.

1958 Marriage and the family among the plateau Tonga. Manchester, University of Manchester Press.

1960 Social organization of the Gwembe Tonga. Manchester, Manchester University Press.

DURKHEIM, E.

1960 The division of labor in society. Glencoe, Illinois, The Free Press. First published 1893.

EVAN, W. M., ed.

1962 Law and society. New York, The Free Press of Glencoe.

EVANS-PRITCHARD, E. E.

1963 The comparative method in social anthropology. London, University of London, Athlone Press.

FALLERS, L. A.

1956 Changing customary law in Busoga district of Uganda. Journal of African Administration 8:139–144.

1962 Customary law in the new African states. Law and Contemporary Problems 27:605–631.

FRAKE, C. O.

1963 Litigation in Lipay: a study in Subanun law. *In* The Proceedings of the Ninth Pacific Science Congress, 1957, Vol. 3, pp. 217–222.

FRAZER, SIR J. G.

1890 The golden bough; a study on magic and religion. London, New York, The Macmillan Co.

FUSTEL DE COULANGES, N. D.

1864 The ancient city: a study on the religion, laws, and institutions of Greece and Rome. New York, Doubleday and Co. Inc., 1956. First published 1864.

GIBBS, J. L., JR.

1963 The Kpelle moot: a therapeutic model for the informal settlement of disputes. Africa 33:1–11.

GLASSE, R. M.

1959 Revenge and redress among the Huli: a preliminary account. Mankind (Sydney) 5(7):273–289.

GLUCKMAN, M.

1955a The judicial process among the Barotse of Northern Rhodesia. Manchester University Press, for the Rhodes-Livingstone Institute.

1955b Custom and conflict in Africa. Glencoe, The Free Press.

1959 The technical vocabulary of Barotse jurisprudence. American Anthropologist 61:743–759.

1962 African jurisprudence. The advancement of Science 75:439–454.

1965a The ideas in Barotse jurisprudence. New Haven and London, Yale University Press.

1965b Politics, law and ritual in tribal society. Chicago, Aldine Publishing Co.

GLUECK, S. and E. GLUECK

1950 Unraveling juvenile delinquency. Cambridge, Harvard University Press.

GULLIVER, P. H.

1963 Social control in an African society: a study of the Arusha, agricultural Masai of Northern Tanganyika. Boston, Boston University Press.

GUTMANN, B.

1926 Das Recht der Dschagga. Mit einem Nachworte des Herausgebers: Zur Entwicklungspsychologie des Rechts. Arbeiten zur Entwicklungspsychologie, F. Krueger, ed., siebentes Stück. Abhandlungen der Sachsischen Staatlichen Forschungsinstitute, Forschungsinstitut für Psychologie, Nr. 7.

HARPER, E. B.

1957 Hoylu: a belief relating justice and the supernatural. American Anthropologist 59:801–816.

HART, H. L. A.

1961 The concept of law. Oxford, Oxford University Press.

HAZARD, J. N.

1962 Furniture arrangement as a symbol of judicial roles. Etcetera 19(2):181–188.

HOBHOUSE, L. T., G. C. WHEELER and M. GINSBERG

1915 The material culture and social institutions of the simpler peoples: an essay in correlation. The London School of Economics and Political Science, No. 3 of the Monographs on Sociology.

HOEBEL, E. A.
1940 The political organization and law-ways of the Comanche Indians. American Anthropological Association Memoir 54. Contributions from the Santa Fe Laboratory of Anthropology, vol 4.
1948 The anthropology of inheritance. *In* Conference on Social Meaning of Legal Concepts, E. N. Cahn, ed. New York, New York University.
1954 The law of primitive man: a study in comparative legal dynamics. Cambridge, Mass., Harvard University Press.
1961 Three studies in African law. Stanford Law Review 13: 418–442.

HOGBIN, H. I.
1934 Law and order in Polynesia: a study of primitive legal institutions. Introduction by B. Malinowski. London, Christophers.

HOWELL, P. P.
1954 A manual of Nuer law. Being an account of customary law, its evolution and development in the courts established by the Sudan government. London, New York, and Toronto, Oxford University Press.

JAYAWARDENA, C.
1963 Conflict and solidarity in a Guianese plantation. New York, The Humanities Press.

JONES, JR., EDGAR H.
1964 Power and prudence in the arbitration of labor disputes: a venture in some hypotheses. UCLA Law Review 2(5):675–791.

KABERRY, P. M.
1941, 1942 Law and political organization in the Abelam tribe, New Guinea. Oceania 12(1):79–95; No. 3:209–225; No. 4:331–363.

KANTOROWICZ, H.
1958 The definition of law. Cambridge, Cambridge University Press.

KAPLAN, I.
1965 Courts as catalysts of change: a Chagga case. Southwestern Journal of Anthropology 21(1): 79–96.

KEUNING, J.
1963 Customary law and customary courts in Yoruba-land. Read at the Nigerian Institute of Social and Economic Research in Ibadan. (Mimeo.)

KLUCKHOHN, C.
1960 The use of typology in anthropological theory. *In* Selected Papers of the Fifth International Congress of Anthropological and Ethnological Science, 1956. A. Wallace, ed., Philadelphia, University of Pennsylvania Press, pp. 134–140.

KROEBER, A. L.
1925 Principles of Yurok law. *In* Handbook of the Indians of California. Washington, D.C., Bureau of American Ethnology, Bulletin 78.

LEACH, E. R.
1954 Political systems of highland Burma: a study of Kachin social structure. London, G. Bell and Sons, Ltd.
1959 Letter to the editor: social change and primitive law. American Anthropologist 61(6):1096–1097.
1961 Rethinking anthropology. London, Athlone Press.

LEWIS, O.
1958 Village life in northern India. Urbana, University of Illinois Press.

LLEWELLYN, K. N. and E. A. HOEBEL
1941 The Cheyenne way: conflict and case law in primitive jurisprudence. Norman, University of Oklahoma Press.

McLENNAN, J. F.
1865 Primitive marriage. Edinburgh, A. & C. Black.

MAINE, SIR H. S.
1861 Ancient law: its connection with the early history of society and its relation to

modern ideas. London, John Murray. Paperback edition printed by Beacon Press, Boston, 1963.

1871 Village-communities in the East and West. London, John Murray.

MALINOWSKI, B.

1922 Argonauts of the western Pacific. New York, E. P. Dutton and Co., 1961.

1926 Crime and custom in savage society. London, Kegan Paul, Trench, Trubner & Co., Ltd.

1934 Introduction to law and order in Polynesia by H. Ian Hogbin. New York, Christophers.

1942 A new instrument for the interpretation of law—especially primitive. The Yale Law Review 51:1237–1254.

MARCH, J. G.

1956 Sociological jurisprudence revisited, a review (more or less) of Max Gluckman. Stanford Law Review 8:499–534.

MARX, K.

1960 Capital: a critique of political economy. Translated from the third German edition by S. Moore and E. Aveling, F. Engels, ed. Revised and amplified according to the fourth German edition by Ernest Unterman. New York, The Modern Library.

1948 The Communist manifesto. Centenary Edition. London.

MAUSS, M. and M. H. BEUCHAT

1906 Les variations saisonnières des societés esquimaux; étude de morphologie social. Anné Sociologique 9:39–132.

MEAD, M.

1961 Some anthropological considerations concerning natural law. Natural Law Form 6:51–64.

METZGER, D.

1960 Conflict in Chulsanto: a village in Chiapis. Alpha Kappa Deltan 30:35–48.

MONTESQUIEU, C. L.

1750 L'esprit de les lois. London, printed for J. Nourse and P. Vaillant in the Strand.

MOORE, S. F.

1958 Power and property in Inca Peru. New York, Columbia University Press.

MOORE, S.

1960 Marxian law in primitive society. *In* Culture in History: Essays in Honor of Paul Radin, Stanley Diamond, ed., New York, Columbia University Press, pp. 642–662.

NADEL, S. F.

1942 A black Byzantium. London, Oxford University Press.

1947 The Nuba. London, Oxford University Press.

1956 Reason and unreason in African law. Africa 26, No. 2:160–173.

NADER, L.

1964a An analysis of Zapotec law cases. Ethnology 3:404–419.

1964b Talea and Juquila: a comparison of Zapotec social organization. University of California Publications in American Archaeology and Ethnology 48(3):195–296.

1965a Choices in legal procedure: Shia Moslem and Mexican Zapotec. American Anthropologist 67(2):394–399.

1965b Communication between village and city in the modern Middle East. Human Organization, Speciál Issue: Dimensions of Cultural Change in the Middle East.

n.d. Variations in Zapotec legal procedure. *In* Homenaje al Ingeniero Roberto Weitlaner. Mexico. (In press.)

NADER, L., K. F. KOCH and B. COX

1966 The ethnography of law: a bibliographical survey. Stanford: Current anthropology, special supplement. (In Press)

NADER, L. and D. METZGER

1963 Conflict resolution in two Mexican communities. American Anthropologist 65:584–592.

NAGEL, S. S.

1962 Culture patterns and judicial systems. Vanderbilt Law Review 16:147–157.

NICHOLAS, R. W. and T. MUKHOPADHYAY

n.d. Politics and law in two West Bengal villages. Bulletin of the Anthropological Survey of India. (In press.)

O'GORMAN, H. J.

1963 Lawyers and matrimonial cases. New York, The Free Press of Glencoe.

POSPISIL, L.

1958a Kapauku Papuans and their law. Yale University Publications in Anthropology 54.

1958b Social change and primitive law: consequences of a Papuan legal case. American Anthropologist 60:832–837.

RADCLIFFE-BROWN, A. R.

1933 Primitive law. *In* Encyclopedia of the Social Sciences, Vol. 9, pp. 202–206. New York, Macmillan. Reprinted in Structure and function in primitive society: essays and addresses by A. R. Radcliffe-Brown, Ch. 12. Glencoe, Illinois, Free Press.

REDFIELD, R.

1950 Maine's ancient law in the light of primitive societies. Western Political Quarterly 3:571–589.

RICHARDSON, J.

1940 Law and status among the Kiowa Indians. American Ethnological Society. Monograph I.

RIESMAN, D.

1954 Individualism reconsidered and other essays. Glencoe, Illinois, The Free Press, pp. 440–466.

RHEINSTEIN, M.

1963 Problems of law in the new nations of Africa. *In* Old Societies and New States, Clifford Geertz, ed., Free Press of Glencoe.

ROTHENBERGER, J. E.

1963 Judicial process and political organization among the Lozi and Tiv. Ms.

SCHAPERA, I.

1938, 1955 A handbook of Tswana law and custom. London, New York, Cape Town, Oxford University Press for the International African Institute.

1943 Tribal legislation among the Tswana of the Bechuanaland Protectorate. London, Lund, Humphries, for the London School of Economics and Political Science.

SCHNEIDER, D. M.

1957 Political organization, supernatural sanctions and the punishment for incest on Yap. American Anthropologist 59, No. 5:791–800.

SCHUBERT, G. A.

1959 Quantitative analysis of judicial behavior. Glencoe, Illinois, The Free Press.

1963 Behavioral research in public law. American Political Science Review 57:433–445.

SCHWARTZ, R. D. and J. C. MILLER

1964 Legal evolution and societal complexity. The American Journal of Sociology 70(2):159–169.

SIEGEL, B. J. and A. R. BEALS

1960 Pervasive factionalism. American Anthropologist 62:394–417.

SIMMEL, G.

1956 Conflict and the web of group affiliations. Glencoe, Illinois, The Free Press.

SIMONETT, J. E.

1963 The common law of Morrison County. American Bar Association Journal 49:263–265.

SKOLNICK, J. H.

1965 The sociology of law in America: overview and trends. Social Problems (summer issue), supplemental monograph.

SMIEGL, E. O.
1964 The Wall Street lawyer. New York, The Free Press of Glencoe.

SMITH, W. and J. M. ROBERTS
1954 Zuni law: a field of values. With an appendix by Stanley Newman. Cambridge, Massachusetts, Peabody Museum Papers 43(1).

STIRLING, P.
1957 Land, marriage, and the law in Turkish villages. Part I. The Reception of Foreign Law in Turkey: International Social Science Bulletin 9:21–33. UNESCO.

STRODTBECK, F.
1962 Social process, the law, and jury functioning. *In* Law and Society, Wm. M. Evan, ed., New York, The Free Press of Glencoe, pp. 152–164.

TAPPAN, P. W.
1947 Delinquent girls in court. New York, Columbia University Press.

TURNER, V. W.
1957 Schism and continuity in an African society: a study of Ndemby village life. Manchester, England, Manchester University Press.

UCHENDU, V. C.
1964 Livestock tenancy among Lgbo of Southern Nigeria. African Studies Quarterly Journal 23(2):89–94.

WEBER, M.
1954 Max Weber on law in economy and society, M. Rheinstein, ed., Cambridge, Harvard University Press.

WHITING, B. B.
1950 Paiute sorcery. New York, Viking Fund Publications in Anthropology, No. 15.

WHITING, J. W. M., *et al.*
1953 Field manual for the cross-cultural study of child rearing. Social Science Research Council, New York.

WINANS, E. V. and R. B. EDGERTON
1964 Hehe magical justice. American Anthropologist 66, 1:745–764.

[2]

Jean Poirier

The current state of legal ethnology and its future tasks

State of research

Vagueness in terminology is a reflection of serious methodological confusion. The place allotted to legal ethnology depends on what one regards as included in ethnological science on the one hand and by the concept of law on the other.

THE MEANING OF LEGAL ETHNOLOGY

The time has come, it seems, to try to overcome the various inconsistencies in order to arrive at a truly international language, in regard not only to the actual terms used, but also to their meaning. The problem is indeed one that concerns the very definition of the social sciences and their interrelationship but it cannot be side-stepped. An effort must obviously be made to reach agreement as to the meaning and precise scope of these disciplines.

The present highly confused situation has arisen due to disagreement as to both terminology and subject-matter. The terms 'ethnology', 'ethnography' and 'anthropology' are often used synonymously. Of even greater concern is the confusion between the scope of all these subjects taken together, and of social psychology and sociology.

Traditionally, these subjects were differentiated according to certain key criteria. To begin with, the first group of subjects (ethnology, ethnography, anthropology) was contrasted with the second (social psychology,[1] sociology), on the basis of a distinction between primitive societies and civilized societies. (Attempts have been made to replace the epithet 'primitive'—felt to have a derogatory ring—by various euphemisms, but they left the basis of the distinction unchanged.) To take the existence of a written language as criterion, though it does make it possible to establish a cultural typology, cannot provide the foundation for a conceptually correct definition. Indeed, orientalists,

1. A formal—though not fundamental—distinction can be made between social psychology and sociology in so far as the former is concerned with the interpretation of relations between individuals belonging to the group.

Int. Soc. Sci. J., Vol. XXII, No. 3, 1970

Islamists and specialists in Indian studies have often felt a closer affinity with ethnologists—the students of pre-literate civilizations—than with sociologists. In the realm of law we shall see that literate civilizations such as Islam, China, India and so on are—despite the existence of written codes of law—in fact more often governed by oral custom.

Nowadays the position has changed, and there are two contending views. One view—apparently that of the majority—is that there are two basic types of society: industrialized and urbanized societies, with which sociology is concerned, and non-industrial societies, which are the province of ethnology. Although this distinction introduces a semblance of order into the field of social studies, the methodological criterion lacks consistency. A minority, on the other hand, with more justification sees the distinction as lying between societies based on the primacy of tradition and those which give paramount importance to the use of reason. Traditionalist societies are the concern of ethnology and rationalist societies that of sociology. The development of this viewpoint owes something to the progress made in the study of folk-lore and its absorption as an integral part of ethnology.

We can adopt—at least as a working premise—the definition based on the concept of tradition. We shall not therefore regard legal ethnology as the science concerned with the laws of pre-literate civilizations, but as that concerned with traditional laws primarily based on custom. It will therefore embrace, in the case of Europe for example, 'local customs', which still govern a major part of rural life.

However, it must be clearly realized that we are rapidly moving towards a merger of the three branches of knowledge concerned with how man is conditioned in society, namely ethnology, social psychology and sociology.[1] An increasing tendency is to fit them into the broader scheme of general anthropology.

It would be an illusion to think that the historical distinctions we have mentioned can be preserved much longer. They appear increasingly artificial, and the development of civilization itself makes them more and more outmoded, since it is only a matter of time before literacy, urbanization and industrialization reach all the peoples of the world. No doubt there will always remain areas where traditional patterns—old ways and customs, the social 'ethos'—will predominate over rationalist patterns, and it is these residual areas that the ethnologist will study in his own right. But the differences between the three disciplines will gradually fade away.

This necessary unification of the three disciplines may be regarded as the indirect result of the general evening-out of differences between human groups. The converging processes of improved inter-racial and inter-cultural relations (revolutionized by the simultaneous advances in transport and the mass media), the growing standardization of the technological infrastructure of social life (e.g. clothing, lighting, communications, information and the

1. To this list we could no doubt add 'socio-analysis', i.e. social psycho-analysis, a newly evolved discipline, which is concerned with group phenomena at the level of the unconscious

press, medical care, even entertainment, etc.) and the growing importance of international law regulating technical matters (broadcasting and telecommunications in general, maritime, commercial and diplomatic law, bilateral and multilateral agreements, extended role of the international organizations) are gradually coming to challenge the compartmentalized approach to the study of man in society.

The already long-recognized truth that 'man is indivisible' (Mauss) and—as its indirect result—the importance given everywhere, in theory if not in practice, to multidisciplinary research also argue in favour of a new approach. A process of rethinking is in fact under way with a view to placing the human sciences on a firm conceptual basis.

We felt it necessary to recall this in order to make quite clear the transitory nature of the present situation. In what follows we shall be using the expression 'legal ethnology' in its most commonly accepted, though methodologically incorrect, meaning as the study of the legal systems of non-industrialized societies.

THE CONCEPT OF THE 'LEGAL IMPERATIVE'

A second preliminary problem arises: what is to be the scope of legal ethnology? How is law to be defined within the over-all context of society?

Here too confusion reigns. Jurists themselves cannot agree on any precise definition of what law is. The trouble is that the problem has been badly formulated, as the 'legal imperative' cannot be defined in terms of law, but must be formulated in sociological terms. The criterion for a rule of law rests in the nature of the sanction; to put it simply, we shall say that the legal sanction is that which is upheld by the sovereign power and automatically applied by the authorities in the event of an infringement of the rules, which in turn raises the question of what we mean by the 'sovereign power'. This should be taken as meaning, regardless how public, constitutional or international law are to be defined, the coercive apparatus that controls the forces of public order and is prepared to use them *vis-à-vis* the citizens of the State. Any reference to a moral code would here be quite beside the point. It would also be a tautology to define law using law as our starting-point. What we have to do is rather to determine on what, in the last analysis, law is based. There can then be no hesitation—law is made by whoever has the authority, even if this has been gained by 'illegitimate' means. In most cases where power is seized by force the régime is subsequently legitimated by parliamentary votes of confidence, referenda, plebiscites or other, at best, somewhat equivocal means. However, this is not the point, and there are moreover many régimes that have not bothered to garb themselves in this cloak of decency. (This concern for legitimacy hardly dates back beyond the nineteenth century. Before that, the conqueror acquired the power of law-maker by the very fact of being in control.) From Napoleon I to Napoleon III, not to speak of various forms of dictatorship of which the modern world offers us several good examples, we can see perfectly clearly the organic relation which undeniably exists between force and law.

This definition is applicable to all forms of written law contained in the codes and legal systems of industrialized societies, but it would be insufficient (though not incorrect) as a means of expressing the basis of custom. An additional criterion here comes into play—the consensus of the community (which is moreover nearly always tacit). Under systems of common law the concept of consensus and the concept of power coincide.

This objective definition embraces the two major types of legal imperative: custom and the law. Much has been said about the content of these two concepts. Their relation is the same as that of tradition and reason, with custom deriving essentially from the former and law from the latter. We would say that custom is 'spontaneous' law, whereas the written law is the result of reflection.

Custom is an integral part of the cultural context: it is not intangible, it is not necessarily oral and it is not uniform. Although custom basically forms part of the permanent cultural pattern to which a group conforms, it can also be a 'continuous creation' of the group.

The nature of the authority on which custom and law are founded is not the same. Common law is *per se* something that has been handed down; it is a sacralized law which all members of the group are bound to respect whatever the political régime may be. Spontaneous behaviour based on assent[1] plays a much greater part than imposed behaviour; social control rests, it might be said, far more on 'order' than on 'power'; but this in no way detracts from the importance attaching to the concept of sovereign power, for sanctions against possible infringements of the rules are enforced by the established institutional apparatus.

If in a particular society there were no continuous creation of custom, nor any action by the authorities to enforce the customary rules, it might be said strictly that such a society did not have any system of 'law'—using this word in the sense defined above—but was living, if not (as has been asserted) in a state of 'anarchy', then at any rate in a situation where the 'rules' give way to 'self-regulation', each member of the group obeying the sacralized tradition. Such rare offenders as there may be are punished by religious and magical sanctions, or banished from their community; this 'pre-law' state (to use Gernet's expression) is the exception today.

Custom itself is gradually giving way to written laws. There remains, however, one important field where common law still applies. If we bear in mind that the written codes of law officially in force among nations that have only recently established or re-established their legal system (People's Republic of China, Ethiopia, newly independent African States, etc.) practically affect only a very small section of the population, while the rural masses continue to be governed by their own customs, we must face the fact that half mankind is still governed by custom. Further, custom retains its full

1. Such spontaneity may be only apparent when behaviour deemed to be spontaneous by those concerned is, in actual fact, the result of social pressures, but such pressures are not consciously experienced.

importance in diplomatic law, in public international law, in rural law and in commercial law.

Legal ethnology will therefore have to study all these legal systems based on tradition, which is itself sanctioned by consensus. Among these the common—or customary—law systems of recently independent countries are of special interest, and it is with them that we shall be concerned in the following pages.

Present situation

It is well known that throughout Europe from the beginning of the twelfth century up to the end of the Middle Ages a great deal of effort was expended on compiling collections of common law or 'customaries'. Since the 1950s a basically very similar movement has developed: here again the aim has been to express in written form a coherent set of oral rules used within a particular ethnic group, but this has been done in conjunction with a programme or blueprint for legal codification elaborated at the national level.

THE COLLECTION OF CUSTOMARY LAWS

Very many of the newly independent countries have undertaken this type of preliminary study, the precedents for which go back to the ancient 'customaries'. One reason for this was the need felt, on gaining independence, for a new legal system, preferably based on a survey of what was actually prescribed by custom; as we shall see, this hope has often been thwarted. The second factor is the transformation that has taken place in the economic and technological spheres, and the extensive resulting social changes; these have undermined custom at many different points, and various calls have been made for an effort to bring together traditional laws that are dying out.

This twofold objective—administrative and scientific—seems to have been pursued with very unequal results. Despite differences in outlook, as far as Africa is concerned, between English-speaking and French-speaking countries (the latter showing a more pronounced tendency towards the codification of laws), the prime distinction that should be made is between the countries of Africa and the countries of Europe.

In Africa the move towards making a systematic collection of customary laws as a necessary preliminary to codification has rapidly been overtaken by events. Governments have been anxious to have at their disposal a body of laws in the shortest time possible; laws and codes have therefore been worked out, not without any reference to custom, but without first making a systematic collection. This process is still far from complete; the lines along which it is developing are very different from those originally intended, everything being, after all, closely patterned on Western models. This is to be explained by reasons of convenience (the 'colonial' tradition and the tendency to follow ready-made patterns) and by practical considerations (European legal models are as a whole carefully elaborated as well as being in fundamental agreement as to how law should regulate the life of the individual—but, of course, in a Western context, which is not the same thing as an African context). It must also be acknowledged that, by following European practice, nations with a composite cultural and ethnic make-up have been able to avoid making difficult—and politically dangerous—choices between different systems of customary law. Perhaps the most typical example of what we mean here is the Ivory Coast. Economically and technologically speaking the most advanced country of the continent, it is, ironically, in relative terms that with the largest number of traditional groups, each of which has its own radically different system of customary laws, even in such essential matters as filiation and inheritance.

It is probably in the Republic of Dahomey that the most sustained effort has been made with a view to the systematic collection of customary laws. This work was carried out over a period of three years throughout the cantons of the country, under the supervision of the 'sub-prefects'. J. Kéké, Minister of Justice, and J. Poirier had some fifty documents, covering pretty well the whole field of customary law, prepared by commissions made up of leading local figures. Though it is not for us to give an appraisal of this inventory, we will merely note that the material it contains is of unequal value, that it has been possible in this way to preserve a heritage of original legal traditions and that it represents the only attempt so far to make such a systematic collection on a nationwide scale. However, the Dahomean Government and the two organizers mentioned above, who were entrusted with the task of drawing up a preliminary draft code of civil law, were obliged in their preparatory document to depart considerably from the norms of customary law.

It is hard to combat the combined effects of the two factors we have already pointed to, namely the internal contradictions in customary laws and their inadequacy to cope with the needs of development. Often, governments are tempted to draw up a modern legal code on radically novel lines, but this is where other difficulties start. Certainly the best example of what we mean here is to be found in Ethiopia's Imperial code of civil law. Professor R. David, of the Paris Faculty of Law, a student of comparative law, was entrusted by H.I.M. Haile Selassie, whose reformist aspirations are well known, with the drafting of this code. A draft was prepared, which aimed at maximum rationality and, technically speaking, was indeed a remarkable document, being very much in advance of the European codes on which it was based. After a number of delays and various minor changes the draft was adopted. A choice was thus made, since a technically perfect code could be applied only to the educated section of the population, that part which was, so to speak, as technically advanced as the code. However, the code is well above the heads of the masses, above their needs and capabilities, and is therefore directed much more at future generations than at the present population. It is in fact arguable whether it is conducive to the development of the country or the reverse. Ethiopia today has one of the best codes of civil law, the most modern and perhaps, technically speaking, the most perfect. But the code has taken over nothing from the body of customary law, having been created outside the Ethiopian legal tradition. It is applied only very incompletely and with great caution. For the present most civil law proceedings are enacted outside it, which will continue for a long time yet.

TRENDS IN TEACHING AND RESEARCH

Naturally, we can here give only a rapid appraisal of current developments. It is regrettable that there is no general study available on the history of legal ethnology, although this gap is shortly to be filled.

In the following pages we propose to give a rough idea of the present situation in France, Belgium and the United Kingdom. This is not to say that efforts in other countries, notably the Federal Republic of Germany and the United States, are to be underrated, but the data presented should suffice to delineate the main trends.

In order that the data may be comparable we shall deal mainly with law in Africa.

Work done in France

The teaching of legal ethnology in France goes back to the inter-war years, when its exponents were Maunier and Labouret. The former, a professor of law, organized in the Faculty of Law at Paris University a seminar on legal ethnology and launched a series of publications which were to include some excellent monographs. At the same time, Henri Labouret, an administrator in the French overseas civil service and subsequently a Governor, instituted at the École Coloniale (which later became the École Nationale de la France d'Outre-mer), the first regular teaching in African customary law and legal ethnology.

After the Second World War Henri Lévy-Bruhl took over the seminar of legal ethnology at the Paris Faculty of Law. In 1955 J. Poirier suggested that African law be taught at the faculty in addition to Moslem law. H. Lévy-Bruhl took up this suggestion and obtained administrative approval. As a result African law (including customary law and modern law) was for a number of years taught by M. Alliot, J. Chabas and J. Poirier, in co-ordination, stressing respectively modern developments, the problems of acculturation and the ethno-sociological foundations of custom. At the École Nationale de la France d'Outre-mer, J. Poirier took over the mantle from H. Labouret, giving his teaching a sociological orientation. The transformation of this institute into an establishment intended primarily to train senior African and Malagasy personnel (under the new name of the Institut des Hautes Études d'Outre-mer) made it possible to enlist the direct participation of the students in the study of customary-law systems, thus foreshadowing a trend which, although slow to develop, now seems decisive. The African and Malagasy students, many of whom were adults already possessing a considerable personal experience of the real problems of Africa, were in this way led to write a large number of papers or reports. These studies are of course of very uneven value; the best ones were produced by students who presented a precise analysis of certain aspects of the customs of their own ethnic group, illustrating their analysis with specific examples often taken from their own personal experience. This therefore represents a considerable source of documentation, which is still largely untapped.

The teaching at the Faculty of Law was further expanded with the setting up of the Department of African Law in 1964 at the instigation of M. Alliot. The department has since run a series of courses of teaching and research into African Moslem law, customary law and modern law. More recently Michel Alliot set up a laboratory of legal anthropology as part of this department and at the same time formed a parallel research team, specializing in African legal anthropology, at the Centre National de la Recherche. The programme worked out is of particular interest to us, as it is centred on the project for compiling a dictionary of legal anthropology relating to black Africa. This will involve making a systematic and comprehensive inventory of the legal terminology used by individual groups. The method used is described as follows by the team, whose work is co-ordinated by Raymond Verdier:[1]

'The study of legal theory and practice, taking the African languages as the starting-point, should make it possible to analyse them in terms of their own categories and classifications, without any explicit or implicit reference to the concepts of Western law. The entry for each term will indicate all meanings, taking into account the sociological, political, economic and religious context. Attention will be paid to changes in vocabulary and in actual conditions during the period of colonial rule and since independence.

'The collection of this material, arranged under ethnic and topical headings, should make it possible to undertake a scientific study of the various legal systems of Africa. This work requires the participation of African research workers and Africanists and the close co-operation of a number of disciplines: law, ethnology, linguistics, sociology, history, etc.'

It should be noted that for the first time African 'ethnojurists' are directly involved as members of a team in the collection and interpretation of customs. In the process of compilation an effort will be made to avoid, as far as possible, injudicious reliance on presuppositions that stem from familiarity with European law, whose 'philosophy' is different, or recourse to irrelevant logical categories. It is hoped that this will in fact be successfully achieved, on the basis of an accurate recording of the facts, by culling the material for the legal glossary and nomenclature at source. The work is at present in progress, and already a substantial amount of material has been published.[2]

1. Private communication.
2. Collections published: Dogon, Nuer, Gusii, Lozi, Nkomi, Duala (in 1966); Tswana, Baga, Tonga, Serer, Fang, Hausa (in 1967); Hausa, Rwanda, Mongo (in 1968); Wolof, Duala (in 1969).

Jean Poirier

A similar effort is being made in the case of Madagascar, which is rightly being treated apart from the African projects. Culturally speaking, the island of course represents a bridge between Africa and Indonesia, but the fundamental values of its civilization are West Oceanian in type. In 1962 the Department of Human Sciences in Tananarive started to carry out an inventory of customary laws.[1] Although this department unfortunately no longer exists, its programme is shortly to be continued by French bodies.[2] There is, however, at the Faculty of Law in Madagascar (Tananarive) a centre for the study of customary law, and under the guidance of A. Rouhette it regularly brings out studies (*Cahiers*) devoted both to customary law and to the analysis of modern law in so far as the latter embodies aspects of customary law. A project is at present under consideration in Paris for getting a mixed team of jurists, ethnologists and sociologists to make a systematic inventory of Malagasy customary laws.

Such are the main trends of research relating to the societies of black Africa, which have received special attention. We may recall here, however, that the legal systems of a great many other societies have long been the object of regular study in France (e.g. Moslem legal systems, studies by Milliot and Massignon in recent times, and the legal systems of South-East Asia, studied by Lengat and Lafont). Comparative law, a companion discipline of legal ethnology, has also been taught for a long time in French universities. R. David has been particularly active in this field of research.

Work done in Belgium

In recent years several major works have been published in Belgium, testifying to this country's interest in the study of customary law. The works, by A. Sohier, Malengreau and Possoz, are well known. In 1953 Judge J. Sohier made a full collection of the case-law of the Congo and Ruanda-Urundi (as it then was). Ethnologists such as J. Vanderlinden, co-Secretary-General of the International African Law Association, have now turned their attention to research in this specialized field.

The Institut Jean Bodin, under the presidency of Count Pirenne, which is concerned with the study of the 'comparative history of institutions', has on a number of occasions manifested its interest in legal ethnology. At the symposia that it has regularly held over the past thirty years it has generally given a prominent place to pre-industrial societies (consolidated studies have for instance been published on the role of the market, the status of women and relations between rulers and ruled[3]).

1. See also *Études de Droit Africain et Malgache*, Paris, 1964, a compendium dealing with various aspects of customary law.
2. The idea of setting up a Centre of Malagasy Studies in Nice, which is 'twinned' with Tananarive, is at present under consideration.
3. cf. the following works, published in Brussels: *Les Liens de Vassalité et les Immunités*; *Le Servage*; *La Tenure*; *Le Domaine*; *La Foire*; *L'Étranger* (3 vols.); *La Femme* (3 vols.); *La Paix* (2 vols.); *La Preuve* (3 vols.); *Gouvernants et Gouvernés* (2 vols.).

The most systematic efforts, however, are due to Professor J. Gilissen, who established in Brussels the Centre d'Histoire et d'Ethnologie Juridiques, of which he is the director. This body has been active in several fields of study with which we are mainly concerned here, including the sociological study of legal pluralism in the developing countries, a survey of disciplinary law and a general bibliography. The centre is also interested in the study of Belgian legislation in the nineteenth and twentieth centuries and is preparing a bibliography on Belgian history.

The broad scheme of the centre's programme of studies is as follows:

Sociological study of legal pluralism in the developing countries. The programme involves an analysis of the problems arising out of the existence of two or more legal systems in most developing countries and the preparation of a general sociological survey. A number of studies prepared for seminars will be brought together in a preliminary mimeographed publication, covering the following subjects: pluralism in African countries (Islam, Ethiopia, Congo, South Africa, Mali); pluralism in Communist countries (U.S.S.R., mainland China); pluralism in the history of law (tenth and eleventh centuries—Western Europe, Middle Ages, modern times); pluralism in the work of legal philosophers and in the work of E. Dupreel; and, lastly, pluralism in domestic Belgian law.

Sociological survey of disciplinary law. As an extension of the study of legal pluralism a research worker undertook a sociological survey involving the collection of material with a view to studying the codes of behaviour imposed by many social groups on their members, as well as of the sanctions which are applied. The survey, which was spread out over several months, was carried out among some 600 social groups.

Bibliographical introduction to the history of law and legal ethnology. The aim of this work is to give legal historians, historians, jurists, ethnologists and sociologists up-to-date bibliographical information on the various aspects of the development of legal studies throughout the world, but not to supersede the many specialized bibliographies which specialists will still have to continue to use.

It is a selective bibliography, whose chronological and geographical scope has been made as wide as possible so as to cover developments in the law and institutions of all five continents from the beginning right up to the present day. Much space has been given to legal ethnology, which is concerned with the law of peoples who have no written language. There will also be sections relating to the bibliography of colonial legal systems, which have often acted as a bridge between two civilizations.

The work will comprise approximately 125 different sections, to be published in eight loose-leaf volumes of which five have now appeared.

Work done in the United Kingdom

Scholars in the United Kingdom have long been interested in the study of anthropology of law. Their efforts have been channelled in three directions.

Jean Poirier

First mention should be made of the research carried out by anthropologists and sociologists, examples being the work done by Anderson on Islamic Africa and by Shapera on South Africa. More recently Max Gluckman published the results of a number of surveys, which quickly became classics.[1]

Secondly, under the guidance of Daryll Forde, the International African Institute has on a number of occasions manifested its interest in the study of African legal systems. In January 1966 a symposium was held at Addis Ababa on the subject 'Concepts and Procedures in African Law', of which the proceedings were recently published.

Lastly, in 1959 Anthony Allott launched the Restatement of African Law Project at the School of Oriental and African Studies in London. The project rapidly gained in importance, especially after the accession of a large number of African States to independence. The aim was to make available to the young nations accurate documentation concerning customary law, which is still the main factor in the law of persons and also governs a large part of land law. It was not the aim of the organizers of the programme to compile a collection of customary laws for individual ethnic groups but to bring together the most important and representative customary laws. In addition to the support lent by the Nuffield Foundation and the School of Oriental and African Studies the project also received the support of African governments, which appointed so-called Customary Law Commissioners to consult with those engaged in the project. By virtue of these arrangements for co-operation between London and the local administrative authorities research has been carried out during the past ten years in Sierra Leone, Ghana, Nigeria (especially the northern and eastern regions), Kenya, Zambia, Malawi, Botswana, Swaziland, Lesotho, Liberia and Cameroon.

The results of the work are being published either in the United Kingdom or in Africa. The first two volumes, dealing with customary law in regard to marriage and to inheritance, have already appeared. Two works on the customary law of Malawi and of Ghana and northern Nigeria are due to be published very shortly. Subsequently, three volumes will deal with the customary law of Botswana. A. Allott has published a comprehensive review entitled *Judicial and Legal Systems of Africa* and finished compiling a bibliography.

The project has come in for a certain amount of criticism both in Europe and in Africa. It has been criticized for its incompleteness, the gaps in its ethno-sociological treatment and the fact that the preparatory work had been scrappy and had not included any field surveys, which would have been useful and in some cases essential. In reply, A. Allott made the point that the project was practical in its objectives, that it answered the needs that had been formulated by African governments and that it was better to have specific data, even if incomplete, than none at all.

This Restatement of African Law, by making it possible to take stock of

1. For example, *Politics, Law and Ritual in Tribal Society*, Oxford, 1965.

a number of systems of customary law, will have made an effective contribution to our knowledge of Africa.

Despite the very interesting achievements mentioned above the task would appear to be beyond the means of individual research workers and even of national bodies, and international co-operation seems to be called for. Such a move was foreshadowed by the setting up in 1955 of the International African Law Association (at the joint instigation of Anthony Allott and Jean Poirier), with headquarters in London. But in spite of the good work done by this body, its attention is confined to Africa, and mainly black Africa. An internationally co-ordinated programme could ensure the carrying through of the inventories that still need to be made, about which two main points should be borne in mind. First, the work should be treated as a matter of urgency, since customary law is now merely a survival and a little more of it is being lost every day. Of course it is not going to disappear completely or everywhere—it is changing, adapting, being assimilated into the new legal systems. However, though codified law incorporates part of customary law, there is no denying that the latter is rapidly dying out. Secondly, the work involves saving a cultural heritage, which is even more important—though perhaps less spectacular—than saving archaeological monuments. This legal heritage forms an essential part of the traditional culture of the developing pre-industrial nations and its disappearance would be a loss to civilization as a whole.

The present situation is, in general, marked by a number of serious shortcomings. For one thing, there are very few courses in legal ethnology. For another, qualified research workers are in short supply. Ethnologists should have at least a grounding in law and jurists a similar grounding in ethnology. Often, legal ethnology either overstresses the legal aspect or the ethnological aspect. Moreover, this discipline does not have the audience it really deserves because it falls between law and ethnology and is classified either as one or the other. Perhaps for this reason international machinery is practically non-existent; there is merely inter-regional machinery in certain spheres (such as the International African Law Association). The situation is all the more disturbing in that there is no coherent programme, as regards either general methodology or the interpretation of the facts. Lastly, a point, which seems to deserve special attention, is the collection of systems of oral law threatened with extinction. Over the past twenty years there has been much discussion of multidisciplinary research; organically speaking, legal ethnology seems to typify this kind of combined research, which is apparently so difficult to conduct in practice.

Programme and methods of work

In the sense that it is a discipline concerned with the study of traditional laws legal ethnology is in an absolutely paradoxical and very disturbing position, as the object of its research may have ceased to exist before there has been time to collect it. There is here therefore a problem of obvious urgency, the real extent of which must be clearly realized.

PARTICULARITY AND RATIONALITY IN LEGAL SYSTEMS

It is evident that human society everywhere is gradually moving towards increased standardization and rationalization. This fundamental trend, even if obscured by delays or particularist tendencies, is specially marked in the field of law, where it operates at three different levels.

In the first place, technology (in the very broad sense of the term) forms a single whole and automatically gives rise to a coherent system of law covering telecommunications law, aviation law and all the other special types of law which, as a matter of vital necessity, spring from and govern the different forms of technology.

Secondly, the spread of international relations implies a rationalized system of communication. There is a kind of administrative technology, less rigorous certainly than the foregoing but which none the less imposes its own criteria. A concerted system of law is therefore developing, founded on the same principles, whether as regards the organization of postal services, passport controls, international driving licence regulations or anything else. The same factors are at work in the obvious proliferation of bilateral and multilateral agreements, such as that of Interpol.

More generally, however, it is within each nation that this process of legal fusion is apparent. The growing 'oneness' of the world and the slow but sure tendency towards a gradual relinquishing of sovereignty constitute an important development, though perhaps basically less significant, as far as we are concerned, than the slow but steady convergence of legal systems. Although the trend is retarded by the basic differences of policy in the social and political fields, we are—consciously or unconsciously, but irreversibly—heading towards an erosion of individual or particularistic features. Whether we consider the law governing archives or that governing traffic there is a certain legal rationality that will continue to gain ground at the expense of traditional modes of behaviour.

This search for rationality obviously raises the question of the gradual disappearance of certain areas of law, and this trend is particularly pronounced in the developing countries, which have until now chiefly been governed by an oral legal tradition. This explains why one of the most urgent priorities must be the collection of customary laws.

AN EMERGENCY PROGRAMME

As the result of a process that has no parallel at any time in history some forty nations have come into being since the end of the Second World War. In every case[1] these nations have sprung from pre-industrial bases and, often

1. Except for Israel, which is a very special case.

also, from pre-literate cultures with an oral legal tradition. This is true even of societies that did in theory have a written language, such as India, Ethiopia and Indonesia, for in fact virtually the whole population lived without any contact with the written language or written law, in accordance with the more or less sacralized traditions of customary law.

A tremendous revolution has therefore occurred, on the legal plane, by their accession to independence, although, for a revolution, it is peculiar in being spread out in time over several decades. A number of consequences arise out of the change-over from oral law to written law. In this study we are concerned with only one of them, though one of the most important—the progressive obsolescence of oral customs. Though it may occasionally be checked, falter or even lose a little ground, this trend definitely seems irreversible. Before long a whole traditional culture is going to disappear. There is a need to see exactly what this means.

Although the figures we give are necessarily highly approximate, we may say that societies governed by oral custom form a vast whole comprising several thousand ethnic groups, subject to several hundred distinct families of customary law. The continent of Africa, for example, alone numbers some three thousand ethnic groups that claim individual identity, as such.[1] The number of legal systems is obviously smaller, since the customs observed by a number of culturally related ethnic groups may differ only on minor points and, consequently, represent a single system, but the number remains appreciable. This one example provides a yardstick by which to gauge the practical importance of the problem.

It is these customs that are threatened with extinction. We mentioned above why legal customs are more fragile than other cultural traditions—they are directly affected by the action of the authorities. No one explicitly forces a particular society to forget a particular myth or to give up circumcision: where action is taken is in the field of law. The administrative authorities do not interfere with marriage or funeral rites, but codes setting out the law of persons or civil law clearly define the conditions of marriage and the rules governing inheritance. Traditional culture no doubt forms a single whole —and social traditions may be affected via legal norms—but it is clear that it is the latter which are directly threatened.

These customary laws must therefore be collected while there is still time. There are not many years left in which to do this. Everywhere we have observed a very distinct generation gap; depending on the country and the ethnic groups involved the gap comes somewhere between the age of 45 and 65. It is less a question of absolute age than of education. In some cases the adult population (or at any rate certain sectors of it) have been acquainted with traditional law by the old people, while in other places they have been severed from their cultural roots and have irremediably lost contact with their culture. But everywhere there are still people versed in customary law—generally old

1. At least if we apply the subjective criterion whereby the term 'ethnic group' is used to denote those individuals who profess to belong to the group.

Jean Poirier

men. These represent our last opportunity of access to the authentic sources; if they are allowed to die off without passing on their knowledge, invaluable evidence will have been lost. These old people are now between 65 and 80 years of age, or more; most of them will be dead within a decade. Knowing what is at stake and the facts being as they are, we have about ten years in which to save a valuable cultural heritage from final extinction.

It is all too little realized in Europe how quickly things are changing. Everything contributes to accelerate the trend of events—the needs of economic development, the new nations' determination to achieve unity, the consequences of the break-up of the extended family unit, a desire to imitate the West and above all to adopt modern solutions. At the same time we find a surprising attachment to tradition among many young people, but it is a sentimental one, mainly concerned with the folk-lore aspect.

This reaction is particularly pronounced among a large section of the intelligentsia trained in Europe, and (although there is no quantitative survey on the subject) it can be reckoned that half of them are in varying degrees opposed to 'abandoning' the customary-law system. However, a similar position is maintained, although less openly, by nearly all the traditional leaders in the villages. On the other hand, the urban middle classes—young and not so young—seem to be in favour of modernization.

One example will perhaps serve to illustrate the true ratio of forces. President L. S. Senghor, the theorist of *négritude* and *africanité*, certainly cannot be suspected of underestimating the importance of African traditions; his attitude to customary law is therefore all the more striking. Dr. Houphouet-Boigny too, who as President of the Ivory Coast has done enough for his country's economic development to be above suspicion of losing sight of its interests, has not hesitated to promote a series of modernizing codes replacing the sixty or seventy systems of customary law prevalent in the country. President Senghor, who has been working in the same direction, said in an interview given some years ago to the periodical *Jeune Afrique*: 'We are at present discussing the code of family law. I am holding discussions with the religious authorities who support the idea of a progressive code that reconciles the code of civil law and the Koran. For there are 70 systems of Moslem customary law in our country. As you can imagine, these 70 systems diverge considerably from the Koran. The aim is to merge them into a single whole that offers a more contemporary interpretation of the Koran.'[1]

The firm opposition of the Western-trained intelligentsia is based, consciously or otherwise, on the rejection of any legislation stemming from outside the country's legal tradition (and sometimes even directed against it). And here we cannot but agree with them that the new legal systems of Africa must not, if they are to be truly African, 'short-circuit' the customary laws, as is too often the case. How can one venture to draw up legal codes without first knowing the legal traditions? Wherever and whenever codes of law have been formulated, it has always been in relation to a pre-existent state of affairs.

1. See *Jeune Afrique*, No. 303, 30 October 1966.

Social dynamics, the innovative element in law, develops only in relation to, and on the basis of, a certain tradition which it educes, supplements or opposes. Quite a different situation, however, exists in the new nations, since their codes of law are worked out practically in ignorance of their customary laws. The problem is therefore partly one of political and administrative expediency. Can new systems of law safely be worked out without investigating the old systems and without identifying the principles on which they operate to guide the legislator? The problem also exists at a purely scientific level. As we pointed out above, with traditional systems of law gradually wasting away from year to year, we shall no longer be able to find out the facts unless remedial action is taken.

But drawing up a set of legal codes suited to the technical requirements of development does not necessarily mean sacrificing custom. We should underestimate neither the profound nature of this return to tradition demanded by certain sectors of the intelligentsia, nor the value of what underlies this demand: for customary law obviously cannot be dissociated from religious thought, or from the system of values, or from the ontological premises. It is not a disembodied corpus of technical rules but the living, everlasting voice of one's ancestors. Consequently, for an African who respects his tradition respect for his customary laws is the only means of remaining faithful to his ancestors and of propitiating them. Two highly commendable reasons can thus be adduced in support of this point of view.

There can therefore be no question of a sudden substitution of a written code for customary law. Various solutions are possible—it can be left to written codes to lay down principles and to local customs to adapt them; it is also possible to restrict written codes to certain fields, leaving customary law competent in others; above all the traditional system of law can be used to breathe life into the new system of law. This clearly shows the practical importance attaching to the collection and analysis of customary laws.

ETHNOLOGY AND THE HISTORY OF LAW

The study of present-day customs already appears to have opened up a new channel for the interpretation of traditional law. One line of research during the coming decade should be to apply to long-established systems of law the methods ethnologists have tried out in their work overseas.

It may be said, without in any way belittling their learning, that legal historians lived in a legal, technical and socio-economic environment which, without their realizing it, acted as a screen between them and the social reality they were studying. These scholars had received a Western legal training and, what is more, found themselves face to face every day with actual situations which arose out of principles quite different from those on which customary law was based. It is no exaggeration to say that primitive Roman law, for example, can for the most part be reinterpreted in the light of the experience gained by the ethnologist. Henri Lévy-Bruhl has shown how productive this method can be, but the example set by him should be followed systematically

The method has a general value that could be fruitfully applied not only to Greek law, but also to the ancient systems of law of the Near East, as well as to the history of European law.

There is in fact a tremendous disparity between the laws of industrialized societies and all other systems; the former are based on the primacy of reason (even taking into account the 'survivals' that may subsist in them), while the latter are based on the primacy of tradition. This is where we get the basic divergence; there is a radical change in environment, mode of life, yardsticks and, generally, system of values. There is of course another relevant distinction which should be made within the law of non-industrialized societies, that between written law and law based on oral custom.

We should therefore like to see collaboration between jurists specialized in the study of ancient law and ethnologists. They have a long-term task ahead of them; as far as we know there is no regular collaboration of this kind anywhere in the world. It is high time that these two complementary fields of study be combined. From such a programme we can expect a veritable renewal of our understanding of the law of the past.

METHODOLOGICAL ASPECTS

For an 'ethno-jurist' to be able to analyse systems other than that in which he has been trained a number of preliminary questions of a methodological nature obviously have to be settled. The research worker must refer in this connexion to the general problems of ethnological inquiry, which it is not for us to examine here. There are, however, two points to which it does seem worth drawing attention.

First, the need for an international glossary is increasingly apparent. We know that most of the new nations engaged in framing their own codes of law need to express in their own language the various concepts arising from modern life. However, this process of developing a new vocabulary can be regulated at the national level. What we are suggesting here is that work should be begun on nothing less than a glossary of comparative law, containing explanations of the main concepts used in the various legal systems together with proposed renderings. The theoretical analysis contained in the explanations should be based on specific ethnographical instances, since in the case of the countries of the Third World, which have no written legal tradition (and no recorded case law), it is only from the realities of contemporary life that the law can be ascertained and the various concepts interpreted.

The work that we are proposing would run on the following lines: (a) designation of the concept (e.g. adoption); (b) illustrative material, drawn from ethnological works, autobiographies or memoirs (ethnobiographies) and case law; (c) theoretical analysis of the concept, synonyms, symbolic significance and religious implications; (d) any relevant legal adages, sayings, witticisms or proverbs; (e) bibliographical references.

Such a glossary would be an invaluable working tool; apart from being extremely useful to legislators, it would above all make it possible to work out an initial theory of customary law, in conditions precluding ethnocentrism or the unjustified extrapolation of Western categories.

Secondly, juristics (a term coined by Henri Lévy-Bruhl) is an essential complement to 'law'; it is concerned not just with the theoretical rule, but with the rule in relation to actual life. It has three major aspects:

The quantification of the legal phenomenon. This involves bringing together facts and figures to illustrate a legal definition. The research worker will not, for example, confine himself to describing how the sale and lease of land, tenant farming and share-cropping operate within a given society but will also bring together such data as may be available on the acreage of land sold and the actual conditions of tenure. The next stage, coupled with statistical analysis of the data, is to relate it to the sociological conditions (i.e. to identify possible correlations between, on the one hand, changing patterns of tenure and the redistribution of estates and, on the other, the current economic situation, technological progress and psychological factors). Law here enters the realm of sociology.

The dynamic study of law through litigation. The research worker will note the various precedents, compile statistics and see if there are any correlations. Law consists not just of the written rule, but also of precedents. Legal ethnology is concerned with the study of the law in its application to life.

The analysis of tacit law, and more generally of law as it is actually practised. The difference between the theoretical rule of law and practice is certainly great; the most striking—even ludicrous—examples of this discrepancy are the work-to-rule strikes which occur from time to time and which involve applying the regulations, not even strictly or draconically, but simply to the letter. All too often the law, however worded, legislates for ideal and absolute conditions, whereas men live in reality, where matters are relative. There is therefore a vast and almost unexplored field which is that of law as it is lived, the field—steadily increasing in importance—of what is tolerated and implicit.

Legal ethnology is a new subject and views still differ from country to country as to the methods it is at this juncture appropriate for it to apply. The problems that it at present raises are threefold.

In the first place, it is still not clear what legal ethnology comprises or its relation to other subjects. There are two tendencies, one to classify it under law, the other to include it in sociology. It seems difficult to make it a mere appendage of the legal disciplines. The best solution—and this appears to be the direction in which we are heading—is to have a general anthropology combining the inseparably linked subjects of sociology, social psychology and ethnology.

Secondly, on the practical plane, legal ethnology, which is at present taught either in faculties of law, in faculties of arts or philosophy or in social science institutes, must affirm the need for parallel training. It little matters how things are arranged administratively, but it seems essential to insist that teaching and research staff be trained as jurists and ethnologists at the same time. A straightforward jurist would be even less qualified to concern himself with ethnology than an ethnologist would be to concern himself with law: in the last resort an ethnologist is qualified to collect and analyse customs as he does with other social phenomena, whereas the jurist finds himself on unknown ground. But a legal training remains essential in order to be able to interpret customary law correctly.

More generally, in the short term, legal ethnology must cope with a vast programme of work, as has been explained above. This would appear to be a pretty unique situation in the field of science, where we have a discipline that must carry out research as a matter of extreme urgency, since the actual object of the research is, in part, on the point of final extinction. Lastly, it will be necessary to win general acceptance for the idea of giving this work absolute priority in terms of equipment and personnel. Although obvious enough, the need for this is still not sufficiently clearly realized.

[*Translated from French*]

Jean Poirier is professor at the University of Nice, has been lecturer at the University of Tananarive in Madagascar and specializes in African questions. He is a member of the editorial board of the Zeitschrift für vergleichende Rechtswissenschaft *in Cologne and author (with A. Leroi-Gourhan) of* Ethnologie de l'Union Française *(1953) and* Les Caractères de la Responsabilité Archaïque *(1961).*

[3]

SUBSTANCE AND PROCESS: REAPPRAISING THE PREMISES OF THE ANTHROPOLOGY OF LAW

Daisy Hilse Dwyer

Anthropologists of law have become somewhat like Joseph K in Kafka's *The Trial.* K must solve the enigma of his prosecution in order to achieve success, which in his case is personal freedom. He sets forth upon a course of action: to discover the essentials of a grievance procedure in a system that he does not yet know and cannot yet negotiate. He seeks to locate his judges, push through adjudicatory levels, and ascertain jurisdictions, but his busy course is in some sense despairing, for one crucial facet of the legal web that entraps him remains more or less unplumbed. What law, if any, has K broken, and why do the authorities and he also seem to require judgement of and expiation for that crime?

In effect, Joseph K, the fictive litigant, shuns the world of substantive law much as do most contemporary legal anthropologists. Instead most opt for a focus upon "procedure" (if one might utilize the substantive-procedural dichotomy that our own folk legal system promotes). And much as the thoughtful reader of fiction might ponder the consequences of K's neglect of substantive issues, the thoughtful anthropologist of law, in search of a maximally dynamic subdiscipline, might mull over the corresponding anthropological avoidance, and might seek out reasons for and effects of the trend. In doing this, he or she must contend with the possibility that the underlying causes are sociocultural, that the effect is an occasional ethnocentrism, and that the first part of a remedy is a clear anthropological explication of the law models of the cultures that have influenced subdisciplinary views. Such an explicitly self-reflective enterprise is especially necessary for the legal ethnographic corpus, for law is a superstructural phenomenon and so has an essential opaqueness upon which specific cultural models, some limiting, can easily be too easily imposed in the effort to describe legal functioning.

Let us return to Joseph K, for from an ethnographic standpoint, the system (a state-level society) in which he operates is not much different from our own when viewed from a cross-cultural perspective, nor are his blindnesses likely to be totally different from ours. We might ask, then, through K about our own legal situations as well as those of other societies: (1) How much do a given society's members know of law substance? (2) When there is a deficiency in substantive law knowledge, is it known and disturbing; if not, why not? (3) If diverse models of substantive law exist within a society, what are the discordances?, and (4) Why do these occur and seem to be maintained?

The legal anthropologist Leopold Pospisil [1] once wrote that each subgroup in a society has its own legal system. I do not take this as a given although ethnographic data points to its insightfulness for many societies, but rather wish to use it as a starting point. Namely, I take as my premise that different subgroups and individuals can and often do have differing legal systems, with the differences being of

Daisy Hilse Dwyer is Assistant Professor of Anthropology at Columbia University.

one or more kinds. There are differences in what might be called density: some groups in a given society have more or less content to the legal models that they hold. There might also be differences in content: these concern discordances in point-for-point principles and premises. There may be differences of clarity, in the precision with which legal models are formulated. Lastly, differences in awareness might also occur, there tending to be variation in the degree to which each group knows the content of the other groups' models, and by extension, knows the degree and placement of dissimilarities. Differences of the last sort strongly underlie the extent to which legal knowledge is strategically usable in struggles between groups, between individuals, or between these in combination. By tying substantive data to strategy through the phenomenon of differential knowledge of the law, this fourth aspect also gives the lie to any stark substantive-procedural dichotomy. Further, the existence of discordances in law models along any of these four parameters indicates that a conceptualization of substantive law as mere statute or document is sterile and misleading, for substantive law, cognitively manipulated, reflects group advantage and disadvantage, and so is more properly a political discourse between groups.

THE LAW LITERATURE IN RETROSPECT

Variability in Law Models

Intrasocietal variability of a behavioral sort occurs in numerous ways in the law realm: in how frequently different individuals seek a judicial solution to conflict situations [2]; in the variability with which persons utilize particular dispute-processing mechanisms [3]; in the judicial treatment which they ultimately receive [4]. Each of these has been rather well documented in the anthropology of law literature. (Nader and Todd [5] provide a broad variety of analyses directed toward precisely these issues in their recent volume.) Intrasocietal variability in cognitive models of law, by contrast, has not; nor has it been typically recognized as a law phenomenon. Gibbs [6] and Collier [7] allude to the phenomenon in their reviews of jurisprudential and anthropological materials. More concretely, Moore [8] has stressed the co-occurrence of alternative rule complexes between which individuals can choose according to situational dictates. Pospisil [9], Llewellyn and Hoebel [10] and Nader and Yngvesson [11] are among those who cite the possibility of co-occurring legal systems operation among different subgroups. The emphasis, in the former case, however, is upon individuals who know their alternatives; in the latter case, it is upon groups that know that they maintain discrete law.

While the latter phenomenon, typically discussed under the rubric of legal pluralism, is certainly important, and particularly so because of the proliferation of nation-states and the convoluted history of colonialism, it also constitutes a relatively transparent phenomenon which corresponds to a more opaque one: the existence of non-isomorphic, intrasocietal representations of "the law," which non-elite members, in some sense, believe are replicas of the dominant model by which those in power operate. That is, they believe that they and one or more other groups, generally the societal elite if there be one can or do function according to a common set of laws, or alternatively that they have free access to those facets of the law system with which they are not immediately acquainted.

The close ethnography of state organized, or political, societies including our own, and also of many traditional societies, reveals that this common folk notion is naive: misinterpretation, error, and ignorance about substantive law often constitute major components of the cognitive "law" models according to which diverse peoples maneuver in the judicial sphere and outside of it. Most Americans, for example, harbor far-reaching misconceptions about divorce and property law, and attach affective "symbolic" value to certain parts of the law corpus when they should not [12]. In one part of the Islamic world, southern Morocco, women are wont to formulate certain laws too stringently, while restating others so as to embody undue safeguards [13]. Similarly, certain Muslim women in Israel do not assert their legal rights in divorce situations when their husbands attempt to circumvent the new procedural protections with which women are afforded: one reason is that they do not fully know the laws that pertain to them [14]. And yet the anthropology of law has not considered the structure and/or functioning of such misinterpretation and/or ignorance. As a starting point, one must certainly ask to what degree the subdiscipline has avoided it, and why.

The Trend Toward "Process"

As numerous recent reviewers of the subdiscipline remind us, the emphasis in the anthropology of law has turned to process [15]. The tendency has been a fruitful one, resulting in landmark studies and methodologies, the extended case method [16] situational analysis [17] and social drama analysis [18] being among them. The tendency, too, has been described as away from substantive law [19]. One might ask, however, what "process" and "substantive law" connote for those anthropologists who have distinguished and defined these areas and to some degree hold to them, and indeed, whether one must reject "substantive law" in order to embrace "process": whether these two aspects of law might not more profitably be explored concurrently as was early attempted, for example, by Schapera [20] and more recently by Moore [21].

A review of the recent literature demonstrates that "process" is too inclusive a cover term for the predominant focus of many "process" studies, for the action and interaction of disputants is their primary focus, making most of these studies more properly behavioral. Adjudication, mediation, arbitration, "lumping it," and other sorts of dispute-processing [22] constitute primary foci. Further, these studies limit the processual domain to the judgement-rendering rather than enforcement aspect of law. (Cochrane [23] and Van Velsen [24] are two of a minority of anthropologists who directly confront the enforcement issue.)

It is not at all clear whether these emphases provide "the most useful and productive focus," as Gulliver [25] suggested early on, for certainly law process has a cognitive aspect and also a coercive one. Certain theorists [26] have recently turned their attention to the cognitive element by examining the psychocultural aspect of decision-making in disputing and dispute-processing, and Collier [27] takes note of this recent tendency as an important return to issues that Bohannan [28] and Pospisil [29] earlier considered. And yet involvement has also been slow, perhaps because a concern with these issues has long labored under the epithet of legalism. What is in the mind cannot as yet be comfortably integrated under the portmanteau of law.

The Impact of Anglo-American Law Models

Most Anglo-American anthropologists have had difficulty in confronting these issues because of the power of certain deep-structural elements in the Anglo-American configuration of law. These elements involve a low level of knowledge about substantive law (low density) among the people at large and a subconscious feeling of appropriateness concerning this tendency (low awareness). The rationale, to the degree that these perceptions are overtly rationalized, lies in a reliance upon a putatively strong, able professionalism in law.

These deep-structural elements, along with the rationale, point to two Anglo-American folk legal models which anthropologists have been wont to project, with attendant insights and limitations. Nader and Yngvesson pinpoint the more apparent one – "anthropologists have been overly influenced by a model of law as defined by the legal profession [30] – and root many of the inadequacies of early anthropology of law studies in its use. Law, they note, was first approached as the corpus of cases and/or rules that legal professionals and paraprofessionals use. Law thereby came to be viewed by many as an elitist phenomenon, and a judicial elite, often conceptualized in too Western a sense, was sometimes conjured up in an effort comfortably to place it in other societies. At times, this resulted in an exaggeration of the authority that legal personages were felt to hold; at times, it promoted an exaggerated concreteness regarding rules [31]. Gulliver [32], in effect, cautioned against both tendencies by forwarding the heuristic device of a spectrum which provided multiple flexibility for description: one endpoint was "judicial" society, in which a judge judged "in accordance with established norms," while the other was "political" society, in which "a decision is reached and a settlement made as a result of the relative strengths of the two parties to the dispute... In this case the accepted norms of behavior relevant to the matter in dispute are but one element involved, and possibly an unimportant one." Through it, Gulliver, like Moore [33] after him, rightly challenged the premises of administrative formalism and a pure rule-oriented decision-making. His ethnographic (Arusha) data, however, do not disprove the strategic role of substantive law principles in dispute-processing and dispute prevention.

The second, less apparent model is the lay counterpoise to the professionalist model. The thrust of this Anglo-American folk model is to distance substantive law from the mind. Law comes to be viewed as an aspect of social life which good citizens need not touch and so the need to commandeer knowledge of it seems minimal. Lawyers are felt properly to hold the requisite expertise should crises arise (See Bohannan and Huckleberry [34] regarding the problems this attitude generates in American divorces).

These two countermodels, one detailed, professional, and case-oriented, the other lay and thin, harken back in United States history to the colonial period and indeed when English groups underwent the socio-cultural transition brought by crossing the Atlantic. United States law developed at times through the manipulation of a low-density, low-awareness lay model, at times through the use of the dense, case-oriented model which law professionals were engaged to employ. The result is a convoluted law history with regard to ideas and behavior, but in any events limitedly substantive. The early settlers in many colonies founded their legal systems upon whatever methods and principles they could remember, which generally were low-density facsimiles of law as practiced in English borough or county courts [35]. Lay settlers' perceptions were clearly far different in content from those of England's law professionals, who manipulated some fifteen sorts of law according to Coke's enumeration [36]. "We had no law of our own and nobody knew what (the law) was," admitted one 1791 New Yorker [37]. An if lay people had little acquaintance with statute and the premises that proceeded from them, lawyers, who especially achieved importance as law-manipulators with the rise of propertied citizenry in the United States, held to their own case-oriented, minimally statutory model, which reflected English law's strong common law basis. Pound [38] records an "attitude of resentment to legislation on the part of the bench and the bar," a resentment which resulted in the use of adjudicated cases as essential material in judgement-rendering rather than the rules underlying them. The emphasis parallels the Anglo-American anthropologists' recent attraction to "process" and sharply avoids the verbalization of generalized rules of any sort (tendencies which certain legal anthropologists trained in the Continental tradition (e.g., Pospisil, Gluckman) do not evince as markedly as their American colleagues).

It is thus not surprising that most anthropologists of law, whether lay or law-professional in origin, have tended to view law in other societies in non-substantive terms. And yet the tendency is clearly dangerous, given the preoccupation which many non-Western peoples have with the law. A host of Africanists have remarked upon the litigious character of many sub-Saharan societies, a character which entails considerable exposure to and command of rules of one sort or another by substantial segments of those populations. My own research [39] in an Arab-Berber region of southern Morocco indicates a comparable involvement which results in relatively high density folk models of varying contents: even non-literate semi-secluded women, who constitute a subordinated and constrained group, are likely to have a working command of the intricacies of who inherits what from whom or how to dissolve an encumbering marriage.

POLITICIZING THE SUBSTANTIVE LAW REALM: PLAUSIBLE DIRECTIONS

Toward the Law Analysis of Groups

The role of supportive groups in various phases of a dispute process has come under increasing scrutiny in the anthropology of law, which now looks as much to conflict networks [40] as to the opposition of disputants, and which has come explicitly to recognize that disputants play to a public which can be formally (e.g., jury, judge) or informally constituted and of variable size. In effect, the anthropology of law has taken to social organizational analysis, a goal long voiced within the subdiscipline. And yet that heightened social organizational concern has moved only haltingly into political analysis, the branch of anthropology of which, ironically, it once was part. Network is, in itself, an apolitical concept, unlike class or caste, for example, to which legal anthropologists have addressed scant attention (See Cohn [41], for example, for commentary on the paucity of law analysis of castes.)

Middle-level socio-political units are badly wanting in the anthropology of law [42], which moves between a focus on the individual (and his coterie) and society at large. Lost, for the most part, is a politico-legal vision of those subgroups that are in some sense "encapsulated" [43], subgroups which can be defined by age, sex, occupation, race, class, or ethnicity. Nader and Yngvesson [44] mention them under the narrower rubric of "ethnic group," although the Bailey definition that they cite (a group that "has a membership which identifies itself, and/or is identified by others, as constituting a category distinguishable from other categories of the same order") points to the fact that such subgroups need not be ethnic. Smith [45] mentions them under the rubric of "corporation". Hoebel [46], Pospisil [47] and Moore [48] have also mentioned the phenomenon of subgroup variability, whether or not ethnicity is taken as the relevant index of differentiation.

One might follow Nader and Yngvesson's suggestion [49] that we examine "shared legal perceptions," this time from the subgroup perspective, using the notion of encapsulation to provide insights. The latter notion calls two basic, generally unstated premises in the anthropology of law literature – the uniform distribution and the free flow of law knowledge – into review. The first takes substantive law knowledge to be evenly distributed among society's members, so that all actors coming under a particular legal systems' purview are presumed to be aware of its rules. Gluckman, for example, defines law as "a set of rules accepted by *all* normal members of the society..." [50] and proceeds in accordance with that view as he describes a complex Barotse political situation involving the interplay of more than twenty ethnic minorities. The second affirms the occurrence of uneven distributions of law knowledge but recognizes no consciously imposed barriers to the free flow of rules and/or interpretations of them. Differences in law models are ascribed to poor education, slow diffusion, or a general law lag. The good will of a political leadership is presumed.

Both premises, of course, are poor approximations of the psycho-dynamics of politics in stratified societies. To one or another degree, power-wielding groups tend to hoard legal knowledge. Weber [51] recognized the tendency among English and French law professionals, who profited socially and economically from it, and Diamond [52] has made a similar point, although in a different context, using political examples from non-Western as well as Western societies. Ehrlich [53] and Pospisil [54] reach a parallel conclusion without ascribing political motivations: the rules that authorities hold are often not those held by the people generally.

There is a second political blindness associated with the free flow postulate: the assumption that the content of law models originates with the politically dominant group and then flows down to the non-elite. The creative thrust of subordinate groups is ignored. And yet evidence points to the more politically salient fact that many subgroups use the actual substantive knowledge that they have in shaping more extensive law models. Elaboration from piecemeal data, extension by logical inference, and creation by simple guesswork provide pathways to formulations which might appear erroneous from the dominant group perspective but which are more nearly attempts at predicting elite behavior in the interests of their own security (see Dwyer [55], Layish [56]).

Reconsidering the Definitional Base

A crucial shortcoming of the anthropology of law to date, then, is that the power politics of coercion and consensus in the law realm have not been sufficiently examined. Rather, consensus in law knowledge has generally been presumed, and coercion has entered the judico-legal picture inconsistently. In no aspect of legal anthropological thinking is this more apparent than in the quest for a definition of law. Broadly, legal anthropologists have forwarded consensus-based and coercion-based definitions, with only a few theorists integrating the two organically. A few scholars [57] point to essential attributes from both facets, but a full appreciation of the problematic existence of societal consensus on the substantive law front is rather unclear (e.g., Pospisil's notion of *obligatio* seems to imply a general knowledge of rights and duties and Bohannan's depiction of double institutionalization stresses restatement more than substitution and modification as subsidiary processes [58]).

The presumption of law as consensus surfaced early and starkly in the equation of law and custom in Malinowski's definition of civil law (law is "a body of binding obligations regarded as a right by one party and acknowledged as a duty by the other [59]). An enraged discipline nullified the equation, but thereafter maintained the somewhat comparable word *norm*. Hoebel thus describes law in the following way: "a social norm is legal if its neglect or infraction is regularly met, in threat or in fact, by the application of physical force by an individual or group possessing the socially recognized privilege of so acting [60]. Weber [61] had similarly provided a (rather guarded) parallel definition: one major thrust (among many) in his thinking is summarized in the developmental schema: usage, convention, law. Similarly, Hart [62] and Fallers [63] after him provide a normative definition of "primary rules of obligation" (substantive law):

these are "norms of social life which are supported not only by institutionalization and internalization in the society at large – by conscience and public opinion – but also by institutions that apply secondary rules" (procedural law) [64].

Much confusion regarding psycho-political processes underlies the conclusion that the general populace must be presumed to accept and know the principles applied by the political elite. "To a certain extent, the interests of the dominant groups must coincide with the interest of the whole association, or at least with those of the majority of the members of the association, for if this were not so, the other members would not obey the norms established by the dominant group," wrote Ehrlich [65] in 1913.

An alternative approach is to sidestep the issue of consensus and to represent law as radiating out from the realm of authority and so to emphasize coercion [66]. It is the well-known current of Weber's thinking: "an order will be called law if it is externally guaranteed by the probability that coercion (physical or psychological), to bring about conformity or avenge violations, will be applied by a staff of people holding themselves specially ready for that purpose" [67]. Austin [68] similarly emphasizes the counterpart notion of "command". Other Austinian definitions, among them Fried's [69] – law involves "a rule of conduct enforced by sanctions administered by a determinate locus of power whether by the sovereign itself or by a surrogate" – follow this notion of coercion. A central dilemma in most of these definitions, which political anthropologists tend to put forward, involves communication and transmissibility: "order" and "command", or equivalent terms, usually circumlocutions, imply a moment of reception by a social audience.

Given the problems posed by the consensus-coercion complex, it is not surprising that present-day theorists have shied away from the definitional dilemma entirely [70], so thoroughly, in fact, that Koch [71] eliminates it from discussion by asserting that it is a very unprofitable ground for debate. And yet if Hart could wonder at the liveliness of the definitional issue during the years prior to 1961, enough to ask why the question "what is law" persisted with such tenacity and indeed so much more so than, for example, "what is chemistry" or "what is medicine" [72], one might ask why it subsequently fell so completely into neglect. The answer, I believe, is that anthropologists are ethnographers in the first instance, and that they have found it increasingly difficult to use these definitions, or the paradigms that underlie them, in representing convoluted, present-day politico-legal situations, such as occur in the new nation-state, in capitalist society, in socialist states, and presently and retrospectively through the colonialist experience.

The anthropology of law, like anthropology generally, has built its paradigms from ethnographic data gathered in the local groups of traditional, including primitive, societies. In societies such as the Tiv [73], Kapauku [74], Cheyenne [75], Ifugao [76], and the Trobriands [77], consensus can be logically presumed. In societies such as the Barotse [78] by contrast, total consensus about legal issues is unlikely, but still the force of political coercion is relatively direct. Full-fledged states, by contrast, show myriad, circuitous pathways for transmitting law knowledge and for controlling their populations, and these require new analytic models of law (and more broadly of social control processes). Nader (Mexico, the Middle East), Moore (Inca), Collier (Latin America), Lowy (urban Ghana), and Layish (Israel), to mention but a few, have analyzed highly complex state systems. Tellingly, all have refrained from the definitional debate in those cases.

Indirect evidence thus indicates that the thorn in the sides of definition-seekers might be the opposite of what has heretofore been supposed. In the history of the anthropology of law, there has been a universalist camp and a particularist camp as well as those who have straddled thoughtfully, with the particularists asserting that the development of law presupposes societal "complexity" while the universalists have worked to enter stateless societies into the law-run category. Contemporary legal anthropology, however, finds its deepest dilemma at the opposite end of the spectrum. There, in the form of complex state organizations that hold extraordinary control potential of varying kinds, legal anthropology finds the situations for which it must go beyond certain narrower perceptions of how law operates, and along with this reconsider its definitions.

CONSENSUS, COERCION, AND LEGAL SYSTEMS

Machiavelli wrote concerning the state: "the main foundations of every state, new states as well as ancient or composite ones, are good laws and good arms, and ... you cannot have good laws without good arms, and where there are good arms, good laws inevitably follow" [79], good, in this instance, meaning effective from the point of view of those who rule. The duality and the relationship Machiavelli posits should pique our attention, for a polity tends to manipulate the ideational realm according to its control powers, so that dispute-processing and breach-management cannot be properly analyzed without the ever-present backdrop of law (and more broadly, order) enforcement. It thus remains for us, in conclusion, to confront the two realms – ideology and order-maintenance – in tandem, and to ascertain their role in the processual sphere by extending the anthropology of law's strong focus on dispute-processing.

Gramsci's [80] emphasis of the difference between the state and civil society, and his perception of how the two interweave are useful as an integrative first framework for this sort of analysis. The state, he submits, operates in the first instance by domination through coercion, so that here one does well to consider the power of law through the courts, which, in turn, have police and army behind them. By contrast, the civil society aspect of the state, he asserts, strives for hegemony through consent, with popular consent being molded explicitly and/or implicitly through "cultural" direction from below and above. In terms of law-related behavior, the shaping of a perception of the law itself and of its content is significant in this second, more hidden social control realm.

It is clear that as institutions of force (Gramsci's state) become more potent and effective, those in power enjoy the option of drawing these forces out of the public view, openly and actively mobilizing them only when dissent reaches critical proportions [81]. The establishment of colonies and the display of armies on potentially hostile territory, two recommendations for successful rulership in *The Prince*, thus becomes less strategically crucial as regions become more tightly controlled and dominated. Instead, the apparently gentler force of "civil society" can take the initial, major role in directing a populace. Coercion can give way, immediately although not ultimately, to the force of persuasion.

Not only do police and army strategically recede according to this formulation but so, too, can courts, taking with them knowledge about the principles that they implement and the mechanisms they employ. Knowledge of a substantive and procedural sort thus is often limited in a powerful state, even among high-breach populations whom outsiders expect know how to "work" the system. Spradley's [82] work with Seattle tramps, for example, indicates that they are moved quickly through the judicial cases that concern them and do not share the norms held by court and police. They remain a manipulated subgroup despite their continuing judical involvement.

Some of the informational barriers which exist within stratified populations obviously serve well, given the goal of those polities and their elites. Galanter [83] interprets the obfuscation of law information politically and economically for the United States case: through an ignorance of substantive (and procedural) law content, "one-shotters" (i.e., those litigants who use the courts only rarely), who are typically "have-nots", suffer a marked disadvantage as opposed to "repeat-players", who are typically "haves", in attaining optimal court settlements.

It is important to note that the perpetuation of low density models among a polity's membership or among certain of its subgroups, is far from the only alternative which societies have for manipulating their citizenry ideationally. "In a sense, the very force of law," asserts Diamond [84], "depends upon ignorance of its specifications," and that ignorance might be fostered by shaping law models along various parameters – content, density, clarity, and awareness being among them. Judicial decisions, being political decisions, often require this careful selection and manipulation of norms [85].

A recognition of the complexity of knowledge control within the law domain thus leads to a greater appreciation of the politics of polities with substantial power and also the variations among them. The United States, for example, is a complex case in which different groups (as defined by occupation, sex, race, ethnicity, and/or class) vary in their substantive and procedural expertise regarding the law, but the predominant tendency appears to be toward low density, low content, low awareness substantive law models among the majority of its citizens. Southern Moroccan urban society, by contrast, sustains a population that is generally better informed (higher density), but certain subgroups (e.g., women) hold a relatively dense law model, which contains important bits of misinformation (mixed content) with low awareness of the fact. A third mix is reflected in the complex politico-legal life of the Kababish Arabs [86]. By virtue of the centralization of power that the colonial experience afforded, the Kababish appear to have high awareness of differences in those aspects of the politico-legal model that relate to an ideology of justice and the legitimacy of the rulership and its courts. At present, however, law data on the Kababish is insufficient to characterize the models of its three political subgroups according to the content, clarity, and density of their substantive law perceptions. Finally, the case of the Arusha [87] points to the likelihood that variability in law models is a phenomenon not only to be examined for state or state-associated societies, but must be seriously considered in terms of its political implications for any society that differentiates subgroups, even if it be according to the basic parameters of age and sex.

CONCLUSION

The anthropology of law works best through the use of the holistic approach that Hoebel [88] recommended in the early stages of the subdiscipline. That approach includes the study of trouble cases, of patterns of actual law-related behavior, and of abstract rules or principles, the last being not the least among them. The quest should ideally be joined, however, so as to generate data that lend themselves to cross-cultural comparison and the formulation of politico-legal principles of a general sort, a goal which numerous anthropologists of law have already espoused in their work. But as Smith and Roberts [89] caution, this is particularly difficult with regard to substantive law content, because substantive law is a "particularly culture bound" domain: there is considerable variability from society to society in its specific content. The structural comparison of substantive law notions as they occur within the boundaries of particular societies, by contrast, presents one fruitful alternative approach, one which carefully reflects the realities of intergroup politics. Through a political analysis of variability in cognitive models of law can better be seen as a reflection of, and an underpinning to, the socio-economic base that correlates with it.

Nader [90] indirectly calls attention to the fact that the law realm is best viewed from an explicitly political vantage. She notes that a lack of interest in substantive law has been accompanied by a relative loss of interest in political development, two tendencies which Koch [91] also cites. But the very element of political developmental dynamics, as has been seen, forms a crucial component in understanding the variability in substantive law models and, more broadly, law's ideational side (see Moore [92]). Polities that wield considerable power potentials can generate and accomodate co-occurring non-isomorphic law models, and, indeed, it seems advantageous from the elite vantage for them to do so. With respect to their political strategies, societies with more modest power potentials also seem to avail themselves of such discordances to some degree. The result is a complex involvement with substantive law in most societies, and certainly at the state level.

NOTES

1 Leopold Pospisil, *Anthropology of Law: A Comparative Theory* (New York: Harper and Row, 1971).

2 See for example, Laura Nader and Duane Metzger, "Conflict Resolution in Two Mexican Communities," *American Anthropologist*, vol. 65 (1963), pp. 584–592; Laura Nader, "An Analysis of Zapotec Law Cases," *Ethnology*, vol. 3, no. 4 (1964), pp. 404–420; Victor Ayoub, "Conflict Resolution and Social Organization in a Lebanese Village," *Human Organization*, vol. 24 (1965), pp. 11–17; and June Starr and Barbare Yngvesson, "Scarcity and Disputing: Zeroing-In on Compromise Decisions," *American Ethnologist*, vol. 2, no. 3 (1975), pp. 553–566.

3 See for example, Jane Collier, *Law and Social Change in Zinacantan* (Stanford: Stanford University Press, 1973); Nancy Tanner, "Disputing and the Genesis of Legal Principles: Examples from Minangkabau," *Southwestern Journal of Anthropology*, vol. 26 (1970), pp. 375–401; and K.F. Koch, *War and Peace in Jalimo: The Management of Conflict in Highland New Guinea* (Cambridge: Harvard University Press, 1974).

4 See for example, Nader, *op. cit.*, 1964; Aharon Layish, *Women and Islamic Law in a Non-Muslim State* (Jerusalem: Israel University Press, 1975); Daisy Hilse Dwyer, "Cultural Conceptions of Conflict and Variability in Conflict Boundaries: A Moroccan Example," *Journal of Conflict Resolution*, vol. 20, no. 4 (1976), pp. 663–686; and Daisy Hilse Dwyer, "Bridging the Gap Between the Sexes in Moroccan Legal Practice," in Alice Schlegel (ed.), *Sexual Stratification* (New York: Columbia University Press, 1977).

6 Jack P. Gibbs, "Definition of Law and Empirical Questions," *Law and Society Review*, vol. 2 (1968), pp. 429–446.

7 Jane Collier, "Legal Processes," *Annual Review of Anthropology*, vol. 4 (1975), p. 130.

8 Sally Falk Moore, *Law as Process: An Anthropological Approach* (London: Routledge and Kegan Paul, 1978).

9 Pospisil, *op. cit.*, 1971, pp. 97ff.

10 K.N. Llewellyn and E. Adamson Hoebel, *The Cheyenne Way: Conflict and Case Law in Primitive Jurisprudence* (Norman: University of Oklahoma Press, 1941), p. 60.

11 Laura Nader and Barbara Yngvesson, "On Studying the Ethnography of Law and Its Consequences," in John Honigmann (ed.), *Handbook of Social and Cultural Anthropology* (Chicago: Rand McNally, 1973), p. 889.

12 Marc Galanter, "Why the 'Haves' Come Out Ahead: Speculations on the Limits of Legal Change," *Law and Society Review*, vol. 9, no. 1 (1974), pp. 95–160.

13 Daisy Hilse Dwyer, *Images and Self-Images: Male and Female in Morocco* (New York: Columbia University Press, 1978), p. 156.

14 Layish, *op. cit.*

15 P.H. Gulliver, "Case Studies of Law in Non-Western Societies," in Laura Nader (ed.), *Law in Culture and Society* (Chicago: Aldine, 1969), p. 13; Nader and Yngvesson, *op. cit.*, p. 884; Collier, *op. cit.*, 1975, p. 139.

16 Max Gluckman, *The Judicial Process Among the Barotse of Northern Rhodesia* (Manchester: Manchester University Press 1954); Max Gluckman, "Ethnographic Data in British Social Anthropology," *Society Review*, vol. 9 (1961), pp. 5–17; Max Gluckman, "Introduction," in A.L. Epstein (ed.), *The Craft of Social Anthropology* (London: Social Science Paperbacks, 1967).

17 J. van Velsen, *The Politics of Kinship* (Manchester: Manchester University Press, 1964); J. van Velsen, "The Extended Case Method and Situational Analysis," in A.L. Epstein (ed.), *op. cit.*, pp. 129–149.

18 Victor Turner, *Schism and Continuity in an African Society* (Manchester: University Press, 1957).

19 Laura Nader, "Introduction," in Nader (ed.), *op. cit.*, p. 2.

20 I. Schapera, *Tribal Legislation among the Tswana of the Bechuanaland Protectorate* (London: Percy, Lund, Humphries, 1943).

21 Sally Falk Moore, *op. cit.*

22 For a summary of procedures see Koch, *op. cit.*, 1974.

23 Glynn Cochrane, "Legal Decisions and Processual Models of Law," *Man*, vol. 7 (1972), pp. 50–56.

24 J. van Velsen, "Procedural Informality, Reconcilliation and False Comparisons," in Max Gluckman (ed.), *Ideas and Procedures in African Customary Law* (Oxford: Oxford University Press, 1969), pp. 137–152.

25 Gulliver, in Nader (ed.), *op. cit.*

26 James Gibbs, Jr., "Law and Innovation in Non-Western Societies," in Nader (ed.), *op. cit.*; J.R. Emshoff and Russell Ackoff, "Explanatory Models of Interactive

Choice Behavior," *Journal of Conflict Resolution*, vol. 14, no. 1 (1970), pp. 77–89; Naomi Quinn, "A Natural System Used in Mfantse Litigation Settlement," *American Ethnologist*, vol. 3 (1976), pp. 331–351; Dwyer, *op. cit.*, 1976.

27 Collier, *op. cit.*, 1975.

28 Paul Bohannan, *Justice and Judgment among the Tiv* (Oxford University Press, 1957).

29 Pospisil, *op. cit.*, 1971.

30 Nader and Yngvesson, *op. cit.*

31 M. Rheinstein, "Problems of Law in the New Nations of Africa," in Clifford Geertz (ed.), *Old Societies and New States* (New York: The Free Press, 1963).

32 P.H. Gulliver, *Social Control in an African Society* (London: Routledge and Kegan Paul, 1963), p. 297f.

33 Moore, *op. cit.*, 1978.

34 P. Bohannan and K. Huckleberry, "Institutions of Divorce, Family and the Law," *Law and Society Review*, vol. 1 (1967), pp. 81–102.

35 George Billias, "Introduction," in Billas (ed.), *Law and Authority in Colonial America* (Barre, Mass.: Barre Publishers, 1965), p. vii.

36 Mark Howe, "The Sources and Nature of Law in Colonial Massachusetts," in Billias (ed.), *op. cit.*

37 Roscoe Pound, *The Spirit of Common Law* (Francestown, N.H.: Marshall Jones, 1921), p. 113.

38 *Ibid.*, p. 45.

39 Daisy Hilse Dwyer, "Law Actual and Perceived: The Sexual Politics of Law Perception in Morocco," *Law and Society Review*, vol. 13, no. 2 (1979), in press.

40 Nader and Yngvesson, *op. cit.*, p. 888.

41 Bernard Cohn, "Anthropological Notes on Disputes and Law in India," *American Anthropologist*, vol. 67, no. 6, pt. 2 (1965), p. 115.

42 Pospisil, *op. cit.*, 1971, pp. 97–126.

43 F.G. Bailey, *Strategems and Spoils* (Oxford: Basil Blackwell, 1969), p. 146.

44 Nader and Yngvesson, *op. cit.*, p. 887.

45 M.G. Smith, *Corporations and Society* (London: Duckworth, 1974).

46 E. Adamson Hoebel, *The Law of Primitive Man* (Cambridge: Harvard University Press, 1954), p. 50.

47 Pospisil, *op. cit.*, 1971, pp. 97ff.

48 Sally Falk Moore, *Power and Property in Inca Peru* (New York: Columbia University Press, 1958), p. 127.

49 Nader and Yngvesson, *op. cit.*, p. 887.

50 Gluckman, *op. cit.*, 1954, p. xv; my italics.

51 Max Weber, *On Law in Economy and Society* (New York: Simon and Schuster, 1954), pp. 198ff.

52 Stanley Diamond, "The Rule of Law versus the Order of Custom," in *In Search of the Primitive: A Critique of Civilization* (New Brunswick, N.J.: Transaction Books – E.P. Dutton, 1974), pp. 255–280.

53 Clarence Morris, *The Great Legal Philosophers: Selected Readings in Jurisprudence* (Philadelphia: University of Pennsylvania Press, 1971), p. 438.

54 Pospisil, *op. cit.*, 1971, p. 196.

55 Dwyer, *op. cit.*, 1979.

56 Layish, *op. cit.*

57 Michael Barkun, "Conflict Resolution through Implicit Mediation," *Journal of Conflict Resolution*, vol. 8 (1964), p. 123f; Paul Bohannan, "Anthropology and the Law," in Sol Tax (ed.), *Horizons of Anthropology* (Chicago: Aldine, 1964), pp. 191–199; Leopold Pospisil, "The Attributes of Law," in Paul Bohannan (ed.), *Law and Warfare* (Garden City, N.Y.: Natural History Press, 1967).

58 Paul Bohannan, "The Differing Realms of Law," in Bohannan (ed.), *op. cit.*, pp. 43–56.

59 Bronislaw Malinowski, *Crime and Custom in Savage Society* (London: Routledge and Kegan Paul, 1926), p. 56.

60 Hoebel, *op. cit.*, p. 28.

61 Weber, *op. cit.*, p. 26.

62 H.L. Hart, *The Concept of Law* (Oxford: The Clarendon Press, 1961).

63 Lloyd Fallers, *Law Without Precedent: Legal Ideas in Action in the Courts of Colonial Busoga* (Berkeley: University of California Press, 1969).

64 *Ibid.*, p. 11.

65 Morris, *op. cit.*, p. 446.

66 Jack Gibbs, *op. cit.*, pp. 429–446.

67 Weber, *op. cit.*, p. 5.

68 John Austin, *The Province of Jurisprudence Determined and the Uses of the Study of Jurisprudence* (New York: Noonday, 1954), p. 133f.

69 Morton Fried, *The Evolution of Political Society* (New York: Random House, 1967), p. 20.

70 Collier, *op. cit.*, 1975, p. 121; Bohannan, *op. cit.*, 1964, p. 193.

71 K.F. Koch, "Law and Anthropology: Notes on Interdisciplinary Research," *Law and Society Review*, vol. 4 (1969), p. 12.

72 Hart, *op. cit.*, p. 1f.

73 Paul Bohannan, *op. cit.*, 1957.

74 Leopold Pospisil, *The Kapauku Papuans and Their Law* (New Haven: Yale University Press, 1958).

75 Llewellyn and Hoebel, *op. cit.*

76 R.F. Barton, *Ifugao Law*, University of California Publications in Archaeology and Ethnology, No. 15 (1919).

77 Malinowski, *op. cit.*

78 Gluckman, *op. cit.*, 1954.

79 Niccolo Machiavelli, *The Prince*, trans. George Bull (London: Penguin, 1972), p. 77.

80 Antonio Gramsci, *Selections from the Prison Notebooks* (New York: International Publishers, 1971), p. 170.

81 Perry Anderson, "The Antinomies of Antonio Gramsci," *New Left Review*, no. 100 (1978–1977), pp. 42ff.

82 J.P. Spradley, *You Owe Yourself a Drunk: An Ethnography of Urban Nomads* (Boston: Little, Brown and Co., 1970).

83 Galanter, *op. cit.*

84 Diamond, *op. cit.*, p. 258.

85 Sally Falk Moore, "Politics, Procedure and Norms in Changing Chagga Law," *Africa*, vol. XL (1970), pp. 321–344.

86 Talal Asad, *The Kababish Arabs* (London: C. Hurst, 1970).
87 Gulliver, in Nader (ed.), *op. cit.*
88 Hoebel, *op. cit.*, 1954, p. 29.
89 Smith and Roberts, *op. cit.*, p. 104.
90 Nader, in Nader (ed.), *op. cit.*, p. 2.
91 Koch, *op. cit.*, 1969, p. 14.
92 Moore, *op. cit.*, 1978.

Dialectical Anthropology 4 (1979) 309–320

[4]

BRITISH JOURNAL OF LAW & SOCIETY
VOLUME 8, NUMBER 2, WINTER 1981

ANTHROPOLOGY, DISPUTE PROCESSES AND LAW: A CRITICAL INTRODUCTION*

FRANCIS G. SNYDER†

ANTHROPOLOGY AND LAW

1. *Purposes and Scope of the Paper*

The relationship between anthropology and law is often viewed as problematic or tenuous.** To examine this relationship more closely, this paper introduces some of the main themes in contemporary anthropological studies of law and dispute processes. In addition it offers a preliminary evaluation of the contributions and limitations of anthropological approaches in relation to legal studies and to the development of social theories of law. It is not possible here to present a full survey of the literature. This review concentrates primarily on selected writings in English and French by scholars in the United States, Britain and continental Europe; the footnotes give references to literature from other countries.

2. *Anthropology and Academic Law*

The influence of anthropological approaches on academic legal studies has so far been marked only in the United States, especially through its elite universities.[1] In contrast to recent trends in sociology and law, the establishment of the anthropology of law as a distinct field of study has rarely resulted in the creation of centres for interdisciplinary research.[2] Anthropological students of law and social control, and legal scholars with similar interests, are bound instead by informal networks, loose professional organisations and a handful of specialist journals.[3] Moreover, collaboration between anthropologists and academic lawyers has always been unusual.[4] This is frequently ascribed to the technical nature of law as a discipline[5], but more convincing reasons lie partly in differences in the training and objectives of anthropologists and lawyers.[6] In the past, most anthropological studies of law concentrated on small-scale communities in Africa, Asia or Latin America, which academic lawyers in North America and Europe generally considered to be of little relevance to their own domestic legal systems.[7] Today many anthropologists, like some sociologists of law, reject Western jurisprudence as a source of analytic concepts or, more importantly, of guidelines for research.[8] Furthermore,

*This article is the third of a series being published in this journal which considers the relationship of law and other disciplines by presenting both the limitations and benefits of their theoretical working association. Each article provides a review of the literature and is structured with the non-specialist in mind. (Editorial Board).

†Senior Lecturer, School of Law, University of Warwick.

the ethnographic, descriptive orientation of many anthropologists, whose theories have usually been implicit or formulated at a very low level of abstraction, has inhibited their making a more significant contribution to social theories of law.[9] In any case, anthropologists often accord a low priority to this theoretical project; many consider that dispute processes, for example, are a less ethnocentric, more cross-culturally valid subject of study than law.[10]

Any general impression that anthropological approaches to legal processes bear little relation to academic legal studies is misleading, however, in at least two respects. First, as will be shown later, anthropological approaches to law-related processes today are extremely diverse, and not all are encompassed within the anthropology of *law*. Some of the broader concerns of legal anthropologists have also preoccupied academic lawyers. Secondly, anthropological approaches to law and related processes raise certain fundamental questions concerning law and social science. These questions, of which some are posed more starkly by anthropological approaches than by other social sciences, have increasingly been debated by academic lawyers and theorists of law.

3. *The Anthropology of Law*

The contrasting characteristics of the disciplines of law and anthropology and other institutional forces, including the development of sociology in different countries[11], have influenced the historical separation between anthropology and academic legal studies. Anthropological approaches to law differ from those in economics or psychology[12] (but resemble those in sociology) in that they are usually considered to constitute an established academic field. The anthropology of law is widely recognised as a subdiscipline of anthropology.[13] Its origins have been traced to Montesquieu[14], but its foundations were laid by nineteenth century historical jurisprudence[15] and cemented during the period of European imperialist expansion and colonialism.[16] Though reflecting this legacy, its principal development is nonetheless relatively recent.[17] This development has occurred primarily in the United States and secondarily on the European continent.[18] For a variety of reasons, anthropological approaches to law have remained on the margins of both legal and anthropological scholarship in the United Kingdom[19], despite numerous important British contributions to the field.[20]

After the publication of Sir Henry Maine's *Ancient Law* in 1861[21], a small number of classic anthropological monographs provided the baseline for contemporary legal anthropology. Malinowski's *Crime and Custom in Savage Society* (1926) and Llewellyn and Hoebel's *The Cheyenne Way* (1941)[22] had a fundamental effect on methods of research. Malinowski's short study, a small part of the published corpus of his research on the Trobriand Islands[23], was a radical innovation at the time in being based on extensive fieldwork, which since then has been considered a precondition of any valid anthropological study of law.[24] In addition, Malinowski insisted on the necessity of emphasising function rather than form and of giving priority to the cultural or ideological categories of the actors themselves[25], thus partly escaping, as Roberts recently argued[26], the ethnocentric misuse of Western legal ideas and institutions in analysing social relations elsewhere. *The Cheyenne Way*, for which Llewellyn, an American legal realist, and Hoebel, a cultural anthropologist, elicited oral accounts of nineteenth century disputes, stands as the prime example to date of interdisciplinary cooperation in the anthropology of law.[27] It was the first systematic anthropological attempt to study law by a careful analysis of "trouble-cases", which has become a standard method of research.

Among other studies published before the mid-1960s, the most significant in the development of the subject in English-speaking countries have been those by Schapera, Hoebel, Gluckman, Bohannan, Pospisil and Gulliver. Schapera's *A Handbook of Tswana Law and Custom* (1938), prepared at the request of the then Bechuanaland Administration, was a clear, precise recording of 'customary' rules based not only on idealised accounts by informants but also on actual disputes.[28] Hoebel's *The Law of Primitive Man* (1954) sought to arrange various groups in an evolutionary sequence embracing social organisation, culture and law and to elucidate the basic jural postulates underlying the law of each group.[29] *The Judicial Process among the Barotse* (1955) by Max Gluckman was the first published anthropological analysis, based on observed cases, of judicial reasoning in a non-Western social group, here the remnant of the Lozi state in the Barotse kingdom in Zambia.[30] Analysing dispute cases and concepts of jural processes in an acephalous social group in Nigeria, Bohannan's *Justice and Judgement among the Tiv* (1957) argued persuasively that it was often difficult, if not impossible, to understand other societies in terms of Western conceptions of law.[31] In *Kapauku Papuans and Their Law* (1958) and other writings, Pospisil elaborated the notion that every society comprised a multiplicity of legal systems, often hierarchically arranged and always dependent on the number of functioning subgroups in the society.[32] Gulliver's *Social Control in an African Society* (1963) compared forms of out-of-court dispute settlement among the Arusha of Tanzania, emphasising the importance of viewing disputes as part of more general social processes.[33]

Many of these studies, however diverse in other respects, shared certain characteristics. They were mainly ahistorical, ethnographic descriptions, based on inductive empiricism and using some form of the case method. All concerned a single ethnic group that was deemed to be relatively homogenous and capable of being isolated, as a "society", for purposes of analysis. Most relied, explicitly or implicitly, on Western conceptions of law, and they considered disputes as the main index of law or its primary locus. Though conducted during the colonial period, they abstracted, by and large, from the processes of colonial domination and from the profound economic and social changes occurring during that period. They were generally functionalist in orientation and concerned with the maintenance of social order.[34] Except for the studies by Malinowski and Gulliver, they considered law primarily as a framework rather than as a process.[35]

These monographs established standards of research method, ethnographic description and limited theoretical generalisation that have profoundly affected contemporary anthropological approaches. Until recently, however, with the exception of Malinowski's book and several other studies, they had relatively little influence on the European continent.[36] Research in the Netherlands, for example, concentrated mainly on practical and theoretical issues raised by colonial policies in Indonesia. It encompassed an immense literature on legal pluralism and *adat* law, including the work by Van Vollenhoven in Leiden.[37] In France, anthropological approaches to law were heavily influenced by Durkheimian sociology and Lucien Lévy-Bruhl's theory of primitive mentality[38], though their more immediate forebearers are Marcel Mauss, Durkheim's nephew and student[39], and Henri Lévy-Bruhl, Lucien Lévy-Bruhl's son.[40] French research and teaching on anthropology of law dates at least from the 1930s; but it was Henri Levy-Bruhl's achievement to establish the sociology of law in the Paris law faculty, which led subsequently to systematic courses in African law, including legal anthropology.[41] These (and other) different continental traditions and Anglo-American approaches have begun to converge only in the last decade or so.

Using several earlier reviews of the literature and other partial syntheses[42] one may roughly distinguish three separate, yet overlapping periods in the development of the field: the publication of the major empirical monographs, mainly in English, before the early 1960s; a shift, especially in the United States after 1965, towards the study of dispute settlement and of law as a process; and, since the mid-1970s, the gradual elaboration of a plurality of approaches, all marked by more explicit concern with theory and greater attention to the role of the state. In each period, of course, diverse strands and traditions co-existed, and scholars drew selectively on earlier work, often including their own, for elaboration and special emphasis. This crude periodisation gives perhaps too much emphasis to literature in English; but it also suggests, rightly, that Anglo-American approaches have been the main beneficiary of recent trends towards the internationalisation of the subject. The first period has already been sketched briefly; the most recent one is treated later. The next part of the paper discusses dispute processes, which have been a central, continuing interest of legal anthropologists for almost two decades.

THE STUDY OF DISPUTE PROCESSES

1. *A Central Theme*

In an important review article in 1965, Laura Nader summarised previous research and proposed new directions.[43] Building especially on earlier studies by Malinowski, Gulliver, Colson[44], Turner[45] and Bailey[46], she suggested that anthropologists should place legal processes more squarely in their social context and aim at empirical and explanatory generalisations. As a basis for achieving these objectives, she proposed the following assumptions:

> 1) there is a limited scope of disputes for any particular society ...; 2) a limited number of formal procedures are used in human societies in the prevention of and/or settlement of disputes ...; 3) there will be a choice in the number and modes of settlement ...[47]

These assumptions reflected changes then occurring elsewhere in anthropology, especially by a greater emphasis on processes, transactions and individual choices[48]; but they formed the basis of a substantially new approach in legal anthropology. They underlay a large number of later studies, especially (but not only) those undertaken by Nader's students in the Berkeley Village Law Project between 1965 and 1975.[49]

This approach takes dispute settlement or dispute processes as its central theme; the latter term denotes clearly that the outcome of disputes is not necessarily a firm resolution of the issues ostensibly at stake.[50] Disputing displaces law as the subject of study. Accordingly, dispute, not law, is a major theoretical concept. Gulliver's 1969 definition of a dispute as the public assertion, usually through some standard procedures, of an initially dyadic disagreement has become widely accepted.[51] Within this framework, definitions of law are often considered to be unnecessary, not only because such definitions are frequently thought to be inevitably ethnocentric but also because this definitional exercise itself is deemed theoretically pointless and sterile.[52] Similarly, the study of substantive concepts and rules is of secondary importance[53], subordinated to the analysis of procedures, strategies and processes, which obviously are not limited to bureaucratic institutions such as courts.

By analysing disputes as social processes through an extended case method or situational analysis[54], this approach shifts the main enquiry from social organisation to processes and also from groups to networks of individuals. It emphasises the actions of parties in disputes just as much as those of negotiators or adjudicators, hence aims to map the perceptions of individual disputants and gives special attention to the cultural meanings and rationalisations of social action. Thus, for example, Collier's study of Mexican Indians concentrated on "defining the range of options open to litigants and ... analyzing the constraints and incentives that channel the choices they make"[55], while Starr's research in Turkey showed how, in disputing, rural villagers formulated strategies to maintain honour or compete for scarce resources.[56] Especially in the context of underdeveloped countries, this perspective has increasingly emphasised the role of political brokers in channelling individual choices, mediating between cultures and maintaining or eroding legal pluralism.[57]

Studies by anthropologists using these and similar approaches to dispute processes are not limited to Africa, Latin America or Asia. Though not concentrating on cases, Spradley used participant observation, formal interviewing and ethnosemantic methods to analyse marginalised urban nomads' perceptions of and relations to courts in Seattle, Washington.[58] More recently, Mather briefly reviewed ethnographic studies of American trial courts; she suggested that the utility of an ethnographic approach lay in raising and answering questions about different groups' knowledge and perceptions of law, about informal social norms and about the relationships between courts and other dispute processes.[59] Within the past decade, studies of dispute processes and informal alternatives to courts have proliferated, especially in the United States but also in Europe; some of these studies are mentioned later.

While unified by a concern with dispute processes and an emphasis on individual actions and perceptions, this approach has in fact tended to be theoretically eclectic[60], though some writers have tried to place it squarely within an empirical interactionist tradition.[61] It is therefore not surprising that recent developments in the study of dispute processes have accentuated previously implicit differences between various theoretical positions and also given rise to new distinctions. Partly reflecting current changes in the political and economic context of scholarship, these developments have fragmented what often appeared in the past to be a fairly uniform approach to dispute processes. In doing so, they have clarified the theoretical and political assumptions that underlay earlier work and, sometimes, resulted in greater theoretical sophistication. It is necessary to mention briefly some of these trends.

2. *Disputes : Processes and Processing*

Despite an emphasis on conflict and disputing as universal processes, anthropological work on dispute processes has, until very recently, been mainly concerned with micro-level studies of the management of conflict and the maintenance of order[62]; the generally conservative implications of this framework is consistent with many studies of law. Although some legal anthropologists have contributed to the analysis of sources of social conflict[63], most have concentrated instead on the characteristics of disputes as processes and/or of the procedural forms by which disputes are handled.

For clarity, I refer to the study of procedural forms as the analysis of dispute processing, a term first used in this sense by Felstiner in 1974.[64] Procedural forms are, of course, often analysed by anthropologists as processes themselves, and the course of a dispute and the means by which an outcome is reached are often intimately connected; but the distinction between dispute processes and dispute processing is nonetheless useful here. The expressions identify two different aspects of ethnographic and theoretical work in legal anthropology: one concerned with social relationships in processes of conflict, and the other with the more or less standardised procedures for reaching an outcome. Both these strands are discussed in this section. The contrast between the dynamic and bureaucratic connotations of the terms "processes" and "processing", respectively, suggests another important point, which raises numerous issues concerning the relationship between scholarship and politics.[65] Though addressed to an increasing variety of issues in anthropological and sociological theory, processual studies still remain primarily academic in orientation; even anthropological studies of the processes by which disputing parties reach outcomes are usually ethnographic or theoretical in purpose and addressed to a social science audience. In contrast, research on dispute processing has increasingly tended to be instrumentalist, often devoted to extension of state control and the implementation of practical, procedural reforms. These studies frequently abstract politics and social relations from the analysis of procedures[66]; and partly for this reason they have, compared to processual studies, been generally (if unfortunately) of more interest to academic lawyers. The next section of the paper considers this literature on informal alternatives to courts.

Anthropologists' definitions, as already noted, frequently postulated that a conflict became a dispute when placed in the public arena. This definition facilitated research on individual decision-making and strategies; but within a processual framework it has also raised questions concerning the effects of prior, pre-dispute relations between parties on the subsequent public confrontation. In order to explore some of these questions, the Berkeley Village Law Project distinguished three phases in the life history of disputes: the preconflict or grievance stage, the conflict stage and the dispute stage.[67] Though most studies concern the dispute stage, some writers have tried to analyse the earlier phases. Yngvesson's study of a Swedish fishing village contrasted social processes in conflicts involving community members with those involving people defined as outsiders. Emphasising the element of time, she showed that the former were marked by a "nonaction" or "cooling" period during which the circumstances, relations between the parties and others and the consequences of formal reactions were considered.[68] Later, she argued that such periods of "bracketed structural time" formed part of dispute processes elsewhere, including an American court.[69] Starr's work on rural Turkish disputing elicited many cases of dyadic negotiation, in which grievances were often not brought to a public arena. Analysing the correlations between social rank and forms of settlement, she suggested that in rural Turkey "[p]ublic confrontation ... is the true forum of the powerless".[70]

Some other work, also emphasising the litigant's perspective, has tried to relate individual choice-making to broader social changes. Thus, Nader has suggested that, in countries such as the United States, individuals often elaborate extra-judicial dispute processes in direct response to the changing functions and increasing bureaucratisation of state law and institutions.[71] Abel's work, drawing on research in both Kenya and the United States, represents the major attempt to develop macro-sociological theory incorporating litigant behaviour as a variable. Using ideal-typical constructs of tribal society and modern society, he offers a number of hypotheses concerning litigant behaviour and argues that the interaction of social structure and institutional structure produces patterns of litigation.[72]

Forms of dispute processing have been the subject of a great deal of research and controversy. This interest formed a natural part of studies of dispute processes, was consistent with the concern with courts and administrative agencies among Anglo-American academic lawyers and has recently been fuelled by governments' preoccupations with informal alternatives to courts. Much of the theoretical work by anthropologists has been stimulated by sociological theories[73]; Gulliver's (1963) conception of the political and judicial modes as two ideal, polar types of processes[74]; Bohannan's (1967) distinction between law and warfare as two basic forms of conflict resolution[75]; and Abel's partial synthesis of the literature.[76] Any typology that distinguishes simply between judicial and political forms of processing is now widely deemed inadequate, as most scholars recognise that both norms and power are pervasive elements in all dispute processes everywhere.[77] Several typologies, using different criteria and often elaborated for different purposes, have recently been proposed. Only a few can be mentioned here.

In 1969 Nader advocated the comparison of procedural styles based on clusters of contrasting features[78], but most scholars have preferred typologies based on fewer, more precise and more institutionally derived criteria. Reconsidering Bohannan's conception, Roberts recently suggested a distinction between fighting and settlement-directed talking as two basic forms, the latter comprising several different types.[79] Danet, who was especially interested in the use of language in disputing, rearranged Roberts' categories into seven different types. She classified physical violence, appeals to the supernatural and the use of magical procedures and avoidance or ostracism as relatively nonverbal modes of processing disputes; shaming, reconciliation rituals, verbal contests and settlement-directed, fact-oriented talking were relatively verbal modes.[80] Using different criteria, Koch distinguished six types of procedure based on, first, the presence or absence of a third party and the mode of its intervention and, secondly, the nature of the outcome; avoidance, negotiation and coercion were dyadic procedures, while mediation, arbitration and adjudication were triadic.[81] Gulliver himself, while recognising the existence of other settlement forms, has concentrated primarily on elaborating a distinction between negotiation and adjudication as the two most common modes. Viewing the presence (as in adjudication) or the absence (as in negotiation) of a third-party decision-maker as the crucial, distinguishing feature, he has presented, in detail, two complementary theoretical models of negotiation as a process.[82] The role of the third party, or "intervenor", was the conceptual focus of Abel's attempt to construct a theory of dispute institutions in society, which proposed a number of hypotheses concerning the effects of increasing functional specialisation, social differentiation and bureaucratisation on dispute processing.[83]

3. *Access to Justice and Informal Alternatives to Courts*

Especially since the mid-1970s, anthropological work on dispute processing has increasingly been incorporated into, yet by no means entirely absorbed by, the ideologically heterogeneous movements concerned with access to justice and informal alternatives to courts. Most legal anthropologists have apparently remained sceptical or simply continued to pursue other, more traditional interests.[84] For many anthropologists and others, however, these movements represented an important, general trend.

Anthropological participation in this trend was influenced by numerous factors, of which two were especially decisive. The first was the fiscal and legitimation crises of the state in advanced capitalist countries, especially the United States, in the late 1960s and early 1970s. The second was the loss of anthropology's protected status in newly independent former colonies and its apparent irrelevance to the demands of emerging post-colonial and neo-colonial states. The former directly affected the amount and orientation of research funds, led to numerous proposals to reform costly, inefficient and often inaccessible court systems and stimulated a growing interest in grassroots movements and popular justice.[85] In conjunction with decreasing funds, the latter signalled a decline in opportunities for anthropological research in underdeveloped countries; and in a period of widespread criticism of traditional anthropological and other social science work[86], it led to calls for "studying up"[87] and for more research on contemporary problems in the United States and Europe.[88] Particularly in the United States, where most legal anthropologists are employed in any event, anthropological research on dispute processing in other countries seemed relevant, though not necessarily directly transferable, to domestic concerns. To many academic lawyers and other social scientists, the ethnography of disputing was one of the elements that suggested the utility of preserving or creating informal alternatives to courts and of fostering non-adjudicatory, yet non-political means of handling conflict.[89] The acceptance of this view, which was encouraged by powerful political forces, was facilitated by the largely ahistorical character of anthropological work[90], its frequent romanticisation of "tribal" societies[91], its relative lack of general theory and its neglect of legal form.[92]

The origins, composition, ideology and consequences of the movements for access to justice and informal alternatives to courts have been extensively described and criticised elsewhere.[93] By 1980, three pilot Neighbourhood Justice Centres and other experiments in more than 100 cities had begun in the United States alone[94]; several studies of alternatives to adjudication in continental Europe were published under the aegis of Cappelletti's large-scale Access to Justice project[95]; and related research was underway at the Oxford Centre for Socio-Legal Studies and elsewhere.[96] In the elaboration of reforms, anthropologists have, with some exceptions, been far less important than other, more powerful, more bureaucratically oriented professionals such as lawyers and administrators. This is due partly to the technical nature of administrative programmes; partly to the different concerns of anthropologists, especially in Europe, and their reluctance to conduct mainly prospective or evaluative research; and also, and most importantly, to the complex web of existing interests, linked to dominant classes and the state, that are at stake in the creation and control of such reforms. Instead, the main contributions of anthropologists have been to outline different forms of dispute processing, provide ethnographic data (usually from other countries) and propose limited generalisations.

Though it is impossible to delimit these contributions precisely, one important strand clearly concerns the influences of social organisation on dispute processing, including informal alternatives to courts. While most of this work has concerned countries outside Europe and America, Felstiner's 1974 paper contrasted forms of dispute processing in two ideal types of society. Criticising a proposal by Richard Danzig of Stanford Law School to establish urban American community moots patterned on rural Liberian institutions[97], Felstiner indicated the difficulty of finding mediators who shared the same experiences as disputants and argued that, in any case, the widespread use of avoidance was a much cheaper, easier way of ending disputes in countries such as the United States.[98] Another influential article was Galanter's discussion of why the 'haves' come out ahead. In addition to drawing a distinction between regular and sporadic users of courts, it outlined various alternatives to the official court system, including inaction or "lumping it", self-help or "exit" (avoidance), recourse to private settlement systems and the use of processes appended to courts.[99] Both these discussions provided points of reference for advocates of informal alternatives. In addition, anthropologists have occasionally evaluated or cooperated in studying American or European institutional alternatives to adjudication.[100] At least one anthropological project, however, has suggested the extreme difficulty of conducting research on less institutionalised forms of dispute processing in England.[101]

A second strand in anthropological work has concentrated on individual perceptions of justice and the means of expressing complaints. Reviewing studies by the Berkeley Law Project, Nader suggested in 1973 that access to justice was a key concept if one took seriously the litigant's perspective. She argued that, in evaluating or ascribing a meaning to this notion, one had necessarily to take account of people's feelings and perceptions.[102] Contrary to the conclusions of some other anthropologists[103], she stated that the view that people in all non-Western societies have access to public forums for resolving grievances "is a romantic one, nothing more".[104] Since 1973, under the aegis of Ralph Nader's Center for the Study of Responsive Law[105], she has directed a large-scale study of the management of complaints among individuals and between individuals and a variety of organisations. The results of this study, which complement the earlier comparative work of the Berkeley Project[106], have recently been published.[107]

Early critics of the movements for access and informal alternatives, and therefore of anthropological work directed towards furthering their diffuse objectives, made essentially two points. First, access meant, in effect, the increasing incorporation of political struggles within the orbit of the state, at least in underdeveloped countries, and their displacement to terrain chosen in the last instance by dominant classes.[108] Secondly, the extension of informal mechanisms would merely permit a further, if decentralised, form of state control.[109] These and other related points are elaborated, and their implications examined, in recent writing that draws on anthropological research but places it in a more general, Marxist theoretical framework. In a review of delegalisation movements, Abel showed that delegalisation assumed rough equality between social actors, a high degree of normative consensus and the existence of adequate informal controls. He concluded that in capitalist societies, where these assumptions did not hold, delegalisation tended to be detrimental to the already underprivileged and powerless.[110] More recently, suggesting that political strategies are more appropriate for dominated classes in capitalist countries, he has argued that informal alternatives to courts (like formal courts) are a means of legalising conflict, a process that extends state control but that is obscured in the movement for informal alternatives by the emphasis on process.[111] Making a similar, though more abstract, argument, Santos suggests that "state sponsored community organisation will be the specific form of disorganisation [of oppressed classes] in late capitalism"; but he warns against viewing these reforms as mere manipulation since an autonomous political movement of dominated classes may be able to take advantage of their popular, potentially liberating elements.[112]

SOME IMPORTANT RECENT TRENDS

1. *General Developments*

For over a decade, as the preceding discussion suggests, anthropological studies of legal processes by Anglo-American scholars have focussed mainly, though not exclusively, on a set of research questions arising from previous work but first articulated clearly in the late 1950s and early 1960s. The central concern has been to elaborate — in different ways and in a changing economic and social context — the ethnographic, theoretical and (sometimes) political implications of the premisses on which these questions were initially based. At the same time, however, anthropological approaches to legal processes have developed and been modified; different themes have also emerged. A sketch of several general developments in anthropological approaches provides a useful background for a discussion of some important recent trends.

First, as already noted, anthropologists today are more concerned than were their predecessors with the study of legal processes in advanced capitalist societies. They have concentrated not only on dispute processes and dispute processing but also on such issues as the creation of urban citizens' groups in contraposition to legal bodies that monopolise information concerning energy decisions in the U.S. and the use of anthropological evidence and similar expertise in American and Canadian Indian litigation.[113] Both anthropologists and lawyers are involved in the work of the Aboriginal Sites Protection Authority in Australia.[114]

Secondly, reflecting the fact that the small communities which were their traditional concerns now often constitute marginalised social groups, anthropological approaches have increasingly sought to place legal processes in their broader national and even international context. This is especially apparent in recent studies of brokers[115], the impact of state law[116], legal pluralism[117] and the political economy of law.[118] Almost all of these themes require more attention to the role of capitalist and neo-colonial states and to the processes of national and international capitalist transformation than was given to such questions in most earlier anthropological research.[119]

Thirdly, closely related to this emphasis on the broader context of small-scale legal processes, and particularly on the state, is the renewed concern with law (in addition to disputes) as a subject of study. This represents a partial shift of interest, even though most anthropologists today, as before, would deny the state's claim to be the sole source of law and hesitate to accept any necessary correlation between the state and all forms of law. During the 1960s and early 1970s, many writers seeking to delimit dispute processes as the primary anthropological terrain showed a marked disinterest in and even neglect of legal forms.[120] While consistent with general anthropological trends, this was also partly a reaction to ethnocentric 19th century assumptions of the universality of Western law[121] and the later misuse by anthropologists of definitions of law derived from Western jurisprudence.[122] Sharing these concerns, recent anthropological studies concerned with law as a theoretical object have generally not followed earlier writers who proposed definitions of law intended to apply across cultures and in all historical periods.[123] They have concentrated instead on elaborating the implications of specific definitions or conceptions of law within different theoretical frameworks[124] and on analysing norms, concepts and processes of social control in specific historical and cultural contexts.[125]

These changes have usually not led to a basic modification of the scale of anthropological research. Though processual or network studies sometimes embody a redefinition of the unit of analysis, anthropologists still tend to concentrate on small groups or groupings amenable to study by individual methods, especially participant observation. These other developments have contributed, however, to a fourth important change, namely a gradual movement towards the explicit use of macro-sociological theory as a source of research questions, working hypotheses and potential explanations. In conjunction with the increasing concentration on specific issues instead of general ethnography, anthropologists within the past decade have drawn explicitly on the works of major theorists such as Weber[126] and Marx[127] in order to learn from and to contribute to the elaboration of social theories of law. This movement is especially significant as an indication of the partial convergence of anthropology and sociology, but its novelty and strength should not be exaggerated: the work of many legal anthropologists has been influenced, at least indirectly, by Durkheim, and most anthropological research uses general theory more implicitly than explicitly and thus differs from much recent sociology of law.

While these general features are noticeable in some contemporary writing on dispute processes, they are characteristic especially of anthropological studies concerning several other recent themes. These themes stem partly from previous work, but they also draw substantially on new interests and on developments in related disciplines and other approaches, such as historical materialism. Three of the most important recent themes are rules and processes, legal pluralism and the political economy of law. Although thus far each topic has been treated from several perspectives, each raises somewhat different analytical problems and theoretical issues; and contrasting theoretical strands in legal anthropology are likely to coalesce around these three different themes in the future.

2. *Rules and Processes*

At least since Gulliver's *Social Control in an African Society*[128], anthropological studies have continually raised questions concerning the role of norms in dispute processes. A distinction between norms and power was the basis of an early (now rejected) typology of dispute processing, and Hamnett recently proposed the concept of executive law to encompass a particular ethnographic conjunction of political and judicial elements.[129] The general issue of freedom versus determinism is of course fundamental to the social sciences; and the specifically anthropological concern with similar issues, though often couched in professional jargon and using apparently exotic examples, closely resembles discussions in both sociology and law of the relationship between freedom and constraint, consent and coercion or substantive and formal justice.[130] In the 1960s and early 1970s, anthropological work concentrated primarily on the processual aspect of disputing, stressing that power was central in all forms of dispute processing including adjudication. Recent studies of rules and processes, however, have examined and thus re-emphasised the importance of norms, whether in triadic processes (e.g., adjudication) or in dyadic ones (e.g., negotiation). In doing so, they have shown that norms do not automatically determine the outcome of a dispute and in fact serve a number of different functions in dispute processes and other social relations.

Legal anthropology has treated the role of norms in several different ways. Two related perspectives represent logical developments of earlier research. One concerns the relationships among concepts, rules and actual behaviour and emphasises the processual nature of all systems of rules. Thus, Sally Falk Moore has analysed the ways in which general concepts are adjusted to specific social circumstances and argued that legal systems are, necessarily, partially indeterminant orders; the same social processes, such as competition, that prevent total regulation of social life by rules also shape and transform attempts at partial regulation.[131] The second perspective, elaborated especially by Gulliver in work on negotiation, is the conception that norms themselves are a form of power, manipulated and used selectively by parties (and third parties) in disputes.[132] Other writers have treated norms as cultural codes, sometimes drawing on Bernstein's work to elucidate the role of brokers in mediating relationships[133], and sometimes emphasising the ways in which people use norms in re-negotiating the bases of inter-personal and wider social order.[134] Another strand has concentrated on the use of norms in argument. Thus, Comaroff and Roberts consider whether any systematic pattern underlies the invocation, manipulation and application of norms in Tswana dispute processes. They argue that, in the instance they discuss, "express invocation of norms ... is associated with efforts to assert control over the paradigm of argument"; and they advocate greater attention to factors intrinsic to the process of argument as distinct from extrinsic factors such as political organisation or institutional structure.[135]

These concerns form part of the increased emphasis in legal (and general) anthropology on the ways in which people conceive, create and sustain definitions of situations, especially through the use of language. While previous anthropological work stressed the phases of disputes and the transformation of social relations and of the issues at stake as a dispute moved from a private context to the public arena, recent research has paid special attention to the role of language in these processes of situational transformation.[136] Danet recently provided a relatively comprehensive review of studies of the use of language in dispute processes.[137] Some writers have also tried to analyse the role of language in disputing within the context of wider social relations. Thus, LeRoy discussed legal reasoning by members of rural councils in dispute processes in Senegal.[138] Santos analyses the use of legal reasoning, argumentative discourse and rhetoric in the construction and reproduction of legality in a Brazilian squatter settlement. He advances the hypothesis that "the verbal content of Pasargada law reflects the CMP [capitalist mode of production] and capitalist legality but actually operates to organise autonomous social action by the working class against the conditions of reproduction imposed by capitalism".[139] Seeking to transcend the dichotomy between rule-centred and processual approaches, Comaroff and Roberts emphasise the dialectical relationship between the sociocultural system and individual action. They show how, in Tswana chiefdoms, the former constitutes a set of normative terms within which disputing occurs and has meaning, while, in turn, disputing and other social processes affect and potentially transform the sociocultural framework.[140]

While giving more attention to the role of norms in disputing and other social processes, some anthropologists have also suggested that the treatment of norms as a code draws basically into question jural models of social relationships.[141] This assertion has two related aspects that should be distinguished. One aspect recognises the limitations or inadequacies of Western jurisprudence in analysing dispute processes and the forms of social order or domination elsewhere. This argument usually rests either on cultural grounds, hence refers generally to all non-Western 'societies'[142], or on economic/historical grounds, hence refers specifically to precapitalist social formations.[143] Many, if not most, contemporary legal anthropologists would accept at least one of the two quite different versions of this general point. The other aspect is the rejection of anthropological or other approaches that view relatively unambiguous rules as the basic constitutive elements in social relationships.[144] It encompasses both legal rules, whether derived from Western jurisprudence or not, and non-legal rules, such as those generally given analytic priority in normative approaches in social science. This second position does not negate a discussion of norms, for they form part of the repertoire used by individuals in social interaction: it simply views the world primarily as a negotiated order in which the relationship between rules and processes is always inherently problematic. Taken to its logical conclusion, this view implies a type of anthropological analysis that gives primary, if not exclusive emphasis to the ways in which individuals construct and manage social relations, including not only relationships among individuals but also those underlying broader social processes. This suggests the close affinity of these recent anthropological approaches to legal processes with the interactionist and phenomenological schools in sociology. It also distinguishes them — in some cases, very sharply — from approaches such as historical materialism that are often concerned with individual actions and conceptions but emphasise in addition the great extent to which these are shaped, limited or determined by fundamental, supra-individual economic laws or forces.

3. *Legal Pluralism*

The view that any society or social group contains a plurality of legal orders or fragments of legal systems is well-known in jurisprudence and sociology of law.[145] It was re-asserted by Llewellyn and Hoebel in *The Cheyenne Way*[146] and has increasingly been elaborated by legal anthropologists. As Griffiths has shown[147], legal pluralism starts from the rejection of the notion of legal centralism—that law necessarily is the law of the state, is uniform and exclusive and is administered by state institutions. Since Furnivall's early work[148], three writers have proposed different conceptions of legal pluralism: Pospisil elaborated the idea of a multiplicity of legal systems and the existence of legal levels in a single society[149];

Smith proposed a structural conception of pluralism based on corporate groups[150]; and Moore has advanced a conception of semi-autonomous social fields based on processual characteristics.[151]

There is, to date, no satisfactory theory of legal pluralism; but Griffiths is concerned to elaborate a descriptive theory of legal pluralism within a positivist sociological framework, while Fitzpatrick has sought to use Moore's notion of semi-autonomous social fields to develop a materialist/structuralist conception of pluralism in underdeveloped countries.[152] Less explicitly theoretical research on this general topic has taken several directions. Roberts distinguishes between two lines of research, one concentrating on the litigant's perspective and especially the choice between one among several potential dispute-handling institutions, and the other focussing on dispute agencies themselves, including both institutional characteristics and the behaviour of third parties.[153] Members of the Berkeley Law Project have been concerned with both strands. Thus, Ruffini, Starr and Witty emphasise primarily litigants' decisions to handle disputes in village institutions rather than going to state courts.[154] Canter and Parnell concentrate mainly on competition between state and local institutions.[155] Both Canter, on the one hand, and Hunt and Hunt, on the other, analyse the ways in which the hierarchy of dispute agencies operates to maintain ethnic stratification and social boundaries.[156] In a number of publications, Van Rouveroy has considered similar questions in the Togolese context;[157] the Stratherns and others have examined the relationships between state and non-state institutions elsewhere.[158]

In addition to emphasising competition between dispute institutions for cases and other resources, anthropologists have stressed the ways in which brokers mediate between rural communities and state agencies. Collier argued in 1975 that brokers primarily accounted for the persistence of rural conciliatory procedures as well as for changes in the substance of rural Zinacanteco (Mexican) settlements towards conformity with state norms.[159] Examining the role of brokers in Zinacantan more recently, Freeman argued that a clear distinction between different legal modes had disappeared in favour of a single, composite system; he concluded that Mexican state officials were seeking to undermine the influence of brokers and establish direct links between individuals and the state.[160] In contrast, Werbner's analysis of centre-periphery relations during an attempted centralisation of villages in Botswana suggested that citizens were not necessarily powerless even in the absence of brokers and were able to use state institutions for their own ends in political power struggles.[161]

Many of these writers have emphasised the continued survival, in both peripheral and central capitalist countries, of dispute-processing institutions relatively independent of the state.[162] Others have discussed the frequently profound disparity between the concepts embodied in state law and those held in many cases by the majority of a country's population.[163] Anglo-American anthropologists have tended to focus on institutional pluralism, while French research has frequently concentrated mainly on concepts. Some of the recent work has drawn on a fundamental, early debate in legal anthropology, of which the most well-known protagonists were Bohannan and Gluckman, that was couched in terms of a discussion of the methodology of description and analysis but in fact concerned the general purposes of research.[164] Consistent with Bohannan's emphasis but drawing mainly on earlier French research, much of the work carried out under the aegis of the Laboratoire d'Anthropologie Juridique in Paris has concentrated on elucidating 'folk' concepts concerning law and social control. For more than a decade and until very recently, its principal focus has been a careful linguistic and semantic analysis of rural African ideas, including, in some instances, comparisons with state legal concepts.[165]

The best such work often reveals the profound ethnocentrism inherent in many anthropological studies of legal pluralism that begin from Western capitalist conceptions of law, but the aim of much recent research on this topic is not merely academic. Some work on legal pluralism by anthropologists falls into an immediately pragmatic, state-oriented tradition. It accepts the ideology and political practice of legal centralism and seeks either to reformulate 'customary laws' to render them amenable for use in state institutions or to argue that they reflect such basic differences in social organisation and values that the groups to which they ostensibly pertain should be accorded a special legal status by the state. Other research which emphasies the continued vitality of concepts, norms and institutions hidden from and often antagonistic to the state apparatus often aims to contribute (if usually indirectly) to popular political struggles.[166] This latter strand encompasses primarily, though not exclusively, research on the political economy of law.

4. *The Political Economy of Law*

Since the mid-1970s, anthropologists reviewing past work and studying legal processes themselves have placed greater emphasis on economic factors, social inequality and forms of domination. [167] Especially in research on brokerage, pluralism and legal change, they have also recognised that the village is generally not an appropriate unit of study; Murray, for example, points out that "piece-meal ethnography can only make sense within its full political, economic and social context".[168] In order to define the salient features of this context in relation to legal processes, some anthropologists have sought to use Marxism as a source of research questions, theoretical concepts and possible explanations.

This work has been stimulated by the general elaboration of Marxist theory since the mid-1960s. Consistent with the general interests of anthropologists, it has drawn particularly on the attempts to elaborate and utilise Marxism in French economic anthropology, British writing on precapitalist modes of production, peasant studies and dependency and underdevelopment theory; I recently gave a survey of this literature.[169] In contrast to sociologists studying central capitalist formations, scholars using anthropological approaches to legal processes have not, with some exceptions[170], made extensive use so far of recent Marxist theories of law. Nor have they been entirely persuaded by earlier and (in their view) overly optimistic calls for the dissolution of anthropology and its annexation by historical materialism[171]; these often amounted ultimately to the absorption of Marxist theory as one among many explanatory models within general anthropology. [172] Instead, though seeking to contribute to Marxist theories of law, scholars using broadly anthropological approaches have been somewhat more cautious, and concerned to explore the implications of different Marxist theories and concepts for the study of legal processes. In contrast to previous research and much contemporary work, however, they tend to be more interested in general theory and to emphasise the economic bases of political and legal institutions, the relationship of law to class formation and the connections between changes in legal processes and the development of capitalism as a distinct historical form.

A central, continuing theme in Marxist approaches is the relationship between the development of capitalism and processes of legal change. Two different strands have thus far emerged, each using a different concept of mode of production. Drawing partly on Banaji's notion of mode of production as an historical/economic category[173], I discuss the ways in which the subsumption of African peasants within capitalist relations of production influenced legal ideas within a formerly precapitalist social formation. I employ Marx's distinction between simple and concrete concepts in arguing that the apparent continuity of simple legal concepts hides the profound transformation of concrete legal forms; thus, for example, the change in the social form of labour power during the colonial period in Senegal resulted in the transformation of a precapitalist conception of "childwealth" into a material and symbolic equivalent of urban labour power as a commodity.[174] This emphasis on the historical specificity of legal concepts is exemplified in my analysis of the relatively recent development of 'customary' law as an ideology of colonial domination and a distinct legal form.[175] In another article, I propose four general theses concerning the changes in rural African legal forms during the 20th century.[176] In contrast, Fitzpatrick employs theories of the articulation of modes of production[177] to argue that, in contemporary underdeveloped countries, one of the functions of law is to conserve the traditional mode of production despite economic forces tending towards its dissolution.[178] He emphasises the ways in which state law is used to restrict the formation of indigenous classes and seeks to show how precapitalist law constitutes, and is constituted by, precapitalist modes of production. He considers the often explicit use of rules as a distinctly legal element in precapitalist social formations.[179]

Such analyses necessarily give special attention to the role of the state; and anthropological approaches have especially emphasised the connections between the state and legal processes in rural and urban communities. Both Fitzpatrick and Paliwala have demonstrated that, despite official pronouncements, the establishment of village courts in Papua New Guinea effectively extended the state apparatus of social control into rural villages and enhanced the formation of class alliances.[180] Fitzpatrick and Blaxter jointly examine the effects of licensing laws on small-scale entrepreneurs and class formation.[181] Discussing Senegalese rural administrative reforms, LeRoy argues that an original form of law, local law, is emerging in certain African countries as a new form of state penetration into rural communities. He discusses the preconditions for the development of local law and proposes that its emergence is related to the intensification of commodity relations and the penetration of transnational capital.[182]

Though sharing with other scholars an interest in legal pluralism, these writers have been especially concerned with the implications of legal pluralism for class formation and the possibility of political action by dominated groups and classes. These questions are considered in articles mentioned in the preceding paragraph; and in a case study I show how the expansion of a rural association with dispute-processing functions was inhibited by consequences of the capitalist, export-oriented economic strategy of the Senegalese state.[183] A recent symposium on African land systems, in which several legal anthropologists participated, discussed the relationships between small-scale legal processes and independent political action.[184] As already noted, Santos considers these issues in his important study on Brazil, several papers on Portugal and a recent theoretical article.[185] Such work takes as a major theme the possibilities and limitations of autonomous political movements within central and peripheral capitalist formations; and it demonstrates the close similarity of concerns between Marxist approaches in legal anthropology and in sociology of law.

CONCLUSION

This review aimed to introduce some of the major themes in anthropological approaches to law and legal processes, especially since the early 1960s. It briefly sketched the major early monographs but, without seeking to minimise the continuing importance of those writers, concentrated mainly on more recent research. Written primarily for an English-speaking audience, it gave special attention to the literature available in English, while also discussing some significant research in France and other countries. In addition, the paper delineated several of the important and continuing debates in the field; but its purposes and scope meant that other, deeper controversies could merely be suggested or were not pursued. Within these limitations, the discussion sought to outline the major recent developments and the principal, if sometimes incipient, theoretical strands. It emphasised particularly the greater attention now paid by anthropologists to Western capitalist societies and the increasing tendency of recent writers to make explicit use of social theory or to situate their work within its terms. The review also indicated the existence of many potentially overlapping interests between proponents of anthropological approaches and either academic lawyers or sociologists of law, though obviously any effective collaboration between people in these groups depends ultimately on factors such as the recognition of common objectives. This conclusion suggests several of the contributions and limitations of anthropological approaches in relation to the study of law and legal processes.

A preliminary caveat is in order, for such an exercise, like any review of the literature, not only reflects personal values and predilections: if it is to go beyond simply recognising the merits and demerits of specific studies or the advantages and disadvantages of particular theoretical positions, it also depends on, and should therefore entail, the isolation of specifically anthropological characteristics of the work being discussed. I would suggest, however, that this is an impossible task. The historical legacy of the initial concern of anthropology (in contrast to sociology) with non-Western social groups or marginalised groups in central capitalist countries remains, of course, important. But if one takes a broad view of anthropological approaches to law and dispute processes, one must recognise that little, if anything, distinguishes this work from the similar and equally diverse theoretical strands in sociology.[186] Virtually all of the studies discussed here could be classified within sociology, though the paper concentrated primarily on work by anthropologists. While perhaps a useful institutional myth, in intellectual terms the separation between anthropology and sociology is an essentially arbitrary distinction that hinders rather than helps collaboration between academic lawyers and other social scientists.

It is possible to accept this general point yet identify some common features of the studies discussed above which, for our purposes, we may consider as exemplifying contemporary anthropological approaches to the study of law and dispute processes. These features are shared with much sociological research, but they distinguish this work from many academic legal studies[187]; and they indicate some potential contributions of anthropological approaches to academic studies of law. Previous writers have suggested that the special contributions of anthropology to academic legal studies lie, first, in research methods and, secondly, in an emphasis on certain aspects of our legal system that academic lawyers sometimes overlook; the latter include the existence of numerous modes of dispute settlement in addition to courts, the critical importance of the litigant's perspective and the general social context of law.[188] This paper showed that both anthropologists and lawyers have recently been concerned with these themes in studies of dispute processing, people's perceptions of access to justice and informal alternatives to courts. From the methodological standpoint, many of the approaches discussed here share an emphasis on micro-analysis and the use of an extended-case method. Though as yet rarely used by academic lawyers, the study of extended-cases has proved useful, especially when combined with other research methods, in showing the actual uses and functions of norms and procedures in continuing social processes, ranging from the maintenance of order to the mobilisation of classes. Another contribution of some recent anthropological approaches is to demonstrate the difficulties and limitations inherent in using the 'society' or 'social formation' as a unit of analysis. Studies that focus especially on disputing or deny the systematic character of law often stress processes which are not necessarily or usually bounded by such social units; and they demonstrate the worth of a processual approach in analysing norms and institutions in the framework of social fields or arenas. To a limited extent, therefore, they overlap with recent Marxist debates on the appropriateness of the social totality as a unit of analysis.

While studies and debates in legal anthropology continue, as before, to be heavily influenced by the predominant legal traditions in different countries, contemporary work has increasingly recognised the disadvantages of accepting these traditions as a source of analytic concepts or of guidelines for social research. As a consequence, most research in legal anthropology is likely to interest sociologists of law more than academic lawyers. The special contributions to sociology of law of anthropological approaches discussed here lie not only in empirical studies but also, and increasingly, in theoretical treatments of such topics as ideologies or cultural conceptions (folk systems), legal pluralism and processes of legal change. Recent anthropological research has concerned the relationships between processes of small-scale social ordering and the role of the state, and the ways in which people construct and maintain local norms and institutions in countries characterised by a plurality of cultures and different forms of class relations. Similarly, some anthropological studies of legal change have moved beyond the evolutionary theories, dichotomous distinctions and conceptions of procedural sequences used in earlier work.[189] Among the significant recent trends are the emphasis on the importance of individual strategies in particular social and cultural contexts and attempts to use historical materialist conceptions of fundamental economic transformations to analyse changes in legal ideas and processes. Some of these studies converge with contemporary sociological work on the state, law and society.

One way in which previous anthropological work has been selectively incorporated into academic legal studies (and state political practice) is exemplified by recent studies of dispute processing. Both lawyers and administrators have drawn on earlier anthropological research on this topic, but they have generally ignored anthropologists' emphasis on the limitations posed by different economic and cultural contexts on the creation of institutions. Nor have they taken account of a central point being made by contemporary anthropologists who have moved from this theme to concentrate on the study of rules and processes. These anthropologists consider that the social meaning of normative doctrines and the operation of institutions arises from the connections between the sociocultural order and individual experience. Law as such is not the object of their study, and they frequently view their work as lying outside the scope of a strictly defined anthropology of *law*. Despite a greater emphasis on context, few academic legal studies go as far as recent anthropological work in defining precisely the features of this context, whether in terms of continuing social processes, the historical specificity of legal ideas or the relationships between modes of production and a plurality of normative forms. This recent work has helped replace debates on universal definitions of law by a greater emphasis on the historical relativity of legal forms; and the anthropological emphasis on process has placed the formulation and use of legal doctrine and the role of legal institutions in continuing political and economic processes instead of viewing law in isolation.[190]

The assumptions underlying mainstream social science approaches to law have been increasingly challenged in the past several decades, raising a number of basic issues concerning the study of legal processes by academic lawyers and social theorists. Anthropological approaches have not been exempt from this challenge and also pose some of these questions more starkly than do other social sciences. The following may be mentioned briefly. Is the role of the social sciences in relation to legal studies best conceived as that of "under-labourer" or of "master-scientist" or, in other words, by whom and how is the subject of study to be defined?[191] How might micro-level studies, such as those common in anthropology, best be integrated with macro-sociological theories of law? To what extent, if at all, are anthropologists' conclusions concerning law or dispute processes in apparently exotic settings applicable to social relations in central capitalist countries? To what extent is the cultural relativism of many anthropologists compatible with social theories of law, including Marxist ones, that claim to be universally valid, though sometimes historically specific? In what ways does a theoretical position that considers virtually all conceptions of law as ethnocentric, or defining law as a sterile exercise, disable a scholar from making a significant contribution to social theories of law? Does the frequent insistence by anthropologists on cultural specificity extend not only to Western jurisprudential ideas but also to Western conceptions of scientific explanation, including explanations of the origin and role of legal forms?

The view of many anthropologists that law and legal processes are not necessarily a monopoly of the state, even in American and European countries, controverts the statist conception of law commonly held by sociologists of law and usually taught by academic lawyers. The latter in particular are likely to regard the pluralist conception of law not only as a central feature but also as a major weakness of many anthropological approaches. Anthropologists, however, would contend that such a perspective raises many important questions, especially concerning intra-group regulation and the relationships of powerful groups to the state, that often are not even asked within the terms of academic legal studies. Moreover, despite an increasing interest in western capitalist legal systems, most anthropological work remains concentrated on small-scale legal processes in other countries. This research is especially pertinent to sociologists of law concerned with underdeveloped countries; but academic lawyers are likely to be deterred by detailed ethnographic data and thus fail to recognise the usefulness of anthropological methods of description and translation[192] in studying their own domestic legal systems. A more fundamental weakness of anthropological approaches concerns the relative absence of comparative research. Anthropologists have often proclaimed their discipline to be inherently comparative. Except in the very limited sense of concentrating on groups or societies other than one's own, however, very few anthropological studies are genuinely comparative, and therefore they offer only implicit contrasts with our own state and its law. Furthermore, many positivist or interactionist anthropological studies tend to concentrate on observable behaviour and the explanations of social actors themselves. These empiricist and idealist approaches often ignore the fundamental economic laws or forces that are emphasised in many recent Marxist contributions to the sociology of law.[193]

Though increasingly concerned with general social theory, legal anthropologists have so far made relatively few contributions to social theories of law. From the standpoint of both academic lawyers and sociologists of law (and indeed of anthropologists interested in law as an object of study), a particular weakness of many recent anthropological approaches is the tendency to reduce law to dispute settlement and to view legal and social processes as not simply inseparable but identical. In 1965 Nader lamented the lack of attention paid by anthropologists to the social context of law[194]; but since then many legal anthropological studies have been concerned with the ethnography of disputes to such an extent that they have either not wanted or been unable to conceptualise law as a theoretical object.[195] This approach has proved valuable in analysing social processes, including the role of norms, and in avoiding or minimising the use of Western legal ideas in studies of non-Western or precapitalist social formations. But it has unfortunately meant that anthropologists concerned with the colonial period or with contemporary Western countries have often neglected state law. Though some anthropologists have disclaimed an interest in law as a subject of study, anthropologists generally have given almost no attention to such questions as, for example, the apparent autonomy of law in capitalist societies. Partly as a consequence of its relative unconcern for law and its emphasis on disputes and process, much recent legal anthropological writing would appear incapable of arriving at a theoretical view of the apparent autonomy of law, or of considering abstractly the relationships between plural legal forms, including those of the state, in different countries. Processual ethnographies sometimes illuminate these issues at the level of individual experience, but they do not provide or suggest more abstract theoretical answers to such questions.

From the standpoint of a genuinely comparative sociology of law, a final limitation of many anthropological studies lies in the ethnocentrism that often appears to be inherent in anthropology, as in other social sciences. Like sociology and economics, the discipline of anthropology is based on Western conceptions of science and developed as a consequence of particular economic and political processes in European and American history. Although the practitioners of anthropology have often claimed it to be the universal science of humankind, they have frequently been unable to envisage social processes or legal forms in ways other than those based ultimately on their own historical and cultural experience. This experience has, of course, become more immediately pertinent to people everywhere with the development of capitalism as a mode of production; but its continuing legacy has been to hinder the elaboration of a more adequate theoretical study of law and related processes, either within mainstream anthropology or within neo-Marxism and historical materialism. The anthropology of law is a myth if conceived as the search for ahistorical and cross-culturally valid features of law or, alternatively, as the reduction of historically and culturally specific normative forms to ethnographic descriptions of individual behaviour. The reformulation of legal anthropology as the study of social order merely displaces these problems of theoretical perspective and in turn raises others, including the difficulty of accounting for the pervasive importance and distinct role of state law. The future development of legal anthropology lies, therefore, not only in elucidating the relationships between social action and cultural ideologies, but also in grasping the extent to which these relationships and the wider social processes of which they form a part are the product of specific historical and economic conditions. In this respect, anthropological approaches, while perhaps offering little to academic lawyers, may contribute to and converge with sociology of law.

NOTES AND REFERENCES

** I wish to thank Peter Fitzpatrick, Etienne LeRoy, Simon Roberts, Avrom Sherr and Siân Snyder for their helpful comments on earlier drafts of this paper; I alone, of course, am responsible for its contents. I am also grateful to Simon Roberts for making available to me the manuscript of his book (with John Comaroff), *Rules and Processes: The Cultural Logic of Dispute in an African Context*, prior to its publication.

[1] A comparison of the (American) *Law and Society Review* with the *British Journal of Law and Society* is instructive in this respect. In addition, for over a decade anthropologists or scholars with strong interests in anthropological approaches have taught in major American law schools. In November 1971, the Yale Law School Program in Law and Modernization held a two-day conference on "The Relevance of Legal Anthropology to Comparative Social Research on Law"; most of the papers were presented by anthropologists, but more than half of the participants were academic lawyers. The anthropologist Laura Nader at Berkeley has consistently maintained links with Boalt Hall (Berkeley) Law School; work on informal alternatives to courts has been carried out at Harvard Law School; and a major project on dispute processing is underway at Wisconsin Law School. Not all of these relations stem from anthropologists, of course; and the influence of such links outside the national law schools in the U.S. should not be overstated.

[2] Among the exceptions is the Laboratoire d'Anthropologie Juridique, Université de Paris I, France. For an early discussion of its activities, see LeRoy, "Reflexions sur une interprétation anthropologique du droit africain: Le Laboratoire d'Anthropologie Juridique" (1972) 26 *Revue Juridique et Politique, Indépendance et Coopération* 427–448. The two major, long-term projects in legal anthropology, one by Max Gluckman and his colleagues and students at the Rhodes-Livingstone Institute and later at Manchester, the other by Laura Nader and her students in the Berkeley Village Law Project, have been based at centres for social science research (excluding lawyers) or at departments of anthropology (and sociology, in the case of Manchester during most of Gluckman's time there).

[3] The major umbrella organisation today is the International Union of Anthropological and Ethnological Sciences Commission on Contemporary Folk Law, established in December 1978, which included 112 members from 34 countries as of 15 July 1981; see (1981) 5 *Commission on Contemporary Folk Law Newsletter* 4. In addition to individual members, the Commission includes the following regional working groups: Northwest Territories Folk Law Workshop (Canada); Working Group on Asian Indigenous Law; Customary Law Group of Australia; Kerukunan Peminat Studi Hukum Adat (Indonesia); Volksrechtskring (Netherlands). The Newsletters of the Commission describe other activities involving legal anthropologists and academic lawyers with similar interests. In the United States, the Association for Political and Legal Anthropology (APLA) was established in November 1976, now includes over 200 members and publishes a newsletter at least twice a year. The Laboratoire d'Anthropologie Juridique in Paris also publishes periodically a *Bulletin de Liaison de l'Equipe de Recherche en Anthropologie Juridique*; and the first issue of *Droits et Cultures* (Cahiers du Centre de Recherche de l'U.E.R. de Sciences Juridiques, Université de Paris X, Nanterre), appeared in 1981. Anthropological articles on law and dispute processes are published in the major anthropological and sociological journals and also form the core of the *Journal of Legal Pluralism*, the successor to *African Law Studies*.

[4] The major exception is Llewellyn and Hoebel's collaboration in *The Cheyenne Way: Conflict and Case Law in Primitive Jurisprudence* (1941). See W. Twining, *Karl Llewellyn and the Realist Movement* (1973), chap. 8, and Twining, "Law and Anthropology: A Case Study of Inter-disciplinary Collaboration" (1973) 7 *Law and Society Review* 561–583.

[5] See D. Riesman, "Toward an Anthropological Science of Law and the Legal Profession" in his *Individualism Reconsidered and Other Essays* (1954).

[6] See Roberts, "Introduction" in *Law and the Family in Africa* (ed. S. Roberts, 1977) and Twining, "Law and Anthropology: A Case Study of Inter-disciplinary Collaboration" (1973) 7 *Law and Society Review* 561–583. On the relationship between anthropologists and lawyers in Britain in particular, see Campbell and Wiles, "The Study of Law in Society in Britain," (1976) 10 *Law and Society Review* 547–578 at 564, which relies on A. Kuper, *Anthropologists and Anthropology: The British School 1922–1972* (1973).

[7] On this view of anthropology, see the two classic descriptions in S. F. Nadel, *The Foundations of Social Anthropology* (1951) and J. Beattie, *Other Cultures: Aims, Methods and Achievements in Social Anthropology* (1964). Different positions concerning contemporary anthropology and law are presented in J. Poirier, "Introduction à l'ethnologie de l'appareil juridique" in *Ethnologie générale* (ed. J. Poirier, 1968) and E. Hill, "Law and Underdevelopment: Conceptualising Legal Formations in Peripheral States", presented at the Annual Conference of the British Sociological Association, University of Warwick, 9–12 April 1979. See also Roberts, "Law and the Study of Social Control in Small-Scale Societies" (1976) 39 *Modern Law Review* 663–679.

[8] Thus, Roberts has argued that legal anthropological studies fall into one of two distinct schools: those that draw their basic concepts from Western jurisprudence and concentrate on law as the subject of study, and those that reject Western jurisprudence as a source of concepts and concentrate on social control, disputing or other social processes deemed to be universal. See Roberts, *ibid.*, and S. Roberts, *Order and Dispute: An Introduction to Legal Anthropology* (1979), chaps. 2 and 11.

[9] Among the discussions of the role of theory in anthropology, see R. A. Manners and D. Kaplan (eds.), *Theory in Anthropology: A Sourcebook* (1968) and I. C. Jarvie, *The Revolution in Anthropology* (1964). See also J. A. Brim and D. H. Spain, *Research Design in Anthropology: Paradigms and Pragmatics in the Testing of Hypotheses* (1974) and R. Naroll and R. Cohen, *A Handbook of Method in Cultural Anthropology* (1973).

[10] The most elaborate theoretical statement of this position is Abel, "A Comparative Theory of Dispute Institutions in Society" (1974) 8 *Law and Society Review* 217–347. See also S. Roberts, *Order and Dispute: An Introduction to Legal Anthropology* (1979).

[11] The division of labour between sociology, concerned with Western societies, and anthropology, focussing on non-Western groups, is well-known, though out-dated and generally recognised to be increasingly irrelevant in contemporary studies; its intellectual foundations have always been shaky. Durkheim in France is the major, and exceptional, example of a sociologist whose work had a lasting influence on anthropological studies. See H. Lévy-Bruhl, "L'ethnologie juridique" in *Ethnologie générale* (ed. J. Poirier, 1968), p. 1119; S. Lukes, *Emile Durkheim, His Life and Work: A Historical and Critical Study* (1973), chap. 20; and D. Goddard, "Anthropology: the Limits of Functionalism" in *Ideology and Social Science: Readings in Critical Social Theory* (ed. R. Blackburn, 1972). Examples of recent work in other disciplines strongly influenced by anthropological research include M. Barkun, *Law without Sanctions: Order in Primitive Societies and the World Community* (1968) and D. Black, *The Behavior of Law* (1976). Some anthropological research discussed later in this paper suggests the common concerns and partial convergence of anthropology and sociology.

[12] Compare my discussion of the anthropology of law with Veljanovski, "The Economic Approach to Law: A Critical Introduction" (1980) 7 *British Journal of Law and Society* 158–193 and Lloyd-Bostock, "Psychology and the Law: A Critical Review of Research and Practice" (1981) 8 *British Journal of Law and Society* 1–28.

[13] See, *e.g.*, Nader, "The Anthropological Study of Law" (1965) 67 (6) (2) *American Anthropologist* (Special Publication on "The Ethnography of Law", ed. L. Nader), 3–32; D. D. Whitney and C. Kobryn, "Ignorance of Legal Anthropology Is No Excuse, or Is It? — A Survey of Introductory Cultural Anthropology Textbooks", Association for Political and Legal Anthropology Occasional Paper No. 3 (March 1981), (1981) 5 (2) *APLA Newsletter and Occasional Papers* 1–29; and C. Greenhouse, "Courses in Political and Legal Anthropology: The APLA Curriculum Survey" Association for Political and Legal Anthropology Occasional Paper No. 4 (July 1981), (1981) 5 (2) *APLA Newsletter and Occasional Papers* 1–14. These sources are useful indications of the general point but are nonetheless limited, Nader's survey to English-language literature and the last two papers to the United States and Canada.

[14] See Levy-Bruhl, *op.cit. supra* n. 11, p. 1116; and Abel, *op.cit. supra* n. 10, p. 219.

[15] The basic work was H. S. Maine, *Ancient Law: Its Connection with the Early History of Society and Its Relation to Modern Ideas* (1861).

[16] See, *e.g.*, Kuper, *op.cit. supra* n. 6; and Gough, "Anthropology and Imperialism" (1968) 19 (11) *Monthly Review* 12–27. For recent discussions, see D. Hymes (ed.) *Reinventing Anthropology* (1969) and T. Asad (ed.), *Anthropology and the Colonial Encounter* (1975).

[17] Thus, Twining recounts Hoebel's difficulty in finding an anthropologist to supervise his postgraduate research on Cheyenne law in the 1930s; see Twining, *Karl Llewellyn and the Realist Movement* (1973), pp. 154–155.

[18] On anthropological research elsewhere, see the *Newsletters* of the IUAES Commission on Contemporary Folk Law.

[19] See Campbell and Wiles, *op.cit. supra* n. 6; Gulliver, "Preface" in *Cross-Examinations: Essays in Memory of Max Gluckman* (ed. P. H. Gulliver, 1978); Roberts, *op.cit. supra* n. 7.

[20] A comprehensive list would include not only work discussed later in this paper but also A. R. Radcliffe-Brown, *Structure and Function in Primitive Society* (1952), especially chap. 11 ("Social Sanctions") and chap. 12 ("Primitive Law"); E. E. Evans-Pritchard, *Witchcraft, Oracles and Magic among the Azande* (1937) and *The Nuer* (1940); H. Cory, *Sukuma Law and Custom* (1953); I. Hogbin, *Law and Order in Polynesia* (1934); and M. Douglas, *Purity and Danger: An Analysis of the Concepts of Pollution and Taboo* (1966).

[21] The continued influence of Maine's work, until recently, was especially apparent in Max Gluckman's writings. See, *e.g.*, his *Politics, Law and Ritual in Tribal Society* (1965) and *The Ideas in Barotse Jurisprudence* (1965); of the latter, Gluckman wrote that "I am not

sure but that 'Footnotes to Sir Henry Maine's Ancient Law' would be a more accurate title for this book" (p. xvi).

[22] Llewellyn and Hoebel's book was sub-titled *Conflict and Case Law in Primitive Jurisprudence.*

[23] Other well-known works include *Argonauts of the Western Pacific* (1922) and *Coral Gardens and Their Magic* (1935). Malinowski's work is discussed in *Man and Culture: An Evaluation of the Work of Bronislaw Malinowski* (ed. R. Firth, 1957).

[24] And indeed in any valid anthropological study. For discussions of Malinowski's contribution to anthropological methods, see Kaberry, "Malinowski's Contribution to Field-work Methods and the Writing of Ethnography" and Leach, "The Epistemological Background to Malinowski's Empiricism" in Firth, ed., *op.cit. supra* n. 23, pp. 71–91 and 119–137, respectively.

[25] Thus, in *Coral Gardens and Their Magic*, Malinowski argued that "the final goal, of which the Ethnographer should never lose sight ... is, briefly, to grasp the native's point of view, his relation to life, to realise *his* vision of *his* world" (p. 25, E. P. Dutton (New York) edition, 1961). See also Malinowski, "A New Instrument for the Interpretation of Law — Especially Primitive" (1942) 51 *Yale Law Journal* 1237–1254 and his "Introduction" to Hogbin, *op.cit. supra* n. 20. For criticisms and a discussion of changes in Malinowski's conception of law, see Richards, "The Concept of Culture in Malinowski's Work" and Schapera, "Malinowski's Theories of Law" in Firth, ed., *op.cit. supra* n. 23, pp. 15–31 and 139–155, respectively.

[26] Roberts, *Order and Dispute, op.cit. supra* n. 8, pp. 190–191.

[27] See the writings by Twining, *op.cit. supra* n. 4. A recent example is J. L. Comaroff and S. Roberts, *Rules and Processes: The Cultural Logic of Dispute in an African Context* (1981); Several scholars have formal training in both law and anthropology.

[28] Schapera also provided major studies of legislation in *Tribal Legislation among the Tswana of the Bechuanaland Protectorate* (1943) and *Tribal Innovators: Tswana Chiefs and Social Change 1795–1940* (1970). A select bibliography of Schapera's writings in legal anthropology is given in (1977) 21 *Journal of African Law* 124.

[29] A bibliography of Hoebel's writing to 1973 appears in (1973) 7 *Law and Society Review* 787–798. Another recent evolutionary study is A. S. Diamond, *Primitive Law, Past and Present* (1971). In sociology, see L. T. Hobhouse, G. C. Wheeler and M. Ginsburg, *The Material Culture and Social Institutions of the Simpler Peoples: An Essay in Correlation* (1915, reprinted 1965). For a useful correction of some conceptions of legal evolution, see Moore, "Legal Liability and Evolutionary Interpretation: Some Aspects of Strict Liability, Self-Help and Collective Responsibility" in *The Allocation of Responsibility* (ed. M. Gluckman, 1972).

[30] See also Gluckman, *op.cit. supra* n. 21. A select bibliography of Gluckman's extensive writings is given in *Cross-Examinations: Essays in Memory of Max Gluckman* (ed. P. H. Gulliver, 1978), pp. 155–157. See also Firth, "Max Gluckman, 1911–1975" in (1975) 61 *Proceedings of the British Academy* 479–496. On Gluckman's continued influence, see LeRoy, "L'anthropologie juridique anglo-saxonne et l'héritage scientifique de Max Gluckman: Un point de vue français", (1979) 17 *African Law Studies* 53–67.

[31] See also his *Social Anthropology* (1963), chap. 17; "'Land', 'Tenure' and Land-Tenure" in *African Agrarian Systems* (ed. D. Biebuyck, 1963) and "Ethnography and Comparison in Legal Anthropology" in *Law in Culture and Society* (ed. L. Nader, 1969).

[32] See also his *Anthropology of Law: A Comparative Theory* (1971); *The Ethnology of Law* (1972; Addison-Wesley Modular Publications, 12, pp. 1–40); and "Legally Induced Culture Change in New Guinea" in *The Imposition of Law* (eds. S. Burman and B. Harrell-Bond, 1979).

[33] See also his *Neighbours and Networks: The Idiom of Kinship in Social Action among the Ndendeuli of Tanzania* (1971); his recent works are mentioned later.

[34] The maintenance of social order has been a continuing theme in legal anthropology. See, *e.g.*, M. Gluckman, *Custom and Conflict in Africa* (1956) and Roberts, *Order and Dispute*, *op.cit. supra* n. 8. Goddard, *op.cit. supra* n. 11 is among the many criticisms of this focus.

[35] Nader and Yngvesson, "On Studying the Ethnography of Law and Its Consequences" in *Handbook of Social and Cultural Anthropology* (ed. J. J. Honigman, 1973), pp. 884–892. The distinction between framework and process, deriving from Durkheim and Malinowski, has been partly reformulated in terms of a distinction between rights and interests. For different criticisms of these dichotomies, see Hamnett, "Introduction" in *Social Anthropology and Law* (ed. I. Hamnett, 1977), pp. 8–10; LeRoy, *op.cit. supra* n. 30; and Comaroff and Roberts, *op.cit. supra* n. 27.

[36] Especially influential were those by Radcliffe-Brown, Evans-Pritchard and Douglas, *op.cit. supra* n. 20. An indication of the general situation, however, the converse of Anglo-American neglect of continental research, is Lévy-Bruhl's assertion, written about 1963, that "l'ethnographie juridique est restée relativement peu dévelopée dans les pays de langue anglaise"; see Lévy-Bruhl, *op.cit. supra* n. 11, p. 1118. The proofs of that paper were corrected shortly before his death in 1964; see Poirier, "Preface" in *Ethnologie générale*, *op.cit. supra* n. 11, p. xv. In contrast, the bibliography prepared by R. Verdier for a course on legal anthropology at the University of Paris in 1969 included numerous references to recent work in Anglo-American anthropology of law.

[37] A translation of part of Van Vollenhoven's work is to be published in late 1981 as *Van Vollenhoven on Indonesian Adat Law — Selections from Het Adatrecht van Nederlandsch-Indië* (ed. J. F. Holleman, 1981). For an earlier discussion of Van Vollenhoven's influence, see Korn, "Past and Future of Indonesian Adat Law" in *The Future of Customary Law in Africa* (1956). In addition to Van Vollenhoven, Schapera and later Llewellyn and Hoebel influenced the work of J. F. Holleman at Leiden; see Holleman, "Trouble-Cases and Trouble-less Cases in the Study of Customary Law and Legal Reform", (1973) 7 *Law and Society Review* 585–586. Holleman's major writings include *Shona Customary Law* (1952); *Chief, Council and Commissioner* (1969); and *Issues in African Law* (1974).

[38] See Lévy-Bruhl, *op.cit. supra* n. 11, pp. 1119–1120. The particular contribution of Lucien Lévy-Bruhl lay not in his specific theories but in posing the question as to the universal validity of Western categories and emphasising the conceptual and symbolic aspects of human thought, according to R. Verdier, "Anthropologie juridique: Sa position dans les Sciences anthropologique. (3) Anthropologie sociale", Cours d'ethnologie juridique, Université de Paris, 1969, p. 4.

[39] Mauss's lectures were published posthumously as *Manuel d'Ethnographie* (1947; 2nd edition 1967); chap. 7 concerns legal phenomena. Among his most important writings in legal anthropology are *The Gift: Forms and Functions of Exchange in Archaic Societies* (trans. I. Cunnison, 1970; orig. pub. 1923–24); "Essai sur les variations saisonnières des societés Eskimos: Etude de morphologie sociale" in *Sociologie et Anthropologie* (1950; 4th edition 1968), pp. 389–476; and (with E. Durkheim) *Primitive Classification* (trans. R. Needham, 1963; orig. pub. 1903).

[40] See my "Introduction" and "Partial Bibliography of the Works of Henri Lévy-Bruhl" in Lévy-Bruhl, "Juridical Ethnology" (trans. C. J. Snyder), Yale Law School Program in Law and Modernization Working Paper No. 16.

[41] *Ibid.*, pp. iii–iv. M. Alliot, Lévy-Bruhl's successor in the Chair of Juridical Ethnology in Paris, established the Laboratoire d'Anthropologie Juridique in 1964–65. See *Ibid.*, pp. iv–v and LeRoy, *op.cit. supra* n. 2. For a more recent discussion of French research, see LeRoy, "Pour une anthropologie du droit" (1978) 1 *Revue Interdisciplinaire d'Etudes Juridiques* 71–100.

[42] Earlier partial reviews of the literature, mainly to 1975, include: Hoebel, "Law and Anthropology", (1946) 32 *Virginia Law Review* 835–854; Bohannan, "Anthropology and the Law" in *Horizons of Anthropology* (ed. S. Tax, 1964); Nader, *op.cit. supra* n. 13; M. Gluckman, *Politics, Law and Ritual in Tribal Society* (1967); Koch, "Law and Anthropology: Thoughts on Interdisciplinary Research", (1969) 4 *Law and Society Review*, 11–27; Moore, "Law and Anthropology" in *Biennial Review of Anthropology* (ed. B. J. Siegel, 1969), reprinted in S. F. Moore, *Law as Process: An Anthropological Approach* (1978), chap. 7; Cox and Drever, "Some Recent Trends in the Ethnography of Law", (1971) 5 *Law and Society Review* 407–415; Nader and Yngvesson, *op.cit. supra* n. 35; Abel, *op.cit. supra* n. 10; Collier, "Legal Processes" in *Annual Review of Anthropology* (eds., B. J. Siegel, A. R. Beals and S. A. Tyler, 1975); M. B. Hooker, *Legal Pluralism: An Introduction to Colonial and Neo-colonial Laws* (1975), chap. 1; Roberts, *op.cit. supra* n. 7; Koch, "The Anthropology of Law and Order" in *Horizons of Anthropology*, 2nd edition (ed. S. Tax and L. G. Freeman, 1977); Roberts, *op.cit. supra* n. 8, chap. 11; Snyder, "Law and Development in the Light of Dependency Theory", (1980) 14 *Law and Society Review* 723 at pp. 775–779. Collections of readings on legal anthropology include: Nader (ed.), *op.cit. supra* n. 13; P. Bohannan (ed.), *Law and Warfare: Studies in the Anthropology of Conflict* (1967); Nader (ed.), *op.cit. supra* n. 31; Gluckman (ed.), *op.cit. supra* n. 29; (1973) 22 *Rural Africana*; (1973) 7 *Law and Society Review*; A. L. Epstein (ed.), *Contention and Dispute: Aspects of Law and Social Control in Melanesia* (1974); Hamnett (ed.), *op.cit. supra* n. 35; (1977) 21 *Journal of African Law*; Gulliver (ed.), *op.cit. supra* n. 30; L. Nader and H. F. Todd, Jr. (eds.), *The Disputing Process — Law in Ten Societies* (1978); and K.-F. Koch (ed.), *Access to Justice, Vol. IV, The Anthropological Perspective — Patterns of Conflict Management: Essays in the Ethnography of Law* (1979). See also L. Nader, K. F. Koch and B. Cox, "The Ethnography of Law: A Bibliographical Survey", (1966) 7 *Current Anthropology* 267–294.

[43] Nader, *op.cit. supra* n. 13.

[44] Especially Colson, "Social Control and Vengeance in Plateau Tonga Society", (1953) 23 *Africa* 199–212.

[45] V. W. Turner, *Schism and Continuity in an African Society: A Study of Ndembu Village Life* (1957).

[46] F. G. Bailey, *Caste and the Economic Frontier* (1958) and *Tribe, Caste and Nation* (1960). In these books, Bailey presented ideas that he has subsequently developed in a number of works.

[47] Nader, *op.cit. supra* n. 13, p. 23.

[48] See especially F. Barth, "Models of Social Organization", Occasional Paper 23, Royal Anthropological Institute of Great Britain and Ireland (1966); M. J. Swartz, V. W. Turner and A. Tuden (eds.), *Political Anthropology* (1966); and van Velsen, "The Extended-Case Method and Situational Analysis" in *The Craft of Social Anthropology* (ed. A. L. Epstein, 1967). These and other influences, especially Malinowski's work, on legal anthropology are discussed in Nader and Yngvesson, *op.cit. supra* n. 35 and in Nader and Todd, "Introduction: The Disputing Process" in Nader and Todd (eds.), *op.cit. supra* n. 42.

[49] See Nader, "Preface" and Nader and Todd, "Introduction: The Disputing Process" in Nader and Todd (eds.), *op.cit. supra* n. 42. Under Nader's direction, fourteen graduate students completed doctoral dissertations on legal anthropology during this decade; essays by ten of them are included in Nader and Todd (eds.), *op.cit. supra* n. 42. See also K.-F. Koch, *War and Peace in Jalémo: The Management of Conflict in Highland New Guinea* (1974); J. Starr, *Dispute and Settlement in Rural Turkey: An Ethnography of Law* (1978); and C. Witty, *Mediation and Society: Conflict Management in Lebanon* (1980).

[50] Though then retaining the expression "dispute settlement", Gulliver was among the first to make this point clearly in his "Case Studies of Law in Non-Western Societies: Introduction" in Nader (ed.), *op.cit. supra* n. 32, pp. 14–15.

[51] *Ibid.*, p. 14. Some of the problems inherent in this definition, especially concerning the requirement that a conflict reach the public arena in order to qualify as a "dispute", are discussed in Epstein, "Introduction" in Epstein (ed.), *op.cit. supra* n. 42, p. 9 and in Starr, "A Pre-Law Stage in Rural Turkish Disputes Negotiations" in Gulliver (ed.), *op.cit. supra* n. 30.

[52] See, *e.g.*, Gulliver, *op.cit. supra* n. 50, pp. 12–13; Koch, "The Anthropology of Law: Notes on Interdisciplinary Research", *op.cit. supra* n. 42, p. 12; Abel, *op.cit. supra* n. 10, pp. 221–224; Roberts, *op.cit. supra* n. 8, chap. 2.

[53] See, *e.g.*, Abel, "Law and Anthropology" (Review of I. Hamnett, ed., *Social Anthropology and Law*, (1980) 28 *American Journal of Comparative Law* 128–135 at p. 131. This was primarily an Anglo-American phenomenon; in that literature, the sole major exception prior to 1975 was L. A. Fallers, *Law Without Precedent: Legal Ideas in Action in the Courts of Colonial Busoga* (1969).

[54] The case method is often viewed as the standard research method in legal anthropology; but anthropologists' conceptions of this method differ substantially from those of lawyers and, in addition, the former are various, have changed substantially since the early 1960s and have recently been attacked on the grounds, *inter alia*, that the study of cases, however defined, is inadequate for some purposes and always needs to be supplemented by other research methods. For discussions of these issues, and especially the important shift in the conception of the case method since the late 1960s, see: Gluckman, "Ethnographic Data in British Social Anthropology", (1961) N.S. 9 *The Sociological Review* 1–17; Gluckman, *Politics, Law and Ritual in Tribal Society*, *op.cit. supra* n. 35, pp. 235–242; van Velsen, *op.cit. supra* n. 48; Epstein, "The Case Method in the Field of Law" in *The Craft of Social Anthropology*, *op.cit. supra* n. 48; Abel, "Customary Law of Wrongs in Kenya: An Essay in Research Method", (1969) 17 *American Journal of Comparative Law* 573–626; Gluckman, "Limitations of the Case-Method in the Study of Tribal Law", (1973) 7 *Law and Society Review* 611–641; Holleman, "Trouble-Cases and Trouble-less Cases in the Study of Customary Law and Legal Reform," *op.cit. supra* n. 37; Abel, "Reply to Max Gluckman", (1973) 8 *Law and Society Review* 157–159; Nader and Yngvesson, *op.cit. supra* n. 35, pp. 892–902; Hooker, *op.cit. supra* n. 35; van Binsbergen, "Law in the Context of Nkoya Society" in *Law and the Family in Africa*, *op.cit. supra* n. 6; and Nader and Todd, *op.cit. supra* n. 49. Other, complementary methods are discussed in Snyder, "The Use of Oral Data in Legal Anthropology: A Senegalese Example", (1973) 17 *Journal of African Law* 196–215; B. E. Harrell-Bond, *Modern Marriage in Sierra Leone: A Study of the Professional Group* (1975), pp. 296–332; and the essays in R. Luckham (ed.), *Law and Social Enquiry: Case Studies of Research* (1981).

[55] J. F. Collier, *Law and Social Change in Zinacantan* (1973), p. 244.

[56] J. Starr, *op.cit. supra* n. 49.

[57] See Collier, "Political Leadership and Legal Change in Zinacantan", (1976) 11 *Law and Society Review* 131–163; Freeman, "Conflict, Law and Lawyers in Chiapas, Mexico" in Koch (ed.), *op.cit. supra* n. 42.

[58] J. P. Spradley, *You Owe Yourself a Drunk: An Ethnography of Urban Nomads* (1970).

[59] Mather, "Ethnography and the Study of Trial Courts" in J. A. Gardiner (ed.), *Public Law and Public Policy* (1977).

[60] See Nader and Todd, *op.cit. supra* n. 49, p. 3.

[61] See Starr, "Different Theories in the Anthropological Study of Law: A Response to Professor Pospisil", (1980) 2 *Zeitschrift für Rechtssoziologie* 253–259 (reply to Pospisil, Review of Starr, *Dispute and Settlement in Rural Turkey: An Ethnography of Law* (1978), 2 *Zeitschrift für Rechtssoziologie* 249–252); Starr, Review of S. Roberts, *Order and Dispute: An Introduction to Legal Anthropology* (1979), (1981) 9 *International Journal of the Sociology of Law* 120–121.

[62] See Roberts, *op.cit. supra* n. 8; Koch, Sodergren and Campbell, "Political and Psychological Correlates of Conflict Management: A Cross-Cultural Study", (1976) 10 *Law and Society Review* 443–466.

[63] Collier, *op.cit. supra* n. 42 discusses some studies; see also LeVine, "Anthropology and the Study of Conflict: An Introduction", (1961) 5 *Journal of Conflict Resolution* 3–15; and A. R. Beals and B. J. Siegel, *Divisiveness and Social Conflict: An Anthropological Approach* (1966).

[64] Felstiner, "Influences of Social Organization on Dispute Processing", (1974) 9 *Law and Society Review* 63–94.

[65] Some of these issues are discussed in papers in Luckham (ed.), *op.cit. supra* n. 54.

[66] See also Abel, "Informal Alternatives to Courts as a Mode of Legalizing Conflict", presented at the Symposium of the IUAES Commission on Contemporary Folk Law, Bellagio, Italy, September 1981; and Abel, "Conservative Conflict and the Reproduction of Capitalism: The Role of Informal Justice" (1981) 9 *International Journal of the Sociology of Law* 245–267.

[67] Nader and Todd, *op.cit. supra* n. 49, pp. 14–15; see also P. H. Gulliver, *Disputes and Negotiations: A Cross-Cultural Perspective* (1979), pp. 268–270.

[68] Yngvesson, "Responses to Grievance Behavior: Extended Cases in a Fishing Community", (1976) 3 *American Ethnologist* 353; and Yngvesson, "The Atlantic Fisherman" in Nader and Todd (eds.), *op.cit. supra* n. 42.

[69] Yngvesson, "The Reasonable Man and the Unreasonable Gossip: On the Flexibility of (Legal) Concepts and the Elasticity of (Legal) Time" in Gulliver (ed.), *op.cit. supra* n. 30.

[70] Starr, *op.cit. supra* n. 51, p. 131.

[71] See Nader, "The Direction of Law and the Development of Extra-Judicial Processes in Nation State Societies" in Gulliver (ed.), *op.cit. supra* n. 30.

[72] Abel, "Theories of Litigation in Society: 'Modern' Dispute Institutions in 'Tribal' Society and 'Tribal' Institutions in 'Modern' Society as Alternative Legal Forms" in *Alternative Rechtsformen und Alternativen zum Recht* (eds. E. Blankenburg, E. Klausa and H. Rottleuthner, 1979) (6 *Jahrbuch für Rechtssoziologie und Rechtstheorie*) 165–191; and Abel, "Western Courts in Non-Western Settings: Patterns of Court Use in Colonial and Neo-Colonial Africa" in Burman and Harrell-Bond (eds.), *op.cit. supra* n. 32.

[73] *E.g.*, Aubert, "Competition and Dissensus: Two Types of Conflict Resolution", (1963) 7 *Journal of Conflict Resolution* 26–42; and Eckhoff, "The Mediator, the Judge and the Administrator in Conflict Resolution", (1967) 10 *Acta Sociologica* 148–172.

[74] Gulliver, *Social Control in an African Society: A Study of the Arusha, Agricultural Masai of Northern Tanganyika* (1963), pp. 297–301.

[75] Bohannan, "Introduction" in Bohannan (ed.), *op.cit. supra* n. 42.

[76] Abel. *op.cit. supra* n. 10.

[77] The debates concerning this typology may be traced in: Gulliver, *loc.cit. supra* n. 74; Moore, "Politics, Procedures and Norms in Changing Chagga Law", (1969) 40 *Africa* 321–343; Gulliver, *op.cit. supra* n. 50, pp. 17–19; Abel, *op.cit. supra* n. 10, pp. 232–239; Gulliver, *op.cit. supra* n. 67, pp. 19–20.

[78] Nader, "Styles of Court Procedure: To Make the Balance" in Nader (ed.), *op.cit. supra* n. 31.

[79] Roberts, *op.cit. supra* n. 8, chap. 9.

[80] Danet, "Language in the Legal Process", (1980) 14 *Law and Society Review* 445 at 493–495.

[81] Koch, *op.cit. supra* n. 49, pp. 27–31; see also Koch, "The Anthropology of Law and

Order", *op.cit. supra* n. 42, pp. 307–311; and Koch, Sodergren and Campbell, *op.cit. supra* n. 62.

[82] Gulliver, *op.cit. supra* n. 67; see also Gulliver, *op.cit. supra* n. 50; Gulliver, "Negotiations as a Mode of Dispute Settlement: Towards a General Model", (1973) 7 *Law and Society Review* 667–691; and Gulliver, "On Mediators" in Hamnett (ed.), *op.cit. supra* n. 35.

[83] Abel, *op.cit. supra* n. 10. Collier, *op.cit. supra* n. 42, p. 134 notes the absence of systematic studies in legal anthropology of the influence on dispute processing of the relationships between the third party and the disputants. M. P. Baumgartner and D. Black are preparing a book on this subject, tentatively entitled "The Theory of the Third Party"; see (1981) 4 *IUAES Commission on Contemporary Folk Law Newsletter* 20.

[84] See, *e.g.*, Whitney and Kobryn, *op.cit. supra* n. 13; Greenhouse, *op.cit. supra* n. 13; and the *Newsletters* of the IUAES Commission on Contemporary Folk Law. Recent French legal anthropological writing suggests the limited impact of these topics on French research. In his survey of socio-legal research in the German Federal Republic, Wilson mentions only a few anthropological studies on this topic: see G. P. Wilson, *Socio-Legal Research in Germany: An Account of Work in the Socio-Legal Field in the Federal Republic* (1980), p. 88.

[85] In the early 1960s, academic lawyers in the United States first became especially interested in popular tribunals, mainly in Cuba, China, the Soviet Union and Eastern Europe: see, *e.g.*, Lubman, "Legal Anthropology and Comparative Social Research on Popular Tribunals: The Search for Function", presented at the Conference on "The Relevance of Legal Anthropology to Comparative Social Research on Law", Yale Law School Program in Law and Modernization, November 1971. For a recent, critical survey by a sociologist, see Brady, "Towards a Popular Justice in the United States: The Dialectics of Community Action", (1981) 5 *Contemporary Crises* 155–192.

[86] See the writings cited in n. 16, *supra*, and Snyder, *op.cit. supra* n. 42, pp. 725–734.

[87] See Nader, "Up the Anthropologist — Perspectives Gained from Studying Up" in Hymes (ed.), *op.cit. supra* n. 16.

[88] See Nader and Singer, "Dispute Resolution" in *Law in the Future: What are the Choices?*, Supplement to (1976) 51 *California State Bar Journal* 281–286 and 311–320; Boissevain, "Introduction: Towards a Social Anthropology of Europe" and Katz, "Village Responses to National Law: A Case Study from the South Tyrol" in *Beyond the Community: Social Process in Europe* (eds. J. Boissevain and J. Friedl, 1975).

[89] See, *e.g.*, Cappelletti, "Foreward" in Koch (ed.), *op.cit. supra* n. 42.

[90] For discussions of this point, see, *e.g.*, Moore, "Archaic Law and Modern Times on the Zambezi: Some Thoughts on Max Gluckman's Interpretation of Barotse Law" in Gulliver (ed.), *op. cit. supra* n. 30; Swartz, "History and Science in Anthropology" (1958) 21 *Philosophy of Science* 59–70, reprinted in Manners and Kaplan (eds.), *op.cit. supra* n. 9; Worsley, "The End of Anthropology?" (1970) 3 *Transactions of the Sixth World Congress of Sociology* 121–129; I. Meszaros, *Marx's Theory of Alienation* (1970), pp. 36–48; and Thompson, "Anthropology and the Discipline of Historical Context", (1972) 1 *Midland History* 41–55. Historical research, often relying especially on oral history, is of course now often conducted by anthropologists but rarely by those interested in law or dispute processes; some exceptions are discussed later. For a related discussion of anthropological theories of culture, see M. Harris, *The Rise of Anthropological Theory: A History of Theories of Culture* (1968).

[91] See, *e.g.*, Abel, "Delegalization: A Critical Review of its Ideology, Manifestations, and Social Consequences" in Blankenburg, Klausa and Rottleuthner (eds.), *op.cit. supra* n. 72, p. 29 For a discussion of the romanticisation of liberal democracy in contraposition to 'tribal society', see Abel, "The Problem of Values in the Analysis of Political Order: Myths of Tribal Society and Liberal Democracy" (A review essay on E. Colson, *Tradition and Contract: The Problems of Order* (1974)), (1978) 16 *African Law Studies* 132–165.

[92] See, *e.g.*, Cox and Drever, *op.cit. supra* n. 42; Abel, *op.cit. supra* n. 53; and Quinney, "Comment" on Lowy, "Modernizing the American Legal System: An Example of the Peaceful Use of Anthropology", (1973) 32 *Human Organization* 213–214.

[93] See, *e.g.*, Friedman, "Access to Justice: Social and Historical Context" in *Access to Justice*, Vol. II: *Promising Institutions* (eds. M. Cappelletti and J. Weisner, 1978); Abel, "Delegalization ...", *op.cit. supra* n. 91; Galanter, "Legality and Its Discontents: A Preliminary Assessment of Current Theories of Legalization and Delegalization" in Blankenburg, Klausa and Rottleuthner (eds.), *op.cit. supra* n. 91. McGillis, "Neighborhood Justice Centers as Mechanisms for Dispute Resolution" in *New Directions in Psycholegal Research* (eds. P. D. Lippsitt and B. D. Sales, 1980); McGillis, "The Quiet (R)Evolution in American Dispute Settlement", (1980) 31 *Harvard Law School Bulletin* 20–25. Studies and criticisms of the movement for informal justice are forthcoming in R. L. Abel (ed.), *The Politics of Informal Justice : The American Experience* (1982) and R. L. Abel (ed.), *The Politics of Informal Justice : Comparative Studies* (1982).

[94] See Abel, *op.cit. supra* n. 65 and sources cited there.

[95] M. Cappelletti (general editor), *Access to Justice*, five volumes (1978–1981); reviewed by Lewis in (1981) 9 *International Journal of the Sociology of Law* 109–112.

[96] See P. J. Wilkinson, *The Social Organisation of Disputes and Dispute Processing and Methods for the Investigation of Their Social, Legal and Interactive Properties: A Bibliography in Three Parts* (1980). A conference on "Formal Courts and Alternative Courts" was organised by the Sociology Department, University of Surrey, in July 1981; and the International Association of Legal Science conference, held in Pau in July 1981, concerned "Settlement of Disputes Out of Court".

[97] Danzig, "Toward the Creation of a Complementary, Decentralized System of Criminal Justice", (1973) 26 *Stanford Law Review* 1–54. Danzig's model was the Kpelle moot described in Gibbs, "The Kpelle Moot: A Therapeutic Model for the Informal Settlement of Disputes", (1963) 33 *Africa* 1–10, reprinted in Bohannan (ed.), *op.cit. supra* n. 42 and in D. Black and M. Mileski (eds.), *The Social Organization of Law* (1973).

[98] Felstiner, "Influences of Social Organization on Dispute Processing", (1974) 9 *Law and Society Review* 63–94. See also Danzig and Lowy, "Everyday Disputes and Mediation in the United States: A Reply to Professor Felstiner", (1975) 9 *Law and Society Review* 675–694; and Felstiner, "Avoidance as Dispute Processing: An Elaboration", (1975) 9 *Law and Society Review* 695–706. A recent study of the use of avoidance is Greenhouse, "Avoidance as a Strategy for Resolving Conflict in Zinacantan" in Koch (ed.), *op.cit. supra* n. 42.

[99] Galanter, "Why the 'Haves' Come Out Ahead: Speculations on the Limits of Legal Change", (1974) 9 *Law and Society Review* 95–160. See also Galanter, "Afterward: Explaining Litigation", (1975) 9 *Law and Society Review* 347–368.

[100] See, *e.g.*, W. L. F. Felstiner and L. A. Williams, *Community Mediation in Dorchester, Massachusetts* (1980); Witty, *op.cit. supra* n. 49; Crowe, "Complainant Reactions against the Massachusetts Commission against Discrimination", (1978) 12 *Law and Society Review* 217–235; Merry, "Going to Court: Strategies of Dispute Management in an American Urban Neighborhood", (1979) 13 *Law and Society Review* 891–925; and two papers in Cappelletti and Weisner (eds.), *op.cit. supra* n. 93: Bierbrauer, Falke and Koch, "Conflict and Its Settlement: An Interdisciplinary Study concerning the Legal Basis, Function and Performance of the Schiedsmann" and Falke, Bierbrauer and Koch, "Legal Advice and the Non-Judicial Settlement of Disputes: A Case Study of the Public Legal Advice and Mediation Center in the City of Hamburg".

[101] See A. Smith, J. Bryant and D. Bond, *A Pilot Study of Dispute Treatment in Leamington : A Report* (Project Director: B. E. Harrell-Bond) (n.d. [1979]).

[102] Nader, "Forums for Justice: A Cross-Cultural Perspective", (1975) 31 *Journal of Social Issues* 151–170 at p. 163.

[103] See Koch, "Introduction. Access to Justice: An Anthropological Perspective" in Koch (ed.), *op.cit. supra* n. 42, p. 2.

[104] Nader, *op.cit. supra* n. 71, p. 92. Among earlier studies on which this conclusion was based are Nader and Metzger, "Conflict Resolution in Two Mexican Communities", (1963) *American Anthropologist* 584–592; Nader, "Choices in Legal Procedure: Shia Moslem and Mexican Zapotec", (1965) 67 *American Anthropologist* 394–399; and Nader, "Powerlessness in Zapotec and U.S. Societies" in *Anthropological Studies of Power* (eds. R. Fogelson and R. Adams, 1977).

[105] A recent paper that indicates the common interests of Laura and Ralph Nader is Ralph Nader, "Consumerism and Legal Services: The Merging of Movements", (1976) 11 *Law and Society Review* 247–256.

[106] Nader and Todd (eds.), *op.cit. supra* n. 42.

[107] L. Nader (ed.), *No Access to Law: Alternatives to the American Judicial System* (1980).

[108] See Lamb, "Marxism, Access and the State", (1975) 6 *Development and Change* 119–135.

[109] This point was made in 1973 by Richard Quinney, *op.cit. supra*. n. 92.

[110] Abel, "Delegalization ...", *op.cit. supra* n. 91.

[111] Abel, *op.cit. supra* n. 66.

[112] Santos, "Law and Community: The Changing Nature of State Power in Late Capitalism", (1980) 8 *International Journal of the Sociology of Law* 379–397; the quotation is from p. 390.

[113] Among the papers scheduled for presentation at a panel on the anthropology of law in complex society at the Law and Society Association Annual Meeting in June 1981 were Wolfe, "The Politics of School Reform: Parent Participation in the Boston Desegregation Case"; Gamburd, "Energy Decisions: Who, What and Why?"; and Joans, "Problems in Pocatello: A Study in Cross-Cultural Misunderstanding"; see (1981) 5 *APLA Newsletter and Occasional Papers* 3. See also Lane, "The Use of Anthropological Evidence in Indian Litigation", presented at the symposium on the Anthropology of Law, Annual Conference of the Canadian Ethnology Society, March 1980 ((1980) 3 *APLA Newsletter and Occasional Papers* 5, 7); and Rosen, "The Excavation of American Indian Burial Sites: A Problem in Law and Professional Responsibility", (1980) 82 *American Anthropologist* 5–27.

[114] See (1981) 5 *IUAES Commission on Contemporary Folk Law Newsletter* 16.

[115] See the sources cited in n. 57, *supra*.

[116] See, *e.g.*, Starr, *op.cit. supra* n. 49; Starr and Poole, "The Impact of a Legal Revolution in Turkey", (1974) 8 *Law and Society Review* 533–560; Craig, "Tradition and Legal Reform in an Iranian Village" in Koch (ed.), *op.cit. supra* n. 42; a much earlier study by Stirling, "Land, Marriage and the Law in Turkish Villages", (1957) 9 *International Social Science Bulletin* 21–33; Sylla, "Le droit: élément essential du changement social en Afrique (Etude de cas)" in *Dynamiques et finalités des droits africains* (ed. G. Conac, 1980). (1979) 1 *African Perspectives* also includes several papers by anthropologists on this theme in the specific context of agrarian reforms. Conversely, the use of "folk law" in state institutions is the subject of papers presented at the IUAES Commission on Contemporary Folk Law symposium, Bellagio, Italy, September 1981. See especially F. von Benda-Beckmann, "Some Comparative Generalizations about the Differential Use of State and Folk Institutions of Dispute Settlement"; Starr, "The Use of Folk Law in the Official Courts of Turkey"; and K. von Benda-Beckmann, "Folk Law and State Courts in West Sumatra, Indonesia".

[117] Hooker, *op.cit. supra* n. 42 discusses legal literature and provides an extensive bibliography on writing on this topic up to 1975.

[118] See Snyder, *op.cit. supra* n. 42, pp. 775–779.

[119] My survey of the literature on underdevelopment and dependency theory in relation to law gave special emphasis to studies of state and classes and of capitalism and peasants (see *Ibid.*, pp. 761–780).

[120] In 1965, Nader, *op.cit. supra* n. 13, p. 6 discerned a shift away from general definitions of law and towards the question, "How is law best conceived of for research purposes?"; but compare the sources cited *supra* n. 52.

[121] See, *e.g.*, Nader, *ibid.*, pp. 4–8.

[122] These are criticised in Roberts, *op.cit. supra* n. 8, especially chaps. 2 and 11; see also F. G. Snyder, *Capitalism and Legal Change: An African Transformation* (1981).

[123] See especially the works by Pospisil, *op.cit. supra* n. 32.

[124] See, *e.g.*, P. Fitzpatrick, *Law and State in Papua New Guinea* (1980); Snyder, *op.cit. supra* n. 122; LeRoy, *op.cit. supra* n. 41; Starr, *op.cit. supra* n. 61; Fallers, *op.cit.*

[125] See, *e.g.*, Snyder, *op.cit. supra* n. 121; LeRoy, "Justice africaine et oralité juridique: Une réinterprétation de l'organisation judiciaire 'traditionnelle' à la lumiere d'une théorie générale du droit oral d'Afrique Noire", (1974) 36 (B) *Bulletin de l'Institut Fondamental d'Afrique Noire* 559–591; R. Verdier, *Terre et Femme dans la Pensée Juridique Négroafricaine* (1968); Wane, "La succession d'états au Fouta Toro", paper presented at the Second Meeting of the Africanist Network, UNESCO Project on the Transfer of Legal Knowledge, Malta, November 1980.

[126] See especially Fallers, *op.cit. supra* n. 53 and his "Administration and the Supremacy of Law in Colonial Busoga" in Hamnett (ed.), *op.cit. supra* n. 42.

[127] See especially Fitzpatrick, *op.cit. supra* n. 124 and Snyder *op.cit. supra* n. 122.

[128] *Op.cit. supra* n. 74.

[129] I. Hamnett, *Chieftainship and Legitimacy: An Anthropological Study of Executive Law in Lesotho* (1975).

[130] See, *e.g.*, Dawe, "Theories of Social Action" and Fisher and Strauss, "Interactionism" in *A History of Sociological Analysis* (eds. T. Bottomore and R. Nisbet, 1978); Hunt, "Dichotomy and Contradiction in the Sociology of Law", (1981) 8 *British Journal of Law and Society* 47–77; Abel, "Delegalization ...", *op.cit. supra* n. 91. See also A. Giddens, *Central Problems in Social Theory: Action, Structure and Contradiction in Social Analysis* (1979).

[131] See, *e.g.*, Moore, "Descent and Legal Position" in Nader (ed.), *op.cit. supra* n. 31; Moore, "Epilogue: Uncertainties in Situations, Indeterminacies in Culture" in *Symbol and Politics in Communal Ideology* (eds. S. F. Moore and B. G. Myerhoff, 1975); and Moore, "Introduction" in S. F. Moore, *Law as Process: An Anthropological Approach* (1978), which includes several of her most important papers; see also my review of *Law as Process* in (1979) 6 *British Journal of Law and Society* 135–139.

[132] See especially Gulliver, *op.cit. supra* n. 67, pp. 190–194; see also Roberts, *op.cit. supra* n. 8, p. 182.

[133] Perry, "Law Codes and Brokerage in a Lesotho Village" in Hamnett (ed.), *op.cit. supra* n. 42.

[134] See, *e.g.*, Roberts, "The Kgatla Marriage: Concepts of Validity" in Roberts (ed.), *op.cit. supra* n. 6; Comaroff and Roberts, "Marriage and Extra-marital Sexuality: The Dialectics of Legal Change among the Kgatla", (1977) 21 *Journal of African Law* 97–123; and Werbner, "Land, Movement and Status among Kalanga of Botswana" in *Studies in African Social Anthropology* (eds. M. Fortes and S. Patterson, 1975).

[135] Comaroff and Roberts, "The Invocation of Norms in Dispute Settlement: The Tswana Case" in Hamnett (ed.), *op.cit. supra* n. 42; the quotation is from p. 106.

[136] See Gulliver, *op.cit. supra* n. 67, p. 20 and sources cited there. For recent work, see, *e.g.*, Mather and Yngvesson, "Language, Audience and the Transformation of Disputes", presented at the Law and Society Association annual meeting, San Francisco, May 1979; Arno, "A Grammar of Conflict: Informal Procedure on an Island in Lau, Fiji" in Koch (ed.), *op.cit. supra* n. 42; and the papers in M. Bloch (ed.), *Political Language and Oratory in Traditional Society* (1975). The emphasis on language and transformation differs from earlier studies of the use of language, either those that merely describe linguistic expressions of cultural concepts or those that aim at more formal ethnosemantic analyses of terms and expressions. See, *e.g.*, P. J. Bohannan, *Justice and Judgement among the Tiv* (1957, reprinted with a new Preface in 1968); S. A. Schlegel, *Tiruray Justice: Traditional Tiruray Law and Morality* (1970); Verdier, "Ontology of the Judicial Thought of the Kabrè of Northern Togo" in Nader (ed.), *op.cit. supra* n. 31; Black and Metzger, "Ethnographic Description and the Study of Law" in Nader (ed.), *op.cit. supra* n. 13, reprinted in *Cognitive Anthropology* (ed. S. A. Tyler, 1969); and Frake, "Struck by Speech: The Yakan Concept of Litigation" in Nader (ed.), *op.cit. supra* n. 31.

[137] Danet, *op.cit. supra* n. 80, pp. 490–546.

[138] See LeRoy, "L'expérience juridique autochtone et le transfert des connaissances juridiques occidentales en Afrique noire" in *Domination ou Partage?* (UNESCO, 1980), and "Concepts-recteurs et pratique juridique dans le droit local en zone arachidière nord (Sénégal)", presented at the Second Meeting of the Africanist Network, UNESCO Project on the Transfer of Legal Knowledge, Malta, November 1980.

[139] Santos, "The Law of the Oppressed: The Construction and Reproduction of Legality in Pasargada", (1977) 12 *Law and Society Review* 5–126; the quotation is from p. 92.

[140] See Comaroff and Roberts, *op.cit. supra* n. 27.

[141] See especially Comaroff, "Introduction" and "Bridewealth and the Control of Ambiguity in a Tswana Chiefdom" in *The Meaning of Marriage Payments* (ed. J. L. Comaroff, 1980). See also the recent debate concerning the Nuer leopard-skin chief in: Gruel, "The Leopard-Skin Chief: An Examination of Political Power among the Nuer", (1971) 73 *American Anthropologist* 1115–1121; Haight, "A Note on the Leopard-Skin Chief", (1972) 74 *American Anthropologist* 1313–1318; and Evens, "Leopard Skins and Paper Tigers: 'Choice' and 'Social Structure' in *The Nuer*", (1978) N.S. 13 *Man* 100–115.

[142] See, *e.g.*, Roberts, *op.cit. supra* n. 8.

[143] See, *e.g.*, Snyder, *op.cit. supra* n. 122.

[144] See, *e.g.*, Comaroff, *op.cit. supra* n. 141; Comaroff and Roberts, *op.cit. supra* n. 27; and Comaroff, "Rules and Rulers: Political Processes in a Tswana Chiefdom", (1978) N.S. 13 *Man* 1–20.

[145] See the discussion of von Gierke, Ehrlich and Weber in Pospisil, *The Anthropology of Law* ..., *op.cit. supra* n. 32, pp. 102–104.

[146] *Op.cit. supra* n. 22, especially pp. 28, 53.

[147] See Griffiths, "What is Legal Pluralism", unpublished paper (n.d.)

[148] J. S. Furnivall, *Colonial Policy and Practice: A Comparative Study of Burma and Netherlands India* (1948).

[149] *Op.cit. supra* n. 22.

[150] See "Institutional and Political Conditions of Pluralism" in *Pluralism in Africa* (eds. L. Kuper and M. G. Smith, 1969), reprinted in M. G. Smith, *Corporations and Society* (1974); and "The Sociological Framework of Law" in *African Law: Adaptation and Development* (eds. H. Kuper and L. Kuper, 1965). For discussion, see Moore, "Introduction" in S. F. Moore, *Law as Process*, *op.cit. supra* n. 131. For criticism of the concept of pluralism, see Legassick, "The Concept of Pluralism: A Critique" in *African Social Studies: A Radical Reader* (eds. P. C. W. Gutkind and P. Waterman, 1977).

[151] See Moore, "Law and Social Change: The Semi-autonomous Social Field as an Appropriate Subject of Study", (1973) 7 *Law and Society Review* 719–746, reprinted in Moore, *Law as Process, op.cit. supra* n. 131, chap. 2. See also Moore, "Individual Interests and Organisational Structures: Dispute Settlements as 'Events of Articulation'" in Hamnett (ed.), *op.cit. supra* n. 42.

[152] See Griffiths, *op.cit. supra* n. 147; Griffiths, "Four Laws of Interaction in Circumstances of Legal Pluralism: First Steps towards an Explanatory Theory", presented at the IUAES Commission on Contemporary Folk Law symposium, Bellagio, Italy, September 1981; and (drawing on Moore's conceptions) Fitzpatrick, "Law, Plurality and Underdevelopment" in *Legality, Ideology and the State* (ed. D. Sugarman, forthcoming).

[153] Roberts, "Introduction" in Roberts (ed.), *op.cit. supra* n. 6, p. 8.

[154] Ruffini, "Disputing over Livestock in Sardinia", Starr, "Turkish Village Disputing Behavior", and Witty, "Disputing Issues in Shehaam, a Multireligious Village in Lebanon" in Nader and Todd (eds.), *op.cit. supra* n. 42.

[155] Canter, "Family Dispute Settlement and the Zambian Judiciary" in Roberts (ed.), *op.cit. supra* n. 6; Canter, "Dispute Settlement and Dispute Processing in Zambia: Individual Choices versus Societal Constraints" and Parnell, "Village or State? Competitive Legal Systems in a Mexican Judicial District" in Nader and Todd (eds.), *op.cit. supra* n. 42.

[156] Canter, *id.*; and E. Hunt and R. Hunt, "The Role of Courts in Rural Mexico" in *Peasants in the Modern World* (ed. P. K. Bock, 1969).

[157] E. A. B. van Rouveroy van Nieuwaal, *A la recherche de la justice: Quelques aspects du droit matrimonial et de la justice du Justice de Paix et du Chef Supérieur des Anufom à Mango dans le Nord du Togo* (1976); "Unité du droit ou diversité du droit: Bases juridiques du droit coutumier au Togo", (1979) 12 *Verfassung und Recht in Übersee* 143–158; "Chieftaincy in Northern Togo", (1980) 13 *Verfassung und Recht in Übersee* 115–121. All give references to van Rouveroy's other writings. Van Rouveroy has also made six films concerning dispute processes and social organisation in Northern Togo; the most recent, giving a list of other films, is "In Search of Justice: Different Levels of Dispute Settlement among the Anufòm in North Togo" (1981)

[158] See, *e.g.*, M. Strathern, *Official and Unofficial Courts: Legal Assumptions and Expectations in a Highlands Community* (1972); A. Strathern, "When Dispute Procedures Fail" in Epstein (ed.), *op.cit. supra* n. 42; Lahav, "The Division of Legal Labor in Rural Haiti", (1975) 8 *Verfassung und Recht in Übersee* 465–481; Roberts, "Tradition and Change at Mochudi: Competing Jurisdictions in Botswana", (1979) 17 *African Law Studies* 37–51.

[159] Collier, *op.cit. supra* n. 57.

[160] Freeman, *op.cit. supra* n. 57.

[161] See Werbner, "Small-Man Politics and the Rule of Law: Centre-Periphery Relations in East-Central Botswana", (1977) 21 *Journal of African Law* 24–39. See also Werbner's forthcoming book on Botswana.

[162] See, *e.g.*, Roberts, "The Survival of the Traditional Tswana Courts in the National Legal System of Botswana", (1972) 16 *Journal of African Law* 103–129. This theme is treated by most anthropologists writing on legal pluralism and, as shown later, by scholars interested in the political economy of law.

[163] See Niang, "Place du droit islamique dans la vie juridique sénégalaise contemporaine: Confrontation des modèles (autochtone, occidental et musulman)", presented at the Second Meeting of the Africanist Network, UNESCO Project on the Transfer of Legal Knowledge, Malta, November 1980; and the papers in (1975) 1 *Kroniek van Afrika* [now *African Perspectives*] on "The Disparity between Law and Social Reality in Africa" (eds. B. E. Harrell-Bond and E. A. B. van Rouveroy van Nieuwaal). See also my review of the latter in (1976) 1 *African Law Studies* 162–168.

[164] A summary of and references concerning this debate are given in Moore, "Comparative Studies: Introduction", Gluckman, "Concepts in the Comparative Study of Tribal Law", and Bohannan, "Ethnography and Comparison in Legal Anthropology" in Nader (ed.), *op.cit. supra* n. 31.

[165] See LeRoy, *op.cit. supra* n. 2; LeRoy, *op.cit. supra* n. 41; *Sacralité, Pouvoir et Droit en Afrique* (1979). On the recent divergence of interests within French anthropology of law, compare (1981) 1 *Droits et Culture* with LeRoy, "Local Law in Black Africa: Contemporary Experiences of Folk Law facing State and Capital in Senegal and Some Other Countries", presented at the IUAES Commission on Contemporary Folk Law symposium, Bellagio, Italy, September 1981. For different approaches to concepts and cultural precepts, see Rosen, "Equity and Discretion in a Modern Islamic Legal System", (1980–81) 15 *Law and Society Review* 217–245 and F. von Benda-Beckmann, *Property in Social Continuity: Continuity and Change in the Maintenance of Property Relationships through Time in Minangkabau, West Sumatra* (1979); and Schott, "Le droit contra la loi: Conceptions traditionnelles et jurisdiction actuelle chez les Bulsa au Ghana du Nord" in Conac (ed.), *op. cit. supra* n. 116.

[166] See the IAUES Commission on Contemporary Folk Law Newsletters and the papers presented at its symposium in Bellagio, Italy, September 1981.

[167] Aspects of Gluckman's work are re-evaluated in Moore, *op.cit. supra* n. 90 and Frankenberg, "Economic Anthropology or Political Economy? (I): The Barotse Social Formation—A Case Study" in *The New Economic Anthropology* (ed. J. Clammer, 1978). See also Starr and Yngvesson, "Scarcity and Disputing: Zeroing-in on Compromise Decisions", (1975) 2 *American Ethnologist* 533–566; Collier, "Stratification and Dispute Handling in Two Highland Chiapas Communities", (1979) 6 *American Ethnologist* 305–328; Dwyer, "Bridging the Gap between the Sexes in Moroccan Legal Practice" in *Sexual Stratification* (ed. A. Schleger, 1977); Dwyer, "Law Actual and Perceived: The Sexual Politics of Law in Morocco", (1979) 13 *Law and Society Review* 739–756; Cutshall, "The Role of Women in Local Disputing among the Ila of Zambia", presented at the symposium on Anthropology of Law, Canadian Ethnology Society annual conference, March 1980.

[168] Murray, "High Bridewealth, Migrant Labour and the Position of Women in Lesotho", (1977) 21 *Journal of African Law* 79–96 at p. 79. See also Snyder, "French Colonial Policy, Law, and Diola-Bandial Society, 1815–1915: Background to Legal Change in Rural Senegal", (1973) 22 *Rural Africana* 69–81; Snyder, "Land Law and Economic Change in Rural Senegal: Diola Pledge Transactions and Disputes" in Hamnett (ed.), *op.cit. supra* n. 42; and Abel, "The Rise of Capitalism and the Transformation of Disputing: From Confrontation over Honor to Competition for Property" (review article on Starr, *Dispute and Settlement in Rural Turkey: An Ethnography of Law* (1978)), (1979) *UCLA Law Review* 223–255.

[169] Snyder, *op.cit. supra* n. 42, pp. 723–804. See also Fitzpatrick, "Law, Modernization, and Mystification" and Greenberg, "Law and Development in Light of Dependency Theory" in 3 *Research in Law and Sociology* (ed. S. Spitzer, 1980).

[170] See Fitzpatrick, *op.cit. supra* n. 124 and Snyder, *op.cit. supra* n. 122. An earlier study is Diamond, "The Rule of Law versus the Order of Custom" in *The Rule of Law* (ed. R. P. Wolff. 1971).

[171] See, *e.g.*, Worsley, *op.cit. supra* n. 90; and Copans and Seddon, "Marxism and Anthropology: A Preliminary Survey" and other papers in *Relations of Production: Marxist Approaches to Economic Anthropology* (ed. D. Seddon, trans. H. Lackner, 1978).

[172] See Copans, "In Search of Lost Theory: Marxism and Structuralism within French Anthropology", (1979) 3 *Review* 45–73; and Kahn and Llobera, "French Marxist Anthropology: Twenty Years After" (review article on D. Seddon, ed., *Relations of*

Production: Marxist Approaches to Economic Anthropology (1978)), (1980) 8 *Journal of Peasant Studies* 81–100.

[173] Banaji, "Modes of Production in a Materialist Conception of History", (1977) 3 *Capital and Class* 1–44. See also Bernstein, "Notes on Capital and Peasantry", (1977) 10 *Review of African Political Economy* 60–73 and Bernstein, "Concepts for the Analysis of Contemporary Peasantries", (1979) 6 *Journal of Peasant Studies* 421–444.

[174] See Snyder, *op.cit. supra* n. 122; Snyder, "Labour Power and Legal Transformation in Senegal", (1981) 21 *Review of African Political Economy*, in press; and Snyder, "'Folk Law' and Historical Transitions: Conceptual and Theoretical Issues", presented at the IUAES Commission on Contemporary Folk Law symposium, Bellagio, Italy, September 1981.

[175] Snyder, "Colonialism and Legal Form: The Creation of 'Customary Law' in Senegal", (1981) 19 *Journal of Legal Pluralism* 44–90; a longer version of this paper appears in *Crime, Justice and Underdevelopment* (ed. C. Sumner, 1981).

[176] Snyder, "Labour Power and Legal Transformation in Senegal", *op.cit. supra* n. 174.

[177] These theories are reviewed in Foster-Carter, "The Modes of Production Controversy", (1978) 107 *New Left Review* 47–77; see also J. G. Taylor, *From Modernization to Modes of Production: A Critique of the Sociologies of Development and Underdevelopment* (1979).

[178] See Fitzpatrick, *op.cit. supra* n. 124; Fitzpatrick, *op.cit. supra* n. 169; Fitzpatrick, "The Political Economy of Dispute Settlement in Papua New Guinea" in Sumner (ed.), *op.cit. supra* n. 175.

[179] See Fitzpatrick, "'Really Rather Like Slavery': Law and Labour in the Colonial Economy of Papua New Guinea" in 3 *Essays in the Political Economy of Australian Capitalism* (eds. E. L. Wheelwright and K. Buckley, 1978); Fitzpatrick, "The Creation and Containment of the Papua New Guinea Peasantry" in 4 *Essays in the Political Economy of Australian Capitalism* (eds. E. L. Wheelwright and K. Buckley, 1980); and Fitzpatrick, *op.cit. supra* n. 152.

[180] See Fitzpatrick, "The Political Economy of Dispute Settlement in Papua New Guinea" and Paliwala, "Law and Order in the Village: Papua New Guinea's Village Courts" in Sumner (ed.), *op.cit. supra* n. 175. See also the papers to be published in A. Paliwala (ed.), *Law and Social Change in Papua New Guinea*, forthcoming.

[181] Fitzpatrick and Blaxter, "Imposed Law in the Containment of Papua New Guinea Economic Ventures" in *The Imposition of Law*, *op.cit. supra* n. 32.

[182] See LeRoy, "L'émergence d'un droit foncier local au Sénégal" in Conac (ed.), *op.cit. supra* n. 116; LeRoy, "Le juge d'instance, le sous-prefet et les paysans: Les détournements de la fonction judiciaire dans le règlement de conflits fonciers au Sénégal", presented to the Seminaire interdisciplinaire d'études juridiques, Facultés Universitaires Saint-Louis, Brussels; and LeRoy, *op.cit. supra* n. 165.

[183] Snyder, "Legal Innovation and Social Change in a Peasant Community: A Senegalese Village Police", (1978) 48 *Africa* 231–247; and Snyder, "Droit non-étatique et législation nationale au Sénégal" in Conac (ed.), *op.cit. supra* n. 116.

[184] See J. P. Chauveau, J. P. Dozon, E. LeBris, E. LeRoy, G. Salem and F. G. Snyder, "Rapport introductif" in *Problèmes fonciers en Afrique Noire: Rapport introductif aux Journées d'études sur les problèmes fonciers en Afrique Noire* (Paris, September 1980).

[185] See Santos, *op.cit. supra* n. 139; Santos, "Popular Justice, Dual Power and Socialist Strategy" in *Capitalism and the Rule of Law: From Deviancy Theory to Marxism* (eds. B. Fine, R. Kinsey, J. Lea, S. Picciotto and J. Young, 1979); Santos, "Law and Revolution in Portugal: The Experiences of Popular Justice after the 25th April 1974", presented at the 4th Conference of the European Group for the Study of Deviance and Social Control, Vienna, September 1976; and Santos, *op.cit. supra* n. 112.

[186] This and related points are discussed in Hymes, "The Use of Anthropology: Critical, Political, Personal" in Hymes (ed.), *op.cit. supra* n. 16. Compare the statement by Kuper, *op.cit. supra* n. 6, p. 238, that "Whichever theoretical model is used, the distinctive anthropological perspective ... is to begin by assuming that the actors' models are part of the data, not useful analyses of the systems being studied".

[187] At least if one accepts the useful stereotypes of "the lawyer" and "the anthropologist" set forth by Twining, "Law and Anthropology ...", *op.cit. supra* n. 4, pp. 572–576.

[188] See Roberts, *op.cit. supra* n. 7, pp. 676–679.

[189] See Moore, *Law as Process, op.cit. supra* n. 42, pp. 215–218.

[190] This is commonly viewed by lawyers as the major contribution of anthropology to legal studies; see Hooker, *op.cit. supra* n. 42, esp. pp. 14, 54.

[191] The relationship of social science to philosophy is discussed in these terms by P. Winch, *The Idea of a Social Science and Its Relation to Philosophy* (1958) and T. Benton, *Philosophical Foundations of the Three Sociologies* (1977). For an analogous discussion concerning sociology and law, see Campbell and Wiles, *op.cit. supra* n. 6, and Abel, "Law Books and Books about Law" (review of M. Rheinstein, *Marriage Stability, Divorce, and the Law* (1972)), (1973) 26 *Stanford Law Review* 175–228.

[192] Koch, "Law and Anthropology ...", *op.cit. supra* n. 42, pp. 15–16 emphasises the translation of cognitive categories as an especially important part of legal anthropological studies. See also the sources cited *supra* n. 31 and n. 164.

[193] These anthropological studies, like some currents in American political studies today, thus differ fundamentally from Marxist conceptions of the method of political economy; see Snyder, *op.cit. supra* n. 42, p. 742–743.

[194] Nader, *op.cit. supra* n. 13, p. 17.

[195] For a similar criticism of anthropological studies as part of contemporary social science, see Thomson, "Law and the Social Sciences — The Demise of Legal Autonomy", presented at the Conference on Critical Legal Scholarship, University of Kent, Canterbury, March 1981.

[5]

Reports

Historical Studies of Legal Change[1]

JUNE STARR AND JANE F. COLLIER
SUNY, Stony Brook, N.Y. 11790/Department of Anthropology, Stanford University, Stanford, Calif. 94305, U.S.A. 12 I 86

An international conference called "Ethnohistorical Models for the Evolution of Law within Specific Societies" was held August 10–18, 1985, in Milan and at the Bellagio Conference Center, Lake Como, Italy, with funding provided by the Wenner-Gren Foundation for Anthropological Research and the Rockefeller Foundation. June Starr and Jane F. Collier were the organizers, Elizabeth Colson (University of California, Berkeley) and William Twining (University College, London) were discussants, Jessica Kuper was editorial advisor, and Longina Jakubowska and Richard Maddox were rapporteurs. Twenty anthropologists, sociologists, and law professors from North America and Europe attended. Theory ranged from functionalism, Marxism, and deconstructionism to cultural analysis and interpretive approaches. Conference goals were to compare case studies of legal institutions changing over time in particular societies and to develop methodologies to direct future research. Because the anthropology of law was once a well-defined subfield within social anthropology, participants wished to make sense of the current diversity of approaches among them. In discussions they focused on the models and methods they were using to analyze the development, change, decay, integration, and articulation of legal systems within specific social units.

Anthropological studies of law in the first half of the 20th century had developed rich descriptions of how social order was maintained in "tribal" and peasant societies that lacked police, a Western-style judiciary, or prisons and jails (Barton 1969 [1919], 1949; Malinowski 1926; Llewellyn and Hoebel 1941). The anthropology of law was a clearly bounded subfield because most anthropologists studying conflict resolution relied on a lawyer's sense of what law was (Bohannan 1957; Gluckman 1955, 1956, 1965; Nader 1969; Gulliver 1963; Van Velsen 1964). By 1960 the evolutionary approach inherited from Maine (1879 [1861]) and Hobhouse, Wheeler, and Ginsberg (1915) had culminated in two publications, one concerned with non-Western legal systems (Hoebel 1954), the other with precapitalist legal forms in relation to economic systems (Fried 1960). Although many anthropologists of law never became involved in evolutionary model building, by 1970 it was clear that legal anthropology would go no farther in this direction for two reasons. First, evolutionary sequences could not capture the increasingly complex legal behavior and "lawlike" forms that had been recorded by legal ethnographers in different world areas for the last five decades. Secondly, the growing interest in conceptualizing law as fully embedded in society meant that to abstract and "purify" legal forms in order to fit them neatly into "stages of sociocultural evolution" did considerable damage to the data.

The early 1970s saw the blossoming of a plurality of approaches. Books in the anthropology of law shared the tradition of detailed description but differed in emphasis on boundaries between disputes and war (Koch 1974:81–82) and between law and nonlaw conflict resolution. Pospisil (1971:113) found law in every social unit from the household to the state, while Starr (1978) found law only in state institutions, treating village "lawways" (Malinowski's term) as nonlaw conflict-resolving forms. Collier (1973) avoided this dilemma by focusing on litigant choice of a legal form. By the end of the 1970s some researchers felt that a dominant focus on processes of resolving extended disputes had emerged (cf. Epstein 1967, Gulliver 1969, Moore 1978, and Nader and Todd 1978). Others debated the advisability of "rule-centered" or "process-centered" studies (Gluckman 1973, Hamnett 1977). Yet, even as this debate was resolved by Comaroff and Roberts (1981), many researchers were abandoning the dispute paradigm as too normative and positivistic and turning to historical research as a way to understand legal change.

The 1985 conference brought together scholars using historical data from texts or their own ethnographic research to consider how dispute-airing forms and power relationships that *changed* over time were affecting legal behavior, legal processes, and other institutions. These ideas stemmed in part from the reading of Giddens (1976, 1979) and Bourdieu (1977) and in part from the influence that political economy and Marxism had had on social anthropology in the 1970s. To focus directly on legal change meant using analytical strategies that differed from those of the earlier community or regional studies. Now, instead of focusing on disputes and attempts at settlement of problems, new objects of study surfaced: how culture mediated legal ideas, the legal strategies of a ruling or a minority group, the negotiation of a dispute across international boundaries, the creation by legislation of new "redistributive" networks, how state-enacted law changed rural agrarian hierarchies, or how less powerful groups struggled to obtain laws representing their interests.

In comparison with earlier ones, these new studies often spanned wider geographical areas and certainly longer time periods. Adding the time dimension altered the sense of place and spatial boundaries of a study. Sometimes hierarchically organized institutions in modern nation-states were studied as political events in the lawmaking process were traced sequentially over time. Some papers examined how power relations shaped the culturally relevant ideas embodied in a legal system, others how outlaw groups appeared and disappeared with the appearance and disappearance of spectacular forms of public punishment. Still others analyzed how weaker groups used ideas available in the wider culture to strengthen their interest in using or avoiding state courts. The conference highlighted common problems; most researchers had had to make decisions concerning how to periodize historical time, how to identify key individuals and groups (the powerless as well as the powerful), and how to understand the relationship between local events, regional dynamics, and world historical processes.

The discussions marked out themes which cut across space and time. One was that "customary" law is not law that stretches back to some distant past or law-giver but "law" that has been negotiated between colonial rulers and those they ruled. A second concerned the analysis of change in power relationships among groups over time and the insight into legal change it might provide. Formulated by Sally Falk Moore, this was labeled "the anthropology of sequences of asymmetrical relations." A third theme was the intertwining of the differing symbolic systems of law and of culture of different groups in a society. Thus, the conference had the cumulative effect of reaffirming the embeddedness of law in culture and culture in law. Culture is adept in shaping different legal forms, and law is powerful in redefining social issues and even in restructuring the relationships among groups in society itself, a fact recognized by both the powerful and the weak.

GIVING UP THEORIES OF LEGAL EVOLUTION

All participants agreed that when the anthropology of law is infused with history, anthropologists studying legal processes must avoid simplistic ideas of legal evolution. The embeddedness of law in culture and of culture in law yields data too rich to meet the criteria of evolutionary stages. Furthermore, evolutionary stages themselves have never provided *dynamic* conceptualizations of socio-legal change. Convened to search for better understanding of how law changes within particular societies through time, participants already recognized that legal forms differed by place and time and could not be correlated with stages in societal evolution or state development. Abandoning a sequential model of customary law, state law, and legal pluralism allowed them to infuse old concepts with new meaning. This is aptly illustrated by the papers and discussions on "customary law."

Papers by Moore and by Joan Vincent argued that "customary law" is not a "folk system" in the consciousness of the people themselves. When placed in historical context, it becomes understandable as the outcome of historical struggles between native elites and their colonial and postcolonial rulers. On the basis of investigation of legal change among the Chagga of Tanzania, Moore showed that "customary rules" are integral elements of the contemporary political order. The relevant context for understanding customary rules is not an ahistorical "cultural system," as delineated by Geertz (1973, 1983), but an ongoing system. Twining supported this assertion and pointed out that "customary law" was invented by British lawyers and colonial administrators for ruling Africa. Among the Chagga, the Christian church, the colonial administration, the Tanzanian national government, and the local coffee-marketing cooperative all affected notions of "customary law" by altering the character of the struggles between the Chagga and their overlords. Underlying these struggles was the issue of which domains of life would be covered by "customary law"—in other words, which areas of life would be defined as within Chagga control. Later, this negotiated law (now called "customary" to legitimate it) was partly embraced by African nationalists who were eager to define autonomous indigenous cultural and political traditions.

Vincent carried this argument to the anthropological model of the "colonial state," saying that it cannot be treated as an ideal type. Any given state is the outcome of a historically specific set of conflicting interests among groups whose reconciliations have been recognized in law. Furthermore, many of the laws passed in Uganda reflect not local interests but the interests of Manchester manufacturers, missionary societies, planters in Kenya, and so forth. Thus, participants agreed that to understand how interests coalesced in shaping legal change within a region over time, one needs to include a much wider geographic arena and institutional framework in the analysis.

With customary law viewed as a colonial invention and "indigenous law" now seen as a "reconstruction" (or an account) of a natives' rule system by an anthropologist, administrator, or writer, some participants recognized the need to deconstruct the viewpoints in all legal texts and ethnographies (cf. Marcus and Cushman 1982). Thus, for example, Starr suggested that Maine's writing about ancient Roman society be viewed in terms of 19th-century thought. She argued that rules concerning guardianship and marriage in 3d-century Roman society constricted women in ways not allowed for in Maine's classic *Ancient Law*. When appellate cases involving women in this time period are examined, the Roman legal system shows no such global shift as Maine postulated from kin-group to private ownership of productive property.

Focusing on how law changes without using evolutionary notions led participants to take stock of what

Volume 28, Number 3, June 1987 | 369

comparative frameworks and ideas might be used in discussing historical similarities across a range of cultures and societies.

IDENTIFYING COMPARATIVE FRAMEWORKS

Out of the discussions grew the notion of an anthropology of sequences that would gloss changes in power relations among status groups, ethnic groups, social classes, or "the dominated" as changes in "asymmetrical relations." The notion of asymmetry is well-suited to cross-cultural and cross-temporal comparisons and is more neutral than "power," over which participants remained deeply divided throughout the conference. Some saw power as based on differential access to strategic resources, while others considered it as embedded in cultural ideas or systems. Power groups had particular characteristics and cultural ideas, "diagnostic features" which distinguished sequences from each other.

Francis Snyder's study of negotiations over sheepmeat production and distribution in the European Economic Community used a time-oriented sequential approach. France, having failed to achieve its aims in initial negotiations on sheepmeat quotas, "stonewalled" by refusing to accept a ruling of the European high court. In this way it was able to force another round of bargaining. Snyder suggested that study of how power arises from tactics (stonewalling, logrolling, and the scheduling of marathon sessions) must complement our analyses of general power relations if we are to understand the politics which leads to lawmaking.

New national land laws changed power and class relations in both a Spanish village studied by George Collier and a village in eastern Ireland studied by Philip Gulliver. Villagers in Ballymacandan, Ireland, were transformed from tenant farmers into small landowners not through their own organized efforts but by acts of British parliaments responding to their larger non-Irish electorates. Spanish national land reform laws in the early 1930s had brought about unexpected alliances in the complex rural agrarian hierarchy, which collapsed into two opposing groups, "workers" and "owners." The two groups struggled for control of the municipal government in order to implement or suppress these new laws. Though the effort became unimportant as the town was drawn into the Civil War, Collier's study demonstrates that legislation from above can produce unpredicted results at the local level.

In postagrarian regions such as New England, legislation (both national and local) sets policy for redistributing money and food. Social scientists do not ordinarily think of household budgets, wages, taxation, unemployment compensation, food stamps, and social security as aspects of a single redistributive system. June Nash argued, however, that market mechanisms and legislated redistribution mechanisms are complexly intertwined and constitute a vast redistributive system determining people's shares in the products of social production. Nash's "redistributive model of law" circumvented a problem that concerned many participants—how to "model" the interconnections among household, community, region, province, and national government. By discussing processes of redistribution that linked a variety of sites and sequences, Nash was able to overcome the weakness inherent in using such concepts as "micro-" and "macro-" systems of interaction.

Building on earlier studies of disputes, a group of papers used detailed case materials to show how the actions of individuals and groups influenced legal change. These papers stimulated discussions concerning how to identify the significant groups and how groups achieve "voice" or are silenced.

Laura Nader proposed a "user theory of law" to analyze the mechanisms triggering and determining the course of legal change within a community court and its regional appellate court. Focusing on "dominant court users" avoids both a top-down approach that highlights social and political processes at the expense of individual action and a bottom-up approach that highlights individuals at the expense of the context in which their claims arise.

Complementing Nader's analysis was Robert Hayden's account of Yugoslav workers' resistance to proposed court reform. Dominated workers sought a legal forum independent of factory managers, while more powerful managers had a vested interest in keeping workers from articulating their dissatisfactions. In 1982, when the government proposed to reform the "overused" labor courts by moving them inside factories, the workers' trade union representatives were able to defeat the proposal and keep the courts free of management control.

Jeremy Boissevain and Hanneke Grotenberg discussed the attempt by recent Surinamese migrants to the Netherlands to establish small shops and businesses in an environment where Dutch shopkeepers have considerable political power, including social and kinship ties to politicians and access to the media for voicing their concerns. Surinamese entrepreneurs organized to subvert a law prohibiting ritual slaughter by helping found a Federation of Muslim Organizations to speak for all Muslim butchers in the Netherlands. This organization was able to have the prohibition repealed, but, in securing legal change, the Surinamese entrepreneurs increased their compliance with other Dutch regulations, thus granting Dutch regulatory agencies more power over their lives and activities. Furthermore, this study raised questions about the role of culture in structuring unequal interactions. Muslim butchers secured the repeal of damaging legislation by emphasizing cultural differences between themselves and Dutch Protestants, which in turn reinforced the Dutch tendency to view Surinamese immigrants as distant, and therefore dangerous, outsiders. This theme of "distancing" certain groups by creating laws that encouraged the view that they were cultural and legal "outsiders" was elaborated in discussions of the dacoits (outlaws) of India and the *Bokkrijders*, robber bands operating in the Low Countries in Europe between 1741 and 1778.

STUDYING THE TEMPORAL ASPECTS OF SYMBOLIC SYSTEMS OF CULTURE AND OF LAW

A number of papers discussed how culture and power coalesced to invest law with a heavy symbolic component. Said Arjomand, for example, described problems encountered by Iran's Ayatollah Khomeini and his supporters in creating a new constitution embodying Shi'ite Islam that would represent the theocratic nature of their new government and demonstrate that the shah and his defeated Western law and government were gone for good. Using Weber's theory of the rationalization of law, Arjomand described the enormous problems the law-makers faced because Shi'ite ideas of statehood had not changed since the Middle Ages. Islamic empires reaching into the modern age (both Ottoman and Arab) were based on Sunni Islam, and so any adaptations that had occurred in Islam statecraft had affected Sunni and not Shi'ite law.

Arjomand's paper highlighted problems all researchers face in deciding what relative weight to assign cultural analysis versus material interests in understanding law-making. He suggested that Khomeini failed to include land reform in the 1979 constitution because Shi'ite sacred law (which originated in a feudal society in the 14th century) provided no justification for equalizing wealth. Others felt that the powerful Iranian landholding classes had blocked reforms that would undermine their hegemony. Still others felt that people cannot have "material interests" apart from a cultural system which gives value to particular material things and rewards particular types of behavior (Sahlins 1981).

Continuing this cultural argument, Lawrence Rosen stated that Islamic law as practiced in Morocco does not aim to build up a body of doctrine distinct from local custom. The ways in which the Islamic court attempts fact-finding and the form of judicial reasoning do not differ greatly from ways in which a person's worth and truthfulness are judged in economic transactions in the bazaar. Thus, Islamic court decisions in Morocco represent attempts to push the litigants back into society so that they will again negotiate with one another within the broad boundaries established by the canons of Islamic law.

The discussion following Rosen's paper revealed deep theoretical divisions between participants emphasizing the role of culture in constructing reality and shaping social practices and those arguing that society can be viewed directly and that factors such as relative power and access to resources can be analyzed with little reference to cultural meanings. Some participants also raised questions about the capacity of cultural analysis to deal adequately with legal change. Doesn't cultural analysis, with its attention to structural aspects of thought and ritual, impute a timelessness to social institutions? Several papers used cultural analysis to probe structural change. Carol Greenhouse found that in the southern town of Hopewell the current Baptist avoidance of state courts could be traced to the period just before the Civil War when conflicts over major issues—states' rights, Cherokee removal, and the abolition of slavery—threatened to split and destroy the community. To save the church, whose membership had been reduced to seven, Baptist leaders preached that conflict was un-Christian and litigiousness the undoing of God's order, and they succeeded. Greenhouse did not portray the Baptists as inventing their repudiation of conflict in order to differentiate themselves from political opponents. Rather, she argued that in experiencing a need for social distance from local populists, Hopewell's Baptists elaborated the idea of nonlitigiousness, a resource available in the wider culture.

Like Greenhouse, who studied the Baptists as a way of understanding wider North American attitudes towards litigiousness, Anton Blok studied the outlaw *Bokkrijders* as a way of understanding a major shift in European legal practices: the transition from public executions to imprisonment that occurred during the 18th century. These outlaws robbed and burned Catholic churches, parsonages, wayside chapels, and farms. They were not, however, social bandits. Most were married, with children and a fixed residence. Almost all were born and bred in the areas where they raided. Skinners were particularly active members, and their regional networks (used for disposing of dead animals) could be mobilized both for raiding and for hiding out. Drawing on Michel Foucault's work, Blok examined historical records which revealed a steady decline in the theatricality of executions but few clues as to the reason for it. He speculated that resistance to public executions was part of a wider movement among town dwellers and literate elites against theatricality in general as promoting idleness and disorder among the lower classes.

Whereas Blok read texts to understand how the powerful used the terrifying symbolism of public dismemberment, burning, and hanging to communicate the awesome power of the state, Sally Humphreys read texts from ancient Greek society that she interpreted as political discourse about changes in society. In archaic Greece, factional divisions within the ruling class gave rise to a concern for protecting the general public from powerful people. By classical times, Athenians were conscious of having man-made laws, and Athenian juries often consisted of 200 adult men rather than single magistrates. Texts from this later period addressed the problem of how to limit the influence of clever and unscrupulous orators on gullible mob juries. Thus, a change in the context and messages of the texts revealed a shift in types of legal institutions and in class structure.

Vilhelm Aubert traced changing meanings of the concept of the "rule of law" from the 19th century to the second half of the 20th. The language of justice remained the same while society underwent vast transformations. In the 19th century the rule of law, an idea from the Enlightenment, referred to penalties imposed by the state in an attempt to discourage unwanted behaviors. Now, the state, still talking about "the rule of law," provides welfare payments and uses pensions to reward people for staying in the labor force. In the 19th century

Volume 28, Number 3, June 1987 | 371

the rule of law signified the state's commitment to provide citizens with access to legal remedies against unlawful exertion of state or private power. Now it refers to distributive justice.

The symbolism of law and power was analyzed by Bernard Cohn, who told how the officers of the British East India Company sought to avoid the direct imposition of British law in 18th-century India. By assembling a group of scholars to translate Sanskrit, Persian, and Arabic texts, Warren Hastings, the first governor general of India, hoped to adapt indigenous legal traditions to British purposes. In their search for an "authentic constitution" of classical India, these scholars contributed to the development of historical linguistics and Indian studies, but Hastings and his successors selected from the ancient texts only principles and doctrines analogous or equivalent to British laws of property, contract, and succession. Thus, despite his intentions, Hastings's search for an ancient Indian constitution led within a hundred years to the utilization of English case law as the law of British India.

Cohn's ideas led participants to consider British ruling strategies in Africa and Ireland as well as India. Noting that the British colonial experience began in Ireland, Cohn drew conclusions concerning the movement of both British administrators and ideas from Ireland to India. Later, Indian colonial officials took many of their symbols of rule and administrative procedures (such as the concept of "customary law" and the institution of the "district officer") with them when they moved to Africa. This sequence was pushed farther back in time when George Collier noted parallels between British ideas of ruling and the 16th-century Spanish debate over how to govern the American civilizations. Both drew on concepts of statehood from the Greco-Roman tradition.

The weaving together of law as a symbolic system and law as encoding asymmetrical power relationships in a number of papers and discussions was a surprise to participants. Yet, this double vision allowed us to compare across cultures, societies, and time periods the growth, florescence, and decline of particular types of social systems in which legal forms were embedded.

CONCLUSION

Analyzing changing power relationships and law in the context of historical studies brought about a new rapprochement between the legal and political anthropologists at the conference. For those who weave together symbols and their referents in the real world, power matters and is felt not only as coercion but as a cultural experience by both individuals and groups. Conceptualizing power as asymmetrical relations helped move participants beyond the notion of conflict as being situated between individual agents and closer to a recognition that as groups become integrated and able to dominate weaker groups this very occurrence becomes a powerful force in legal change.

When time, space, and power relationships are conceptualized as the "study of sequences of asymmetrical power relations," terms like "macro-" and "micro-" studies can be abandoned. These terms pose the false problem of how to "integrate" synchronic analyses at the two levels, and focus on time makes them irrelevant. An analyst now would specify "when" and "how" small-scale or local developments are influenced by more hegemonic forces. No longer do we need to confine patterns of political, cultural, or economic interrelationships to arbitrary, discrete levels. By focusing on sequences of "redistribution," for example, domestic, community, industrial, and governmental processes can be understood as partly articulated and partly disjunctive dimensions of a single complex system.

Participants also reached implicit agreement in rejecting the notion of dual, multiple, or plural legal systems. Where "customary law" is found, it is not a survival from a traditional past but an integral part of an ongoing asymmetrical order. Societies may be characterized as having dual or multiple legal systems, but these systems are never autonomous. Historical analysis inevitably reveals that such systems have been negotiated in relation to an encompassing political structure.

The final conference discussions were characterized by controversy as well as by agreement, but most found this liberating, as it confirmed the validity of a variety of theoretical approaches within the anthropology of law. The goal of the conference was not to reach a unified perspective but to understand differences in approaches and to confirm convergences. Some emphasized the ordering dimension of law, focusing on ways in which groups holding power seek to create or oppose governmental structures. Others focused on the communicative and symbolic dimensions of law, viewing law as discourse or even as theater. Still others adopted an instrumental perspective, focusing on individuals' use of legal resources and how those disadvantaged by lack of power used available legal resources to obtain a forum for voicing their concerns. The lively discussions signaled a healthy field of inquiry.

Current interests, questions, and methods have diverged considerably from the contemporary legal scholarship that had inspired some earlier anthropologists (see Barton 1949, 1969 [1919]; Malinowski 1926; Radcliffe-Brown 1934; and Gluckman 1961). Although earlier anthropologists of law made legitimate claims for the separateness and boundedness of legal anthropology, this conference confirmed that it is no longer a separated subfield but an integral part of contemporary social anthropology. With the new emphasis on how culture, history, and power relations shape legal forms and practices and how forms and practices shape culture and power relations, the anthropology of law has set itself an agenda closely allied with major interests and theory in the discipline as a whole.

References Cited

BARTON, R. F. 1949. *The Kalingas, their institutions and customary law.* Chicago: University of Chicago Press.

———. 1969 (1919). *The Ifugao.* Berkeley and Los Angeles: University of California Press.

BOHANNAN, P. 1957. *Justice and judgment among the Tiv.* London: Oxford University Press for the International African Institute.

BOURDIEU, PIERRE. 1977. *Outline of a theory of practice.* London: Cambridge University Press.

COLLIER, JANE F. 1973. *Law and social change in Zinacantan.* Stanford: Stanford University Press.

COMAROFF, JOHN L., AND SIMON ROBERTS. 1981. *Rules and processes: The cultural logic of dispute in an African context.* Chicago: University of Chicago Press.

EPSTEIN, A. L. 1967. "The case method in the field of law," in *The craft of social anthropology.* London: Tavistock Publications.

FRIED, MORTON. 1960. "On the evolution of social stratification and the state," in *Culture in history.* Edited by S. Diamond, pp. 713–31. New York: Columbia University Press.

GEERTZ, CLIFFORD. 1973. *The interpretation of cultures.* New York: Basic Books.

———. 1983. *Local knowledge.* New York: Basic Books.

GIDDENS, ANTHONY. 1976. *New rules of sociological method.* New York: Basic Books.

———. 1979. *Central problems in social theory.* Berkeley and Los Angeles: University of California Press.

GLUCKMAN, MAX. 1955. *The judicial process among the Barotse of Northern Rhodesia.* Manchester: Manchester University Press.

———. 1956. *Custom and conflict in Africa.* Oxford: Basil Blackwell.

———. 1961. African jurisprudence. *Advancement of Science* 74:1–16.

———. 1965. *Politics, law, and ritual in tribal societies.* Oxford: R. A. Mowbray.

———. 1973. Limitations of the case-method in the study of tribal law. *Law and Society Review* 7:611–41.

GULLIVER, P. H. 1963. *Social control in an African society: A study of the Arusha, agricultural Masai of North Tanganyika.* Boston: Boston University Press.

———. 1969. "Dispute settlement without courts: The Ndendeuli of southern Tanzania," in *Law in culture and society.* Edited by Laura Nader. Chicago: Aldine.

HAMNETT, IAN. 1977. *Social anthropology and law.* London: Academic Press.

HOBHOUSE, L. T., G. C. WHEELER, AND M. GINSBERG. 1915. *The material culture and social institutions of the simpler peoples.* London.

HOEBEL, E. A. 1954. *The law of primitive man.* Cambridge: Harvard University Press.

KOCH, KLAUS-FRIEDRICH. 1974. *War and peace in Jalemo: The management of conflict in Highland New Guinea.* Cambridge: Harvard University Press.

LLEWELLYN, KARL N., AND E. A. HOEBEL. 1941. *The Cheyenne way.* Norman: University of Oklahoma Press.

MAINE, SIR HENRY. 1879 (1861). 3d American edition. *Ancient law: Its connection with the early history of ideas, and its relation to modern ideas.* New York.

MALINOWSKI, B. 1926. *Crime and custom in savage society.* London: Kegan Paul, Trench, Trubner.

MARCUS, GEORGE E., AND DICK CUSHMAN. 1982. Ethnographies as texts. *Annual Review of Anthropology* 11:25–69.

MOORE, SALLY FALK. 1978. *Law as process: An anthropological approach.* London: Routledge, Kegan Paul.

NADER, LAURA. Editor. 1969. *Law in culture and society.* Chicago: Aldine.

NADER, LAURA, AND HARRY TODD. 1978. *The disputing process: Law in ten societies.* New York: Columbia University Press.

POSPISIL, LEO. 1971. *Anthropology of law: A comparative theory.* New York: Harper and Row.

RADCLIFFE-BROWN, A. R. 1934. "Sanction, social." *Encyclopaedia of the Social Sciences,* vol. 13, pp. 531–34.

SAHLINS, MARSHALL. 1981. *Historical metaphors and mythical realities: Structure in the early history of the Sandwich Islands kingdom.* Ann Arbor: University of Michigan Press.

STARR, JUNE. 1978. *Dispute and settlement in rural Turkey: An ethnography of law.* Leiden: E. J. Brill.

VAN VELSEN, J. 1964. *The politics of kinship: A study in social manipulation among the lakeside Tonga.* Manchester: Manchester University Press.

Part II
Legal Theory, Anthropology, Anthropological Theory and Law

[6]

ANTHROPOLOGY AND LEGAL THEORY

I WOULD like to explore, in a general and to some extent tentative fashion, the help which anthropology may provide for those inquiring into the nature of law. It is necessary first to define the material relevant to the inquiry. Anthropologists study societies of widely different types. From the Western point of view they are technologically simple, with agricultural or pastoral economies. But they often have complex forms of social organisations, and some have elaborate political structures. On the whole I have not found relevant studies of societies with forms of central government. This is because anthropologists studying them have not had to think very precisely about problems of the nature of law. Problems, of course, do arise, especially in relation to what is often called custom, that is, a collection of rules not derived from the enactments of the central government or its agencies.[1] But it has been relatively easy to avoid problems of the " What is law?" type, because it has seemed obvious that there is law in the enactments of the chief and the decisions of the courts. On the other hand, studies of societies which lack central government, especially those which lack any form of political institution (which I call " simple " societies), are relevant to my inquiry. There are two reasons for this: (i) if the anthropologist is interested at all in law he is forced to give some attention to the problem of classification and determine whether and how the legal is to be identified in a situation where the usual criteria supplied by legislature and courts are missing; (ii) a study of these societies allows one to discern the minimum forms of behaviour that need to be observed if a group is to be viable. This has important implications for some versions of natural law.

These two reasons supply the theme of this paper. First I consider what may be learnt as to the operation of " law " in simple societies. It is essential to make a preliminary distinction which may seem obvious and yet is often overlooked or not sufficiently observed. This is the distinction between the external and the internal approach to the study of a society other than one's own. The external approach may be manifested in a number of ways. At its most extreme it takes the form of the application to the

[1] *Cf.* the discussion of customary law in I. Hamnett, *Chieftainship and Legitimacy*, Chap. 1.

society under investigation of a theory of law formulated in the context of a different society or culture.[2] But it may take less overt forms; an investigator after describing the social life of a people may use a criterion not recognised by the people themselves to divide the legal from the non-legal.[3] The internal approach is adopted where an investigator, working without preconceptions, attempts to discover the classifications which members of the society use in applying normative notions to behaviour.

There is nothing startling in the proposition that an investigator of a society different from his own should adopt the internal approach. But its implications require some thought. In order to understand and make intelligible the data he discovers, the investigator has to use some concepts derived from his own culture. He would find it impossible to avoid altogether the words "ought," "rule," "right" and "duty." The point is that such words, although indispensable, need to be used with caution. The investigator must try to make sure that the word he chooses to describe a state of affairs does not convey an impression which is misleading. A particular danger arises with the use of the words "rule," "right" and "duty." These are terms with which the investigator is so familiar from his own culture that he may take them as a self-evident means of describing what he finds in the society investigated. But in fact these terms may not be suitable, because of the implications which they carry. A rule implies the existence of conduct which ought to be followed where "ought" has a mandatory or imperative sense. Likewise a right implies strongly that one may require another to behave in some particular way, and duty has a corresponding implication. These terms may be unsuitable for application to behaviour observed in simple societies, both because of their strongly imperative overtones and because they convey a sense of a clearly defined aspect of behaviour to which a mandatory "ought" attaches. If one says there is a rule which requires X to be done, or that people are under a duty to do X, one implies that the range of behaviour which is mandatory (expressed by X) is clearly understood.

I hope I can illustrate what I mean from the way in which a

---

[2] A recent interesting example is supplied by S. Schlegel's application of Hart's rule of recognition theory to the Tirurary, a Philippine people: *Tirurary Justice* (1970).

[3] B. Malinowski, for example, in his study of the Trobriand islanders uses both the principle of reciprocity and rules placing limits on man's fundamental drives as criteria of law. See especially *Crime and Custom in Savage Society*, and his introduction to H. Ian Hogbin, *Law and Order in Polynesia*.

North Alaskan Eskimo community looks at dealing with property. Among this community it is expected that normally one person will not take or destroy another's property. Cases occur in which A believes rightly or wrongly that he has a grievance against B. To work off the grievance A may destroy some valuable piece of property (a canoe) belonging to B. A typical reaction on the part of B is to take no steps against A, but to proclaim to the community in general that he has all along acted properly. He is satisfied if he is able to get public opinion on his side. I think that it would be a distortion to attribute to this community a rule requiring people to refrain from destroying or taking the property of others, or a rule requiring compensation or return if another's property is taken or destroyed. One needs instead to speak of the way in which people are expected to behave, and to recognise that a certain degree of vagueness or fluidity attaches to what is expected. It would be misleading to impose a sharp dividing line between behaviour which ought to be observed with respect to property and that which ought not to be observed, and to describe such behaviour in terms of rights and duties.[4]

Once the investigator has completed his analysis and unravelled so far as he can the indigenous modes of classification, he will be faced with a variety of behavioural patterns to each of which an "ought" may be attached. In some cases he may conclude that the behaviour forms the subject-matter of a rule, or rights and duties, in others that the "ought" is less prescriptive and justifies a description more in terms of expectations than in terms of rules prescribing behaviour. Expectations may be, and commonly are, generated by rules. But these need to be distinguished from expectations derived from the belief that a particular form of behaviour is proper or appropriate. His problem is to decide which part of his material is to be classified as legal or as constituting the law. To solve the problem he will, I suggest, have to resort to the external approach. In other words, the investigator in constructing his "test" for law has to take into account matters other than the conditions of the society he has studied. But he cannot present his test as self-evident; he needs to recognise the fact that he has adopted an external approach, and to give reasons for the particular approach adopted.

---

[4] R. F. Spencer, *The North Alaskan Eskimo*, pp. 97 *et seq.* The author wisely does not use the language of "rules," "rights" and "duties," although he does speak of "social norms."

Anthropologists who have adopted the internal approach have not, it seems, been fully aware of the problems involved.[5] It is difficult for anyone who has not conducted fieldwork to judge the accuracy of the data presented, but one cannot escape a suspicion that some of the complexities arising in the description of normatively-regarded behaviour have been overlooked. There does not always seem to have been sufficient attention paid to the distinction between rules and other "ought" statements which, with little violence to the facts, might be used to describe beliefs and evaluations of conduct. Further, when applying what is in effect an externally-constructed criterion for the identification of law, anthropologists neither make clear that they are applying an external approach nor give reasons to justify the criterion selected. Thus one sometimes finds an anthropologist taking law to be a set of rules deemed by the members of the society to be the most important. Importance is evidenced by the fact that the rules have the backing of the whole community.[6] What is happening is that the anthropologist takes rules falling within one of the categories he has found operating in the society and deems these to be law. But he has not said why such a category should be singled out as the hallmark of law.

Suppose one wishes to construct a theory of law applicable to simple societies. One first has to conduct an internal investigation designed to uncover the indigenous approaches to normatively-regarded behaviour. This will yield for each society investigated information on the extent to which it has adopted rules which prescribe behaviour, the way in which it classifies such rules and the varieties of behaviour to which a less prescriptive "ought" attaches. The investigation will necessarily include the study of procedures for the settlement of disputes, since it is through disputes that reliable information relating to rules and other "ought" statements is most readily obtained. Once the information has been gathered the investigator will have to adopt an external approach, and select a criterion by which to distinguish the legal from the non-legal phenomena in the material before him. His most difficult task will be to justify the criterion which he selects.

---

[5] *Cf.* the remarks of S. Roberts, "Law and the Study of Social Control in Small-Scale Societies" (1976) 39 M.L.R. 667 *et seq.*

[6] *Cf.* D. Tait, *The Konkomba of Northern Ghana*, pp. 62 *et seq*, 141 *et seq.*, speaking not of law but of "jural activities," "quasi-legal" or "para-legal methods"; M. Fortes, *Kinship and the Social Order*, p. 89; J. G. Peristany, "Pokot Sanctions and Structure" (1954) 24 *Africa* 25.

It is perhaps worth considering some of the possible approaches that might be taken. One approach is to select the dispute process, or an element of it, as the criterion of law.[7] Although there is some attraction in the argument that the way in which a society resolves its conflicts is an essential, if not the essential, element in law, there are reasons for regarding this approach as inadequate. The problem may be put in this way: why should a procedure for the settlement of disputes be singled out as the hallmark of law? The answer might be that the main task of "law" in society is to prevent and control the outbreak of conflict between members of the society. If this is not done the society is likely to disintegrate. Hence the procedures which the society evolves for the treatment of "trouble cases" may properly be called "law" in that society.

An answer along these lines is not entirely satisfactory. The reason is that insufficient attention is paid to the rules or expectations regarding behaviour current within the society. This is obvious in those versions of the dispute approach which seeks to locate law in the actual decisions of the person resolving the dispute. But even the more flexible theories which stress the need to consider the whole history of a dispute are still too narrowly based. They recognise that a dispute arises because people think that they have not received their due, or that others have behaved wrongly towards them. To understand the cause of the dispute, the investigator has to establish the standards of behaviour accepted by the society and determine the degree of "obligation" attached to them. In establishing these standards the investigator of dispute processes has collected part of the material which needs to be scrutinised before a judgment on the nature of law within the society can be made. The difficulty lies in the fact that investigators of dispute processes are generally more interested in giving an account of the relationship of the parties than in examining the way in which the society evaluates conduct to which an "ought" is attached. One can see the reason for the emphasis on the actual course of the dispute. If one wishes to investigate the rules or other

[7] For a variety of approaches, see A. L. Epstein, "The Case Method in the Field of Law," in Epstein, *The Craft of Social Anthropology*, p. 205; P. H. Gulliver, "Case Studies of Law in Non-Western Societies" (Introduction), in L. Nader, *Law in Culture and Society*, p. 11; K. F. Koch, "Law and Anthropology: Notes on Interdisciplinary Research" (1969) 4 *Law and Society Review* 11; V. W. Turner, "Law, Primitive," in *New Catholic Encyclopaedia*; N. Tanner, "Disputing and the Genesis of Legal Principles: Examples from Minangkabon" (1970) 26 *Southwestern Journal of Anthropology* 375; L. Pospisil, *Anthropology of Law*, Chaps. 2, 3; G. Cochrane, "Legal Decisions and Processual Models of Law" (1972) 7 *Man* (N.S.) 50.

" ought " statements accepted by a society it is natural to start with a dispute. A situation in which people have quarrelled about the behaviour either has observed or failed to observe towards the other is likely to focus sharply on such rules as either party alleges the other has not observed. Yet the fact of the quarrel provides merely an appropriate start to an investigation of normatively-regarded behaviour. Where the main object of the investigation is the nature of law, the emphasis should be on the manner in which conduct is evaluated within the society and not on the circumstances which give rise to particular disputes and the methods by which they are resolved.

A better approach is to cast one's net more widely, and consider the rules and other " ought " statements accepted by a society. If, for the moment, one concentrates on rules, can one say that the rules which the members of a particular society regard as most important constitute law for that society? An obvious difficulty is the selection of a criterion by which to determine degrees of importance. One is unlikely to find within a society a neat division of rules into those regarded by the society as important and those regarded as of significantly less importance. Certainly one can look at the way the society employs sanctions for breach, and conclude that the most important rules are those which engage the whole society in their maintenance. This looks well in theory, but in practice even an anthropologist might find it extraordinarily difficult to determine when the society as such is operating a sanction.

A different standpoint might be adopted, and one might look at the advantages of a criterion supplied by the notion " essential to the survival of society." Where one is looking at a simple society, can it be said that its law consists of those rules whose maintenance is essential for its survival? It is again necessary to distinguish between such rules as the external observer finds to be essential for the survival of a particular society, and such rules as the members of the society deem to be essential for its survival. If one presents the rules devised by an external observer as law, one has to accept that the members of the society may themselves not be conscious of these rules. On this view there may be a significant difference between the rules which constitute the law of the society and the rules which the members of the society deem themselves to be following. On the other hand, an investigation of the rules which the members of the society regard as essential for its survival is also not without difficulty. In particular the investigator may find that the members of the society do not explicitly use the notion of " essential for survival " as a criterion by which one group of rules may be distinguished from another. Hence he will be forced to substitute " most important " for " essential for survival."

An alternative approach is to concentrate on the notion of a rule as such, rather than upon the division of the class of rules into distinct categories. From this point of view it may be possible to draw a distinction between rules and a wide range of expectations to which are attached the notion of " ought." The essence of the distinction lies in the degree of prescription conveyed by the " ought." In the case of a rule the " ought " is mandatory. Where a rule states that a particular form of behaviour ought to be followed, those subject to the rule are required to behave in the way defined. Normally compliance with the requirement is secured through the availability of sanctions. Indeed, in a society which lacks a legislature and a court, it is difficult to see how one could speak of behaviour required of members of the society unless sanctions to secure compliance are available and regularly applied. In the case of an expectation one might still say that behaviour ought to be followed, but one would not go so far as to say that it was prescribed or required or mandatory. Evidence that behaviour was regarded as the object of an expectation and not as a rule may be found in the lack of sanctions. Members of a society might regard certain behaviour as proper, and yet there might exist no means specifically designed to ensure that the behaviour was observed, even though adverse reaction such as criticism might follow upon a failure to behave in the way expected.

An illustration may be taken from J. M. Meggitt's account of the Walbiri, an aboriginal people of central Australia.[8] He attributes to this people a distinction between an obligation entailed by a particular status, and the manner in which such an obligation is performed. Failure to perform the obligation is treated as a breaking of the law; performance of the obligation in an unusual way is treated as odd, but not as a breach of the law. The difference is reflected in the nature of the community's reaction. For example, a man is under an obligation to give meat to his wife. If he fails to do this he will be physically coerced by his wife's male relations; if he gives her meat derived from an improper source (payment for

[8] J. M. Meggitt, *Desert People*, pp. 251 *et seq.*

a circumcision) he will be exposed to ridicule but not to physical pressure.

A further difference between a rule and an expectation relates to the content of the behaviour prescribed or expected. In a simple society, one would not say that behaviour was required by a rule unless there was general agreement on the specific kind of behaviour required. This does not mean that there would not be cases in which it was unclear whether the rule applied or not. But there should be a clear understanding of the central features of the behaviour required by the rule. Where behaviour is expected but not prescribed, there may also be a clear understanding among the members of the society of the specific content of the behaviour. But I think it will often be the case that considerable vagueness and flexibility are found. There may be an expectation that people should behave in a proper or appropriate way towards their kin. But what in a particular instance is regarded as proper or appropriate behaviour may be the subject of legitimate doubt, that is, there may be a wide range of responses each of which arguably qualifies as proper or appropriate. There will, consequently, be greater scope for disagreement about whether behaviour conforms to what is expected than about whether it complies with what is prescribed.

Personally I am inclined to think that an approach which distinguishes between rules and other "ought" statements governing human behaviour,[9] and locates law in the former, is the most fruitful. I realise that it may not be easy for the anthropologist investigating a simple society to discern whether the behaviour which he observes is the object of a rule or an expectation. But the attempt to classify normatively-regarded behaviour in accordance with such a distinction seems to me a more realistic enterprise than the attempt to classify rules according to the degree of their importance.

An important point still needs to be stressed. Such conclusions as one reaches on the basis of societies which lack legislatures and courts cannot be applied to societies which possess these legal institutions and therefore can be said to possess legal systems. In so far as one wishes to defend the conclusion that the law of a society is those rules which regulate human behaviour, one must accept that it is inapplicable to societies which have legal systems. Once

[9] I am not considering "ought" statements relating to the behaviour of natural phenomena: *cf.* the reference cited in the previous note.

a society has developed specific criteria for the identification of rules of law (for example by means of a law-enacting or a law-enforcing body), the investigation of law in that society is determined, though not exclusively so, by the boundaries inherent in the criteria of identification.

Although I have suggested that anthropologists in their studies of simple societies have not always distinguished with sufficient care between rules and other " ought " statements regarding human behaviour, I think that they do have a significant contribution to make with respect to the analysis of normatively-regarded behaviour. Not until anthropologists have scrutinised a number of societies from this point of view does it seem possible to say anything conclusive about the law of those societies. A rather different type of contribution that anthropology has to make is the opportunity it provides for an empirical verification of some versions of natural law theory.[10] The versions I have in mind are those which offer a set of rules deduced by reason and grounded upon the natural characteristics of man. As an illustration of this approach I have taken the version of natural law put forward by Professor Hart in *The Concept of Law*, which in turn draws heavily on the work of Hobbes and Hume.[11]

In offering what he calls a description of " the minimum content of natural law," Professor Hart's starting-point has been the use of reason in establishing conditions relating to human behaviour which must be met if man as a species is to survive. So far as I can see, his argument is that man, impelled by a wish to survive, has reasons for establishing such rules of behaviour as are necessary to ensure his survival. Since man lives in groups, these rules are those which permit co-existence within the group. In order to arrive at the content of the rules, Professor Hart combines man's wish to survive and certain fundamental facts of his nature and environment in the following way. The fundamental facts are human vulnerability, approximate equality, limited altruism, limited resources and limited understanding and strength of will. Of these the most significant is the " approximate equality " of man with man. No individual possesses by nature such physical and mental superiority over his fellows that he is able to keep them in a permanent state of subjection. If he is to live at peace with his

10 See also the remarks of M. Mead, " Some Anthropological Considerations concerning Natural Law " (1961) 6 *Natural Law Forum* 51.

11 H. L. A. Hart, *The Concept of Law*, pp. 181–195.

neighbours and so fulfil his wish to survive, he has to pursue a policy of co-operation and not domination. Man's wish to survive, together with the fundamental facts of his nature and environment, supply reasons for holding that men should adopt certain rules in their relations with each other. Viewed as a whole these rules constitute what Professor Hart describes as "a system of mutual forbearance and compromise."

The rules constructed in this fashion by Professor Hart relate to an individual's person, property and promises. There should be rules which prohibit indiscriminate killing or infliction of violence, and rules which ensure a man's peaceful enjoyment of his property. The latter require a short comment. Professor Hart specifically mentions rules which impose respect for such property as an individual acquires. He does not say anything about rules which ensure the more or less equal distribution of a group's resources among its members. Possibly one is entitled to infer from his remarks on "approximate equality" and the need for "a system of mutual forbearance and compromise" that he would have included such rules in "the minimum content of natural law." With respect to promises, Professor Hart's argument is that the division of labour obtaining in all but the smallest groups, together with the need for co-operation, supply reasons for the development of rules about the exchange of goods and the keeping of promises. Finally Professor Hart adduces the fact that men are prone to temptation and to prefer their own interests to those of others. In this may be seen a reason for the establishment of an organised system of coercion, to ensure that those willing to observe the rules of the society will not be exploited by a dissident minority. A coercive system is required in all societies except small closely-knit groups.

In putting forward his version of natural law, Professor Hart is careful not to commit himself to any particular view of social evolution, or to a view which treats the development of certain rules as necessarily entailed by the occurrence of certain social conditions. He concerns himself merely with the question: given certain facts about man's nature and environment, what rules would it be rational for man to adopt, granted that he wishes to survive? Professor Hart's thesis allows for the fact that men in any particular society might adopt rules which are not rational, and certainly this could be shown to be true in societies where the fact of "approximate equality" was not the dominant characteristic. In societies where power is monopolised by a few, it is possible for the rulers to govern the society in accordance with rules that would conflict with Professor Hart's "minimum content of natural law." Those with the power may be in a position to reserve for themselves the bulk of the society's resources and to treat in a cavalier fashion the persons and property of those who do not have the power.

However, in societies where there is no power structure and no monopoly of power in the hands of a few, the dominant characteristic is the "approximate equality" of man with man. Consequently one would expect the rules adopted by the members of such a society to be those for whose adoption Professor Hart adduces reasons. His thesis is not disproved should it turn out that the members of a society have adopted rules different from those included in the "minimum content of natural law." But should it be the case that these societies commonly adopt rules not included by Professor Hart in his account, or commonly do not adopt rules which are included, the thesis loses something of its general persuasiveness. One might be able to put the position more strongly. It is difficult sometimes to resist the inference that Professor Hart does suppose there to be a necessary connection between given social conditions and the adoption of certain rules.[12] That is, it seems to be implied in his account that a society based on "approximate equality" of man with man would not be viable unless the rules which he specifies were observed. If one does interpret Professor Hart's thesis as a thesis about the viability of societies which lack power structures, it is possible to seek verification through the investigation of such societies which have existed in the past or still exist today.

Anthropological studies of simple societies, those without power structures, are relevant to Professor Hart's thesis in two ways. If one limits the thesis to a statement of rules derived by reason from man's wish to survive and certain facts about his nature and environment, one may assess its persuasiveness against the results obtained by anthropologists. If the thesis is interpreted as a statement of the rules relating to human behaviour which a society of this type needs to adopt, its accuracy can be verified by reference to these results. The former interpretation I shall call version A and the latter version B.

The question is: how do versions A and B fare in the light of

[12] *Cf.* the remarks on primitive societies at p. 89 of *The Concept of Law.*

data obtained from the anthropological studies of simple societies? Anthropologists have not been explicitly concerned to prove or disprove theories of natural law. Where they have been interested in law they have concerned themselves with the question: what counts as law within a particular society or range of societies? Yet the result of their investigations is often to produce a list of rules which can be construed as necessary conditions for the survival of the human group.[13] In many other writings which are not specifically concerned with law, one can find relevant material. From studying accounts of a large number of simple societies one is able to compile modes of behaviour common to all. Where common modes of behaviour are found, the suggestion appears reasonable that they constitute necessary conditions for the survival of the society.[14]

The first proposition that may be asserted is that all societies without power structures have a rule prohibiting one member of the society from killing another.[15] I think it is reasonable to state the position in this apparently dogmatic manner. A full discussion of the topic would need to investigate such difficult questions as the way in which the boundaries of the society or group were to be drawn, and the actual attitudes exhibited in particular groups to the killing of one member by another. For my purpose I hope that these questions may be left aside. It also has to be recognised that the rule prohibiting killing is frequently qualified. The group accepts that certain categories of person may be killed with impunity. Nevertheless in all simple societies, even those much given to fighting and aggressive activities, the killing of one member by another is regarded as wrong. The same attitude may not be taken to killings which occur between groups. There may be no rule which prohibits the members of one group from killing the members of another, at least where the groups are not closely connected through blood or marriage. Thus one may say that version B of the natural law thesis receives confirmation in respect of a rule prohibiting killing, and that what version A puts forward as a rule derived from reason is in fact observed.

---

13 Apart from the works of Malinowski cited in note 3, *cf.* the approach to law taken by K. N. Llewellyn and E. A. Hoebel, *The Cheyenne Way*, Chaps. 10, 11; and M. G. Smith, *Corporations and Society*, pp. 87 *et seq.*, 94 *et seq.*

14 Colin Turnbull's study of the Ik, a nomadic, hunting people of the Sudan, is instructive: *The Mountain People*. He shows how a prolonged famine, which leads to a policy of each for himself and a breakdown of normal family and communal life, is causing the dissolution of the whole society.

15 *Cf.* Mead (1961) 6 *Natural Law Forum* 52.

Physical injuries are not treated in quite the same way as killings. They naturally give rise to quarrels and provoke retaliation, and there may be scales of compensation applicable to different types of injury. But at least in some societies the infliction of an injury is not treated as a serious matter unless it is likely to lead to death.[16] Consequently I think it doubtful whether one can postulate a rule prohibiting the infliction of physical injury as common to all simple societies. As against version B it cannot be said that a general rule prohibiting violence is necessary for the viability of a society or group, and with respect to version A it has to be said that there are societies in which men have not appreciated the reasons for adoption of a rule prohibiting violence in general.

In relation to resources, the most significant point that emerges is the equal distribution and the emphasis on sharing to be found in simple societies.[17] For example, members of the society have equal opportunities to obtain food. There is commonly found a great deal of co-operative activity in cultivating crops, gathering roots, nuts and berries, herding cattle and hunting animals. The products of this co-operative activity are commonly shared among those taking part and their kin. Within the group no one is allowed to go without food unless he is ejected from it. If one were to speak of a rule or rules with respect to resources, I think that the formulation would be in terms of a requirement for co-operation in obtaining food and for sharing what was obtained. Of course one could say that each was entitled to keep such food as he was allocated. But it seems to me that it would be a mistake to treat as primary a rule requiring respect for property acquired by the individual. The emphasis should be placed not on what the individual is entitled to keep, but on what he is expected to share with or contribute to others. Hence, if one were considering the conditions necessary for a viable society, one would have to include a rule requiring co-operation and sharing with respect to resources, even though one were not disposed to exclude a rule requiring respect for property obtained by an individual. Likewise, if one

16 See W. Goldschmidt, *Sebei Law*, Chap. 8.

17 A great deal of material on food sharing has been collected by Marshall Sahlins in the appendices to "On the Sociology of Primitive Exchange," in M. Banton, *The Relevance of Models for Social Anthropology*, p. 139. Much variation is found in the degree of co-operation and sharing practised in simple societies. In most there seems to have been considerable emphasis on co-operation but some appear to have been more "individualistic." But even in these support and help were given to those in need. *Cf.* R. Landes, "The Ojibwa of Canada," in M. Mead, *Co-operation and Competition among Primitive Peoples*, p. 87. The other essays in this volume also contain relevant material on the allocation of resources.

were thinking of rules for the adoption of which good reasons could be advanced, the rule about co-operation and sharing should be included.

Promises and organised sanctions form part of Professor Hart's "minimum content of natural law," though their inclusion is subject to qualifications not made in connection with the rules concerning person and property. One of the facts that supplies a reason for the keeping of promises is the division of labour, a fact not present in the smallest groups. Consequently Professor Hart allows for the fact that in some groups there may not exist a reason for the keeping of promises. One problem in assessing this argument is the vagueness of the phrase "division of labour." In all groups there is at least a division of labour between man and woman and adult and child. It is only if one restricts the notion of division of labour to work undertaken by men, that one may say many simple societies have no division of labour and therefore, on Professor Hart's argument, no reason for the development of a rule requiring the keeping of promises. As will be seen, on both interpretations difficulties are created for Professor Hart's thesis.

The anthropological evidence shows that neither the most simple societies nor sometimes even those that technologically and politically are more advanced have explicit rules about the keeping of promises. This does not mean that promises or agreements are not made, or that, when made, they are never kept. Nor does it mean that a person who fails to do what he has said he would do incurs no censure. Occasionally, indeed, the matter can be put more strongly. Among the Ifugao a person who makes a promise to sell land is held to be bound by the promise, and to be liable in damages where he had been the first to broach the matter with the prospective buyer.[18] One notes, however, that even here it is only within strictly defined conditions that a promise is held to create an enforceable obligation. The point is that promises as such do not play a significant role in simple societies. Accordingly, one cannot say that these societies have a rule that promises should be kept. The reason is that emphasis is placed upon something more tangible, namely the giving and receipt of property. People are expected to give to others, not because they have promised or agreed to give, but because of the relationship of blood or marriage which exists between them. This expectation, and often one might

[18] R. F. Barton, *Ifugao Law*, p. 52.

be able to describe it as an obligation, is reinforced by the "obligation" to make a return for what has been received.[19]

If all simple societies are held to have division of labour, at least in the sense that the men do different work from the women, version B of Professor Hart's thesis requires modification and version A becomes less cogent. If Professor Hart were right in arguing that reason suggests the development of a rule about the keeping of promises, it is at least odd that no society characterised primarily by the fact of "approximate equality" should have appreciated and acted upon reason. If the notion of division of labour is applied only to work undertaken by men, many simple societies can be held to have no division of labour. In these societies there is, on Professor Hart's argument, no reason for the development of a rule requiring that promises be kept. The evidence supports this conclusion. But there remains a difficulty. There are societies in which the men specialise and perform different tasks and yet no clear rules about the keeping of promises are found.[20] If, as I suspect, quite a number of such societies have existed, one would again have the oddity of a widespread failure to appreciate the reason for the adoption of a rule requiring promises to be kept. A further difficulty also arises on this interpretation. The "minimum content of natural law" is constructed by reference to two types of group: that with and that without division of labour. Why should the inquiry be restricted to just these groups?

In so far as Professor Hart distinguishes between small, closely-knit groups which lack organised sanctions and other groups which require them, the same objection may be taken. If one is constructing a "minimum content of natural law" on the basis of fundamental facts of human nature, it is not easy to see why groups other than the simplest which allows for the survival of man should be relevant. The simplest societies in fact cannot be said to operate organised sanctions or systems of coercion. They do have sanctions, in the sense that people who do not behave in the way prescribed by rules are subjected to physical compulsion or other forms of pressure specifically designed to ensure compliance or to impose a punishment for breach. But such sanctions are imposed by various persons related to the offender or the

19 Some of the relevant literature is mentioned in my article on "Reciprocity" (1976) 11 *Man* (N.S.) 89.

20 *Cf.* M. Gluckman's discussion of contract among the Lozi: *The Ideas in Barotse Jurisprudence*, pp. 180 *et seq.*

victim, or sometimes by members of the group as a whole. They are not activated by a particular person or body whose duty it is to institute sanctions under defined circumstances. On the other hand, what the simplest societies do all possess is some procedure for the settlement of disputes. Each society needs to evolve or practise some means by which disputes between its members may be contained or settled. No group can be viable unless it has a means of permitting the continuation of co-operation despite the occurrence of disputes. And if one is thinking of rules for the conduct of life suggested by reason on the basis of "approximate equality," rules providing procedures for the settlement of disputes have a stronger claim on one's attention than rules establishing a system of organised coercion.[21] The point is that once a society develops an organisation for the infliction of sanctions a power structure emerges and the natural fact of "approximate equality" ceases to be of primary importance.

In general, consideration of the anthropological evidence suggests that version B of Professor Hart's thesis requires modification and that version A loses something of its persuasiveness, since members of simple societies have not always appreciated the reasons said to stem from man's wish to survive and the fundamental facts of his nature and environment. I do not want to say anything further of the relevance of anthropology to the particular thesis presented by Professor Hart. But I should like to pose two questions which require answers if one attempts generally to utilise the results obtained by anthropologists for the construction of a "minimum content of natural law." The first question concerns the distinction between rules observed by members of the same group and rules observed by members of different groups in their dealing with each other. On the basis of studies made by anthropologists, one may be able to construct a set of rules which needs to be observed by the members of a group if the group is to survive. An argument that these rules constitute "a minimum content of natural law" has to meet the objection that the rules have a restricted ambit. They apply only to members of a group in their dealings with each other. How can they be relevant where one is considering relationships between groups? A possible line of argument is the following. Just as life within the group can be maintained only if certain rules are observed, so can the group

[21] In some societies, as in a number of those found in Papua and New Guinea, it is difficult even to detect *rules* which establish procedures for the settlement of disputes.

itself, once it has come into contact with other groups, survive only if it is able to apply similar rules to its relationship with these groups. For example, as between groups indiscriminate killing has to be avoided, and in so far as they are competing for the same resources the distribution must be more or less equal. If these conditions are not observed, in the long run one or perhaps both groups will break up and their members either die or merge with another group or found a new group.

The second question concerns the nature of the data utilised by the person wishing to construct a "minimum content of natural law." Is it the behaviour alone which is relevant, or is it the rules observed by the members of the groups? Does the investigator argue that everywhere members of the groups studied refrain on the whole from killing each other, and that therefore everywhere man ought to refrain from killing man? Or does he argue that all groups studied accept a rule that members should refrain from killing each other, and that therefore such a rule forms part of the minimum content of natural law? In fact the investigator will have to adopt both approaches. He has to start by looking at the way members of the groups actually behave. In so far as he is able to isolate behaviour common to all groups, he will find it impossible to separate the question of what is done from the question of what ought to be done. Members of the group practise the behaviour because they regard it as behaviour which ought to be practised. One might press the investigation further, and ask why they attach an "ought" to the behaviour, but the answer does not seem to be relevant to the construction of a set of natural laws. What is relevant is the investigator's conviction that the behaviour is necessary for the survival of the group.[22] *

G. MacCormack

[22] I am most grateful to my colleague Dr. M. Dalgarno, for his searching criticisms of an earlier version of this paper.

* This paper was presented to the World Congress on Philosophy of Law and Social Philosophy, Sydney-Canberra, August 1977. It is now published with the permission of the Organising Committee of the Congress.

[7]

LEGAL PLURALISM

SALLY ENGLE MERRY

I. INTRODUCTION

The intellectual odyssey of the concept of legal pluralism moves from the discovery of indigenous forms of law among remote African villagers and New Guinea tribesmen to debates concerning the pluralistic qualities of law under advanced capitalism. In the last decade, the concept of legal pluralism has been applied to the study of social and legal ordering in urban industrial societies, primarily the United States, Britain, and France. Indeed, given a sufficiently broad definition of the term legal system, virtually every society is legally plural, whether or not it has a colonial past. Legal pluralism is a central theme in the reconceptualization of the law/society relation.

Early twentieth century studies examined indigenous law ways among tribal and village peoples in colonized societies in Africa, Asia, and the Pacific. Social scientists (primarily anthropologists) were interested in how these peoples maintained social order without European law (e.g., Malinowski, 1926). As they documented the rich variety of social control, social pressure, custom, customary law, and judicial procedure within small-scale societies, these anthropologists gradually realized that colonized peoples had both indigenous law and European law. Colonial law was reshaping the social life of these villages and tribes in subtle ways, even when it seemed remote. Indeed, as Chanock observed for colonial Africa, "The law was the cutting edge of colonialism, . . ." (1985: 4). Tribes and villages had some law developed over the generations on to which formal rational law was imposed by the European colonial powers. The imposed law, forged for industrial capitalism rather than an agrarian or pastoral way of life, embodied very different principles and procedures. Scholars termed these situations legal pluralism. They recognized that the introduction of European colonial law created a plurality of legal orders but overlooked, to a large extent, the complexity of previous legal orders.

For the proponents of empire in the nineteenth century, this imposition of European law was a great gift, substituting civilized

---

This article was completed in February, 1988 and covers literature from 1978 to early 1988. I am grateful to Peter Fitzpatrick, John Griffiths, Christine Harrington, Robert Hayden, Stuart Henry, and June Starr for helpful suggestions and comments on earlier drafts.

LAW & SOCIETY REVIEW, Volume 22, Number 5 (1988)

law for the anarchy and fear that they believed gripped the lives of the colonized peoples, freeing them from the scourges of war, witchcraft, and tyranny (Ranger, 1983). In Africa, the British and the French superimposed their law onto indigenous law, incorporating customary law as long as it was not "repugnant to natural justice, equity, and good conscience," or "inconsistent with any written law," (Okoth-Ogendo, 1979: 160; Adewoye, 1986: 60; Bentsi-Enchill, 1969). The repugnancy principle was used to outlaw unacceptable African customs. That the European legal system also helped to mold a cooperative labor force to serve the new extractive industries or to produce cash crops for export was probably not lost on the colonial administrators (cf., Chanock, 1985; Comaroff, 1985; Comaroff and Comaroff, 1986; Moore, 1986a).

Yet, legal pluralism goes far deeper than the joining of European and traditional forms of law. We are only now beginning to explore the extent to which previously colonized societies are legally and culturally plural. The Europeans were not the first outside influence bringing a new legal system to many Third World peoples. Indigenous law had been shaped by conquests and migrations for centuries. For example, Geertz describes the legal complexity of Java as the product of the encounters of an original group of settlers from South China and north Vietnam with India states, Chinese trading communities, Islamic missionaries, Dutch and British colonizers, Japanese occupation forces, and presently, the Indonesian state (1983: 226). As we engage in careful historical study, we throw off the notion that the pasts of traditional societies were unchanging (Ranger, 1983; Chanock, 1985).

What is legal pluralism? It is generally defined as a situation in which two or more legal systems coexist in the same social field (Pospisil, 1971; Griffiths 1986a; Moore, 1986a).[1] Pospisil, in his pioneering work on legal levels, claims that "every functioning subgroup in a society has its own legal system which is necessarily different in some respects from those of the other subgroups" (1971: 107). By subgroups he means units such as family, lineage, community, and political confederation that are integral parts of a homogenous society, hierarchically ranked, and essentially similar in rules and procedure. Recent work defines "legal system" broadly to include the system of courts and judges supported by the state as well as nonlegal forms of normative ordering. Some of these are part of institutions such as factories, corporations, and universities and include written codes, tribunals, and security forces, sometimes replicating the structure and symbolic form of state law (Macaulay, 1986; Henry, 1983). Other normative orders are informal systems in which the processes of establishing rules, securing

[1] In an important essay on the definition of legal pluralism, Griffiths defines it as "that state of affairs, for any social field, in which behavior pursuant to more than one legal order occurs (1986a: 2)."

compliance to these rules, and punishing rulebreakers seem natural and taken for granted, as occurs within families, work groups, and collectives (Abel, 1982; Henry, 1985). Thus, virtually every society is legally plural. This approach runs the risk of defining legal system so broadly that all social control forms are included (see further Comaroff and Roberts, 1981).

Griffiths distinguishes between the "social science" view of legal pluralism as an empirical state of affairs in society (the coexistence within a social group of legal orders that do not belong to a single "system") and what he calls a "juristic" view of legal pluralism as a particular problem of dual legal systems created when European countries established colonies that superimposed their legal systems on preexisting systems (1986a: 5, 8). A legal system is pluralistic in the juristic sense when the sovereign commands different bodies of law for different groups of the population varying by ethnicity, religion, nationality, or geography, and when the parallel legal regimes are all dependent on the state legal system. This situation creates a range of complex legal problems, such as the need to decide when a subgroup's law applies to a particular transaction or conflict, to what group particular individuals belong, how a person can change which law is applicable to him or her (educated Africans in the colonial era, for example, chafed at being judged under African law rather than European law), choice of law rules for issues between people of different groups, and determinations of which subjects, particularly family law, and in which geographical areas subgroup law should be accepted (Griffiths, 1986a: 7). It is often difficult to determine what the subgroup's rules are, particularly when they are not part of a written tradition. As we will see below, even those legal systems with written codes, such as Islamic law, are often embedded in very different ways of thinking about the fact/law dichotomy, the nature of evidence, and the meaning of judging (Rosen, 1980–81; Geertz, 1983; Messick, 1986).

Hooker provides a masterful and comprehensive overview of legal pluralism in this sense, surveying plural legal systems in Asia, Africa, and the Middle East (1975). He defines legal pluralism as circumstances "in the contemporary world which have resulted from the transfer of whole legal systems across cultural boundaries" (Ibid.: 1). Legal problems of the juristic kind confront leaders of many post-colonial societies, who widely regard their complex legal systems as frustrating, messy, and obstructive to progress (Bentsi-Enchill, 1969; Griffiths, 1986a). Contemporary elites in Africa see modernization and nation-building as requiring a unified legal system, often drawing on models of European law (Okoth-Ogendo, 1979: 165).[2] As post colonial societies endeavor to adopt uniform state law, however, they meet with pockets of in-

[2] To this extent, they appear to have accepted the dominant legal ideology of Western society (see Merry, 1986).

tense resistance from those groups whose law has been preserved in some fashion (see further, Geertz, 1983: 228).

This review discusses primarily the social science version of legal pluralism. According to the design of the Fifth Issue, the review focuses on literature from the past decade, although I have included earlier work when it is important for my argument. I focused on materials published in English, although there is a substantial non-English literature. Central resources in the study of legal pluralism are the new *Journal of Legal Pluralism and Unofficial Law*, created in 1981,[3] and several important international conferences along with the books they have generated.

II. CLASSIC LEGAL PLURALISM AND THE NEW LEGAL PLURALISM

Research on colonial and post-colonial societies produced a version of legal pluralism I call "classic legal pluralism." This is the analysis of the intersections of indigenous and European law. Beginning in the late 1970s, there has been an interest among sociolegal scholars in applying the concept of legal pluralism to noncolonized societies, particularly to the advanced industrial countries of Europe and the United States. This move produces a version of legal pluralism I call the "new legal pluralism." A number of studies explore contemporary legal pluralism in the United States (e.g., Moore, 1973; Forer, 1979; Merry, 1979; Engel, 1980, 1984, 1987; Nader, 1980; Greenhouse, 1982, Buckle and Thomas-Buckle, 1982; Macaulay, 1986), Britain (e.g., Henry, 1983; 1985), and the Netherlands (e.g., van den Bergh *et al.*, 1980; Strijbosch, 1985; van den Bergh *et al.*, 1980). There are also several historical studies of legal pluralism in these countries (e.g., Auerbach, 1983; Arthurs, 1985; Bossy, 1983). Case studies on legal pluralism presented at a conference on the imposition of law included the American Indians, Hungarian farm cooperatives, British trade unions, British game laws, and the American death penalty along with the more traditional topics of legal pluralism in New Guinea, Kenya, and Niger (Burman and Harrell-Bond, 1979). Legal pluralism has expanded from a concept that refers to the relations between colonized and colonizer to relations between dominant groups and subordinate groups, such as religious, ethnic, or cultural minorities, immigrant groups, and unofficial forms of ordering located in social networks or institutions (Woodman,

[3] This journal, under the editorship of John Griffiths in the Netherlands, incorporates international scholarship on legal pluralism to a far greater extent than the *Law & Society Review*. The *Journal of Legal Pluralism* includes important theoretical articles, book reviews, and case studies on diverse subjects such as the role of public letter writers in the development of the legal profession in Ibadan, Nigeria between 1904 and 1960 (Adewoye, 1986), the coexistence of indigenous, Islamic, British colonial, and post-colonial Nigerian law in Northern Nigeria (Salamone, 1983), and the acquisition of indigenous Hawaiian lands through legal means (Lam, 1985).

1987–88: 3–4; Macaulay, 1986). Moore provides a useful summary of concepts of legal and social pluralism in her overview of ways of comparing legal systems of the world (1986b: 15–24).

According to the new legal pluralism, plural normative orders are found in virtually all societies. This is an extraordinarily powerful move, in that it places at the center of investigation the relationship between the official legal system and other forms of ordering that connect with but are in some ways separate from and dependent on it. The new legal pluralism moves away from questions about the effect of law on society or even the effect of society on law toward conceptualizing a more complex and interactive relationship between official and unofficial forms of ordering. Instead of mutual influences between two separate entities, this perspective sees plural forms of ordering as participating in the same social field. In his remarks at the Bellagio Conference on People's Law and State Law (see Allott and Woodman, 1985), Francis Snyder argues that any dualistic distinction, such as that between folk and state law, is misleading because plural normative orders are part of the same system in any particular social context and are usually intertwined in the same social micro-processes (Griffiths, 1985: 17–18). The particulars of the relationship in any social location are historically derived and unsettled.

The new legal pluralism draws on the rich ethnographic and theoretical work from classic legal pluralism. Among the significant contributions of classic legal pluralism there are, I think, three of particular importance. First is the analysis of the interaction between normative orders that are fundamentally different in their underlying conceptual structure. Second is an attention to the elaboration of customary law as historically derived. Third is the delineation of the dialectic between normative orders. In classic legal pluralism, this dialectic takes place in situations in which different orders are readily identified and the dynamics of resistance and restructuring by groups experiencing the imposition of a very different normative order are relatively easy to see. When Pospisil reports the Kapauku Papuans' response to the introduction of Dutch law, for example, it is relatively easy to identify the actors, since Kapauku law and Dutch law are quite distinct. In this situation there are clearly limits to the penetration of Dutch law, areas in which the Kapauku have taken Dutch law and made it their own, and areas in which Dutch law has become part of the political struggle between different factions, some more attuned to the colonial order than others (1981).

In societies without colonial pasts, however, the nonstate forms of normative ordering are more difficult to see. They blend more readily into the landscape and, aside from some notable exceptions (such as Ehrlich's concept of "living law," (1913), Gurvitch's "social law," (1947) and Macaulay's work on private ordering (1963)) were generally ignored until the mid 1970s. To recognize legal pluralism at home required rejecting what Griffiths calls the "ideology of legal centralism," the notion that the state and the system of lawyers, courts, and prisons is the only form of ordering (1986a). Indeed, scholars trained in legal positivism are taught that law and ordering take place in courthouses and law offices, not in corporate gossip, university regulations and tribunals, or neighborhood bars (on this point, see Arthurs, 1985). It is probably no accident that many of the prominent scholars in the new legal pluralism, such as Richard Abel, David Engel, Marc Galanter, Peter Fitzpatrick, Sally Falk Moore, Boaventura de Sousa Santos, and Francis Snyder began their sociolegal research in postcolonial societies in which legal pluralism was an obvious and unambiguous fact of life.

In sum, research on legal pluralism began in the study of colonial societies in which an imperialist nation, equipped with a centralized and codified legal system, imposed this system on societies with far different legal systems, often unwritten and lacking formal structures for judging and punishing. This kind of legal pluralism is embedded in relations of unequal power. The concept has been expanded in recent years to describe legal relations in advanced industrial countries, but here, discussions of legal pluralism are quite different. They center on a rejection of the law-centeredness of traditional studies of legal phenomena, arguing that not all law takes place in the courts (e.g., Nader and Todd, 1978; Arthurs, 1985). The concern is to document other forms of social regulation that draw on the symbols of the law, to a greater or lesser extent, but that operate in its shadows, its parking lots, and even down the street in mediation offices. Thus, in contexts in which the dominance of a central legal system is unambiguous, this thread of argument worries about missing what else is going on; the extent to which other forms of regulation outside law constitute law.

These two contexts make odd companions. Their central adversaries, the positions against which they are arguing, are quite different. They come out of different scholarly traditions. The nature of the relationship between the systems seems quite different. In the former, there is an unambiguous imposition or dominance of one system over the other; in the latter, the nature of the linkage is more fluid and opaque. Yet, on closer inspection, even dominant colonial legal orders failed to penetrate fully, encountered pockets of resistance, and were absorbed and co-opted, as Kidder has shown clearly in the Indian case (1974; 1979). Further, in industrial societies, despite the apparent autonomy of nonjudicial spheres, the legal system stands in a relation of superior power to other systems of regulation as the ultimate source of coercive power (Abel, 1982; Merry, 1986; Yngvesson, 1985). Thus, there are ways in which joining these two contexts of legal pluralism enhances our understanding of the interaction of plural orders rather than obstructing it.

III. FOLK LAW, INDIGENOUS LAW, STATE LAW, LAWYER'S LAW: DEFINING THE TERMS

There are a wide variety of terms used to discuss the parts which make up legally plural societies: the systems or normative orders that make up a legally plural situation. Each is discredited in various ways because the term carries with it unwanted perjorative implications. The terminological debate concerning state law is the easier one: commonly used terms are law, state law, lawyers' law, official law, and bourgeois legality. Names for nonstate law form a far greater tangle. The early work in classic legal pluralism referred to a distinction between law and custom. Diamond, in an influential article, described the relations dichotomously (1973: 322–323):

> Custom—spontaneous, traditional, personal, commonly known, corporate, relatively unchanging—is the modality of primitive society; law is the instrument of civilization, of political society sanctioned by organized force, presumably above society at large, and buttressing a new set of social interests. Law and custom both involve the regulation of behavior but their characters are entirely distinct; no evolutionary balance has been struck between developing law and custom, whether traditional or emergent.

Rejecting the notion that custom is a form of primitive law that will gradually develop into state law, Diamond argues instead that the advance of law contradicts and extinguishes custom.

But what is custom? In colonial settings, pre-colonial law recognized or accepted by the colonial rulers after conquest or takeover was labeled customary law (e.g., Hooker, 1975). This law was often predominantly oral rather than written and derived from sources of authority outside the colonial state (Snyder, 1981b: 49). Yet, a rich body of recent ethno/historical research in Africa, Indonesia, and Papua New Guinea argues that the notion of an unchanging custom or even customary law was a myth of the colonial era, while customary law itself was a product of the colonial encounter (Colson, 1976; Benda-Beckmann, 1979; Fitzpatrick, 1980; Snyder, 1981a, 1981b; Ranger, 1983; Chanock, 1985; Gordon and Meggitt, 1985; Moore, 1986a; Starr and Collier, 1987, 1989).

Snyder, for example, argues that customary law was not simply an adapted or transformed version of indigenous law, but a new form created within the context of the colonial state (1981b). Through a detailed history of the changing social position of the rain priest among a group of rice farmers in Senegal, Snyder shows how customary law was created. Senegalese more familiar with European languages and customs served as intermediaries, interpreters of indigenous law to Europeans. The Europeans, in turn, accepted those versions of customary law which meshed best with their own ideology of land ownership as well as other legal relations. Snyder concludes (Ibid.: 74, 76):

876 LEGAL PLURALISM

> Customary law in the Casamance [Senegal], as elsewhere, was a concept and a legal form that originated in specific historical circumstances, namely the period in the transformation of pre-capitalist social relations that saw the consolidation of the colonial state. . . . Produced in particular historical circumstances, the notion of 'customary law' was an ideology of colonial domination. The concept of 'customary law' itself manifested an attempt to reinterpret African legal forms in terms of European legal categories, which formed part of the ideology of those classes most closely associated with the colonial state. The designation of African law as 'customary' because it was oral, though apparently technical, embodied and masked an essentially political conclusion that it was subordinate to the colonial law of European origin.

Snyder urges a full reanalysis of the role law plays in post-colonial societies from the perspective of dependency theory rather than from that of modernization theory (1980). Rather than viewing plural legal orders as barriers to modernization, he suggests that their creation was a product of the expansion of the European capitalist order throughout the world over the last 400 years, an expansion which has gradually incorporated the most remote societies into a single economic system despite its fractionated political structures. These traditional forms of law were constructs of the European expansion and capitalist transformation, as were also the tribes, villages, chiefs and many other features of apparently traditional social systems (Wolf, 1982). Ranger argues, for example, that the vision of a traditional, unchanging African past ruled by long-established custom was a creation of colonial administrators of the early twentieth century in an effort to restore some order after the chaotic years of the nineteenth century (1983: 250–251).

If the nonstate forms of social ordering in legally plural situations are not customs or customary law, then what can we call them? A symposium in 1978, The Social Consequences of Imposed Law, debated using imposed law but abandoned the term as inadequate since all law is experienced as imposed in some ways, yet all law is also to some degree accepted rather than simply imposed (Burman and Harrell-Bond, 1979: 2). Kidder, pointing to the enthusiasm with which Indians adopted British law, suggested instead the concept of external law, which takes into account the "sources of power at different levels of externality" (1979: 296). He suggests thinking of multiple layers of legal organization at various levels of externality with struggles between these levels, rather than just law and custom (Ibid.: 299).

In a later paper, Galanter suggests the terms indigenous ordering and indigenous law to refer to forms of ordering outside the official system (1981: 17). But recent work indicates that even those societies analyzed as if they were untouched by European culture, and in that sense "indigenous," were vulnerable to outside influences at the time of early ethnographic research (Fitzpatrick, 1985). Indeed, Pospisil, an anthropologist who worked during the early contact period between a group of New Guinea peoples and the Dutch government and authored a classic text on indigenous law, points out that he himself was an important pawn in local politics, co-opted by one faction (1979). On a second trip to the Kapauku, he was surprised to find that the Dutch colonial administrators were using his book on Kapauku law as the basis for their determinations of customary law (Ibid.: 132). As anthropologists examine more carefully the situations in which early ethnographic accounts were produced they discover ways in which these accounts were structured by the colonial encounter (Marcus and Fisher, 1986).

At a 1981 conference on people's law and state law, participants discussed using the term folk law, but there was concern over whether the term romanticized folk law or minimized it (Roberts, 1986). The participants concluded that there is no such type of law as folk law distinct from state law, but instead a continuum of differentiation and organization of the generation and application of norms, a conception suggested by Galanter (Allott and Woodman, 1985).

Within the new legal pluralism, Macaulay proposes the concept of "private government," which he defines as that governing done by groups not part of federal and state constitutions but which may mimic symbols and structures of the public legal system (1986). He advocates a "private government perspective," which recognizes private associations that affect governing and also treats distinctions between public and private as problematic (1983: 2). He envisions a private government landscape as follows: ". . . While it may be necessary to draw a sharp line between public and private government even to think about law, actually there is no such line but situations of interpenetration, overlapping jurisdictions, and opportunities for harmony and conflict (Ibid.: 1)." Henry suggests the term "private justice" to refer to nonstate systems that "include practices of such institutions as the disciplinary bodies, boards, and councils of industrial and commercial organizations, professional and trade associations and unions, down to the peer sanctioning of relatively amorphous voluntary associations such as local self-help and mutual aid groups (1985: 89)."

Private justice does not exist in isolation but interrelates with the more formalized state order in a semiautonomous way (Henry, 1985: 89). As with Macaulay's private governments, private justice institutions can be formally constituted with written rules and procedures or informally constituted, generated spontaneously by members who share only tacit assumptions and who do not necessarily recognize that they are part of a system of normative ordering. Private government or private justice often replicates aspects of the legal order, such as security forces and tribunals, and mimics its symbols with similar police uniforms, lights, codes, and systems of judgment. However, there are also occasions when it takes an oppositional form, as it does with the law of cooperatives in a capitalist society (Henry, 1985; 1987).

The most enduring, generalizable, and widely-used conception of plural legal orders is Moore's notion of the semiautonomous social field, a concept developed to describe multiple systems of ordering in complex societies (1973). The semiautonomous social field is one that (Ibid.: 720):

> can generate rules and customs and symbols internally, but that . . . is also vulnerable to rules and decisions and other forces emanating from the larger world by which it is surrounded. The semi-autonomous social field has rule-making capacities, and the means to induce or coerce compliance; but it is simultaneously set in a larger social matrix which can, and does, affect and invade it, sometimes at the invitation of persons inside it, sometimes at its own instance.

The advantages of this concept are that the semiautonomous social field is not attached to a single social group, that makes no claims about the nature of the orders themselves or their origin (whether traditional or imposed), and that it draws no definitive conclusions about the nature and direction of influence between the normative orders. The outside legal system penetrates the field but does not dominate it; there is room for resistance and autonomy.

Galanter, building on this model, argues that indigenous ordering persists not in bounded groups so much as in more open social networks that are regulated largely by reciprocity and shared but tacit understandings (1981: 22). Societies contain many partially self-regulating sectors organized along geographical, ethnic, or familial lines, often in fragmentary and overlapping social networks (Ibid.: 19–20). Galanter states (Ibid.: 22):

> If we have lost the experience of an all-encompassing inclusive community, it is not to a world of arms-length dealings with strangers, but in large measure to a world of loosely joined and partly overlapping partial or fragmentary communities. In this sense, our exposure to indigenous law has increased at the same time that official regulation has multiplied.

Macaulay's conception of private government is very similar: he envisions ordering through open social networks as well as within more organized and established institutional frameworks (1986).

Why is it so difficult to find a word for nonstate law? It is clearly difficult to define and circumscribe these forms of ordering. Where do we stop speaking of law and find ourselves simply describing social life? Is it useful to call all these forms of ordering law? In writing about legal pluralism, I find that once legal centralism has been vanquished, calling all forms of ordering that are not state law by the term law confounds the analysis. The literature in this field has not yet clearly demarcated a boundary between normative orders that can and cannot be called law. I think one of the difficulties lies in the tremendous variation in normative orders and the diversity of particular situations. The move to include noncolonized societies under the framework of legal pluralism adds to the complexity. However, there is general agreement that pluralism does not describe a type of society but is a condition found to a greater or lesser extent in most societies, with continuous variation between those that are more and those less plural (Galanter, 1981; Griffiths, 1986a).

Defining the orders which make up legal pluralism raises other issues as well. Does it make a difference that these plural legal orders vary greatly in power, in coercive potential, in symbolic strength, in attachment to class groupings? Are state and nonstate forms of ordering similar, or are there ways in which the state-law system is fundamentally different from all other forms of ordering? I think it is essential to see state law as fundamentally different in that it exercises the coercive power of the state and monopolizes the symbolic power associated with state authority. But, in many ways, it ideologically shapes other normative orders as well as provides an inescapable framework for their practice.

IV. RELATIONS BETWEEN NORMATIVE ORDERS: EXPLORING THE INTERACTIONS

Legal pluralism not only posits the existence of multiple legal spheres, but develops hypotheses concerning the relationships between them. The existence of legal pluralism itself is of less interest than the dynamics of change and transformation. Historically, there has been a shift in the way the interaction between legal orders, particularly between state law and nonstate law, has been described. Early research in classic legal pluralism saw normative orders as parallel but autonomous. During the 1960s and early 1970s, several studies demonstrated the power of state law to reshape the social order, suggesting the dominance of this form of law over other normative orders (e.g., Massell, 1968; Diamond, 1973; Burman and Harrell-Bond, 1979). Law appeared to be a potent tool for modernization in Third World countries (see Gardner, 1980; Lynch, 1983) and for creating social justice in the First World during this period.

But, it has not always worked that way, as law and development scholars discovered and as American social reformers found (Trubek and Galanter, 1974). In the 1970s, a more cautious and limited view of law's potential to reshape other social orders emerged. Some studies showed limits to the capacity of law to transform social life. The comparative examination of imposed law showed that sometimes it had powerful consequences for change but that at other times the consequences were unexpected or negligible (Burman and Harrell-Bond, 1979). In contrast to Massell's analysis of the revolutionary impact of new laws on the status of women in the Islamic societies of Soviet Central Asia (1968), for example, Starr and Pool showed that the drastic law reforms introduced into Turkish society in 1926 that swept away Islamic Ottoman law in favor of the Swiss civil code produced relatively little change in the normative ordering of local villages (1974: 534). The vast majority of the Turkish population continued to follow customs incompatible with the new codes (Ibid.). Instead of revolutionary transformation, Starr and Pool document gradual, incremental change as, for example, women began to use the courts more frequently for family problems.

The creation of customary law, to give another example, was an ongoing, collaborative process in which power was clearly unequal, but subordinate groups were hardly passive or powerless. For example, Adewoye describes the development of public letter writers in Ibadan, Nigeria, between 1904 and 1960 (1986). These Africans drafted and produced legal documents in the absence of trained lawyers, shaping the forms of sale and land ownership contracts. Moore's model of the semiautonomous social field was in part an effort to explain why new laws or other attempts to direct change did not always produce the anticipated results or brought unplanned or unexpected consequences (1973: 723):

> This is partly because new laws are thrust upon going social arrangements in which there are complexes of binding obligations already in existence. Legislation is often passed with the intention of altering the going social arrangements in specified ways. The social arrangements are often effectively stronger than the new laws.

Moore's careful historical study of customary law among the Chagga of Tanzania documents this process more fully (1986a). Here she defines customary law as a cultural construct with political implications, a set of ideas embedded in relationships that are historically shifting (Ibid.: xv). Franz von Benda-Beckmann points out that the particular areas of resistance or acquiescence to imposed colonial law are complex and historically situated, depending to some extent on the processes of imposition themselves, which are highly variable (1981).

Research in the 1980s has increasingly emphasized the dialectic, mutually constitutive relation between state law and other normative orders. I think this reflects a new awareness of the interconnectedness of social orders, of our vulnerability to structures of domination far outside our immediate worlds, and of the ways implicit and unrecognized systems of control are embedded in our day-to-day social lives. Moreover, analysis of this dialectic is enriched by recent interpretations of law as a symbolic and ideological system (c.f., *Law & Society Review Special Issue on Law and*

Ideology, 1988). Research in the 1980s emphasizes the way state law penetrates and restructures other normative orders through symbols and through direct coercion and, at the same time, the way nonstate normative orders resist and circumvent penetration or even capture and use the symbolic capital of state law. In a final turn, some research explores the way nonstate normative orders constitute state law. Beyond well-known research on phenomena such as plea bargaining and courtroom workgroups, however, this study is in its infancy.

I will begin by describing research that focuses on the ways state law shapes other normative orders. Auerbach's study of the history of nonjudicial forms of dispute resolution in the United States demonstrates how state law gradually infiltrates and restructures alternatives so that they come to resemble state law (1983; see also Arthurs, 1985). This and other studies of the progressive reconstitution of alternatives as legalistic forums illuminate the expansion of state law into other normative orders over time (Nader, 1984; Harrington, 1985; Arthurs, 1985). But, subordinate groups may also choose to draw on the symbols and meanings of the state legal system. Santos's well-known study of law in the *favelas* of Brazil describes how residents of an illegal squatter settlement create their own legality using the forms and symbols of state law, the "law of the asphalt," as they call it (1977). Here, legal orders are attached to classes. Legal pluralism describes the relations between a dominant class and an oppressed urban class, relations that reflect the class hierarchy of Brazilian society, its structure of domination and unequal exchange. Squatters pursue a strategy of implicit confrontation at the same time as they adapt in order to survive (1977).

In another context, Westermark documents the practices of new village courts in Papua New Guinea, created in 1973 as informal, conciliatory alternatives to the state courts (1986). But the courts he studied replicated the state courts in architecture and furniture, using tables, chairs, the national flag, notes, and stone-lined walkways to an enclosed building (1986). Equipped with handbooks and badges, the magistrates pressed for uniforms and handcuffs. These village courts dispense what they call government law.

In an American study, John Brigham argues that legal discourse constitutes the discourse and practices of some American social movements (1987). Using examples from the gay rights movement, the anti-pornography movement, and the alternative dispute resolution movement, Brigham shows how references to rights or to the failures of law enter into and thus constitute movement discourse and even the strategies and tactics of the movements. Other studies have begun to explore the widespread legal consciousness of American society (Scheingold, 1974; Merry, 1986;

Macaulay, 1987) but there has been relatively little investigation of how this consciousness shapes other normative orders.

Symbolic appropriation works the other way around as well: state law may borrow the symbols of other normative orders. Government reformers sometimes promote new state judicial institutions with traditional symbolic trappings, claiming to reinstitute traditional law. The Philippine *katarungang pambarangay*, (neighborhood justice) or Indian *nyaya panchayats* (justice village councils) (Silliman, 1985; Meschievitz and Galanter, 1982; Hayden, 1984) illustrate this practice. The Philippine system is called neighborhood justice but is administered by state officials called neighborhood captains (Silliman, 1985). Many have argued that American neighborhood justice is another example of state law masquerading under the symbolic trappings of nonstate normative orders (Santos, 1982; Abel, 1982; Harrington, 1985; Harrington and Merry, 1988). New state judicial institutions clothed in revolutionary symbols have been created in the service of social transformation, as in Allende's Chile (Spence, 1978) and Castro's Cuba (Salas, 1983).

Studies of the micro-level processes of legal action, disputing, and case processing describe the dynamics of the symbolic radiation and imposition of state law, its appropriation within other normative orders, and forms of resistance to its penetration. The rich ethnographic studies of local dispute processes reported in Nader and Todd (1978) provide numerous examples of individuals pursuing dispute strategies in legally plural arenas (see, e.g., Ruffini, 1978). Even when state law is not used, it constitutes bargaining and regulatory endowments, to use Galanter's terms (1981). In these situations, the contours of local disputing are inextricably connected with local political struggles between those whose authority claims rest on kinship or religion and those whose claims rest on knowledge of the state, education, or connections with the government. Moore's description of a dispute among the Chagga illustrates this dynamic, pointing to the linkage between local political competition for power and knowledge of and access to village and state legal systems (1977). Based on her analysis of disputing in a legally plural arena in Indonesia, Keebet von Benda-Beckmann proposes a model of forum shopping and social change that provides a way of understanding how local processes of disputing reshape legally plural situations (1981). Disputants shop for forums for their problems and forums compete for disputes, which they use for their own local political ends (Ibid.: 117). There are constraints on disputants, however. For example, state courts refuse to hear claims by women for rice plots since only the official representative of the lineage is entitled to sue, thus preventing women from appealing to the state courts to escape the control of the lineage head over their land (Ibid.: 143).

Abel (1979a) and Merry (1982) also develop models of disputing and legal change which argue that the cumulative effect of litigant choice of forum affects dispute institutions at the same time as dispute institutions are themselves changing along with developments in the political economy. Starr's analysis of disputing strategies during a period of capitalist transformation in Turkey carefully analyzes this process as well (1974; see also Abel, 1979b). Peter just explores the manipulation of evidence as a strategy for providing justice while conforming to law (1986).

Another new area of research examines how state law both constitutes and is constituted by the normative orders of which it is composed. Fitzpatrick's concept of "integral plurality" focuses on the interaction between normative orders, positing that state law is integrally constituted in relation to a plurality of social forms (1984). His work draws on Foucault's analysis of the emergence of modern law (Fitzpatrick 1983a: 176). Fitzpatrick argues that we need to look at law not simply as domination but also as constitutive of social life. Both state law and semiautonomous social fields are constituted in significant part by their interrelations with one another: the family and its legal order are shaped by the state, but the state in turn is shaped by the family and its legal order because each is a part of the other (Ibid.: 159). Here, Fitzpatrick makes the turn from seeing the semiautonomous social field as constituted by state law to seeing state law shaped by its constituent normative orders and vice versa.

In Fitzpatrick's theory, state law takes identity from and derives support from other social forms, but these forms both support and oppose state law. Bourgeois legality, for example, depends on social forms such as the prison and capitalist labor relations that both support and undermine it. The prison is a condition of the existence of bourgeois legality, since prison serves both as the ultimate enforcer of law and as an example of a pervasive disciplinary power that typifies modern society, yet it cannot itself incorporate bourgeois legality in its functioning. It coerces outside this structure while leaving bourgeois free to be equal and universal (1984: 116).

Integral relations of mutual support between law and other social forms tend toward convergence as elements of law are elements of the other social forms and vice versa. For example, science is incorporated into elements of law, and law supports and reinforces science: the two take identity from each other in positively supportive ways (Fitzpatrick, 1984). Similarly, custom, when penetrated by state law, changes its nature fundamentally and becomes part of state law. In his words, "Custom supports law but law transforms the elements of custom that it appropriates into its own image and likeness. Law, in turn, supports other social forms but becomes, in the process, part of the other forms" (1984: 9). Not a unitary phenomenon, law is constituted by a plurality of social forms. Since law is constituted in relations of opposition and support to other social forms, however, there is a gap between law and other social forms that cannot be bridged; law depends on these opposed social forms. Integral pluralism is part of a dialectic of power and counter power. Fitzpatrick concludes, that "law is the unsettled resultant of relations with a plurality of social forms and in this law's identity is constantly and inherently subject to challenge and change" (Ibid.: 138).

Henry's work on law in collectives and cooperatives in Britain further develops this model of integral plurality (1983; 1985; 1987; see also Nelken, 1986). Henry argues that the relations between state law and other normative orders now appear very complicated, requiring attention to history, human agency, local contexts, and culture (1985: 315). Conflicting normative orders, such as those of the cooperative and the capitalist state, may challenge and oppose each other, both by outright rejection (when the state prohibits conflicting normative orders, for example), or by accepting and recognizing the autonomy of a separate normative order within that sphere. Thus, the law refuses to intervene in the cooperative because some matters are seen as the private concern of the co-op (Ibid.: 314). The members of the cooperative, on the other hand, can reject and to some extent undermine capitalist legality. Henry proposes a dialectical model, in which "[a]lternative institutions and their associated normative orders do not work transformations on capitalist structures and rule systems but instead interact with them in a dialectical way such that both the alternative system and the capitalist order are vulnerable to incremental reformulations" (Ibid.: 324). Drawing on Giddens' analysis of structure and action according to which action shapes structure and structures constrain and enable actions, an integrated theory that provides some space for individual actions to "make a difference," even for the powerless, Henry adds the dimension of individual action to Fitzpatrick's model of integral plurality. Individuals within communitarian organizations, he argues, are likely to interject communitarian elements into capitalist society as long as they are not totally marginal or separated from that society. Thus, the impact of communitarian organizations within capitalist society may be greater than that of marginal collectives (Ibid.).

Of particular interest, yet also particularly unstudied, is the way constituent normative orders shape state law. Yet, this describes how groups in power attempt to control state law and shape it to their ends at the same time as they are limited by the plural normative orders of which they are a part. Careful empirical work such as Henry's study of workplace discipline (1983) or Silbey's and Bittner's study of consumer protection reveal the importance of constituent normative orders within regulatory activities (1980–81, 1982). Yngvesson's ethnographic studies on local-level legal processes in American courts demonstrate how court clerks constitute the legality of the lower courts through their understanding of community norms of justice (1985, 1988). Sarat and Felstiner, listening to the way lawyers talk to clients, hear the construction of a vision of legality for the client which seems to reflect the local normative order of lawyers (1986).

David Sugarman develops the mutually constitutive understanding of state law and nonstate normative orders in his edited volume, *Legality, Ideology, and the State* (1983). State law is itself plural: it contains procedures for establishing facts, general substantive rules that guide citizen action, enforcement of judgments, provisions for physical punishment, modes of appeal, insurance against loss, ideological and symbolic dimensions, and the ability to provide a degree of private ordering through facilitative laws (1983: 230–231). Law and legal institutions mean different things to different people. There are tensions between local and central regulation, indigenous and state conceptions of legality, discretionary practices and enforcement, and arbitration and other extralegal mechanisms for dispute resolution. In eighteenth and nineteenth century Britain, there were struggles between local courts, special courts, and the formal state system of courts. Arthurs demonstrates these struggles in British administrative law (1985) and Provine describes analogous debates over local lay judges in the United States (1986).

Sugarman explores the plurality of law through his discussion of facilitative law, law that functions not by imposing obligations but by providing individuals with facilities for realizing their wishes through conferring legal powers on them, such as the powers to construct marriages, wills, contracts, companies, trusts, and so forth (1983). This law permits private law-making and affords the opportunity to bypass the legal obligations of the state. Facilitative laws simultaneously define and constrain permissible conduct and enable individuals to expand or contract their autonomy, thus promoting, qualifying, or subverting state policy (Sugarman, 1983: 217).

In his review of this book, Freeman sees the move in British critical legal scholarship toward seeing law as pluralistic—as having many sides and many determinations—as analogous to the American critical legal studies' move to deconstruction (1986: 840). Freeman claims that, in an effort to avoid simple reductionist views of law as the product of the ruling class, British critical legal studies scholars argue that law is pluralistic just as Americans argue that it is indeterminant and incoherent. Yet, Freeman concludes, pluralism, just as deconstruction, ultimately ends in immobilization, since if everything is complex and variable, just as if everything is a matter of interpretation, how can one say anything?

The turn toward a dialectic analysis of the relations between plural legal orders, particularly between state law and other normative orders, comes primarily from work within the new legal pluralism: that is, from those who have used the model of legal pluralism to understand legality in the First World. Yet, this dialectic analysis is equally fruitful for a reanalysis of classic legal pluralism materials, as the example of the reanalysis of customary law demonstrates. In none of these analyses, however, is there an implication that the power relations between plural legal orders are equal: the theme instead is the penetration and dominance of state law and its subversion at the margins.

V. PLURAL LEGALITIES AND LOCAL KNOWLEDGE

Another aspect of legal pluralism is the study of law as a system of meanings, a cultural code for interpreting the world. Geertz, a preeminent spokesman for this perspective, has developed an interpretive view of legal pluralism, one richly evocative of cultural diversity (1983). Law is understood as a system of symbols, of meanings. Unlike the research tradition discussed above, there is little attention here to relations of power or to the political economy of legal pluralism, but there is a substantial interest in history and context.

In *Local Knowledge*, Geertz urges a focus on structures of meaning, especially on the symbols and systems of symbols through whose agency such structures are formed, communicated, and imposed, in the comparative analysis of law as in the comparative analysis of myth, ritual, ideology, art, or classification systems (1983: 182). In his words, . . . " 'law' here, there, or anywhere, is part of a distinctive manner of imagining the real (Ibid.: 184)." He conceives of law as a species of social imagination. Starting with basic words or concepts, he compares the "legal sensibilities" of three cultures, using these words to orient the reader to different senses of law. This is a hermeneutic project; the words are keys to understanding the social institutions and cultural formulations that surround them and give them meaning (1983: 187). For example, in the Islamic world he discusses the concept *haqq* which means reality, truth, or validity, and in various permutations and combinations, God, fact, actuality, right, duty, claim, obligation, fair, valid, just, or proper (1983: 188). In Islamic legal sensibility, to determine the empirical situation is to determine the jural principle. Facts, in other words, are normative; there is no fact/law dichotomy. Facts are estimates of character assumed by background and demeanor as much as they are weightings of notarized documents presented (Rosen, 1980–81: 231; see also Messick, 1986).[4] Because the law itself is certain and comprehensive, although what is just and unjust is not, it is in the recounting of incident and situa-

[4] The *qadi* or judge takes into account the relationship between the parties, their social background, each person's location in the system of ordering, their kin connections, residence, and occupation as evidence as to the likely way that the person acted in any situation (Rosen, 1980–81: 229). The standard of conduct to which a person is held depends on who he or she is.

tion that value balancing comes in. To achieve the proper recounting of a situation, the court needs morally upright people who can testify about cases. In classical times these people were chosen by the *qadi* and appeared before the court over and over (Geertz, 1983: 191–192). Geertz argues that even in secular courts, one can see the lingering influence of the notion of the virtuous witness speaking moral truth in the persistence of certified truth bringers and other examples of normative witnessing in these courts (Ibid.: 193).[5] A hermeneutic approach applied to legally plural situations describes sets of meanings joined together in a "polyglot discourse" (Ibid.: 226). These views do not cohere into a systematic position, but bounce off one another. This means viewing the situation as one of several, incommensurate local expressions of legal sensibilities. The diversity and mingling of legal sensibilities is not likely to end, in Geertz's opinion, but may increase; it is something that Indonesians and other Third World peoples live with as they try to construct principled lives, as do many First World peoples as well.

In a recent paper that develops these themes, Santos asserts that legal pluralism is the key concept in a postmodern view of law (1987: 297). Using the metaphor of the map to discuss law, he suggests that law is a system of signs that represents/distorts reality through the mechanisms of scale, projection, and symbolization. As do maps, different legal orders have different scales, different forms of projection and centering, different systems of symbolization. Thus, another way of discussing legal pluralism is to talk about the different symbolic systems inscribed in each normative order.

Santos delineates two ideal-typical sign systems by means of which law symbolizes reality. The first he labels the Homeric style, in which (to shorten his description) everyday reality is described in abstract and formal terms through conventional cognitive and referential signs. A second, the biblical style, presupposes an image-based legality in which (again condensed) interactions are inscribed in multilayered contexts and described in figurative and informal terms through iconic, emotive, and expressive signs (1987: 295). These styles are perpetually in tension, with variations in dominance during particular historical periods. He suggests that the modern state legal order is predominantly Homeric. In Cape Verde, the tension between these two types of legal symbolization appears in the system of popular justice, which fuses both customary law and state law (Ibid.: 296). The tension crops up in the way judges settle disputes: some judges adopt one, some the other, some shift from one to another depending on the case and their familiarity with it. He concludes that the legal pluralism he is

[5] Hayden provides an analysis of forms of speaking and consideration of facts in Indian caste panchayts, government courts, and United States courts (1984; 1987).

describing is not the legal pluralism of traditional legal anthropology (what I have called classic legal pluralism) but (Ibid.: 297–298)

> rather the conception of different legal spaces superimposed, interpenetrated, and mixed in our minds as much as in our actions. . . . Our legal life is constituted by an intersection of different legal orders, that is, by *interlegality*. Interlegality is the phenomenological counterpart of legal pluralism and that is why it is the second key concept of a postmodern conception of law.

Bentley develops the culturally constructive role of law in his analysis of disputing among the Maranao in the Philippines (1984). He argues that disputing is an expression of competing visions of social reality, an arena for constructing and expressing alternative visions of the world. In the society he studied, which combines custom (*adat*), Islamic law, and Philippine civil and criminal law, the manipulation of the different legal systems is part of the effort to construct an interpretation of truth in the world in a way that others will accept. He argues that the complexity and fluidity of the arenas of contest appears to enhance the range of manipulation and contest. In the same vein, O'Connor makes the intriguing argument that law is an indigenous social theory, using Thai ethnography (1980).

Foucault's conceptions of the forms of power and discipline of modern society provide yet another take on legal pluralism (1979), a perspective that is being developed by Fitzpatrick (1983b). If the nature of law that has emerged in the wake of capitalism is fundamentally different from that of pre-capitalist societies in what Foucault refers to as its "disciplinary technologies"—productive forms of power such as the timetable, the cell, and the panopticon—the encounter between these forms of power and discipline and those of noncapitalist societies takes on new meaning. Power, in Foucault's theory, is not simply based on prohibition but also on the positive formation of norms and shaping of individuals to fit these norms (Fitzpatrick, 1983b: 50). Law gives shape to institutions that supervise rather than contain; it creates new technologies of discipline that stretch from the prison to the factory to the military to the school (Fitzpatrick, 1983b; Foucault, 1979).

In an intriguing illustration of the meaning of these shifts in forms of power and discipline, Pospisil describes the dismay of the Kapauku Papuans at the use of jail as a punishment, one that to them seems extraordinarily severe since it separates the individual from the essential cooperation of soul and body, the linkage between one's actions and one's own free decisions (1979: 141). In their words, in jail, "The man's vital substance deteriorates and the man dies" (Ibid.: 142). Indeed, the Dutch colonial administrators found that Kapauku tended to pine and die if imprisoned long, despite the administrators' conviction that prison had a positive, civilizing effect.

VI. CONCLUSIONS AND DIRECTIONS FOR FUTURE RESEARCH

What are the implications of focusing on legal pluralism for future sociolegal research? My review of this literature suggests at least five ways in which viewing sociolegal phenomena as plural expands the research framework. First, a concern with legal pluralism moves away from the ideology of legal centralism—the predisposition to think of all legal ordering as rooted in state law—and suggests attention to other forms of ordering and their interaction with state law. It highlights competing, contesting, and sometimes contradictory orders outside state law and their mutually constitutive relations to state law.

Second, this perspective requires a shift away from an essentialist definition of law to an historical understanding since any situation of legal pluralism develops over time through the dialectic between legal systems, each of which both constitutes and reconstitutes the other in some way. Defining the essence of law or custom is less valuable than situating these concepts in particular sets of relations between particular legal orders in particular historical contexts. Plural normative orders, once created, can persist with tenacity justifying themselves by appeals to tradition, or they can be radically reformed in the contest between opposing orders, a process exemplified by the creation of customary law in colonial societies.[6] Or they may change incrementally through small additions, subtractions, and reinterpretations. The papers from a recent conference, Ethnohistorical Models for the Evolution of Law within Specific Societies, provide rich descriptions of these historical processes of change and transformation in legally plural societies (Starr and Collier, 1988).[7]

Third, viewing situations as legally plural leads to an examination of the cultural or ideological nature of law and systems of normative ordering. Rather than focusing on the particular rules applied in situations of dispute, this perspective examines the ways social groups conceive of ordering, of social relationships, and of ways of determining truth and justice. Law is not simply a set of rules exercising coercive power, but a system of thought by which certain forms of relations come to seem natural and taken for granted, modes of thought that are inscribed in institutions that exercise some coercion in support of their categories and theories of explanation.

Fourth, examining the plurality of legal situations facilitates

---

[6] Starr and Collier describe this process in terms of "historical struggles between native elites and their colonial and postcolonial rulers" (1987: 368).

[7] As the twenty participants in this 1985 conference concluded, societies may be characterized as having multiple legal systems that are not autonomous but negotiated in relation to an encompassing political structure and particular assymetrical relations of power (Starr and Collier, 1987: 371; see further, Starr and Collier, 1989).

the move away from an exclusive focus on situations of dispute to an analysis of ordering in nondispute situations (see further, Collier, 1973; Engel, 1980). Holleman suggests the study of "troubleless cases" rather than situations of trouble, arguing that disputes are exceptional events and therefore misleading guides to the nature of ordering (1986).[8] The study of facilitative law and historical studies of legal change similarly move away from an exclusive focus on dispute.[9]

Fifth, the dialectical analysis of relations among normative orders provides a framework for understanding the dynamics of the imposition of law and of resistance to law, for examining the interactive relationship between dominant and subordinate groups or classes. It offers a way of thinking about the possibilities of domination through law and of the limits to this domination, pointing to areas in which individuals can and do resist. This is a difficult area for research. On the one hand, attention to law in its ideological role points to its power to construct modes of thinking and implicit understandings as a central aspect of its power. On the other hand, attention to plural orders examines limits to the ideological power of state law: areas where it does not penetrate and alternative forms of ordering persist, groups that incorporate the symbols of state law but oppose it, perhaps becoming expert in its intricacies and forms of power as in colonial India, and situations in which other forms of ordering are so embedded in the administration of law that they subvert its actual implementation. Here, of course, we are on the familiar terrain of plea bargaining, courtroom workgroups and agency capture, but instead of explaining why the law on the books and the law in action differ according to gap theory, we could understand this well-documented characteristic of legal life as one of plural legal orders within the courthouse, the police station, or the regulatory agency, some of which are organized around standards of community justice, others around rule-of-law standards, and others around the cultural predispositions of particular groups in power. Indeed, state law is itself plural. Despite efforts to root out pluralism such as attacks on "rough justice," on lay justices of the peace (Provine, 1986), and on police discretion, new plural orderings continually spring up. These plural orderings constitute state law.

[8] The Dutch tradition of the anthropology of law, which is premised on assumptions of legal pluralism, indicates the potential of an approach to sociolegal phenomena that looks at systems of ordering within arenas of social life such as the family, land tenure, inheritance, commercial transactions, and so forth, examining day-to-day peace rather than rare moments of trouble (Griffiths, 1986b). Griffiths suggests that perhaps the Anglo-American common law tradition leads British and American anthropologists to focus on moments of dispute rather than on systems of ordering embedded in the wider domain of uncontested social life (1986b; see also Ietswaart, 1986).

[9] As Starr and Collier point out, the dispute paradigm has become too normative and positivistic for many researchers, leading to a turn to historical research as a way of considering legal change (1987: 367).

However, for some problems the concept has limitations. One is in the analysis of change within a single social field and a second is in the attention to the specific characteristics of particular social locations. A legal pluralist analysis tends to emphasize changes that occur through interactions between social fields but not those taking place within a social field. It is likely to miss the way a particular social field is gradually reshaped by a variety of ideological and political forces both within and outside it. For example, in their study of the impact of European missionaries on South Africa during the colonial period, Comaroff and Comaroff argue that the missionaries introduced new concepts of time, space, work, personhood, and so forth, at a variety of particular locations throughout the country over a period of years, gradually shifting the consciousness of the Africans they encountered and converted and paving the way for the colonial conquest of these people despite the missionaries' efforts to oppose it (1986).[10] Although this historical shift in consciousness could be described in terms of legal pluralism—the interaction between the African and the missionary legal orders—the concept tends not to highlight the intricate relations between ways of thinking and knowing within a social field, the ways they change over time, and the ways symbols seep into and out of legal systems in large cities, small towns, and provincial places.

Moreover, the concept of legal pluralism can press too quickly toward analyses of systems to the neglect of the variation in particular local places. It is difficult to understand the particularity of small situations and the interaction of large systems at the same time. Thinking of legal pluralism seems likely to get us out of the courtroom and the lawyers's office, but once outside, legal pluralist analyses could lead away from detailed examinations of particular local places. To examine the ever-changing conceptions of the normal and the cultural and the constant struggle of interpretation of the symbols and forms of legality in small places and large legal systems at the same time is, at the least, challenging.

In sum, the new legal pluralism has opened up questions of dialectic and resistance that build on the sophisticated theoretical traditions and rich ethnography of classic legal pluralism. There is much in these traditions that could serve as the basis for exciting new directions in law and society research. However, the concept requires refinement as we work to develop it, including attention to the specificity of each situation, to the variations in minute so-

---

10 By introducing new symbols such as the moral worth of work, wealth, belief in free choice, liberal democracy, impersonal forms of regulation such as the clock, and conceptions of political authority as distinct from religious authority and power, the missionaries gradually transformed the taken-for-granted world of the Tswana people and, despite their explicit opposition to taking political power or fostering imperialist expansion, facilitated the political absorption of the Tswana into the colonial state (Comaroff and Comaroff, 1986; see also Comaroff, 1985).

cial processes, and to the complex texture of ideological meanings formed within particular historical situations. This is no small project.

SALLY ENGLE MERRY is Associate Professor of Anthropology at Wellesley College, Wellesley, Mass. She is the author of a monograph on urban crime, *Urban Danger: Life in a Neighborhood of Strangers*, and numerous articles on legal ideology and legal consciousness, mediation in American society and in cross-cultural perspective, and urban social order. She is currently completing a manuscript describing the people who bring interpersonal problems to court and the nature of their legal consciousness.

REFERENCES

ABEL, Richard L. (1982) *The Politics of Informal Justice*, 2 Vols. New York: Academic Press.

——(1979a) "Western Courts in Non-Western Settings: Patterns of Court Use in Colonial and Neo-Colonial Africa," in Sandra B. Burman and Barbara E. Harrell-Bond (eds.), *The Imposition of Law*. New York: Academic Press, pp. 167–200.

——(1979b) "The Rise of Capitalism and the Transformation of Disputing: from Confrontation over Honor to Competition for Property," 27 *UCLA Law Review* 223.

ADEWOYE, Omoniyi (1986) "Legal Practice in Ibadan, 1904–1960," 24 *Journal of Legal Pluralism* 57.

ALLOTT, A.N., and G.R. WOODMAN, (eds.). (1985) *People's Law and State Law: The Bellagio Papers*. Dordrecht: Foris.

ARTHURS, H.W. (1985) *Without the Law: Administrative Justice and Legal Pluralism in Mid 19th-Century England*. Toronto; University of Toronto Press.

AUERBACH, Jerold S. (1983) *Justice Without Law?* New York: Oxford University Press.

BENDA-BECKMANN, Franz von (1981) "Some Comments on the Problems of Comparing the Relationship between Traditional and State Systems of Administration of Justice in Africa and Indonesia," 19 *Journal of Legal Pluralism* 165.

——(1979) *Property in Social Continuity: Continuity and Change in the Maintenance of Property Relationships through Time in Minangkabau, West Sumatra*. The Hague: Nijhoff.

BENDA-BECKMANN, Keebet von (1981) "Forum Shopping and Shopping Forums—Dispute Settlement in a Minangkabau Village in West Sumatra," 19 *Journal of Legal Pluralism* 117.

BENDA-BECKMANN, Keebet von, and Fons STRIJBOSCH (eds.) (1986) *Anthropology of Law in the Netherlands: Essays in Legal Pluralism*. Dordrecht and Cinnaminson: Foris.

BENTLEY, G. Carter (1984) "Hermeneutics and World Construction in Maranao Disputing," 11 *American Ethnologist* 642.

BENTSI-ENCHILL, Kwamena (1969) "The Colonial Heritage of Legal Pluralism," 1 *Zambia Law Journal* 1.

BOSSY, John (ed.) (1983) *Disputes and Settlements: Law and Human Relations in the West*. Cambridge: Cambridge University Press.

BRIGHAM, John (1987) "Right, Rage, and Remedy: Forms of Law in Political Discourse," in *Studies in American Political Development*. New Haven: Yale University Press.

BUCKLE, Leonard, and Suzann R. THOMAS-BUCKLE (1982) "Doing unto Others: Dispute and Dispute-Processing in an Urban American Neighborhood," in Roman Tomasic and Malcolm Feeley (eds.), *Neighborhood Justice*. New York: Longman.

BURMAN, Sandra, and Barbara E. HARRELL-BOND (eds.) (1979) *The Imposition of Law*. New York: Academic Press.

CHANOCK, Martin (1985) *Law, Custom, and Social Order: The Colonial Experience in Malawi and Zambia*. Cambridge: Cambridge University Press.

COLLIER, Jane (1973) *Law and Social Change in Zinacantan*. Stanford, CA: Stanford University Press.

COLSON, Elizabeth (1976) "From Chief's Court to Local Court: The Evolution of Local Courts in Southern Zambia," in M.J. Aronoff (ed.), *Freedom and Constraint*. Amsterdam: Van Gorcum, pp. 15–29.

COMAROFF, Jean (1985) *Body of Power: Spirit of Resistance: Culture and History of a South African People*. Chicago: University of Chicago Press.

COMAROFF, Jean, and John L. COMAROFF (1986) "Christianity and Colonialism in South Africa," 13 *American Ethnologist* 1.

COMAROFF, John L., and Simon ROBERTS (1981) *Rules and Processes*. Chicago: University of Chicago Press.

DIAMOND, Stanley (1973) "The Rule of Law versus the Order of Custom," in Donald Black and Maureen Mileski (eds.), *The Social Organization of Law*, New York: Seminar Press, Pp. 318–344. Reprinted from (1971) 38 *Social Research* 42.

EHRLICH, E. (1913) *Fundamental Principles of the Sociology of Law*, trans. W.L. Moll. Cambridge: Harvard University Press.

ENGEL, David M. (1987) "Law, Time, and Community," 21 *Law & Society Review* 605.

——— (1984) "The Oven Bird's Song: Insiders, Outsiders, and Personal Injuries in an American Community," 18 *Law & Society Review* 549.

——— (1980) "Legal Pluralism in an American Community: Perspectives on a Civil Trial Court," 3 *American Bar Foundation Research Journal* 425.

FITZPATRICK, Peter (1985) "Review Article: Is it Simple to be a Marxist in Legal Anthropology?," *Modern Law Review* 472.

——— (1984) "Law and Societies," 22 *Osgoode Hall Law Journal* 115.

——— (1983a) "Law, Plurality, and Underdevelopment," in D. Sugarman, (ed.), *Legality, Ideology, and the State*. London: Academic Press, pp. 159–183.

——— (1983b) "Marxism and Legal Pluralism," 1 *Australian Journal of Law and Society* 45.

——— (1980) *Law and State in Papua New Guinea*. London: Academic Press.

FORER, Norman (1979) "The Imposed Wardship of American Indian Tribes: A Case Study of the Prairie Band Potawatomi," in Sandra B. Burman and Barbara E. Harrell-Bond (eds.), *The Imposition of Law*. New York: Academic Press, pp. 89–114.

FOUCAULT, Michel (1979) *Discipline and Punish: The Birth of the Prison*. New York: Vintage.

FREEMAN, Alan (1986) "The Politics of Truth: On Sugarman's *Legality, Ideology, and the State*," 1986 *American Bar Foundation Research Journal* 829.

GALANTER, Marc (1981) "Justice in Many Rooms: Courts, Private Ordering, and Indigenous Law," 19 *Journal of Legal Pluralism and Unofficial Law* 1.

GARDNER, James A. (1980) *Legal Imperialism: American Lawyers and Foreign Aid in Latin America*. Madison, Wis.: University of Wisconsin Press.

GEERTZ, Clifford (1983) *Local Knowledge: Further Essays in Interpretive Anthropology*. New York: Basic Books.

GORDON, Robert J., and Mervyn J. MEGGITT (1985) *Law and Order in the New Guinea Highlands: Encounters with Enga*. Hanover: University Press of New England (for University of Vermont).

GREENHOUSE, Carol (1982) "Nature is to Culture as Praying is to Suing: Legal Pluralism in an American Suburb," 20 *Journal of Legal Pluralism* 17.

GRIFFITHS, John (1986a) "What is Legal Pluralism?," 24 *Journal of Legal Pluralism* 1.

——— (1986b) "Recent Anthropology of Law in the Netherlands and its Historical Background," in Keebet von Benda-Beckman and Fons Strijbosch (eds.), *Anthropology of Law in the Netherlands: Essays in Legal Pluralism*. Dordrecht and Cinnaminson: Foris.

——— (1985) "Introduction," A. Allott and G. Woodman (eds.), *People's Law and State Law: The Bellagio Papers*. Dordrecht: Foris, pp. 13–20.

GURVITCH, Georges (1947) *The Sociology of Law*. London: Routledge and Kegan Paul.

HARRINGTON, Christine (1985) *Shadow Justice: The Ideology and Institutionalization of Alternatives to Court*. Westport, Conn: Greenwood Press.

HARRINGTON, Christine, and Sally Engle MERRY (1988) "Ideological Production: The Making of Community Mediation," 22 *Law &Society Review*.

HAYDEN, Robert M. (1987) "Turn-taking, Overlap, and the Task at Hand: Ordering Speaking Turns in Legal Settings," 14 *American Ethnologist* 251.

——— (1984) "A Note on Caste Panchayats and Government Courts in India: Different Kinds of Stages for Different Kinds of Performances," 22 *Journal of Legal Pluralism* 43.

HENRY, Stuart (1987) "The Construction and Deconstruction of Social Control: Thoughts on the Discursive Production of State Law and Private Justice," in J. Lowman, R. Menzies, and T. Palys (eds.), *Transcarceration*. Farnborough: Gower.

——— (1985) "Community Justice, Capitalist Society, and Human Agency: The Dialectics of Collective Law in the Cooperative," 19 *Law & Society Review* 303.

——— (1983) *Private Justice*. Boston: Routledge and Kegan Paul.

HOLLEMAN, J.F. (1986) "Trouble-Cases and Trouble-Less Cases in the Study of Customary Law and Legal Reform," in Keebet von Benda-Beckman and Fons Strijbosch (eds.), *Anthropology of Law in the Netherlands: Essays in Legal Pluralism*. Dordrecht and Cinnaminson: Foris. Reprinted from 7 *Law & Society Review* 585.

HOOKER, M.B. (1975) *Legal Pluralism: An Introduction to Colonial and Neo-Colonial Laws*. Oxford: Clarendon Press.

IETSWAART, Heleen (1986) "Review of Keebet von Benda-Beckmann and Fons Strijbosch (eds.) *Anthropology of Law in the Netherlands: Essays in Legal Pluralism*," 24 *Journal of Legal Pluralism* 161.

JUST, Peter (1986) "Let the Evidence Fit the Crime: Evidence, Law, and Sociological 'Truth' among the Dou Donggo," 13 *American Ethnologist* 43.

KIDDER, Robert L. (1979) "Toward an Integrated Theory of Imposed Law," in Sandra B. Burman and Barbara E. Harrell-Bond (eds.), *The Imposition of Law*. New York: Academic Press, pp. 289–306.

——— (1974) "Formal Litigation and Professional Insecurity: Legal Entrepreneurship in South India," 9 *Law & Society Review* 11.

LAM, M. (1985) "The Imposition of Anglo-American Land Tenure Law on Hawaiians," 23 *Journal of Legal Pluralism* 103.

LYNCH, Dennis O. (1983) "Hundred Months of Solitude: Myth and Reality in Law and Development?," 1983 *American Bar Foundation Research Journal* 223.

MACAULAY, Stewart (1987) "Images of Law in Everyday Life: The Lessons of School, Entertainment and Spectator Sports," 21 *Law & Society Review* 185.

——— (1986) "Private Government," Disputes Processing Research Program Working Paper 1983–86. Madison, Wis.: University of Wisconsin Law School. Reprinted in (1986) *Law and the Social Sciences*, ed. by Leon Lipson and Stanton Wheeler. New York: Russell Sage Foundation.

——— (1963) "Non-contractual Relations in Business: A Preliminary Study," 28 *American Sociological Review* 55.

MALINOWSKI, Bronislaw (1926) *Crime and Custom in a Savage Society*. Paterson, N.J.: Littlefield, Adams.

MARCUS, George E., and Michael M.J. FISHER (1986) *Anthropology as Cultural Critique: An Experimental Moment in the Human Sciences*. Chicago: University of Chicago Press.

MASSELL, Gregory (1968) "Law as an Instrument of Revolutionary Change in a Traditional Milieu: The Case of Soviet Central Asia," 2 *Law & Society Review* 179.

MERRY, Sally Engle (1986) "Everyday Understandings of the Law in Working-class America," 13 *American Ethnologist* 253.

——— (1982) "The Articulation of Legal Spheres," in Margaret Jean Hay and Marcia Wright (eds.), *African Women and the Law: Historical Perspectives.* Boston: Boston University African Studies Center, pp. 68–89.

——— (1979) "Going to Court: Strategies of Dispute Management in an American Urban Neighborhood," 13 *Law & Society Review* 891.

MESCHIEVITZ, C.S., and Marc GALANTER (1982) "In Search of Nyaya Panchayats: The Politics of a Moribund Institution," in R. Abel (ed.), *The Politics of Informal Justice: Comparative Studies.* New York: Academic Press.

MESSICK, Brinkley (1986) "The Mufti, the Text, and the World: Legal Interpretation in Yemen," 21 *Man* n.s. 102.

MOORE, Sally Falk (1986a) *Social Facts and Fabrications: Customary Law on Kilimanjaro, 1880–1980.* Cambridge: Cambridge University Press.

——— (1986b) "Legal Systems of the World: An Introductory Guide to Classifications, Typological Interpretations, and Bibliographic Resources," in Leon Lipson and Stanton Wheeler (eds.). *Law and the Social Sciences.* New York: Russell Sage Foundation.

——— (1977) "Individual Interests and Organizational Structures: Dispute Settlements as 'Events of Articulation,'" in I. Hamnett (ed.), *Social Anthropology and Law.* New York: Academic Press.

——— (1973) "Law and Social Change: The Semi-Autonomous Social Field as an Appropriate Subject of Study," 7 *Law & Society Review.* 719.

NADER, Laura (ed.)(1980) *No Access to Law.* New York: Academic Press.

NADER, Laura (1984) "The Recurrent Dialectic Between Legality and Its Alternatives," 132 *University of Pennsylvania Law Review* 621.

NADER, Laura, and Harry F. TODD (eds.) (1978) *The Disputing Process–Law in Ten Societies.* New York: Columbia University Press.

NELKEN, David (1986) "Review Essay: Beyond the Study of 'Law and Society'? Henry's *Private Justice* and O'Hagen's *The End of the Law?,*" 1986 *American Bar Foundation Research Journal* 323.

O'CONNOR, R.A. (1980) "Law as Indigenous Social Theory," 8 *American Ethnologist* 223.

OKOTH-OGENDO, H.W.O. (1979) "The Imposition of Property Law in Kenya," in Sandra B. Burman and Barbara E. Harrell-Bond (eds.), *The Imposition of Law.* New York: Academic Press, pp. 147–166.

POSPISIL, Leopold (1981) "Modern and Traditional Administration of Justice in New Guinea," 19 *Journal of Legal Pluralism* 93.

——— (1979) "Legally Induced Culture Change in New Guinea," in Sandra B. Burman and Barbara E. Harrell-Bond (eds.), *The Imposition of Law.* New York: Academic Press, pp. 127–146.

——— (1971) *The Anthropology of Law: A Comparative Theory of Law.* New York: Harper and Row.

PROVINE, Marie Doris (1986) *Judging Credentials: Non-lawyer Judges and the Politics of Professionalism.* Chicago: University of Chicago Press.

RANGER, Terence (1983) "The Invention of Tradition in Colonial Africa," in Eric Hobsbawm and Terence Ranger (eds.), *The Invention of Tradition.*

ROBERTS, Simon (1986) "Book Review: A.N. Allott and Gordon R. Woodman, *People's Law and State Law: The Bellagio Papers,*" 24 *Journal of Legal Pluralism* 171.

ROSEN, Lawrence (1980–81) "Equity and Discretion in a Modern Islamic Legal System," 15 *Law & Society Review* 217.

RUFFINI, J.L. (1978) "Disputing over Livestock in Sardinia," in L. Nader and H. Todd (eds.), *The Disputing Process–Law in Ten Societies.* New York: Columbia University Press.

SALAMONE, Frank A. (1983) "The Clash Between Indigenous, Islamic, Colonial and Post-Colonial Law in Nigeria," 21 *Journal of Legal Pluralism* 15.

SALAS, Louis (1983) "The Emergence and Decline of the Cuban Popular Tribunals," 17 *Law & Society Review* 587.

SANTOS, Boaventura De Sousa (1987) "Law: A Map of Misreading; Toward a Postmodern Conception of Law," 14 *Journal of Law and Society* 279.

——— (1982) "Law and Community: The Changing Nature of State Power in

896 LEGAL PLURALISM

Late Capitalism," in Richard Abel. (ed.), *The Politics of Informal Justice*, Vol. I. New York: Academic Press.

——— (1977) "The Law of the Oppressed: The Construction and Reproduction of Legality in Pasagarda," 12 *Law & Society Review* 5.

SARAT, Austin (1988) "The 'New Formalism' in Disputing and Dispute Processing," 21 *Law & Society Review* 695.

SARAT, Austin, and William FELSTINER (1986) "Law and Strategy in the Divorce Lawyer's Office," 20 *Law & Society Review* 93.

SCHEINGOLD, Stuart A. (1974) *The Politics of Rights: Lawyers, Public Policy, and Political Change*. New Haven, Conn.: Yale University Press.

SILBEY, Susan S. (1980–81) "Case Processing: Consumer Protection in an Attorney General's Office," 15 *Law & Society Review* 849.

SILBEY, Susan S., and Egon BITTNER (1982) "The Availability of Law," 4 *Law and Policy* 399.

SILLIMAN, G. Sidney (1985) "A Political Analysis of the Philippines' Katarungang Pambarangay System of Informal Justice through Mediation," 19 *Law & Society Review* 279.

SNYDER, Francis G. (1981a) *Capitalism and Legal Change: An African Transformation*. New York: Academic Press.

——— (1981b) "Colonialism and Legal Form: The Creation of 'Customary Law' in Senegal," 19 *Journal of Legal Pluralism* 49.

——— (1980) "Law and Development in the Light of Dependency Theory," 14 *Law & Society Review* 723.

SPENCE, Jack (1978) "Institutionalizing Neighborhood Courts: Two Chilean Experiences," 13 *Law & Society Review* 139.

STARR, June (1978) *Dispute and Settlement in Rural Turkey* Leiden: E.J. Brill.

STARR, June, and Jane F. COLLIER (1989) *History and Power in the Study of Law: New Directions in Legal Anthropology*, Ithaca, N.Y.: Cornell University Press.

——— (1987) "Historical Studies of Legal Change," 28 *Current Anthropology* 367.

STARR, June, and Jonathan POOL (1974) "The Impact of a Legal Revolution in Rural Turkey," 8 *Law & Society Review* 533.

STRIJBOSCH, F. (1985) "The Concept of Pela and its Social Significance in the Community of Moluccan Immigrants in the Netherlands," 23 *Journal of Legal Pluralism* 177.

SUGARMAN, David (1983) "Law, Economy, and the State in England, 1750–1914: Some Major Issues," in David Sugarman (ed.), *Legality, Ideology and the State*. London and New York: Academic Press, pp. 213–267.

TRUBEK, David, and Marc GALANTER (1974) "Scholars in Self-Estrangement," 1974 *Wisconsin Law Review* 1062.

VAN DEN BERGH, G.C.J.J. et al. (1980) *Staphorst en zijn Gerichten* (Staphorst and its Popular Tribunals). Amsterdam: Boom Meppel.

WESTERMARK, George D. (1986) "Court is an Arrow: Legal Pluralism in Papua New Guinea," 25 *Ethnology* 131.

WOLF, Eric R. (1982) *Europe and the People Without History*. Berkeley: University of California Press.

WOODMAN, Gordon R. (1987–88) "What is the Commission About?," 14 *Newsletter of the Commission on Folk Law and Legal Pluralism* 3.

YNGVESSON, Barbara (1988) "Private Nuisance, Public Crime: The Clerk, the Court, and the Construction of Order in a New England Town," 22 *Law & Society Review*.

——— (1985) "Legal Ideology and Community Justice in the Clerk's Office," 9 *Legal Studies Forum* 71.

[8]

Theory in Anthropology since the Sixties

SHERRY B. ORTNER

University of Michigan

Every year, around the time of the meetings of the American Anthropological Association, the *New York Times* asks a Big Name anthropologist to contribute an op-ed piece on the state of the field. These pieces tend to take a rather gloomy view. A few years ago, for example, Marvin Harris suggested that anthropology was being taken over by mystics, religious fanatics, and California cultists; that the meetings were dominated by panels on shamanism, witchcraft, and "abnormal phenomena"; and that "scientific papers based on empirical studies" had been willfully excluded from the program (Harris 1978). More recently, in a more sober tone, Eric Wolf suggested that the field of anthropology is coming apart. The sub-fields (and sub-sub-fields) are increasingly pursuing their specialized interests, losing contact with each other and with the whole. There is no longer a shared discourse, a shared set of terms to which all practitioners address themselves, a shared language we all, however idiosyncratically, speak (Wolf 1980).

The state of affairs does seem much as Wolf describes it. The field appears to be a thing of shreds and patches, of individuals and small coteries pursuing disjunctive investigations and talking mainly to themselves. We do not even hear stirring arguments any more. Although anthropology was never actually unified in the sense of adopting a single shared paradigm, there was at least a period when there were a few large categories of theoretical affiliation, a set of identifiable camps or schools, and a few simple epithets one could hurl at

This essay contains much of my own intellectual history. There will be no more appropriate context in which to thank my teachers, Frederica de Laguna, Clifford Geertz, and David Schneider for having turned me, for better or for worse, into an anthropologist. In addition, I wish to thank the following friends and colleagues for helpful contributions to the development of this essay: Nancy Chodorow, Salvatore Cucchiari, James Fernandez, Raymond Grew, Keith Hart, Raymond Kelly, David Kertzer, Robert Paul, Paul Rabinow, Joyce Riegelhaupt, Anton Weiler, and Harriet Whitehead. Parts of this work were presented at the Department of Anthropology, Princeton University; the Department of Social Anthropology, University of Stockholm; the Social Science History Seminar (founded and coordinated by Charles and Louise Tilly), University of Michigan; the Humanities Seminar, Stanford University; and the Seminar on Theory and Methods in Comparative Studies (coordinated by Neil Smelser) at the University of California, Berkeley. I received valuable comments and reactions in all of these contexts.

0010-4175/84/1709-0100 $2.50

one's opponents. Now there appears to be an apathy of spirit even at this level. We no longer call each other names. We are no longer sure of how the sides are to be drawn up, and of where we would place ourselves if we could identify the sides.

Yet as anthropologists we can recognize in all of this the classic symptoms of liminality—confusion of categories, expressions of chaos and antistructure. And we know that such disorder may be the breeding ground for a new and perhaps better order. Indeed, if one scrutinizes the present more closely, one may even discern within it the shape of the new order to come. That is what I propose to do in this article. I will argue that a new key symbol of theoretical orientation is emerging, which may be labeled "practice" (or "action" or "praxis"). This is neither a theory nor a method in itself, but rather, as I said, a symbol, in the name of which a variety of theories and methods are being developed. In order to understand the significance of this trend, however, we must go back at least twenty years and see where we started from, and how we got to where we are now.

Before launching this enterprise, however, it is important to specify its nature. This essay will be primarily concerned with the *relations* between various theoretical schools or approaches, both within periods of time, and across time. No single approach will be exhaustively outlined or discussed in itself; rather, various themes or dimensions of each will be highlighted insofar as they relate to the larger trends of thought with which I am concerned. Every anthropologist will probably find his or her favorite school oversimplified, if not outright distorted, insofar as I have choosen to emphasize features that do not correspond to what are normally taken, among the practitioners, to be its most important theoretical features. Thus readers seeking more exhaustive discussions of particular approaches, and/or discussions pursued from a point of view more interior to the approaches, will have to seek elsewhere. The concern here, again, is with elucidating relations.

THE SIXTIES: SYMBOL, NATURE, STRUCTURE

Although there is always some arbitrariness in choosing a starting point for any historical discussion, I have decided to begin in the early 1960s. For one thing, that is when *I* started in the field, and since I generally assume the importance of seeing any system, at least in part, from the actor's point of view, I might as well unite theory and practice from the outset. It is thus fully acknowledged that this discussion proceeds not from some hypothetical external point, but from the perspective of this particular actor moving through anthropology between 1960 and the present.

But actors always wish to claim universality for their particular experiences and interpretations. I would further suggest then that, in some relatively objective sense, there was in fact a major set of revolutions in anthropological theory, beginning in the early sixties. Indeed it appears that such revisionist upheaval was characteristic of many other fields in that era. In literary criticism, for example,

> by the 1960's a volatile mixture of linguistics, psychoanalysis and semiotics, structuralism, Marxist theory and reception aesthetics had begun to replace the older moral humanism. The literary text tended to move towards the status of phenomenon: a socio-psycho-culturo-linguistic and ideological event, arising from the offered competencies of language, the available taxonomies of narrative order, the permutations of genre, the sociological options of structural formation, the ideological constraints of the infra-structure. . . . [There was a] broad and contentious revisionist perception (Bradbury 1981:137).

In anthropology at the close of the fifties, the theoretical *bricoleur's* kit consisted of three major, and somewhat exhausted, paradigms—British structural-functionalism (descended from A. R. Radcliffe-Brown and Bronislaw Malinowski), American cultural and psychocultural anthropology (descended from Margaret Mead, Ruth Benedict, *et al.*), and American evolutionist anthropology (centered around Leslie White and Julian Steward, and having strong affiliations with archaeology). Yet it was also during the fifties that certain actors and cohorts central to our story were trained in each of these areas. They emerged at the beginning of the sixties with aggressive ideas about how to strengthen the paradigms of their mentors and ancestors, as well as with, apparently, much more combative stances vis-à-vis the other schools. It was this combination of new ideas and intellectual aggressiveness that launched the three movements with which this account begins: symbolic anthropology, cultural ecology, and structuralism.

Symbolic Anthropology

"Symbolic anthropology" as a label was never used by any of its main proponents in the formative period—say, 1963–66. Rather it was a shorthand tag (probably invented by the opposition), an umbrella for a number of rather diverse trends. Two of its major variants appear to have been independently invented, one by Clifford Geertz and his colleagues at the University of Chicago, and the other by Victor Turner at Cornell.[1] The important differences between the Geertzians and the Turnerians are probably not fully appreciated by those outside the symbolic anthropology scene. Whereas Geertz was primarily influenced by Max Weber (via Talcott Parsons), Turner was primarily influenced by Emile Durkheim. Further, Geertz clearly represents a transformation upon the earlier American anthropology concerned mainly with the operations of "culture," while Turner represents a transfor-

[1] For the discussion of the sixties and the seventies, I will for the most part invoke only the most representative figures and works. In an article of this length, many interesting developments must be by-passed. One important figure of this period who gets left by the wayside is Gregory Bateson (e.g., 1972), who, though himself clearly a powerful and original thinker, never really founded a major school in anthropology.

mation upon the earlier British anthropology concerned mainly with the operations of "society."

Geertz's most radical theoretical move (1973b) was to argue that culture is not something locked inside people's heads, but rather is embodied in public symbols, symbols through which the members of a society communicate their worldview, value-orientations, ethos, and all the rest to one another, to future generations—and to anthropologists. With this formulation, Geertz gave the hitherto elusive concept of culture a relatively fixed locus, and a degree of objectivity, that it did not have before. The focus on symbols was for Geertz and many others heuristically liberating: it told them where to find what they wanted to study. Yet the point about symbols was that they were ultimately vehicles for meanings; the study of symbols as such was never an end in itself. Thus, on the one hand, Geertzians[2] have never been particularly interested in distinguishing and cataloguing the varieties of symbolic types (signals, signs, icons, indexes, etcetera—see, in contrast, Singer 1980); nor, on the other hand (and in contrast with Turner to whom we will get in a moment), have they been particularly interested in the ways in which symbols perform certain practical operations in the social process—heal people through curing rites, turn boys and girls into men and women through initiation, kill people through sorcery—and so forth. Geertzians do not ignore these practical social effects, but such symbols have not been their primary focus of interest. Rather, the focus of Geertzian anthropology has consistently been the question of how symbols shape the ways social actors see, feel, and think about the world, or, in other words, how symbols operate as vehicles of "culture."

It is further worth noting, in anticipation of the discussion of structuralism, that Geertz's heart has always been more with the "ethos" side of culture than with the "worldview," more with the affective and stylistic dimensions than with the cognitive. While of course it is very difficult (not to say unproductive and ultimately wrong-headed) to separate the two too sharply, it is nonetheless possible to distinguish an emphasis on one or the other side. For Geertz, then (as for Benedict, especially, before him), even the most cognitive or intellectual of cultural systems—say, the Balinese calendars—are analyzed not (only) to lay bare a set of cognitive ordering principles, but (especially) to understand how the Balinese way of chopping up time stamps their sense of self, of social relations, and of conduct with a particular culturally distinctive flavor, an ethos (1973e).[3]

[2] E.g., Ortner 1975; M. Rosaldo 1980; Blu 1980; Meeker 1979; Rosen 1978.

[3] If culture itself had been an elusive phenomenon, one may say that Geertz has pursued the most elusive part of it, the ethos. It may also be suggested that this, among other things, accounts for his continuing and broad-based appeal. Perhaps the majority of students who go into anthropology, and almost certainly the majority of nonanthropologists who are fascinated by our field, are drawn to it because they have been struck at some point in their experience by the "otherness" of another culture, which we would call its ethos. Geertz's work provides one of the very few handles for grasping that otherness.

The other major contribution of the Geertzian framework was the insistence on studying culture "from the actor's point of view" (e.g., 1975). Again, this does not imply that we must get "into people's heads." What it means, very simply, is that culture is a product of acting social beings trying to make sense of the world in which they find themselves, and if *we* are to make sense of a culture, we must situate ourselves in the position from which it was constructed. Culture is not some abstractly ordered system, deriving its logic from hidden structural principles, or from special symbols that provide the "keys" to its coherence. Its logic—the principles of relations that obtain among its elements—derives rather from the logic or organization of action, from people operating within certain institutional orders, interpreting their situations in order to act coherently within them (1973d). It may be noted here, however, that while the actor-centered perspective is fundamental to Geertz's framework, it is not systematically elaborated: Geertz did not develop a theory of action or practice as such. He did, however, firmly plant the actor at the center of his model, and much of the later practice-centered work builds on a Geertzian (or Geertzo-Weberian) base, as we shall see.

The other major figure in the Chicago school of symbolic anthropology has been David Schneider. Schneider, like Geertz, was a product of Parsons, and he too concentrated primarily on refining the culture concept. But his efforts went toward understanding the *internal logic* of systems of symbols and meanings, by way of a notion of "core symbols," and also by way of ideas akin to Claude Lévi-Strauss's concept of structure (e.g., 1968, 1977). Indeed, although Geertz prominently used the phrase "cultural *system*" (emphasis added), he never paid much attention to the systemic aspects of culture, and it was Schneider who developed this side of the problem much more fully. Schneider in his own work cut culture off from social action much more radically than Geertz did. Yet, perhaps precisely because social action ("practice," "praxis") was so radically separated from "culture" in Schneider's work, he and some of his students were among the earliest of the symbolic anthropologists to see practice itself as a problem (Barnett 1977; Dolgin, Kemnitzer, and Schneider 1977).

Victor Turner, finally, comes out of quite a different intellectual background. He was trained in the Max Gluckman variant of British structural-functionalism, which was influenced by Marxism, and which stressed that the normal state of society is not one of solidarity and harmonious integration of parts, but rather one of conflict and contradiction. Thus, the analytic question was not, as for the straight line descendants of Durkheim, how solidarity is fine-tuned, reinforced, and intensified, but rather how it is constructed and maintained in the first place over and above the conflicts and contradictions that constitute the normal state of affairs. To the American reader, this may appear to be only a minor variant on the basic functionalist project, since for both schools the emphasis is on the maintenance of integration, and specifically on the maintenance of the integration of "society"—actors, groups, the social whole—as opposed to "culture." But Gluckman and his students (including Turner) believed their differences from the mainstream to be quite deep. Moreover, they always constituted a minority within the British establishment. This background may account in part for Turner's originality vis-à-vis his compatriots, leading ultimately to his independently inventing his own brand of an explicitly symbolic anthropology.

Despite the relative novelty of Turner's move to symbols, however, there is in his work a deep continuity with British social anthropological concerns, and, as a result, profound differences between Turnerian and Geertzian symbolic anthropology. For Turner, symbols are of interest not as vehicles of, and analytic windows onto, "culture"—the integrated ethos and worldview of a society—but as what might be called *operators* in the social process, things that, when put together in certain arrangements in certain contexts (especially rituals), produce essentially *social* transformations. Thus, symbols in Ndembu curing or initiation or hunting rituals are investigated for the ways in which they move actors from one status to another, resolve social contradictions, and wed actors to the categories and norms of their society (1967). Along the way toward these rather traditional structural-functional goals, however, Turner identified or elaborated upon certain ritual mechanisms, and some of the concepts he developed have become indispensable parts of the vocabulary of ritual analysis—liminality, marginality, antistructure, communitas, and so forth (1967, 1969).[4]

Turner and the Chicago symbolic anthropologists did not so much conflict with one another as simply, for the most part, talk past one another. Yet the Turnerians[5] added an important, and characteristically British, dimension to the field of symbolic anthropology as a whole, a sense of the *pragmatics* of symbols. They investigated in much more detail than Geertz, Schneider, *et al.*, the "effectiveness of symbols," the question of how symbols actually do what all symbolic anthropologists claim they do: operate as active forces in the social process (see also Lévi-Strauss 1963; Tambiah 1968; Lewis 1977; Fernandez 1974).

In retrospect, one may say that symbolic anthropology had a number of significant limitations. I refer not to the charges that it was unscientific, mystical, literary, soft-headed, and the like leveled at it by practitioners of cultural ecology (see below). Rather, one may point to symbolic anthropol-

[4] Another point of contrast between Turner and Geertz is that Turner's concept of meaning, at least in those early works that launched his approach, is largely referential. Meanings are things that symbols point to or refer to, like "matriliny" or "blood." Geertz, on the other hand, is primarily concerned with what might be called Meaning, with a capital M—the purpose, or point, or larger significance of things. Thus he quotes Northrop Frye: "You wouldn't go to *Macbeth* to learn about the history of Scotland—you go to it to learn what a man feels like after he's gained a kingdom and lost his soul" (Geertz 1973f:450).

[5] E.g., Munn 1969; Myerhoff 1974; Moore and Myerhoff 1975; Babcock 1978.

ogy's lack, especially in its American form, of a systematic sociology; its underdeveloped sense of the politics of culture; and its lack of curiosity concerning the production and maintenance of symbolic systems. These points will be discussed more fully in the course of this article.

Cultural Ecology[6]

Cultural ecology represented a new synthesis of, and a further development upon, the materialist evolutionism of Leslie White (1943, 1949), Julian Steward (1953, 1955), and V. Gordon Childe (1942). Its roots go back to Lewis Henry Morgan and E. B. Tylor in the nineteenth century, and ultimately back to Marx and Engels, although many of the 1950s evolutionists, for understandable political reasons, were not encouraged to emphasize the Marxist connection.[7]

White had been investigating what came to be labeled "general evolution," or the evolution of culture-in-general, in terms of stages of social complexity and technological advancement. These stages were subsequently refined by Elman Service (1958), and by Marshall Sahlins and Elman Service (1960), into the famous bands-tribes-chiefdoms-states scheme. The evolutionary mechanisms in White's framework derived from more or less fortuitous events: technological inventions that allowed for the greater "capture of energy," and population growth (and perhaps warfare and conquest) that stimulated the development of more complex forms of social/political organization and coordination. Steward (1953) attacked both the focus on the evolution of culture-in-general (as opposed to specific cultures), and the lack of a more systematically operative evolutionary mechanism. Instead, he emphasized that specific cultures evolve their specific forms in the process of adapting to specific environmental conditions, and that the apparent uniformity of evolutionary stages is actually a matter of similar adaptations to similar natural conditions in different parts of the world.

If the idea that culture was embodied in public, observable symbols was the key to the liberation of symbolic anthropology from earlier American cultural anthropology, the concept that played a similar role in cultural ecology was "adaptation." (See Alland 1975 for a summary.) Just as Geertz had trumpeted that the study of culture as embodied in symbols removed the problem of getting inside people's heads, so Sahlins proclaimed the focus on adaptation to environmental factors as the way around such amorphous factors as cultural *gestalten* and historical dialectics (1964). There was a large-scale rejection of the study of the inner workings of both culture in the American sense and society in the British sense. Internal dynamics were seen as hard to

[6] This section is partly based on readings, partly on semiformal interviews with Conrad P. Kottak and Roy A. Rappaport, and partly on general discussions with Raymond C. Kelly. Absolution is extended to all of the informants.

[7] White and Childe were fairly explicit about the Marxist influence on their work.

measure, and even harder to choose among for purposes of assigning causal primacy, whereas external factors of natural and social environment were amenable to treatment as fixed, measurable, "independent variables:"

> For decades, centuries now, intellectual battle has been given over which sector of culture is the decisive one for change. Many have entered the lists under banners diverse. Curiously, few seem to fall. Leslie White champions technological growth as the sector most responsible for cultural evolution; Julian Huxley, with many others, sees "man's view of destiny" as the deciding force; the mode of production and the class struggle are still very much in contention. Different as they are, these positions agree in one respect, that the impulse to development is generated from within. . . . The case for internal causes of development may be bolstered by pointing to a mechanism, such as the Hegelian dialectic, or it may rest more insecurely on an argument from logic. . . . In any event, an unreal and vulnerable assumption is always there, that cultures are closed systems. . . . It is precisely on this point that cultural ecology offers a new perspective. . . . [I]t shifts attention to the relation between inside and outside; it envisions as the mainspring of the evolutionary movement the interchange between culture and environment. Now which view shall prevail is not to be decided on a sheet of paper. . . . But if adaptation wins over inner dynamism, it will be for certain intrinsic and obvious strengths. Adaptation is real, naturalistic, anchored to those historic contexts of cultures that inner dynamism ignores (Sahlins 1964:135–36).[8]

The Sahlins and Service version of cultural ecology, which was also adhered to by the mainstream of the archaeology wing of anthropology, was still fundamentally evolutionist. The primary use of the adaptation concept was in explaining the development, maintenance, and transformation of social forms. But there was another variant of cultural ecology, which developed slightly later, and which came to dominate the materialist wing in the sixties. Its position, expressed most forcefully by Marvin Harris (e.g., 1966) and perhaps most elegantly by Roy Rappaport (1967), drew heavily on systems theory. It shifted the analytic focus away from evolution, and toward explaining the existence of particular bits of particular cultures in terms of the adaptive or system-maintaining functions of those bits. Thus, the Maring *kaiko* ritual prevented the degradation of the natural environment (Rappaport 1967), the Kwakiutl potlatch maintained a balance of food distribution over tribal segments (Piddocke 1969), and the sacredness of the cow in India protected a vital link in the agricultural food chain (Harris 1966). In these studies, the interest has shifted from how the environment stimulates (or prevents) the development of social and cultural forms to the question of the ways in which social and cultural forms function to maintain an existing relationship with the environment. It was these latter sorts of studies that came to represent cultural ecology as a whole in the sixties.

One would have had to be particularly out of touch with anthropological

[8] This was the programmatic position. In practice, Sahlins did pay a good deal of attention to internal social dynamics.

theory at the time not to have been aware of the acrimonious debate between the cultural ecologists and the symbolic anthropologists. Whereas the cultural ecologists considered the symbolic anthropologists to be fuzzy-headed mentalists, involved in unscientific and unverifiable flights of subjective interpretation, the symbolic anthropologists considered cultural ecology to be involved with mindless and sterile scientism, counting calories and measuring rainfall, and willfully ignoring the one truth that anthropology had presumably established by that time: that culture mediates all human behavior. The Manichean struggle between "materialism" and "idealism," "hard" and "soft" approaches, interpretive "emics" and explanatory "etics," dominated the field for a good part of the decade of the sixties, and in some quarters well into the seventies.

That most of us thought and wrote in terms of such oppositions may be partly rooted in more pervasive schemes of Western thought: subjective/objective, nature/culture, mind/body, and so on. The practice of fieldwork itself may further contribute to such thinking, based as it is on the paradoxical injunction to participate and observe at one and the same time. It may be then that this sort of polarized construction of the intellectual landscape in anthropology is too deeply motivated, by both cultural categories and the forms of practice of the trade, to be completely eliminated. But the emic/etic struggle of the sixties had a number of unfortunate effects, not the least of which was the prevention of adequate self-criticism on both sides of the fence. Both schools could luxuriate in the faults of the other, and not inspect their own houses for serious weaknesses. In fact, both sides were weak not only in being unable to handle what the other side did (the symbolic anthropologists in renouncing all claims to "explanation," the cultural ecologists in losing sight of the frames of meaning within which human action takes place); both were also weak in what neither of them did, which was much of any systematic sociology.[9]

Indeed, from the point of view of British social anthropology, the whole American struggle was quite meaningless, since it seemed to leave out the necessary central term of all proper anthropological discussion: society. Where were the social groups, social relationships, social structures, social institutions, that mediate *both* the ways in which people think ("culture") *and* the ways in which people experience and act upon their environment? But this set of questions could not be answered (had anybody bothered to ask them) in terms of British social anthropological categories, because the British were having their own intellectual upheavals, to which we will return in due course.

[9] The early Turner is a partial exception to this point, but most of his successors are not.

Structuralism

Structuralism, the more-or-less single-handed invention of Claude Lévi-Strauss, was the only genuinely new paradigm to be developed in the sixties. One might even say that it is the only genuinely original social science paradigm (and humanities too, for that matter) to be developed in the twentieth century. Drawing on linguistics and communication theory, and considering himself influenced by both Marx and Freud, Lévi-Strauss argued that the seemingly bewildering variety of social and cultural phenomena could be rendered intelligible by demonstrating the shared relationships of those phenomena to a few simple underlying principles. He sought to establish the universal grammar of culture, the ways in which units of cultural discourse are created (by the principle of binary opposition), and the rules according to which the units (pairs of opposed terms) are arranged and combined to produce the actual cultural productions (myths, marriage rules, totemic clan arrangements, and the like) that anthropologists record. Cultures are primarily systems of classification, as well as the sets of institutional and intellectual productions built upon those systems of classification and performing further operations upon them. One of the most important secondary operations of culture in relation to its own taxonomies is precisely to mediate or reconcile the oppositions which are the bases of those taxonomies in the first place.

In practice, structural analysis consists of sifting out the basic sets of oppositions that underlie some complex cultural phenomenon—a myth, a ritual, a marriage system—and of showing the ways in which the phenomenon in question is both an expression of those contrasts and a reworking of them, thereby producing a culturally meaningful statement of, or reflection upon, order. Even without the full analysis of a myth or ritual, however, the sheer enumeration of the important sets of oppositions in a culture is taken to be a useful enterprise because it reveals the axes of thought, and the limits of the thinkable, within that and related cultures (e.g., Needham 1973b). But the fullest demonstration of the power of structural analysis is seen in Lévi-Strauss's four-volume study, *Mythologiques* (1964–71). Here the method allows the ordering of data both on a vast scale (including most of indigenous South America, and parts of native North America as well), and also in terms of explicating myriad tiny details—why the jaguar covers his mouth when laughing or why honey metaphors describe the escape of game animals. The combination of wide scope and minute detail is what lends the work its great power.

Much has been made of the point that Lévi-Strauss ultimately grounds the structures he discerns beneath society and culture in the structure of the mind. Both the point itself, and the criticism of it, are perhaps somewhat irrelevant for anthropologists. It seems incontrovertible that all humans, and all cultures, classify. This suggests in turn an innate mental propensity of some sort, but it does not mean that any particular scheme of classification is inevitable, no more than the fact that all humans eat motivates some universal system of food categories.

The enduring contribution of Lévi-Straussian structuralism lies in the perception that luxuriant variety, even apparent randomness, may have a deeper unity and systematicity, derived from the operation of a small number of underlying principles. It is in this sense that Lévi-Strauss claims affinity with Marx and Freud, who similarly argue that beneath the surface proliferation of forms, a few relatively simple and relatively uniform mechanisms are operating (DeGeorge and DeGeorge 1972). Such a perception, in turn, allows us to distinguish much more clearly between simple transformations, which operate *within* a given structure, and real change, revolution if you will, in which the structure itself is transformed. Thus, despite the naturalistic or biologistic base of structuralism, and despite Lévi-Strauss's personal predilection for considering that *plus ça change, plus c'est la même chose*, the theory has always had important implications for a much more historical and/or evolutionary anthropology than that practiced by the master. The work of Louis Dumont in particular has developed some of these evolutionary implications in analyzing the structure of the Indian caste system, and in articulating some of the profound structural changes involved in the transition from caste to class (1965, 1970; see also Goldman 1970, Barnett 1977, Sahlins 1981).[10]

Structuralism was never all that popular among American anthropologists. Although it was seen at first (mostly by the cultural ecologists) as a variant of symbolic anthropology, its central assumptions were in fact rather distant from those of the symbolic anthropologists (with the partial exception of the Schneiderians). There were a number of reasons for this, which can be only very briefly sketched: (1) the very pure cognitive emphasis of Lévi-Strauss's notion of meaning, as against the Americans' interest in ethos and values; (2) Lévi-Strauss's rather austere emphasis on arbitrariness of meaning (all meaning is established by contrasts, nothing carries any meaning in itself), as against the Americans' interest in relations between the *forms* of symbolic constructs and the *contents* for which they are vehicles;[11] and (3) the explicitly abstract locus of structures, divorced in every way from the actions and intentions of actors, as against the symbolic anthropologists' fairly consistent, if variably defined, actor-centrism (again, Schneider is a partial exception to this point). For all these reasons, and probably more, structuralism was not as much embraced by American symbolic anthropologists as might

[10] Dumont is another of those figures who deserve more space than can be afforded here.

[11] This is not to imply that American symbolic anthropologists deny the doctrine of arbitrariness of symbols. But they do insist that the choice of a particular symbolic form among several possible, equally arbitrary, symbols for the same conception, is not only not arbitrary, but has important implications that must be investigated.

have appeared likely at first glance.[12] It was granted what might be called fictive kinship status, largely because of its tendency to focus on some of the same domains that symbolic anthropologists took as their own—myth, ritual, etiquette, and so forth.

The main impact of structuralism outside of France was in England, among some of the more adventurous British social anthropologists (see especially Leach 1966). Lévi-Strauss and the British were in fact more truly kin to one another, born of two lines of descent from Durkheim. In any event, structuralism in the British context underwent a number of important transformations. Avoiding the question of mind, and of universal structures, British anthropologists primarily applied structural analysis to particular societies and particular cosmologies (e.g., Leach 1966, 1969; Needham 1973a; Yalman 1969; the point also applies to Dumont (1970) in France). They also focused in more detail on the process of mediation of oppositions, and produced a number of quite original ruminations upon anomaly and antistructure, especially Mary Douglas's *Purity and Danger* (see also Turner 1967, 1969; Leach 1964; Tambiah 1969).

However, there was also an important way in which many of the British purged structuralism of one of its more radical features—the eradication of the Durkheimian distinction between the social "base" and the cultural "reflection" of it. Lévi-Strauss had claimed that if mythic structures paralleled social structures, it was not because myth reflected society, but because both myth and social organization shared a common underlying structure. Many of the British structuralists (Rodney Needham is the major exception), on the other hand, went back to a position more in the tradition of Durkheim and Marcel Mauss, and considered myth and ritual as reflecting and resolving "at the symbolic level" oppositions taken to be fundamentally social.[13] As long as British structuralism was confined to the study of myth and ritual, then, it was possible for it to fit nicely into British anthropology without having a very profound effect upon it. It became their version of cultural or symbolic anthropology, their theory of superstructure. It was only later, when a structural (i.e., structural-Marxist) eye was turned on the British concept of social structure itself, that the sparks began to fly.

In a number of fields—linguistics, philosophy, history—there was a strong reaction against structuralism by the early seventies. Two interrelated features—the denial of the relevance of an intentional subject in the social and

[12] James Boon (e.g., 1972) has devoted a fair amount of effort to reconciling Lévi-Strauss and/or Schneider on the one side, with Geertz on the other. The outcome is generally heavily in favor of structuralism. (See also Boon and Schneider 1974.)

[13] Lévi-Strauss himself moved *from* a Durkheim/Mauss position in "La Geste d'Asdiwal" (1967) *to* the more radical structuralist position in *Mythologiques*. It is no accident that Leach, or whoever made the decision, chose to present "La Geste d'Asdiwal" as the lead essay in the British collection, *The Structural Study of Myth and Totemism* (1967).

cultural process, and the denial of any significant impact of history or "event" upon structure—were felt to be particularly problematic, not to say unacceptable. Scholars began to elaborate alternative models, in which both agents and events played a more active role. These models did not, however, get much play in anthropology until the late seventies, and they will be discussed in the final section of the essay. In anthropology during most of that decade, structuralism itself, with all its flaws (and virtues), became the basis of one of the dominant schools of theory, structural Marxism. We move now to that decade.

THE SEVENTIES: MARX

The anthropology of the 1970s was much more obviously and transparently tied to real-world events than that of the preceding period. Starting in the late 1960s, in both the United States and France (less so in England), radical social movements emerged on a vast scale. First came the counterculture, then the antiwar movement, and then, just a bit later, the women's movement: these movements not only affected the academic world, they originated in good part within it. *Everything* that was part of the existing order was questioned and criticized. In anthropology, the earliest critiques took the form of denouncing the historical links between anthropology on the one hand, and colonialism and imperialism on the other (e.g., Asad 1973, Hymes 1974). But this merely scratched the surface. The issue quickly moved to the deeper question of the nature of our theoretical frameworks, and especially the degree to which they embody and carry forward the assumptions of bourgeois Western culture.

The rallying symbol of the new criticism, and of the theoretical alternatives offered to replace the old models, was Marx. Of all the great nineteenth-century antecedents of modern social science, Marx had been conspicuously absent from the mainstream theoretical repertoire. Parsons's *Structure of Social Action*, one of the sacred texts of the Harvard-trained symbolic anthropologists, surveyed the thought of Durkheim and Weber, and of two economic theorists, Alfred Marshall and Vilfredo Pareto, whose main significance in that context seemed to be that they were Not Marx. The British, including both the symbolic anthropologists and the structuralists, were still firmly embedded in Durkheim. Lévi-Strauss claimed to have been influenced by Marx, but it took a while for anyone to figure out what he meant by that. Even the cultural ecologists, the only self-proclaimed materialists of the sixties, hardly invoked Marx at all; indeed Marvin Harris specifically repudiated him (1968). One does not need to be an especially subtle analyst of the ideological aspects of intellectual history to realize that the absence of a significant Marxist influence before the seventies was just as much a reflex of real-world politics as was the emergence of a strong Marxist influence in the seventies.

There were at least two distinct Marxist schools of anthropological theory: structural Marxism, developed mainly in France and England, and political economy, which emerged first in the United States, and later in England as well. There was also a movement that might be called cultural Marxism, worked out largely in historical and literary studies, but this was not picked up by anthropologists until recently, and will be addressed in the final section of the essay.

Structural Marxism

Structural Marxism was the only one of the schools developed entirely within the field of anthropology, and probably for that reason was also the earliest in its impact. Within it, Marx was used to attack and/or rethink, or at the very least to expand, virtually every theoretical scheme on the landscape—symbolic anthropology, cultural ecology, British social anthropology, and structuralism itself. Structural Marxism constituted a would-be total intellectual revolution, and if it did not succeed in establishing itself as the only alternative to everything else we had, it certainly succeeded in shaking up most of the received wisdom. This is not to say that it was necessarily the actual writings of the structural Marxists themselves (e.g., Althusser 1971; Godelier 1977; Terray 1972; Sahlins 1972; Friedman 1975) that had this effect; it was simply that structural Marxism was the original force within anthropology for promulgating and legitimating "Marx," "Marxism," and "critical inquiry" in the discourse of the field as a whole (see also Diamond 1979).

The specific advance of structural Marxism over its antecedent forms of materialist anthropology lay in its locating the determinative forces not in the natural environment and/or in technology, but specifically within certain structures of social relations. Ecological considerations were not excluded, but they were encompassed by and subordinated to the analysis of the social, and especially political, organization of production. Cultural ecology was thus attacked as "vulgar materialism," reinforcing rather than undoing the classical capitalist fetishization of "things," the domination of subjects by objects rather than by the social relations embodied in, and symbolized by, those objects (see especially Friedman 1974). The critical social relations in question, referred to as the mode(s) of production, are not to be confused with the surface organization of social relations traditionally studied by British social anthropologists—lineages, clans, moieties, and all the rest. These surface forms of what the British called "social structure" are seen as native *models* of social organization that have been bought by anthropologists as the real thing, but that actually mask, or at least only partially correspond to, the hidden asymmetrical relations of production that are driving the system. Here, then, was situated the critique of traditional British social anthropology (see especially Bloch 1971, 1974, 1977; Terray 1975).

In addition to critiquing and revising both cultural ecology and British social anthropology, structural Marxists turned their attention to cultural phenomena. Unlike the cultural ecologists, the structural Marxists did not dismiss cultural beliefs and native categories as irrelevant to the real or objective operations of society, nor, alternatively, did they set about to show that apparently irrational cultural beliefs, such as the sacred cow, actually had practical adaptive functions. Just as the New Left in the real world took cultural issues (life style, consciousness) more seriously than the Old Left had done, so the structural Marxists allocated to cultural phenomena (beliefs, values, classifications) at least one central function in their model of the social process. Specifically, culture was converted to "ideology," and considered from the point of view of its role in social reproduction: legitimating the existing order, mediating contradictions in the base, and mystifying the sources of exploitation and inequality in the system (O'Laughlin 1974; Bloch 1977; Godelier 1977).

One of the virtues of structural Marxism, then, was that there was a place for everything in its scheme. Refusing to see inquiries into material relations and into "ideology" as opposed enterprises, its practitioners established a model in which the two "levels" were related to one another via a core of social/political/economic processes. In this sense, they offered an explicit mediation between the "materialist" and "idealist" camps of sixties anthropology. The mediation was rather mechanical, as we will discuss in a moment, but it was there.

More important, to my mind, the structural Marxists put a relatively powerful sociology back into the picture. They cross-fertilized British social anthropological categories with Marxist ones, and produced an expanded model of social organization ("mode of production") which they then proceeded to apply systematically to particular cases. Whereas other Marxisms emphasized relations of political/economic organization ("production") almost exclusively, the structural Marxists were, after all, anthropologists, trained to pay attention to kinship, descent, marriage, exchange, domestic organization, and the like. They thus included these elements within their considerations of political and economic relations (often giving them a more Marxist ring by calling them "relations of reproduction") and the total effect was to produce rich and complex pictures of the social process in specific cases. Given the relative paucity, mentioned earlier, of detailed sociological analysis in the various sixties schools, this was an important contribution.

All this having been said, one may nonetheless recognize that structural Marxism had a number of problems. For one thing, the narrowing of the culture concept to "ideology," which had the powerful effect of allowing analysts to connect cultural conceptions to specific structures of social relation, was too extreme, and posed the problem of relating ideology back to more general conceptions of culture. For another, the tendency to see culture/ideology largely in terms of mystification gave most of the cultural or ideological studies in this school a decided functionalist flavor, since the upshot of these analyses was to show how myth, ritual, taboo, or whatever maintained the status quo. Finally, and most seriously, although structural Marxists offered a way of mediating the material and ideological "levels," they did not actually challenge the notion that such levels are analytically distinguishable in the first place. Thus despite criticizing the Durkheimian (and Parsonian) notion of "the social" as the "base" of the system, they merely offered a deeper and allegedly more real and objective "base." And despite attempting to discover more important functions for the "superstructure" (or despite claiming that what is base and what is superstructure varies culturally and/or historically, or even occasionally and rather vaguely that the superstructure is part of the base) they continued to reproduce the idea that it is useful to maintain such a set of analytic boxes.

In this sense, it may be seen that structural Marxism was still very much rooted in the sixties. While it injected a healthy dose of sociology into the earlier scheme of categories, and while this sociology was itself relatively originally conceived, the basic pigeonholes of sixties thought were not radically revised. Further, unlike the political economy school and other more recent approaches to be discussed shortly, structural Marxism was largely nonhistorical, a factor which, again, tied it to earlier forms of anthropology. Indeed one may guess that it was in part this comfortable mix of old categories and assumptions wrapped up in a new critical rhetoric that made structural Marxism so appealing in its day. It was in many ways the perfect vehicle for academics who had been trained in an earlier era, but who, in the seventies, were feeling the pull of critical thought and action that was exploding all around them.

Political Economy

The political economy school has taken its inspiration primarily from world-systems and underdevelopment theories in political sociology (Wallerstein 1976; Gunder Frank 1967). In contrast to structural Marxism, which focused largely, in the manner of conventional anthropological studies, on relatively discrete societies or cultures, the political economists have shifted the focus to large-scale regional political/economic systems (e.g., Hart 1982). Insofar as they have attempted to combine this focus with traditional fieldwork in specific communities or microregions, their research has generally taken the form of studying the effects of capitalist penetration upon those communities (e.g., *American Ethnologist* 1978; Schneider and Schneider 1976). The emphasis on the impact of external forces, and on the ways in which societies change or evolve largely in adaptation to such impact, ties the political economy school in certain ways to the cultural ecology of the sixties, and indeed many of its current practitioners were trained in that school (e.g., Ross 1980). But whereas for sixties cultural ecology, often studying relatively "primitive" societies, the important external forces were those of the natural environment, for the seventies political economists, generally studying "peasants," the important external forces are those of the state and the capitalist world system.

At the level of theory, the political economists differ from their cultural ecology forebears partly in showing a greater willingness to incorporate cultural or symbolic issues into their inquiries (e.g., Schneider 1978; Riegelhaupt 1978). Specifically, their work tends to focus on symbols involved in the development of class or group identity, in the context of political/economic struggles of one sort or another. The political economy school thus overlaps with the burgeoning "ethnicity" industry, although the literature in the latter field is too vast and too amorphous for me to do more than nod to here. In any event, the willingness of the political economists to pay attention, in however circumscribed fashion, to symbolic processes, is part of the general relaxation of the old materialism/idealism wars of the sixties.

The emphasis of this school upon larger regional processes is also salutary, at least up to a point. Anthropologists do have a tendency to treat societies, even villages, as if they were islands unto themselves, with little sense of the larger systems of relations in which these units are embedded. The occasional work (e.g., Edmund Leach's *Political Systems of Highland Burma*) that has viewed societies in larger regional context has been something of an unclassifiable (if admired) freak. To ignore the fact that peasants are part of states, and that even "primitive" societies and communities are invariably involved in wider systems of exchanges of all sorts, is to seriously distort the data, and it is the virtue of the political economists that they remind us of this.

Finally, the political economists must be given leading credit for stressing very strongly the importance of history for anthropological study. They are not the first to have done so, nor are they the only ones doing so now, and I will say more about anthropology's rapprochement with history in the conclusions of this essay. Nonetheless, it is certainly the members of this school who appear the most committed to a fully historical anthropology, and who are producing sustained and systematic work grounded in this commitment.

On the negative side of the ledger, we may complain first that the political economy model is too economic, too strictly materialist. One hears a lot about wages, the market, the cash nexus, economic exploitation, underdevelopment, and so forth, but not enough about the relations of power, domination, manipulation, control, and the like which those economic relations play into, and which for actors constitute much of the experienced pain of economic injustice. Political economy, in other words, is not political enough.

My main objection, however, is located deeper in the theoretical model of political economy. Specifically, I find the capitalism-centered view of the world questionable, to say the least, especially for anthropology. At the core of the model is the assumption that virtually everything we study has already been touched ("penetrated") by the capitalist world system, and that therefore much of what we see in our fieldwork and describe in our monographs must be understood as having been shaped in response to that system. Perhaps this is true for European peasants, but even here one would want at least to leave the question open. When we get even further from the "center," however, the assumption becomes very problematic indeed. A society, even a village, has its own structure and history, and this must be as much part of the analysis as its relations with the larger context within which it operates. (See Joel Kahn (1980) for a more balanced view.)

The problems derived from the capitalism-centered worldview also affect the political economists' view of history. History is often treated as something that arrives, like a ship, from outside the society in question. Thus we do not get the history *of* that society, but the impact of (our) history *on* that society. The accounts produced from such a perspective are often quite unsatisfactory in terms of traditional anthropological concerns: the actual organization and culture of the society in question. Traditional studies of course had their own problems with respect to history. They often presented us with a thin chapter on "historical background" at the beginning and an inadequate chapter on "social change" at the end. The political economy study inverts this relationship, but only to create the inverse problem.

The political economists, moreover, tend to situate themselves more on the ship of (capitalist) history than on the shore. They say in effect that we can never know what the other system, in its unique, "traditional," aspects, really looked like anyway. By realizing that much of what we see as tradition is in fact a response to Western impact, so the argument goes, we not only get a more accurate picture of what is going on, but we acknowledge at the same time the pernicious effects of our own system upon others. Such a view is also present, but in modes of anger and/or despair rather than pragmatism, in a number of recent works that question philosophically whether we can ever truly know the "other"—Edward Said's *Orientalism* is the prime example (see also Rabinow 1977; Crapanzano 1980; Riesman 1977).

To such a position we can only respond: try. The effort is as important as the results, in terms of both our theories and our practices. The attempt to view other systems from ground level is the basis, perhaps the only basis, of anthropology's distinctive contribution to the human sciences. It is our capacity, largely developed in fieldwork, to take the perspective of the folks on the shore, that allows us to learn anything at all—even in our own culture—beyond what we already know. (Indeed, as more and more anthropologists are doing fieldwork in Western cultures, including the United States, the importance of maintaining a capacity to see otherness, even next door, becomes more and more acute.) Further, it is our location "on the ground" that puts us in a position to see people not simply as passive reactors to and enactors of some "system," but as active agents and subjects in their own history.

In concluding this section, I must confess that my placement of the political economy school in the seventies is something of an ideological move. In fact political economy is very much alive and well in the eighties, and it will probably thrive for some time. My periodization is thus, like that of all histories, only partly related to real time. I have included political economy and structural Marxism within this period/category because both schools continue to share a set of assumptions distinct from what I wish to emphasize for the anthropology of the eighties. Specifically, both assume, together with earlier anthropologies, that human action and historical process are almost entirely structurally or systemically determined. Whether it be the hidden hand of structure or the juggernaut of capitalism that is seen as the agent of society/history, it is certainly not in any central way real people doing real things. These are precisely the views from which at least some anthropologists, as well as practitioners in many other fields, appear to be struggling to break free as we move into the present decade.

INTO THE EIGHTIES: PRACTICE

I began this article by noting the apparent accuracy of Wolf's remarks to the effect that the field of anthropology is disintegrating, even granting the low degree of integration it had in the past. I also suggested that one could find scattered over the landscape the elements of a new trend that seems to be gathering force and coherence. In this final section I call attention to this new trend, sketch it, and subject it to a preliminary critique.

For the past several years, there has been growing interest in analysis focused through one or another of a bundle of interrelated terms: practice, praxis, action, interaction, activity, experience, performance. A second, and closely related, bundle of terms focuses on the doer of all that doing: agent, actor, person, self, individual, subject.

In some fields, movement in this direction began relatively early in the seventies, some of it in direct reaction to structuralism. In linguistics, for example, there was an early rejection of structural linguistics and a strong move to view language as communication and performance (e.g., Bauman and Sherzer 1974; Cole and Morgan 1975). In anthropology too there were scattered calls for a more action based approach. In France, Pierre Bourdieu published his *Outline of a Theory of Practice* in 1972. In the United States, Geertz attacked both hypercoherent studies of symbolic systems (many of them inspired by his own programmatic papers) and what he saw as the sterile formalism of structuralism, calling instead for anthropologists to see "human behavior . . . as . . . symbolic action" (1973a:10; see also Dolgin, Kemnitzer, and Schneider 1977; Wagner 1975; T. Turner 1969). In England, there was a minority wing that criticized traditional views of "social structure" not from the point of view of structural Marxism, but from the perspective of individual choice and decision making (e.g., Kapferer 1976).[14]

[14] The transactionalist tradition in British anthropology may of course be traced back further,

For much of the seventies, however, the structural Marxists and, later, the political economists, remained dominant, at least within anthropology. For them, social and cultural phenomena were to be explained largely by being referred to systemic/structural mechanisms of one sort or another. It was only in the late seventies that the hegemony of structural Marxism, if not that of political economy, began to wane. An English translation of Bourdieu's book was published in 1978, and it was at about that time that the calls for a more practice-oriented approach became increasingly audible. Here is a sampler:

> The instruments of reasoning are changing and society is less and less represented as an elaborate machine or a quasi-organism than as a serious game, a sidewalk drama, or a behavioral text (Geertz 1980a:168).

> We need to watch these systems [of kinship] in action, to study tactics and strategy, not merely the rules of the game (Barnes 1980:301).

> . . . gender conceptions in any society are to be understood as functioning aspects of a cultural system through which actors manipulate, interpret, legitimize, and reproduce the patterns . . . that order their social world (Collier and Rosaldo 1981:311).[15]

> What do actors want and how can they get it? (Ortner 1981:366)

> If structural/semiotic analysis is to be extended to general anthropology on the model of its pertinence to "language," then what is lost is not merely history and change, but practice—human action in the world. Some might think that what is lost is what anthropology is all about (Sahlins 1981:6).

As was the case with the strong revisionist trend in the sixties, the present movement appears much broader than the field of anthropology alone. In linguistics, Alton Becker, in a much-cited article, has emphasized issues of text building over and against reification of The Text (1979). In sociology, symbolic interactionism and other forms of so-called microsociology appear to be attracting new attention,[16] and Anthony Giddens has dubbed the relationship between structure and "agency" one of the "central problems" of modern social theory (1979). In history, E. P. Thompson has railed against theorists (everything from Parsonians to Stalinists) who treat "history as a 'process without a subject' [and] concur in the eviction from history of human agency" (1978:79). In literary studies, Raymond Williams insists that literature must be treated as the product of particular practices, and accuses those who abstract literature from practice of performing "an extraordinary ideological feat" (1977:46). If we push further—and here we skirt dangerous

to Barth and to Bailey in the sixties, to the earlier works of Leach (e.g., 1960), and ultimately to Raymond Firth (e.g., 1963 [1951]). See also Marriott (1976) in the United States.

[15] I would argue, if I had more space, that feminist anthropology is one of the primary contexts in which a practice approach has been developing. The Collier and Rosaldo (1981) article is a good example. See also Ortner (1981).

[16] Mayer Zald, personal communication, at the Social Science History Seminar (University of Michigan), 1982.

ground—we might even see the whole sociobiology movement as part of this general trend, insofar as it shifts the evolutionary mechanism from random mutation to intentional choice on the part of actors seeking to maximize reproductive success. (I should probably say, right here and not in a footnote, that I have a range of very strong objections to sociobiology. Nonetheless, I do not think it is too far-fetched to see its emergence as part of the broad movement to which I am drawing attention here.)

The practice approach is diverse, and I will not attempt to compare and contrast its many strands. Rather I will select for discussion a number of works that seem to share a common orientation within the larger set, an orientation that seems to me particularly promising. I do not wish to canonize any single one of these works, nor do I wish to provide a label for the subset and endow it with more reality than it has. What I do here is more like beginning to develop a photograph, to coax a latent form into something recognizable.

We may begin by contrasting, in a general way, this (subset of) newer practice-oriented work with certain more established approaches, especially with symbolic interactionism in sociology (Blumer 1962; Goffman 1959; see also Berreman 1962, and more recently Gregor 1977 in anthropology) and with what was called transactionalism in anthropology (Kapferer 1976, Marriott 1976, Goody 1978, Barth 1966, Bailey 1969). The first point to note is that these approaches were elaborated *in opposition to* the dominant, essentially Parsonian/Durkheimian, view of the world as ordered by rules and norms.[17] Recognizing that institutional organization and cultural patterning exist, the symbolic interactionists and transactionalists nonetheless sought to minimize or bracket the relevance of these phenomena for understanding social life:

> From the standpoint of symbolic interaction, social organization is a framework inside of which acting units develop their actions. Structural features, such as "culture," "social systems," "social stratification," or "social roles," set conditions for their action but do not determine their action (Blumer 1962:152).

The newer practice theorists, on the other hand, share a view that "the system" (in a variety of senses to be discussed below) does in fact have very powerful, even "determining," effect upon human action and the shape of events. Their interest in the study of action and interaction is thus not a matter of denying or minimizing this point, but expresses rather an urgent need to understand where "the system" comes from—how it is produced and reproduced, and how it may have changed in the past or be changed in the future. As Giddens argues in his important recent book (1979), the study of

[17] Parsons and his colleagues gave the term "action" central place in their scheme (1962 [1951]), but what they meant by this was essentially *en*-actment of rules and norms. Bourdieu, Giddens, and others have pointed this out, and have cast their arguments in part against this position.

practice is not an antagonistic alternative to the study of systems or structures, but a necessary complement to it.

The other major aspect of the newer practice orientation, differentiating it significantly from earlier interactionist and transactionalist approaches, resides in a palpable Marxist influence carrying through from the seventies. Partly this is visible in the way in which things like culture and/or structure are viewed. That is, although the newer practice theorists share with sixties anthropology a strong sense of the shaping power of culture/structure, this shaping power is viewed rather darkly, as a matter of "constraint," "hegemony," and "symbolic domination." We will come back to this position in greater detail later. More generally, the Marxist influence is to be seen in the assumption that the most important forms of action or interaction for analytic purposes are those which take place in asymmetrical or dominated relations, that it is these forms of action or interaction that best explain the shape of any given system at any given time. Whether it is a matter of focusing directly on interaction (even "struggle") between asymmetrically related actors, or whether it is more broadly a matter of defining actors (whatever they are doing) in terms of roles and statuses derived from asymmetrical relations in which they participate, the approach tends to highlight social asymmetry as the most important dimension of both action and structure.

Not all of current practice work manifests the Marxist influence. Some of it—like symbolic interactionism and transactionalism themselves—is more in the spirit of Adam Smith. The members of the subset with which I am concerned, however, implicitly or explicitly share at least the critical flavor of seventies anthropology, if not a systematic allegiance to Marxist theory per se.

Yet to speak of a Marxist influence in all of this is actually to obscure an important aspect of what is going on: an interpenetration, almost a merger, between Marxist and Weberian frameworks. In the sixties, the opposition between Marx and Weber, as "materialist" and "idealist," had been emphasized. The practice theorists, in contrast, draw on a set of writers who interpret the Marxist corpus in such a way as to render it quite compatible with Weber's views. As Weber put the actor at the center of his model, so these writers emphasize issues of human praxis in Marx. As Weber subsumed the economic within the political, so these writers encompass economic exploitation within political domination. And as Weber was centrally concerned with ethos and consciousness, so these writers stress similar issues within Marx's work. Choosing Marx over Weber as one's theorist of reference is a tactical move of a certain sort. In reality, the theoretical framework involved is about equally indebted to both. (On theory, see Giddens 1971; Williams 1976; Avineri 1971; Ollman 1971; Bauman 1973; Habermas 1973; Goldmann 1977. For substantive case analyses in this Weberian-Marxist vein, see Thompson 1966; Williams 1973; Genovese 1976.)

I will proceed to explicate and evaluate the "new practice" position by way of posing a series of questions: What is it that a practice approach seeks to explain? What is practice? How is it motivated? And what sorts of analytic relationships are postulated in the model? Let me emphasize very strongly that I do not offer here a coherent theory of practice. I merely sort out and discuss, in a very preliminary fashion, some of the central axes of such a theory.

What is Being Explained?

As previously indicated, modern practice theory seeks to explain the relationship(s) that obtain between human action, on the one hand, and some global entity which we may call "the system," on the other. Questions concerning these relationships may go in either direction—the impact of the system on practice, and the impact of practice on the system. How these processes work will be taken up below. Here we must say a few words about the nature of "the system."

In two recent works in anthropology that explicitly attempt to elaborate a practice-based model (Bourdieu 1978 [1972]; and Sahlins 1981), the authors nominally take a French structuralist view of the system (patterns of relations between categories, and of relations between relations). In fact however both Bourdieu's *habitus* and Sahlins's "cosmological dramas" behave in many ways like the American concept of culture, combining elements of ethos, affect, and value with more strictly cognitive schemes of classification. The choice of a French or an American perspective on the system does have certain consequences for the shape of the analysis as a whole, but we will not pursue these here. The point is that practice anthropologists assume that society and history are not simply sums of ad hoc responses and adaptations to particular stimuli, but are governed by organizational and evaluative schemes. It is these (embodied, of course, within institutional, symbolic, and material forms) that constitute the system.

The system, further, is not broken up into units like base and superstructure, or society and culture, but is rather a relatively seamless whole. An institution—say, a marriage system—is at once a system of social relations, economic arrangements, political processes, cultural categories, norms, values, ideals, emotional patterns, and so on and on. No attempt is made to sort these components into levels and to assign primacy to one or the other level. Nor, for example, is marriage as a whole assigned to "society," while religion is assigned to "culture." A practice approach has no need to break the system into artificial chunks like base and superstructure (and to argue over which determines which), since the analytic effort is not to explain one chunk of the system by referring it to another chunk, but rather to explain the system as an integral whole (which is not to say a harmoniously integrated one) by referring it to practice.

But if the system is an integral whole, at the same time all of its parts or dimensions do not have equal analytic significance. At the core of the system, both forming it and deforming it, are the specific realities of asymmetry, inequality, and domination in a given time and place. Raymond Williams, a Marxist literary/cultural historian, sums up both the insistence upon holism and the privileged position of domination characteristic of this view. Picking up Antonio Gramsci's term "hegemony" as his label for the system, he argues that

> "hegemony" is a concept which at once includes and goes beyond two powerful earlier concepts: that of "culture" as a "whole social process," in which men define and shape their whole lives; and that of "ideology" in any of its Marxist senses, in which a system of meanings and values is the expression or projection of a particular class interest.
>
> "Hegemony" goes beyond "culture" in its insistence on relating the "whole social process" to specific distributions of power and influence. To say that men define and shape their whole lives is true only in abstraction. In any actual society there are specific inequalities in means and therefore in capacity to realize this process. . . . Gramsci therefore introduces the necessary recognition of dominance and subordination in what has still, however, to be recognized as a whole process.
>
> It is in just this recognition of the *wholeness* of the process that the concept of "hegemony" goes beyond "ideology." What is decisive is not only the conscious system of ideas and beliefs, but the whole lived social process as practically organized by specific and dominant meanings and values. . . .
>
> [Hegemony] is in the strongest sense a "culture," but a culture which has also to be seen as the lived dominance and subordination of particular classes (Williams 1977:108–109, 110).

What a practice theory seeks to explain, then, is the genesis, reproduction, and change of form and meaning of a given social/cultural whole, defined in—more or less—this sense.

What is Practice?

In principle, the answer to this question is almost unlimited: anything people do. Given the centrality of domination in the model, however, the most significant forms of practice are those with intentional or unintentional political implications. Then again, almost anything people do has such implications. So the study of practice is after all the study of all forms of human action, but from a particular—political—angle.

Beyond this general point, further distinctions may be introduced. There is first of all the question of what are taken to be the acting units. Most practice anthropology to date takes these units to be individual actors, whether actual historical individuals, or social types ("women," "commoners," "workers," "junior siblings," etcetera). The analyst takes these people and their doings as the reference point for understanding a particular unfolding of events, and/or for understanding the processes involved in the reproduction or change of some set of structural features. In contrast to a large body of work in the field of history, there has been relatively little done in anthropology on concerted collective action (but see Wolf 1969; Friedrich 1970; Blu 1980; see also the literature on cargo cults, especially Worsley 1968). Even in studies of collective action, however, the collectivity is handled methodologically as a single subject. We shall be discussing, throughout this section, some of the problems that arise from the essential individualism of most current forms of practice theory.

A second set of questions concerns the temporal organization of action. Some authors (Bourdieu is an example) treat action in terms of relatively ad hoc decision making, and/or relatively short-term "moves." Others suggest, even if they do not develop the point, that human beings act within plans or programs that are always more long range than any single move, and indeed that most moves are intelligible only within the context of these larger plans (Sahlins (1981) implies this, as do Ortner (1981) and Collier and Rosaldo (1981); for an older example, see Hart and Pilling (1960)). Many such plans are culturally provided (the normative life cycle, for example), but many others must be constructed by actors themselves. Even projects generated ("creatively") by actors, however, tend to take stereotyped forms, insofar as the constraints and the resources of the system are relatively constant for actors in similar positions. In any event, an emphasis on larger "projects" rather than particular "moves" underlines the point that action itself *has* (developmental) structure, as well as operating *in*, and in relation *to*, structure.

Finally, there is the question of the *kinds* of action taken to be analytically central to the current approach. Everyone seems to agree in opposing a Parsonian or Saussurian view in which action is seen as sheer en-actment or execution of rules and norms (Bourdieu 1978; Sahlins 1981; Giddens 1979). Moreover, everyone seems also to agree that a kind of romantic or heroic "voluntarism," emphasizing the freedom and relatively unrestricted inventiveness of actors, will not do either (e.g., Thompson 1978). What is left, then, is a view of action largely in terms of pragmatic choice and decision making, and/or active calculating and strategizing. I will have more to say about the strategic model in the next section, when I discuss the views of motivation entailed in practice theory. Here, however, I wish to question whether the critique of en-actment or execution may not have gone too far. Indeed, despite the attacks on Parsons by Bourdieu and Giddens, both recognize the central role of highly patterned and routinized behavior in systemic reproduction. It is precisely in those areas of life—especially in the so-called domestic domain—where action proceeds with little reflection, that much of the conservatism of a system tends to be located. Either because practice theorists wish to emphasize the activeness and intentionality of action, or because of a growing interest in change as against reproduction, or both, the degree to which actors really do simply enact norms because "that was the way of our ancestors" may be unduly undervalued.

What Motivates Action?

A theory of practice requires some sort of theory of motivation. At the moment, the dominant theory of motivation in practice anthropology is derived from interest theory. The model is that of an essentially individualistic, and somewhat aggressive, actor, self-interested, rational, pragmatic, and perhaps with a maximizing orientation as well. What actors do, it is assumed, is rationally go after what they want, and what they want is what is materially and politically useful for them within the context of their cultural and historical situations.

Interest theory has been raked over the coals many times before. Here it is sufficient simply to note a few points that have particular relevance for anthropological studies of practice.

Insofar as interest theory is, even if it pretends not to be, a psychological theory, it is clearly far too narrow. In particular, although pragmatic rationality is certainly one aspect of motivation, it is never the only one, and not always even the dominant one. To accord it the status of exclusive motivating force is to exclude from the analytic discourse a whole range of emotional terms—need, fear, suffering, desire, and others—that must surely be part of motivation.

Unfortunately, anthropologists have generally found that actors with too much psychological plumbing are hard to handle methodologically, and practice theorists are no exception. There is, however, a growing body of literature which explores the variable construction of self, person, emotion, and motive in cross-cultural perspective (e.g., M. Rosaldo 1980, 1981; Friedrich 1977; Geertz 1973a, 1975; Singer 1980; Kirkpatrick 1977; Guemple 1972). The growth of this body of work is itself part of the larger trend toward an interest in elaborating an actor-centered paradigm, as is the fact that the subfield of psychological anthropology seems to be enjoying something of a renaissance (e.g., Paul 1982; Kracke 1978; Levy 1973). One may hope for some cross-fertilization between the more sociologically oriented practice accounts, with their relatively denatured views of motive, and some of these more richly textured accounts of emotion and motivation.

If interest theory assumes too much rationality on the part of actors, it also assumes too much active-ness. The idea that actors are always pressing claims, pursuing goals, advancing purposes, and the like may simply be an overly energetic (and overly political) view of how and why people act. We may recall here the distinction, underscored by Geertz, between interest theory and strain theory (1973c). If actors in interest theory are always actively striving for gains, actors in strain theory are seen as experiencing the complexities of their situations and attempting to solve problems posed by those situations. It follows from these points that the strain perspective places greater emphasis on the analysis of the system itself, the forces in play upon actors, as a way of understanding where actors, as we say, are coming from. In particular, a system is analyzed with the aim of revealing the sorts of binds it creates for actors, the sorts of burdens it places upon them, and so on. This analysis, in turn, provides much of the context for understanding actors' motives, and the kinds of projects they construct for dealing with their situations (see also Ortner 1975, 1978).

While strain theory does not rectify the psychological shortcomings of interest theory, it does at least make for a more systematic exploration of the social forces shaping motives than interest theory does. Indeed, one may say that strain theory is a theory of the social, as opposed to psychological, production of "interests," the latter being seen less as direct expressions of utility and advantage for actors, and more as images of solutions to experienced stresses and problems.

Finally, an interest approach tends to go hand in hand with seeing action in terms of short-term tactical "moves" rather than long-term developmental "projects." From a tactical point of view, actors seek particular gains, whereas from a developmental point of view, actors are seen as involved in relatively far-reaching transformations of their states of being—of their relationships with things, persons, and self. We may say, in the spirit of Gramsci, that action in a developmental or "projects" perspective is more a matter of "becoming" than of "getting" (1957). Intrinsic to this latter perspective is a sense of motive and action as shaped not only by problems being solved, and gains being sought, but by images and ideals of what constitutes goodness—in people, in relationships, and in conditions of life.

It is a peculiarity of interest theory that it is shared across a broad spectrum of analysts, Marxist and non-Marxist, "old" and "new" practice theorists. The popularity and durability of the perspective, despite numerous attacks and criticisms, suggest that especially deep changes in our own practices will be required if anything is to be dislodged in this area.

The Nature of Interactions between Practice and the System

1. *How does the system shape practice?* Anthropologists—American ones, anyway—have for the most part long agreed that culture shapes, guides, and even to some extent dictates behavior. In the sixties, Geertz elaborated some of the important mechanisms involved in this process, and it seems to me that most modern practice theorists, including those who write in Marxist and/or structuralist terms, hold an essentially Geertzian view. But there are certain changes of emphasis, derived from the centrality of domination within the practice framework. For one thing, as noted earlier, the emphasis has shifted from what culture allows and enables people to see, feel, and do, to what it restricts and inhibits them from seeing, feeling, and doing. Further, although it is agreed that culture powerfully constitutes the reality that actors live in, this reality is looked upon with critical eyes: why this one and not some other? And what sorts of alternatives are people being dis-abled from seeing?

It is important to note that this view is at least partly distinct from a view of culture as mystification. In a mystification view, culture (= "ideology") tells lies about the realities of people's lives, and the analytic problem is to understand how people come to believe these lies (e.g., Bloch 1977). In the approach under discussion here, however, there is only one reality, and it is culturally constituted from top to bottom. The problem is not that of the system telling lies about some extrasystemic "reality," but of why the system as a whole has a certain configuration, and of why and how it excludes alternative possible configurations.

In any event, in terms of the specific question of how the system constrains practice, the emphasis tends to be laid on essentially cultural and psychological mechanisms: mechanisms of the formation and transformation of "consciousness." Although constraints of material and political sorts, including force, are fully acknowledged, there seems to be general agreement that action is constrained most deeply and systematically by the ways in which culture controls the definitions of the world for actors, limits their conceptual tools, and restricts their emotional repertoires. Culture becomes part of the self. Speaking of the sense of honor among the Kabyle, for example, Bourdieu says:

> . . . honour is a permanent disposition, embedded in the agents' very bodies in the form of mental dispositions, schemes of perception and thought, extremely general in their application, such as those which divide up the world in accordance with the oppositions between the male and the female, east and west, future and past, top and bottom, right and left, etc., and also, at a deeper level, in the form of bodily postures and stances, ways of standing, sitting, looking, speaking, or walking. What is called the sense of honour is nothing other than the cultivated disposition, inscribed in the body schema and the schemes of thought (1978:15).

In a similar vein, Foucault says of the discourse of "perversions":

> The machinery of power that focuses on this whole alien strain did not aim to suppress it, but rather to give it an analytical, visible, and permanent reality: it was implanted in bodies, slipped in beneath modes of conduct, made into a principle of classification and intelligibility, established as a *raison d'être* and a natural order of disorder. . . . The strategy behind this dissemination was to strew reality with them and incorporate them into the individual (1980:44).

Thus insofar as domination is as much a matter of cultural and psychological processes as of material and political ones, it operates by shaping actors' dispositions such that, in the extreme case, "the agents' aspirations have the same limits as the objective conditions of which they are the product" (Bourdieu 1978:166; see also Rabinow 1975; Barnett and Silverman 1979; Rabinow and Sullivan 1979).

At the same time, however, those authors who emphasize cultural domination also place important limits on the scope and depth of cultural controls. The extreme case is never reached, and often never even approached. Thus while accepting the view of culture as powerfully constraining, they argue that hegemony is always more fragile than its appears, and never as total as it (or as traditional cultural anthropology) would claim. The reasons given for this state of affairs are various, and relate directly to the ways in which the different authors conceptualize systemic change. This brings us to our final set of questions.

2. *How does practice shape the system?* There are really two considerations here—how practice reproduces the system, and how the system may be changed by practice. A unified theory of practice should ideally be able to account for both within a single framework. At the moment, however, it is clear that a focus on reproduction tends to produce a rather different picture from a focus on change, and we will thus take these issues separately.

Beginning with reproduction, there is of course a long tradition in anthropology of asking how it is that norms, values, and conceptual schemes get reproduced by and for actors. Prior to the sixties, at least in American anthropology, emphasis was laid upon socialization practices as the primary agents of this process. In England, however, the influence of the Durkheimian paradigm generated an emphasis on ritual. It was through the enactment of rituals of various kinds that actors were seen as coming to be wedded to the norms and values of their culture, and/or to be purged, at least temporarily, of whatever dissident sentiments they might harbor (e.g., Gluckman 1955; V. Turner 1969; Beidelman 1966). The ritual focus, or what might be called for focus on extraordinary practice, became even stronger in the sixties and seventies. American symbolic anthropologists took up the view that ritual was one of the primary matrices for the reproduction of consciousness (Geertz 1973b; Ortner 1978), even if they dissented from certain aspects of the British approach. And the structural Marxists too placed great weight on the power of ritual to mediate social structural contradictions and mystify the workings of the system. Ritual in fact is a form of practice—people *do* it—and to study the reproduction of consciousness, mystified or otherwise, in the processes of ritual behavior is to study at least one way in which practice reproduces the system.

The newer practice approaches, by contrast, place greater emphasis on the practices of ordinary living. Although these were not by any means ignored in earlier work, they assume greater prominence here. Thus despite his stress on the highly intentionalized moments of practice, Bourdieu also pays close attention to the little routines people enact, again and again, in working, eating, sleeping, and relaxing, as well as the little scenarios of etiquette they play out again and again in social interaction. All of these routines and scenarios are predicated upon, and embody within themselves, the fundamental notions of temporal, spatial, and social ordering that underlie and organize the system as a whole. In enacting these routines, actors not only continue to be shaped by the underlying organizational principles involved, but continually re-endorse those principles in the world of public observation and discourse.

One question lurking behind all of this is whether in fact *all* practice, everything everybody does, embodies and hence reproduces the assumptions of the system. There is actually a profound philosophic issue here: how, if actors are fully cultural beings, they could ever do anything that does not in some way carry forward core cultural assumptions. On the more mundane level, the question comes down to whether divergent or nonnormative practices are simply variations upon basic cultural themes, or whether they actually imply alternative modes of social and cultural being.

These two formulations are grounded in two quite different models of systemic change. One is the classic Marxist model, in which the divisions of labor and the asymmetries of political relations create, in effect, incipient countercultures within the dominant system. At least some of the practices and modes of consciousness of dominated groups "escape" the prevailing hegemony. Change comes about as a result of class struggle in which formerly dominated groups succeed to power and institute a new hegemony based on their own distinctive ways of seeing and organizing the world.

There are a variety of problems with this model that I will not review here. I will simply note that it appears to overstate the differences of conceptual, as opposed to tactical, orientations between classes or other asymmetrically related entities. The model seems to work best when class differences are also, historically, cultural differences, as in cases of colonialism and imperialism (e.g., Taussig 1980). It works less well for many other sorts of cases with which anthropologists typically deal—culturally homogeneous systems in which inequities and asymmetries of various kinds (based on gender, age, or kinship, for example) are inseparable from complementarities and reciprocities that are equally real and equally strongly felt.

Recently, Marshall Sahlins has offered a model which derives systemic change from changes in practices in a rather different way. Sahlins argues that radical change need not be equated with the coming to power of groups with alternative visions of the world. He emphasizes instead the importance of changes of meaning of existing relations.

In a nutshell, Sahlins argues that people in different social positions have different "interests" (a term Sahlins worries over, and uses in an extended sense), and they act accordingly. This does not in itself imply either conflict or struggle, nor does it imply that people with different interests hold radically different views of the world. It does imply, however, that they will seek to enhance their respective positions when opportunities arise, although they will do so by means traditionally available to people in their positions. Change comes about when traditional strategies, which assume traditional patterns of relations (e.g., between chiefs and commoners, or between men and women), are deployed in relation to novel phenomena (e.g., the arrival of Captain Cook in Hawaii) which do not respond to those strategies in traditional ways. This change of context, this refractoriness of the real world to traditional expectations, calls into question both the strategies of practice and the nature of the relationships which they presuppose:

> . . . the pragmatics had its own dynamics: relationships that defeated both intention and convention. The complex of exchanges that developed between Hawaiians and Europeans . . . brought the former into uncharacteristic conditions of internal conflict and contradiction. Their differential connections with Europeans thereby endowed their own relationships to each other with novel functional content. This is structural transformation. The values acquired in practice return to structure as new relationships between its categories (Sahlins 1981:50).

Sahlins's model is appealing in a number of ways. As already noted, he does not equate divergence of interest with an almost countercultural formation, and is thus not forced to see change in terms of actual replacement of groups (although there is some of this, eventually, in the Hawaiian case too). Further, in arguing that change may come about largely through (abortive) attempts to apply traditional interpretations and practices, his model unites mechanisms of reproduction and transformation. Change, as he says, is failed reproduction. And finally, in stressing changes of *meaning* as an essentially revolutionary process, he renders revolution itself less extraordinary (if no less dramatic, in its own way) than the standard models would have it.

One may nonetheless register a few quibbles. For one thing, Sahlins is still struggling with the interest perspective. He confronts it briefly, and he offers a formula that attempts to soften some of its more ethnocentric qualities, but he does not really grapple with the full range of thought and feeling that moves actors to act, and to act in complex ways.

Further, one may suggest that Sahlins makes change appear a bit too easy. Of course the book is short, and the model only sketched. Moreover, the relative "openness" of any given system, and of different types of systems, is probably empirically variable (see, e.g., Yengoyan 1979). Nonetheless, Sahlins notes only in passing the many mechanisms that tend, in the normal course of events, to hold a system in place despite what appear to be important changes in practices. The moves to maintain the status quo by those who have vested interests are perhaps the least of these, and in any event they may backfire or produce unintended novel results. More important is the sort of "drag" introduced into the system by the fact that, as a result of enculturation, actors embody the system as well as living within it (see Bourdieu 1978). But mature actors are not all that flexible. An adequate model of the capacity of practice to revise structure must thus in all probability encompass a long-term, two- or three-generation developmental framework.

A related point derives from the fact that much of systemic reproduction takes place via the routinized activities and intimate interactions of domestic life. To the degree that domestic life is insulated from the wider social sphere (a degree generally much greater than is the case in Polynesia), important practices—of gender relations and child socialization—remain relatively untouched, and the transmission of novel meanings, values, and categorical relations to succeeding generations may be hindered. At the very least, what gets transmitted will be significantly—and conservatively—modified.

In short, there are probably far more linkages, and far more possibilities of slippage, in the route leading back from practice to structure than Sahlins's relatively smooth account allows for. Nonetheless, if the course of structural change is more difficult than he makes it appear, Sahlins presents a convincing account of how it may be easier than some would claim.

I close this final section with two reservations beyond those already expressed. The first concerns the centrality of domination within the contemporary practice framework, or at least within that segment of it upon which we have focused here. I am as persuaded as many of the authors that to penetrate into the workings of asymmetrical social relations is to penetrate to the heart of much of what is going on in any given system. I am equally convinced, however, that such an enterprise, taken by itself, is one-sided. Patterns of cooperation, reciprocity, and solidarity constitute the other side of the coin of social being. In this post-seventies context, views of the social in terms of sharing, exchange, and moral obligation—in David Schneider's famous phrase, "diffuse, enduring solidarity"—are treated largely as ideology. Often of course they *are* ideological. Yet a Hobbesian view of social life is surely as biased as one that harks back to Rousseau. An adequate model must encompass the full set.

My second point is not so much a critical reservation as a kind of fingering of an irony at the core of the practice model. The irony, although some may not feel it as such, is this: that although actors' intentions are accorded central place in the model, yet major social change does not for the most part come about as an *intended* consequence of action. Change is largely a by-product, an *un*intended consequence of action, however rational action may have been. Setting out to conceive children with superior mana by sleeping with British sailors, Hawaiian women became agents of the spirit of capitalism in their society. Setting out to preserve structure and reduce anomaly by killing a "god" who was really Captain Cook, the Hawaiians put in motion a train of events that ultimately brought down their gods, their chiefs, and their world as they knew it. To say that society and history are products of human action is true, but only in a certain ironic sense. They are rarely the products the actors themselves set out to make.[18]

[18] Michel Foucault, whose later work (1979 and 1980) is certainly part of the current practice trend, and who is making an impact in at least some quarters of anthropology, has put this point nicely: "People know what they do; they frequently know why they do what they do; but what they don't know is what what they do does" (quoted in Dreyfus and Rabinow 1982:187). I regret having been unable to incorporate Foucault into the discussions of this section. In particular, he has been struggling against some of the ramifications of the individualism at the heart of much of practice theory, although he has wound up tying himself into other knots—such as "intentionality without a subject, [and] a strategy without a strategist" (*ibid.*)—in the process.

CONCLUSIONS AND PROSPECTS

It has not been my intention, as I said earlier, to give an exhaustive account of any single school of anthropological thought over the last two decades. Rather I have been concerned with the relations between various intellectual trends in the field, within and across time. Nor has this been, as is surely obvious, a wholly disinterested inquiry. The strands of thought I have chosen to emphasize are those which I see as being most important in bringing the field to a certain position today, and my representations concerning where we are today are themselves clearly selective.

Much of what has been said in this essay can be subsumed within Peter Berger and Thomas Luckmann's little epigram: "Society is a human product. Society is an objective reality. Man is a social product" (1967:61). Most prior anthropologies have emphasized the second component of this set: society (or culture) has been regarded as an objective reality in some form or another, with its own dynamics divorced in large part from human agency. The American cultural and psychocultural anthropologists, in addition, have emphasized the third component, the ways in which society and culture shape personality, consciousness, ways of seeing and feeling. But until very recently, little effort has been put toward understanding how society and culture themselves are produced and reproduced through human intention and action. It is around this question, as I see it, that eighties anthropology is beginning to take shape, while at the same time maintaining—ideally—a sense of the truths of the other two perspectives.

I have thus taken practice as the key symbol of eighties anthropology. I am aware, however, that many would have chosen a different key symbol: history. Around this term clusters notions of time, process, duration, reproduction, change, development, evolution, transformation (see Cohn 1981). Rather than seeing the theoretical shift in the field as a move from structures and systems to persons and practices, it might thus be seen as a shift from static, synchronic analyses to diachronic, processual ones. Viewing the shift in this way, the practice approach comprises only one wing of the move to diachrony, emphasizing microdevelopmental processes—transactions, projects, careers, developmental cycles, and the like.

The other wing of the move to diachrony is macroprocessual or macrohistorical, and itself comprises at least two trends. On the one side, there is the political economy school already discussed, which attempts to understand change in the small-scale societies typically studied by anthropologists by relating that change to large-scale historical developments (especially colonialism and capitalist expansion) external to the societies in question. On the other, there is a more ethnographic sort of historical investigation, which pays greater attention to the internal developmental dynamics of particular societies over time. External impingements are taken into account, but there is greater effort to delineate forces of both stability and change at work within a given system, as well as the social and cultural filters operating to select and/or reinterpret whatever may be coming in from outside (e.g., Geertz 1980b; Blu 1980; R. Rosaldo 1980; Wallace 1980; Sahlins 1981; Ortner, in preparation; Kelly n.d.).

Anthropology's rapprochement with history is in my view an extremely important development for the field as a whole. If I have chosen in this essay not to emphasize it, it is only because, at the moment, the trend is too broad. It covers, rather than reveals, important distinctions. Insofar as history is being amalgamated with virtually every kind of anthropological work, it offers a pseudointegration of the field which fails to address some of the deeper problems. As argued in this essay, those deeper problems were generated by the very successes of systems and structuralist approaches, which established the reality of the thinglike nature of society, but which failed to ask, in any systematic way, where the thing comes from and how it might change.

To answer these questions with the word "history" is to avoid them, if by history is meant largely a chain of external events to which people react. History is not simply something that happens to people, but something they make—within, of course, the very powerful constraints of the system within which they are operating. A practice approach attempts to see this making, whether in the past or in the present, whether in the creation of novelty or in the reproduction of the same old thing. Rather than fetishizing history, a practice approach offers, or at least promises, a model that implicitly unifies both historical and anthropological studies.[19]

There have, of course, been attempts to put human agency back in the picture before. These attempts, however, yielded either too much or too little to the systems/structures perspective. In the case of Parsons's "general theory of action," action was seen almost purely as en-actment of the rules and roles of the system. In the cases of symbolic interactionism and transactionalism, systemic constraints were minimized, the system itself being viewed as a relatively unordered reservoir of "resources" that actors draw upon in constructing their strategies. The modern versions of practice theory, on the other hand, appear unique in accepting all three sides of the Berger and Luckmann triangle: that society is a system, that the system is powerfully constraining, and yet that the system can be made and unmade through human action and interaction.

[19] It might be objected that the political economists themselves put practice in a central position in their model. As external events impinge, actors in a given society react and attempt to deal with those impingements. The problem here is that action is primarily re-action. The reader might object in turn that re-action is central to Sahlins's model too. But the point in Sahlins is that the nature of the reaction is shaped as much by internal dynamics as by the nature of the external events.

All of which is not to say either that the practice perspective represents the end of the intellectual dialectic or that it is perfect. I have touched upon many of its defects in the present essay. Like any theory, it is a product of its times. Once, practice had the romantic aura of voluntarism—"man," as the saying went, "makes himself." Now practice has qualities related to the hard times of today: pragmatism, maximization of advantage, "every man," as the saying goes, "for himself." Such a view seems natural in the context of the failure of many of the social movements of the sixties and seventies, and in the context of a disastrous economy and a heated up nuclear threat. Yet however realistic it may appear at the moment, such a view is as skewed as voluntarism itself. A lot of work remains to be done.

REFERENCES

Alland, Alex. 1975. "Adaptation," in *Annual Review of Anthropology*, 4. Palo Alto: Annual Reviews, Inc.

Althusser, Louis. 1971. *Lenin and Philosophy*, Ben Brewster, trans. New York and London: Monthly Review Press.

American Ethnologist. 1978. Special issue on *Political Economy* (5:3).

Asad, Talal, ed. 1973. *Anthropology and the Colonial Encounter*. London: Ithaca Press.

Avineri, Shlomo. 1971. *The Social and Political Thought of Karl Marx*. Cambridge: Cambridge University Press.

Babcock, Barbara, ed. 1978. *The Reversible World: Symbolic Inversion in Art and Society*. Ithaca, New York: Cornell University Press.

Bailey, F. G. 1969. *Strategems and Spoils*. New York: Schocken.

Barnes, J. A. 1980. "Kinship Studies: Some Impressions on the Current State of Play." *Man*, 15:2, 293–303.

Barnett, Steve. 1977. "Identity Choice and Caste Ideology," in *Symbolic Anthropology*, J. Dolgin, D. Kemnitzer, and D. Schneider, eds. New York: Columbia University Press.

Barnett, Steve, and Silverman, Martin G. 1979. *Ideology and Everyday Life*. Ann Arbor: University of Michigan Press.

Barth, Fredrik. 1966. "Models of Social Organization." Royal Anthropological Institute of Great Britain and Ireland, Occasional Papers 23.

Bateson, Gregory. 1972. *Steps to an Ecology of Mind*. New York: Ballantine Books.

Bauman, Richard, and Sherzer, Joel, eds. 1974. *Explorations in the Ethnography of Speaking*. Cambridge: Cambridge University Press.

Bauman, Zygmund. 1973. *Culture as Praxis*. London and Boston: Routledge and Kegan Paul.

Becker, A. L. 1979. "Text-Building, Epistemology, and Aesthetics in Javanese Shadow Theater," in *The Imagination of Reality*, A. L. Becker and A. A. Yengoyan, eds. Norwood, New Jersey: Ablex.

Beidelman, Thomas. 1966. "Swazi Royal Ritual." *Africa*, 36:4, 373–405.

Berger, Peter, and Luckmann, Thomas. 1967. *The Social Construction of Reality*. Garden City, New York: Doubleday.

Berreman, Gerald. 1962. *Behind Many Masks: Ethnography and Impression Management in a Himalayan Village*. Monograph 4. Ithaca, New York: Society for Applied Anthropology.

Bloch, Maurice. 1971. "The Moral and Tactical Meaning of Kinship Terms." *Man*, 6:1, 79–87.

———. 1974. "The Long Term and the Short Term: The Economic and Political Significance of the Morality of Kinship," in *The Character of Kinship*, J. Goody, ed. Cambridge: Cambridge University Press.

———. 1977. "The Disconnection between Power and Rank as a Process." *Archives Européene de Sociologie*, 18:107–48.

Blu, Karen. 1980. *The Lumbee Problem: The Making of an American Indian People*. Cambridge: Cambridge University Press.

Blumer, Herbert. 1962. "Society as Symbolic Interaction," in *Human Behavior and Social Processes*, A. M. Rose, ed. Boston: Houghton Mifflin.

Boon, James A. 1972. "Further Operations of 'Culture' in Anthropology: A Synthesis of and for Debate." *Social Science Quarterly*, 52 (September), 221–52.

Boon, James A., and Schneider, David M. 1974. "Kinship vis-à-vis Myth: Contrasts in Lévi-Strauss' Approach to Cross-cultural Comparison." *American Anthropologist*, 76:4, 794–817.

Bourdieu, Pierre. 1978 [1972]. *Outline of a Theory of Practice*, Richard Nice, trans. Cambridge: Cambridge University Press.

Bradbury, Malcolm. 1981. Comment on "Modern Literary Theory: Its Place in Teaching." *Times Literary Supplement*, (6 February), 137.

Childe, V. Gordon. 1942. *What Happened in History*. New York: Penguin.

Cohn, Bernard S. 1981. "Anthropology and History in the 1980's." *Journal of Interdisciplinary History*, 12:2, 227–52.

Cole, P., and Morgan, J., eds. 1975. *Syntax and Semantics 3: Speech Acts*. New York: Academic Press.

Collier, Jane, and Rosaldo, Michelle Z. 1981. "Politics and Gender in Simple Societies," in *Sexual Meanings: The Cultural Construction of Gender and Sexuality*, Sherry B. Ortner and Harriet Whitehead, eds. Cambridge and New York: Cambridge University Press.

Crapanzano, Vincent. 1980. *Tuhami: Portrait of a Moroccan*. Chicago: University of Chicago Press.

DeGeorge, Richard, and DeGeorge, Fernande, eds. 1972. *The Structuralists from Marx to Lévi-Strauss*. Garden City, New York: Doubleday.

Diamond, Stanley, ed. 1979. *Toward a Marxist Anthropology*. The Hague: Mouton.

Dolgin, J.; Kemnitzer, D.; and Schneider, D. M. 1977. "As People Express Their Lives, So They Are . . ." in their *Symbolic Anthropology*. New York: Columbia University Press.

Douglas, Mary. 1966. *Purity and Danger*. New York: Frederick A. Praeger.

Dreyfus, Hubert L., and Rabinow, Paul. 1982. *Michel Foucault: Beyond Structuralism and Hermeneutics*. Chicago: University of Chicago Press.

Dumont, Louis. 1965. "The Modern Conception of the Individual: Notes on Its Genesis." *Contributions to Indian Sociology*, 8:1, 13–61.

———. 1970. *Homo Hierarchicus: An Essay on the Caste System*, M. Sainsbury, trans. Chicago: University of Chicago Press.

Fernandez, James. 1974. "The Mission of Metaphor in Expressive Culture." *Current Anthropology*, 15:2, 119–45.

Firth, Raymond. 1963 [1951]. *Elements of Social Organization*. Boston: Beacon Press.

Foucault, Michel. 1979. *Discipline and Punish: The Birth of the Prison*, Alan Sheridan, trans. New York: Random House.

———. 1980. *The History of Sexuality*. Volume I, Robert Hurley, trans. New York: Vintage.

Friedman, Jonathan. 1974. "Marxism, Structuralism, and Vulgar Materialism." *Man*, n.s. 9:3, 444–69.

______. 1975. "Tribes, States and Transformations," in *Marxist Analyses and Social Anthropology*, M. Bloch, ed. New York: John Wiley and Sons.

Friedrich, Paul. 1970. *Agrarian Revolt in a Mexican Village*. Englewood Cliffs, New Jersey: Prentice-Hall.

______. 1977. "Sanity and the Myth of Honor: The Problem of Achilles." *Ethos*, 5:3, 281–305.

Geertz, Clifford. 1973. *The Interpretation of Cultures*. New York: Basic Books.

______. 1973a. "Thick Description: Toward an Interpretive Theory of Culture," in Geertz, *Interpretation of Cultures*.

______. 1973b. "Religion as a Cultural System," in Geertz, *Interpretation of Cultures*.

______. 1973c. "Ideology as a Cultural System," in Geertz, *Interpretation of Cultures*.

______. 1973d. "The Cerebral Savage: On the Work of Claude Lévi-Strauss," in Geertz, *Interpretation of Cultures*.

______. 1973e. "Person, Time and Conduct in Bali," in Geertz, *Interpretation of Cultures*.

______. 1973f. "Deep Play: Notes on the Balinese Cockfight," in Geertz, *Interpretation of Cultures*.

______. 1975. "On the Nature of Anthropological Understanding." *American Scientist*, 63:1, 47–53.

______. 1980a. "Blurred Genres: The Refiguration of Social Thought." *The American Scholar*, 49:2, 165–79.

______. 1980b. *Negara: The Theater-State in Nineteenth Century Bali*. Princeton: Princeton University Press.

Genovese, Eugene D. 1976. *Roll, Jordan, Roll: The World the Slaves Made*. New York: Random House.

Giddens, Anthony. 1971. *Capitalism and Modern Social Theory*. Cambridge: Cambridge University Press.

______. 1979. *Central Problems in Social Theory: Action, Structure and Contradiction in Social Analysis*. Cambridge: Cambridge University Press.

Gluckman, Max. 1955. *Custom and Conflict in Africa*. Glencoe, Illinois: The Free Press.

Godelier, Maurice. 1977. *Perspectives in Marxist Anthropology*, Robert Brain, trans. Cambridge: Cambridge University Press.

Goffman, Erving. 1959. *The Presentation of Self in Everyday Life*. Garden City, New York: Doubleday.

Goldman, Irving. 1970. *Ancient Polynesian Society*. Chicago: University of Chicago Press.

Goldmann, Lucien. 1977. *Cultural Creation in Modern Society*, Bart Grahl, trans. Oxford: Basil Blackwell.

Goody, Esther N., ed. 1978. *Questions and Politeness: Strategies in Social Interaction*. New York: Cambridge University Press.

Gramsci, Antonio. 1957. *The Modern Prince and Other Writings*, Louis Marks, trans. New York: International Publishers.

Gregor, Thomas. 1977. *Mehinaku: The Drama of Daily Life in a Brazilian Indian Village*. Chicago: University of Chicago Press.

Guemple, Lee. 1972. Panel on "Cultural Basis of Social Relations: Kinship, Person, and Actor." Annual Meetings of the American Anthropological Association, Toronto.

Gunder Frank, Andre. 1967. *Capitalism and Underdevelopment in Latin America.* New York and London: Monthly Review Press.

Habermas, Jürgen. 1973. *Theory and Practice,* John Viertel, trans. Boston: Beacon Press.

Harris, Marvin. 1966. "The Cultural Ecology of India's Sacred Cattle." *Current Anthropology,* 7:1, 51–64.

———. 1968. *The Rise of Anthropological Theory.* New York: Crowell.

———. 1978. "No End of Messiahs." *New York Times* (26 November), sec. 4, p. 21.

Hart, Keith. 1982. *The Development of Commercial Agriculture in West Africa.* Cambridge: Cambridge University Press.

Hart, C. W. M., and Pilling, Arnold R. 1960. *The Tiwi of North Australia.* New York: Holt, Rinehart, Winston.

Hymes, Dell, ed. 1974. *Reinventing Anthropology.* New York: Vintage.

Kahn, Joel S. 1980. *Minangkabau Social Formations: Indonesian Peasants and the World Economy.* Cambridge: Cambridge University Press.

Kapferer, Bruce, ed. 1976. *Transaction and Meaning: Directions in the Anthropology of Exchange and Human Behavior.* Philadelphia: ISHI Publications.

Kelly, Raymond. n.d. "The Nuer Conquest: A Case Study in the Structure of Non-equilibrium Systems." Manuscript.

Kirkpatrick, John T. 1977. "Person, Hierarchy, and Autonomy in Traditional Yapese Theory," in *Symbolic Anthropology,* Dolgin, Kemnitzer, and Schneider, eds.

Kracke, Waud H. 1978. *Force and Persuasion: Leadership in an Amazonian Society.* Chicago: University of Chicago Press.

Leach, Edmund. 1954. *Political Systems of Highland Burma.* Boston: Beacon Press.

———. 1960. "The Sinhalese of the Dry Zone of Northern Ceylon," in *Social Structure in Southeast Asia,* G. P. Murdock, ed. London: Tavistock.

———. 1964. "Anthropological Aspects of Language: Animal Categories and Verbal Abuse," in *New Directions in the Study of Language,* E. H. Lenneberg, ed. Cambridge: MIT Press.

———. 1966. *Rethinking Anthropology.* London School of Economics Monographs on Social Anthropology, no. 22. New York: Humanities Press.

———. 1969. *Genesis as Myth and Other Essays.* London: Jonathan Cape.

Leach, Edmund, ed. 1967. *The Structural Study of Myth and Totemism.* London: Tavistock.

Lévi-Strauss, Claude. 1963. "The Effectiveness of Symbols," in his *Structural Anthropology,* C. Jacobson and B. G. Schoepf, trans. New York: Basic Books.

———. 1964–71. *Mythologiques (Introduction to a Science of Mythology).* 4 vols. Paris: Plon.

———. 1967. "La Geste d'Asdiwal," in *Structural Study of Myth and Totemism,* Leach, ed.

Levy, Robert. 1973. *Tahitians: Mind and Experience in the Society Islands.* Chicago: University of Chicago Press.

Lewis, Gilbert. 1977. "A Mother's Brother to a Sister's Son," in *Symbols and Sentiments,* I. Lewis, ed. London: Academic Press.

Marriott, McKim. 1976. "Hindu Transactions: Diversity without Dualism," in *Transaction and Meaning,* Kapferer, ed.

Meeker, Michael E. 1979. *Literature and Violence in North Arabia.* Cambridge: Cambridge University Press.

Moore, Sally Falk, and Myerhoff, Barbara G., eds. 1975. *Symbols and Politics in Communal Ideology.* Ithaca, New York: Cornell University Press.

Munn, Nancy. 1969. "The Effectiveness of Symbols in Murngin Rite and Myth," in *Forms of Symbolic Action*, R. Spencer, ed. Seattle: University of Washington Press.

Myerhoff, Barbara G. 1974. *Peyote Hunt: The Sacred Journey of the Huichol Indians*. Ithaca, New York: Cornell University Press.

Needham, Rodney. 1973a. "The Left Hand of the Mugwe: An Analytical Note on the Structure of Meru Symbolism," in *Right and Left*, Needham, ed.

Needham, Rodney, ed. 1973b. *Right and Left: Essays on Dual Symbolic Classification*. Chicago: University of Chicago Press.

O'Laughlin, Bridget. 1974. "Mediation of a Contradiction: Why Mbum Women do not eat Chicken," in *Woman, Culture and Society*, M. Rosaldo and L. Lamphere, eds. Stanford: Stanford University Press.

Ollman, Bertell. 1971. *Alienation: Marx's Conception of Man in Capitalist Society*. Cambridge: Cambridge University Press.

Ortner, Sherry B. 1975. "Gods' Bodies, Gods' Food: A Symbolic Analysis of a Sherpa Ritual," in *The Interpretation of Symbolism*, R. Willis, ed. London: Malaby Press.

______. 1978. *Sherpas through their Rituals*. Cambridge: Cambridge University Press.

______. 1981. "Gender and Sexuality in Hierarchical Societies: The Case of Polynesia and Some Comparative Implications," in *Sexual Meanings*, S. Ortner and H. Whitehead, eds. Cambridge: Cambridge University Press.

______. In preparation. "High Religion: An Interpretive History of Sherpa Buddhism." Manuscript.

Parsons, Talcott. 1949 [1937]. *The Structure of Social Action*. New York: The Free Press of Glencoe.

Parsons, Talcott, and Shils, Edward A., eds. 1962 [1951]. *Toward a General Theory of Action*. New York: Harper and Row.

Paul, Robert A. 1982. *The Tibetan Symbolic World: Psychoanalytic Explorations*. Chicago: University of Chicago Press.

Piddocke, Stuart. 1969. "The Potlatch System of the Southern Kwakiutl: A New Perspective," in *Environment and Cultural Behavior*, A. P. Vayda, ed. Austin: University of Texas Press.

Rabinow, Paul. 1975. *Symbolic Domination: Cultural Form and Historical Change in Morocco*. Chicago: University of Chicago Press.

______. 1977. *Reflections on Fieldwork in Morocco*. Berkeley: University of California Press.

Rabinow, Paul, and Sullivan, William M. 1979. "The Interpretive Turn: Emergence of an Approach," in their *Interpretive Social Socience, A Reader*. Berkeley: University of California Press.

Rappaport, Roy A. 1967. *Pigs for the Ancestors*. New Haven: Yale University Press.

Riegelhaupt, Joyce. 1978. "The Revolt of Maria da Fonte: Peasants, 'Women,' and the State." Manuscript.

Riesman, Paul. 1977. *Freedom in Fulani Social Life: An Introspective Ethnography*. Chicago: University of Chicago Press.

Rosaldo, Michelle Z. 1980. *Knowledge and Passion: Ilongot Notions of Self and Social Life*. Cambridge: Cambridge University Press.

______. 1981. "Towards an Anthropology of Self and Feeling." Manuscript.

Rosaldo, Renato. 1980. *Ilongot Headhunting, 1883–1974*. Stanford: Stanford University Press.

Rosen, Lawrence. 1978. "The Negotiation of Reality: Male-Female Relations in

Sefrou, Morocco," in *Women in the Muslim World*, L. Beck and N. Keddie, eds. Cambridge: Harvard University Press.

Ross, Eric B., ed. 1980. *Beyond the Myth of Culture: Essays in Cultural Materialism*. New York and London: Academic Press.

Sahlins, Marshall, 1964. "Culture and Environment," in *Horizons of Anthropology*, S. Tax, ed. Chicago: Aldine.

———. 1972. *Stone Age Economics*. Chicago: Aldine.

———. 1981. *Historical Metaphors and Mythical Realities: Structure in the Early History of the Sandwich Islands Kingdom*. Ann Arbor: University of Michigan Press.

Sahlins, Marshall, and Service, Elman R., eds. 1960. *Evolution and Culture*. Ann Arbor: University of Michigan Press.

Said, Edward W. 1979. *Orientalism*. New York: Vintage.

Schneider, David M. 1968. *American Kinship: A Cultural Account*. Englewood Cliffs, New Jersey: Prentice-Hall.

———. 1977. "Kinship, Nationality, and Religion in American Culture: Toward a Definition of Kinship," in *Symbolic Anthropology*, Dolgin, Kemnitzer, and Schneider, eds.

Schneider, Jane. 1978. "Peacocks and Penguins: The Political Economy of European Cloth and Colors." *American Ethnologist*, 5:3, 413–47.

Schneider, Jane, and Schneider, Peter. 1976. *Culture and Political Economy in Western Sicily*. New York: Academic Press.

Service, Elman, R. 1958. *Profiles in Ethnology*. New York: Harper and Row.

Singer, Milton. 1980. "Signs of the Self: An Exploration in Semiotic Anthropology." *American Anthropologist*, 82:3, 485–507.

Steward, Julian H. 1953. "Evolution and Process," in *Anthropology Today*, A. L. Kroeber, ed. Chicago: University of Chicago Press.

———. 1955. *Theory of Culture Change*. Urbana: University of Illinois Press.

Tambiah, Stanley J. 1968. "The Magical Power of Words." *Man*, n.s. 3:2, 175–208.

———. 1969. "Animals Are Good to Think and Good to Prohibit." *Ethnology*, 8:4, 423–59.

Taussig, Michael T. 1980. *The Devil and Commodity Fetishism in South America*. Chapel Hill: University of North Carolina Press.

Terray, Emmanuel. 1972. *Marxism and "Primitive" Societies*, Mary Klopper, trans. New York: Monthly Review Press.

———. 1975. "Classes and Class Consciousness in the Abron Kingdom of Gyaman," in *Marxist Analyses and Social Anthropology*, M. Bloch, ed. New York: John Wiley and Sons.

Thompson, E. P. 1966. *The Making of the English Working Class*. New York: Vintage.

———. 1978. *The Poverty of Theory and Other Essays*. New York: Monthly Review Press.

Turner, Terence S. 1969. "Oedipus: Time and Structure in Narrative Form," in *Forms of Symbolic Action*, R. Spencer, ed. Seattle: University of Washington Press.

Turner, Victor. 1967. *The Forest of Symbols*. Ithaca, New York: Cornell University Press.

———. 1969. *The Ritual Process*. Chicago: Aldine.

Wagner, Roy. 1975. *The Invention of Culture*. Chicago: University of Chicago Press.

Wallace, Anthony F. C. 1980. *Rockdale: The Growth of an American Village in the Early Industrial Revolution*. New York: W. W. Norton.

Wallerstein, Emmanuel. 1976. *The Modern World System*. New York: Academic Press.
White, Leslie A. 1943. "Energy and the Evolution of Culture." *American Anthropologist*, 45:3, 335–56.
______. 1949. *The Science of Culture*. New York: Farrar Straus.
Williams, Raymond. 1973. *The Country and the City*. New York: Oxford University Press.
______. 1976. *Keywords: A Vocabulary of Culture and Society*. New York: Oxford University Press.
______. 1977. *Marxism and Literature*. Oxford: Oxford University Press.
Wolf, Eric R. 1969. *Peasant Wars of the Twentieth Century*. New York: Harper and Row.
______. 1980. "They Divide and Subdivide and Call it Anthropology." *New York Times* (30 November), Ideas and Trends Section, p. E9.
Worsley, Peter. 1968. *The Trumpet Shall Sound: A Study of "Cargo" Cults in Melanesia*. New York: Schocken.
Yalman, Nur. 1969. "The Structure of Sinhalese Healing Rituals," in *Forms of Symbolic Action*, R. Spencer, ed. Seattle: University of Washington Press.
Yengoyan, A. A. 1979. "Cultural Forms and a Theory of Constraints," in *The Imagination of Reality*, A. L. Becker and A. A. Yengoyan, eds. Norwood, New Jersey: Ablex.

Note: This article was originally submitted in July 1982. A number of relevant works have been published since then which could not be incorporated into the discussion or the bibliography.

[9]

THE INDIVIDUAL, COMMUNITY AND SOCIETY: RIGHTS AND RESPONSIBILITIES FROM AN ANTHROPOLOGICAL PERSPECTIVE

COLIN M. TURNBULL*

Contents

I. INTRODUCTION 77

II. THE RETRIBUTION-RESTITUTION DICHOTOMY 78

III. AMERICAN COURTS AND TRADITIONAL AFRICAN TRIBUNALS ... 81

IV. AMERICAN CONCEPTS OF INDIVIDUAL, COMMUNITY AND SOCIETY RE-EXAMINED 85

V. INDIVIDUAL, COMMUNITY AND SOCIETY IN ANTHROPOLOGICAL CONTEXT 88

- A. *Concepts and Definitions* 88
- B. *A Specific African Culture: The Mbuti* 92
- C. *The Western Concept of "Community"* 99
  - 1. The Size and Nature of a "Community" 99
  - 2. A "Community" in Virginia 101
- D. *The Mbuti Again* 105
- E. *The Amish and the Mbuti* 111
- F. *Community-Society Conflict* 117
  - 1. The Reciprocity Issue 117
  - 2. The Factor of the Sacred in Amish and Mbuti Communities 117
  - 3. The Poletown Conflict in Detroit 121

VI. A WORKABLE BASIS FOR A RELATIONSHIP AMONG INDIVIDUAL, COMMUNITY AND SOCIETY 125

I. INTRODUCTION

As a social anthropologist, my concern and interest in the topic is not only with various levels of social integration and their structures, but also

* Professor, George Washington University. B.A. 1947, Oxford University; M.A. 1948, Oxford University; D. Phil. 1964, Oxford University.

with the law and with legal institutions as they exist and function in American society. The institutions of one society may better be understood by cross-cultural comparison, a technique that stimulates our thinking about the legal, social and moral aspects of specific issues in our own society. In comparing two contrasting forms of society, loosely described as "primitive" and "civilized," we discover different concepts as well as different practices relating to the three social units under consideration in this article. Primitive usage suggests that our own system, while well adapted to our own specific context, still may be suffering from certain deficiencies. This article will present examples from other cultures not with any thought that the examples in themselves may serve as models which can be adopted elsewhere, but because the examples throw new light on the basic principle at work, on the social process, and hence on our own law and legal institutions.

The justification for such a study lies, at least in part, in the evident dissatisfaction with our legal system and with the disjunction between law and justice. This dissatisfaction is expressed both in and out of court, by the general public as well as by practitioners of the law, by victims as well as criminals. This article will examine how it is that other cultures are able largely to avoid this malaise and to arrive more easily at a harmony between the exercise of authority and achievement of justice. Sometimes other cultures arrive at a greater degree of order without law than we often seem to achieve with it, perhaps thereby achieving a greater degree of justice for all. This article will also confront the issue of what the terms "individual," "community," and "society" really imply, their structural relationship with each other, and the rights and responsibilities of each.

First, however, from the vantage point of having lived and worked with a variety of "primitive" societies, I will start by looking at a few specific aspects of our own society to make the comparison more productive. No value judgment is implied on the fact that I ignore our society's obvious merits and select only those aspects of our system that merit adverse criticism. Space and time alone demand selectivity. The anthropologist is not interested in making any judgment against one form of social organization or for another, since he recognizes that each society tends to develop the system best suited to its particular context. Our own system, however, has been undergoing such far reaching changes over such a short period of time that we may not have had time to develop what is suited to our context, for our needs and context are in a constant state of flux. And if public dissatisfaction is any measure, the system is not even what we want.

II. The Retribution-Restitution Dichotomy

My most intimate contact with the legal system in our country comes from teaching and research in a number of prisons. Many of those I have interviewed in prison, even when they admit their guilt (that is, admit that they committed what the law has determined to be a crime, which is a rather different thing from admitting moral culpability), genuinely feel that they have been done an injustice even while they recognize their responsibility in consciously committing the act.

We must put aside the temptation to dismiss this as irrational self seeking or self pity. Regardless of its validity, the sentiment is very real indeed. Such sentiment has profound social implications and must be dealt with. The injustice often stems from comparison with judgments passed on others of different social, economic or religious origins for the same offense, sometimes in the same court. Comparison with judgments for comparable acts in neighboring counties or states aggravates the sense of injustice. With or without justification the law is in this way brought into disrepute and even invites disrespect from the individual. Yet, among a comparable class of individuals on the African societies, this sense of injustice is almost totally absent even among those whom we would say were penalized most heavily. Part of the reason is that the "penalty" is not regarded as such, but rather as a welcome means of making restitution and of being restored to society. Moreover, judgments earn respect because they are not valid until they are accepted by all. The only exceptions have occurred when traditional customary expectation has been replaced by western law, which takes judgment out of the hands of the community.

In our own society, the prison system illustrates the malaise most clearly. The malaise is not confined to those serving in prisons, but the prison is perhaps the most obvious and most disturbing by-product of our legal system. We know prisons to be breeding grounds for discontent and social maladjustment, and hence of future crime. Prisons are even more insidiously breeding grounds for discontent with and abuse of the legal process itself. This discontent makes itself felt far beyond the prison walls, permeating society at large. When those convicted and their families view the convictions as marked by chance and caprice, if not by wilful bigotry and prejudice, their demand for "justice" is frequently no more than a demand for vengeance, for self satisfaction. Ultimately, the prison system even victimizes its own employees, creating yet other grounds not only for discontent but also for disrespect for the law.

Many nearly illiterate inmates voice an observation that would be precisely the one made by almost any anthropologist comparing our legal system with a typically "primitive" manner of resolving conflict. The inmates I have interviewed unanimously have observed that our system seems to be primarily concerned with retribution, and even denies the person convicted the possibility of making restitution. This is one of the most deeply felt sources of the pervasive sense of injustice, not only among petty thieves who say they would see more sense to their incarceration if in some way it enabled them to make restitution, but even among murderers on death row. Of course, capital punishment is the institution in which our system most effectively excludes any possibility of atonement. Yet, even in murder cases, traditional African societies often strive for and effect not only reconciliation, but restitution.

It is worth taking a moment to look at how this works in Africa because it highlights the relationship between the individual, community and society. Thus, among the Bira of Zaire, as among many other such rural farming societies, the real victim is not the murdered person, nor even his or her family, but society itself. Nor is the act of murder in itself necessarily and inherently right or wrong. In assessing such rightness or wrongness not only the intent must be considered, but also the result. The result in question is not merely the death of an individual, but the social import of that death for society. Thus, the death of a healthy child might be considered as more serious than that of an aged and sick person who has become a burden to society, while conversely the death of a weak or deformed child would be weighed lightly against the death of a wise elder who had much to give society. In determining the appropriate societal response to an act of murder, the objective is not to hit upon a "fair" or "just" penalty, but to have the murderer take the steps necessary to repair the damage to the social fabric.

Further, while murder generally is considered "wrong" (i.e., harmful to society), murder also is considered unnatural for much the same reason as leads our courts to presume "innocence" until otherwise proven. So, much of the inquiry among the Bira centers on the *cause* of this unnatural condition in an otherwise perfectly natural (and social) person. In our courts the accused is allowed to introduce "mitigating circumstances," but in other societies instead of being peripheral or secondary, such circumstances are central. Only when the full social implications of a murder have been assessed, including the conscious motive, the cause or causes, and the damage to society, is any decision reached.

Such a decision is always related directly to the individual case and tailored precisely to the need for effective restitution. Economic damage must be repaired, but so must personal, familial, and even emotional damage. Damage to narrowly individual rights ranks lowest, much as individual responsibility ranks lower than collective responsibility. The assessment of "cause" almost invariably serves to distribute responsibility for the act. Family or friends may in this way be judged as "accomplices." The victim or the victim's family and friends can be held to share in the "guilt." But even family rights and responsibilities are held subordinate to those of community, and so on up through various levels of integration such as lineage and clan, to the rights and responsibilities of society itself.

These rights and responsibilities are social, economic, political and religious. All four of these must be taken into account, in such societies, when assessing damage and restitution. A man who has killed a woman obviously cannot bear children in her place, but if he has female kin they could and would undertake that role for the bereaved husband (and his family). Instead, he could name any children subsequently born to him as if they had been born to the murdered woman, and they would be brought up as such with full rights in her family and that of her widower, but none in those of their biological parents. If a boy is killed before he has been circumcised, if he was close to the age of circumcision, the operation is performed with all the ritual and social obligations, again shared by those judged to be causal factors as well as by the murderer himself and his family. Among the Bira this satisfies specific political and religious niceties essential to the continuity of political and religious life, and it also satisfies what would otherwise be a major source of emotional stress, the failure of the boy to complete this important stage of the life cycle.

In these and many other similar ways the "criminal" as well as those who contributed to the cause of the crime (and this always includes immediate kin) all share in the task of restitution in all four areas of social life. Ultimately, this must result in the restoration of previously existing social relationships between all involved. Fines, and even exile where (rarely) imposed are not considered as punishments, but rather as obligations and/or opportunities for restitution and atonement. In similar ways, most traditional community-oriented societies achieve justice for both victim and offender by seeking, finding and coercing a restoration of the original *status-quo*, including as far as possible the restoration of the normal social, interpersonal and intergroup relationships vital for the ongoing life of the society.

III. American Courts and Traditional African Tribunals

Comparisons between a county court and a traditional African tribunal or council, its nearest equivalent, are also instructive. Generalizations about either society are of course dangerous, but perhaps permissible here since we are looking for general principles. While my sample in this country admittedly is small, numbering fewer than two hundred inmates with whom I have had personal contact and/or maintained more than casual correspondence, I have not met a single one who has been able to associate a court or court procedure with either honor or justice. This is in sharp contrast to the Bira, where even those unfavorably adjudged by village tribunals may come away with understandable feelings of personal embarrassment, disappointment, even anger, but with their respect for the "law" (i.e., for the ideal way of life and its rights and responsibilities) reaffirmed by the actions of others, and even heightened by the ritual and religious elements of the procedure.

The reasons cited for the unfavorable attitude of inmates in this country vary from accusations of blatant prejudice to judicial incompetence. Discretionary powers are seen as vested in magistrates and justices who not only may be ill-versed in the law, but who too often see the position as one enabling them to impose their own private and individual view of what society (and the individual) should be upon the community under their jurisdiction. Since the position is regarded by some as a moderately lucrative and prestigious form of retirement, we could in some cases add senility to the complaints of imcompetence, bigotry and megalomania. This may sound like an overstatement of reality, however limited. If anything it is an understatement of the opinion held by many of those processed through our judicial system, an opinion spread outwards through them to their families, friends, and others of the public who have not experienced the courts as they *can* function, with honor and justice.

Without looking for these unfortunate characteristics, I have seen them at work in five states in both civil and criminal courts, in cases ranging from failure to pay rent to capital murder. The very appointment of Supreme Court Justices can be interpreted as being a matter of political whim rather than of concern with justice. Even if this allegation is not true, the fact that it is made and taken seriously threatens the good repute of the overall system.

The variable competence of judges, as with their variable predisposition to allow personal opinion and belief to enter into the proceedings, results from many factors, educational ones included. The one the general public would be least likely to recognize as prime, but which any village African would pick out at once, is the failure of some judges to separate the social self from the individual self, the office from the person. Yet the ritual of separation is there, clear for all to see if only we were more ritually conscious, in court dress, insignia, paraphernalia, in the use of horizontal and vertical orientation with their connotations of right and left, up and down, with good and bad, and so on. We readily fail to see the function of the "primitive" mask, often worn by judges as a public demonstration that the judgment rendered is not theirs, but that of the sacred authority they represent. Similarly, we fail to accept the function of our judicial robes and insignia and ritual procedure. So, I suspect, do some of the judges I have seen in action.

That, of course, is largely an educational problem, particularly aggravating in a plural society such as ours in which it is difficult to find symbols that have the same significance for all, just as it is impossible to find a common belief system. One might contrast the great strength of the traditional African court, the appeal to a common Sacred, accepted by all because it is believed in by all. Our society is not without religious fervor by any means, but it is fervor that divides rather than unites.

Another factor that we tend to neglect when we consider court composition has the same potential for us that it does for the traditional small-scale society. The factor is family, and the associated concept of individual rights and responsibilities as being morally, if not legally, interconnected with the rights and responsibilities of family. We tend to expect, and often prefer, to be heard in a court composed of strangers, suspecting that personal prejudice is likely to be more of a factor in a court composed of kith and kin. A village African would find it virtually impossible to accept that justice was being done in any court unless his kith and kin were not only present, but made an integral part of the enquiry, giving evidence and taking part in the adjudication. At the village level, in Africa and elsewhere in small-scale societies, the court is composed almost exclusively of kith and kin, including the judge or judges. In our own country, in some small, rural courts, we find something of the same process at work. Here the similarities as well as the differences are instructive. We shall examine them more closely in our discussion of "community."

In our own society the secularization of the court and its officials has weakened authority by removing the sense of infallibility associated with the sacred, and by placing authority openly in the hands of fallible humans. If respect is shown in court, it well may be for power rather than authority. The fact that our courts are composed of strangers rather than kith and kin aggravates any potential lack of confidence or suspicion of prejudice or incompetence. While the jury system helps, our Bira critic would say it is a poor substitute. By his standards a jury of strangers is necessarily a jury of incompetents, the more so since they typically have no training or experience in critical analysis and evaluation, have no first hand knowledge of the parties or problems before them, and do not have unlimited time with which to study the issues.

By contrast, even at the crucial upper level of the Bira process, the final decision-making process involves all parties, and a system of checks and balances operates to make the exercise of individual prejudice or self-interest impossible. Perhaps most dramatically of all, the participation of the entire community often is required. As a result, not only is the objective of the tribunal different from that of our courts (that is, restitution rather than retribution), but so is the entire process.

We place different values on objectivity and subjectivity. We claim than an "impartial" jury of strangers can be more objective, having no personal stake in the outcome of the case. The Bira would deny that this is so, since the beliefs and convictions of each member of the jury are at stake, and they may be very different from those of the litigants. Much of the "objectivity" is thus a pretense, however honest the effort. Far better, the Bira would say, to be judged by those who know you well and whose welfare intimately is bound up with yours and that of others involved in the proceedings. If that effective interdependence is reflected in the court composition, the Bira would say, it is unquestionably in the court's interest to resolve the case in such a way that is satisfactory to all by restoring and reinforcing the human relationships, the social bonds of rights and responsibilities, that are manifestly in the interests of all. Again, he would say, one of the major problems with our system is the value we place on the individual and on independence, rather than on society and interdependence.

Another factor worth comparing is the relationship between the accuser and the accused, in the context of their objectives and the objectives of the court. While in our society economic restitution increasingly is being written into judgments given in criminal cases, it is a far cry from what is meant by restitution in the African tribunal we have been looking at. Moreover, economic restitution is generally considered only in minor cases with some highly significant, if controversial, exceptions involving major corporations. The more serious the offense, and certainly when the offense involves violence, the less likely it is that a solution will be found that will be satisfactory to both parties and will effect *any* kind of restitution, economic or otherwise. Accuser and accused are cast as antagonists. Our court process can be seen by the anthropologist as a kind of game in which each side seeks to defeat the opposing side. Both agree only to follow certain prescribed rules in achieving that goal. In fact, the rules are often broken or circumvented. Formal rules govern that procedure, as when there is "inadvertent" introduction of inadmissible evidence, or equally "inadvertent" leading of a witness at the cost of a perfunctory apology or a meaningless instruction to a jury to "ignore" what has been said as though their memories selectively can be erased. In every case of this kind the loser, be it the accusor or the accused, is likely to feel dissatisfaction with the legal process and to feel that the court has, albeit unwittingly, committed a "wrong."

This is in direct contrast to a comparable process of conflict resolution in a "primitive" society in which the court proceeding, or "hearing," is more analogous to a ritual than to a game. A ritual suggests that we are dealing with sacred authority rather than secular power, with the infallible rather than the fallible. Moreover, another essential difference exists between a game and a ritual. In a game both sides start theoretically equal and the objective, or at least the effect, is to end unequal. In a ritual the participants start theoretically unequal and the objective is the restitution of equality. In our system the focus is on the act, its criminality as defined by law, and whether or not the defendant was responsible for that act. In other cultures, in the absence of a legal code, there is nothing necessarily right or wrong in the action itself, as we have seen, and the objective of the court is the equalization of whatever inequities the action may have wrought, consciously or unconsciously. No anthropologist would say that one system is "better" than another. Nevertheless, while primitive systems are consistent in aiming for and achieving the social equality and harmony that are the communally accepted ideals, in our system we systematically seek and impose an inequality that is inconsistent with our ideals. In this way, we further rend, rather than repair, the social fabric.

In making these comparisons we should look for consistency between the nominally held ideals and the actual practice of the law. We certainly cannot suppose that fragments of one system that we deem "good" can be grafted onto another system, especially when, as here, the two contexts being compared are obviously at almost polar extremes. In the farming, fishing, and hunting communities and societies of the tropical rain forests of Africa, the communities are small enough to allow for every individual to participate in major hearings, or at least for every individual to be represented by a close kinsman. Further, the subsistence economy allows for prolonged discussion in which all members of the community are meant to participate, each being allowed to state his own opinions about the case in his own way and at whatever length he or she chooses. Indeed, that is an essential part of the process and perhaps is not so time consuming as it may at first seem, since any one case is made a pretext for informally bringing into the open all other disputes, latent or manifest. This serves a much wider social need than the resolution of one specific dispute. In our modern society, pressures of time and money, coupled with the overwhelmingly high incidence of anti-social behavior, mean that our courts face enormous backlogs of cases awaiting attention. These cases must be dealt with as expediently as possible. The irony is that when the legal system demands that courts deal with the greatest number of cases in the shortest possible time, a disservice results to society at large.

This all suggests two classifications by which we can tentatively distinguish the "primitive" system from our own, with the one being moralistic and the other legalistic. In the one society the rules of behavior are internalized, voluntarily accepted and perceived as sacred, if not god-given. They are sanctioned by some supernatural power. In our own society the rules are imposed rather than arising from within, and are man-made, secular. We have already noted that punishment is not an objective in African cultures. When punishment is considered in those cultures, it is invoked rather than imposed, being left in the hands of the supernatural. The human court concerns itself only with the problem of restitution. We have replaced this essentially moral coercion, perhaps necessarily given the size and complexity of our society, with physical coercion. The question raised by the comparison is whether we have not in this way lost a major, perhaps vital, force toward social order by neglecting the role of moral coercion as a necessary part of our social and legal structure. We leave such coercion to individual conscience or religious conviction rather than making it an integral part of our daily lives, including the educational system.

The "primitive" would indeed have to wonder at our inconsistency throughout the system, but most particularly at the separation of church and state. Even when we insist on the oath of truth being taken upon the Bible, the process of cross-examination seems to assume that the oath is ineffective. And while we invest the judge with evident symbols of near-divinity, at least of wisdom and justice and overall excellence, we then relegate him to the role of overseer and bind him to the decision of a jury that is secular and necessarily less qualified, often singularly unqualified.

The malaise that characterizes our legal system derives not only from the material pressures of time and economy, however important these and other material factors are. Nor does it derive primarily from the built-in reality of inequality so directly in conflict with our stated ideal of equality. The system and the malaise both have their roots in our ideals and in the concepts associated with those ideals. We vociferously hold to the ideal of equality, yet not only does our society tolerate grotesque inequalities, it even encourages them. A major source of national pride lies in games and sports through which we publicly honor and advocate competition and its resultant, inevitable inequality. It might even be said that our very emphasis on and aspirations towards equality of opportunity legitimize ultimate inequality. We talk, sincerely, about social responsibility, cooperation, harmony, brotherhood and love; yet in the same breath we honor the antithetical ideals of independence, individual initiative, and competition, and we acclaim as an American folk hero the "self-made man." Self sufficiency becomes an ideal in itself. One might ask whether such inconsistency is the mark of a healthy society, or the inevitable price we have to pay for having traveled too far too fast.

IV. American Concepts of Individual, Community and Society Re-Examined

We need to rethink our concepts of individual, community and society. Insofar as justice reflects ideals, when a society's ideals are in conflict with each other and cannot be practiced, the conflict between law and justice becomes inevitable at a certain level.

The inherent conflict between ideal behavior and expected or required behavior has been seen, for example, in the trials of those who refused to register for the draft. In some cases, at least, the refusal was clearly an honorable and courageous act that happened to be illegal. While Sassway said that "an individual should have some means to challenge the law," the prosecutor said that in Sassway "we have an individual who wanted to set himself above the law and that is not what society is about." Both of course were right, for one was thinking of justice and the other of law. Sassway's parents made an emotional appeal, which brings us to the crux of the issue. They claimed that while Sassway broke a man-made law, he held to a higher law, God's law. We shall need to return to the concept of a "higher law" when we attempt to define community as distinct from society. For the moment I want to use this case to illustrate an inherent weakness in our concept of the individual. It is plain that we have a problem when it can be illegal to be honorable, or when it is considered honorable to commit an illegal act. Plainly also we have a problem when the pursuit of freedom to follow religious belief, guaranteed by the constitution, can be considered as deserving of imprisonment. The problem is associated not only with our view of individuality but also with our particular individual-oriented concepts of guilt and innocence and their occasional confusion with the concepts of right and wrong. We suffer from a lack of clarity that is not found in any "primitive" system known to me. More important still, is the contrast between the two conceptual worlds.

I have already had to place "guilt" in quotes when using it in the African context, because in the African societies and languages known to me, the concept does not translate, though a very superficial observation of the village tribunal in action might suggest that it does. While every adult has a duty to seek the "right" way of life, to make the effort to follow the way of the ancestors, this is plainly different from a mere duty to obey the law. Failure to succeed in the effort is not wrong, it is merely the cost of human fallibility and should be corrected rather than punished.

Even in our society there is some ambivalence. "Guilt" has been applied at different times to describe some general fault in an individual, a dereliction of duty, the commission of a crime, later the commission of a sin, and later still "the state of being justly liable to penalty." The connotations of "guilt" today are primarily secular and suggest a human offense against a human law. The formal opposite used in handing down a verdict is not guilty. Yet, the opposite in common parlance is *innocent*, which implies much more than the mere non-commission of a crime, more than adherence to some man-made law. The state of innocence suggests uprightness, virtue, purity and morality. A guilty verdict indicates illegality, yet the moment a non-guilty verdict is translated by the word "innocent" it conveys with it an aura of righteousness, a far cry from mere legality. Are we being merely careless, or evasive, in such conflicting usage? If we accept "innocent" as an alternative for "not guilty," why do we never hear of "sinful" being used as an alternative for "guilty"? It is not such a small point as it seems, and is certainly symptomatic of the conflict and confusion inherent in our system. Do we really mean and believe "guilty," or do we mean "fallible"? Do we mean "legal" or do we mean "righteous," "illegal" or "sinful"? Perhaps our separation of church and state has not been as complete as we thought, otherwise why this ambivalence?

The issue of dual meaning, significant in itself, is indicative of two other, more immediately relevant and vital considerations revealed by a comparison between the two systems. The first, already discussed, is that unlike others, we concentrate on the notion of individual guilt. The second consideration is that when the illegal act is committed by several individuals, each may be held to be wholly guilty and responsible, whereas in a small-scale society the responsibility probably would be shared. In both instances, moreover, we hold the total person responsible and adjudge that person totally guilty. It seems logical and just to us that when a crime is committed by more than one person in equal partnership they should both suffer the full penalty rather than share it. This is in contrast to the traditional African approach partly because we have codified behavior and defined acts as right or wrong, legal or illegal. We have slipped into what such an African would say is the grossly unjust, unrealistic and usually unwarranted assumption that any person who commits an illegal act is therefore also morally "wrong" or "sinful."

In many other cultures the blame for the commission of an anti-social act invariably and systematically is shared between the perpetrator(s) and others in the community whom we would hold to be totally innocent. As often as not the accuser is found, in our terms, to be guilty as the acused, sometimes more so. It is thus rare, if ever, that an individual is held to be totally guilty, even if he cannot plead self defense, insanity, or mitigating circumstances, devices employed in our own society to come closer to justice in spite of the law. It is equally unlikely that any individual would be held totally bad or totally good, totally right or wrong. Thus, in such a society, it would be unjust to put all the blame on any one individual or to place on any single person the total burden of restitution. Similarly, it would be unjust to incarcerate an entire human being, since no human is totally without merit. The problem is resolved not by the cutting off of the guilty hand, letting the other remain, which is one primarily symbolic resolution. It is resolved in such societies by the avoidance of a penal system. The responsibility is shared by all those found to be causal factors. They also share the burden of restitution, without in any way being denied the right to continue to pursue their positive activities for the continued benefit of society, much as we penalize the innocent families of convicted criminals by incarcerating their kin.

In a Bira tribunal the hearing almost consciously sets out to distribute the blame so as to allow the offender every opportunity to pursue more socially acceptable forms of behavior without stigmatizing him as "guilty." The issue of whether or not someone committed a certain act is seldom in question. Thus, one of the first steps is to establish the positive attributes of the "accused" as a good father, a good son, a good brother, a good friend, a good farmer, and so forth. To this end the entire community is expected to testify. Any "badness" that is left over, and which became manifest in the anti-social act, is thus fractional and is by equally diligent enquiry apportioned among those who however indirectly or unconciously contributed to the manifestation of that latent badness: the wife who burned his breakfast that morning, the friend who refused to repay a debt, the child who laughed at him when he tripped and fell, the fact that his best piece of cloth was caught by the current and swept away while being washed. All these and many more I have heard listed as contributing factors for purposes of sharing responsibility. If it were a case of theft of food, for instance, it might well be held that as a good neighbor the accuser should have known the accused was hungry and should have offered food. I have heard it held that the "thief" was doing his victim a good service by compelling him to do the socially and morally correct thing (sharing his food with others) by taking it when it was not offered freely. In cases like this, the Bira say it is more important publicly to reaffirm an ideal for all to benefit, than to harm a weak and foolish individual.

The crucial difference in such communities is that what is at stake is not individual guilt or innocence, for we all have a potential for both, but rather the social and communal good. This will be defined differently from one population to the next, but basically it involves the recognition of reciprocal obligations for each other's welfare, material and/or spiritual. In his analysis of traditional law in southern Africa, among peoples organized into states rather than the less centralized tribal societies to which I mostly have been referring, Max Gluckman, himself trained in British law, identified the concept of "the reasonable man" as being the central concept in the jural process. In considering any action brought before the tribunal the issue was whether or not that action was "reasonable," and that in turn was defined in terms of social responsibility. Again the objective of the tribunal, as in tribal societies, was to effect a restitution of the sociality that was intended to be the all-pervasive norm. In such a society no room exists for the concept of individual guilt or innocence.

This is consistent with the belief in such societies that truly independent individual action is as impossible as exclusively individual responsibility. Thus, a man is not capable of truly independent action, they would say, since his actions are always influenced by the actions, thoughts, desires and manipulations of others. If he is not capable of truly independent action, he can never exclusively be held responsible for his actions save in a few exceptional cases where it can be shown that by consciously evil manipulation of the supernatural an individual has overcome these external influences and achieved true independence. In a true society, they would say, in which members are bound to each other in mutual need, respect, and consideration, the individuality and independence we value so highly are anathema, the mortal enemies of sociality and of society itself.

V. Individual, Community and Society in Anthropological Context

A. *Concepts and Definitions*

We are now in a position to consider the concepts of individual, community and society in a way that will throw light on the malaise that affects all of us, including our legal system. Part of our trouble is that we have taken our sociality for granted, it being a commonly accepted myth that humans are innately social. A "society" by definition implies some form of social organization, involving various techniques of social control in the quest for both order and survival. All forms of social control involve coercion of some kind and impose limitations on individual freedom. This is where the major potential for conflict arises. The extent of that potential depends on how effectively individuals are encouraged to perceive their individual survival as synonymous with the survival of society as a whole; how far their self perception is that of independent isolates or of vital, necessary, integral parts of a whole; and the extent to which they are taught the values of independence or interdependence. The foundations of social behavior are laid upon these values. They determine the relative importance and success of moral and physical coercion. It is primarily an educational problem. Such an education takes place in domestic life and through the system of religious belief and practice, not only in schools, if it is to become a truly vital and effective force toward social order in our lives.

The problem is magnified in plural societies with a significant internal differential in the form or structure of domestic or religious life. The variables, however, that determine the potential for conflict remain essentially the same. This latent primal conflict between the individual good and the good of society, between the individual self and the social self, underlies much of the conflict that manifests itself in crime and violence in any society, plural or small-scale. By looking to exotic societies for comparisons we not only are likely to uncover the basic principles at work in any society, but we are compelled to reassess our concepts of both individual and society and to perceive the importance of that intermediate unit here called community. A preliminary attempt at definition immediately shows that the relationship between individual, community and society is much more complex than might have been thought, and demonstrates the cogency of a relativistic approach to conflict in any plural society.

The concept of individual, which would at first seem the simplest to define, is in fact the most difficult. Self awareness is one thing, self perception is clearly something totally different. Perhaps in our educational system the significance of self perception is underestimated. Self perception may even be with and subordinated to the crude fact of self awareness. Self awareness is sensory, self perception is intellectual. The one is a fact evidenced with undeniable and vital clarity by each and every sense; the other is a construct of our mind, and therefore changeable and questionable. Not only is self awareness vital and undeniable, it persists for the duration of our conscious lives and provides us with a sense of continuity, a sense of individual identity that persists in some way without change. The only variation in such awareness is largely one of intensity. Self perception, on the other hand, is constantly subject to change as we grow older, as we alter our social context, move from one environment to another, and as we engage in increasingly complex interrelationships with other individuals. Just as self awareness isolates us as individuals, so self perception joins us to and makes us a part of the world around us. The primacy of self awareness is biologically determined; sometimes its power and vitality are borrowed falsely by the more strictly sociologically determined construct of self perception, giving it a seeming primacy and unquestionability that it does not deserve. By the same token, however, this process can be an invaluable positive force by which self perception is molded by cultural factors into culturally accepted form.

In considering the concept of individual we are concerned with self perception, but with the knowledge that the quality of self perception may, particularly in unthinking moments, be unwarrantably enhanced by confusion with the unquestionable fact of the perceiving individual's existence. Let us not enter for the moment into the even more complex realm of one individual's perception of another.

Our self perception as individuals is conditioned by many factors. I have suggested that two major realms of influence lie in our domestic and religious organization, and for the purpose of this discussion I include philosophy as a part of religious life. Depending upon the cultural context in which we are born and nurtured during the first few critical years of life even our most basic perceptions, such as those of time and space, will vary enormously. For instance, in the western industrial world we have a linear sense of time and space; others have a cyclical sense of the two phenomena, and for some they are both conceived in spherical terms. While our system supposes a unilinear, non-repetitive progression from one mundane point to another, through life to death, others posit a cycle of birth and rebirth, and still others explain the phenomena of life and death by a belief in two realms of existence that are paralleled, simultaneous and eternal. These varied perceptions necessarily bring about variations in perceptions of self, and necessarily have social implications.

In the last mentioned system the individual coexists with his other self in the "other" world. Since the two worlds are believed to be in constant interaction a double set of sanctions is at work, natural and supernatural. The incentive to social order is extremely high, particularly given the belief that this eternal interplay between the two worlds, and within each, results in an effective system of reciprocal obligations and responsibilities between all those within the same "sphere" at any given moment. This ordering system is prescribed not by law but by belief and perception, coerced not by threat of physical or supernatural punishment but by what is perhaps the most basic urge of all, the urge to survive. When social order is seen not as a duty or legal requirement but as a logical necessity and a prerequisite for survival, a powerful inner incentive drives the individual self to try to become a social self.

In cyclic systems the individual sees his present existence as conditioned by the past and as conditioning the future. This results in identification with and hence obligation toward the past as well as the future, a process virtually incomprehensible to those with a spherical sense of time and space. Identification with the past lends power to the social prescriptions and proscriptions attributed to the ancestors. These correspond in many respects with our legal principles, but they have greater flexibility. Identification with the future provides for effective, active concern for the unborn, with predictable consequences for property law, rules of inheritance, and so forth. But again the coercion is from within, deriving from this particular form of self perception, rather than from without. The concept of "the way of the ancestors" serves more as an explanation than as a coercive element.

In linear systems individual existence becomes more central since it is seen as being brief, unique, limited and non-repetitive. In such systems the quest for social order demands reassurance or reward, often through religious belief in after-life. It is in proportion to the strength or weakness of that belief system that we find the absence or emergence of secular law resting on the threat and use of physical coercion. When we have a plurality of belief systems, adhered to with varying degrees of intensity, the perceived need for secular law and respect for it will vary accordingly.

The cyclic and linear cultural models represent extremes to highlight the degree of variability possible, but even within any one culture the sub-cultural variations are by no means insignificant. We have only looked at one aspect of self perception, in relation to culturally determined concepts of time and space. Nevertheless, the implications for our understanding of the legal process are clearly fundamental, particularly when we talk of "individual" rights and responsibilities.

We now are able to expand on our understanding of the social implications of the concept of individual, thus beginning to come to grips with the concept of community. As generally understood the term has distinct *qualitative* connotations implying not only a special degree of conformity of behavior and belief, but also suggesting a communality of individual self perception that makes conformity and order a matter of choice. This minimizes the need for the threat of physical coercion or secular law. In general usage "community" invariably is used to connote a very different kind of social unit than is understood by the word "society." Equally general but widespread is the notion that "community" is smaller than "society," more highly integrated, characterized by greater conformity and order. It is also often thought that community, perhaps because of its apparently more cohesive sense of identity, possesses a special power that helps to bring about a measure of social order related directly to the perceived needs of the community. All these are partial truths, as is our uncomfortable awareness that the needs of community are not always in conformity with the needs of society. Yet so powerful is the qualitative aura attached to the very word "community" that in spite of the lack of any clear, unequivocal definition of what "community" is, the word is often used to win support in both legal and political arenas, the implication being that "communities" have special rights to which other social units are not privileged.

In fact, there is far more to "community" than the general qualities listed above. Conformity, order and uniformity, however voluntary, do not make a community any more than does the mere assertion by a given social unit, be it a rural village or an inner city ghetto or block association, that it is a "community." Such an assertion may just be wishful thinking, or a conscious attempt to claim special consideration. And it may well be a mistaken extension of individual self *awareness* to group *awareness*, whereas what really defines a true community is the nature of its self *perception*. The same distinction is made in the kinds of exotic societies I have been referring to, between a "good" person and a "bad" person, one who is socially responsible and one who is not. The socially responsible person is one who has realized the all important difference between the narrow but intensely vital and demanding individual, biological self, and the wider, less tangible but potentially much greater social self.

I have referred to an educational problem in dealing with various legal and social issues. Here it is important to pursue the cross-cultural examination by seeing how other cultures deal with the specific educational problems of socialization, of transforming the individual self into the social self. Into this task they put an enormous amount of time and energy. It starts with the birth of an individual and does not end until death. The educational process involves both formal and informal techniques; it is private and public; it is constant and ongoing at all levels of life. This is because without such sustained effort, as they see it, there would be no community, and without community there would be no society. Graphically, in their own terms, "[w]e would all be animals."

B. *A Specific African Culture: The Mbuti*

I shall from now on be very specific in my cross-cultural examples, referring to the northeastern corner of the Republic of Zaire, where I have spent many years of field work. It is a tropical rain forest, the Ituri. The area under consideration is about 50,000 square miles, bisected by a single road running west to east, connecting the navigable head of the Congo River, at Kisangani, with Uganda. This road follows the old slave trail, a trail that was followed and enlarged by Stanley in his journeys across the forest barely a hundred years ago. It was not made into a "motorable" road until the nineteen twenties, under Belgian colonial rule. Even today it is only barely motorable and often impassable. Further, since the Ituri was not an economically productive area, the Belgians left it largely undeveloped though by no means "untouched." Traditional ways of life continued through all the time of my researches, which were begun in 1951 and are ongoing; and yet there was sufficient contact with the colonials and their way of life for the Africans to make cross-cultural comparisons of their own.

Finally, for our purposes this area is ideal in another respect, for its population includes diverse and culturally interesting groups. One is an extremely early indigenous population of nomadic hunters, the Mbuti, who are organized at the band level of social integration, without any form of centralization. Among the Mbuti, a hunting band of from three to a maximum of thirty families is the largest effective social unit. At the other extreme are recently immigrant empires and kingdoms such as those of the Azande and Mangbetu in the north. At an intermediate level, and best known to me after the hunters, are a number of tribal groups who are either farmers or fishers. Each tribe is divided into relatively autonomous villages loosely linked in a clan system, the village headman being subordinate to the clan head, and all clan heads being (more or less) subordinate to the tribal chief. All these tribes are at the subsistence level of economy, and again are relatively recent immigrants, the forest having been the preserve of the hunters until some four hundred years ago. The migration came from all directions, composed of populations with very different cultural backgrounds, speaking different languages, holding to different religious beliefs, with very different political and economic systems. Some were fleeing from persecution, others from mere population pressure, and now with the new cash economy, a new wave of immigrants seeking personal gain has come. There are, therefore, some special reasons for making a comparison between this area and the United States though there is absolutely no simple equation between specific segments of each population.

I shall refer to the wider process of social integration later, but for an example of how at the smallest, narrowest level the individual is socialized into a perception of being a part of the much wider whole, I here refer to the Mbuti hunters. They are by far the longest established population in the area, numbering about 40,000. They occupy the entire central part of the forest, the immigrants being settled around the periphery. They have had probably at least ten thousand years to adapt to this tropical rain forest environment and have evolved a system of socialization that encourages the child, almost from birth onwards, to see itself as a functioning and therefore necessary part of the total ecological system. A child's first lessons teach the value of dependence, and the very teaching reinforces the same value for all others. From the first lesson of dependence upon the mother's breast for milk the child's social horizons are widened, together with its horizons of rights and responsibilities, by being shown that it profits enormously from increasing those horizons. For instance, it allows itself to be fed by other "mothers." As the child grows older he or she quickly learns the reciprocal nature of the relationship, and by the crawling stage already seems to sense the reality of mutual interdependence. It will by then have classified all other adults in the camp as either fathers or mothers, and will address them by the same form used for its biological parents. It will recognize that this terminology, and with it the corresponding system of rights and responsibilities, is only effective for as long as those fathers and mothers (and grandparents and siblings, for everyone in the camp is considered as kin) are actually residing in that camp and hunting and gathering with that band. Thus the very system of kinship terminology is a powerful lesson in the realities of reciprocal rights and obligations, teaching that these primarily operate among all those bound together by common residence, the economically cooperative band. When biological kin leave the territory (and every month the camp moves with some people leaving and others coming in) they are no longer referred to as kin, but by their personal names, removing them from that intimate circle of effective inter-dependencies.

By the time the child is old enough to make its way to the adjoining *bopi*, or children's play area, it is aware that children have a special role to play in the life of the band. Unless the children light the morning hunting fire nearby, the adults and youths will not be able to go off hunting. They may not yet know that this is because they are considered as "pure" and therefore able to mediate and propitiate the forest for the killing to follow, but the children certainly realize that this gives them a measure of social control, for while they can stop the hunt by refusing to light the ritual fire, causing others to go hungry, they can then go and get for themselves certain foods forbidden to others. The rest of the camp goes hungry but they do not. They also learn to exercise this control wisely, for other age levels have controls that they can exert. Even in the *bopi* activities, the Mbuti children are learning essential lessons of social behavior, of the profit to be found in dependence rather than independence. There is, for instance, a total absence of competitive games, though there are plenty of pastimes by which each individual may in a sense compete with himself to develop skills, but never in competition with the others. Some pastimes indeed demonstrate the very real dangers inherent in any attempt to be independent, or to assert oneself over another. A young sapling climbed by ten children will bend down until it almost touches the ground. A Mbuti pastime is to do this, then for all to jump together and watch the sapling spring upright like an arrow from a bow. Sometimes, not very often, a solitary child will stay clinging to the branches a second longer than the others, perhaps to show his bravery, perhaps just to find out what it is like to be different. The child gets thrown upwards with the tree, and is lucky to escape with no more than a few scratches and bruises.

By the time youth is reached, every child has found that the greatest satisfaction, as well as security, lies in cooperation rather than isolation, in the sharing of thoughts and tasks rather than in individual initiative and effort. Each has discovered how to explore and develop that which is uniquely her or him (the aware, the individual self) in such a way that it can express that separate individuality most satisfactorily in cooperation with others. This is a lesson that is sharpened during youth and reinforced for the rest of life in many ways, of which the most graphic is perhaps music-making. Music is not made very often with conscious educational intent, but the anthropologist would be tempted to say that for the Mbuti that is its prime function. Thus, on entering youth and approaching the age of puberty the Mbuti learn something of the social consequences of gender by taking part in songs in which the boys may sing in antiphony to the girls, and in which the girls sing in parallel seconds rather than in unison. In these puberty songs, as in songs associated with gathering, the female part dominates. Similarly, in an almost literal reflection of real life, the technique required for singing hunting songs demands just the same pattern of cooperation between the gender and age groups as is demanded by the hunt. In no songs (except the lullaby) are there soloists and this is how it should be in real life, for the Mbuti.

This could be elaborated in much greater detail, not only for song, but also for dance, story telling, and other forms of entertainment and pastime.

In fact there is probably not a single recreational activity that does not have clearly recognizable educational value and play an important role in the constant revitalization of the social values that bind all the individuals in the hunting band together as a single, cooperative, corporate being with a vitality of its own.

But the Mbuti are no paragons of virtue. Just as in childhood a child may be tempted to find out what it is like to stay on the sapling after all the others have jumped, so in later life any Mbuti may be tempted to do something that is not in keeping with the social good. Such individual actions, however, are explained rather than punished, for the innate conflict between the individual self and the social self is well recognized. If the action is harmful to society, the action is blamed, not the actor.

Take an example. When Kenge awakened his girl friend's father as he crawled into bed with her, and the father awakened the rest of the camp with his shouts of outrage, what was at fault was the noise ... and as Kenge slyly pointed out, the father was making more noise than anyone else, so if any *person* was at fault it was he. All that was needed to put an end to the harm being done was for an old man to say that everyone was making too much noise, and had given him a headache; for who wants a headache? In muttered discussions to which I was privy, individual blame of a sort was apportioned; on Kenge for having been careless enough to wake the father; much more on the father for having made so much noise that he awakened the entire camp; but most of all the noise itself was blamed for having given an old man a headache, and for having threatened to do the same for others.

So it is with other disputes. If Kenge had gone on being "careless," corrective action would have been taken, and that knowledge was enough to encourage him to avoid "noise." The action would have been some form of ostracism, from mild ridicule to temporary exile. The latter is mild for a nomadic people whose bands change in composition every month, and who have a "kinship" system that classifies everyone as family who takes up residence in any camp and participates fully in its life, according to age, gender and ability. Ridicule within a camp is a powerful sanction, almost more powerful than exile, except that it gives the offender an opportunity to cure himself. But rather as with the case of Kenge's flirtation, the focus of attention is gradually weaned away from the initial act, which we could call the offense, and even from the actor (or offender) so the blame is placed in such a way that many more than the original offender are held to be responsible.

In the case of the flirtation, when "noise" became the offense, almost everyone was shouting, at Kenge to be more careful, at the girl to choose less clumsy friends, at the father to go back to sleep. Thus, it could be said that almost the entire camp was at fault. But when Kelemoke slept with his first cousin, a profitless rather than sinful thing to do, he was endangering more than sound sleep. Premarital sex is encouraged, but always with the end of settling down to a lasting marriage and raising a family. Marriage is a means be which the Mbuti expand their social horizons, acquiring in this way whole new sets of kin with whom they can interact accordingly. So why sleep with your cousin, particularly in the same band, and so called "sister"? To marry her would not enlarge one's area of sociality at all, either for you or, much more importantly, for the band as a whole.

Because the band, the grand "family," stood to lose or gain as much as Kelemoke by his courtship and ultimate marriage, he was subject to the band's most extreme sanction (with one exception), exile. He had threatened the welfare of all, so he no longer deserved to be a part of the family he served so ill. He was immediately driven from the camp, into the forest, that very night. But then it was recognized that Kelemoke had no intention of marrying the girl, so he intended no harm to the group as a whole. His individual needs had merely taken momentary precedence over his (and the group's) social needs. He was allowed to slip back into the camp and resume his place, without direct comment, after three days. The only comment was a question as to his health, which in their language referred to his social and spiritual as much as to his physical and mental health. His answer meant both "I am well" and "I am cured." As with the case of Kenge's flirtation, any attention given to the affair beyond the initial reaction was concentrated on the noise created by various family members who, with rather less justification than Kelemoke, were voicing individual and private concerns at the cost of *ekimi* (peace and quiet) for all. As in the other case, they were induced to waive these personal complaints by being shown that they were creating widespread *akami* (noise) and were in danger of giving the entire camp a headache.

It is not the nature of the disputes, nor even of their resolution, that is important to us, but rather the restitutive and diffusive process at work. In particular, the value of the social good has been so thoroughly assimilated and learned by all that it is necessary only to point out that their actions are harmful to the larger group. At that point they abandon such actions without further coercion. If anyone feels that his action was justified and posed no threat to society at large, the Mbuti always have the solution of leaving the band temporarily, until the dispute blows over, on the pretext of visiting some friend or relative in another hunting territory. I have found that such movement was an almost invariable indication of some latent dispute.

Two more cases need to be described to complete the picture, for if the Mbuti were without conflict they would not serve our purposes very well. Some cases are severe enough to warrant stronger action than mere ridicule, ostracism or temporary exile. Such a case involved one of the most popular hunters, Njobo. Unfortunately, for a number of reasons, including his familiarity with western ways, Njobo was aware that he possessed certain abilities that others did not. He knew how to deal with colonial administrators on the rare occasions when it was necessary, just as he knew how to deal with the village farmers like the Bira, with their incessant demands for forest products and for help in their fields. He also happened to be a particularly clever and brave hunter, and as a mere youth fulfilled every Mbuti male's dream of killing an elephant single handedly. That is more of a symbolic act than an act of bravery, for to the Mbuti the elephant represents the forces of destruction. It was the only animal capable of destroying the forest, until the advent of the village farmers, and of course the colonials. But Njobo went on and killed another elephant single handedly, and another, and another. He was plainly boastful of his prowess and his bravery, and more concerned with that than with the symbolic fight against destruction. Worse, he began using his excellence as a hunter to *tell* others how and where they should hunt, instead of discussing with them, as is the Mbuti custom. Rather as with the tree-clinging pastime, Mbuti children learn that all decisions affecting the group as a whole are taken by the group as a whole, that there are no leaders. Children that are beautiful are given ugly nicknames, those that are ugly are given beautiful nicknames. The slow are called "lightening," and the speedy "tortoise." All are trimmed to the same size, while allowing for full individual development nonetheless.

Njobo threatened the system, not so much by merely being a better hunter than others, but by wanting to make it *his* hunt and by thinking that this would make it a better hunt. In addition, he refused openly to acknowledge that in other ways he was less than perfect, and should be subordinate. At first people tried telling him that all he was doing in this way was to create *akami*, but Njobo would point to the pots full of food. Then ridicule was tried, picking on the slightest mistake Njobo made during the hunt. Youths and adults and elders all took part. Njobo paid no attention. Finally, the children, those who have just come from "the other world" and are therefore close to purity and power, even if they did not know it, began to ridicule Njobo. But instead of picking on his hunting ability, or his tendency to give orders or dominate discussions, they diverted attention away from this painful reality and "cured the sickness" in a masterly way. For anyone else, which means for the band as a whole, to have told Njobo to pack up and leave would be unthinkable, for he was a good man, and well loved. But his departure was all that could save the situation.

It so happened that Njobo only had one child, a boy who was born crippled. He had been able to get no other children, though he tried with three successive wives. Other Mbuti would have accepted the fact of their sterility or barrenness and simply have accepted adoptive children offered them by others with already large families. But not Njobo. When the children started to ridicule Njobo, it was not at the expense of the boy, Nyange, but it was by a graphic mime, performed in mid-camp for all to see, of Njobo engaged in the act of copulation. It suggested that the reason he was so unlucky with children was that he did not have the slightest idea of how to copulate. Each day we came to look forward to the afternoon performance, to see what new impossible and unproductive positions, postures and antics the children would have dreamed up as a parody of Njobo's private sexual life. That was more than Njobo could stand. His self (*individual* self!) esteem was his biggest fault, standing in the way of his social self, and the children wounded his self esteem. After a short time Njobo announced that he was leaving. He would take crippled Nyange out of the band, out of the forest, and go to the colonial hospital to try and have Nyange cured. Nobody reminded him that he had refused medical help from outside the day Nyange was born. Everyone wished him well. But the day he left he ceased to exist.

I took Njobo and Nyange to the hospital in Bunia. That was just before independence with the Simba Revolution and the mercenary warfare that tore the Ituri apart for the following years. It was eleven years before I could return. Nyange was back with the hunting band, still crippled, but occupying an honorable role. He and all the others said that Njobo had died. But months later, when I was visiting a colleague who was working in a different part of the forest, a villager who knew me from the old days told me that Njobo was alive and well, living in that part of the forest with another band. But he had changed his name, adopted children, and was known as having only killed one elephant.

The other "offense" is the most extreme of all. I have never even heard of it actually occurring. Yet it is most significant that such essentially non-violent people without any penal system, should have one penalty that at least in theory could be imposed on an individual, and that the penalty should be death. This capital sin, for such it is, rather than a crime, is refusal or failure to sing during the *molimo* festival. This is a sacred festival, most often occasioned by death. It is a way, as the Mbuti see it, of "making the death good," of making sure that the dead person has made the transition satisfactorily to the "other world," that the forest is happy. They believe the festival to be absolutely essential, since otherwise the death might have come unknown to the forest, which is the impersonal deity of the Mbuti (or perhaps better, which is their symbol for the creative force that animates all living things).

Extending their family system outwards, the Mbuti refer to the forest as "mother" and "father," and claim that just as parents look after their children, so the forest looks after the Mbuti. They call themselves *bamiki bandura*, children of the forest. So, they say, if the forest intended the death, it is good, but if the forest was asleep and did not know, then death could strike again, anywhere and at any time. The *molimo* is designed to make sure the forest is awake. This is done by song using a technique that incorporates "forestness" by making use of the echo, and by using a trumpet into which the song of the *bamiki bandura* is sung and carried off into the depths of the forest in the dead of night, carried in all directions, to reach forestness wherever it might be. For the song to be heard, for it to awaken the forest if the forest is asleep, and when it is awake to "rejoice" in it so that the good life can continue for the band, the song must be unanimous. *All* must contribute, especially the men who as hunters daily threatened the *ekimi* of the forest by bringing death to forest animals. So for one whole month, every night, from dusk to dawn, *all* men in the camp must sing. Any man not doing so renders the song ineffective, and thus threatens the entire band with further death or disaster.

During the night, a dance takes place during which a singer arms himself with two spears, one under each arm, and followed by the others, all singing, prowls around the camp looking for any sleeping man. The *molimo* trumpet makes noises like a leopard one moment, like an elephant the next, just as the two spears are made to look like the fangs of a human leopard one moment, and like the tusks of a human elephant the next. They say that if a man is found sleeping anywhere in the camp, the "elephant" will kill him with his tusks; the body will be buried beneath the *molimo* hearth, and that person's name will never again be mentioned. He will have no place in this world or the other world. To put it shortly, the death penalty is warranted only by blasphemy, by an insult against the Divine, an action that threatens directly to bring down Divine wrath on the entire society. The counterpart in a secular nation-state would be treason.

This is perhaps the clearest indication of the extent to which the Mbuti focus on restitution, not just in economic terms, nor even merely in terms of the restoration of the essential effective network of human relationships by which their society survives. Their focus is on the reestablishment of the highest demand of all, unanimity of devotion to the forest and "its" way of *ekimi*. If anyone were just to nod off at the *molimo* fire, he would merely be awakened, with some caustic jokes at his expense. But for someone to leave the molimo hearth and go to another part of the camp and deliberately lie down and go to sleep would be to demonstrate a deliberate, conscious lack of concern for the common good. It would be a blatant affront to the spirit of "forestness," for that is really synonymous with the common good. The death of such a hypothetical sinner would not be a punishment, but a purification, in Mbuti terms of "curing," or "making good." The removal of the name effectively removes any stigma that would otherwise have attached, through the system of diffusion, to kith and kin.

Thus, we have an example of how, in another culture, a community has established and maintained social order without a penal system. It has done so through the conscious and ongoing education of all its members in social awareness and obligation. Much (one might almost say *all*) of this education is "religious" in nature, in that it makes an ultimate appeal not so much to what is good for society as to what is good for the forest, i.e., the supernatural. This is the Spirit God, whatever it might be called elsewhere. The Mbuti clothe their supernatural in "forestness," referring to it simply as Mother Forest or Father Forest, so that at every moment of every day they are surrounded by their deity, dependent upon it, deriving all their benefits from it, living in the shelter it provides, eating the food it allows them. They are even clothed in forestness, bark cloth. And we have also seen how as part of their system for maintaining social order, the focus is on restitution of the social order, of the social norm, and on diffusion of blame so that no individual ever can be seen as "better" or "worse" than another.

These are all some of the factors that, in a rather less consistent and systematic way, we tend to acknowledge with respect to our concept of "community."

C. *The Western Concept of "Community"*

1. The Size and Nature of a "Community"

In a rather inconsistent way, we acknowledge some of the factors the Mbuti demonstrate when we think of "community." Yet in spite of our frequent appeal to the concept of "community," it has little if any legal or political significance as a social concept. Definitions are so broad that the entire United States of America could be called a "community." The criteria that limit community to a group of people sharing common residence, common interests, common policy, who interact with each other and are a part of a larger society, can be applied at any level from the nuclear family to the nation. Yet clearly when we talk of the nation as a community we imply that nationality demands more than we commonly give it by way of loyalty, unity, and responsibility. While a community can, theoretically, be of any size, the intimacy, the *degree* of communality of interests, rights and responsibilities that we imply by the term "community" are only to be found in relatively small populations and geographical areas. Thus, the concept of a national community may only be an ideal, rather than an empirical reality. We must work from that to see if studies of other cultures permit us to discover at least a structural reality.

This is important. While as a mere ideal "community" serves a useful function, if it *does* or *could* have empirical reality, we are losing an enormous potential force toward social order. What *does* have reality is the powerful sense of belonging to a community, affecting a wide range of social relationships. This exists in some urban areas just as strongly as it exists in rural areas. Where it exists, moreover, the sense of rightness or wrongness of social behavior is heightened so that insofar as community interests (as they are perceived by individuals) do not coincide with the greater social interests, we have a basic potential for conflict with any law that does not take "community" into cognizance. When a sufficient number of citizens, territorially discrete, share such interests and also share political power, the potential for conflict becomes all the greater.

The potential for conflict reaches its greatest proportions when the community can define itself in terms of religious belief. We have already noted the vital importance of communality of religious belief, and the consequent acceptance of common religious symbols that convey a sense of unity that is also economic, political, social, as well as spiritual, affecting each individual equally. In our society we have examples of what for the moment we might call "religious communities" in both urban and rural contexts, such as the Hassidim in New York, and the Amish in Pennsylvania. It is precisely when religious belief becomes a factor that such social groups acquire the greatest legitimacy within the wider society, almost *because of* their difference in religious belief. Such groups are allowed privileges not allowed to other common-interest residential groups that are secular rather than religious, such as block associations, ethnic neighborhoods, rural hamlets, villages or counties, though all of these frequently use the word "community" in describing themselves. They may have well established legal identities, but remain well within the law of society. Religious communities on the other hand, are given special consideration and allowed to maintain a life style that is not only distinct from that of society at large, but almost counter to it. This is possible only when there is a structure that enables such religious communities to exist (at times) in opposition to society at large, but without ever being in conflict with it. We will see how the Mbuti achieve this, as a religious community with a highly distinctive style of life and thought, with distinctive behavioral expectations (approximating to our moral code), existing within a series of wider societies. They retain their integrity at each level, but do not come into conflict.

In our own society the conflict arises not when the opposition is the most consistent and explicit, as with the Hassidim and Amish, but when members of the self-styled community, while claiming to be different in some respects, also claim *not* to be in opposition to society at large and to subscribe to that society's law. It seems to be much healthier and more constructive, in fact, for a "community" to run counter to the law of wider society, at times, than for it to operate, as often happens, *in spite of* that law, either by consciously circumventing it or by ignoring it, treating it as a regrettable political reality but one with little or no moral justification. Such would-be communities frequently appeal to morality as though it were indeed a "higher law," and try to validate their independence still further by claiming communality of religious interests. When this fails it is probably because they mistake communality of church membership for communality of religious interests, even when such a communality does exist outside that membership. Such seems to the outsider to be the case in the rural county in which I have lived in Virginia for the past fifteen years or so. It is from the outsider's point of view that I shall describe it.

2. A "Community" in Virginia

Lancaster County is a relatively isolated county at the southern tip of what is known as "The Northern Neck of Virginia." Its population is just over ten thousand, now rather more white than black, who traditionally all have survived by farming and fishing. Forty acres is considered a reasonable sized farm. In addition to this "native" population is a steadily increasing population of wealthy retirees. When I first came to know Lancaster, over twenty years ago, it had all the outward appearances of being a "community," which was indeed how it perceived itself. There was a great deal of communality of interests at all levels, social, economic, political, and religious. While primarily Baptist, a certain elite related to the earliest settlers formed an Episcopalian minority with considerable prestige. Methodists probably ranked next in acceptability, then Roman Catholics and "others," but strictly Christian "others." The economic differential was not highly marked, though nearly all the business in the county was in the hands of whites. It seemed, at that time, that there was little racial or religious conflict, and that what segregation there was either existed because of some "foreign" law, or was voluntary. There was a fair degree of inter-racial socialization, both legal and illegal, in both business and pleasure. The churches were completely segregated, however.

Such was the expectation of communality of interest in those days that the sheriff's department and the court both worked to try and avoid disputes from being brought to trial. The sheriff himself was known to drive around and try to mediate between parties to a dispute. There was a common understanding that outside or foreign interference, however legal, was unnecessary and unwelcome. If an issue arose in the county, that was where it should be settled. Stories circulated freely to support this view, and functioned (regardless of their validity) to coerce a certain degree of conformity to "the Lancastrian Way" (not incomparable to the African "Way of the Ancestors," though it was not recognized as being in any sense a religious communality). One such story concerned a young teen age neighbor of mine who claimed to have been raped, but at first could not say by whom. Since she was white, the immediate fear expressed, by black and white alike, was that her assailant was black, and there was general relief when a white was arrested and jailed. Nobody seemed unduly surprised when the story circulated, a few days later, that the young man had died "of a heart attack" in the county jail, so there would be no need for an unpleasant trial, bringing foreign lawyers, media and others into the county.

"Outside" law (state and federal) was sometimes avoided by a court bringing lesser charges that could be dealt with at the county level such as by construing as a misdemeanor what might be a felony, if that were considered in the interest of the "community." But increasingly it was said that this preferential treatment was selective and worked against certain segments of the community, notably blacks and those classified as "white trash." Blacks were afraid to go to a certain clinic because of stories about blacks who had died after the most minor treatment there. It was thought that the court and the sheriff's office were in complete collusion and that their protection was denied those deemed by them to be "undesirable members of the community." As an outsider living in the county, I found that my personal experience was more than enough to cause me to give some credence to such allegations.

Over the past few years the county has been invaded by an ever increasing number of wealthy retired people, many buying up waterfront property and adding to the general decline of oystering, crabbing and fishing as an almost universal way of life, in conjunction with small farming. This immigration also brought a flow of cash unknown before, and an economic differential began to form quite clearly, particularly along racial lines. Individual interests now were manifest as against community interests, and economic considerations took precedence over religious. Whereas it used to be a requirement of "community acceptability" that residents were churchgoers, this criterion became lowered to mere church membership. Even this vestige of what used to be one of the prime requirements of "acceptability" has been further reduced by the now overt repudiation of commonly stated church values, particularly those concerning drink, sex and gambling, by nominal church members. Lancaster County is thus in the process of transformation from a quasi-religious community into a secular district in which increasingly individual and economic values take precedence over communal and religious values. Since the county is still strongly influenced, if not directly controlled, by those with a vested interest in the old concept of "community," we may expect further discontent and disorder.

My own subjective appraisal of the situation in Lancaster County is in many ways in accord with that of those who remain faithful to the old community ideals, even though I differ from them in background and political and religious beliefs. They frequently refer to the effective and affective human relationships that used to pertain in the county, transcending race and religion, and to the customary expected behavior of mutual aid in the occupations of farming and fishing. They made such references as if these relationships and this behavior were religiously ordained, if not actually spiritual in nature. Both the affectivity and the effectivity of the relationships have all but disappeared, and with them the spiritual bond. What symbols there were, though few recognized them as such, are blurring or vanishing. These symbols not only used to separate insiders from outsiders, but also made it possible to recognize some of the ranking system at work within the "community." Thus predictability of behavior is lessened, and predictability appears to be one of the factors that connotes an "effective" community as distinct from a merely self-styled community.

For example, it was considered right to eat certain kinds of food, wrong to eat others, and very definitely wrong not to eat the right kind. Thus food was used to effect both negative and positive sanctions. Much of this was associated with the sentiment attached to fishing, oystering and crabbing, vanishing standbys that formerly assured all against hunger. The anthropologist would be quick to note the universality of food taboos, prescriptions and proscriptions in religious observances, and would use this as partial evidence that "religion" at least contributed to Lancastrian communality. There were distinctive forms of greeting, even between pedestrians and automobile drivers that signified "community" membership and implied unspecified mutual obligations.

With the symbol of dress, there was also a right way and a wrong way, and this varied for different segments of the population. There was a significant period during which it became "right," at least in the sense of expedient, for black and white to dress differently, particularly when not at work. It became as wrong for a black to dress well, drive a good car, and demonstrate a good education, as it was for a white to dress poorly and manifest a lack of education; one was "uppity" and the other was "trashy." These are distinctions common in the South, but such distinctions were newcomers to this county and represented an intermediate stage in the process being described. But this stage was quickly superseded by open confrontation which, while having certain racial overtones, was perhaps equally part of individual assertiveness against the community, and individual competition in the quest for individual success, defined differently by each individual. So also, the common sanctions continued against outsiders or those who became unacceptable or undesirable, but were imposed along lines of individual conflict and competition. Such sanctions included a certain amount of ridicule, but were and still are primarily in the nature of withholding of services, even at some economic cost. But most dangerous of all is the lingering feeling held by some, at least, that the power structure still represents the old values of now defunct "community," and that any who flaunt those values, however much it is their legal right to do so, can expect no support or protection from "the law,"and may indeed expect systematic harassment.

The rights and wrongs, even if this be true (and I believe it to be partly true, at the very *least*) are not what need concern us here. The interesting point is that the county demonstrates the subtle way in which a general malaise can permeate a healthy community within a larger society when that community insists on isolation and an unrealistic degree of autonomy in the name of "community." There is clear hierarchy of sentimental social identities, but it is without effective significance. Loyalty is first to the county, then to the Northern Neck, then to the eastern, coastal part of Virginia, then to the Commonwealth in opposition to neighboring states, and thence to the "south" and finally to the nation. What some of the older Lancastrians do not realize, having grown up at a time when migration in and out of the county was minimal, is that the community values, and the community version of "law," had to change as the isolation broke down. But they had become fixed and inviolable in the minds of some, and are increasingly inconsistent and hence in conflict with the values and law of the wider society of which Lancaster, perhaps grudgingly, is a part. The genius of "community" in small scale societies is the way in which its values and law are sufficiently conservative to ensure continuity of distinctive identity while being flexible enough to adapt to changing social horizons, usually expanding. The common manifestation here of "community" identity in the form of intercommunity competition through sports or otherwise, does not help towards the creation of a wider, integrative structure, nor do the economic and political rivalry, nor the rivalry of sectarian interests passing for "religion."

For instance, a Baptist church may organize a rummage sale on the same day and at the same time as a Methodist church sale held two miles further up the road. While the motives may be good and ostensibly in community interest, bad feelings, even hostility, are engendered at both locations by the recognition that people either wishing to support the cause or to purchase some inexpensive items from their own group are likely to stop first at the other if approaching from that direction. Again, the vital and indisputable communal volunteer fire departments increasingly raise the necessary money by setting up what amount to road blockades in such a way as to make it all but impossible for automobiles to evade the outthrust nets. The point made by this practice is not only that the community does not support its volunteer departments adequately, but that it has to be coerced in an aggressive manner to general inconvenience at the cost of much goodwill.

Lancaster County also points to other hazards that a would-be community within a wider society has to face. By focusing on the necesity of economic survival it has lost touch with the equally vital necessity of survival of identity, the centerpiece of the "religious" factor to which I have so frequently referred. It has virtually lost anything that can be called a common "sacred," and has consequently lost the all pervasive unifying and socially binding power of a shared religious sentiment. There has been a process of fission into smaller units, church and otherwise, that has only further heightened the spirit of divisiveness and competition. The retirement population has not effectively been integrated into what is left of community, but stands outside it in some respects while assuming control in others. In some ways the retirees take an increasing interest in county affairs while older residents sink further into apathy, yet in other respects, such as matters pertaining to schools, the retirement community—without children of its own to send to those schools—shows less than adequate interest.

Above all there is a lack of clarity in the authority structure. That structure, however informal flexible, must be established clearly if a community is to survive as such. Given the lack of homogeneity of church membership, there is no central spiritual leader, no priest or prophet such as one might find in a community within a small-scale society. But equally there is no charismatic figure either to lead or advise. The constitution does not encourage this, there being at least five authority figures that are responsible to the Commonwealth rather than to each other or to the community or any central community representative. The Commonwealth Attorney, thought by many (probably by most) to be the most powerful authority figure, and indeed thought by many to have authority over the others, is himself isolated; similarly with the sheriff, the clerk of the court, the treasurer and the board of supervisors. If these virtually independent elective officers choose to work together, there might be a greater sense of community than there is, but to be effective such cooperation would demand more time than is available. The best that can be expected under such conditions is for the county to operate as a mere geographical administrative segment of the Commonwealth, in rivalry for the attention of the Commonwealth with other segments. Many of the others are closer to Richmond, wealthier, more prestigious for historical or other reasons.

In these circumstances, rivalry again takes the place of that essential feeling of religious unity, a shared identity and common destiny, that is the hallmark of the true community. When community, in this sense, is lost, the larger society is ultimately the loser. Common adherence to a wider secular law can be more or less coerced and enforced, but the shared, voluntary will to unify, arising through various levels of recognizable and ritualized common identity, can never be imposed. It can only arise from within, at the smallest, familial level of social organization.

D. The Mbuti Again

Let us return for the last time to the Ituri Forest, briefly reassess just what "individual" and "community" mean there, and see how the Mbuti consciously work to integrate communities into the wide society while leaving them free to pursue separate sets of religious beliefs and practices in such a way as to bring about order without law. As we have seen, in such societies it is the common good (at whatever level) that is sacred, not the individual. Clearly what defines a "community," making it an effective social unit, is that its members share a common moral code rooted in a common religious belief. But we now have to add one other factor. That is the factor of *faith*, the essentially non-rational quality of direct knowledge, direct awareness of truth. This faith is of course encouraged by very rational and material means, notably the consistent use of sacred symbols to which I have referred several times. It thus can be induced, whereas it cannot be intellectually taught.

The *belief* system, which is taught and learned, formally and informally, is every bit as real and as effective as our legal code and any ethical code to which we might subscribe. The shared *faith*, which is acquired in infinitely subtle but detectable ways from birth onwards, is what activates the belief system, making it a living way to be followed (the indigenous term often used is "pathway" or "road"). The neat trick is that any individual following it (as well he should, for its obvious individual rewards) unwittingly finds that it is also for the *social* good. Thus, the almost inevitable tendencies of the individual self to assert itself are turned to good advantage through what is no less and no more than a remarkably straightforward, perceptive, socially oriented, educational system.

By puberty boys and girls alike have learned that their individual welfare is synonymous with that of their community, which for the Mbuti we have seen is regarded as a kind of extended "family." Shortly after puberty, on entry into adulthood, the social horizons are likely to be enlarged still further since the various populations can no longer fight to maintain their isolation from each other. That is no longer possible, given the existence of a central national government and its delegation of authority to provinces and districts.

The situation is comparable to that in Lancaster County in that in the Ituri there is also a succession of geographical identities to which any individual can claim membership. When in relationship with a member of adjoining Northumberland County a Lancastrian would be just that. But in relationship with someone from Richmond, say, a Lancastrian would be more likely to define himself as coming from The Northern Neck, and would join with anyone from Northumberland who would adopt the same wider identity; and of course all would be Virginians in opposition to outsiders from North Carolina. Thus, the concept of "outsider" is relative. But these are sentimental, affective identities rather than effective; that is, there is no corresponding succession of rights and responsibilities.

In the Ituri a member of the Epulu hunting band is just that at one moment, but he is an Mbuti when in relationship with the farming and fishing sedentary villagers, and he is a member of the *nkumbi* confederation when in relationship with the provincial or central government. However, the individual does not remain the same in each of these very different contexts. This is sometimes indicated by the fact that he will be known by a different name in each different situation, indicating a different personality. That is indeed the reality. What might otherwise pass for systematic schizophrenia is really no more that the recognized difference between individual and social self at work. This is exactly the same process by which bias is virtually eliminated in juridical proceedings in some African societies by a judge wearing a mask and/or assuming and giving judgment under a different (sacred) name. So also a tribal chief may well use one name when he is being a husband to his wife or father to his children, but when being a chief will use an ancestral name that will link him equally to all his kindred subjects.

We do not have the same versatility, though we do differentiate between the usage of first and last names in both address and reference, to indicate or even assert proximity or distance. But by comparison with the small scale society, it is our techniques that are primitive; they are inconsistent, unsystematic, unpredictable. It is our failure to reconcile our various levels of social identity with corresponding and clear-cut levels of social integration (reciprocal obligations) that contributes to the ultimate failure of a would-be community, such as Lancaster, and the success of "recognized" communities such as the Amish and the Hassidim.

The Mbuti boy, say, is born and for a fleeting moment is an individual (I rather think the Mbuti would question even that), with individual parents and an individual home. Within three days, however, the mother presents the child to the camp, and it immediately is classified by all camp members collectively as *our* child, grandchild, sibling. In interpersonal interaction each adult will refer to the child as *my* child. As soon as the child can talk it learns that it has a plurality of sociological parents, and that this relationship is both effective and affective. All the time the child retains the clear distinction between them and its biological parents. That distinction, however, is more affective than effective as he grows older, interacting more with his wider "family." Then, through the necessarily nomadic nature of life the child learns that he has many potential such families, and that if his parents leave one band to join another (perhaps as part of conflict avoidance) his affective life will remain as full as ever. While the names and relationships remain the same, the faces will be different. He may have different looking fathers and mothers but since they have the same names as in any other camp ("father" and "mother") the relationships will also be unchanged. At the same time he learns that his former fathers and mothers are now "outsiders," and this will be manifest by referring to them by personal names rather than by kinship terminology. Of course, with the change in terminology, there is a change in the effective relationship, in the expected system of reciprocal obligations.

By the time the boy reaches puberty he has undergone many such contextual changes. He has learned to adjust his social identity accordingly, so that he is an integral part of his present situation, wherever it is. He will have learned what it is to be "an Mbuti," for although he will only have visited and become a part of a few of the hundreds of hunting bands that make up the Mbuti population, he will know that effectively he has similar access to all of them, with absolute predictability as to what his role would be. His identity as an Mbuti also will have been sharpened by the occasional visits that all Mbuti bands make to neighboring villages on the periphery of their hunting territories. He will have seen how different life styles can be.

While in the village he will have had to eat very different foods, participate in different forms of work and different forms of recreation, and deal with different religious beliefs, different rules of behavior. Through all of this he learns to retain his identity not as an individual, but as an Mbuti. To this end he takes a different name when in the village, and with it, to some extent, a different personality, one that is able to accept and live with the new way of life. But there is no pretence at assimilation, and the fact that the Mbuti are visibly distinct, averaging only just above four feet in height, is not nearly as significant in this respect as is their conscious and overt ridicule of village life. They do this even while participating in it, emulating it, and, in their own way, enjoying it. This ridicule is expected by the villagers, who reciprocate, thus firmly establishing *their* collective identity in opposition to that of the Mbuti. But the rules of behavior change the moment the Mbuti return to the forest, as do the causes of pleasure and thus the various forms of recreation. Highly significant here is that the Mbuti, whose highest and most sacred ritual is song, never bring their sacred song out of the forest. Territorially the sacred remains inviolable, and is left behind with the Mbuti names and Mbuti identities.

This all makes for good neighborly relationships and for a mutually satisfactory exchange of goods and services. But amongst themselves the villagers face similar problems, for while each village is relatively autonomous, rather like the hunting bands of the Mbuti, they too need to interact, primarily for courtship and marriage, but also for trade. Thus villages associate with those on each side for such purposes, forming marriage and trade "circles." And this overlapping exchange system is now used to link formerly hostile tribes together, villages on the border trading and even marrying across the border. Just the same process of identity change takes place during all of this, and consistent with that, a change in rules of behavior in each different social context: the village, the "marriage/trade circle" of villages, and the tribe (or subdivision, if it has them). Ultimately all the village farming and fishing tribes are linked together in this way, around the periphery of the forest, and all of them are also linked to each other by their common links inwards to the Mbuti who occupy the whole of the central forest. This process provided much greater security than the earlier isolation during the days of slavery, and was an effective political force in opposition to the colonial administration. Today it is an equally effective force in opposition (but not in conflict with) the still wider social unit, the national province of which the Ituri is a part.

Probably most Mbuti and villagers could verbalize all this if called upon to do so, but they would find such rationalization difficult and highly tedious, since for them it is a supra-rational reality, having been consecrated by sacred ritual and become integrated with their religious life. Once again we see religion as if it were consciously being used to make a political ideal an effective reality. To this end there is one social institution, not incomparable with our school system, but overtly religious and ritual in nature. It is called *nkumbi. Nkumbi* involves the circumcision of boys between the ages of eight or nine and eleven. As a rite of passage this separates each boy from his individual past and from the narrow loyalties felt to his nuclear family. It prepares the boy for his future social identity as a man, which means as a member of the wider clan and tribal societies. By a simple extension today the same ritual is used to expand that identity right through the circumcising confederation of forest tribes to national identity. When a *nkumbi* camp is built, each house pole of the boys' shelter must be set in the ground by a member of a different village, thus bringing about the necessary cooperation between adjoining villages. And today, when a government post is within reach, a member of that is invited to take part, symbolically bringing the government into the confederation. Thus, this major political step forward was taken by the smaller political unit reaching out, once it saw the necessity, and incorporating the larger unit into itself, rather than the other way around.

The *nkumbi* takes place once every three years, and therefore serves not only to effect the social transformation of the boys, and to reinforce and reify the social norms for all regardless of age or gender, but to establish the various effective levels of social integration from family to nation and the corresponding rules of legitimate behavior. Just as it integrates the individual with the community, so it integrates community with society. And while its prime functions may be said to be political or economic, the prime conscious objective, the goal and the motivation, are unquestionably religious, ritual in nature and spiritual in content. It might be thought that this would diminish the essentially and uniquely religious nature of each community, but that is not so. The *nkumbi* provides a means by which a wide diversity of religious beliefs can retain their autonomy and distinctiveness, within their separate contexts, while coming together and forming a wider political unit sanctioned by a community of religious belief at a much wider level. It does this by finding a theoretical (religious) answer to a self-evident problem (territorial propinquity and all its attendant potential for conflict). Each of the tribes within itself recognized the need for progressive circles of socialization and met this need in its own way.

The *nkumbi* was the specific response of one tribal group, which it brought as it migrated into the Ituri from the southwest. For whatever reason this one institution proved adaptable enough to serve as a model in which all the various populations, except possibly the Mbuti, could see reflections of their own institutionalized response to the need for ongoing socialization. Adaptability was crucial, and this was possible by focusing attention on the process rather than on dogma and ritual precision. Thus, peoples who did not circumcise but had comparable institutions were given a kind of junior membership, opening the door to their eventual full admission. The political upheaval of the Simba Revolution provided an incentive, effectively completing the circumcision circle.

In some tribal cultures women are prohibited from even touching the ritual paraphernalia; in others it is they who *must* play the sacred drums, and in at least one, women openly ridicule the ritual performance of the men. The variants are all expressions of different belief systems at work, but underlying all is the common process, because there is a perceived common need for wider unity. Even the very word *nkumbi*, as with the various ritual acts, has a different meaning in the different cultures, being interpreted according to the local belief system. The process, however, remains the same.

The degree of religious diversity that can flourish in such a system is best illustrated by reference again to the Mbuti's concept of "forestness" as the ultimate sacred, and the way in which they measure "good" and "bad" by whether it is good or bad for the forest, such as the values of *akami* and *ekimi*. The economic determinist might well say that this is obviously because of the fact that the Mbuti are hunters, and at their pre-stone age level of technology are entirely dependent upon the forest. A sociological explanation of their specific religious beliefs, as of the general belief in "forestness," would be that they are reflections of sociological needs as well as answers to individual and emotional or intellectual needs. Whatever the explanation, the Mbuti see themselves as totally dependent upon the forest and say that without it they would die; and obviously as hunters and gatherers they are right. Yet their neighbors, the farmers such as the Bira, can only survive by cutting the forest down, and as fast as they cut it down it tries to grow up again and choke out their tiny plantations. Consequently, the Bira have a very different set of beliefs about "forestness"; for them it is evil, a consciously malevolent force that seeks their destruction (as in growing up and choking out healthy fields).

At first glance the two systems seem totally opposed and necessarily in conflict, but that is not so. They both share the concept of forestness, though they interpret it differently. Some villagers, like the Ndaka, are less hostile to the forest, have adapted part way to the indigenous Mbuti system of belief, live by fishing as much as by farming, and are far less compulsive than the Bira about cutting the forest down all around them. On the other side of the Bira, the Lese have been almost as much at home in the forest as in the village, and were considered by the Bira almost to be Mbuti themselves. Historically, each segment of the population has retained its isolation for as long as is expedient, but has not hesitated to expand its social and political horizons when necessary. It has done so by expanding its ritual and religious horizons.

Africa alone can provide innumerable examples of this process, even up to the nation-state level. All that needs to be done to unite two formerly hostile nations, after all, might be to invent a sort of *ur*-ancestor. Each tribe or nation having defined itself as descended from some real or mythical ancestral hero, was as distinct and inviolable as a biological kinship group. Not for nothing were queens called Mother and kings (and later, presidents) called Father. When political expediency dictated, it was suddenly "discovered" that those ancestors, formerly thought to be totally unrelated (which condition permitted warfare), were in reality siblings, jointly descended from an even earlier common ancestor. The process is by no means unknown to us in western civilization. It is just that we do not always recognize forces such as belief and faith, name and family, when they are at work, and we have separated religious life from secular just as we have separated church from state, making it difficult if not impossible for religion to play its uniquely integrative role in the way that it does in almost all other cultures. At least, I suppose, it would have to be admitted that this is consistent with our ever-increasing focus on individuality and competition, rather than on sociality and cooperation.

Something else that aggravates the problem of social integration for us is our tendency to think in terms of absolutes and our passion for rank-ordering.

This again is consistent with our emphasis on competition, but it makes far more problems than it solves. Exclusivity in religious belief, and in community membership, is perhaps not only acceptable, but necessary, provided it is not associated with any concept of superiority. It is that concept that prevents the enormous degree of sociality found in any true community from spreading and manifesting itself at wider levels of social integration. When the Mbuti move from their forest hunting camp to a village, they feel neither superior nor inferior, but they are aware that they are in a different world and are willing to accept that, however strange or even repugnant it may seem, the religious belief and practice of that world may be best suited to its specific needs. The mutual ridicule that takes place does not serve to establish any sense of superiority, merely of difference.

Another factor at play here is that in cultures such as those thriving in the Ituri, centralization is a recognizably recent phenomenon, whereas we tend to take it for granted. And whereas in those small-scale societies socialization is an upward movement, with us it is downward. There the biologically determined dependence of child on parents rigorously and systematically is expanded into ever-increasing circles of communal and social interdependence so that, as we have seen, not only the tribe but even a whole nation, may be perceived as a vast extended family. But with us, social order is seen more as filtering downwards from the apex. Even here we do not have conformity. Some perceive the apex as secular while others see it as divine, and among those who give priority to divine law there is further disagreement as to the nature of that law, resulting in fission of society rather than fusion of community.

E. The Amish and the Mbuti

The Amish of Pennsylvania are an excellent example of how community can and does operate within a national framework, even though it persists in holding to ideals that are almost in open conflict with those held by society at large. While not much is to be gained at this stage by comparison with the small rural would-be community such as Lancaster County in Virginia, one general observation is pertinent. The Amish are all united by a single religious belief, and are bound together by a corresponding community of faith, which demands that the belief be put into action in daily life as fully and consistently as possible. Internal divisions in such a system are likely to occur not through any difference of belief or faith, but rather through the ability of some to deal more successfully than others with the inroads of change.

Members of Lancaster County, however, are united more by secular considerations such as common residence and (formerly more so than now) a shared economy and political position. If anything, "religion" serves to divide rather than unite in Lancaster County, and faith would be difficult to demonstrate at anything but the individual level. So would the implementation of belief in practice. This is by no means a gratuitous criticism of Lancastrians, for it is but part of a widespread national phenomenon; on the contrary it is tantamount to saying that the closer Lancaster County was to being isolated and exclusive and united in church membership, the closer it probably was to being a community and deserving of consideration as such. While resistant to outside influence, in some ways Lancaster County was not resistant enough and admitted the seeds of its own destruction as a community. We may have to consider exclusivity as a necessary characteristic of "community."

The Amish certainly display this characteristic. They not only seek to exclude foreign influences by forbidding television and forbidding or restricting the use of a number of other outside inventions that would interfere with the style of their life or thought, but they also exclude non-believers in the single belief system that is permissible for them. The exclusivity does not mean that there can be *no* movement in and out of the community. Rather like the Mbuti, the community consists of whoever is there at the time, and all of those, at that moment, subscribe to the common set of beliefs that define the Amish, regardless of what they might subscribe to in other contexts.

Tourist attraction to the Amish is in itself evidence of the positive contribution the community makes to society at large, quite apart from its economic contribution. Tourists are attracted by the unusual. One of the most unusual things about the Amish, though this may not be in the tourist's mind at first, is that their whole way of life is a manifestation of their determination to practice what they preach, to live out in daily life their religious ideals. The tourist may be attracted by the strange clothing and the use of horse carriages, but tourists do not merely look; they feel, they think, and like anthropologists, they compare. So the Amish can be said to function, consciously or otherwise, as a kind of sacred community within a secular society, reminding the rest of society of its own ideals, and of the distance that may develop between ideals and practice. It also serves to demonstrate that difference, even exclusivity of a kind, is a richness rather than a weakness, when that difference defines a community that is a functioning part of wider society, neither superior nor inferior.

Just as the Mbuti have considerable, even fundamental differences of belief (such as with respect to "forestness") from the villagers, so do the Amish differ on some very fundamental issues from the rest of society. Yet because society recognizes these differences of practice to be related to differences of belief, and see (in Amish willingness to sacrifice the individual good) the extent to which the belief is supported by faith, society is willing to negotiate and to grant exceptions from its norms for some educational and other practices.

Since society does recognize an overtly religious group such as the Amish as a true community, let us consider the values, beliefs and practices of the Amish, and see how far they enlighten us and clarify our tentative list of criteria for whatever a true community might be.

For the moment "true community" means one that functions both within itself and in relation to other communities around it and/or within any greater society of which it is a political part (i.e., in which it is subject to some form of external governmental control). Such a community may not call itself a true community. It may call itself a church or a village or a county or a block or an inner city or a neighborhood, or many other things, but it must, for our purposes, be more than an ideal; it must have an actual, interactive part in the overall social structure. Our interest in the concept of community is that in some societies, notably the small-scale societies often called "primitive," such communities play a vital role in socializing the individual so that he is prepared for socially responsible life not only within the community, but in any wider context of which the community is a part.

An "outsider's" view of Lancaster County, shared by some "insiders," seemed to indicate that whereas under this definition Lancaster County might once have been a community, it now is not. It may be more important to test this than to demonstrate that an overtly religious group like the Amish represents a community, since Lancaster County is much more representative of the situation throughout the United States than are the Amish. Nevertheless, the Amish will help us to establish a model. And against the criticism that the Amish are a self serving group who make little or no contribution to society at large, it could be argued that at least one positive function of the Amish is to serve as a model.

The position of the Amish in the United States is not unlike that of the Mbuti in Zaire. In a sense they are a community of communities, like the Mbuti having no central political head, but nonetheless being bound together tightly in an effective network of reciprocal obligations that to a large measure averts conflict and the need for the imposition of an outside legal and penal system. Like the Mbuti, they draw this cohesion from their faith in a supernatural or divine power to which they owe allegiance. For them, it is the Christian God; for the Mbuti, it is Forestness. And the Amish have their very clearly defined form of the Mbuti Way of ("what is pleasing to") the Forest, or the villagers' Way of the Ancestors, in Matthew 18. There is no question that as a community the Amish are a community of believers, activated and unified by a deep personal, individual faith. Hostetler captures it when describing how lawyers for the Amish "were able to demonstrate to the courts that their religion was not simply a matter of worship, but a way of life expressed in the community—religion is community and community is religion."[1]

The Amish also have a very clear idea as to what the other criteria of community are, and they correspond interestingly to some of these we have tentatively established for our small-scale societies, namely: "(1) A world view requiring the maintenance and functioning of a redeeming community, (2) a cooperative relationship with the soil and creation, (3) effective socialization in the practical arts, with strong emphasis on family and community responsibility, and (4) the practice of humility and simplicity."[2] While the first of these establishes the overtly and consciously religious nature of the community (like the Mbuti, the Amish make the analogy between Community and Family), the second corresponds to the way in which the Mbuti see themselves as part of the natural world around them, having with it a reciprocal

1. HOSTETLER & HUNTINGTON, CHILDREN IN AMISH SOCIETY (1971).
2. *Id.*

relationship just as they do with each other. It is perhaps the all-inclusiveness of this self perception that is as important as the specific relationship with "nature," and this would allow the same criterion to be applied to a strictly urban context. The third Amish criterion, of effective socialization, we have also seen to play a major role among the Mbuti. There is a striking similarity between the Amish focus on "social coherence on the one hand, and the critical analytic method stressing ego fulfillment on the other" and the Mbuti focus on social self as distinct from individual self.

Similar also, and vitally important, is the fact that for the Amish the process of socialization is not confined merely to the formal and informal education of children. It is an ongoing process that uses symbols and rituals (including what others might consider to be secular festivals) constantly to reify the community code of behavior (be it Matthew 18 or Forestness or whatever) for *all* members of the community, regardless of age, gender or other differentiation. Nevertheless, it emphasizes the proper and necessary role for such structured divisions as there might be. For the Mbuti, age was the major structural division that functioned as a basis for division of labor, authority and responsibility; for the Amish, gender seems at least as important as age in serving the same function, but the process is clearly the same. Both groups, as part of the ongoing process of socialization, reaffirm their specific rights and responsibilities to each other in ways that visibly distinguish them from other social groups or communities. Dress, body decoration and adornment (including hair style), manner of speech and manner of behavior are all used by both communities, but not as isolated techniques. All are integrated with and have their justification in the belief system, establishing a religious as well as social identity.

At this point, since "religion" is clearly one prime criterion of "community," we must clarify what is meant by the word, at least for the purposes of this argument. It is plainly more than church going or church membership, which may or may not be religious. For our purposes, "religion" involves both faith and belief in a spiritual or supernatural power that influences, or can influence, human and earthly affairs, and upon which humans are seen as being at least in part dependent. For our purposes it is irrelevant whether or not that power has any actuality in existence, or is merely the expression of sociological needs, or is the result of wishful thinking. The belief and the faith are social facts with far reaching and highly pragmatic consequences in the establishment and maintenance of social order. Moreover, when used in conjunction with the anthropological concept of "function," a form of behavior might well be classified as religious even though that is not the motivation or understanding of the "actors." So while the Amish religious belief in community makes it obligatory for members to join together to "raise" a neighbor's house that has been burned down, many attending may be there for the conscious motive of having fun, to socialize, rather than because of any "religious" commandment. All, however, would be able to point to the religious "function" of the house raising, and rather like the Mbuti would be rather surprised that such a question should be asked, because for them that aspect would be most obvious.

Even architecture has indisputably religious connotations as well as communal significance for both the Amish and the Mbuti. The Amish add to their home to take care of elders, just as a Mbuti camp changes in shape and size as necessary to accommodate the "family" of the moment. Neither culture has a "church" in which religious services are held; for the Amish it is the family home, just as for the Mbuti it is the center of the family camp. Whereas for many of us the sacred is something distant and distinct, for these communities (and we may suspect for others) the sacred is essentially and necessarily familiar as well as familial. It is an integral part of all aspects of everyday life, domestic, economic, and political as well as ritual. The very process of living in such a community is an act of worship; so while religion may have its formal moments, it is also largely informal. The very concept of family is sacred in such communities.

The fourth requirement of the Amish, the practice of humility and simplicity, is a little less easy to relate to the Mbuti. Humility is not a concept they would understand, and while we might say they practice simplicity, they would not. However, there are related and comparable values which are essential to Mbuti communality. Far from practicing humility, the extrovert Mbuti are almost diametrically opposed to the Amish in their boastfulness both as individuals and as a group (for instance, when a hunting band visits a farming village). Yet the individual boastfulness is just that, it is an expression of the lesser individual self, and is almost invariably in a form of self ridicule as much as it is an expression of self awareness; if anything it serves to avert pride, which would certainly be the Amish objective, rather than to encourage it. If the boaster does not ridicule himself, his boasting will be taken up by others and exaggerated to the point of absurdity, and the individual effectively reduced to socially acceptable size. When there is group boastfulness, such as when Mbuti emerge from the forest bringing forest foods and products to the village world, telling stories of their bravery and how weak and cowardly and ignorant the villagers are for not being able to get these things for themselves, the stories are always exaggerated to such an extent that the villagers are laughing as much as the Mbuti. Such apparent demonstrations of pride serve the vital and positive function of maintaining a clear separation between the identities of the two groups while doing so in such an entertaining and obviously good-natured fashion as to avert the potentially disfunctional formation of mutual feelings of superiority. It is indeed a form of ritual and is therefore equalizing.

As for simplicity, the Mbuti do indeed shun all but a very few of the luxuries and amenities of western civilization, including those readily accessible to them in the villages on their periphery. They do not do this with the moral conviction of the Amish, nor in response to any specific religious belief; they do it primarily because to them, in their forest world, these things would be hindrances rather than luxuries, and bring nuisance rather than convenience.

The similarity is in the sacredness of their reference point: the Mbuti reject those manifestations of the outside world that would bring *akami*, that would be displeasing to the forest, that would result in "unforestness." Hostetler's comment that "pocket calculators or battery operated razors are no threat to *family solidarity*"[3] among the Amish could be applied to the Mbuti, pointing out that the little metal knives and miniature axes they get from the villagers are totally incapable of cutting down the *forest*. At the same time, the Mbuti totally reject the use of the larger axes with which the villagers fell fully grown forest trees and the guns with which they kill game. The Amish are very conscious of the effect that mechanical convenience can have on patterns of cooperation, and they have found scriptural justification for their preference for cooperation and community over convenience and individuality. The Mbuti do not have a body of written scriptures, but ultimately their appeal is equally to the sacred, their yardstick being the quality of their communal life in the forest.

Here a most important comparison is evident, one that leads us towards our consideration of society. Hostetler says that the Amish "see no contradiction in forbidding a telephone in the home but permitting its use from a pay station."[4] The Mbuti see no contradiction in smoking marijuana when in a village, but forbidding its use in the forest. It is both a matter of keeping an appropriate distance between the sacred and the profane, and a highly perceptive awareness of the complex realities of behavioral function and disfunction. Again, for both communities, reference is to the sacred. But Hostetler says that the Amish go beyond this, and that some even encourage their young, particularly at the critical time just before marriage, to test their faith and enter the outside world, taste it, and then either voluntarily reject it and return to the Amish way, or become part of it and give up the Amish way. Some believe that the mixing of young Amish children with others may also serve, by contrast, to demonstrate the advantages of the Amish way. All children grow up with some familiarity with the outside world so that when they consciously reject it, by baptism, they know what they are rejecting.

The Mbuti, similarly, while keeping their sacred world apart from the profane village world, accomplish far more even than the vital reaffirmation of their communal belief. Like the Amish, the Mbuti explicitly recognize the reality of the outside world simply by the fact of opposing it, or dealing with it in any way whatsoever, and by not trying to convert that outside world to their own way of life and thought. They take pains not to interfere with that foreign way; both communities implicitly recognize the equal right of others, however distinct, to exist. So at the very least, it is perfectly possible for social groups, however distinct, to form a community of communities, given each group's ability to retain its own distinct way without interfering with the right and ability of the others to do the same. That does not constitute a society, but it points the way.

---

3. *Id.* (emphasis added).
4. *Id.*

F. *Community-Society Conflict*

1. The Reciprocity Issue

The problems that rise between community and society mostly arise when each is unwilling or unable to respect fully the rights and interests of the other, when they seem to or do necessarily run counter to each other, and when separation is not possible. What binds communities together into a single society is some necessity for mutual reciprocity, which can be in one or all areas of life. Such a necessity demands the establishment of a common code of behavior defining the relationship, at least; it need not always define behavior within the communities. One factor that in our society makes it necessary for the common code to reach into the communities and define to *some* extent what behavior shall be throughout, is the possibility, likelihood, and even necessity in our society for mobility. In the Ituri, a member of one community who does not like it, or is disliked, can with relative ease move to another without any stigma, and will be perfectly welcome wherever he can be a good community member. The standard and the quality of life does not vary that much, except between the farmers, fishers, and hunters. Between such dramatically different life style communities there is less mobility. All that is required, however, is the willingness and ability to practice the appropriate way. Consequently, it was by no means unknown, although rare, for village farmers to live in the forest among the Mbuti hunters. They were then, however, subject to the forest code, not that of the village.

In our society such total fragmentation and autonomy of communities is not possible. Nevertheless, each community had its own inner conflict between communal self awareness and communal self perception. Near-communities, like Lancaster County, feel a divided loyalty to two laws, not precisely those of God and Mammon, but certainly those that in our terms are sacred (communal) and secular (social). Individuals can and do utilize whichever set of "laws" suit their needs, but this practice would be totally impermissible in a small-scale society in which the context would define which set of laws was applicable. The issue is compounded in proportion to the strength with which any community believes that its survival as such depends on adherence to its "way."

2. The Factor of the Sacred in Amish and Mbuti Communities

The Mbuti and the Amish make it very clear, conscious and overt, that their ways of life and thought are their very being, that without the possibility of pursuing those ways they would cease to be Mbuti and Amish. Such conviction is the mark of a true community, and while it opens the door to confrontation by its very uncompromising nature, it also opens the door to negotiation and a conflict-free resolution by at least clarifying the situation. If then a community finds it cannot come to terms with the needs and demands of the society of which it is a part, the only option is for it to leave. This does not happen frequently in our society, but the voluntary self-exile of the Jonestown community (however mistaken thinking was on both sides) is one example. Better that than for a community to compromise merely for the sake of compromise, without conviction, for then it loses the religious integrity and vitality that is its prime justification for existence.

Adaptation, modification and reconciliation can take place without being compromised only if the belief systems involved are flexible. There is nothing more destructive of society or of communities within societies than the religious arrogance that claims both absolute superiority and absolute uniqueness, and consequently refuses to depart from the letter of its own law. Such inflexibility may well be a sign of inner weakness rather than strength, but nonetheless the damage it does to the fabric of society is real and powerful. The success of the Amish in the United States is an example of how a people totally and uncompromisingly dedicated to their religious ideal, to their chosen way of life, can still be flexible enough to make their presence in a very different society perfectly workable. If there is any danger in that relationship, between the Amish and the state or the nation, it is likely to be due to inflexibility on the part of the latter.

For one thing, like the Mbuti their very dedication to their way of life, which for them is their "law," inculcates and demands a respect for "law" in general. Thus, state and federal law are respected insofar as the respect is mutual. Very significantly (and very differently from the multitude of near-communities like Lancaster County of Virginia), the Amish do not take their internal problems to courts of law, and indeed decline to appear in such courts even when accused of violating state or federal law. But they accept the consequence, even though that may be jail. This is not how the system need work, any more than truly conscientious objectors should be jailed because of their religious beliefs. The specific beliefs of the Amish make theirs an extreme case, for to be Amish is a matter of belief, not a matter of preference. You could only be Amish if you could not be anything else. Living is stated to be "a redemptive process"; the focus is on right effort, and failure it expected since the perfection aimed at is superhuman.

In such a system, be it Mbuti or Amish, there is no place for crime, courts, or penal systems. The weak must be strengthened and the community must be protected from harm, so we are dealing with sin rather than crime, and with purification rather than punishment. Plainly the secular courts of society and its secular laws must be seen by such a community as the Amish as having little if any authority over them. It would be wrong, however, to think the Amish deny that the courts and law of the outside world, of "society," have any authority. The Amish are certainly aware of the power of those courts, and it is at that crucial point that the two worlds, community and society, may come into conflict.

Community, as represented by the Amish, achieves social order through spiritual and moral coercion, with the goal of individual redemption *through community redemption*. Hence its focus is on restitution. Society, as represented by the state and federal governments, courts and law, achieves social order through physical coercion and the threat of such coercion in the form of physical incarceration. It is essentially punitive rather than restitutive (regardless of the ongoing debate as to how far, if at all, the system has any deterrent effect), and focuses primarily on the individual. The social good is more of a remote ideal than the immediate concern of the law. While in Community the model for order is established deeply and indelibly at the outset through family order, and is expanded upward and outward to the prime focus in adult life on communal order, with society it is the reverse. There the state (or nation) establishes itself as the model and its order filters down through successive levels to the individual. The fact that the government is theoretically of, for and by the people does not result in anything like the same immediate and directly perceived relationship between the individual good and social order as is perceived in community. Nevertheless, these differences are far from irreconcilable, and the two systems can work effectively together, as seen in the Ituri, where many communities, differing radically from each other in way of life and in religious belief and practice, nonetheless form a single political entity. This is what elsewhere I have called the *nkumbi* confederation that effectively corresponds to the provincial legal entity.

The Amish, within themselves, are sufficient in number and widely enough dispersed (not only in Pennsylvania, but in other states and in Canada) to require some form of effective centralization, though they would in the interests of the smaller discrete localized communities shun even an Amish "government." So territoriality and community of residence, as in the Ituri, are clearly shown to be prime criteria of "community" just as are religion and community of belief, and community of life style (which derives almost inevitably from the other two.) Given the permissible mobility from one Amish community to another, a mobility that may well be utilized (as it is by the Mbuti) to every conflict that would be disruptive to the community, there has to be some form of inter-community communication. This is far from approaching any form of central Amish government imposing a secular law. At the most it seems more like a religious council that exists to ensure that all communities are indeed adhering to the same "ancestral," or divine, spiritually ordained way. Thus, when mobility occurs, it can occur without danger of pollution. It would be wrong to mistake this for the rigid conformity too often and wrongly thought to be synonymous with "community." In fact, it allows for a large measure of individual freedom within the community.

The Amish among themselves, recognize the need for some form of coordination, if not government, and they certainly recognize the need for government in the modern nation state. In no way do they deny the obligations and responsibilities of citizenship, though they make relatively scant use of its rights, even resisting welfare. They perceive their social self to be necessarily a mere extension of their communal self. Thus, they accept state and federal law, their rights and responsibilities as citizens, only insofar as these do not conflict with the higher, spiritual law that, they believe, should govern *all* human behavior, including that of governments. At first it might seem that this position, although understandable, is hardly tenable in a modern state, least of all a plural society such as the United States. On the contrary, the Amish instance demonstrates that in fact the two units, Amish community and state/federal society, conflict on remarkably few points, though those points are emotionally and structurally crucial. On the side of society there may be feelings that the Amish are a parasitical population, pursuing their own good at the expense of others, contributing little or nothing to the wider national good. They refuse to join the armed services for the defense of the nation, and they resist more localized state needs, as for instance when these impinge on Amish owned land and its usage. The Amish, on the other hand, see certain central legislation as directly interfering with their religious duty to the higher law of God, though others normally would not think of taxation and land development or the Department of Highways as having much to do with "religion." However, most of these issues have been negotiated and settled with the secular authorities. The Amish do not deny the right of others to live as they wish, in accord with their conscience. They merely seek a central government and law that will allow such freedom equally for all. The government's position is not that far removed, if we accept Warren Burger's ruling that a way of life that does not interfere with the rights and wants of others is not to be condemned merely because it is different. And the Amish acceptance of central secular government (insofar as it does not interfere with their sacred way) is not an empty posture: a sizeable proportion of the Amish population register and actively participate in the local and central electoral process, in full keeping with their conscience. They also contribute in many direct and practical ways to the welfare of the non-Amish communities living around them.

The ongoing, crucial area of conflict concerns education. Throughout this examination of individual, community and society we have come against the central importance of the educational process. Hostetler discusses this detail, showing that initially the Amish took advantage of local rural elementary education, seeing its value in providing their children with necessary contact with the outside world. Thus their decision to be Amish, when it came time for baptism, was not made in ignorance. The Amish resisted higher education, for this took their children away from the communally vital educational process that could only be had by full time residence at home and on the farm, where the Amish had their own secondary level schools. This is precisely the time in life, around puberty, when the *nkumbi* plays such a vital role in the socialization process in the Ituri, making possible the ordered relationship *between* communities while encouraging the continuation of disparate ways of living *within* those communities. What makes it possible for "community" to thrive within a wider society, as seems now to be the case, in the Ituri, is that the wider society, while not favoring the religious belief of one community over another, is not irreligious. On the contrary, the wider society, being yet another outward expansion from the nuclear family, accepts the existence and value of a diversity of religious beliefs, regards each community in this sense as a sacred community, and is therefore itself sacred.

The implications of this are simple, yet absolutely crucial to the coexistence of community and society. The main implications for our purposes are that the areas of responsibility and authority are clearly defined, and that in such definition society fully recognizes the sanctity of community, as "family writ large," and its inviolable right to practice its religious belief. Community, similarly, must accept the defined authority of society, provide its own members with ample opportunity to know enough of the outside world to make community membership not only voluntary but well considered, and ensure that its own form of religious belief and practice in no way interferes with that of others. In this sense, all that is preventing Lancaster County in Virginia from being a "community" is its own self perception as a secular rather than sacred unit, as being composed of individuals and families rather than as itself being a family in both effect and affect. As a result it accepts individual good as distinct from communal good. There is also no possibility for the unanimity of decision making that is another hallmark of the Ituri and Amish communities. This of course derives at least in part from the diversity of religious belief within the county. That diversity of church affiliation, even of "religion" in the wider sense (Jewish, Islamic, Christian, whatever) need be no barrier to the kind of religious unity demanded by "community," though a broad diversity might result in sub-families or sub-communities. What is more necessary than nominal affiliation is a common belief in a prime common sacred. That for the Amish is the community itself, just as for the Mbuti it is "Forestness." At best, Lancaster County's *overall* self perception is secular. While this enables it to fit into the state and federal system of secular law, it is with some reluctance because of its powerful sense of self awareness, as though it felt that it had certain *independent* rights but was unable to articulate them.

3. The Poletown Conflict in Detroit

This inherent possibility of conflict begins with the conflict between the individual self and the social self, and may be enlarged into conflict between nuclear family and community, and ultimately between community and society. It becomes most troublesome in the United States when it arises in an urban context. Despite our too often repeated assertion of the separation of church of state, and the fact that we are an industrial nation, we allow a measure of "freedom" in the rural context, as though a village or county had some valid claim to being a sacred, religious unit, whereas the urban context is almost by definition secular, if not profane. Yet ethnic neighborhoods in all our major cities may come a lot closer to being communities, as we are defining the term, than many a rural village or county. It is not unrelated that the very term, "ethnic," originally had almost exclusive religious connotations, referring to populations and cultures who were gentile, or at best neither Jewish nor Christian.

When we come to consider social issues such as the proposal by General Motors to take over the northern section of "Poletown" in Detroit, as part of its massive modernization plan in 1980, we are once again having to deal with a "religious" issue. General Motors turned down offers of other sites in Detroit, and increasingly insisted on Poletown as the location for its new plant. One of Poletown's chief defenses was, in effect, that it was a "community" and, in practice if not in law, untouchable. Perhaps the most immediate weakness of the claim lay in the usage of the term "Poletown," which for most outsiders has national rather than religious connotations. Indeed the crucial issue should have been *is* Poletown a true community, that is bound by a community of religious belief, or is it merely a secular (however viable and distinctive) neighborhood? The study by Bukowczyk enables us, after the fact, at least to use the unhappy coup of corporation over community to help resolve our own dilemma in trying to define the rights and responsibilities of society as distinct from those of community.

There were three major interested parties: General Motors, which wished to acquire a tract of land for its expansion program; the City of Detroit, in which the tract was located; and the residents of that tract. There was resistance from at least a sizeable segment of the residents (so either there was no communal unanimity or the area should not have been considered, as it was, as being a single neighborhood, let alone a "community"). This resistance publicly raised the issue of the public good (that of the residents) being sacrificed for private interests (those of General Motors). This obscured what was really the prime issue, whether or not the residents did form a "community," and placed the focus on the shifting sands of private and public interests, shifting because what is private interest in one context may be public interest in another.

For Detroit, badly in need of an economic shot in the arm, the proposed takeover of some 465 unproductive acres meant not only the preservation of 6,000 jobs that would be lost if General Motors relocated elsewhere, but also a massive increase in tax revenue. For General Motors the acquisition of the particular tract of land was part of a vast program of expansion, and for a number of reasons the site was its first choice but by no means the only possible choice. Partly because of the complex multiple reasons that made this, for General Motors, the most advantageous site, it was possible for the media to play on the fact that General Motors was a private corporation, and to imply that this was a classic conflict between private and public interests, assuming that the interests of the residents were *ipso facto* "public." What lay concealed in most media accounts was the fact that it was by no means clear what was private and what was public. Further obscuring the underlying issue of whether or not the area was a "community" were the distinctions made between purpose and usage, both private and public. In substituting the terms individual and social, for private and public, the issue takes on a different and less equivocal appearance.

For the third party to the dispute, the residents of the area, it was even more uncertain as to what was at stake. The issue was generally presented as being a conflict between a private corporation and "the public." Not only did this ignore the fact that any private corporation, particularly one the size of General Motors, is an integral and potentially profitable part of the wider society, just as it is an integral part of the same social structure that incorporates "the public" (individuals), but it diverted attention from the fact that the conflict was really one of city versus neighborhood. The neighborhood *claimed* to be a community and was an integral a part of the city as General

Motors Corporation was of the state of Michigan, and the state of the nation. General Motors was merely a vehicle through which this inherent conflict was able to manifest itself. In the manifestation there was revealed an extraordinary lack of clearly defined rights and responsibilities at different levels of social integeration. We have already posited clarity of these definitions as one of the chief requirements if the interrelationship between individual, community and society is to minimize conflict. Each of the participants viewed the issue rather as if they were competitors in a game, each playing the game according to different rules. Each had the same goal of an exclusive, individual victory in which its interests would win over the interests of the other participants, though not necessarily at the expense of those other interests.

Two factors emerge here that are important for our interest in the rights and responsibilities of individuals and groups at different levels of social integration. One was that all three participants claimed that their interests were also in the public interest. This was an appeal to both law and morality, to what might be held to be a "religious" right. The other factor was that similarly, but much more specifically, the case for the residents involved the claim that they constituted a "community." Thus, they made an appeal to a clearly felt but hopelessly ill-defined sanctity—one that, if accurately defined, would vest in a residential unit whose members are bound together by more than mere common residence, a shared economy, a mutually acceptable life style and political position. They are bound by a community of religious belief, a bond that can almost be made to sound mystical. What is interesting is that, at that point, when the mystical or even spiritual aspect is played up, the case for community begins to lose credibility in the eyes of many, including those of the law. This is important because all along I have been saying that not only is "religion" an important factor in defining community, but that there is far more to "religion" than mere church membership, or adherence to a moral code supported by a belief system. To understand the power of "community" as an effective structural entity we have to take sentiment into account, and consider faith as a phenomenon at least as important as, and quite different from, belief.

In media accounts the terms "neighborhood" and "community" were at first used interchangeably, but the word "community" was used increasingly when the writer wished to support the case of the residents. Presumably, then, if a community is entitled to more protection in the popular view than a neighborhood (and presumably a neighborhood to more protection than a mere subdivision, and so on), one wonders why so little energy was given to determining whether or not the area of the proposed General Motors development was indeed the community it claimed to be. In fact, the issue was played out in such a way that the victory went to the best strategists, and from the outset the residential strategy was poor. Their best strategy was in claiming to be a community, though if they had been questioned on that they might have been hard pressed to substantiate the claim. But even more untenable was the claim implicit in their resurrection of the old name for that part of Detroit, "Poletown," implying that what was at stake was an ethnic neighborhood, if not a community. Also remarkably weak in their strategy was the lack of any substantial argument that they represented any real public interest. The very private corporation the neighborhood council attacked, in precisely those terms, could with much greater justification demonstrate that in practice, if not as a prime objective, it operated for the good of the public. It could make that argument at the level of the national good, or interest, right down to the good of the individual worker. The position of the city was even less ambivalent in claiming that it properly represented the interests of a greater good than that of any of its parts.

From our point of view, the position of the neighborhood council that claimed to represent the residents was the most untenable. Many of the residents were in favor of the takeover, some standing to gain as part of the labor market that would benefit by the creation of 6,000 jobs, and some standing to gain by accepting the city's offer to pay more than market value for rapidly depreciating property. In addition, the claim implied in the resurrection of the old name "Poletown" did not reflect the actual ethnic composition of the district, which was primarily black American and secondarily Polish. It also had a substantial number of residents from East Europe and from such places as the American South and the Philippines. Although the district had a ratio of one church for every eighty-five households, that does not suggest a very tight-knit single "community," nor even a "neighborhood" of any effective homogeneity. Divided as it was by race, class, national background and religion, the use of the name Poletown was clearly a tactic to win popular support and favor in court. It was also designed to win the support of the powerful Roman Catholic Church, headed locally by a Polish Archbishop and, of course, in Rome by a Polish Pope.

Historically, the district first began to assume a residential ethnic character with its settlement by German workers; ever since there have been successful waves of immigrants, including German Poles, Russian Poles, Austrian Poles, and presumably some Polish Poles. During this period it acquired the name Poletown; it was a period when it might have been able to lay claim to being a community, with Polish schools, churches using the Polish language, and festivals that expressed the shared spiritual heritage. That was a far cry from the shared spiritual heritage. That was a far cry from the cultural scene as it was at the time of the dispute, in 1890.

In fact the population of the area designated for demolition did have some justification for their claim to be a community, but it was ill-formulated and falsely presented. First, there was a common attachment to territory, and territoriality is one of the criteria we have suggested as determining what is and what is not "community." That the territory was, in the eyes of others, dilapidated, run down, a "wasteland" (as it was described with remarkable insensitivity), in no way affects the reality and strength of the sentiment felt by the residents. The Mbuti hunters regard the forest as all that is good, yet it is perceived as dark and full of evil by their village neighbors. Again we are dealing with the reality of self perception. This common attachment to territory transcended the nominally "religious" and ethnic and class divisions of Poletown.

Second, "family," another major criterion of "community," was also present, though not (as presented by the critics of General Motors) through any common Polishness, nor even common formal religious affiliation. Rather, it was in the form of union fraternity. There was certainly an economic cohesiveness, though in trying to establish the validity of a claim to being a community, any researcher would want to know a lot more about the system of economic rights and obligations as it bound (or did not bind) individual households into a single corporate entity.

While all this would have lent strength to an argument for preserving the area as a community, there were other factors crucial to the concept of community that were lacking. There was no unanimity. And while relocation of individuals and families would have made it difficult or impossible for some affective bonds to be retained, it does not seem that such relocation would have broken any bonds that were both effective and necessary. Nor is it clear that there was anything approaching an effective socialization system that provided a common loyalty to a common communal good, a common good that would be recognized and ranked by all as greater than that of the individual good. Union membership would have achieved this to some extent, but it does not seem to have been represented in the formal educational system nor in the home (through common child-rearing practices), and above all there was little if any ongoing socialization in the form of rituals of revitalization. At best such revitalization and sharing of common symbols of sociality might have been found at the smaller parish level, but not at the community or neighborhood level.

These are just some of the factors that relate to whether or not "Poletown" was a "community," but they are the same factors that pertain to the relationship of community to society, and in fact one of the most poignant facts is that many residents who saw themselves as members of a community did not object to the sacrifice of their community if it was indeed for the wider good of the city. What they objected to, and one of the factors that encouraged them to resist, was the way that their neighborhood was described as a wasteland. Yet that appellation was not intended to be derogatory, it was merely a highly insensitive assessment that was perfectly correct in one context (that of society) and totally incorrect in another context (that of neighborhood).

VI. A Workable Basis For a Relationship Among Individual, Community and Society

Once we have established the duality of individual identity, we have implied the duality of community identity. Once we accept the possibility of the individual moving from one set of values to another in the making of decisions, applying the values appropriate to the context, we should be able to accept the same process as a workable basis for the relationship between community and society. At this stage we are not thinking of "community" as a theoretical construct, but as a living entity composed of rational (and well socialized) individual human beings. Its relationship with society is thus organic rather than mechanical, moral rather than legal, but supported by and formalized through structure and law. Society also, of course, is composed of human individuals, but it is useful to think of it as a theoretical entity, mechanical rather than organic (though by no means exclusively so), for the very good reason that the interpersonal and inter-group relations within the wider human society become less direct and less personal, more diffuse and mechanical, the larger the society. The same process of mechanization of human relationships, and of the law itself, is proportionate to the degree to which the society is composed of communities rather than neighborhoods, for ultimately the nature of any given society is determined by the nature of these smaller social units. The reciprocal rights and obligations that pertain between community and society should be such that society does not have the power to determine the nature of any of its communities, and such that no one community has the power to determine the nature of society.

The word "society" can be made to mean almost anything we want it to. It is used, as are many other crucial words, with almost unbelievable carelessness and irresponsibility, and not uncommonly (as with "community") as a lever to effect some kind of behavioral or attitudinal coercion. This implies that as with "community" there is a widespread belief that the individual as well as groups of individuals are under some moral obligation to "society." As convenient as it would be to define community as sacred and society as secular, it is not quite that simple. Since no one usage of the term can claim absolute precedence it is useful here to recapitulate briefly and review how we have used the terms for our own purposes in this discussion. In light of that usage and that purpose we can find a meaning in the concept of society that will be consistent with the meaning we attach here to individual and community, and will help us to understand better the importance of greater precision in the usage, both common and legal, of such terms.

To recapitulate, as a social anthropologist I am concerned with social institutions and with social structure, and as a humanist I am concerned with *all* the forces that influence human relationships, interpersonal or intergroup, and help to bring about social order or social disorder. Among those forces, then, I must consider those loosely called emotional and religious, though without any pretension of being able to do so as thoroughly as might a psychologist, a theologian or philosopher. Finally, as a member of one particular society, the United States, my prime ultimate concern is with social order and disorder at home. To this end I use the comparative method, making comparisons both within our own society and between ours and others far removed in space and kind. My motivation is that as an individual resident in what refers to itself as a "community," and with legally binding rights and responsibilities in a nation that is sometimes referred to as a "society," I am not only aware of what I referred to as a general malaise, but a part of it. My position is, therefore, subjective as well as objective. I bring my understanding of other ways of life and thought to bear not with the slightest suggestion that they are directly applicable, but rather to enlighten first by juxtaposition, then to suggest new and specific ways of reassessing our own social system. The reassessment includes some of those concepts we so readily take for granted, such as the three under consideration here.

In the Ituri Forest of the Republic of Zaire, then, we find a sizeable number of peoples and cultures of great diversity, yet throughout there is a common perception of "society." For them this means at least "the largest political unit" of which they are an effective part, which for some would be the forest, for others the province, and for fewer the nation, depending on their education. So for them society is not bounded by size, but by efficacy, by the fact (rather that the theory) of interaction and interdependence. I suggest that this limitation would be inappropriate in a different educational context, such as our own, in which we *might* wish to accept theoretical interdependence rather than demand actual interdependence.

Another conceptual point that all these people share is their view of human society as an expanding universe, expanding outward from the individual through an ever-widening succession of different levels of "family." At the same time they all accept that in a kind of mirror image of the same model, but flowing in the reverse direction, authority flows downwards and outwards from a single divine, supernatural, or spiritual source. Thus, the total population understands that "family" provides the basic model for all relationships, human and suprahuman, natural and supranatural. The individual is aware of himself as an isolate, distinct from all others in certain respects, but to him those respects are insignificant by comparison with the respects in which he is similar to all others at the outward extension of his universe. In such a world he can relate himself to any other individual by the simple process of tracing the two ancestries back to a common ancestor. The extent to which he has to go to find such a common ancestor will determine the precise extent and nature of their reciprocal rights and responsibilities concerning each other, their effective social relationship. While he has a single self awareness, he has an ongoing and ever changing self perception of himself as a social self rather that an individual self, with the crucial recognition that each "self" has clearly defined reciprocal rights and responsibilities. These are not ranked hierarchically in order of merit. All are equally binding; they are merely different in nature.

Similarly with his perception of the different social groups to which he belongs, varying in size and composition, the smallest is the nuclear family, and just as the emotional bonds are at an early stage the most intense, so are the rights and responsibilities. Deriving from the natural felt dependence of the infant on the mother, and its later perceived dependence upon the father, the associated rules of behavior are thought of as "natural." They are also thought of as being desirable since, if followed, they lead to satisfaction and survival. From the earliest moment onward the infant's experience is that certain forms of behavior are associated with reward, with satisfaction, and others are not. Reward is not contrasted with punishment, merely with non-satisfaction.

The next step outward from nuclear family is usually into a wider kin-group such as lineage (thence into clan and tribe, the exact divisions varying from culture to culture). This wider kin group, however, includes affines, those to whom the individual is only related through the marriage of one of his own kin, or later through his own marriage. But in the Ituri, as in many other small-scale societies, this wider group, this association of nuclear families, has all the emotional cohesion of being a kin group and also has the cohesive strength of being a corporate economic group. Whether it is the hunting band of the Mbuti, a fishing camp of the Ndaka or a village of the agricultural Bira, *all* residents are seen as contributing in an effective way to the common good. Residents of the village, or whatever the territorial unit is, may not all actually be directly related, since some may have joined to avoid dispute elsewhere. But in that case they usually can trace some kinship if they go back far enough. Even if not, such immigrants are *classified* as kin and this way brought into exactly the same system of rights and responsibilities as others, into the same effective world and into the same affective world. This is a world in which all have a common stake in a common, shared territory, just as they share common kinship—be it real or classificatory. The members of this "family" are structured in such a way as to unite all the individuals and nuclear families as equal members in one single corporate unit that is essentially sacred in nature since all members subscribe to the same belief. The belief may be in the sanctity of the ancestor from which they are all descended, or in the sanctity of the territory that is uniquely theirs and which provides them their sustenance. Finally, members of this corporate family see themselves as distinct from similar units, even those with which they may interact. With other such corporate units they do not share the same *proximity* of kinship, nor are they as absolutely and necessarily economically interdependent; they do not share the same residential and economic territory, nor do they participate in the same rituals at the same time and in the same place. Each group is distinct and sacred in its own right, and the prime obligation of the members of each is to maintain that uniqueness and sacredness.

These communities share the same model of an expanding universe, based on the universal phenomenon of family. Consequently, when these communities come together, they merely shift horizons, in time and space, and become a larger community, we might say. Between immediate neighbors, who are likely to be interrelated through marriage anyway, and who interact most often for mutual economic and political advantage, the bonds binding them together may be almost as strong and vital as those binding members of the smaller territorial communities. Obviously, both the affective and effective bonds decrease in strength as the universe expands, and this is when reinforcement is needed. In place of "law and order," however, this society utilizes ritual and belief, and can do so because all communities share a common sacred which they all see, though perhaps in different ways, as being manifest in society itself. Such a society thus is not less sacred than its communities, but its sanctity is more distant and that much less direct and effective. Invariably such societies, like the sacred communities, make use of rituals and symbols to reaffirm their authority while limiting that authority to the regulation of inter-community relationships.

In such interrelationships communities need to be represented, but the representation is significantly different in nature and quality from that known in our political system. There may or may not be choice, but whether the representative comes to be that through rules of inheritance such as primogeniture (thus the senior living representative of the common sacred ancestor) or through an electoral process, perhaps based on charisma (as would be the case with the Mbuti), the representative is of the same "family" as all those he represents. He shares the same name, and therefore has the same social identity, regardless of his own individual identity. The larger the community, the more likely that the representative will be "strengthened" by rituals reaffirming this shared identity. To us that might seem like insufficient safeguards against the possibility of corruption. That is where we have to recognize the importance of the phenomenon of faith in such communities and societies, for faith, being suprarational, is inherently unquestionable (though not immune from the process of change). This may help us to realize the extent to which our system is impoverished by the absence of such well-inculcated systems of belief and faith. Since the oath taken in a courtroom is not considered any longer to have binding power in itself or through any invocative power it might have, it is little more than a public, secular, rational affirmation of the acceptance of the secular law pertaining to perjury. Were it otherwise there would be little or no need to question the veracity of any witness. If a witness did depart from the truth, there would be no place for punishment since breaking the oath would have been a blasphemy, subject to supernatural rather than mortal sanctions.

In a curious way, small-scale societies work as well as they do not by any means because they are composed of saints and angels, and certainly not because the individual members are endowed with any excess of altruism. On the contrary, they work well largely because the individuals, who are as interested in the survival of the individual self as in any society, have been socialized into accepting a system in which the individual good is best, if not only, achieved through prior achievement of the social good. Moreover, this is a self-evident truth at the level of community (perhaps that should be another criterion of true "community") and its extension to the wider society involves at most a change in degree, not in nature. Finally, all communities within such a society must be bound by effective rather than theoretical bonds, by a system of mutual interdependencies, so that in larger societies in which interaction by one community with all others is impossible, all must be interrelated by common and necessary interaction with society. This can occur in an amorphous ritual confederation of believers as in the Ituri, or in a nation-state with a central government.

Historically states have developed out of such societies. When we can trace that development on one single continent, as we can in Africa, we see that even the most powerful, centralized, populous and diverse nations and empires have retained the familiar imagery of the family, both sacred and secular. The state is then something very familiar and real even to the least educated peasant, for he see it, if over-simply, as a superfamily, and consequently knows how to relate to it.

Even in our own world, in which the process has been going on for much longer, the same imagery may be found. We still talk of fatherlands and motherlands, and even of a "family of nations." God Himself is seen as a Father, or Herself as a Mother. We have the same tendencies to think of the *land* as sacred. Unanimity, while plainly impossible in our nation, even at a county level, is nonetheless an ideal. The importance of religion is recognized, though perhaps not the presence of Spirit, as manifest in the Constitution and the laws relating to religious belief and practice. It is manifest again in the deep-seated and highly emotional attitude of the public to any religious issue at almost any level. Further, religion is present in many symbols and forms of behavior most of us take to be secular. So the very elements that make order without law possible in small-scale societies are all present in our own, but largely unformulated and unsystematized, subject to abuse and exploitation for private ends, it often seems, as much as subject to application toward the common good.

We do not recognize clearly the duality of individual identity, the coexistence of the individual and private self with the social and public self, and we fail to distinguish between the rights and responsibilities of these two entities. Our malaise is agravated by our highly dangerous, undiscriminating focus on inherently non-social values such as "individual" success, "individual" freedom, "individual" rights and responsibilities. Without the clear distinction between rights and responsibilities of the individual and social self, we are not really in a position to associate with each other in communities. In true communities, individual interests of both kinds are subsumed in the communal interest, through the mere expansion of the social self through the family model to "community." Even our concept of family is rapidly shrinking, both in terms of its size and of its being a network of necessarily effective and interlocking social relationships. If the nuclear family is not a corporate unit working toward a single common goal, it is plainly impossible to expect to have a community as we have defined it. Yet few would deny the ideal that a family should be working together rather than for disparate individual interests, and the constant manipulation of the word "community" is clear indication that here too our ideals are far distant from the actuality we have created.

In place of "communities" we have "neighborhoods." That term also is value laden, and is a kind of secular version of community, with most criteria either shrunken or modified and that of common belief generally abandoned. We are also more comfortable with other, more secular criteria for "neighborhood," material criteria such as architecture, occupation, economic status, social services and facilities, and perhaps a representative body. In many neighborhoods, indeed, individual families compete with each other so that rivalry ("living on opposite banks") easily becomes a more common characteristic than territorial fraternity. Neighborhood fetes and festivals are notoriously competitive. Yet at the same time neighborhoods are also known for their neighborhood organizations, such as those for security, health or welfare, that thrive on voluntary labor and are dedicated to the common good. These frequently serve to equalize some of the inequalities. What is most lacking by contrast with the African communities we have examined is the carefully institutionalized mandatory socialization of children in or approaching their early teens. Junior and senior high school education can in no way be said to serve this function in their present form.

Since a child growing up in a nuclear family and living in a neighborhood, progressing from one school to another, does not have the experience of mutual interdependence that an African child living in the Ituri would, there is no consistent model for the systematic enlargement of those nuclear interdependencies, no matter how strong and effective the family model might be. The wider social rights and responsibilities come to the child in the form of theory; he is instructed rather than experienced in the desirability of sociality. Being rationalized, sociality is therefore questionable, as are the rights and responsibilities learned in other cultures through unrationalized experience from birth onwards, so that by puberty, when they can successfully be rationalized, they are already the only acceptable norms. The only choice of any reasonable person in such a society is the choice to be social.

Perhaps the first spiritual and social experience of any human is the dependency of the infant upon its mother. That experience is necessarily (given the physical condition of the brain) at least nonrational, if not supranatural. Much of the enormous importance of early childhood is its sensory nature, it being a time for experimentation, for discovery, and above all for wonder together with a simple acceptance that certain things simply are. In no known society do we humans go through all of life like this. Western society tends to replace this mode of apprehension by reason, but in societies such as that of the Ituri, reason is considered to be merely yet another mode of apprehension that is added to the modes already learned, rather than replacing then. So acceptance of the unknown, including the perceived power and reality of the unknown (increasingly rationalized as the "supernatural," or perhaps better as "Spirit") becomes a matter of course. This is why it is possible to talk in very real terms of such communities as being "sacred," possible to refer to their members as sharing community of belief, as being irrevocably bound together by community of faith (a direct mode of apprehension so unfamiliar in our social life that we seldom hear the word, and if we do it is all too often confused with mere belief). If anything is to be learned from these kinds of comparisons it is that religion (not mere formal membership in a church or adherence to a specific body of rational belief, but these things built on top of an unshakable personal faith in the existence of some form of suprahuman power) is indispensable for the proper creation and maintenence of community, and of any society that is an association of communities. Even for the rationalist here also lies a perfectly rational way of resolving the inherent conflict that plagues our society, that of the private good against the public good, of self against society.

Any rational African traditionalist, looking at our society, would be likely to react with horror at the totality of our separation of church and state, the proscription against religious education in our schools, and its absence in so many homes. He would be likely to see that in denying an equal place to religion in our society we are denying our very essence, our vital force, an inner reality that is our greatest potential source of common identity and social cohesion. As an anthropologist who has looked at many different kinds of social systems, I have found the greatest sense of security as well as the greatest degree of sociality in societies in which religious faith is deeply embedded. I believe that until we find a way of restructuring our religious belief and practice so that they broaden our sense of individual and social self awareness, using all the educational forces at our disposal, the conflict will flourish between individual rights and responsibilities, and those of society. Without some medial social unit between the individual and society, such as community, the law will continue to be faced with the impossible task of achieving social order through the threat of physical coercion. It will deal only with bodies and minds, ignoring that vital core in all of us that will always demand recognition, and cry "injustice" as long as it is not recognized. We must recognize the spiritual self that is the union of the individual and the social selves.

References and Suggested Further Reading

J. Bukowczyk, The Decline and Fall of a Detroit Neighborhood: Poletown vs. G.M. and the City of Detroit, 41 Wash. & Lee L. Rev. 49 (1984).

T. Elias, The Nature of African Customary Law (1956) (an analysis of the basic concepts underlying African Law).

M. Gluckman, Custom and Conflict (1955).

M. Gluckman, The Judicial Process among the Barotse of Northern Rhodesia (1955).

M. Gluckman, *Reasonableness and Responsibility in the Law of Segmentary Societies*, in M. Gluckman, African Law: Adaptation and Development (Kuper & Kuper eds. 1965).

J. Hostetler, Amish Society (1980).

J. Hostetler, The Amish as a Viable Community (1980) (unpublished manuscript).

J. Hostetler, American Legal Systems and the Amish (1982) (unpublished manuscript).

Hostetler & Huntington, Children in Amish Society (1971).

C. Turnbull, The Forest People (1961) (a descriptive account of the Mbuti).

C. Turnbull, Wayward Servants; The Two Worlds of the African Pygmies (1965) (a more detailed account of the relationship between the Mbuti and their village neighbors).

C. Turnbull, *The Politics of Non-Aggression*, in Learning Non-Aggression: The Experience of Non-Literate Societies (A. Montagu ed. 1978).

C. Turnbull, *Society and Sociality: An Expanding Universe*, in Ethnicity in Modern Africa (B. du Toit ed. 1978).

C. Turnbull, *Death by Decree: An Anthropological approach to capital punishment*, 87 Natural History 50 (May 1978).

Part III
The 'New' Ethnography

[10]

International Journal of Law and Psychiatry, Vol. 9, 295–319, 1986
Printed in the U.S.A.

0160-2527/86 $3.00 + .00

Personal Control, Social Responsibility, and Image of Person and Self Among the Bimin-Kuskusmin of Papua New Guinea

Fitz John Porter Poole*

This essay will explore certain aspects of a confluence of interests of anthropology, law, and psychiatry in the complex nexus of agency, control, judgment, responsibility, and related capacities of person and self that are ultimately articulated with basic notions of deviance—especially when deviance is deemed severe, a trait of character rather than circumstance, and debilitating and disruptive or dangerous to personal or community life. Indeed, images or schemata of deviance—and the kinds or degrees of breach and restraint that they entail—may bound, bracket, and otherwise mark and inform images or schemata of agency, control, judgment, responsibility and other capacities that enter variously into instructions or instantiations of personhood and selfhood in a "culturally constituted behavioral environment" (Hallowell, 1955; see also Black, 1976; Poole, 1985f). If personhood and selfhood are centered in understandings about the ethical foundations of a socio-moral order, ideas about deviance often mark the periphery, the fragility and the negation of that order (cf. Poole, 1983, 1985d; see also Read, 1955; Shotter, 1984; Shweder & Bourne, (1982; Shweder & Miller, 1985).

An analysis of person, self and deviance has some significant general implications for comprehending the personal and social contours of "madness" and the cultural manner of its recognition, evaluation and management in a community.[1] Such analytic concerns are inevitably interwoven—albeit often tacitly—in the fabric of debates which focus on the utility of ideas about the

---

*Associate Professor of Anthropology, Department of Anthropology, University of California, San Diego, La Jolla, CA 92093, U.S.A.

[1]The legal, moral, political and other social complexities of defining, diagnosing and attributing "madness" as a variously sanctioned form of deviance have been extensively examined by Black (1976), Maeder (1985), Morris (1982), Scheff (1984), Tancredi (1983) and Warren (1982). In all of these works there is an explicit or implicit concern with the legal, moral and political consequences of the socio-cultural "labelling" of deviance (see Scheff, 1984; cf. Gove, 1980; Kitsuse, 1980; Warren, 1982), and an emphasis on the tensions between biomedical ideas of (mental) disease and socio-cultural notions of (mental) illness (see Murphy, 1976; Romanucci-Ross, 1983; Simons, 1985; Tancredi, 1983; Warren, 1982; Westermeyer, 1985), in the conceptualization of what jurally constitutes the phenomenon of "insanity" as a legally recognizable and salient incapacity.

"reasonable man" in the anthropology of law,[2] the distinctions between the "normal" and the "abnormal" in ethnopsychiatry,[3] and the efficacy of processes of cultural "labelling" of personal behavior and experience in social contexts as understood in recent sociological theory.[4] In accordance with some preliminary insights of Epstein (1973, pp. 663–664) and Tancredi (1983, p. 287) on the matter, it is suggested here that these apparently related analytic notions are variously predicated on, and also entailed by, fundamental concepts of personhood and selfhood, which are organized and represented as complex schemata in *common sense* systems of cultural "meaning" (Geertz, 1985a) and are variously instantiated in different configurations in a diversity of events that mark the course of personal experience and community life.

In general, therefore, this essay is concerned with probing the nuances of the cultural form, psychological salience, and social force of those common sense schemata that bound, focus and otherwise shape notions of personhood and selfhood, which encompass and articulate concepts of agency, control, judgment, responsibility and other basic capacities of the sentient human actor in a socio-moral order, and which also implicate and bracket ideas of deviance.[5] In particular, this essay will examine—through the analytic lenses of personhood, selfhood and deviance—an unusual and illuminating case of hostility, aggression, and homicide among the Bimin-Kuskusmin of the West Sepik hinterland of Papua New Guinea.[6] This case is explicitly focused through local idioms on

[2]The concept of the "reasonable man" in legal anthropology was formulated most cogently by Gluckman (1955–1956, 1966) to refer to those cultural expectations and social norms that are brought to bear on jural assessments of intention, judgment, agency, responsibility and related capacities of a person of particular status in the commission (or omission) of specifiable acts under ascertainable personal and social circumstances (cf. Epstein, 1973; Seidman, 1965; Yngvesson, 1978). Despite its ambiguities, this notion has been deployed with profit in numerous studies of traditional legal systems, introduced concepts of law, and socio-legal change in Papua New Guinea (see Brown, 1964; Chalmers, 1975; Hookey, 1969; O'Regan, 1972).

[3]The subtle problems of universalistic and/or relativistic discriminations that beset a cross-culturally comparative, yet intra-culturally sensitive differentiation of "normal" and "abnormal" have been usefully—albeit quite differently—explored by Benedict (1934), Devereux (1980), Murphy (1976), Romanucci-Ross (1983), Simons (1985) and Westermeyer (1985). Yet Murphy (1976, p. 1019) notes that "in widely different cultural and environmental situations sanity appears to be distinguishable from insanity by cues that are very similar to those used in the Western world." With Simons (1985), this author supports the view—at least as a hypothesis—that all abnormalities of "mental" functioning are bound up with complex interactions of biological, cultural, psychological and social factors which theoretically admit of comparative alignment, but that diagnostic efforts—usually focused on behavioral presenting complaints—easily become mired in socio-cultural differences which shape such behavior, and thus readily resort to a relativistic classification by local labels or "culture-bound syndromes" (but see Murphy, 1976; Simons, 1985; Westermeyer, 1985). For purposes of this analysis, however, this author is concerned primarily with socio-cultural dimensions of personhood and selfhood as they become salient in a "culturally constituted behavioral environment" (Hallowell, 1955) and in local reckonings of normality and abnormality.

[4]See especially Scheff (1984) and Warren (1982) on the insights of labelling theory; cf. Gove (1980) and Kitsuse (1980) on some problems and limitations of this approach.

[5]Consequently, this essay is not concerned with the more formalized, esoteric, and philosophically elaborate schemata of person and self that are instantiated in, and largely have reference to ritual contexts (but see Poole, 1982b, 1982c, 1985e).

[6]Field research among the Bimin-Kuskusmin (1971–1973) was generously supported by the National Institutes of Health, the Cornell University/Ford Foundation Humanities and Social Sciences Program, and the Center for South Pacific Studies of the University of California, Santa Cruz. The New Guinea Research Unit of the Research School of Pacific Studies of the Australian National University and the Department of

culturally elaborated emotions and more ambiguous "feelings" (*agetemkhraan*) of "anger" (*guur*), subtle matters of "internal control" (*faatebeemiin*), and complex ideas of "shame" (*fiitom*) that circumscribe the remarkable image of the "man of perpetual anger" (*kunum atuur*),[7] although it intricately implicates the nexus of person, self and deviance in terms of those schemata brought to bear on its interpretation that it instantiates. The image of the man of perpetual anger is associated with a rare, congenital and incurable affliction of "sharp, uncontrollable anger twisted together" (*atuur fuugamiin*), which soon erodes the very capacities upon which a morally proper personhood and an experientially cohesive selfhood are predicated. The focal event of this extraordinary case is the sudden murder of a "man of timidity" (*kunum tiinaar*), the usually meek Kotiik, by a renowned man of perpetual anger—the ferocious and feared killer Baariin.[8]

Ideas of person, self and deviance are complexly and subtly embedded or articulated in what Moscovici (1984) terms "social representations" (in the Durkheimian tradition) or what D'Andrade (1981, 1984, 1985a, 1985b) calls either "folk models" or "cultural schemas" (in the cognitive science tradition).[9] Shared cultural schemata are fundamentally involved in perception, recognition, interpretation, problem-solving, planning, and other modes of processing information that facilitate representation of, and enable or guide action in those situations in which particular crystallizations of the schemata are instantiated (cf. Holy & Stuchlik, 1981, 1983). A schema usually consists of a small number of variables or conceptual elements and their relations to one another as they are linked in networks. The variables or conceptual elements of a schema exhibit a typical or normal range of values, can be variously interlinked within the schema and among schemata, and can be variously bound to different aspects of the environment on different instantiations of the schema.[10] The

Anthropology and Sociology of the University of Papua New Guinea provided much valuable assistance. The primary debt of gratitude, however, is owed to the Bimin-Kuskusmin people, in general, and to Baariin and his kith and kin, in particular, for endless patience and kindness and sensitivity in the face of all manner of tedious inquiry and observation.

[7]Note that there are a large number of terms that refer to states or processes of "thinking/feeling" or to mental states or processes that represent different combinations and balances of cognition and affect, which tend not to be distinguished normally, easily or sharply in Bimin-Kuskusmin discourse. Thus, "to think/feel" (*taakhriinaniin*) anger emphasizes cognitive considerations of motivation, provocation and justification that underlie or are otherwise articulated with a culturally encoded emotion, while "to feel/think" (*duurakhaa-niin*) anger stresses more uncognized, inchoate "feelings" (*agetemkhraan*). "To think/feel" (*tobuukhuniin*) shame, however, represents an emphasis on a more or less symmetrical balance between cognition and affect (see Poole, 1985b, 1985f).

[8]Both the names of the protagonists and the details of the event have been altered to disguise the identities of participants in a vivid historical case.

[9]When adapted to considerations of cultural knowledge and inference, the conceptual development of the idea of cognitive schemata is a significant theoretical advance on the seminal insights of Durkheimian notions of collective or social "representations" (cf. Moscovici, 1984). However, it should be noted that, in cognitive science, both "parallel distributed processing models" (McClelland, Rumelhart, & the PDP Research Group, 1985) and "mental models" (Johnson-Laird, 1983) exemplify attempts to remedy perceived deficiencies in schema theory with respect to representing knowledge structures and their deployment in information processing, but these complications will not intrude on the immediate concerns of this essay.

[10]The schema embodies a prototype sense of "meaning" in that its typical articulation of linkages among the nodes of a network of concepts is encoded in normal situations—most readily retrieved from memory and

typical or normal constraints on the variables or concepts of a schema—that is, on their values and interrelationships—serve two critical functions: (1) they facilitate the use of the schema as an hypothesis about the identity or conceptual properties of an event or situation; and (2) they permit an interpretation to proceed beyond the information given in guiding inferences about unobserved, tacit or ambiguous aspects of the situation or event. Yet each conceptual element or variable of a schema may itself be a complex schema, for schemata encompass sub-schemata in an hierarchical mode of organization that may be simultaneously activated *both* from the top down (that is, from whole to part) and from the bottom up (that is, from part to whole) as the construction of an instantiation and an interpretation proceeds.[11]

As D'Andrade (1981, 1984, 1985a) implies, a distinctive attribute of most cultural schemata is that they are not precisely specified or explicit in all respects as they are represented in natural discourse.[12] Indeed, certain aspects of folk models remain tacit, ambiguous, or even opaque. Tacit dimensions presume other schemata that are implicated by, but are not explicitly embedded in or otherwise articulated with the focal folk model, and thus require the activation of implicit criteria of relevance and processes of inference to interconnect and to interpret these covert schemata. By virtue of the intersubjective sharing of these cultural schemata in a community, certain aspects of folk models are often perceived as being obvious and "natural" facts of the world and need not be made explicit (D'Andrade, 1985a). These implicit aspects, however, are commonly the premises of the more explicit features of folk models. Ambiguous aspects of cultural schemata leave unresolved the problem of which of several potentially linked schemata, each with somewhat different implications for the hierarchical organization of *relevant* schemata, may be implied. Opaque features are lacunae in the structure of the folk model that are not readily articulated with other available cultural schemata and mark certain disjunctive aspects of the linkages between those concepts that are articulated by a schema. These several characteristics of cultural schemata suggest that the interwoven net-

---

recognized in the environment—that instantiate those concepts. Yet the schema provides only a skeleton or lattice around which a situation is interpreted through a more or less flexible binding of concepts and their interrelations to their instances and an assessment of the "fit" between the pattern of the schema and the pattern of the event. Thus, the idea of a schema accommodates a looseness of structure, irrelevant variation and innovative interpretation, while maintaining an essential sense that the schema is being instantiated within certain parameters.

[11]Schemata seem to guide such constructions in the following manner. The environmental occurrence of some event somehow activates—perhaps automatically through some kind of perceptual "readiness"—certain elemental or lower level schemata that are sensitive to the detection of features or patterns of features in the perceived event. In turn, the lower level schemata activate—given the recognized features or patterns of features of the event—the most probable higher level schemata of which they are constituents. Then, the higher level schemata activate other lower level schemata not already activated, in an evaluation of the fit between the structure of the nested or hierarchically organized schemata and the perceived structure of the event. These higher level schemata might also activate still higher level schemata, which would then activate a wider network of lower level schemata as bottom-up and top-down activations are interwoven in the interpretation.

[12]As D'Andrade (1981, 1984) notes, this lack of explicitness may be bound up with how folk models are learned, communicated, shared and used (see Poole, 1985b, 1985c, 1985d, 1985f). The nexus between folk models and processes of enculturation, however, remains a largely unexplored domain.

works of concepts that constitute the schemata may variously exhibit strong and weak, complex and simple, dense and diffuse, and other variable qualities of connectivity or even gaps of articulation.

It is essential to recognize that these "loose linkages" of cultural schemata are significantly in accord with our field intuitions about how people engage, construe, and act upon the ordinary circumstances of everyday life, and involve—in most of their many manifestations—what Geertz (1985a) vividly describes as *common sense* systems of cultural "meaning." Geertz (1985a, p. 85) maintains that, "'Naturalness', 'practicalness', 'thinness', 'immethodicalness', and 'accessibleness' are the somewhat unstandard properties . . . [of] . . . common sense generally, as an everywhere-found cultural form." Indeed, these common sense understandings do not appear to place an emphasis upon the systematic, the coherent, and the tightly and smoothly articulated aspects of the cultural constitution of "meaning" that are usually the central features of anthropological portrayals of the structure of folk models. In contrast, common sense understandings—and the cultural schemata that underlie and represent them—often seem to tolerate considerable contradiction, inconsistency, ambiguity, hedging, simplification, idealization, shortcutting, "looseness" in the integrity of semantic connections, and other forms of messiness that emphasize their flexibility and capacity to accommodate myriad manifestations of the ideal, canonical, probable and normal, yet may pose problems for comprehending understandings of the atypical, improbable and unexpected that inevitably punctuate the ebb and flow of community life. The intrusive shock of Baariin's sudden murder of Kotiik is a case in point.

Common sense systems of meaning, therefore, are perhaps best understood in certain respects by recognizing that they are importantly structured through those complex kinds of analogical mappings that are characteristic of metaphor—mappings which both constitute what structure such *systems of meaning* do exhibit, and mark the inferential pathways of common sense reasoning in those more or less mundane and recurrent, but experientially rich situations that constitute most social life (Poole, 1985f). It may well be the case that analogical or metaphoric modes of reasoning enable the bridging inferences which render the atypical, the improbable and the unexpected understandable by variously linking them to the commonsensical. Thus, the metaphoric constructions so richly embedded in natural discourse may reveal densely packed traces of the concepts and imply the variable conceptual relations that together constitute the common sense cultural schemata being instantiated in those particular situations that are being interpreted. From such metaphoric allusions, common sense cultural schemata or folk models of the nexus of person, self and deviance must be analytically unraveled if most events or situations in any society are to be sensitively deciphered, and if Bimin-Kuskusmin understandings of the case of Kotiik and Baariin are to be explicated.

The total set of shared folk models that members of a collectivity have available for interpreting their "culturally constituted behavioral environment" (Hallowell, 1955) in a sense comprises their theory of the nature of reality, and the subset of schemata that are instantiated at a particular moment in time constitutes a cultural model of the event(s) or situation(s) encountered at that moment. Cultural schemata which focus on various crystallizations of the nexus of person, self and deviance are among the most complex and pervasive folk models in any society, for they are intricately—albeit often tacitly—implicated in some manner in almost every facet of social life. Indeed, conceptions of personhood are complexly and centrally embedded in fundamental matters of world view and ethos, having reference to the moral codes entailed by known human "forms of life," and are subtly bound up with most cognitive-affective modes of organizing or making sense of socio-cultural reality (Geertz, 1985b; Shotter, 1984; Shweder & Bourne, 1982,; Shweder & Miller, 1985).

By personhood, following Fortes (1973), Harris (1980), and Read (1955), this essay refers to those attributes, capacities and signs that mark a moral career and its jural entitlements in a particular society. An interest in personhood invokes a concern with the cultural forms and social forces that together publicly render the individual present in a culturally constituted "human nature" that is socially encompassed, and in some array of social positions that are the entitlements and the emblems of the achievement of particular kinds and degrees of personhood. Indeed, social personhood endows the culturally recognized individual with those powers or capacities upon which human agency depends, enables and constrains his proper actions, casts him as possessed of judgment and thus responsibility, and calls him to account in a legal-moral-political-social order. Although the capacities of personhood may be anchored to the powers and limitations of the human body and thus seen as "natural" attributes, they are at once judgmental, social and mystical capacities (see Harris, 1980; Poole, 1982b, 1985b, 1985d, 1985f); and persons are essentially social beings who develop in different ways and to differing degrees over the course of the social lifecycle. Thus, a person is fundamentally a social being with a certain moral status and is a legitimate bearer of rights and obligations. A person has a sense of self, a notion of the past and the future; he can hold values, perceive goals, recognize resources, acknowledge constraints, make choices, and thus adopt plans that are attributable to him as a being with the conscious, reflective capacity to frame culturally appropriate representations of phenomena and to have purposes, desires and aversions which require judgment. To be a person, or a moral agent, is to be sensitive to certain standards of the socio-moral order of the community and to suffer a sense of shame when their breach may be attributed to one's personal judgement and responsibility.

In turn, concepts of selfhood are also importantly culturally constituted (Hallowell, 1955); but the self is a concept that variously attends to nuances of an actor's awareness of himself, construction of his identity over time, reckoning of his locus and continuity in time, space and the social life-cycle, and interpretation of his personal, private, or subjective experience. The concept implicates the actor's recognition of himself as a feeling, thinking, experiencing, reflecting, communicating, interacting being who can be located in significant measure—as an "I" and a "me" (in James' sense)—in a "culturally constituted behavioral environment" (Hallowell, 1955). The concept invokes the capacity and the right to express first-person, present-tense, self-descriptions or "avowals" (in Ryle's sense). As Harris (1980, p. 3) notes, the self is "the locus of conscious experience, created processually by the exercise of second-order monitoring." Such monitoring may significantly respond to what others say and do in the construction of a "looking-glass self," but "the self *as such* is generated by reflexivity" (Harris, 1980, p. 3). Concepts of self often focus on complex matters of boundedness in time and space, continuity, discontinuity, coherence, cohesiveness and the like, whether or not the self is seen to be an inner state or to be embodied. Yet the self is bound up with the person and with socio-moral affect, cognition, motivation and behavior.

Notions of self and person are importantly predicated upon each other and thus may be conceptually linked in a number of ways (Fortes, 1973; Harris, 1980; Poole, 1982b, 1984a, 1984b, 1985b, 1985d, 1985f), and there are contexts in which particular constructions of self and person—each being constituted out of a more or less common cultural repertoire of concepts articulated in linked sets of schemata, but often deployed to rather different ends—tend almost to merge and in some ways to become synonymous. Thus, concepts of person and self both typically involve considerations of the primary loci of affective, cognitive, motivational and behavioral control (Lefcourt, 1982), although these loci of control tend to be somewhat differently constituted and distributed with respect to each concept in most contexts. The issue of control and its locus provides a critical focus and fulcrum for considering how notions of person and self come to figure prominently in discourse on the constitution and maintenance of a moral order; most constructions in this discourse recognize some significant balance (or imbalance) between self control and social control in the constitution and maintenance of both person and self. Yet the matter of control necessarily implicates ideas of deviance, which, in its sense of moral aberrance, is often seen to be erosive of the integrity of personhood and selfhood. To the extent that concepts of person and self are bound up—albeit somewhat differently—with ideas of moral order, integrity, principles, understandings, rules and the like, notions of deviance that have moral import mark the boundaries, the foundations, the ambiguities, and the vulnerabilities of personhood and selfhood; and deviant feelings, thoughts, motives and acts may be judged to be indices of moral lapse or deviant character, with implications for the constitution of person and self (D'Andrade, 1985b). It is in this complex, culturally constructed nexus of person, self, and deviance among Bimin-Kuskusmin that the significance of the case of Kotiik and Baariin must be unraveled.

The protagonists of the case, Kotiik and Baariin, are both adult and fully initiated men of the same patriclan and are expected to be publicly supportive of each other in most contexts and especially in contexts of inter-clan ceremonial exchange. The contexts of ceremonial exchange, which are bound up with myriad clan rites, give particular emphasis to male solidarity with the clan. Yet, during one episode of a formal exchange involving their common clan, Baariin strode to the center of the exchange ground amidst a large audience of men and shouted that his clan brother, the "little pig" (*kaing gerger*) known as Kotiik, had been weak and lazy and, therefore, the feast presented by the host clan would be meager. Startled by this unexpected and severe insult, the meek Kotiik uncharacteristically rose and forcefully denied the humiliating accusation of sloth, stammering an expression of "justifiable anger" (*kuur-dam ken*) which should have elicited a sense of "shame" (*fiitom*) in Baariin. But, perhaps encouraged by murmurs of surprise and apparent approval from the audience, Kotiik escalated the force of his rhetoric in moving beyond justifiable anger to the public challenge—seemingly unintended—of an expression of "controlled anger" (*ursaak*). Realizing that he may have provoked Baariin unnecessarily, Kotiik mumbled an apparent apology for his outburst and hurriedly retreated. In a rage, Baariin lept to the center of the exchange ground and responded in a highly insulting manner embedded in the style of "veiled speech" (*weeng niim-teywa*), but devoid of the tactful ambiguities of metaphor and delivered in a slow, low monotone.[13] Rapidly striding from the exchange ground into the forest, Baariin turned his back on Kotiik.[14] The formal exchange was brought to an abrupt halt, and the men of the two clans dispersed to spread the gossip of the encounter between Baariin and Kotiik. Late that very afternoon, as Kotiik shared a meal in his men's house, Baariin suddenly entered the hamlet, ran to the plaza of the men's house, and screamed for Kotiik to appear.[15] As Kotiik emerged into the plaza, Baariin struck him dead with violent blows of a war-club and then anointed his own body with Kotiik's blood before disappearing into the forest.[16] In stunned silence, members of the hamlet gathered around the bloody corpse. Then, an elderly man muttered, "Kotiik was a fool and brought death upon himself. He was a fool to provoke a 'man of perpetual anger.' Such men are like wounded boars in the forest. They will kill you if you turn toward them."

Why was the responsibility for this murder allocated to Kotiik? Among Bimin-Kuskusmin, Kotiik and Baariin represent, or are characterized by, two extreme and contrasting images of masculinity—the "man of timidity" (*kunum tiinaar*) and the "man of perpetual anger" (*kunum atuur*), respectively. In turn, these images are bound up with the culturally elaborated emotion "anger" (*guur*) and the less differentiated and more inchoate feeling "gentleness" (*bu-ruutnaam*).[17] The man of perpetual anger is believed to be dominated by a form of "thinking/feeling" (*agetuukhraanaak*) known as "perpetual anger" (*atuu-riin*), which is contrasted with "innate anger" (*guuraan*), "mindless anger" (*tiibi-saak guur*), "controlled anger" (*ursaak*), and "justifiable anger" (*kuur-daam ken*). The man of timidity, in turn, is said to be enveloped by another form of "thinking/feeling" (*diinuruutaak*) known as "gentle smoothness" (*tiinaariin terotero*), which is contrasted only with "twisted gentleness" (*buruutiin wer-*

[13]Both the lack of figurative disguise in and the low monotone of Baariin's speech are strongly indicative of a severe threat of impending violence. It is generally believed that no man would speak in this manner without aggressive intention.

[14]To turn one's back on a person being addressed explicitly in speech is considered to be a dire insult.

[15]To disrupt the afternoon commensal meal in a hamlet of one's own clan is more than a breach of etiquette and verges on sacrilege, for this meal—ideally taken in the men's house—symbolizes the common substance shared by clansmen which is the foundation of their solidarity and sense of moral community.

[16]To kill a clansman with a weapon of war and to come into deliberate contact with his blood represent the most heinous offenses against the moral order of the patriclan, and constitute proper grounds for performing the rare rite of "severing bonds of kinship" (*taakgom-karaak*), which symbolically dissolves the moral and jural bonds of clanship and casts a man adrift beyond the pale of clan nurturance, support, security and protection.

[17]Both emotions admit of kinds and degrees, but "gentleness" is less elaborated in both respects. See Footnote 7 on the phenomena of thinking/feeling cognitive-affective states and processes. It should be noted here, nevertheless, that the form of "thinking/feeling" (*agetuukhraanaak*) known as "perpetual anger" is relatively uncognized, with an emphasis on matters of feeling. In contrast, the form of "thinking/feeling" (*diinuruutaak*) known as "smooth gentleness" represents a greater symmetry of cognition and affect.

naam).[18] As a consequence of smooth gentleness, the man of timidity presents a decidedly unmasculine image, for he is thought to be soft, weak, meek, malleable, passive, timid, fearful, cowardly, complaining, and yet always most gentle and compliant – being apparently willing to accommodate others even at risk of much personal humiliation.[19] His gentleness is both "smooth" (*terotero*) and "taut" (*terotero*); for it rarely changes, is uniform in its public expression, is seemingly devoid of affect, and remains under firm "internal control" (*faatebeemiin*). Yet, this form of stoicism is associated with some image of the beleaguered woman, who grimaces and endures her fate at the hands of others.[20] As a result of some fundamental failure in the lessons of boyhood socialization and the ordeals of male initiation (Poole, 1982b), the man of timidity is flawed in both personhood and selfhood, and cannot hope for prominence in the economic-political-ritual realm of male prestige. Such men cannot contend and win respect, it is said, in the myriad trials of manhood that mark the adult careers of all Bimin-Kuskusmin men. Indeed, the meek become targets for a contempt which they can only endure in anguish and in a perpetual and deeply felt state of shame.[21] Thus, the man Kotiik was seen to have overstepped his own limitations and thus to have hastened his own death because, by his very nature, he could not manage an aggressive confrontation with any forceful man – much less a man like Baariin. Nevertheless, men of timidity are known on occasion to unleash some unexpected burst of anger, for they are subject to "permanent frustration" (*taak babuur*), as are men of perpetual anger (see Poole, 1984a).[22]

As a consequence of perpetual anger, however, the man of perpetual anger is said to be hard, tough, unyielding, forceful, tenacious, aggressive, brave, bold, inured to pain and generally stoic in most respects – all admired traits of masculinity. Yet, these masculine characteristics are highly exaggerated and markedly rigid, and are not tempered by compassion, reason, gentleness or internal control. Indeed, the man of perpetual anger is known to be highly sensitive to ridicule and other forms of real or imagined slight, diffusely and dangerously paranoic, devoid of empathy, quick to anger and long to hate – an unforgiving, suspicious, ferocious killer who must be feared and avoided.[23] There is much

[18]For a detailed discussion of Bimin-Kuskusmin kinds of anger and gentleness and their interconnections, see Poole (1984a, 1985b, 1985c, 1985f).

[19]Thus, in rising to his own defense in the face of an insult, Kotiik was seen to have acted "out of character" (*kaaranegaar*).

[20]Note, however, that this particular characterization draws on only certain facets of gender constructs concerning femininity, and contrasts with more forceful images of women (see Poole, 1981a, 1981b, 1985d).

[21]In contrast, the man of perpetual anger is believed not to experience shame.

[22]Indeed, both men of timidity and men of perpetual anger share certain flaws of personhood and selfhood resulting from critical imbalances of personal constitution, a distorted masculine identity, an impoverishment of supportive social relationships, and a state of permanent frustration that leads to a debilitating "anxiety" (*saakhiik*). In the case of the exaggerated masculinity of the man of perpetual anger, however, there is no internal control and no experience of shame, and anxiety often leads to a massive number of homicides ultimately ending in suicide. In the case of the diminished masculinity of the man of timidity, a rigid mechanism of internal control and an overwhelming and enduring sense of shame often lead through a thicket of dreams and fantasies of homicide directly to suicide (see Poole, 1985a).

[23]Baariin was reputed to have killed some 74 men in individual assaults. If living legend is somewhat tempered by an examination of genealogical data and other kinds of ethnohistorical materials, the number of homicides attributed to Baariin still does not fall below 45. Indeed, in 1971–1973 during the course of field research, Baariin almost certainly killed four men, including Kotiik.

ambivalence and anxiety about the image and the person of the man of perpetual anger. On the one hand, his renowned capacity for extraordinary violence can be a political resource to be exploited by his clan, and he may become a legendary warrior in his own time and a living exemplar of *certain* admired aspects of masculinity. Baariin was the subject of many songs and tales portraying his enormous courage and ferocity against quite formidable odds, and his truly startling yet much deserved reputation for almost unprovoked violence was acknowledged far beyond the pale of Bimin-Kuskusmin territory.[24] Men of his clan often basked vicariously in the exaggerated masculinity of his audacious exploits and sometimes voiced excessive bravado to strangers when he was near, but they were almost always unusually deferential in his presence.[25] Baariin himself took some pride in the power of intimidation that he wielded, and sometimes used this power to extract all manner of support from his cowering fellows.

On the other hand, the man of perpetual anger is also a threat and liability to his community, and a living reminder of the failure of the collective responsibility of his clansmen to ensure proper masculine socialization in both secular and ritual contexts.[26] The idea of "perpetual anger" itself is tightly bound to two cultural images—the "man of perpetual anger" and the "female witch" (*waneng tamam*)—that represent perhaps the most minimal and defective forms of personhood and selfhood within any semblance of the Bimin-Kuskusmin sociomoral order. Cast in these embodied forms, perpetual anger is a very considerable danger, for there is no sure means of predicting whether the "force" (*araartaan*) of anger will be directed within or beyond the community. Neither the man of perpetual anger nor the female witch can be brought under certain community control, and both are lacking in internal control and in shame (see Poole, 1981a, 1983). Thus, both are believed to attack close kith and kin without a sense of moral discrimination or a need of justifiable provocation. Consequently, it is said that they "crack the hearth" and "eat their own pigs" in reference to their wanton disregard of the dense moral bonds among close agnates. In these regards, the man of perpetual anger is believed to be "like a woman."[27]

[24]Indeed, Baariin took special delight in travelling unarmed across the frontier into the territory of enemy groups and in watching the panic that quickly followed his sudden appearance from the forest. Yet he was also a fighter of great skill and cunning, and he had thwarted many vengeful assaults on his person, often killing one or more of his fearful attackers. A number of "clinical" interviews with Baariin suggest that he was well aware of the advantages of his rather awesome image of unbridled ferocity.

[25]One astonishing feature of Baariin's reputation was that he had killed three men of his own clan prior to his encounter with Kotiik, for intra-clan homicide—especially in the form of a public assault with weapons of war—is almost unknown. Yet in other ways Baariin seemed deliberately to overturn fundamental moral understandings in a personal assertion of power. He had twice committed rape under circumstances of both incest and adultery without apparent fear of lethal retribution or pollution. He defecated in public areas, taunting witches to use his feces as a medium of attack. He insulted kith and kin with abandon, and honored obligations of sharing and reciprocity seemingly at whim. He flaunted the deliberate breach of taboos of many kinds on numerous public occasions. He had a particularly gruesome reputation as a cannibal (Poole, 1983).

[26]In fact, however, to the extent that a predisposition toward perpetual anger is a consequence of the mystical "ancestral destiny or fate" (*kwan werkhaak*), it remains unclear whether any mode of socialization can effectively overturn its force.

[27]Note that the reference here is to the woman only as a "female witch," and that there are many female images which are significantly different (see Poole, 1981a, 1981b, 1982b, 1984b, 1985d).

The lack of predictability and the raging anger of the man of perpetual anger are said to be manifested in several ways. Although he is unquestionably a fearsome warrior, he often fights alone, neither protecting his kinsmen nor avenging them. He takes pride in not acting in concert with others in warfare, but he may disrupt the social coordination of successful battle. In turn, his many acts of individual assault and homicide inevitably bring acts of retaliation in their wake, and these revenge killings are usually inflicted most heavily on his lineage and clan agnates.[28] His anger is known to disrupt the affairs of hamlet life in sudden, unexpected and dangerous ways, and he has no apparent tolerance for the moral suasion of community consensus in which he has not joined. Thus, he is often not asked to participate in the close community of a hamlet men's house, and he lives in isolation in the forest.[29] His marriages are generally difficult to arrange, for he has little promise of being a gentle husband or a worthy affine. Indeed, his temperament is such that his marriages are known to be conflict-ridden, fragile, and short-lived.[30] He may gain limited honor from his reputation for ferocity, but he is denied access to those economic, political, and ritual pathways that lead to ordinary forms of male prestige and has little more than momentary sway in the affairs of his lineage and clan. He is often barred from participation in the rites of male initiation, for his brutal disposition might damage the efficacy of the rituals for the novices (Poole, 1982b). Furthermore, his very status as a man of perpetual anger indicates that his own experience of initiation was ineffectual, and thus his presence in subsequent rites would be deemed inauspicious. He has only the most peripheral position in local networks of trade and exchange because he seems too preoccupied with paranoic violence to establish enduring social relationships of any kind. In childhood he gained a reputation as a quarrelsome loner. As an adult he has become an isolated, frustrated, depressed, anxiety-ridden killer who can live only at the edges of the socio-moral order, for he can experience neither internal control nor shame. Suffering from the incurable affliction of "sharp, uncontrollable anger twisted together" (*atuur fuugamiin*), he is expected to end his life in a lonely suicide—an act which will cause his name to be obliterated from genealogical memory, prevent his spirit from entering the ancestral underworld, and deny him ancestral status in his clan (Poole, 1985a).

In order to understand the complex image of the man of perpetual anger that had come to envelop Baariin, it is necessary to explore how certain key concepts of ethnopsychology among Bimin-Kuskusmin are crystallized in a particular configuration to represent this disfigured image of personhood and selfhood, and how the particular deviance of the man of perpetual anger is bound up in this critical disfigurement. At the most complex level of cultural conceptualization, the idea of "perpetual anger" is intricately articulated with Bimin-Kuskusmin notions of person and self—of the *finiik* and the *khaapkhabuurien* "spirits or life-forces." The *finiik*, strengthened by male substance, experience, ritual,

[28]The author recorded 31 deaths over a 12-year period in Baariin's clan that were attributable in some way to vengeance for homicides that he had committed.

[29]Baariin lived at some distance from the nearest hamlet, having been asked to move further into the forest on more than one occasion when attacks on him threatened nearby communities.

[30]Now widowed, Baariin had been twice married. After a succession of brutal beatings, his first wife departed in divorce. His second wife was killed in an ambush intended for him.

and knowledge, is a male procreative contribution to the formation of the mystical and bodily constitution of a fetus of either sex.[31] It emanates from an ancestral clan corpus of spirit substance, which it re-enters when it is transformed into an ancestral spirit at death. Thus, the *finiik* is the idiom of intergenerational continuity and of the social regeneration of lineage, clan, and ritual moiety. Ideally, it is located in the heart, which is the focal organ of the "male anatomy" in any person and the complex site of myriad processes of thinking/feeling (see Footnote 7). The heart, and the *finiik* embedded in it, are nourished by semen, bone marrow, bone, male foods, and the experiences and substances of male ritual, and thus the *finiik* is normally stronger and more active in men than in women. In many respects, the *finiik* represents some of the more social dimensions of personhood—the ordered, moral, proper, restrained aspects of the person that are ideally learned in ordained ways and settings which are associated with the very foundations of Bimin-Kuskusmin tradition. Hence, it is the *finiik* that absorbs the vital experiences of a decade of male initiation and other ritual performances, and that encompasses capacities of internal control and shame (Poole, 1982a, 1982b, 1982c, 1985a, 1985e). The *finiik* is the valued intellect, judgmental capacity, and Durkheimian *conscience* of the person, and it is strengthened by all ritual enhancement of masculinity or male parts of the anatomy. It is the substantial link that connects a person to a socio-moral order, and it is the idiom in terms of which rights and obligations are phrased. Its dominance over the wily *khaapkhabuurien* ensures the proper development of *la personne morale* in a manner that precludes the emergence of perpetual anger.[32]

The *finiik* contrasts with its antithesis—the *khaapkhabuurien*— which gains vigor from female substance, experience, ritual and knowledge and represents the more unruly, unmodulated, idiosyncratic character of women. Unlike the *finiik*, the *khaapkhabuurien* has no unambiguous means of ritual enhancement and no certain anatomical loci, although it does not normally occupy the heart and commonly clings in fragmented form to various aspects of the "female anatomy" in any person. Being of uncertain prenatal origin and *tabula rasa* at birth, the *khaapkhabuurien* simply takes an indiscriminate imprint of the full range of all biographical experiences that are more or less idiosyncratic. In proximity to menstrual blood and other polluting female substances and influ-

[31]During the course of prenatal development, the gender of the unborn is believed to change constantly due to various mystical influences in the environment and to deliberate ritual attempts to influence the matter. At the moment of birth, the final such influence is said to determine the gender of all children except the "male pseudo-hermaphrodite" (*yomnok-min*), in whom the final transformation occurs on the eve of adolescence.

[32]It is said that the *finiik* and *khaapkhabuurien* are engaged in a constant struggle for dominance, and that only the exercise of certain proper modes of affect, cognition, motivation and behavior—collectively known as "heart activity" (*kwan iboorop*)—under the influence of traditional, ancestral forces will strengthen the *finiik* sufficiently. A variety of taboos and ritual acts encompass such heart activity. Any debilitation of body or of thinking/feeling processes, however, can provoke the temporary dominance of the *khaapkhabuurien*, which then enters the heart and proceeds to influence the course of all heart activity. During dreams, illnesses and hallucinations, however, the strength of the *finiik* wanes, the *khaapkhabuurien* gains temporary dominance, and perpetual anger—if it is present—may emerge in heart activities, changing the apparent shape of moral character. Thus, divinations focused on suspected but latent perpetual anger—as in the case of an unusually aggressive, but quite immature child—often occur during sleep, sickness, or trance.

ences, it becomes most active and receptive to all manner of impressions. It is the source of unintended and uncontrollable "impulses" (*yaamyaam*) that intrude upon morally ordered "heart activities" (*kwan iboorop*), and of "nightmares" (*iraamrasiik*), which are believed to portray frightening, semi-human creatures and horrible monsters dwelling beyond the pale of the known moral order (Poole, 1983). Indeed, in dreams, illnesses or hallucinations, the *khaapkhabuurien* is said to flee the body, the *finiik*, and the moral community and to travel to strange, monstrous and amoral places near the edges of the world. At the other moments, the internal force of the wily *khaapkhabuurien* may "lure" (*bagaa'iin*) hunters in the deep forest into the dangerous realm of amoral beings—a realm from which none have returned. It is the *khaapkhabuurien* that subtly encompasses, protects and activates perpetual anger; and when perpetual anger becomes lodged in or "clings" (*ferabiinamin*) to the *khaapkhabuurien*, the latter migrates to and becomes embedded in the gall bladder. The gall bladder is a mysterious organ of somewhat uncertain procreative origin that is believed to invigorate the *khaapkhabuurien* with a form of highly irrational and erratic "thinking/feeling" (*kuurkuuranaak*), which enhances the strength of perpetual anger and causes it to "pulsate" (*fiitfiitamiin*).[33]

The rapid, strong pulsations of perpetual anger are said to "beat" (*tantaniin*) in a distinctive manner like that of the heart, causing the moral capacities associated with the *finiik* and manifested in heart activities to be weakened and somewhat dislodged. As a consequence, the *khaapkhabuurien* gradually comes to dominate the *finiik*, and perpetual anger becomes a dominant force in processes of thinking/feeling and modes of behavior. Although the phenomenon of perpetual anger is irrevocably caused by "ancestral fate or destiny" (*kwan werkhaak*) for largely unfathomable reasons, its inexorable development takes time;[34] for the imbalance of *khaapkhabuurien* and *finiik* must emerge and become stable, and the *khaapkhabuurien* must migrate to the gall bladder. When these critical developments have occurred, perpetual anger is dominant, and the capacity of internal control is eroded by a lack of proper "attachment" (*adetera'fefebaanam*) between the dominant *khaapkhabuurien* and the weakened *finiik*. This loose articulation between the *finiik* and the *khaapkhabuurien* is gradually strengthened as the "roots" (*kiimkiim*) of perpetual anger become entangled with "innate anger" (*guuraan*), which is an unalterable trait ordained by clan ancestors, set from the moment of conception, and only modestly and negatively modified in early infancy by post-natal trauma or exposure to contaminating female substances. The form of innate anger is attached to the *finiik*, which is now in a weakened state. Normally, because of its association with the *finiik*, the temperamental range of innate anger is believed not to exceed the proper limits of moral personhood except under circumstances when

[33]These pulsations are believed to diffuse aspects (fragments of refractions?) of the form of perpetual anger throughout the body, including the heart, where the *finiik* is ideally located.

[34]Some Bimin-Kuskusmin maintain that such consequences of ancestral fate or destiny as perpetual anger are perhaps provoked before conception by mortal indiscretions in the conduct of rites of couvade, sacrifices and mortuary rituals. Such comments often seem to implicate some ambiguous sense of ancestral anger, which is never explicated except in reference to the capacity of ancestors to "take revenge" (*tiikamiin*) on agnates.

it is modified by "justifiable anger" (*kuur-daam ken*). Under the present circumstances of being linked to perpetual anger, however, the condition of innate anger is such that it expands the intensity and scope of its hostility and can no longer be bound to any form of justifiable anger, which requires the capacities of internal control and shame that have been eroded by perpetual anger. In turn, and by virtue of the linkage between perpetual anger and its condition of "sharp, uncontrollable anger twisted together" (*atuur fuugamiin*), the form of "mindless anger" (*tiibisaak guur*)—a condition of the anxious, depressed, or deranged—also becomes implicated. Mindless anger is often associated with images of the male and female "tricksters" (*gabruurian* and *kamdaak waneng*), who inhabit the fringes of the moral order and are often dominated by their unruly and irrational *khaapkhabuurien*. Such mindless anger, which cannot be predicted in any usual manner, is believed to be a form of "thinking/feeling" (*kiinkiinmaakhraan*) in which "judgmental capacity" (*yegaar*) is severely lacking and unintended impulses akin to those associated with perpetual anger tend to prevail. These three forms of anger—that is, perpetual anger, innate anger and mindless anger—inevitably become entangled to constitute the permanent affliction of sharp, uncontrollable anger twisted together that marks the man of perpetual anger.

The condition of sharp, uncontrollable anger twisted together is dominated by the form of perpetual anger, which is said to exhibit "scars of misfortune" (*guur iruumaar*) and to be "hot" (*mamiin*), suggesting a lack of social encompassment and internal control and a contrast with the "hot" (*kaarkaar*) quality of "ritual anger" (*guur aiyem*).[35] Thus, perpetual anger and its linked forms—innate anger and mindless anger—contrast with both justifiable anger and "controlled anger" (*ursaak*). These last forms attend to the nuances of moral sensitivities and social negotiations, and they are founded on a properly asymmetrical balance between the *finiik* and the *khaapkhabuurien*. They reveal "scars of pride" (*guur anaariit*) and are "cold" (*giriir*), suggesting the essential capacity of internal control. Indeed, subtly tempered expressions of these forms of anger are considered to be indices of the moral fiber of an underlying personhood and selfhood. The powerful form of perpetual anger, nonetheless, is *not* bound up with moral sensitivity or social negotiation and is viewed as a unique kind of Bimin-Kuskusmin anger. Even the form of mindless anger, which shares with perpetual anger a dominance of unintended impulses and a lack of judgmental capacity, is believed to be under the control of the person as an agent, even if the capacity of agency is erratic on occasion. In contrast, perpetual anger is endowed with a special and more or less autonomous form of "perpetual anger agency" (*atuuriin kiipdaak*) that increasingly comes to dominate the person.[36]

---

[35]Note that the vernacular term for the generic sense of "anger" is *guur*, which also denotes a "scar." The sense of anger as a scar seems to suggest both a cause and a consequence of anger, and an emphasis on some indelible trace of an associated affliction, pain or wound. Indeed, anger is said to "cut" (*karaakiin*). The notion of "ritual anger" (*guur aiyem*) is a specially marked and context-bound genre that, in certain senses, may represent the ritual complement of ordinary justifiable anger.

[36]Thus the man of perpetual anger is not held to be responsible for his perpetual anger, which was caused by an ancestral fate or destiny determined before his conception and is governed by its own capacity for

With the sole exception of perpetual anger, all forms of anger are said to be present in every person as a "reservoir" (*ok kumun*), which is represented by the bodily liquids discovered in the abdominal cavity at death in mortuary divinatory "autopsies." The presence of this reservoir of anger is a more or less "natural" state, always shaped within the proper limits of moral personhood by the endowment of innate anger. There is no emphasis, however, on some hydraulic metaphor of anger somehow being in a kind of bodily container, under pressure and ready to erupt or burst forth. Anger is always present, but it tends to be quiescent until imbalances of substance, spirit, milieu, and so forth (coded in terms of *finiik* and *khaapkhabuurien*) cause it to be expressed in modes of thinking/feeling, motivation and behavior. But then it does not erupt, burst or explode into action. Instead, it seeps, flows, drips, oozes, drifts, spreads and settles in the manner of a viscous liquid. It gently and slowly overflows the reservoir; it begins gradually to expand. It submerges the veneer of gentleness that normally exists as a thin and delicate canopy covering the reservoir of anger.[37] It issues forth and spreads to become connected to various anatomical loci associated with *finiik* and *khaapkhabuurien*, which are bound up with modes of thinking/feeling, motivation and behavior. It cannot be readily blocked or suppressed.[38] But it can be brought under internal control, which then either deflects it harmlessly in an "oath" (*tuubii*) or directs it toward more or less intended and usually human "targets" (*khraimiin*).[39] When encompassed by the distinctive force of internal control, anger is intricately bound up with and tempered by the proper configuration of a dominant *finiik* and a subordinate *khaapkhabuurien*, and therefore is shaped by socially learned and shared moral understandings and by shame. Otherwise, anger is believed somehow to direct its own flow because it tends to be endowed with a mysterious agency of its own when a person is too "stoic" (*biriir saaninam*)—in regard to ordinary processes of thinking/feeling. But then the only form of anger having agency is perpetual anger. So this unfathomable form of agency is perpetual anger, and a person of this stoic and unstable character is a man of perpetual anger.[40]

In contrast to all other forms of anger, perpetual anger is not covered by the

---

agency. This "perpetual anger agency" (*atuuriin kiipdaak*) is believed ultimately to provoke suicide. Some Bimin-Kuskusmin claim that this perpetual anger agency is similar to a spirit and returns to a cavern in the ancestral underworld when a man of perpetual anger dies by suicide—a cavern from which it may again emerge in the form of another person's ancestral fate or destiny.

[37]In the case of the man of timidity, however, the canopy of gentleness is said to be thick and "matted together" (*duunduun*), encasing all processes of thinking/feeling.

[38]Indeed, it can only be slowed or diverted through the exercise of internal control.

[39]For all forms of anger except perpetual anger, the metaphor of an "arrow" (*on*) coursing toward a "target" is common in ordinary discourse. This metaphor often seems to imply some sense of "intention" (*agiirikhaar*), "purposeful direction" (*unaakuur*) and "will" (*faaran*), all of which implicate the dominance of the *finiik* and the capacity of internal control. Because perpetual anger is endowed with its own agency and is bound up with erratic *khaapkhabuurien*, however, it is not believed to be propelled in this manner, and the metaphor of an arrow does not properly apply.

[40]Note that it is considered to be a "natural" impossibility for a woman to be possessed of perpetual anger despite the putative dominance of the unruly *khaapkhabuurien* in women. Indeed, women are rarely the focus of ancestral fate or destiny of any kind beyond a few matters associated with capacities of fertility, childbirth and childrearing.

canopy of gentleness, which is believed to have been incompletely formed as a consequence of ancestral fate or destiny and to have been eroded during an increasingly irascible childhood. Thus perpetual anger is to be found "on the surface" (*utaan kerook*), remains "visible" (*kiin diim kemaanin*), and appears "on the skin" (*kaar aar-ker*).[41] It is always interwoven with thought, feeling, motivation and behavior—often in some startling and terrifying expression of seemingly wanton hostility. It does not behave in the manner of a viscous liquid, for it is said to be like the mysterious "death adder" (*mesanaariik*)—always present, gliding slowly, darting quickly, pausing nervously, hiding in the foliage, turning abruptly and unexpectedly and striking suddenly without warning or apparent reason. It is similar in form and force to the rage associated with a cornered, trapped or wounded animal—beyond the bounds of normal reason and restraint. Indeed, the man of perpetual anger is known to be extremely "short-tempered" (*atuur ket*) in a special sense—unpredictable, uncontrollable, easily provoked and highly dangerous.[42] He is often compared to the fearsome wounded boar attacking any passerby in the dark of the forest. His ever-present and overwhelming perpetual anger represents a threat to all on his path—kith and kin, stranger and enemy—and even to himself, for his corpse-strewn "path of life" (*daib kwan*) often leads to the "hanging tree" of suicide (Poole, 1985a). His raging perpetual anger is sometimes compared to a "clump of friable earth" (*boor biinaar*), for it cannot be firmly held together or controlled and readily crumbles into many "fragments" (*giitakhaa*) which may sweep beyond the "target," and inadvertently strike and injure anyone near him. Yet it is also embedded in the incurable affliction of sharp, uncontrollable anger twisted together—a condition and complication of perpetual anger which may sometimes be portrayed as a compact "lump of moist clay" (*taam ok-toor*), and which cannot be made "smooth" (*terotero*) or "calm" (*saankhaarinaak*) because it cannot be properly "disentangled" (*miirtomiin*), dominated by the powers of the *finiik*, brought under internal control, and articulated with shame.[43]

The complex, metaphoric notion of sharp, uncontrollable anger twisted together often suggests that perpetual anger follows a "crooked path" (*daib wernaam*) as it is highly erratic and out of control, and that this path is "blocked" (*duugamiin*) from being properly "straightened" (*teroterakhaaniin*) by any form of moral influence—presumably because of the weakened state of the *finiik*.[44] Thus perpetual anger is not usually susceptible to persuasion, either

[41]Note that shame (*fiitom*), which is believed to be lacking in the man of perpetual anger who does not possess a normal semblance of "moral character" (*kugaar kemataak*), is ordinarily "on the skin" and is firmly connected to the *finiik* through "skin roots" (*kaar kiimkiim*).

[42]Bimin-Kuskusmin descriptions of "short-tempered" in this unusual sense suggest an extreme and permanent state, which contrasts markedly with the much milder, relatively common and more context-bound, controllable and transient state of being "short-tempered" (*agetuun*). Both states are characterized, however, by somewhat similar *expressive* traits and rather different *underlying* causes and structures, and they are commonly linked through comparison by Bimin-Kuskusmin.

[43]Note that perpetual anger, innate anger, and mindless anger—that is, those forms of anger *not* bound up with socio-moral sensitivities, negotiations and adjustments—have become "entangled" (*werkhuukiin*) under these circumstances.

[44]Indeed, the metaphor of a lonely, twisted, dark, treacherous "path" is often used to describe the life passage of the man of perpetual anger. Note that a similar metaphor is used to describe the life course of the suicidal, which the man of perpetual anger is believed to be (Poole, 1985a).

through internal modes of thinking/feeling associated with the powers or capacities of the *finiik* or through the social force of "moral speech" (*kenraan weeng*). On the one hand, the man of perpetual anger is dominated by the idiosyncratic, unruly *khaapkhabuurien* and the mysterious perpetual anger agency in a manner that erodes and ultimately extinguishes morally sensitive modes of thinking/feeling and senses of shame which emanate from an intact and dominant *finiik*, and that precludes, therefore, the proper establishment of "moral character" (*kugaar kemataak*). He can neither identify nor evaluate the causes or the consequences of his ferocious acts as others do, and he cannot avoid the difficult course of the crooked path that has been set by his ancestral fate or destiny as the source of his perpetual anger. On the other hand, he is afflicted by the condition of permanent frustration which has been growing in force since early childhood and which now alienates him from the moral voice of his community—a voice which, due to his much diminished moral capacities, he can no longer "hear" (*tiinangkhamiin*). Indeed, he is now fundamentally "isolated" (*asiitiik*) in several senses, both from his fellows and from himself. It is commonly noted that a man of perpetual anger is "blinded by his rage" (*kiin miriirebokiin*) and looses all sense of "reason" (*magaam*).[45] He is said to have a diminished sense of responsibility for his acts—diminished by his weakened *finiik*, his strengthened *khaapkhabuurien*, and his afflictions of sharp, uncontrollable anger twisted together and permanent frustration. Indeed, the ultimate responsibility for "his" acts is commonly allocated to his mysterious, yet forceful perpetual anger agency which comes to pervade and to dominate his thought, feeling, motivation and behavior, and he is not held accountable in any ordinary manner for *its* actions. In the various dissociative forms of locution that encompass the matter, the man of perpetual anger is more the object than the subject of his anger in certain respects. He too is a victim—a victim of a powerful ancestral fate or destiny for which he is believed to bear no personal responsibility, yet which may lead to his ostracism and to violent death. His dangerous perpetual anger is not volitional—except perhaps in the limited sense of being an impulse of the erratic *khaapkhabuurien*—and is not under internal control, which is a distinctive capacity of the intact and dominant *finiik*.

The concept of "internal control" is inevitably bound up with the complex idea of the *finiik*, and thus is believed to be motivated by learned and shared moral understandings and to be manifested in stable and "well anchored" (*ken kuurkaakiin*) modes of thinking/feeling which are intricately embedded in the *finiik*. Such internal control is said to emanate from those socially ordained experiences that give shape and strength to the *finiik*, and to be projected outward in those presentations of self that are the mark of socio-moral sensitivity and the focus of social negotiation. Consequently, internal control is subtly connected to that form of "external control" (*tuukhaamiin*) which involves the insights and skills necessary to the constitution of influence or power in social negotiations. Internal control is most elaborately expressed in the social arenas

[45]Sometimes the sense of "blinded" (*kiin dagaariin*) involves a more unusual metaphor which suggests that the condition is permanent and is only exacerbated by circumstances. The idea of being "blind to a situation" (*kiin kuubabesiin*) is also used on occasion.

of the political-jural domain and articulated with ideas of masculinity, which are associated with a strong, dominant *finiik*. The man of perpetual anger, however, is said not to possess any semblance of internal control despite his exaggerated masculinity in other regards. His apparent stoicism is only a mask obscuring a weakened *finiik*, strengthened *khaapkhabuurien*, affliction of sharp, incontrollable anger twisted together, condition of permanent frustration, and powerful perpetual anger agency, which together make him irredeemably deviant and beyond the pale of the socio-moral order of the Bimin-Kuskusmin community. The constitution of his personhood is "weak" (*tuuk-menaam*), and therefore his culturally constituted self—wrought from the deviant, idiosyncratic experiences of the crooked path of his life—is fundamentally and irredeemably flawed. His *finiik* and *khaapkhabuurien* are in a precarious state of imbalance yielding homicidal and suicidal impulses, and they cannot properly represent or guide understanding, experience and action in a community. He is seen not to possess proper "moral character," which is predicated upon a proper balance between the *finiik* and *khaapkhabuurien*, and which enables and constrains the normal course of social interaction. These severe defects of person, self and character are believed to be most dramatically apparent in the inability of the man of perpetual anger to experience the significant force of shame.

It is commonly noted that although the amoral or immoral misbehaviors of the man of perpetual anger may result in justifiable anger on the part of his antagonists, this justifiable anger and the censure that it unleashes do *not* elicit normally expectable shame in the man of perpetual anger. The personhood of the man of perpetual anger is so essentially diminished in its proper moral attributes, capacities and signs that there is no apparent sensation or recognition of possible wrongdoing of any kind, and his rigid and aberrant sense of self is unresponsive to his image reflected from social others and is largely incapable of reflexivity in any ordinary manner. Indeed, the mere suggestion of *justifiable* anger and reprimand on the part of others may provoke instant rage and violent retribution on account of an implied insult, but perpetual anger is not dissipated by acts of retribution because there is no clear understanding of reciprocity in human affairs and no predictable abatement of this form of anger. The slightest form of provocation—often a seemingly benign, innocuous act—may result in an unpredictable, sudden and unending "flood" (*faago-tereem*) of perpetual anger, which is often manifested in homicidal violence. The powerful confluence of the weakened *finiik*, the strengthened *khaapkha-buurien*, the forceful perpetual anger agency, and the highly abnormal conditions of sharp, uncontrollable anger twisted together and permanent frustration implies that there can be neither meaningful internalization nor conscious acknowledgement of the moral understandings and social norms of the community. Thus, in the remarkable instance of the man of perpetual anger, there is no certain sense of shame that might deter any morally significant misbehavior or provide an instrument of social control. By remaining markedly unaffected and unencumbered by shame, the man of perpetual anger remains unencompassed by the socio-moral order of the community in a manner quite similar in some respects to that of the dreaded female witch, who is also sometimes said to be dominated by fearsome and uncontrollable perpetual anger (Poole, 1981a, 1983).[46]

Consequently, in their tragic and incurable states of moral deviance, both the man of perpetual anger and the female witch remain anomalous, dangerous and much feared "strangers within" (*igaar mutuuk*) the community.[47] Bereft of any normal, stable capacity for moral responsibility and accountability, they must be carefully and tactfully avoided whenever possible and *never* confronted with a forceful demand of any kind, for they are said to recognize only an impulsive and self-centered sense of their rights and to have no appreciation of obligations in sharing and in exchange. They cannot enter the myriad and subtle understandings that inform and guide the course of everyday social interactions, and they must dwell at the edges of the community where the force of their threat to social life is perhaps diminished or blunted. Their remarkable incapacity for shame—a delicate barometer and powerful sanction of moral sensitivity—is the most commonly cited cultural index of those fundamental flaws of the *finiik* and *khaapkhabuurien* that mark certain extreme forms of deviance among Bimin-Kuskusmin, and the concept of perpetual anger is the exemplar *par excellence* of the extremes of moral aberrance. Indeed, tales narrated to inculcate moral messages about the nature of masculinity and femininity, of shame and internal control, of the capacities of the *finiik* and *khaapkhabuurien* and of extraordinary deviance may often portray vivid images of the man of perpetual anger and the female witch, and may point to the many complexities and nuances of the phenomenon of perpetual anger (Poole, 1985d). Thus the idea and the image of the "man of perpetual anger" is a common point of cultural reference in discourse on matters of ethics and morality in the Bimin-Kuskusmin community.

In the aftermath of Kotiik's murder by Baariin, the scattered hamlets of the entire Bimin-Kuskusmin community were swept up in interpreting and judging the astonishing events of the day. Late into the evenings, fires burned brightly in the hearths and in front of men's houses, casting solemn shadows into the more lively circles of women gossiping in the hamlet plazas below. From Kotiik's hamlet came the keening wail of mourning amidst a torch-lit frenzy of activity as lineage agnates began the preparations for the funerary observances soon to follow. The highly inauspicious nature of Kotiik's death at the hand of a clansman required special sacrifices to appease clan ancestors and brought the full weight of many onerous taboos to bear on the members of his clan, but it was generally expected that Baariin would stand entirely and angrily aloof from all mortuary proceedings. Indeed, Baariin remained secluded in his house in the forest for several weeks, avoiding the hamlets when he wandered abroad and ventured forth to hunt and to garden alone in his usual manner.[48] Yet, there was

[46] Note that the *tamam* "witch" is the only woman believed to be capable of possessing perpetual anger (cf. Footnote 40), although the structure of related notions of agency, responsibility and accountability is different from the structure of such ideas in the case of the man of perpetual anger (cf. Footnote 49).

[47] The Bimin-Kuskusmin notion of "stranger" is invariably bound up with the idea of being beyond the pale of the moral order and somehow representing a threat to that order.

[48] He was reported, however, to roam near the boundaries of hamlets and gardens at night in the manner of a *tamam* witch, who also possesses perpetual anger.

virtually no discussion of taking vengeance against him for Kotiik's murder or of seeking some form of "death compensation" (*kawii*) from Baariin or his lineage.[49] In marked contrast, the lineage of Baariin made a formal request for "injury compensation" (*yaan*) from the lineage of the murdered Kotiik for the long periods of mourning, costly sacrifices, bothersome taboos and onerous stigmata that they must endure as a consequence of the unfortunate incident. This seemingly unusual request was immediately honored, for there was complete unanimity in the view that Kotiik was both responsible and accountable for the homicide—his own! He was understood to have committed an act closely akin to suicide in some respects. He had deliberately provoked a known man of perpetual anger whose flaws of moral personhood had been revealed in many divinations over decades, and whose reputation for wanton killing was awesome. With such diminished capacities of personhood and known deficiencies of self and moral character, Baariin had simply acted in the only manner possible, in accordance with the perpetual anger agency that had long controlled his thought, feeling, motivation and behavior. This mysterious force or agency had *acted*, almost autonomously in a certain sense, to commit the horror of intra-clan murder. The "provocation" (*biikbok*) of this act, however, had been the fault of the meek Kotiik, who should have known that Baariin was a man of perpetual anger and that such men are dominated by unreasoning capacities for anger and violence.

Beyond these matters of community interpretation, Baariin himself seemed to understand and to accept to some extent the label of man of perpetual anger.[50] Unquestionably, he perceived the considerable power that accrued to his canny wielding of this culturally constituted identity, and he used this resource to extract various kinds of limited support from others. Indeed, his best remembered *modus operandi* in a range of social situations was a barely veiled threat of violence. In some respects, he took much pride in his legendary status as a warrior and was a splendid raconteur of grisly tales of battle, but he deeply resented his reputation as a mindless, irresponsible killer. He was indeed "angry" about his constant exclusion from almost all male activities but fighting as a consequence of this reputation, and he had become bitterly and resentfully lonely. Yet, even by his own reckoning, Baariin did have a long history of being asocial or violent. Critical divinations in his middle childhood had offered consistent prognoses, it was said, of his becoming a man of perpetual anger. He recalled a lonely childhood of many fights and few friends. He had fared poorly in enduring the ordeals of initiation, although he had duly completed the ritual cycle. He had not been seen as a promising young man in many domains of social life, for his reputation as a fearsome killer was secure before the age of

[49]Even though intra-clan homicide creates numerous moral and jural complications, both vengeance and compensation are possible in this situation, but under other circumstances. Note that a *tamam* witch would be held responsible and accountable for an act of homicide and would be killed, with no possibility of offering "death compensation." The critical difference is bound up with the matter of *agency*, which is subject to varying cultural constructions in the cases of the man of perpetual anger and the *tamam* witch.

[50]These brief comments on how Baariin made sense of his own identity are based on some 12 hours of clinical interviews with Baariin, who was also given a set of projective tests (e.g. Rorschach, T.A.T., Machover's Draw-A-Person, and story completion protocols). Dream reports and life-history materials were also examined.

twenty and the termination of male initiation. These recounted patterns of life history, however, accord well with the stereotypic developmental patterns that are attributed to an incipient man of perpetual anger. Both Baariin and his local biographers almost certainly shaped aspects of his life history with respect to these developmental patterns.

Despite the analytic difficulties of cross-cultural psychiatric diagnosis (Hughes, 1985; Murphy, 1976; Westermeyer, 1985), detailed "clinical" examinations of interviews with Baariin and the results of his projective tests suggested that he was not only functional in many ways and often lucidly and insightfully self-reflective, but also that he had developed an increasingly coherent and pervasive, yet highly aberrant personal belief system that supported strongly paranoid tendencies, which were also apparent in life history accounts and in dream reports. These paranoid delusions seemed to serve him both as a sudden stimulus to kill and as a publicly articulated—albeit delusional—defense against accusations of wanton homicide, for he could always point to known instances of attempted revenge directed against him as the basis of a much overgeneralized justification for killing. Although Baariin drew adequately upon the cultural repertoire of appropriate concepts to represent himself intelligibly as a man of perpetual anger, his personal schemata concerning his identity articulated such concepts in an idiosyncratic manner that lent legitimacy to his acts and agency to himself and avoided the issue of the moral deviance of perpetual anger. Others often attributed the idiosyncracy of his personal models of his identity as a man of perpetual anger to the weakened *finiik* and unstable modes of thinking/feeling that culturally characterize his very condition. In their view, Baariin was dominated by those peculiar modes of aberrant thinking/feeling that mark the phenomenon of perpetual anger, which is both a special form of "possession" (*duubaraarminaam*) and a particular genre of "insanity" (*iruum-karaak*) because of the highly mysterious force of perpetual anger agency. In turn, Baariin constructed his personal schemata in an attempt to preserve some sense of public dignity in an assertion of masculine normalcy and pride, and simultaneously to illuminate his deeply felt "anxiety" (*sakhiik*) and "suspicion" (*naanuup*) by lending cultural shape to inchoate and subjective thoughts and feelings.

In the publicly negotiated interpretation and judgment of the case of Baariin and Kotiik, however, there was a general agreement that certain cultural concepts are central to making local sense of this extraordinary incident. These concepts invariably include the *finiik* and *khaapkhabuurien* spirit entities, the forces of "internal control" and "shame," the unusual and aberrant conditions of "sharp, uncontrollable anger twisted together" and "permanent frustration," the powerful and mysterious influence of "ancestral fate or destiny," and the focal phenomena of "perpetual anger" and the ambiguous "perpetual anger agency." The notions of *finiik*, *khaapkhabuurien*, "internal control," "shame," and "ancestral fate or destiny" are very complex, pervasive and general purpose cultural schemata which are widely incorporated into myriad cultural schemata developed for special purposes. One could understand almost nothing of ethnopsychology among Bimin-Kuskusmin without having knowledge of these concepts and being familiar with how they are "packaged" in instantiated schemata. In contrast, the concepts of "sharp, uncontrollable anger twisted together" and "permanent frustration" refer to a relatively limited range of deviant phenomena bound up with matters of thought, feeling, motivation and behavior. The ideas of "perpetual anger" and "perpetual anger agency," however, are only articulated with the images of the "man of perpetual anger" and the "female witch," albeit in different ways and with distinctive consequences. Within a range of possible semantic networks, each of these concepts implicates or entails an array of other concepts that may be articulated with one another in a variety of hierarchical modes of interlinkage. As the interpretive and judgmental effort proceeds and instantiates cultural schemata by "binding" their conceptual elements and relations to perceived features or patterns of the ethnographically complex case of Baariin and Kotiik, these conceptual elements and relations become subtly, intricately and often tacitly crystallized in particular configurations that constitute the instantiated cultural schemata.

These cultural schemata do not exist as abstractions, but are adapted to and embedded in the complex contingencies of the ebb and flow of social life which they shape, focus and interpret; and they are analytically extracted from figurative speech which inevitably has tacit or ambiguous reference to underlying corpora of cultural knowledge that are only implicated. The carefully wrought explication of the ethnopsychology of perpetual anger set forth in this essay draws upon the intertwined metaphors, metonyms, propositions and images that are revealed, entailed, implied, inferred or otherwise cast in the nuances of local discourse on the cultural meaning of this startling murder, its sequence of acts and its protagonists. Indeed, the analysis attempts to indicate the complete pattern of local explanations of the case while alluding to matters of inconsistency, ambiguity, contradiction, fluidity, strong or weak linkages, and other characteristics of the common sense systems of meaning that are brought to bear on the phenomenon of perpetual anger and its implications for understanding the nexus of person, self and deviance among the Bimin-Kuskusmin.

Whatever the other clinical realities that underlie the phenomenon may be, perpetual anger—the key concept in this case—exists largely in terms of certain concepts articulated in cultural schemata that are instantiated in social situations which are bounded, focused and otherwise rendered recognizable as contexts in the community of Bimin-Kuskusmin. These cultural framings of social experience are invoked to interpret, evaluate, rationalize, legitimate, highlight, disguise and otherwise shape aspects of perpetual anger in a manner that accommodates the perceived salient patterns of the particular case, which may then serve as an exemplar of perpetual anger in a particular and perhaps prototypical crystallization of the idea. In this instance, other incidents from Baariin's career as man of perpetual anger served as significant exemplars in the service of illuminating particular facets of the present instance of murder. Yet, different aspects of the relevant cultural knowledge are drawn upon for different purposes and at different times in the construction and instantiation of the schemata that provide the lenses for interpretation and judgment, and various aspects of such cultural knowledge are more or less, or differently accessible—being variously explicit, tacit, ambiguous or even opaque. Organized as a common sense system of meaning, the coherence of the ideas about perpetual anger is neither rigid nor complete, but rather is sufficiently flexible and "open" to accommodate various instantiations of the relevant cultural schemata in different but more or less related events or situations. The several cultural schemata that variously encode the repertoire of cultural knowledge brought to bear on the phenomenon of "perpetual anger" in this instance are drawn upon and deployed differently by Baariin and by the community at large in making sense of critical events from significantly different vantage points and with markedly different ideological, moral, and personal investments in these perspectives.

One the one hand, the case of Baariin and Kotiik may be seen to represent an extreme of moral aberrance in its special marking of certain defects and deficiencies of the person and of the self. On the other hand, the case provides an elaborate cultural reference point for subtly assessing the "normal" (as normalcy is constituted in the nexus of person and self) and for rendering ordinary experience intelligible, for it implicates and illuminates fundamental notions of personhood and selfhood in a socio-moral order and sets them in particular cultural relief by reference to an elaborate genre of deviance. Above all, however, the case and its analytic explication demonstrate the intricate web of cultural meanings that lend significance to socially embedded events, the ways in which cultural meanings are structured in the form of schemata, and how such schemata begin to illuminate the "hidden conceptual models" (Lazare, 1973) that are embedded in the cultural, psychological and social dimensions of human experience. It has been suggested that the schemata which variously articulate the cultural nexus of person, and deviance will require prominent analytic attention at the confluence of anthropological, legal and psychiatric interest in the human condition.

References

Benedict, R. F. (1934). Anthropology and the abnormal. *Journal of General Psychology, 10*, 59.

Black, D. (1976). *The behavior of law*. New York: Academic Press.

Brown, B. J. (1964). The "Ordinary Man" in provocation: Anglo-Saxon attitudes and unreasonable non-Englishmen. *International and Comparative Law Quarterly, 13*, 203.

Chalmers, D. (1975). Human rights and what is reasonably justifiable in a democratic society. *Melanesian Law Journal, 3*, 92.

D'Andrade, R. G. (1981). The cultural part of cognition. *Cognitive Science, 5*, 179.

D'Andrade, R. G. (1984). Cultural meaning systems. In R. A. Shweder & R. A. LeVine (Eds.), *Culture theory*. Cambridge: Cambridge University Press.

D'Andrade, R. G. (1985a). A folk model of the mind. In D. Holland & N. Quinn (Eds.), *Cultural models in language and thought*. Cambridge: Cambridge University Press.

D'Andrade, R. G. (1985b). Character terms and cultural models. In J. W. D. Dougherty (Ed.), *Directions in cognitive anthropology*. Urbana: University of Illinois Press.

Devereux, G. (1980). Normal and abnormal. In G. Devereux (Ed.), *Basic problems of ethnopsychiatry*. Chicago: University of Chicago Press.

Epstein, A. L. (1973). The reasonable man revisited: Some problems in the anthropology of law. *Law and Society Review, 7*, 643.

Fortes, M. (1973). On the concept of the person among the Tallensi. In G. Dieterlen (Ed.), *La notion de personne en Afrique noire*. Paris: Editions du Centre National de la Recherche Scientifique.

Geertz, C. (1985a). Common sense as a cultural system. In C. Geertz (Ed.), *Local knowledge*. New York: Basic Books.

Geertz, C. (1985b). "From the native's point of view": On the nature of anthropological understanding. In C. Geertz (Ed.), *Local knowledge*. New York: Basic Books.

Gluckman, M. (1955-1956). The reasonable man in Barotse law. *Journal of African Administration, 7*, 51, 127; *8*, 101, 151.

Gluckman, M. (1966). Reasonableness and responsibility in the law of segmentary societies. In H. Kuper & L. Kuper (Eds.), *African law*. Berkeley: University of California Press.

Gove, W. R. (1980). The labelling perspective: An overview [and] postscript. In W. R. Gove (Ed.), *The labelling of deviance* (2nd ed.). Beverly Hills: Sage Publications.

Hallowell, A. I. (1955). The self and its behavioral environment. In A. I. Hallowell (Ed.), *Culture and experience*. Philadelphia: University of Pennsylvania Press.

Harris, G. G. (1980). *Universal elements in concepts of the person: The Taita case*. Paper presented at the 79th Annual Meeting of the American Anthropological Association, Washington, D.C.

Holy, L., & Stuchlik, M. (1981). The structure of folk models. In L. Holy & M. Stuchlik (Eds.), *The structure of folk models*. London: Academic Press.

Holy, L. (1983). *Actions, norms and representations*. Cambridge: Cambridge University Press.

Hookey, J. F. (1969). The "Clapham Omnibus" in Papua New Guinea. In B. J. Brown (Ed.), *Fashion of law in New Guinea*. Sydney: Butterworths.

Johnson-Laird, P. N. (1983). *Mental models*. Cambridge: Harvard University Press.

Kitsuse, J. I. (1980). The "New conception of deviance" and its critics. In W. R. Gove (Ed.), *The labelling of deviance* (2nd ed.). Beverly Hills: Sage Publications.

Lazare, A. (1973). Hidden conceptual models in clinical psychiatry. *The New England Journal of Medicine, 288*, 345.

Lefcourt, H. M. (1982). *Locus of control* (2nd ed.). Hillsdale: Lawrence Erlbaum.

Maeder, T. (1985). *Crime and madness*. New York: Harper & Row.

McClelland, J. L., Rumelhart, D. E., & the PDP Research Group. (1985). *Parallel distributed processing* (2 vols.). Cambridge: M.I.T. Press.

Morris, N. (1982). *Madness and the criminal law*. Chicago: University of Chicago Press.

Moscovici, S. (1984). The phenomenon of social representations. In R. M. Farr & S. Moscovici (Eds.), *Social Representations*. Cambridge: Cambridge University Press, Paris: Editions de la Maison des Sciences de l'Homme.

Murphy, J. M. (1976). Psychiatric labeling in cross-cultural perspective. *Science, 191*, 1019.

O'Regan, R. S. (1972). Ordinary mena and provocation in Papua and New Guinea. *International and Comparative Law Quarterly, 21*, 551.

Poole, F. J. P. (1981a). *TAMAM*: Ideological and sociological configurations of "Witchcraft" among Bimin-Kuskusmin. *Social analysis, 8*, 58.

Poole, F. J. P. (1981b). Transforming "natural" woman: Female ritual leaders and gender ideology among Bimin-Kuskusmin. In S. B. Ortner & H. Whitehead (Eds.), *Sexual meanings*. Cambridge: Cambridge University Press.

Poole, F. J. P. (1982a). Cultural significance of "drunken comportment" in a non-drinking society: The Bimin-Kuskusmin of the West Sepik. In M. Marshall (Ed.), *Through a glass darkly*. Boroko: Papua New Guinea Institute of Applied Social and Economic Research.

Poole, F. J. P. (1982b). The ritual forging of identity: Aspects of person and self in Bimin-Kuskusmin male initiation. In G. H. Herdt (Ed.), *Rituals of manhood*. Berkeley: University of California Press.

Poole, F. J. P. (1982c). Couvade and clinic: Birth among the Bimin-Kuskusmin. In M. W. deVries, R. L. Berg, & M. Lipkin, Jr. (Eds.), *The use and abuse of medicine*. New York: Praeger Scientific.

Poole, F. J. P. (1983). Cannibals, tricksters, and witches: Anthropophagic images among Bimin-Kuskusmin. In P. Brown & D. Tuzin (Eds.), *The ethnography of cannibalism*. Washington, D.C.: Society for Psychological Anthropology.

Poole F. J. P. (1984a). *Frustration, sickness, and anger among Bimin-Kuskusmin*. Paper presented at the 13th Annual Meeting of the Association for Social Anthropology in Oceania, Molokai.

Poole, F. J. P. (1984b). Symbols of substance: Bimin-Kuskusmin models of procreation, death, and personhood. *Mankind, 14*, 191.

Poole, F. J. P. (1985a). Among the boughs of the hanging tree: Male suicide among the Bimin-Kuskusmin of Papua New Guinea. In F. X. Hezel, D. H. Rubinstein, & G. M. White (Eds), *Culture, youth, and suicide in the Pacific*. Honolulu: Pacific Islands Studies Program of the Center for Asian and Pacific Studies of the University of Hawaii at Manoa and Institute of Culture and Communication of the East-West Center.

Poole, F. J. P. (1985b). Coming into social being: Cultural images of infants in Bimin-Kuskusmin folk psychology. In G. M. White & J. T. Kirkpatrick (Eds.), *Person, self, and experience*. Berkeley: University of California Press.

Poole, F. J. P. (1985c). *Cultural images, social scripts, and personal displays of "anger" among the Bimin-*

Kuskusmin of Papua New Guinea. Paper presented at the 14th Annual Meeting of the Association for Social Anthropology in Oceania, Salem.

Poole, F. J. P. (1985d). Morality, personhood, tricksters, and youths: Some narrative images of ethics among Bimin-Kuskusmin. In L. L. Langness & T. E. Hays (Eds.), *Anthropology in the high valleys*. Novato: Chandler & Sharp.

Poole, F. J. P. (1985e). Ritual rank, the self, and ancestral power: Liturgy and substance in a Papua New Guinea society. In L. Lindstrom (Ed.), *Drugs in Western Pacific societies*. Lanham: University Press of American.

Poole, F. J. P. (1985f). *The surfaces and depths of Bimin-Kuskusmin experiences of "Anger": Toward a theory of culture and emotion in the constitution of self*. Paper presented at the 84th Annual Meeting of the American Anthropological Association, Washington, D.C.

Read, K. E. (1955). Morality and the concept of person among the Gahuku-Gama, Eastern Highlands, New Guinea. *Oceania, 25*, 233.

Romanucci-Ross, L. (1983). On madness, deviance, and culture. In L. Romanucci-Ross, D. E. Moerman, & L. R. Trancredi (Eds.), *The anthropology of medicine*. South Hadley: J. F. Bergin.

Scheff, T. J. (1984). *Being mentally ill* (2nd ed.) New York: Aldine.

Seidman, R. B. (1965). Mens rea and the reasonable African: A problem of society under radical social change. *Modern Law Review, 28*, 46.

Shotter, J. (1984). *Social accountability and selfhood*. Oxford: Basil Blackwell.

Shweder, R. A., & Bourne, E. J. (1982). Does the concept of the person vary cross-culturally? In A. J. Marsella & G. M. White (Eds.), *Cultural conceptions of mental health and therapy*. Dordrecht: D. Reidel.

Schweder, R. A., & Miller, J. G. (1985). The social construction of the person: How is it possible? In K. J. Gergen & K. E. Davis (Eds.), *The social construction of the person*. New York: Springer-Verlag.

Simons, R. C. (1985). Sorting the culture-bound syndromes. In R. C. Simons & C. C. Hughes (Eds.), *The culture-bound syndromes*. Dordrecht: D. Reidel.

Tancredi, L. R. (1983). Psychiatry and social control. In L. Romanucci-Ross, D. E. Moerman, & L. R. Tancredi (Eds.), *The anthropology of medicine*. South Hadley: J. F. Bergin.

Warren, C. A. B. (1982). *The court of last resort*. Chicago: The University of Chicago Press.

Westermeyer, J. (1985). Psychiatric diagnosis across cultural boundaries. *American Journal of Psychiatry, 142*, 798.

Yngvesson, B. (1978). The reasonable man and unreasonable gossip: On the flexibility of (legal) concepts and the elasticity of (legal) time. In P. H. Gulliver (Ed.), *Cross-examinations*. Leiden: E. J. Brill.

[11]

JOURNAL OF LAW AND SOCIETY
VOLUME 12, NUMBER 2, SUMMER 1985
0263–323X $3.00

Discovering 'Social Control'

MARILYN STRATHERN*

Law, states Black, is governmental social control. As he is forced to add, "By this definition, then, law is only one kind of social control". Later he proposes that "law varies inversely with other social control".[1]

It is an anthropological platitude that the institutions of 'law' do for societies with government what other forms of social control do elsewhere. Or conversely that the sense of social order enshrined in legal/governmental institutions is simply a more complex, rigid and systematic version of what people do everywhere to sustain an ordered life. A battery of further concepts — regulation, sanction, conflict resolution — registers the diminished governmental aspects of peacekeeping activities in systems where these draw instead on political or religious processes, or on other regulatory forces such as 'reciprocity'.

The platitude is served by the notion that societies do not just exhibit structure, they also sustain themselves as social orders. People make this order known through their formulation of norms (in Black's words, "social control is the normative aspect of social life"[2]). Indeed, anthropological discussion about the nature of normative and sanctioning behaviour turns readily from the issue of whether or not the X 'have law' to the more interesting one of how the X maintain social control. The permeability of the two themes shows in the quasi-legal metaphors which have penetrated descriptions of social regularity itself. There is more in this than simply the elucidation of rule-like formulations. Thus Geertz writing of culture as a whole, uses the notion of control by way of analogy; culture "is best seen not as complexes of concrete behavior patterns — customs, usages, traditions, habit clusters — . . . but as a set of control mechanisms — plans, recipes, rules, instructions. . . — for the governing of behavior". He

**Trinity College, Cambridge CBZ 1TQ, Great Britain.*

This is part of a paper originally prepared at the request of William Wormsley in conjunction with the Law and Order Project being conducted in the Enga Province of Papua New Guinea. Its companion, which continues the argument, will appear in his book, *Conflict and Control in the New Guinea Highlands*. Versions of the original were presented to Anthropology Departments at the Universities of Sydney, London (L.S.E.) and Hull, and I am grateful for the criticism they received. The present version benefits from and in some cases directly incorporates the detailed comments of John Comaroff, Peter Fitzpatrick, Lisette Josephides, Laurence Goldman and Alan Rumsey. I also appreciate the encouragement of Aletta Biersack, Paula Brown, Jane Collier, Donald Denoon, Rena Lederman, Harriet Whitehead and Anna Yeatman. I must thank two other sources: the Gender Research Group at the Australian National University, Canberra, in whose company the original was written, and Francis Snyder (reader for the Journal of Law and Society).

then adds a note about man's nature: "man is precisely the animal most desperately dependent upon such extragenetic, outside-the-skin control mechanisms, such cultural programs, for ordering his behavior".[3]

To follow Comaroff and Roberts' analysis of Tswana litigation, however, there seems no reason on the face of it why disputing as such should concern the imposition of order and exercise of control. The authors deliberately dislodge Tswana dispute processes from the simple implementation of norms.[4] When they refer to 'sociocultural order', they intend order in the sense of system or structure, in dialectical relation with practice, and not as a matter of normative control. On the contrary, they distinguish their analysis from two separate paradigms in anthropological approaches to social control, the 'rule-centered paradigm', and the 'processual paradigm' which postulates "the dynamics of order in the social process itself".[5]

Yet again, on the face of it, whereas Comaroff and Roberts avoid the elision of dispute processes with dispute settlement, for ethnographic material from Papua New Guinea Highlands which I wish to discuss here, a whole class of disputes emerge specifically in the context of their apparent 'settlement'. They are made public at the point at which parties come to talk about the issues between them and seek adjustments to their relations through compensation payments. These 'settlements' appear to reconcile differences, and thus to have a regulatory force. Like many others, I have in the past assumed that such procedures are part of what is meant by 'social control', and if I go over old ground in the anthropology of law, it is as much to understand previous assumptions of my own. It will be clear that I am dealing with only one strand of anthropological thinking on the subject, as I deal with only one interpretation of law to which such thinking is related.[6]

The interesting question is why the idea of the social control is so compelling. For anthropologists this comes, I think, not simply from their interests in elucidating normative order, or order as system and structure, but from an interest in the activity of making representations of social life.[7] As in the case of symbolism, parts of social life are seen to offer commentaries on other parts, much as the social scientist's job is to offer commentary. Social control-like mechanisms perhaps draw us for the reason that they appear to validate the act of describing behaviour as an endeavour separate from the behaviour itself. This hierarchism inheres in western social science. I would argue, then, that one impulse to discover social control in institutionalised form, and thus set apart as a realm of interaction which deals with, modifies and above all comments on other realms (such as conflict or the 'normal' state of affairs), lies in its hierarchical analogue to the activity of describing society as such.

It is worth considering this process of discovery. Social control is frequently discovered in other cultures as the specific counterpart to regulatory mechanisms in western society. In the form of 'law', such mechanisms are presented as having a transformative effect on social life and as adjudicating both on what the sources of conflict are and on social order itself. Thus even where we cannot find counterparts in other societies to our formal judicial structures we nevertheless like to discover regulatory mechanisms, in however a diffuse or generalised form.[8] They may be uncovered as 'customary law'. Yet it is not always appreciated, perhaps, the extent to which such discoveries simultaneously underwrite western law as a specialised and sophisticated mechanism whose primitive counterparts are uncoverable everywhere, and also underwrite the legitimacy of such law as dealing with fundamental human processes. Societies everywhere are seen to have similar regulatory problems. For certain styles of anthropology, this model is a double validation of the assumption that society is describable.

The model does not have to look at alien societies for cross-cultural support: in extra-legal areas of western life it uncovers regulating mechanisms which are held to replicate the controlling functions of law.[9] Non-legal instruments of social control thus support naturalist assumptions that law is only doing in a governmental context what elsewhere is contrived through a variety of other means but remains directed to the same ends of societal regulation and order. A particular view of human nature is involved here. In this view, what is regulated is disorderly behaviour; as Epstein observes, "universally men have differences and quarrels with their neighbours and fellows".[10] Quarrels, disputes, conflicts in stateless systems thus become the counterparts to litigation over offences, torts and so on in western society, or to informal western processes of conflict managment. Interpersonal violence and warfare may be classed as a 'breakdown' of order. Thus, there is a general assumption that customary dispute settlement procedures have an interest in the regulations of social life which is comparable to western 'law and order' interests.

At least for the Papua New Guinea case, however, it may pay us to regard dispute settlement in another light. For the very idea that law is a societal mechanism which meets *basic human needs* for regulation is part of the ideology of law. This ideology in turn draws on a model of social life and human behaviour which belongs very much to the industrial west, as well as to state systems of government. I am referring to that self-description of law which upholds the notion that order is the proper state of society, and society itself is imposed upon individuals who are by natural propensity asocial beings. Indeed 'society' is evinced in the regulation of individual behaviour. As expanded by anthropologists, this model classifies societies as everywhere attending to the same ends,[11] including the management of disruptive behaviour manifested at the level of individual conflict. The introduction of novel judicial institutions into third world countries is consequently regarded as a matter of 'law' supplanting indigenous dispute-settlement procedure, on analogy with the new social order supplanting the old. Yet for cultures, as in the Highlands of Papua New Guinea, who do not define 'society' as the regulation of 'individual behaviour', assumptions about social order and control may underestimate the direction of indigenous interests. They may also lead to misunderstandings about the impact of introduced judicial procedures and the nature of local dispute seettlement processes alike.

THE IMPOSITION OF LAW

A naturalist interpretation of western law, that it serves universal human needs for regulation, hardly needs expounding. The interpretation has been thoroughly aired in the context of the imposition of law.

Among the questions posed by Burman and Harrell-Bond's book of this name is the extent to which *all* law is imposed law.[12] Kidder criticises the assumption that if people were left to their own devices then they would not impose on one another.[13] He himself suggests that law should be treated as an arena for the promotion of interests; the issue then becomes levels of interest. Interests by their nature lead people to impose on one another, and one could not describe social life without 'impositions' of this sort. Yet this leaves us with a further problem of description. Even if they are about the promotion of interests why should some arenas, and not others, be conceptualised as to do with the regulation of behaviour?

Kidder is sceptical about defining law "as a manipulable device for producing social control".[14] However, a number of the contributors to this volume take as axiomatic the propostion that law itself is a behaviour which 'controls' other behaviour. Thus Aubert, distinguishing between norms (means) and values (ends), states:

> By norm I refer to a rule of behavior. The tendency in traditional law is to demarcate the borderline between acceptable and non-acceptable behavior . . . The law deals with marginal behaviour; it sets the minimum standards of conduct.[15]

The whole vocabulary of norms, regulations, standards speaks to the postulate that one type of behaviour has to be controlled by another type. Certain institutions, such as the judicial institutions of governments, specifically present themselves as specialised instruments of control. They might promote administrative or class interests, yet are regarded as essentially in competition with other means of behaviour control.[16]

The contributors not only draw attention to the question of 'imposed' law, but to basic behavioural assumptions which underlie the notion of imposition. It is pointed out that law is regarded either as imposed in the sense of dominating other interests, or else as a mechanism of self-regulation.[17] These dichotomised views, I would add, share a common conception of human behaviour. Whether, as the editors observe, "man is a social animal, most fully realizing his potential in a society ordered for the common good and in which there is a general consensus on the laws" or is "an atomized individual pursuing his own selfish goals, on whom any social control is an imposition", the human being in each instance ('man') is analytically separable from the social order.[18] Thus the editors are careful to say apropos the first instance that the consensual tradition constitutes true freedom for the individual: "laws preventing individual action that interferes with social cohesion are not an imposition on people's freedom, but an aid to it".

One source of these ambiguities must rest in the attempt to delineate non-European social formations through the concepts of the European Enlightenment: "how men can order their social relations and still remain 'free'".[19] Aubert points to the roots of this question in the twin developments of eighteenth century natural law, through the science of economics and the less successful sociology of legislation. Both Adam Smith's market place and Jeremy Bentham's utilities solve the dilemma of regulation versus freedom through the notion of self-interest. Self-regulation becomes a social phenomenon, since if individual behaviour is regulated, then society is regulated. Individuals bear within themselves, their conduct, the model of the regulated society of which they are part.

In this constitutional paradigm the individual becomes the site of social interest, the selector (market place) and regulator (legislation) who will shape society at large. Enlightened self-interest means that the individual does not compromise his freedom in pursuing social goals. But this apparent resolution of the legal paradox, between the imposition/enforcement of law and law as depending on the will of the people, works (Aubert argues) for the market place better than it works for legislation. The market place offers a common measure of values where the legal system does not. One could add furthermore that the market place is represented as regulating needs and desires it also creates; whereas the legal system is held to respond more directly to the demands for regulation itself — and thus plays itself out against what needs to be regulated, viz. human behaviour. This requires that the origins of human behaviour lie outside it.[20] 'Law' in this interpretation does not set itself up as only creating needs it then fulfills (as one might regard the market place) but also responding to a need to regulate behaviour which arises from other conditions. It implements a theory of 'behaviour', then, which requires that persons emerge as social agents when they are able to be in control (of themselves, property, others).

On this premise, westerners have no problems in visualising continuity between criminal and civil law. Individual and state in an adversary confrontation, the one seeking to 'control' the other, is imaginably analogous to two individuals each controlling the influence the other has on his or her person. This extraordinary if common analogy leads Hamnett to question the ease with which legal anthropologists focus on control. He would oppose the dissolution of law into the general category of social control.[21] Control recalls criminal law and neglects the operations of civil law. Hamnett wishes to argue that customary law provides 'normative' without necessarily 'controlling' mechanisms. Actors make normatively clothed abstractions from practice; the abstractions are both descriptions of practice and are invested with 'binding authority'; one may understand these as facilitations rather than regulations. His model is thus of a civil order.

Yet Hamnett reintroduces the assumption that order in the sense (1) of structure, regularity, the ground rules for expectations, the definitive contextualisation of actions, implies order in the sense (2) of normative non-contradictory, non-conflictual, non-violent regulation. The whole purpose of the 'political' debate within the anthropology of law, including the development of the processual paradigm, was of course to separate conflict in the sense (1) of opposed interests not open to reconciliation from conflict in the sense (2) of a breakdown of social order. Conflict in the first sense could well be part of order in the first sense. An antithesis between conflict and order (sense 2) only emerges when order is defined as peaceable regulation, and thus defined as the opposite of conflict. Conflict and order then become antonyms, and belong to ideologies which promote a transformational view of the relationship between 'society' so conceived and individuals/events/acts. This ideology equates the regulatory ends of both criminal and civil law, in the interests of a social order seen at rest.

The premise of those western models which inform much social science thinking on the matter is (a) that individuals reflect society, either as its subject of domination, or else in the sense of regulating themselves as society is also regulated, so that they internalise its norms, and (b) that behaviour has to be regulated — people have to be made or have to make themselves behave. What is taken for granted is the normatively 'civil' or peaceable dimension of such regulation: the second proposition (b) can be re-written, on this model, as [unbridled self-interested/violent] behaviour has to be [peacably] regulated. Regulation, then, implies modification of interaction *of a particular kind.* These processes may be discerned in other societies. Thus Abel describes tribal systems in terms of the extent to which conflict or dispute may be frequent, polycentric, may preserve relationships, urge 'behavioural reform' and so on. He gives a fine description of the vagueness and inconsistency which widespread consensus allows in 'judgements'. But in the end his subject matter is social control:

> Social control operates through special deterrence — convincing each wrongdoer not to repeat his error — rather than through general deterrence, making an example of one wrongdoer in order to influence the behavior of others.[22]

It is possible to move from talking about 'control' to talking about 'influence' only if one has a theory of human interaction which sees a certain type of 'regulation' (regulation in the interests of social order) as the outcome in either case.

I have argued elsewhere that while we may use problems of our own to explore those of other peoples, it often turns out a totemic illusion to 'discover' those problems within the symbolic and ideational systems of those we study. Perhaps we are doing just this when we juxtapose the formal law of our society against the informal legal procedures of other societies, and thus discover a realm of social control which apparently operates according to principles and ideas not dissimilar to extra-judicial processes in our own. What is discovered is 'more' or 'less' attention (cf. Black) to formal judicial procedure. Yet western law can be interpreted as a microcosm of society only because in the end its regulative functions bear analogy with all 'social' activity. Whatever distinctions exist between formal judical institutions and their informal social control counterparts, as common regulative mechanisms these together operate to differentiate social from non-social behaviour.

It is integral to this interpretation of law that it at once attempts to recapitulate a whole order and remains a partial description of it. 'Law' as a microcosm of society forever has to work against asocial forces. Moore begins her book:

> A conventional self-image of law in the American legal profession is that the law constitutes the intentionally constructed framework of social order. Yet everyone in the profession knows that the practice of lawyers is by and large an exercise in the manipulation of 'the system'.[23]

Given a self-description of contemporary legal process as dealing with an ordering and organisation of rules in the interests of social order as such (order as both regularity and regulation), it is not surprising that the historical origins of law (a source other than itself in its present form) should be seen to come from a different arena, custom. Custom is held to promote regulation, but in a primitive manner:

> In capitalist countries the dichotomy between 'law' and the residual category, 'rules that are not law', is encapsulated in the notion of 'government' as opposed to 'private' regulation. The preservation of the division between the state-regulated sector and the private sector is an ideological point of honour.[24]

Whence the ideology?

Fitzpatrick identifies this ideology in the constitution of the state. The notion of state law as a unifying, universalising institution necessarily precipitates a plurality of social forms; "state law stands in opposition to and in asserted domination over social forms that support it".[25] That is, law creates its own boundaries, the area to which it is applied and from which it stands apart, and even those areas to which it is not applicable. It "sets and maintains an autonomy for opposing social forms".[26] Thus the concept of coercion depends equally on the concept of consent (coercion is consent overridden). At the risk of oversimplifying Fitzpatrick's argument, I suggest that such dialectical constructions result from the effort of self-description, which is itself a cultural activity of a particular kind. We belong to a 'society' which describes itself as a 'society' over and against other entities, nature, the individual etc. The relation is a transformative one:

> In terms of mentalitites and the supportive complicities of scholarship, law becomes associated with what is effective, that which acts and controls, rather than that which is acted on and controlled. It dominates rather than reflects nature.[27]

Its origins are regarded as lying in the partial move towards such domination which also constitute 'custom' and 'private regulation'. The area of custom may thus be seen as either a primitive domination of nature, analogous to modern law, or as itself closer to nature, to be encapsulated by or set against modern law. A plurality of social forms is integral to the bourgeois world of which formal law is a part. Fitzpatrick raises the issue of whether the genesis of this plurality should be sought in state or class formation. For my purposes the source is irrelevant. My interest in the manner in which such ideas have formed the screen through which western European anthropology has discovered social control, of a more or less formal kind, in other societies. The notion of extra-judicial dispute settlement, of non-governmental self-regulation, is of course part of the screen.

I turn to interpretations of customary dispute settlement procedures in Papua New Guinea. A caveat is necessary. At issue is the extent to which certain western models of society also become the basis upon which western observers discover legal mechanisms in other systems than their own. This means that I am not in any sense comparing social organisation in Papua New Guinea with that of a specific western country. To take on board a proper comparison of legal systems, for instance, would lead into an analysis of judicial practice, informal settlements, and so on. It has also been necessary to subordinate the ethnographic account to the ends of my argument. Material dating originally from the 1960s and early 1970s is drawn mainly from one central Highlands society, Hagen. Descriptions of the state of affairs at specific historical junctures are already published, and I deal only with certain generalisations drawn from these.[28] Finally, attention is paid to the area of formal dispute settlement in which men alone are prominent, although the character of their transactions here cannot be fully understood without appreciation of the adjustment of relations among kin of both sexes and in the domain of domestic production where women are as significant as men. This is a contrast I mention but cannot develop here.

PAPUA NEW GUINEAN DISPUTE SETTLEMENT

Dispute settlement procedures comprise a special type of social activity in Papua New Guinea; but they do not mark themselves off as regulating or overriding behaviour considered in some sense anti-social or non-social in nature. This observation is indirectly supported by the strong tradition in anthropological analyses of the area which points to continuities between such procedures and other features of social life. Approaches which concentrate on interests reveal this well. Nevertheless, it will be seen that for Hagen society I distinguish my arument from that truism noted by Fitzpatrick which takes "the legal" as "embedded indistinguishably in the totality of social relations".[29] There are very particular characteristics of the sphere in which Hagen 'dispute settlement' emerges as a social form.

Epstein remarks generally for Papua New Guinea on the characteristic reliance on the principle of self-help.[30] Lawrence uses the term self-regulation.[31] A person seeks his own redress, whether for himself or on behalf of a group with whom he is identified.[32] Self-help is perhaps more accurately rendered self-interest, since what is generally at stake is the acknowledgement of an injury sustained to interests. Others come to a person's aid insofar as interests are seen to be shared. The value of these interests can be commuted into wealth or compensation items under certain conditions, as happens in many Highlands societies.

By comparison with approaches which take some kind of 'trouble' as their focus,[33] conflict in Papua New Guinea situations may be interpreted much more neutrally. Epstein himself offers an open formula: "I shall treat as a dispute any kind of behaviour that points to contention based on opposing claims and involves the taking of sides".[34] Interference in the alleged 'rights' of one party (a 'disagreement' or 'quarrel' arising) turns into a 'dispute' by being brought into the public arena. Koch uses almost identical language. "I view a conflict or dispute as a confrontaion arising from at least partially incompatible interests of opposing parties.'[35] The incompatibility of interests, and people's mobilisation in relation to them, leads the analysis back into politics.

Fitzpatrick takes anthropologists to task, however, for tending to subordinate dispute settlement to political issues, and for failing to address the concept of legality — the constitution of the rights and powers of persons which derive from relations of production. By legality he means "individual right and the recognition or constituting of the legal subject".[36] This gives him a strong purchase in discriminating between situations where principles of legality do and do not apply. Thus, apropos Papua New Guinea, he writes:

> aspects of legality . . . can be discerned in absences of their application to some people. If legality were based in production, we could expect that because of women's subordinate place in production . . . legality would have an attenuated application to them. This was indeed so.[37]

He argues that (among men) freedom and equality in formal terms are firmly embedded in production; it is exchange that serves "to create relations of subordination and inequality".[38] But we need to know whose evaluation of 'equality' this is. As far as Hagen is concerned, there is a whole rhetoric of egalitarianism which belongs to the exchange sphere. I here take exchange as constituting political process in its widest sense. In the context of public, political transactions, men assess themselves in terms of *both* equality *and* inequality.

The demarcation of persons in respect of legality may discriminate between social categories to perpetuate fundamental diferences in people's access to remedies. But differences constituted on these grounds cannot be the same as those constituted through *competing* claims.[39] The interests which divide Papua New Guinea men often include those of competitive self-advancement. Insofar as 'equal' persons and groups are in competition with one another, in the creation of inequalities, they are divided only by the success with which they can pursue their goals in the face of competitors. When the issue is presented as restoring balance, assertions of equality between disputants acquire the character of vociferous claims. Pursuit of redress thus feeds into adjustments of agonistic relations. Indeed 'settlements' as public event often only work where there is a presumption of bargaining parity.[40] As Reay emphasises, it is within the framework of egalitarianism that contestants in fact pitch their strengths against one another.[41] This is the sense in which dispute settlement is seen to be part of ongoing political processes.

Dispute settlements occur, as Fitzpartick notes, precisely in those spheres also characterised by ceremonial exchange. This is the sphere in which persons perceive they have certain interests in maintaining relations but, not being materially interdependent, are not bound to do so. Dogmas of reciprocity help sustain these relations, and maintain the fiction of potential equality between exchanging partners. Ideas such as reciprocity and equality, then, are ones through which the actors think about aspects of public life. But the principles of collective life to which Hagen men at least give voice turn out to be very partial depictions of 'society' as such. Here I wish to advance a specific argument for Hagen. Their representations demarcate a public arena of social action, involving men in politics of various kinds. Assumptions are made about the way people will behave, especially as far as the issues of motivation and intention are concerned. These representations also set up an evaluation of other areas of social life and may see their ends as to some extent subordinated to the demands for collective interaction. But this political arena is not I think held to replicate all social interaction. The conduct which 'regulates' relations between political competitors is not a microcosm of societal regulation at large. By the same token, what goes on in dispute-settlement arenas cannot be taken as crystallisations of general sanctioning behaviour. Hagen courts, traditional or otherwise, were not a focus for the implementation of general regulatory principles. In short, Hagen dispute-settlement does not stand to Hagen social regulation as legal and judicial institutions in state societies such as our own stand to social control. Settlements are not informed by an overriding concern to discriminate 'social' from 'non-social' human behaviour, and thus do not see all social behaviour as conspiring towards a common end (order, regulation).

This throws some light on the comments above. For although the conflict-of-interest model is one we have known since Evans-Pritchard's analysis of the Nuer feud, there seems to be a self-adjusting mechanism which steers even this model towards ultimate formulations of 'social order'. In the Papua New Guinea case, this shows in the awkwardness of analyses dealing with the close relation between conflict and violence. Anthropological accounts of dispute settlement have been successful in their delineation of a whole range of social interests bar those represented in violence itself. This comes from, I think, mistaking the relationship between violent and non-violent action. Because we take people's interests as directed towards gaining returns, we tend to assume that in the long run such interests are promoted and rewards enjoyed in a peaceable fashion. Violence is interpreted as a means to an end. We thus also assume that people have an interest in non-violent action as such, including the regulation of violent actions. One of the problems, as the next section suggests, may be the way in which the one substitutes for the other.

Let me press the point through Koch's description of Jalémó in West Iran.[42] Koch suggests that almost any Jalé conflict can be settled by restitution or indemnification, or equally that almost any conflict can escalate into war. His analysis is directed towards the extent to which peaceable settlement is possible. Conflicts can be 'managed' peacefully under certain conditions; people try to prevent violent reprisals, however, not because violence as such is abhorred, but because they may see particular benefits in turning the event other ways. Yet in his final analysis violence is explained away through an assumption, that feelings of hostility and desire for revenge will prevail unless other factors intervene; there is no real account of the values of violent reprisal as such. If "peaceful relations within a community" really are so "precarious" then it is questionable the extent to which 'peacefulness' is an appropriate description for the general state of affairs.[43] The language of "brakes" and "constraints" will not do. And to assert that "All warfare . . . follows from an absence or breakdown of peaceful means to settle the dispute" is not only a generalisation that goes against his own data, but describes Jalé conflict management in terms of political aims quite alien to their world.[44]

Jalé are thus credited with certain interests that lead to conflict in the first place, and with certain other interests that violent conflict endangers, but the analysis stops short of attention to special interests which violent behaviour itself might embody. Koch is squeezing what he more usefully calls 'conflict management' into the frame of reparation and regulation. Yet if conflict arises when an opposition of interests becomes the focus of public action, then these can be channelled, as Young indicates, without being 'reconciled'.[45] Where relationships are defined by an opposition of interest, it follows that they cannot be 'broken' when they are mobilised along these lines. Black took social control as evinced in 'problems' which achieve certain 'solutions' in respect of several different 'standards' — prohibition, obligation, normality and harmony.[46] Koch's analysis of Jalémó is set in a theoretical frame which regards violence itself as a 'problem'. He asks what measures would regulate it. This problem however really turns out to be ours: his interest in the fact that Jalé have "very few and very ineffective methods . . . to transform a dyadic confrontation into a triadic relationship which could secure a settlement by the intervention of the third party" is related to the needs of the modern world to avoid war in the interests of "a higher political unity of mankind" as a common goal.[47] In spite of Chowning's comment that small scale communities do not need to conceptualise their relations as harmonious,[48] writers on Papua New Guinea affairs continue, in the words of one, to use the terminology of law and order, that "disputes are ruptured social relationships", and what must be found is "the wherewithal for repairing these relationships".[49]

The model that a dispute is a kind of disruption and that procedures are taken to repair the disrupted relationships rests on the further concept that social order is a system at rest, an arrangement of relationships describable apart from the behaviour and interaction of persons — 'behaviour' either acts out such relationships or disrupts them. The problem with this analytical model is that it pre-judges the nature of violent confrontations, as they occur in the Papua New Guinea Highlands. If we do not pre-judge the nature of 'violent' behavior, than we need not pre-judge the nature of 'peaceable' behaviour either. Metaphors of order are misleading in linking the relationship of violent and non-violent behaviour to issues of control and regulation.

The argument is not simply that we have underestimated the political dimensions of dispute settlement, that some cultures are more litigious than others, or that we need a conflict theory of society. There is more to the Highlands material than that. Men place value on themselves and on what they do through the construction of mediating items (wealth objects), and it is to the character of these wealth exchanges that we should look. It has been received anthropological wisdom that after formal pacification, the ceremonial exchange of wealth items between clan groups became a substitute for competition and hostility through fighting. However, this political interpretation of wealth exchange has been largely insulated in anthropological accounts from the role of compensation and exchange in the local settlement of disputes. The possibility of converting injury or loss into wealth items acceptable as compensation draws on traditonal procedures for the adjustment of relations, and provides the basis for settlement through unofficial courts and through the official Village Courts. Yet wealth exchanges (compensation) cannot simply be put into the slot of non-violent solutions which restore relationships and mend torn social fabric.

Comaroff and Roberts' argument is suggestive in this regard. The sociocultural order which the authors analyse for the Tswana comprise what they call a constitutive order, that is, a set of value oppositions and structural elements, and the lived-in universe, a "shifting, enigmatic, and managerial world in which persons repeatedly negotiate their relations in terms of a set of constant referents encoded in categorical labels".[50] Although the character of the lived-in world is shaped by the constitutive order, Twsana conceive of their society as simultaneously norm-governed and manipulable. 'Process' cannot simply be set against 'norm', as the old debates had it. One might argue an analogous point for certain New Guinea Highlands societies, especially those such as Hagen which are characterised by large scale organised warfare and ceremonial exchange. 'Disputes' can not be simply set against their 'resolution'. It is not just that

Wealth exchanges afford a facility for the mobilisation of allies in warfare. They also appear to provide a facility for peaceful resolution, both in inter-group confrontation and in disputes between individual litigants. This rests on a general mechanism: the mediation of relations between persons and thus the value they have for one another, through material items. A. Strathern puts the point directly for Hagen: "in one sense the payments *are* the relationships . . . wealth goods . . . 'represent' people".[52] Injuries inflicted upon people can thus be transmuted into wealth equivalents. But the overall process has to be understood systemically.

Each settlement which takes the form of a translation of one value into another facilitates the mutability of values. If wealth can compensate for theft, then theft is translated into a wealth-depriving action; if a theft mobilises clan support for the victim, it is redefined as a political act; if an exchange can affect people's feelings, then they become a vehicle for them. In other words, the constant pitting of one act against another, one item against another, sustains their convertibility. In terms of the political aims of group confrontation, this need have little to do with peace-keeping in any abstract sense. Thus when Modjeska refers to high production societies of the Hagen type which create "an exchange-value cycle (of social causalities) in which increasing potentials for violent social conflict are mediated by the substitution of pigs as compensation for loss of life",[53] the reverse is at least as plausible, that the system develops a dual capacity for large-scale ceremonial exchange *and* large-scale warfare.

Collier's comparison of two different value schema is to the point.[54] In 'brideservice' societies debts and obligations between persons; take the form of service, that is, unmediated labour; disputes are characterised by episodes of violence and constraint. However, in 'bridewealth' societies wealth may come to stand for persons and/or labour, and injury be redressed through compensation. Such is Hagen, where persons and their relations with others are mediated in the flow of items between social categories. Transactions are definitive of social power, for one may dominate through giving gifts as well as blows. The dispute settlement considered briefly here involves the public confrontation of interested parties, in a setting seen by them as analogous to government courts.[55] The event is constituted by talk about the quarrel in question and by the suggestion of remedies which generally take the form of compensation of some kind. Men as opposed to women are the managers of these events. The publicity and the handing over of wealth make cultural sense only between parties who are divided by social interest; the forum is not suitable for matters which arise among close kin not differentiated in terms of wealth holding or wider interests.

In the public handling of disputes as they occurred then (see p.118) many compensation payments had two parts. There was a component which matched the injury — which translated personal value into material value — and there was a component 'to shake hands', restore good relations. The first was constructed on a premise of substitutability and thus negotiability: the value of things stolen or injury done. Frequently this was yielded with bravado; that the offender replaced the value of something he had taken did not detract from the fact that he had taken it. In overt political offences, it was often judged to be worth inflicting this or that injury, even if it were paid for afterwards. The second item, however, was a gesture towards mutuality — to soothe disturbed emotions. This looks like reparation but is perhaps better understood as a public evaluation of relationships. For reparation is not the right word if it implies that these transfers of wealth had as their object the restoration of something perceived as broken. The image of an entity whole or broken is a western one, and rests on definitions of 'whole' persons, 'whole' societies, susceptible to shattering. Between 'partible' persons, who constantly circuate items amongst themselves, what counts less than the repair of a broken connection (our own metaphor) is the conversion of one type of flow (e.g. of blood) into another type (e.g. of pigs).[56] Power is shown in the ablility to effect conversions. Some of the motivation behind making such conversions (compensating with wealth; avenging through war) can be attributed to men's desire to be seen to be effective in a public arena.

Indeed the conduct of compensation payments and the settlement of 'disputes' through them specifically advertise the collective life of men. It is part of their self-representation as managers of affairs. Time and again, orators (mediators, dispute settlers) comment that to exchange wealth is better than to fight: an underlying premise is that the two activities are convertible. It is not simply that the exchange of gifts enables people to settle their differences peaceably, but that either exchange or warfare can indeed turn into its alternative. Exchange enhances the visibility of big men; warfare enhances the display of clan strength. The values of these activities are not identical — but in the pursuit of inter-group competition, each sustains the other as an alternative. Dispute settlement is thus a form of public, collective activity which mobilises support and contributes towards a definition of inter-group relations predicated on reciprocity. Reciprocity is to be understood as framing such equalising relationships, and underpinning revenge as well as other forms of exchange.

Meggitt's account of warfare among the Mae Enga, western neighbours of Hagen, is illuminating in this regard.[57] Intermarrying Mae clans are linked to one another through obligations to protect the lives of their consanguines. When a man is injured his agnates must make reparation to his maternal kin. Valuables flow against injury and death. Given the hostility and rivalry which characterise relations between intermarrying clans, it seems likely that such payments also serve as a measurement of affliction. Meggitt points out how clans always "strive to utilize prestations to sustain their reputations, while at the same time placing their rivals at a disadvantage. Naturally enough, the manipulation of homicide compensation payments, themselves a consequence of overt political competition, plays an important part in this ceaseless struggle."[58] In other words, so-called reparation for loss suffered is also a registration, a measurement, of loss inflicted. It does not necessarily cancel out the loss; it inevitably draws attention to it. Its hardly hidden message may well be a reminder of imbalance under the rubric of an ostensibly balancing action: that one side can afford to pay in wealth what its allies have suffered as injury to their persons.

Ability to pay for offences is certainly a component of Hageners' attitudes towards compensation. The astute manager is one who does nothing he cannot pay for. Valuables are 'on the skin' — they are part of him, and he suffers to lose them; but they also are not part of him — they are the facilitating currency of his interactions with others. Men sometimes speak as though they have weighed up what offences they can afford to commit, a calculation of resources in terms of their ability to act with effect against others. Having wealth to dispose of supports personal efficacy. At the same time ambivalence is built into relationships mediated through all wealth transactions. The prestation itself is a vehicle for tension, and can bear a whole set of political statements — and, like words, does so with ambiguity.[59]

Wealth transactions are regarded by the actors as making statements about people's states of mind. Let me turn briefly to the management of emotions. Precisely because of its symbolic qualities, as standing for persons and the relations between them, wealth as a vehicle for feelings inflames as well as soothes. This observation goes against Hagen idiom which dwells on the capacity of wealth to make people's feelings 'good'. I offer it on systemic grounds. The very fact that emotions are mediated through wealth means not only that persons can adjust their relations towards one another through indirect means (such as through compensation) but that emotions can become inflated as attributes of whole groups who then come to face one another with collective feelings and desires.

States of feeling can be blown up to collective proportions: thus a group of dancers may feel shame in public; whole clans, hundreds strong, may be mobilised to seek revenge through anger, and allies are moved to sympathy with one another. This is not a vague, behaviourist observation. There are two significant systemic features here. First, the structural context of such expressions of emotion is reciprocal relations between formally equally social entities. Public gift giving is said to inflame as well as soothe people within the sphere of conversions upheld by reciprocity. That is, politics involves among other things a constant circulation of messages between formally independent groups who seek to balance out or aggrandise their fortunes in relation to one another.[60] They may exchange aggressive acts, or friendly ones, or take pleasure for themselves in inflicting pain on others. That feelings can be mediated through injury or through wealth transfers facilitates this circulation. The only measure of satisfaction is of course the claim to have equalled or bettered one's rivals. Dispute settlement procedures are part of this circulation. Second is the precise mechanism of mediaton. Mediation is necessary because collectivities do not, in the Hagen view, have 'minds'; there has to be an instrument which will set the individual minds of its members on a common course. When by contrast these emotions are experienced in the context of complementary relations between unequals (as in the sphere of domestic kinship), they are presented through a range of non-competitive means. Here it is possible to acquire unmediated information about the states of people's minds, and adjustments in such relations do not require the facilitations of wealth exchange and public talk.

Three points can be made in summary. First, wealth exchanges, like fighting, enable emotional states to be converted into political acts. That is, since a whole group can be seen to be liable for its actions, and to be indemnified for injury, it is also held to be emotionally unified in its anger or pleasure. But, second, political groups are related through negotiated reciprocity and strenuously sustained independence, not through relations of dependency; intermarriage, for instance, is seen as a matter of exchange rather than interdependence. In so far as feelings of anger or pleasure circulate to promote reciprocity (positive or negative) between these groups, they operate very differently from their contribution to domestic kinship relations where they underpin asymmetrical relations of dependency. Finally, group appropriation of emotional states makes them, as it were, lethal instruments of self-aggrandisement. The mediated display of emotion does not feed into long-term dependency, but into those assertions of independence which create an endless cycle of exchanges of mutual hostility or mutual assistance.

'Mediation' generally connotes mediatory adjustments, that is, the avoidance of confrontation through the mediation role of a third party or mediation substances (such as compensation). The term is used almost exclusively in anthropological accounts of dispute settlement to refer to the socialising intervention of a third party or principle which prevents naked confrontation. Yet in the kind of society I have been describing, where kinpersons, for instance, are held to have direct, unmediated influence on one another (manifested in bodily health), the capacity to mediate relations may not necessarily represent a superior sociality. Rather,

CONCLUSION

I do not see myself as having entered the hustings in the debate over the nature of social control charcterised by Hamnett as between 'order' and 'interaction'.[61] Jousters on both sides of that debate seem to be interested in normative behaviour and the kinds of sanctioning pressures brought to bear on disputants. An assumption of such accounts has to be that people are aware that their relationship is broken; the further factor to be considered in Hagen is that people regard themselves as chronically unable to read off the intentions of others. They may be uncertain as to whether they have been injured or not (in the social sense: who is the cause of the injury) and need to test the situation to see what effect the next move will have. The handing over and receiving of wealth items offers a contestable interpretation of the social relationships in question rather than unambiguously 'expressing' or 'reflecting' them. Much the same may be said of the talk which accompanies such transactions, and which is itself a major component in dispute settlement. It is a helpful point upon which to conclude, for 'talk' is both a medium into which and from which wealth may be converted, and raises similar problems about regulation. As one might expect the occasions on which Hageners talk out conflict cannot be reduced to the imposition of norms. They test the meaning of incidents in the light of its penetration of people's intentions.

But even the formula of testing in my description implies too much of the second-order event. The anthropology of law started out with investigating how far customary procedures were specialised or non-specialised instruments of regulation. In concentrating on the degree of specialisation (did the x have courts?) observers assumed that regulation had to be a feature of social life. Anthropology itself specialises in the elucidation of social regularities. Thus people's self-consciousness about 'norms' (values, interests, idoeologies) are held to represent society as it 'normally' exists — to be a description of a society the actors themselves conceive of as an order. Arenas in which norms are given voice (as dispute settlement and so on) thus attract analysis as second-order commentaries on the nature of social order itself. I have said enough to indicate that this is not useful framework in the Hagen case.

As a set of events, the Hagen dispute settlement process is on a continuum with those it also describes — the antecedent thefts, say, and the exchanges which follow. It is one among several arenas for public re-definition. Each arena recontextualises the translation of intent into action. Litigants' talk cannot be abstracted as a commentary on acts already completed as it were — that is, as not part of the acts themselves. When third parties offer their own views, these stand juxtaposed; they do not necessarily encompass or summarise and thus displace (redescribe) previous statements.[63] In the same way, the norms promulgated in the context of such hearings are not special to those hearings: they are not second-order framings. They draw on the same rhetoric by which people appeal to solidarity or confrontation in other contexts. The prospects of settlement through talk brings in concrete possibilities for action (to do with compensation and indemnity) bypassed when violent reprisals are taken. The social context thus provides for nonviolent solutions if the parties want it; but the norms implemented in that context are not of themselves concerned with the issues of violence or peace. They do not constitute a description of society as norm-bound in the interests of peaceful coexistence.[64] There are no norms that could not also be used to justify actions of a different kind (including the perpetuatuion of dispute itself — quarrelling, conflict, suicide). One cannot thus gather up all the apparently normative statements uttered during a Hagen court hearing and come out with a depiction of a social order 'disrupted' by conflict.

Neither the talk, then, which give a particular character to indigenous dispute settlement mechanisms nor the norms appealed to in the context of such talk can be seen as second-order abstractions from 'practice' (as Hamnett put it). That is, they do not have an authority beyond the fact that they offer a special arena for men's collective display. Men certainly promote the advantages of entering that arena — "Let us exchange wealth rather than fight" — but those advantages do not afford some kind of privileged access into the normative workings of society overall.

In western society judicial processes may be seen as having exactly that funcion. To describe one's social world as apart from the actions which constitute it, to set up procedures which deal with events as already enacted and closed to further modification, to see adjudication as not itself participating in the events under scrutiny all participate in a common philosophical position within western cosmology. Life is understood in terms of a split between representations (descriptions) of it, and as it really is. This promotes a parallel conceptual split between social action which incorporates the ideal, the normative, and what that action controls/regulates/modifies.[65] Certain types of behaviour thus have the potential for transforming others. In the adjustment of relations described here for Hagen, it is not transformations which occur so much as conversions. Within the public/political sphere actions, either violent or non-violent, can be converted the one into the other.

Public speech operates among other major conversions, notably wealth exchange and warfare, to register the effects of people's actions upon one another. Transactional metaphors which emphasise currency switches would be more apposite than the transformational metaphors suggested by resolution or reparation. These are not systems which operate a logic of social transformation. Wrong-doers cannot be reformed; they can only 'feel' the effects of their own faults. Similarly, enemies cannot be transformed into peaceable neighbours. On the contrary, enemies are always enemies; but if the relationship is conducted in that political zone where enemies are also allies, people with whom one exchanges as well as fights, then the currency of interaction may be converted by events.

The mediation of conflict through wealth exchanges (compensation) of the Hagen sort cannot be taken simply, then, as non-violent solutions to potential or actual violent eruptions.[66] Mediation, effecting the mutability of values, must also be seen as an instrument for specifically political interaction between clan groups; it helps define relations between such entities as a matter or reciprocity. Reciprocity involves a constant strain towards balancing or out-balancing exchanges. Added to this, the mediatory character of wealth allows the inflation of emotions to collective dimensions; it thus sustains the circulation of violent as well as non-violent interchange.

Much of the paper has been taken up with a critique of traditional approaches to dispute settlement, and the imposition of law, because I wished to detach public dispute settlement processes as they occur in Hagen from the representational place they often occupy in anthropological analyses. Obviously they cannot be read as implementations of a separately constituted and normative social order. One dichotomy derived from the idea of social order is that between violent and peaceable forms of interaction, a view of society as a state. We may equate society with the internal regualtion of violent behaviour, so there is a sense in which it is coterminous with the operation of social control. Yet in stateless systems such as those of the Highlands, 'control' does not figure as a second-order imposition on 'behaviour'. I have tried to suggest that violent outcomes from talk and wealth exchanges in Hagen are not a matter of practical affairs impinging on the ideal, of politics interfering with government, or the irregularities of behaviour disrupting an order. The mutability of values is a technical mutability, a characteristic of a system of conversions. What they really interfere with is the observer's ability to see parts of their social life as commentary and adjudication on other parts, and thus incorporating a descriptive activity which echoes his or her own descriptive endeavours.

NOTES AND REFERENCES

[1] D. Black, *The Behavior of Law* (1976) pp.2, 107.

[2] *Op.cit.*, pp.1-2.

[3] C. Geertz, "The impact of the concept of culture on the concept of man" (1966) in *The Interpretation of Cultures* (1973; ed. C. Geertz) p.44.

[4] J. Comaroff and S. Roberts, *Rules and Processes: The Cultural Logic of Dispute in an African Context* (1981).

[5] *Op.cit.*, p.5. The authors raise a number of criticisms in relation to this latter paradigm, and suggest that society is no more a field of endemic conflict than it is a moral universe. The important thing, they argue, is to know what is represented normatively, and what is open to negotiation, so that "to account for the relationship between conflict and the social order . . . we have found it necessary to formulate a particular analytical conception of the sociolcultural system itself" (*id.*, p.248).

[6] I attend neither to the whole range of folk models of 'law' nor to theoretical/political critiques which would provide very different starting points for discussion. The orthordox interpretation taken up here is pertinent insofar as its central ideas have had impact on common social science thinking. Fitzpatrick refers to it as bourgeois legality.

[7] I follow Comaroff and Roberts' point that dispute processes are not an instantiation or icon of social processes at large, but integral to them, to wonder if the attraction of a social control analysis does not lie in its analogue to the controlling efforts of analysis itself. This 'interest' in making representations is an implicit rather than explicit component of anthropological practice.

[8] Referring to the Bedouin of Cyrenaica, the Lugbara of Uganda and so on, Black states: "Anarchy has its own kinds of social control" (*Op.cit.*, p. 126).

[9] Black, for instance, refers to 'family control' (*Op.cit.*, p. 108).

[10] A.L. Epstein, "Introduction" in *Contention and Dispute: Aspects of Law and Social Control in Melanesia* (1974) p. 10; on the point which follows, cf. P. Gulliver, *Disputes and Negotiations: a Cross-Cultural Perspective* (1979).

[11] This observation is derived ultimately from R. Wagner's critique in *The Invention of Culture* (1975).

[12] S.B. Burman and B.E. Harrell-Bond, *The Imposition of Law* (1979).

[13] R.L. Kidder, "Towards an Integrated Theory of Imposed Law" in Burman and Harrell-Bond, *op.cit.*

[14] *Id.*, p.296.

[15] V. Aubert, "On Methods of Legal Influence" in Burman and Harrell-Bond, *op.cit.* p.34.

[16] See for instance R.L. Abel, "Western Courts in Non-Western settings: Patterns of Court Use in Colonial and Neo-Colonial Africa" in Burman and Harrell-Bond, *op.cit.*

[17] Aubert *op. cit.*, p.28.

[18] S.B. Burman and B.E. Harrell-Bond, "Introduction" in Burman and Harrell-Bond, *op. cit* p.3.

[19] *Id.*, p.1.

[20] Aubert, *op. cit.*, pp.37-9.

[21] I. Hamnett, "Introduction" in *Social Anthropology of Law* (1977; ed. I. Hamnett).

[22] Abel, *op. cit.*, p.171.

[23] S.F. Moore, *Law as Process. An Anthropological Approach*, (1978) p. 1.

[24] *Id.*, p.21.

[25] P. Fitzpatrick, "Law and Societies" (1984) 22 *Osgoode Hall Law J.* 115, p.116.

[26] *Id.*, p.126.

[27] *Id.*, p. 133. Fitzpatrick goes on to observe that law thus partakes of the rationality

constructivist rather than the organic and of the universalist rather than particularist; "Law is an encompassing of the individual and general social relations formalized in universal and equal rule. As such, it is integrally set against social relations of a lesser scale or of a particularistic nature" (*id*).

[28] E.g. M. Strathern, *Women in Between. Female Roles in a Male World* (1972); "Official and Unofficial Courts" *New Guinea Research Bulletin* (1972); "Managing Information" in *Contention and Dispute* (1974; ed. A.L. Epstein). See also A. Strathern, "When dispute procedures fail" (*id*); "Compensation Payments in the Highlands" in *Lo Belong Ol Manmeri* (1975; eds. J. Zorn and P. Bayne); "Compensation: Should There be a New Law?" in *Homicide Compensation in Papua New Guinea* (1981; ed. R. Scaglion).

[29] P. Fitzpatrick, *Law and State in Papua New Guinea* (1980) p. 103.

[30] Epstein, *op. cit.*, p.25.

[31] P. Lawrence, "Law and Anthropology, the Need for Collaboration" (1970) 1 *Melanesian Law J* 40; see also *The Garia. An Ethnography of a Traditional Cosmic System in Papua New Guinea* (1984).

[32] I use the male pronoun advisedly, since the observation is specifically applicable to men, not women.

[33] For instance, L. Nader and H.F. Todd jr, *The Disputing Process: Law in Ten Societies* (1978) p.8: "all societies have developed procedures that can be called into operation when trouble arises".

[34] Epstein, *op. cit.*, p.9.

[35] K-F Koch, *War and Peace in Jalémó. The Management of Conflict in Highland New Guinea* (1974) p.26.

[36] P. Fitzpatrick, "The Political Economy of Dispute Settlement in Papua New Guinea" in *Crime, Justice and Underdevelopment* (1982; ed. C. Sumner) p.235.

[37] *Id.*

[38] *Id.*, p.229.

[39] Women's restricted access to remedies differentiates them "judicially" from men (cf. M. Strathern *Women in Between. Op. cit.*). However, in a companion paper to appear in *Conflict and Control in the New Guinea Highlands* (ed. W.E. Wormsley) I expand this into an argument about methods of domestic conflict management involving men as well as women; the remedies for any wrongs among close kin form a class of their own.

[40] See M. Reay, "Changing Conventions of Dispute Settlement in the Minj Area" in *Contention and Dispute* (1974; ed. A.L. Epstein) p. 198; M. Young, "Private Sanctions and Public Ideology" *id.*, p.48.

[41] Also D. and D. Counts, "The Kaliai Lupunga: Disputing in the Public Forum" *id.*, pp.124–25. R. Gordon, "The Decline of the Kiapdom and the Resurgence of 'Tribal Fighting' in Enga" (1983) 53 *Oceania* 205, pp.212–13, notes that the idea of two parties pitting their strengths against one another characterises the relationship between litigants in the post-independence Village Courts.

[42] Koch *op. cit.*; also "Pigs and Politics in the New Guinea Highlands: Conflict Escalation among the Jalé" in *The Disputing Process* (1978; eds. L. Nader and H.F. Todd jr).

[43] Koch *id.*, p.48.

[44] Koch *op. cit.*, n. 35, p. 174. He reports that Jalé themselves "conceptualize their patterns of conflict management according to five distinct modes of *antagonistic* interaction: altercation, scuffle, sorcery, avoidance, and warfare" (*id.*, 67; my emphasis).

[45] In reference to my general argument, the context of Young's reflections on his own earlier analysis are worth quoting in full:

> In my book *Fighting with Food*, I characterised Kalauna people as . . . given to 'endemic conflict' . . . and divided rather than united by a configuration of values which stress competition rather than cooperation. A general problem . . . was how the consolidated community of Kalauna manages to withstand internal rifts and tensions. . . . My analysis was influenced by assumptions of homeostasis characteristic of much political anthropology; for example, that there *must* be institutionalised modes of conflict resolution in order that the social system may persist. While this and similar views still appear to me to be generally valid, I would not now accept them so uncritically . . . Kalaun people . . . tend to enjoy disputation and they accept it as a normative mode of conducting certain social relationships outside the domain of kinship. Even so, disputes have to be dampened if not settled, conflicts contained if not resolved, and it seems to me that competitive food-exchanges serve these ends admirably . . . by channelling conflicts into contests which allow people to take sides and arbitrate issues by appeal to common moral attitudes and cultural values (original emphasis) (*op. cit.*, 41).

[46] Black, *op. cit.*, p.5.

[47] Koch, *op. cit.*, n. 35, pp. 159, 175. The notion of global harmony and common goals has to be put into the context of 'conflict management' between nations with vast populations armed with the means of total destruction. Jalé conflict management is an instance not of a common human predicament but of specific mechanisms produced out of specific times and places, and on a specific scale. I repeat the point that it is legal ideology which makes us see 'human behaviour' as everywhere dealing with the same problems.

[48] Chowning, "Disputing in Two West New Britain Societies: Similarities and Differences" in *Contention and Dispute* (1974; ed. A.L. Epstein) p.153. She notes that "in some Melanesian societies there is considerable enjoyment to be derived from quarrels, and as long as they are regulated — that is, do not lead to killing within the community — there may be little general interest in really establishing peace". She adds the important rider that simply because people do not habitually fight (within a community), we cannot make any presumption that they expect to live in harmony. They may expect to live with trouble, dispute, conflict. This can carry on at low cost — reparation if needed at all is not expensive. In cases of intercommunity conflict, however, one enters an arena where *all* actions cost more. Gift exchange, compensation payments, fighting are likely to be conducted at an inflated level.

[49] Gordon, *op. cit.*, n.41, p.212. Earlier he observed: "social order is achieved through exchange relationships whereby people (essentially men) are controlled", and that "social order is ultimately generated through the personal power of big men", a rendering of the way big men would no doubt like to see their influence. *id.*, p.207.

[50] Comaroff and Roberts, *op. cit.*, p.68.

[51] E.g. Epstein, *op. cit.*, p.11; D. Tuzin, "Social Control and Tambaran in the Sepik" in *Contention and Dispute* (1974; ed. A.L. Epstein) p.318.

[52] A. Strathern, "Compensation: Should There be a New Law?" *op. cit.*, n. 28, p.7; also N. Modjeska, "Production and Inequality: Perspectives from Central New Guinea" in *Inequality in New Guinea Highlands Societies* (1982; ed. A. Strathern).

[53] *Id.*, p.54.

[54] J.F. Collier and M.Z. Rosaldo, "Politics and Gender in Simple Societies", in *Sexual Meanings* (1981; eds. S.B. Ortner and H. Whitehead); "Social control in bands and tribes: inequality and folk models of social structure" in *Toward a General Theory of Social Control* (in press; ed. D. Black).

[55] The way in which dispute settlers both drew on traditional practices and regarded themselves as borrowing power from the then Administration is treated in my account of official and unofficial courts in the early 1970s, M. Strathern, *op. cit.*, n. 28. Where it is relevant, the ethonographic present refers to this period. Were dispute processes as such the subject of this paper, precise historical contextualisation would be necessary.

[56] Cf. R. Wagner, "Analogic Kinship: a Daribi Example" (1977) 4 *American Ethnologist* 623; A. Biersack, "Ginger Gardens for the Ginger Woman: Rites and Passages in a Melanesian Society" (1982) 17 *Man* 239.

[57] M. Meggitt, *The Lineage System of the Mae-Enga of New Guinea* (1965); *Blood is their Argument: Warfare among the Mae-Enga Tribesmen of the New Guinea Highlands* (1977).

[58] *Id.*, p. 123.

[59] The point is effectively recapitulated by R. Gordon, "Some Notes Towards Understanding the Dynamics of Blood Money" in *Homicide Compensation in Papua New Guinea* (1981; ed. R. Scaglion); see also Reay *op. cit*; A. Strathern, "Veiled Speech in Mount Hagen" in *Political Language and Oratory in Traditional Society* (1975; ed. M. Bloch).

[60] M. Reay argues this for these Wahgi neighbours of Hagen; see "Lawlessness in the Papua New Guinea Highlands" in *Melanesia: Beyond Diversity* (1982; eds. R.J. May and H. Nelson).

[61] Hamnett, *op. cit.*

[62] As seems to be the implication of the exchange-of-information model offered by Gulliver, *op. cit.*, n. 10, p. 79.

[63] Goldman's account of Huli disputations is highly pertinent here, though I cannot do justice to it; see L. Goldman, *Talk Never Dies: the Language of Huli Disputes* (1983).

[64] The extent to which they constitute a description of men's collective power will be discussed elsewhere (see n. 39).

[65] R. Poole attributes the modern origins of such formulae to certain conceptions of society such as lay behind Kantian morality:

> The sphere of material life [commercial society] . . . does not constitute a morally coherent whole. One way of bringing out this incoherence is to show the way in which self-interest and the form of practical rationality appropriate to it are self-destructive. This incoherence is resolved by positing a form of reason which is not that of means to ends, but which emphasises the notions of universality and consistency. This form of rationality is ideally embodied both in the legal and administrative structures of civil society and in the motivations of its individual members. Civil and material life will constitute two symbiotically related spheres of human existence. Particular self-interest must be constrained by universalistic legal and motivational structures; in this sense, the formal rationality of civil society must dominate the substantive rationality of material life ("Reason, Self-interest and 'Commercial Society': the Social Content of Kantian Morality" (1984) 1 *Critical Philosophy* 24, p. 42.

Reason has the capacity to describe itself — the very notion of civil life, with its legal and administrative structures, implies an other order of practice. "(T)he role of reason is to provide a criterion by which already existing principles of action might be evaluated" (*id.*, p. 29). G. Lloyd traces some of the symbolic dimensions of this ordering, with its internal structure of domination. In particular she delineates the concern of Baconian science with matter "no longer to be seen as what had to be dominated in order to attain knowledge; but as the proper *object* of knowledge, now construed as the power to manipulate and transform" (original emphasis); "History of Philosophy and the Critique of Reason" (1984) 1 *Critical Philosophy* 1, p. 14 Knowledge involves a practical self-knowledge — including the ability to describe the activity of the pursuit of knowledge ('science') as distinct from mind itself (*id.*, p. 16).

Finally, western binarisms are thrown into relief in D. Tuzin's account of Arapesh horror at Japanese wartime cannibalism. Their refusal to accept an explanation in terms of starvation is to be contrasted with the way 'we' seize on such acts as evidence of a return to nature, or as a response provoked by fundamental need. Society or humanity as such is not threatened because normally society *controls* such behaviour: here the controls were simply absent. For the Arapesh, however, proper humanity is sustained in contra-distinction to a non-human realm, so that the blurring of the distinction becomes a terrible threat to the idea of humanity ("Cannibalism and Arapesh Cosmology: A Wartime Incident with the Japanese" in *The Ethnography of Cannibalism* (1983; eds. P. Brown and D. Tuzin).

[66] My discussion on the mutability of values is not of course to be read as suggesting that ceremonial exchange, dispute settlement and the like 'encourages' warfare such that if the former were to disappear so would the latter. On the contrary, the argument has to be that if ceremonial exchange and compensation payments were discouraged, then men's collective life would be channelled into other forms. The cessation of warfare in the 1950s and 1960s brought about an escalation of exchange. An immediate effect of discouraging exchange would no doubt be an escalation of war or increasing competition along sharpened class lines.

[12]

Bobotoi and *Pulu* Melanesian Law : Normative Order or Way of Life ?

by

Peter SACK *

1. The Tolai of East New Britain in Papua New Guinea have a tradition of *bobotoi*, the time of darkness. Today its passing is often identified with the arrival of the first missionaries in the area (who were also the first European settlers). Yet, *bobotoi* and the ' new order ' replacing it have little to do with the bad, old, heathen days and a conversion to Christianity. *Bobotoi* is timeless, primordial chaos, when people lived like animals, grunting like pigs and fornicating with their mothers, daughters and even sisters. Nor are Christian beliefs the essence of the ' new order ' ; rather, it is characterised by the creation of the true Tolai language, the *tinata tuna*, and of the traditional, matrilineal, social organisation.

These are the two main pillars of Tolai humanity : language and exogamy. Both are not divine gifts but man-made, although the new messengers of God, as individual human beings, are now often allocated a major role in their creation. Moreover, they remain the responsibility of man ; like everything else, they are subject to change and not assumed to have eternal or universal validity.

It is appropriate to introduce a story at this point ; for it is, from the Tolai perspective, a conglomerate of stories rather than a system of theories which gives meaning and structure to human life. It was told to me, about ten years ago, by Pius Pio Toratoro, probably the oldest Tolai I ever met, whose life spanned almost the entire century of his people's colonial history.

> The first Tolai were a man and his wife, called Mina and Adellman. They left Sodom and Gomorrah after the troubles there and went to Siar, in New Ireland. After further troubles in Siar, they came to New Britain, where they had seven daughters with perfectly ordinary Tolai names, like la Taal or la Kuburam. The old man, Tagogo, who died when I was a small boy, could have told you more stories about them, since he was alive at the time of the seven sisters. But you would not have understood him. People spoke very differently in the olden days, before the Mission came. I helped Pater Dicks and Pater Kleintitschen to work out the proper Tolai language. Also, in the olden days people married everybody, brother could even marry sister. When the population grew, the people decided it was better to divide them into two groups so that members of one could only marry members of the other [1]

Toratoro stopped short of claiming responsibility for this decision himself or of attributing it to one of his old people, like Tagogo, although that would have been in Tolai character. However, he took it for granted that it had been made fairly recently, most likely during his parents' generation.

It is remarkable that Tolai insist on the newness of the most central ingredients of their life. Coconut palms were introduced to their villages by the Germans. The first expeditions to central New Britain to collect *nassa* snails for their shell money were undertaken in boats purchased from the Chinese boat builder, Ah Tam. Outrigger canoes were first built by the Methodist mis-

* Australian National University, Canberra.

1. This is, of course, a selective paraphrase not a verbatim quotation.

sion teachers from Samoa. Even revenge magic came to them only after the arrival of the *lotu* [Christianity], for the simple reason that ' the government ' was stopping people from fighting so that they had no choice but to resort to sorcery instead.

Tolai see no contradiction in their fathers embracing magic after their conversion to Christianity, are not impressed by eyewitness accounts of precolonial *nassa* snail expeditions, and seem to treat the introduction of moiety-exogamy as being on a par with the adding of European vegetables to their food crops. At the same time there is a general feeling — although, perhaps, less strong than in other parts of Melanesia — that things have always been the way they are now and that they must stay this way to preserve the fragile balance of the universe. *Bobotoi* is still lurking in every cave and can return at any moment, turning man again into an unpredictable wild beast.

In other words, Tolai are most concerned with ' order ' as opposed to chaos. But the ' order ' they have given themselves is not perceived as a normative order ; it is quite unlike the ' legal ' order introduced by the colonial state, which is perceived as the coercive aspect of government, a price to be paid for roads and schools and hospitals and not as a charter of a human society.

Melanesians, including the Tolai, often describe their law, in contrast to that of the government, as *pasin bilong mipela*, that is " our fashion " or " the way we do things ". This does not mean to imply that Melanesian law constitutes an order which is automatically followed in every case ; quite the contrary. On the other hand, the words used are significant. They indicate that Melanesian law is different from a normative order as a series of commands which demand obedience and are enforced by various sanctions. Melanesian law does not express itself in obligatory norms but in the actual social organisation of the people.

2. In a study of Karavara, a small island in the neighbouring Duke of York Group, whose inhabitants are closely related to the Tolai of New Britain, the anthropologist F. K. Errington [2], gives the notion of *bobotoi* or *momboto* (which he translates as ' the failure to see clearly ', *ibid.* : 19) a central position. He describes the state of *momboto* and its supersession in terms similar to those used above to characterise *bobotoi* :

In the momboto, the Karavarans say, men looked and behaved like wild animals. They did not shave or cut their hair ; they had red eyes " like wild pigs " ; they were cannibals and ate even those now considered to be their kinsmen as though their kinsmen were animals. There was no kinship ; there was no regulation of sex. Men had sexual relations with women who would now be considered their sisters or sisters' daughters ; men did not purchase brides nor did they pay adultery fines. In the absence of regulation, men simply fought each other to get women. Their image of the momboto is a statement of the Karavaran view of basic human nature, a nature of greed and violence, characterized by the untrammeled exercise of individual interest. The expression of unrestrained human nature is seen as a chaos of conflicting desires and activities. The Karavarans refer frequently to the momboto in conservation with each other and with me.

The momboto, as an image of disorder, tells the Karavarans about the nature of order. The momboto is the reference point which shows indirectly the principles on which their current society rests. What has changed since the momboto is not human nature itself but the means by which human nature can be regulated and social order thereby established.

The momboto, in the Karavaran view, ended a few days after the arrival of George Brown, a Methodist clergyman who was the first missionary to settle in this area. It is said that when he first arrived he saw that those on shore wanted to spear him ; consequently he and his companions stayed on their boat singing hymns continuously for three days. At the end of that time he dipped his hand into the sea. The water had been hot when he arrived but now it was cool : this indicated that the passions of those on shore had been cooled. Brown went ashore, no longer afraid. With his arrival the momboto ended and the modern era began.

Specifically, Brown and the other Europeans — all of whom are seen as arriving at virtually the same time — ended the momboto by bringing to the Duke of York Islands *divara* (shell money) and the principle of moiety [*ibid.* : 21-22].

Errington's subsequent interpretation of the impact of *momboto* on Karavaran society differs markedly from my picture of Tolai society. It is at the same time more shapeless and more singleminded and dualistic. This is mainly the result of Errington's dimissal of social structure and individual morality as irrelevant for Karavaran social practice and world view. This leaves him with an unspecified notion of ' power ' as his only focal point. Power in turn is exclusively controlled (and exercised) by means of shell money, and all this takes place in a strictly dualistic world,

2. *Karavar : Masks and Power in a Melanesian Ritual*, Cornell University Press, 1974.

defined by the dichotomies between *mom-boto* and order, between the two moieties, between males and females, and, in particular, between leader and followers (see *ibid.* : 23-29.

I find this interpretation fascinating but difficult to accept. But it is not my intention to criticise Errington ; rather, I have been referring to his study to show that my own emphasis on *bobotoi* is not a personal fancy. Moreover, there is a common base : like Errington I was struck by the central role the notion of ' power ' — or ' powers ' — plays in Melanesian society. However, from my legal perspective, it was natural to view this not in contrast to structure (or morality), but in contrast to the place the notion of ' laws ' occupies in modern Western societies. In addition it appeared to me that the significance of the notion of power in Melanesia — like that of laws in the West — is not restricted to interhuman relations but operates for the whole universe, social and natural, deeply affecting Melanesian attitudes to ' order ' as well as to ' freedom ' and to ' control ', ' regulation ' and so on. This is why I regard the Tolai emphasis on the links between the end of *bobotoi* and the acquisition of language — rather than of shell money — as crucial. Tolai perceive humans primarily as talking animals and the ' new order ' as a product of talk. For Toratoro the establishment of the two exogamous moieties was the result of talk between people which led to a decision by them. More importantly, exogamy itself is first and foremost, a way of forcing different groups to talk to each other in order to acquire marriage partners and thus to procreate themselves. The creation of this and other artificial interdependencies — which must be worked out through talk — is the core of the ' new order '.

I fully endorse Errington's stress [*ibid.*] on the centrality of ' relations ' and ' juxtapositions ' for the operation of Melanesian society and thought. The Melanesian aim is to balance rather than to regulate. ' Order ' is not a positive ideal but a means of preventing chaos. It defines a social framework within which a limited manipulation of interpersonal relations is possible. Autonomy of individuals or groups is hubris — not a desirable goal. Hence interdependence is more than a necessary evil — and this is where I take issue with Errington's interpretation, certainly as far as its applicability to the Tolai of New Britain is concerned. For him Karavarans are amoral, greedy and violent and can be controlled only through fear ; they are fiercely competitive and obsessed by divisive dualisms. All this is, to some extent, unquestionably true, but I am also sure that it is, even in Karavara, only part of the story. There is competition, but there is also, for example, the satisfaction of sharing (the positive side of reciprocity). It is simply not true that Melanesians, on Karavara or elsewhere, are totally amoral, and Errington's concentration on the competition for political power produces, for me, a dangerously lop-sided picture [3]. Still *momboto* differs, perhaps, significantly from *bobotoi*, and we are concerned with the latter rather than with the former, and with law rather than with politics.

3. I claimed above that *bobotoi* stood for primordial chaos. I now have to clarify this statement. *Bobotoi* does not refer to a state of affairs in the world as a whole but relates solely to the prehuman condition of man as a social being. Consequently the ' new order ' is exclusively a *social* order. It is not concerned with the paths of the stars, the ways of the animals or with the meaning of human life. It does not regulate the universe. On the contrary, it assumes that nature continues in its distinctly ' disorderly ' fashion-without man, or anyone else, being able to do anything about it. But man or, more precisely, human society, can escape from *bobotoi*, although it has to remain constantly alert and ready to remake itself to avoid having to rejoin the pigs in the bush.

The ' new order ' does not consist of commands by an omnipotent creator to his creatures — but it actually exists, instead of merely being obligatory. Man is not free to opt out of this order as long as it functions. The will of the individual is as immaterial in this respect as the will of God. A Tolai cannot decide for himself that he rejects matrilineal descent and that he is thus henceforth no longer a member of his mother's group. He can change this social fact as little as the biological fact that she is his mother. The ' new order ' is a social and not a moral order — which does not mean that the people living under it must be in other respects amoral or

3. I am stressing this point because I too will in this paper avoid the question of traditional Tolai morality. I therefore want to make clear that by highlighting the fact that Tolai social order is not concerned with moral postulates I do not wish to imply that all interpersonal relations among the Tolai are dominated by self-interest.

that it cannot itself create secondary obligations which are felt to be binding.

By the same token, since the 'new order' is not a divine charter but more like a 'social contract' it is 'negotiable'. It is not an ideal order, not even necessarily a good order, but simply order as opposed to non-order. Tolai, as social groups, are free to switch from matrilineal to patrilineal descent ; they would not thereby interfere with the will of God or with universal moral postulates — although a single group which made such a decision would certainly come under various pressures and face considerable pratical difficulties.

Nevertheless, it is crucial to appreciate that the 'new order' is not claimed to be ideal or necessary. As a result, Tolai have no difficulty in accepting that other societies have different orders (without feeling morally affronted by them and compelled to attempt conversion). Their attitude towards members of their own society who breach the social order also differs significantly from attitudes shown if a moral or religious code is breached. On the one hand, such a breach does not have to produce a feeling of guilt or sin in the perpetrator ; on the other hand, it is independent of his individual responsibility and it endangers existence of the entire social order. This last characteristic is a major disadvantage of a purely social order. The flexibility, amendability and tolerance it permits causes a general fragility. Since it is not rooted in the will of God, or universal moral postulates, it cannot stand unblinkingly until eternity, striking down those who offend against it, and gathering additional strength from each punished offence. Instead it needs for its survival the continuing acceptance and confirmation by the action of those to whom it applies : it simply ceases to exist when it is no longer practised, because it has no other than its actual social existence.

4. From the Tolai perspective the basis of social order is beyond question : it is the notion of matrilineal descent which determines that every Tolai is automatically, by birth, a member of his or her mother's group. While there are many stories about the introduction of the moiety system — usually attributing it to the two culture heroes, To Kabinana and To Purgo (who are an alternative way of explaining the Tolai's emergence from *bobotoi*), there is, as far as I know, not a single one dealing with the introduction of matrilineality. Tolai mythology takes matrilineality so much for granted that the first women the culture heroes 'create' cannot possibly be their daughters. They act, so to speak, on behalf of their mother (who figures in other stories) and can really only produce members of her matrilineal group. The women they create thus 'ought' to be their sisters. In some versions they manage to create wives for themselves, but even this is regarded as 'improper', because wives must be 'bought' from other groups. In other words, some form of exogamy is also presupposed.

The primary significance of the matrilineage is therefore, somewhat paradoxically, negative : it unites the 'we' who are *not* permitted to marry (or to have sexual intercourse). The matrilineage can — by definition — only exist because there are the 'they' who are marriageable and necessary for its survival. As a social ordering principle matrilineality is almost incidental. What counts in this respect is not that the Tolai are matrilineal rather than patrilineal but that they are *unilineal*. It is this unilineality which gives the matrilineage its capacity to act as a clearly defined corporate body since under a bilineal system a child belongs simultaneously to the two 'groups' of its parents, the four 'groups' of its grandparents and so on. It is also *descent*, rather than *matrilineal* descent, as the only 'official' recruiting principle, which prevents the absorption of the foreign spouse into the 'group' — with the result that even the nuclear family must contain the members of two kinship groups. Although the position among the Tolai is further complicated by the fact that matrilineality is combined with male domination, there is no question that the former provides, together with the exogamy principle it implies, the main 'inner logic' of Tolai social order.

The Tolai carry the exogamy principle to an extreme by super-imposing a dual moiety organisation over these individual matrilineages which groups them together into two large exogamous sections. This is not as divisive as it may sound. Indeed, it works against exclusivity and ultimately unites the whole of mankind into a single society — at least in principle — for the moiety organisation not only encompasses all Tolai, but extends indefinitely beyond the horizon. The

4. The most extensive published collection of Tolai myth and stories is still A. Kleintitschen, *Mythen und Erzählungen eines Melanesierstammes*, Anthropos Monographs, Vol. 2, No. 4.

' we ' in the moiety sense thus do not add up to a single, politically active unit — although shared moiety membership can bring together two or more matrilineages for certain purposes. Nonetheless, every Tolai shares his moiety ' we-ness ' with people whom he has never seen and with whom he will never have social dealings of any kind. This openness and flexibility, which complements the harsh and, in theory, immutable dividing line between the ' we ' and the ' they ', also shapes Tolai attitudes towards other social groups, including the matrilineage : they can all expand and contract according to the context and are meant to supplement each other ; no Tolai ever owes his whole allegiance to a single group.

Secondly, all ' they ' in the moiety sense, however distant, share the ' we-ness ' of one's father, whose role is (as a positive consequence of male domination) of considerable importance in Tolais' lives. From their vantage point the whole of mankind consists either of one's own or of one's father's people. There are no strangers. The ' they ' are not enemies but primarily one's ' fathers ' or one's (actual or potential) spouses. Exogamy, it must always be remembered, is not just the prohibition of endogamy, its positive social purpose is intermarriage : it promotes, and, necessitates, social intercourse between groups ; it makes interdependence, instead of autonomy, the key to social survival. This means, *inter alia*, that the idea of law as an autonomous field is not only alien but antagonistic to traditional Tolai culture.

5. Although unilineal descent is the most important ingredient of Tolai social order, it has, like that of all other human societies, also to deal with questions of territory, locality and residence. This is the context in which male domination asserts itself ; for the Tolai are, in principle, virilocal ; that is to say a couple after marriage, lives together at the husband's rather than the wife's place and with his rather than with her group. It is the woman and not the man who is to be the outsider, who must garden on another group's land etc. But this arrangement has other, more practical reasons : virilocal residence keeps the adult male members of a matrilineage, the warriors, spatially together to defend ' the group ' and its territory. Yet, this group — as a residential unit — consists, apart from the warriors, primarily of their wives and children who belong to kinship groups in the opposite moiety. Thus, each moiety depends on the other not only for the ' fathering ' of its children but also for their physical protection during the early stages of their lives.

As a consequence of virilocal residence all adult female members of a residential unit, the ' wives ', are sexually ' available ' to all adult males — because their ' sisters ' (who belong to the same moiety) are, as wives of the males of the other moiety, resident elsewhere. By contrast, the residential unit includes no females who are sexually available to the adolescent boys since they are all either ' mothers ' or their ' sisters ' and thus members of their own moiety [5]. This provides a strong incentive for young males, upon reaching puberty, to join — as is the ' custom ' — their own group and their uncles, whose wives and daughters are — theoretically — sexually available to them. There is also no wonder that adultery is a major problem among the Tolai, and that a widow is expected to return from her husband's to her brother's place, instead of being a constant sexual temptation to the former's brothers.

It is obvious that I have been pointing to only some of the consequences of even this oversimplified model, but they are sufficient to demonstrate what I have called the ' inner logic ' of Tolai social order. It is not a system of explicit, prescriptive rules which opts for one particular set of choices, excluding all others, but it encourages certain tendencies and discourages others, and it has far-reaching, quasi-normative effects which a Westerner who is used to different forms of social and legal organisation tends to overlook and rarely ever ' instinctively ' appreciates.

6. The position sketched so far must create the impression that matrilineages and moieties were physically neatly separated, in the sense that the whole area of Tolai settlement is divided into two parts, each inhabited by the adult males of one moiety together with the females and children of the orther. This was, of course, never the case, although there is some evidence that matrilineages originally had single territories, and that matrilineages belonging to the same moiety tended to congregate geographically. Nevertheless, even then we are talking about contiguous moiety ' territories ' of, at the most, a few square kilometres. Still, kin-exogamy unquestionably implies a tendency towards at least small-scale local exogamy. But there are counter-acting ten-

5. I am using — as the Tolai do — terms like mother, sister, daughter etc. in their ' classificatory ' sense.

dencies at work in Tolai society. Here I would like to look briefly at one which stems from the acknowledgement of the social significance of father/child and especially father/daughter relations.

The Tolai have a tradition of regarding the oldest daughter as a ' gift ' of the mother and her group to the father and his people [6]. This does not affect the group membership of the girl but ' entitles ' the father to receive her ' bride price ' which is normally paid to her own group. In turn, he becomes ' obliged ' to provide her with land which will usually come from his own group (and will pass permanently to the other moiety). This obviously encourages the daughter to stay with her father's group upon reaching adulthood instead of returning to her mother's group (and its land), especially since it provides her children with a basis on which to continue living in their maternal grandfather's locality [7].

Under these circumstances it is natural for the daughter's group to arrange a marriage with a male already living in her father's locality, so that she can continue using her own as well as her husband's land after her virilocal marriage. As a result of such cases the landholdings of the two moieties become interspersed and other incentives for local endogamy can begin to operate : daughters no longer have to move physically far away from their own group ; they can visit, seek support when they fight with their husbands etc. A locally endogamous marriage also permits fathers and (virilocally living) mothers to keep in close touch with their daughters after marriage.

7. This is probably all the information needed for setting the scene for a discussion of *pulu*, the Tolai equivalent of incest, to which we will now turn, since it is the most serious disturbance of the social order known to them. We can therefore assume that it also marks the area where notions of prescription, guilt, sin, punishment etc., are most likely to play a decisive role — in short, the area where Tolai social order is at its most normative.

To understand Tolai attitudes towards *pulu* we must appreciate first of all that it deals with intra-moiety incest, so that ideas of biological closeness or genealogical proximity, which shape the Western approach, are irrelevant. The ' condemnation ' of *pulu* is the negative side of the exogamy principle it is meant to protect. Hence it is not so much concerned with sexual intercourse as with marriage and procreation. The paradigm case of *pulu* is the public marriage between brother and sister, not secret sexual acts between father and daughter. Indeed, even marriage between father and daughter is ' technically ' not *pulu* because they belong to different moieties (and Oedipus is quite out of place in Tolai mythology) [8].

On the other hand, it makes ' technically ' no difference whether the individuals involved in a case of *pulu* are actually the offspring of the same father and mother. *Pulu* committed with a classificatory sister — however distant genealogically — is just as ' bad ' as that committed with a ' true ' sister. Nor does it technically matter whether the ' offenders ' know that they are members of the same moiety : *pulu* is independent of subjective elements. It is also not because it involves the misuse of parental authority or filial trust that it is ' bad ' : *pulu* is typically committed by consenting adults.

When and in what sense is *pulu* then ' bad ' or ' wrong ' ? There is neither an explicit rule prohibiting it nor one which requires ' culprits ' to be put to death — which was the traditional ' punishment ' — simply because norms are not the verbal form Tolai use to talk about such matters. They do not say that *pulu* is morally bad or legally wrong. Nor do they say that individual cases of *pulu* are not inherently objectionable but merely require action because *pulu*, generally speaking, undermines the socially useful exogamy principle. Rather, Tolai say that in the past people committing *pulu* were killed. This is a statement of fact, but it also indicates that killing people under these circumstances was in itself the ' proper ' thing to do. It was not murder justified by way of exception as being ' punishment in accordance with the law '.

6. I am grateful to Jim Fingleton for drawing my attention to the importance of this ' custom ' (see ' Changing Land Tenure in Melanesia : The Tolai Experience ', Ph.D. Thesis, The Australian National University, 1985).

7. The position is significantly different in the case of male children' who are incapable of starting new group segments because their own children always belong to those of their wives. This consequence of matrilineality is particularly visible in cases of adoption : a man cannot adopt a ' son and heir ' but has to arrange with one of his sisters to do so ; and if he has none, his group is doomed to extinction.

8. Since making this rash remark, I read M. E. Spiro's *Oedipus in the Trobriands*, University of Chicago Press, 1982. I was, as usual, fascinated by the seemingly unlimited capacity of psychologists to advance grand, transcultural theories. Nevertheless, I remain unconvinced, although I must postpone the development of a counter-argument until a more appropriate occasion.

Pulu itself is compared to eating excrement or poisonous fruit. Like poison, it makes people rotten inside ; it spoils them as people. *Pulu* is not a sin committed by an individual but a ' social disease '. Tolai are less worried about the act of *pulu* than about the altered state of affairs it brings about and which affects every member of society, including the members of the other moiety. *Pulu* which remained ' unpunished ' by the offenders' kin is, for this reason, said to have attracted the attention of the *iniet* sorcerers in the past : they would ' finish them off ' by their own magical means because they were offended by the ' poison ' they smelt inside the incestors.

At this point another story may be helpful in illustrating the Tolai point of view. It deals with the man Tadakai who was caught committing *pulu* with one of his sisters. He was to be ' eaten ' by a *tubuan*, a powerful ancestral mask.

> His people sent Tadakai from Tingenavudu, where he lived, to To Inia in neighbouring Vunamami, whose *tubuan*, Ia Mareve and Ia Bagubagu, were to perform the task. But To Inia refused, because Tadakai was his *bar maku*, his in-law, and sent him on to Turlom in Keravi, who also refused because Tadakai was a member of his *vunatarai* [matrilineage]. He sent Tadakai to Talok in Vunakambi, for his *tubuan*, Ia Marinata. Talok too refused because he ' felt sorry ' for Tadakai. He kept him for a few days on his *taraiu* [the meeting place of the *tubuan* society] and went to see To Ragat in Gunanba, in Reber, where the traditional enemies of Tadakai's people lived. To Ragat accepted Tadakai for his *tubuan*, Ia Muruna. So Ia Marinata took Tadakai to Ia Muruna's *taraiu*. After some days he was decorated with lime and leaves and feathers and with the special design of Ia Muruna. Then Tadakai knew he was finally going to be killed. He was very sad and composed and sang a beautiful song expressing his sadness, which is still remembered and sung today (compiled from my 1975 field notes).

Tadakai is not seen as a despicable criminal but as a hero struck by fate who must be sacrificed. He is not expected to be weighed down by guilt. Nor is he seen as having redeemed himself by facing his death courageously (although he is admired for it). He just did the ' proper ' thing, and to kill him was also the ' proper ' thing ; for where there is no guilt, there can be no forgiveness.

8. More recently incestors survive and sometimes even marry. Those ' in the know ' will try to send them to distant parts, using moiety connections, to terminate the embarrassment caused by the presence of this unnatural union. But arrangements are also made to adjust the moiety membership of one of the spouses so that they no longer live in the state of *pulu* at their new home [9].

This is not a fiction. Instead, it expresses the belief that by agreement of those who have the ' legitimate ' power social facts can be adjusted to what is ' proper ' if there are ' good ' reasons. The leaders who make these arrangements do not see themselves as hiding criminals behind a screen of make-believe. They actually change social reality so that things can again be done ' properly '. They terminate an unnatural state of affairs instead of protecting an ongoing illegal activity. But they can only change the future. They neither condone past behaviour nor rectify it retrospectively. The spouses did commit *pulu*, and they, as well as their (' innocent ') children, remain individually affected by it — but they no longer disturb the social order.

This is different in the still extremely rare cases in which matrilineal relatives marry and remain in their own locality because they are sufficiently powerful and brazen to do so. In one such case a man married his ' true ' sister's daughter — the next worse thing to marrying one of his sisters. The reaction of people who learn and talk about this case is a mixture of horror, helplessness and mirth. Since the extreme traditional measures are no longer permitted and since their propriety is also no longer unquestioningly accepted, the people prefer to bewail the passing of the good old days and to see the funny side of *pulu* — which is made easier by the fact that it never did create a sense of moral outrage. The idea of being, at the same time, the maternal greatuncle of one's children and the son-in-law of one's sister has always been hilarious as well as frightening to Tolai. It is a source of jokes, but these jokes also reinforce the social order the incestuous marriage is threatening.

Moreover, it must not be overlooked that Christianity and the modern Western state are profoundly changing Tolai perceptions of *bobotoi* and their social order : they not only provide additional sources of stability in human affairs but also strengthen the traditional social order which they are trying to undermine. The Tolai have managed to establish — and so far to maintain — a traditional kind of interdependence between these modern,

9. I am again grateful to Jim Fingleton for case material used in this section.

Western imports and the traditional order, making the former in the process more open and pluralistic. Nonetheless, theyare, in turn, altering the way in which Tolai see and talk about their own institutions. Tolai can now perceive, for example, the *tubuan* society as equivalent of government and law-enforcement, just as the early European observers did a hundred years ago. They are even beginning to adjust indigenous values and aspirations to Christian morality and Western materialism. Yet, fundamental differences remain. They show up clearly in Tolai attitudes towards forms of quasi-incest, where a ' closeness ' between members of the opposite moiety makes marriage and sexual intercourse nevertheless ' improper '.

9. The father/daughter relationship is the extreme case in point, but the propriety of marriages between true cross-cousins or to true patrilateral uncles or aunts is also doubted. Tolai even feel uneasy about a man being married to two true sisters or to a woman and her true daughter (by somebody else). This indicates that the ultimate source of uneasiness is not biological closeness (nor the notion of sex-free social spheres) but the feeling that it is ' bad ' to mix different social roles and to diminish the range of social relationships available to a person. Both circumstances make people permanently less human — hence, again, the emphasis on the state of marriage rather than on individual sexual acts.

By marrying his daughter a man deprives her of either her father or her husband because he cannot possibly perform both roles simultaneously. A woman cannot be the co-wife of her daughter because mother/daughter and co-wife relationships are different. Other relationships too are ' proper ' only if they link people belonging to different generations : one does not marry ' children ' or father or mother ' siblings ' — not because it is immoral or illegal but because it is inhuman to do so.

In short, our entire legal and moral vocabulary and the practical responses it suggests are basically inappropriate in the Tolai context. Although it is tempting to say that the Tolai have a rule prohibiting *pulu* and that an act breaching it traditionally attracted the death penalty, it tells us nothing about Tolai social reality but merely reinforces our own ideological and conceptual prejudices.

10. At some stage during work on this paper the motto *divide et impera* became a kind of unwanted but inescapable counterpoint. I first tried to silence it by stressing that Tolai dichotomies are not meant to divide but to create interdependencies : they do not separate people but establish the potential for different relations between them. But this was, by itself, an inadequate response, because it did not address itself to the *impera* component of the counterpoint. To put it to rest as well, I must end on a different note.

Traditional Tolai social order does not establish divisions (or interdependencies) to enable to rule but to prevent this from happening. It is inconsistent with the emergence of an all-powerful ruler who is at the same time the mother and the father and the maternal uncle and the brother and the sister of his people. Traditional Tolai social order is horizontal rather than vertical — pluralistic instead of hierarchical — and Tolai society therefore ungovernable [10]. Tolai law, and Melanesian law in general, reflects this and precludes its translation into a normative, sovereign-oriented, legal system. Melanesian law is a way of life. It is neither totally amoral, nor does it lack normative and coercive elements. It has an ' inner logic ', but it does not aspire to be an exclusive order which is free of internal contradictions.

Man does not escape from *bobotoi* by centralising power in the hands of the state but by diffusing it among as many people as possible, and in such a way that it maximises their interdependence and thus their need for cooperation. For Tolai the humanity of man is not the product of his individual freedom but of the social bonds which link him to other people. These bonds are not shackles — although their restraining force is certainly felt — but means of expanding and differentiating the network of interpersonal relationships. Tolai social order — and this is the core of Tolai law — defines a framework for individual action ; it gives choice by limiting its range, but it does prescribe what is good or prohibit what is bad ; it does not tell people to do only the right thing ; it does not want to bring about a state of affairs where reality matches an ideal ; it does not presume to be an ideal order. It is an actual order which permits people to live as human beings — which, as far as Melanesians are concerned,

10. Although it should go without saying, it is perhaps better to spell out that ungovernability is *not* the same as anarchy.

is all that mankind can possibly hope to achieve.

RÉSUMÉ

Cet article utilise les notions de *bobotoi* (le temps de l'obscurité) et *pulu* (l'inceste) afin d'analyser les attitudes des Tolai face à « l'ordre » social. Tout d'abord il se propose de démontrer que les Tolai ne perçoivent pas leur propre « loi » comme un système « normatif », ensuite l'auteur analyse les effets d'une société ayant une position tolérante à l'égard des comportements individuels déviants mais également attentive au maintien de la cohésion sociale de la communauté.

SUMMARY

This paper uses the notions of *bobotoi* (the time of darkness) and *pulu* (incest) to explore Tolai attitudes to social ' order '. It is primarily concerned to demonstrate that the Tolai do not perceive their own ' law ' as a *normative* system and to indicate what consequences their alternative position has for the treatment of individual deviant behaviour as well as for the maintenance of general social cohesion.

[13]

Just in Time: Temporality and the Cultural Legitimation of Law

Carol J. Greenhouse†

Introduction: Time, Culture, and Society

This Article is about the relationship between cultural conceptions of time—"social time"—and the organization and management of legal institutions. As an idea, time has profound consequences in its capacity to encode and systematize otherwise disparate and unreferenced events and relationships. Concepts of time vary widely around the world, and Western ideas about time—including the conventional formulation that time moves in a straight line from past to present, through one's own lifetime—acquired shape and force entirely apart from the scientific "discovery" of time.[1] This Article focuses in particular on Western ideas about time, and, even more particularly, on the ways in which temporality suffuses popular understandings of law. Specifically, after some preliminary ethnological and historical discussion, it offers an analysis of the ways in which specific indeterminacies in Western notions of time are worked out in the legal context. Its central thesis is that temporality and legality are conceptually fused in the West through their mutual implications of a total order in relation to which social life acquires meaning.

Among the ways in which cultural systems differ—and anthropology is the study of the significance of cultural difference—are the ways in which they engage different temporal logics as fundamental rationales of social organization. Social structure, which preserves essential principles, purposes and institutional forms over the generations, is itself a kind of timekeeping.[2] Anthropologists and scholars in other disciplines have longstand-

---

† Associate Professor of Anthropology, Cornell University. An earlier version of the first two sections of this article was presented to the Anthropology Department Colloquium of Cornell University in April, 1988. Any research project that has been in the making for as long as this one benefits from numerous conversations; mine is no exception, and I express appreciation here for my colleagues and students at Cornell. I feel particularly indebted to Professors A.C. Aman, James Boon and Nancy Lutz. The preliminary research for the larger project from which this article derives was funded by a summer stipend from the National Endowment for the Humanities in 1983. I gratefully acknowledge their support.

1. *See* J.G.A. Pocock, Politics, Language and Time: Essays on Political Thought and History 233-72 (1989) (discussing time as social and historical questions and "geochronic" or "cosmochronic" times as scientific concerns).

2. *See* Evans-Pritchard, *Nuer Time-reckoning*, 12 Afr. 189-216 (1939); Fortes, *Time and Social Structure: An Ashanti Case Study*, in Social Structure: Studies Presented to A. R. Radcliffe-Brown 54 (M. Fortes ed. 1949).

ing interests in the connections between social structures and the temporalities they involve. When sociologists Sorokin and Merton[3] coined the term "social time," they sought an idiom that would capture the multiple meanings of time beyond the technology of time-reckoning. The idea of "social time" provides one starting point for this Article.

A second starting point is in the ethnology of law. Ethnology is the comparative study of sociocultural systems. The ethnology of law and academic law share a common intellectual ancestor in Sir Henry Maine, whose *Ancient Law* explores the sources and meanings of legal innovation in Roman society and culture.[4] His modern inheritors on the anthropological side are, in general, concerned with the construction and reproduction over time of normative orders and their social significance in contemporary societies.[5] As the cross-cultural sweep of anthropological studies of law widens, scholars are increasingly confronted with the fundamentally different meanings and arrangements that social order entails in the modern world. Simply stated, notions of what law is and how it operates are far from universal. While this observation adds to the interest of ethnological studies, it also confounds the question of where the starting point of productive comparison might lie.[6]

These two points—the social nature of time and the cultural ramifications of law—converge in issues of the regulation of social processes. In practice, this means that every culture has some constantly dynamic code (or, more probably, a set of rival codes) for controlling competition, contradiction, and irony. In effect, such codes are systems of accountability, for it is through notions of accountability that societies formally attach social meaning to individual experience. To this we must add the observation that social systems never sit still, but constantly improvise, negotiate, contest, celebrate, and lament change. Where institutionalized law exists, it claims for itself many formal roles in managing normative change.

Time is about many things, but it is always ironic; it always implies that there is meaning beyond lived experience that nevertheless constitutes a commentary on lived experience. Time, whatever its "shape," calls forth loyalties of various kinds: to God, land, descent group, king, nation, employer, one's children, and so on. Concepts of time might be dominated by

---

3. Sorokin & Merton, *Social Time: A Methodological and Functional Analysis*, 42 AM. J. SOC. 615-29 (1937).

4. H. MAINE, ANCIENT LAW (1986) (1st ed. 1861).

5. For synoptic views of this literature, see Collier, *Legal Processes*, in ANNUAL REVIEW OF ANTHROPOLOGY 121; Moore, *Law and Anthropology*, in BIENNIAL REVIEW OF ANTHROPOLOGY 1969, at 252-300 (B. Siegel ed. 1970); Nader, *The Anthropological Study of Law*, 67 AM. ANTHROPOLOGIST 3 (1965); Snyder, *Anthropology, Dispute Processes and Law: A Critical Introduction*, 8 BRIT. J.L. & SOC'Y 141 (1981); Starr & Collier, *Introduction: Dialogues in Legal Anthropology*, in HISTORY AND POWER IN THE STUDY OF LAW 1-28 (J. Starr & J. Collier eds. 1989)

6. *See generally* J. COMAROFF & S. ROBERTS, RULES AND PROCESSES: THE CULTURAL LOGIC OF DISPUTE IN AN AFRICAN CONTEXT 3-21 (1981); C. GEERTZ, LOCAL KNOWLEDGE 167-234 (1983).

one "shape" or another (e.g., a circle, line, or pendulum motion) or by no shape at all (later, I call one version of shapeless time "all-times"), but all concepts of time are flexible, permeable, and capable of proliferation. Thus, to refer to time's form is inevitably merely a shorthand for referring to cultural strategies for managing the ***multiple*** forms of time that are simultaneously available in any single social context.[7] For the same reason, social structures are never permanently fixed or free of internal contradictions that are potentially undermining.

Time could never be socially neutral, even where it appears to Western eyes to be closest to the "givens" of birth and death. Time is not everywhere thought to be about the interval between birth and death,[8] nor everywhere about "lifetimes" or even individuals.[9] The ethnological literature shows that many concepts of time may be immanent in any single social system, and even in any single situation. Temporal discourse varies sometimes with age[10] and gender,[11] sometimes with status,[12] and, generally, with differing forms of social participation. Institutions that regulate social change must also, therefore, regulate the play and contestation of the multiple temporal logics that inhere in situations, and make temporal commitments themselves. Thus, the "shapes" of time are not inscribed as fixed geometric blueprints in a culture's *mentalité*, but are contested, negotiated, defended, and transformed in the juxtaposition of personal and institutional forms that comprise social life anywhere.

To put this more directly: "We" moderns are supposed to know that time is "really" linear and infinitely so. We are supposed to know that time is about motion, change, mortality, and progress. We are supposed to know that linear time rationalized the periodicity of cyclical time and lifted the veils of timelessness from the now-visible face of human experience, and that the clock is the essential technology of modern life.[13] But "we" have also devised a strategy for resisting linear time: we imagine

---

7. One of the premises of this article is that time concepts are always implicitly multiple. In some contexts, the simultaneity of explicitly competing or divergent temporal forms makes an interesting subset of the anthropological literature. *See* C. GEERTZ, *Person, Time, and Conduct in Bali*, in THE INTERPRETATION OF CULTURES 360 (1973); A. ORTIZ, THE TEWA WORLD (1969) (on the Tewa Pueblos of New Mexico); LeGoff, *Au Moyen Age: Temps de l'Eglise et Temps du Marchand*, 15 ANNALES: E.S.C. 417 (1960) (on medieval Europe); Turton & Ruggles, *Agreeing to Disagree: The Measurement of Duration in a Southwestern Ethiopian Community*, 19 CURRENT ANTHROPOLOGY 585 (1978) (on tribal Ethiopians).

8. The dreamtime of the Australian aborigines is not. *See, e.g.*, W. STANNER, WHITE MAN GOT NO DREAMING: ESSAYS 1938–1973, at 23 (1979).

9. Time is about social collectivities among the Merina. *See, e.g.*, Bloch, *Death, Women and Power*, in DEATH AND THE REGENERATION OF LIFE 211 (M. Bloch & J. Parry eds. 1982).

10. *See, e.g.*, H. HAZAN, THE LIMBO PEOPLE 89–117 (1980).

11. *See, e.g.*, L. DOOB, PATTERNING OF TIME (1971).

12. *See, e.g.*, LeShan, *Time Orientation and Social Class*, 47 J. ABNORMAL SOC. PSYCHOLOGY 589–92 (1952).

13. *See generally* S. TOULMIN & J. GOODFIELD, THE DISCOVERY OF TIME (1965); Goody, *Time: Social Organization*, in 16 INTERNATIONAL ENCYCLOPEDIA OF THE SOCIAL SCIENCES 30 (D. Sills ed. 1968).

that there exist people not preoccupied with change; we are supposed to know that some of *them* are happier, more sociable, more provincial, more attuned to nature and less skeptical of their rituals.[14] If we are romantics, we imagine ourselves experiencing this liberation in love, faith, or travel to exotic places. If we are *post*-moderns, though, we also know that we are not supposed to think this.[15] The difficulty of developing intellectual strategies for dismantling the privileges of linear time cross-culturally and, even more so, in the examination of more familiar cultural terrain, is compounded by such contemporary Western engagements with the idea of time.

I. Linear Time

The idea of linear time that now dominates public life in the West (and elsewhere) was not indigenous to the West. Linear time came to Europe with Christianity.[16] It was the concern of specialists—theologians—and became a popular idea by a long, slow, and interesting process. European conceptions of time underwent a major transformation beginning in the late twelfth century. It was then that the popularization of linear time was greatly accelerated by a wide variety of changes in thought and public life.[17] The European invention of the mechanical clock (though this was not the first mechanical clock) in 1354 gave impetus and definition to new ideas about time.[18]

The expansion of Christianity into Europe brought with it two ideas about time that had long roots in Jewish and autochthonous Christian tradition: first, the origin of time in Creation, and second, the end of time in a Day of Judgment. The linearity of time derives simply from the geometric connection between these two endpoints.[19] These arrived as new ideas to Europe, and it is difficult to know how they affected ordinary people as they encountered them in the long process of Europe's conversion to Christianity.[20]

---

14. *See generally* Bloch, *The Past and the Present in the Present*, 12 MAN 278-92 (1977).

15. *See* J. FABIAN, TIME AND THE OTHER: HOW ANTHROPOLOGY MAKES ITS OBJECT (1983).

16. *See* LeGoff, *supra* note 7. The idea of linear time as the segment between creation and Judgment Day was initially a theological concern, and gradually became laicized. O. CULLMANN, CHRIST and TIME: THE PRIMITIVE CHRISTIAN CONCEPTION OF TIME AND HISTORY 51-60 (F. Filson trans. 1964).

17. *See, e.g.*, J. HUIZINGA, THE WANING OF THE MIDDLE AGES (1924) (new humanism and industrial workshops).

18. *See* L. MUMFORD, TECHNICS AND CIVILIZATION 13 (1934).

19. *See* O. CULLMANN, *supra* note 16, at 51.

20. Goody's analysis of changes in family structure and inheritance as a result of early Church conversion efforts beginning in the fourth century suggests that local populations responded to Church doctrine fairly quickly. J. GOODY, THE DEVELOPMENT OF THE FAMILY AND MARRIAGE IN EUROPE 33, 44-46 (1983). But other social historians suggest that the idea of one's own lifetime as personal property came much later. E. LADURIE, MONTAILLOU (1978); J. LEGOFF, POUR UN AUTRE MOYEN AGE: TEMPS, TRAVAIL ET CULTURE EN OCCIDENT (1977); Thompson, *Time, Work-Discipline and Industrial Capitalism*, 38 PAST & PRESENT 56-97 (1967). This is not necessarily a contradiction, in that there is no reason to think that the implications of linear time were fully worked out or unchang-

The early theologians wrote about time as "a segment of eternity"; eternity is "endless time."[21] Time was believed to belong to God, a belief which had numerous practical consequences as well as theoretical ones.[22] The keystone of medieval philosophy was the proposition that God is not only the unique "total being" (*totum esse*) but also the unique "true being" (*verum esse*); hence, the visible, sensible world was by definition (since God monopolizes all authenticity) "mere appearance."[23] Time, which was limited to the world of humankind, *represents* this incompleteness in this worldview. Individuals could aspire to completion only in salvation, that is, in joining God. God, always (and uniquely) total and true, existed outside of time, since there was nothing else that he could become, or could have been. Thus, the social logic of linear time took shape.

Late medieval Christianity was by no means a single entity,[24] but historians stress the prevalence and persistence of ideas of time and eternity.[25] All of time was the history of salvation; therefore, the very idea of duration was charged with sacred significance.[26] Linear time became the constant marker of the contingent and incomplete nature of human society and of every individual's life.[27] The advancement of time, always toward Judgment Day, represented the advancement of human perfectibility, always relative to the perfect completeness of God. Time was "a certain mode of existence proper to contingent things, unable to realize themselves all at once in the permanence of a stable present."[28] The instant was drenched in the poignancy of impossibility: the impossibility of refusing the struggle for perfection, and the impossibility of succeeding in it. This irony became the very meaning—the enduring meaning—of the idea of a life*time*.[29]

---

ing (they continue to be worked out and to change now), or that they were experienced simultaneously.

21. *See* O. CULLMANN, *supra* note 16, at 62–63; *see also* LeGoff, *supra* note 7, at 419.

22. *See* J. LEGOFF, LA CIVILISATION DE L'OCCIDENT MÉDIÉVAL 169-248 (1965); R. TAWNEY, RELIGION AND THE RISE OF CAPITALISM (1962).

23. *See* E. GILSON, THE SPIRIT OF MEDIEVAL PHILOSOPHY 64 (A.H.C. Downes trans. 1940).

24. *See* G. LEFF, HERESY IN THE LATER MIDDLE AGES: THE RELATION OF HETERODOXY TO DISSENT C. 1250–C. 1450, at 26 (1967).

25. *See* J. LEGOFF, *supra* note 22, at 211–12; Dales, *Discussions of the Eternity of the World During the First Half of the Twelfth Century*, 57 SPECULUM 495–508 (1982).

26. *See* LeGoff, *supra* note 7, at 420.

27. *See* E. GILSON, *supra* note 23, at 385.

28. *Id.*

29. However great the significance and anxiety about the impending day of judgment, ordinary medieval Europeans were unconcerned with time-keeping and recording time, *see* 1 M. BLOCH, FEUDAL SOCIETY ch. 5, § 1 (1964); M. GILMORE, THE WORLD OF HUMANISM 1453–1517, at 201 (1952); E. LADURIE, *supra* note 20; J. LEGOFF, *supra* note 22, at 222, though medieval time-keeping methods are not well understood today. Wolff, *Le Temps et Sa Mesure au Moyen Age*, 17 ANNALES: E.S.C. 1141–45 (1962). The idea of life as a measurable property received an incalculable impetus from the invention of the mechanical clock in the middle of the fourteenth century. L. MUMFORD, *supra* note 18, at 14. Although the inspiration for this innovation may have been the needs of clerics, *id.* at 12, its widespread use facilitated the laicization of time, J. LEGOFF, *supra* note 20, at 67. The clock rapidly became an urban phenomenon, a key symbol of secular power. Debates over the connection between forms of power and technologies of time-reckoning suggest that the connection is con-

Eventually, clocks moved from steeples to palaces and town halls, as potent symbols of dominion. The ticking clock was not only a *memento mori*, but a reminder of the ownership of time. The fact that debates over wages, interest payments and secular government in general took place in these terms underscores the extent to which linear time calls forth a declaration of the ultimate instrumentality of time in social terms.[30] Linear time is time with a purpose: a time-for-the-sake-of-God, -state, -shop, -self, among other possibilities. The linearity of time reproduces both the cry for redemption and redemption's form in its fundamental proposition that the individual can find completion only by participating in a cosmic order—through social institutions that await the end of time.

II. The Indeterminacies of Linear Time

One way of summing up this discussion of linear time in Europe is to say that linear time's most powerful claim is that of its own redemptive power in relation to an individual's life (for example, fulfillment always implies a passage of time in this worldview). *There* is where the redemptive promise of linear time lies. *There* is where linear time provides a reservoir of symbols with which the legitimacy of hierarchies can be defended and reproduced. But *there* is precisely where linear time must defend itself conceptually, since any life entails multiple and simultaneous engagements involving competing priorities and loyalties. Linear time intrinsically demands a single principle of selection (or a single hierarchy of principles; for example, a subject simultaneously serves the king and God, because the king serves God), but real life is not so neatly arranged.

Linear time did not displace indigenous time concepts in Europe so much as it added itself to them in the life of the new institutions which made linear time socially relevant. As we have already seen, to the extent that people cared about time at all, their temporality was cyclical, organized in terms of binary oppositions (day/night, summer/winter, et cetera) between which time moved in pendulum fashion.[31] As new institutional forms developed—industrial workshops, the state, contracts and courts—different forms of time multiplied as they were juxtaposed in contiguous social fields. Such proliferations continue today, in the West as well as the other places where different temporalities come into contact as social tensions—for example, work and family life, the market and faith, aspiration and consolation.

vincing in general, but controversial in detail; for additional data and discussion of these controversies, see D. Landes, The Revolution in Time (1983); J. Needham, W. Ling & D.J. DeSolla Price, Heavenly Clockwork: The Great Astronomical Clocks of Medieval China (1960). In any event, L. Mumford, *supra* note 18, at 14–17, ascribes the symbolic power of the clock to its dissociation of time from human events; time-keeping became time-serving.

30. *See* J. LeGoff, *supra* note 20; R. Tawney, *supra* note 22, at 44–55; Thomas, *Work and Leisure in Pre-industrial Societies*, 29 Past & Present 50–62 (1964).

31. *See* E. Leach, Rethinking Anthropology 124 (1961).

If linear time dominates our public lives it is because its primary efficacy is in the construction and management of dominant social institutions, not because it is the only "kind" of time that is culturally available. Linear time in the West was popularized by the church, by monarchs, and eventually by other elites who found in an image of time's unidirectional progress the central symbol of their legitimacy. Linear time, however, cannot fulfill its own claims to redemptive completeness without borrowing from the other temporal idioms that express other, equally sacred meanings from other domains, for example, the idioms of cyclical time. Cyclical time idioms suffuse Western concepts of private life and personal life: birth and death, the generations, dust to dust, the ages of man, marriage, parenting—all of these cultural images invoke cyclical time.

Indeed, cyclical and linear time compete with each other in Western culture. Their clearest competition is in cultural notions of the individual life, which is itself an intersection of two domains: ideas about the *creation* of life (birth, maturity, aging, death), and other ideas about the *meaning* of life. Cyclical time offers the primary idiom of life's creation as the reciprocal of personal death. Linear time makes a person's life just another segment in the larger progress of time in relation to eternity (to the extent that modern secular thinking does not utterly conflate time and eternity). Cyclical time emphasizes substance in its constant alternation (in the Western case) between opposed and reciprocal states (for example, life and death, hot and cold, day and night). Linear time emphasizes historical form in its continual juxtaposition of equivalent intervals.

Both forms of time share and express a long Indo-European cultural tradition that stresses the reciprocal relationship of society and cosmos, the eternity of matter, the infinity of time and the inevitability of change,[32] although they do so in substantially different ways. Where cyclical time makes death the source of life, linear time makes God the source of time. Where the infinity of time is represented as an unending cycle or pendular motion, it can also be expressed as an unending line. Where constant change can be conceptualized as cyclic, linear time expresses a unique cycle (the world being said to have been created only once, by God, a "big bang" or whatever) that is itself a manipulation of the idea of cyclicity.

Linear time does not so much replace cyclical time, as literally reform it within its same general framework. But the reformulation of time can be achieved only if the crucial differences among time's forms can be effectively suppressed. The difference between death as a source of life, and death as the marker of an ineluctable ending, or the difference between life as an event and life as a condition—these differences must somehow be blurred. By rendering the differences indeterminate, this blurring of

32. *See* B. Lincoln, Myth, Cosmos and Society: Indo-European Themes of Creation and Destruction 140 (1986).

particular points of competition among forms of time can be effectively managed. Linear time involves two crucial kinds of indeterminacy—one in the construction of the lifetime (as reciprocal or interval), and the other in the representation of the completeness time claims to represent (linear versus cyclical infinity). Perhaps these are only two sides of the same conceptual coin, in that both involve the "sites" where the respective geometries of linear and cyclical time most conspicuously converge in the individual on the one hand and in ultimate things on the other.

The affirmative power of linear time is in its ability to resolve tensions among priorities, loyalties, and accountabilities. But such power is lost if rival temporalities lose *their* power to create tension. To put this another way, linear time can dominate a society only if its beneficiaries carefully manage the indeterminacies discussed here, loosening time's "line" to engage the widest possible array of human commitments, but tightening it again when the efficacy of public institutions is at stake. We will return to this idea later.

III. Time, Law and Other Institutions

Although the discussion so far makes use of historical data, the analysis is not historical, but cultural. That is, it is about relationships among systems of ideas rather than about events and motives. Cultural analysts stress the self-referential aspects of systems of ideas, but this is not to say that ideas are born in vacuums. A single idea may have many expressions, and so anthropologists are as concerned with how principles of selection develop in relation to the myriad possible enactments of cultural propositions as they are with the propositions themselves. In the case of Europeans' popularizations of linear time, the context is important in shedding light on how the meanings of linear time have become what they are. Hence the discussion in the previous Section. This Section highlights three aspects of that context that have particular bearing on the modern meanings of law in the West.

First, the secularization of linear time—moving the clock from the church steeple to the palace turret—represented a major strategic innovation of medieval statecraft. In effect, by borrowing the church's idiom that situated time in relation to eternity, secular temporal discourse achieved a reification of society by locating the end of time outside of any individual or collective social experience. "Society" thus became a conceptual union of time and place (here is to there as now is to then). This analogy is by no means universal around the world, since its underlying premise (the differentiation of places in terms of the passage of time) is not universal. It is worth noting in passing that society reified in this way cannot escape at least a rhetorical commitment to "progress" as a way of connecting "societies" at different points in time.

Second, secular monarchies eventually resolved the contradictions between an enduring kingship and a mortal king with the notion of "the king's two bodies," that is, differentiating between the office of the king and the occupant of the office.[33] This conceptualization of incumbency is not universal, either, though it is by no means unique to Europe.[34] Before the idea of the King's two bodies was established, the king had become the symbol of the state, as shown by the idea of treason, new in Edward III's time in England.[35] Treason in England acquired statutory definition before any other crime (in 1352); that is, the symbolic status of the state was (and had to be) established before acts could be prosecuted in "its" name. The important point here is that this symbolic status was achieved by regularizing the temporal contradictions of kingship by embracing *both* the king's mortal person *and* the enduring kingship within a single institutional form. The scholarly assessment that Europe's legal development was revolutionary in the medieval period appears to be widely accepted.[36]

Third, by the time the modern period began, law had become the dominant image of conflict resolution,[37] linking king and subject—at least hypothetically—in the integument of everyday life. Extensive changes in European legal institutions and law were but one element of wider patterns of social and cultural change. This was the era that saw the development of cities,[38] major changes in church doctrine,[39] and profound changes in the structure of the economy. By the end of the medieval period, Europe had the common law, written contracts, juries, academic law, and, more generally, a wider use of the law, in the prosecution and defense of individual interests.[40] In any event, both legal institutions and their pattern of use at the end of the medieval period seem relatively more familiar to the modern eye than what preceded it.[41]

---

33. *See* E. KANTOROWICZ, THE KING'S TWO BODIES (1963).

34. *See, e.g.*, J. GOODY, SUCCESSION TO HIGH OFFICE (1966).

35. *See* 3 W. HOLDSWORTH, A HISTORY OF ENGLISH LAW 287-89 (3d ed. 1927).

36. *See, e.g.*, M. GIBBS, FEUDAL ORDER 106 (1949). For a discussion of the development of English common law, see A. HARDING, A SOCIAL HISTORY OF ENGLISH LAW 13 (1966).

37. *See* J. BOSSY, DISPUTES AND SETTLEMENTS: LAW AND HUMAN RELATIONS IN THE WEST 287 (1983) (discussing images of feud, charity, and law).

38. *See* C. CIPOLLA, BEFORE THE INDUSTRIAL REVOLUTION 143-49 (2d ed. 1980).

39. *See, e.g.*, J. LEGOFF, LA NAISSANCE DU PURGATOIRE 9 (1981) ("invention" of Purgatory).

40. *See* 1 M. BLOCH, *supra* note 29, at 113-20. The fifteenth century was "the golden age of litigation," Kagan, *A Golden Age of Litigation: Castile 1500-1700*, in DISPUTES AND SETTLEMENTS: LAW AND HUMAN RELATIONS IN THE WEST 145-66 (J. Bossy ed. 1983) [hereinafter DISPUTES AND SETTLEMENTS], so widespread had it become—and the most frequent litigant was the king.

41. Anglo-Saxon law was kin-based. *See* 1 F. POLLOCK & F. MAITLAND, THE HISTORY OF ENGLISH LAW BEFORE THE TIME OF EDWARD I 31 (2d ed. 1959). Land disputes were regularly resolved through trial by battle, A. HARDING, *supra* note 36, at 41, and the blood feud persisted in northern Europe until "well into the medieval period." Wormald, *The Blood Feud in Early Modern Scotland*, in DISPUTES AND SETTLEMENTS, *supra* note 40, at 101, 102. An early role of the church in local dispute settlement in sixth-century Gaul was to intervene to end blood feuds; records from this period also show the legal use of ordeals and oaths. *See* James, *'Beati pacifici': Bishops and the Law in Sixth-Century Gaul*, in DISPUTES AND SETTLEMENTS, *supra* note 40, at 25, 32-33. The ancient law of Belgium and northern France distinguished not personal rights but family rights. 1 E.M.

The common law, which developed at this period, in some respects reflects perfectly a logic of linear time, in its reliance on precedent, its commitment to reform, and its acknowledgment of individual persons and rights. But the common law also involves larger claims beyond linear time. Reasoning by analogy to precedent creates a *false* historicity in that it perpetually reclaims the past for the present: in theory, a dispute in 1989 can be resolved by reference to cases from 1889 or 1389. "The law" thus accumulates, but it never passes; at any instant, it represents a totality. It is by definition complete, yet its completeness does not preclude change. It is a human achievement, yet, by its reversible and lateral excursions, and by its collective voice, it is not identifiably the product of any *particular* individual or group. Symbolically, it stands at the border between the two great zones of Indo-European thinking—the human-made (the anthropogonic) and the divine (cosmogonic)—and is nourished by the indeterminacy of the distinction between events in linear time and possibilities (all-times).[42]

Law[43] has a mythic dimension, in its self-totalization, its quality of being in time (in that it is a human product) but also out of time (where did it or does it begin or end?) and in its promise of systematic yet permutable meaning. This myth is essentially a temporal one. Specifically, the law's implicit claim is to invoke the total system of its own distinctions simultaneously in a way that both individualizes subjects/citizens and orients them toward particular forms of action.[44] That such symbolism has been effective only since the late Middle Ages reveals the continued capacity of modern society to generate myth. For the myth to remain viable, the law must continually reiterate the distinctions between law and interests, the ephemeral and the enduring, the political and the sacred.

MEIJERS, ÉTUDES D'HISTOIRE DU DROIT 228 (1956). The same could be said of England, where the early state had to compete against the family. *See* 1 F. POLLOCK & F. MAITLAND, *supra*, at 31. After the Normans appeared concepts of absolute liability, *id.* at 54, both apparently successfully directed at strengthening and extending the power of the king over a hostile countryside. The regularization of law in England under the Normans is credited with resolving serious problems of disorder which had persisted since the break-up of tribal kingdoms in the eighth century. M. GIBBS, *supra* note 36, at 60.

42. Berman argues that the critical formative issue in modern Western law is its origins in canon law, and the canon law's embedded premises about the contingencies of the Last Days. Thus, the modern nation would involve conceptions of transcendence. H. BERMAN, LAW AND REVOLUTION: THE FORMATION OF THE WESTERN LEGAL TRADITION 49–119 (1983).

43. I use the word "law" in the broad sense here and below, acknowledging distinctions to be drawn in some contexts (but not, I think, in this Article) among the common law, constitutional law, and statutory interpretation. *See* Monaghan, *The Supreme Court, 1974 Term—Foreword: Constitutional Common Law*, 89 HARV. L. REV. 1, 4–5 (1975). In general, my usage emphasizes cultural ideas about law, which may or may not be descriptive of legal operations.

44. I take this definition of myth from the work of Claude Lévi-Strauss. *See, e.g.*, C. LÉVI-STRAUSS, THE JEALOUS POTTER (1988).

IV. The Law and Its Times

So far, this Article has focussed on general issues of social structure, temporality, and law in Europe and the West. In effect, the argument has been that, given the social context in which linear time was received and popularized in Europe, linear time is "about" the crucial indeterminacies between the individual lifetime and the enduring public institutions which claim an individual's consciousness and, potentially, service. These indeterminacies are essential in that they go to the very crux of what linear time is "for" in the West, that is, the redemption of individual lifetimes through participation in the social and cosmic order. Further, they must be preserved as indeterminacies for the system to work. In the West, it is the law's cultural role to do just this. The law represents itself in ways that situate it at precisely these indeterminate points, resolving conflicts one at a time while gesturing toward the totality of all resolutions of all hypothetically possible conflicts. (The contrast at issue in that gesture is that of an actual human being, as opposed to the printed words "plaintiff" and "defendant.") Western cultural notions of law give it this mythic aspect, which is by no means universally the "property" of the law.

Let us turn now to a modern, familiar social field in which these themes are expressed, negotiated, and reproduced. The remainder of this Article offers an extended illustrative case, and that is in the general domain of judicial succession at the United States Supreme Court. I have chosen the Supreme Court because it is the highest court of the nation, and so by its very nature must be concerned with strategies for defining and protecting its own unique status as the ultimate *national* legal authority. I focus on succession because it is there that anthropologists look to find the most explicit cultural definition of office in relation to social structures and groups. An office is a scarce resource, and the cultural concerns that surround its allocation are highly revealing of indigenous conceptions of social structure.[45] Eligibles may be determined in any number of ways—from primogeniture to battle to popular election and so on—but they are determined somehow, and that is key. Installation may be marked with ceremony, or it may not, and these rituals are laden with significance for anyone interested in the wider meanings encoded in systems of statuses and roles. The ethnological literature is helpful on each of these points.

Judicial succession is particularly relevant to the general problem of this Article in that it is precisely in succession that multiple temporalities—of the law, personal lifetimes, and public lives—and their indeterminacies must be worked out. I must stress that I refer here to cultural

45. *See* J. Goody, *supra* note 34, at 2.

representations of succession—the ideal—and, eventually, the sorts of practical problems that those ideals generate.

The law in the United States (but not only there) must juggle at least three essentially different forms of time. First, at least in public life, Americans inherit a dominant temporal culture that stresses the linear, infinite nature of time and simultaneously the finite irreversibility of any individual's lifetime. This means that while modern secular thought suspends the beginning and end points of time as indeterminate, it nonetheless celebrates them in the "certainty" of time's passage from past to present. No two moments repeat, and the passage of time is both regular and regulated according to international standards.[46] This is the kind of time of ethnic and national histories.[47]

But a second temporality is in the law itself. As we have already proposed, the law involves the constant expansion of a linear time framework (in the production and use of "precedent," for example, but not only by extending the "time-line" further forward or back). This is a form of timelessness, or, more accurately, *all-times*, a form of time which stipulates time as social, but not with geometric metaphors. Importantly, the endpoint of the law in time is neither fixed nor envisioned. Significantly, though, it is symbolically coterminous with a national social life, and it represents that national life in temporal terms.[48] As mentioned earlier, the mythic aspects of law that inhere in this conception of things set the law apart from the many other institutions in which conflicts can be resolved and the normative repertoire adjusted. The mythic aspects of the law that inhere in its special expanded temporality are essential to its claims to neutrality, both in the sense of being capable of balancing competing interests, and engaging in a values discourse.[49] If linear time is the time that connects individual interests to the state, then neutrality in a linear time idiom requires a symbolism of all-times.[50]

The time of the law is distinctive not only for its cumulative aspect, but also because it is reversible. The law exists in reversible time in two senses, that is, in that prior decisions can control present ones, and also in

---

46. *See* Zerubavel, *The Standardization of Time: A Sociohistorical Perspective*, 88 AM. J. SOC. 1 (1982).

47. *See* Chock, *The Outsider Wife and the Divided Self: The Genesis of Ethnic Identities*, in DISCOURSE AND THE SOCIAL LIFE OF MEANING 185–204 (P. Chock & J. Wyman eds. 1986); Kahn, *Reason and Will in the Origins of American Constitutionalism*, 98 YALE L.J. 449, 509 (1988). For a discussion of neutrality in the ethnology of law, see Greenhouse, *Mediation: A Comparative Approach*, 20 MAN 90–114 (1985).

48. *See* Kahn, *supra* note 47, at 508–16.

49. That justices themselves must struggle with the meaning of neutrality is also relevant here. *See* Kahn, *The Court, the Community and the Judicial Balance: The Jurisprudence of Justice Powell*, 97 YALE L.J. 1 (1987).

50. Neutrality is defined differently around the world, as well as in different situations in the same context, along several converging continua: knowing or not knowing the parties, having an interest in the outcome or not, participating as an equal or as a superior—the anthropological literature on law offers multiple examples of each of these possibilities.

that prior decisions can be reversed. The reversible aspect of the law is another important hallmark of its mythic nature. It symbolically underscores its claims to transcend any particular era or individual's life (more on this below). It also symbolically connects the law to nature itself—that peculiarly reasoned and authored nature of the late eighteenth century that made God, law, reason, and nature share a single set of principles.[51] I will argue later that the law's particular temporality generates the key symbols of the American judiciary—even though the law has many sources, and modern skepticism has challenged the specifics (though not the symbols in the civic culture) of the enlightenment view of things.[52]

But finally, there is a third kind of time embedded in the law, and that is the judges' own lifetimes. In stark contrast—the starkest possible—to the law's self-totalizing, reversible, and boundless accumulations, judges' lives are finite. This problem is by no means unique to judicial succession in the United States. Any conception of time that has shape and direction focuses attention on the incongruities of sustaining the legitimacy of the system while vesting individuals with its authority. In the special time of the law, which is multidirectional rather than nondirectional, qualification becomes a particular cultural dilemma as well as a practical problem that goes to the very heart of the judiciary's cultural legitimacy.

In the process of filling a vacant seat on the Supreme Court, all three of these times come vibrantly into play. A vacancy is ordinarily caused by the death of the incumbent, or anticipated age- or health-related decline of competence. Life tenure potentially secures long service from an individual Justice, and yet his or her performance can involve no conspicuous apprenticeship. The new Justice will be selected by the two "other," political branches of government, and is in itself a partisan, if not political, event.[53] The special temporal symbolism of the law requires a special "kind" of person, one who will find the law, not make it; know the law, but not preach it; be a representative of the national community, but have no causes of his or her own. These three temporal charters are by no means easily reconciled. Their reconciliation is possible only with the deft management of essential temporal symbols, that is, by downplaying or

51. M. Horwitz, The Transformation of American Law 1780-1860, at 7 (1977).

52. Ferguson notes that this particular equation (linking law, reason, and nature) emerged in American culture only after the Revolution. R. Ferguson, Law and Letters in American Culture 15-16 (1984). By the time Chief Justice Marshall retired in 1835, the Supreme Court had become "the great oracle of Americanism." *Id.* at 23.

53. The fact that the confirmation hearings for Supreme Court nominees are now televised, and widely viewed, reinforces several aspects of the process from a cultural perspective. As Gitlin suggests in his discussion of the impact of the televised Watergate hearings, public participation in the process via television tends to sharpen the cultural distinction between an office and its incumbent. T. Gitlin, Watching Television 31 (1986). Yet the media "transform the great silence of things into its opposite" by means of a narrative of "what's-going-on." M. de Certeau, The Practice of Everyday Life 185 (S. Rendall trans. 1984). This is radically at odds with the public silence the Justices conventionally preserve about the development and negotiation of judicial opinions.

suppressing altogether aspects of a judicial "career" that entail *becoming*. It is in *becoming* a judge that any tensions between individuality and a judicial persona would be most evident.[54]

V. LAW, LIFE, AND TIME

Regular succession to office calls not only for institutionalizing the principles by which competition for office can be controlled (this is what succession means), but also for sequencing eligibility for office. Another way of stating this is that we speak of "succession" when it is a question of the incumbent's fitting the role, rather than the other way around. The ethnological literature offers highly diverse examples of modes of succession and their accompanying ritualizations.[55]

Before reopening the cross-cultural questions, though, we must consider what sort of person is culturally considered to be qualified for the Supreme Court.[56] The answer would not stir much controversy; what follows is literally a textbook definition:

> One, demonstrated judicial temperament. Two, professional expertise and competence. Three, absolute personal as well as professional integrity. Four, an able, agile, lucid mind. Five, appropriate professional educational background or training. Six, the ability to communicate clearly, both orally and in writing, especially the latter.[57]

Several things are striking about this set of criteria: first, they are presented as if they describe an *exceptional* individual, yet they evoke attributes that one might assume are widely and positively valued in society. Second, the list is evenly balanced among general statements of professional experience and personal attributes that are not aspects of experience. Third, the description implies that a judicial temperament is reinforced by the ability to reason; furthermore, while communication skills are clearly important, it is not ordinary social conversation that is key, but "especially" one's writing ability. Murphy offers a metaphor for this personal and professional elite when he refers to the Justices' "performance of their priestly duty of expounding the meaning of that holy writ [the Constitution]."[58] The metaphor is perhaps at the heart of the matter: in the United States, the judiciary is the only robed branch. The robes (like those of American academics in procession) are those of (medieval) clerics.

54. Kantorowicz describes parallel debates over kingship in ancient Greece, as to whether the person who becomes king does so by receiving grace at the moment of installation, or by imitating the divine. E. KANTOROWICZ, *supra* note 33, at 500.

55. *See infra* text accompanying notes 61-69.

56. Again, I must stress that this is not the same as asking what sorts of persons have actually been considered for the Supreme Court; this article is about idealizations and symbols.

57. H. ABRAHAM, JUSTICES AND PRESIDENTS: A POLITICAL HISTORY OF APPOINTMENTS TO THE SUPREME COURT 4 (2d ed. 1985).

58. W. MURPHY, ELEMENTS OF JUDICIAL STRATEGY 16 (1964).

In effect, in terms of the symbolic claims of their office, Justices must literally embody neutrality; they are literally "judicial bodies." That their relationship to the law is metonymic rather than metaphoric implies important cultural constraints on the notion of representation as an aspect of the judicial role. In the case of the Supreme Court, the kind of neutrality that is culturally valued is a very particular one, in that the Justices are accountable "to the people" but in a way that precludes any legitimate scope for the expression of their own interests or personal views. Indeed, they are "supposed" to have no interests; this renunciation of particular private interests symbolically inverts to become, in effect, an embrace of all public interests.[59] The alternative (renunciation as other-worldly) would contradict the other stipulations that a Justice be an exemplary individual without being a hero. A Justice should reason, without the exercise of will;[60] a Justice must be the law, but he must also be society without representing either. Such are the symbolic prescriptions of the judicial office.

While the prescription for eligibility to the Court clearly demands an exceptional individual, it is mute on the question of how and when an individual comes to be inscribed with these qualities. This is an important cultural silence: at stake in it are other, larger questions about the nature of social life. For example, if Justices are literally to be found, then the implication is that there is a natural hierarchy of men and women that makes some fit for service and others not, and the authority and power of the President and Senate are symbolically downplayed. On the other hand, if Justices are made at the moment of their nomination—if it is then, and only then, that their renunciation of private interests takes place—then the conceptualization of the law is democratized and the authority and power of the President and Senate to select the Justice are symbolically emphasized. This is something of a dilemma for a society culturally committed to ideals of egalitarianism as well as the equality of the three branches of government. In effect, the time of the nation (linear, progressive time) and the time of the law (linear, cumulative time) compete for symbolic dominance over the process.

The installation of new Justices is so minimally ritualized—American civic ritual is characteristically truncated—that one must look elsewhere for signs of how the explicit negotiation of the law's multiple temporalities might proceed. Here, the ethnological literature is helpful, particularly where the temporal indeterminacies of law are roughly congruent. Such

59. *See* Kahn, *supra* note 49, at 56–57.

60. *Id.* at 4–5. Kelman develops Unger's discussion of the distinction between desire and reason in liberal thought; desire individuates and reason universalizes. M. KELMAN, A GUIDE TO CRITICAL LEGAL STUDIES 65 (1987). Later, Kelman relates this world view to a vision of law and truth as being beyond history. *Id.* at 229. *See also* Mensch, *The History of Mainstream Legal Thought*, in THE POLITICS OF LAW: A PROGRESSIVE CRITIQUE 19-26 (D. Kairys ed. 1982).

congruence can be found in the traditional ritual chieftainships of central and western Africa, which also symbolically addressed incongruities among simultaneous temporalities, in ways that make their juxtaposition to American Justices productive. A brief excursion follows.

Chiefs, who ordinarily were members of a royal or chiefly clan or lineage, were understood to be otherwise ordinary mortal men. The chiefship, on the other hand, was associated with the regulation of the rains and other enduring natural cycles. Thus, the two salient temporalities were those of individual lifetimes and the larger cyclical idioms that expressed the society's relationship to nature.[61] Furthermore, at least among the Bashu of Eastern Zaire, the chiefship itself (as opposed to the chief) marked the cycles of time. When the ritual chief died, or failed to ritually protect the land, pollution (which is always present) accumulated along with other negative social effects, and famine resulted; in practice, the one was literally the sign of the other: "The power of chiefship . . . is thus seen as fluctuating through time. It is, in fact, viewed as an almost organic substance that grows, declines, and is reborn. . . . Thus the waxing and waning of the land, cycles of plenty and famine, are directly tied to the waxing and waning of chiefship."[62] The role of the ritual chief was complex; at its core, he absorbed the pollution that otherwise would have poisoned the community by fixing it in his own body.

Central African chiefs came to their offices by a combination of factors, both ascribed and achieved. While they might become eligible for the chiefship by virtue of their birth, their actual candidacy was a function of their performance skills in the conduct of the community's affairs.[63] A central political arena (where such skills could be appropriately displayed) in traditional villages was the court, where royal representatives, or the king himself, heard disputes in a public forum.[64] Chiefdoms and kingdoms identified strongly with their own law; many indigenous African cultures had an explicit cultural category for law.[65] The law and the social existence of the community were symbolically coterminous, in contrast to power, which was the property of the royal lineage or the kingship itself.[66]

---

61. *See* M. FORTES, RELIGION, MORALITY AND THE PERSON: ESSAYS ON TALLENSI RELIGION 94 (1987); R. PACKARD, CHIEFSHIP AND COSMOLOGY: AN HISTORICAL STUDY OF POLITICAL COMPETITION 24-32 (1981).

62. *See* R. PACKARD, *supra* note 61, at 31.

63. *See* J. COMAROFF & S. ROBERTS, *supra* note 6; M. FORTES, *supra* note 61, at 87; Jones, *Chiefly Succession in Basutoland*, in SUCCESSION TO HIGH OFFICE 57, 61 (J. Goody ed. 1966); Southwold, *Succession to the Throne in Buganda*, in *id.* at 82, 91-92.

64. *See* M. GLUCKMAN, THE JUDICIAL PROCESS AMONG THE BAROTSE OF NORTHERN RHODESIA 1-34 (1967).

65. *See, e.g.*, *id.*; J. COMAROFF & S. ROBERTS, *supra* note 6.

66. *See* Southwold, *supra* note 63, at 82-126.

I use the past tense here because it is temporally accurate, not because the nature of "traditional" or indigenous law is in any way a settled question wherever it has been described. Chanock examines at length the indigenous referents of contemporary "customary" law in Malawi and Zambia. M.

Thus, at stake in succession were not only the symbolic efficacy of the law, but also the literal health of the chiefdom—perhaps each was the corollary of the other. The investiture ceremony among the Bashu unfolded around the central imagery of the new ritual chief's social rebirth.[67] The candidate was given a funeral, and then a surrogate mother, and finally a new social identity as ritual chief. Indeed, throughout central and west Africa the dominant mode of the investiture ceremony appears to have been that of the funeral; at death, the subject-candidate died, the chief was born.[68] These societies addressed the dilemma of the incumbent's single lifetime in relation to the law by symbolically dividing it, letting the ordinary man with his private interests die, and setting the stage for the birth of the new ritual chief who served the entire community. He was symbolically—which is to say literally—not the same person.

The installation ceremony among the Bashu also addressed the other dimension of the law's temporality, and that is its identity with the ebb and flow of nature and society. To be more accurate, that ebb and flow is the circulation of pollution, from the bush to the village and back again. When all is well, the ritual chief kept the pollution at bay by means of his ritual expertise and his ability to absorb (literally to incorporate) the pollution that would otherwise poison the community. The installation ceremony commented on this theme in detail. Since the installation followed the death of a ritual chief who was by definition polluted by virtue of his performance of office, that pollution had to be discharged in a purification rite. Eventually, the new chief, as part of his ceremonial, took on this pollution and transferred it to the bush, leading the way to his own purification. Pollution could not be purified but only ritually displaced; hence the importance of maintaining the succession of the ritual chief,[69] and the succession ritual itself.

Let us return now to the American case, reiterating briefly some parallels with the African contexts briefly described above, and then some contrasts. First, in both the American and African contexts, law is equated with social health.[70] Second, in both contexts law is distinguished from

---

CHANOCK, LAW, CUSTOM AND SOCIAL ORDER: THE COLONIAL EXPERIENCE IN MALAWI AND ZAMBIA (1985). Moore challenges the notion that customary law was in any sense of the word traditional or indigenous. S. MOORE, SOCIAL FACTS AND FABRICATIONS: "CUSTOMARY" LAW ON KILIMANJARO, 1880-1980 (1986).

67. I refer particularly to the Bashu because their ceremony is described in rich detail by Packard. *See* R. PACKARD, *supra* note 61, at 34-42.

68. In addition to Packard, see Forde, *Death and Succession*, in ESSAYS ON THE RITUAL OF SOCIAL RELATIONS 89-123 (M. Gluckman ed. 1962).

69. This is also true among the Tallensi and Ashanti. *See* M. FORTES, *supra* note 61, at 94.

70. There is also an interesting difference at this juncture. Where the African cultures do not define conflict in itself as antisocial or asocial, they do define the community in terms of controlling its antithesis, that is, nature. American culture, too, locates the antithesis of community in nature. In the American case, however, it is conflict that is considered antisocial or asocial, a sign of the "untamed" and therefore, symbolically devalued. *See* Greenhouse, *Courting Difference: Issues of Interpretation*

politics, even though legal officials might in practice be important political actors. Third, legal officials, by their office, mark their distinction from the rest of the community from which they have come. Finally, both systems address parallel temporal incongruities in that the incumbent of a legal office is mortal, yet the law is identified with a larger temporality. In the African case, this larger temporality is cyclical. In the American case, it is cumulative and reversible.

In contrast to American judicial succession, the African succession rituals referred to here illuminate a cultural armature that is less evident in the American setting. The African succession rituals negotiate specific tensions between the incumbent's lifetime and the time of the law, in effect, by separating his *person* from his *body*. The office of the ritual chief begins with the birth of the new chief—a second birth that brings him to the world as chief. His body is unchanged, but his person is now the chief who occupies and uses his body differently than he did before. The chief can die; the chiefship is time itself.

In the American context there is no public imagery of rebirth to mark the formation of a new Justice—of new justice. To do so would be symbolically dangerous, as I have already mentioned, as it would denote the subordination of the judiciary to the first and second branches, and of law to politics. The Justices are not politically accountable, yet remain accountable by the same indirection as the Tallensi chiefship: the Tallensi chief is accountable to the ancestors, and—only through them—to their living clansmen.[71] Similarly, the Supreme Court Justices are accountable to the American people—an ancestral, or mythic/historical invocation—but not to *particular* people. The Justices no longer live in a single time dimension, but in all the times that have been and are the law. This is one sign of their altered personhood, and it is consistent that they conventionally be held to a public silence, that they forbear from narrating their own decisions and indecisions as personal events, and that their primary discourse be written, not spoken. And, as has already been noted. they must selectively leave the world.

Another sign of their changed personhood, of their second birth—or is it a first death in the American case?—is the subtle transformation of the meaning of their physical bodies. The illnesses of the Justices are strikingly downplayed in the press in relation to those of the president, for example. Their gender, until Justice O'Connor's appointment, was unmarked (male). Their race, until recently, was unmarked (white), and now the refraction of this standard creates new *generic* markers: the public refers to "the Jewish seat," "the black seat." Their bodies are seats.

---

and Comparison in the Study of Legal Ideologies, 22 LAW & SOC'Y REV. 687-707 (1988).

71. M. FORTES, *supra* note 61, at 101.

just as the African chiefships are stools.[72] The only public relevance of their bodies, in other words, is in their occupancy (or not) of a seat. This is not ordinary mortality, with maturation and decline; it is the mortality of gods, as if Justices were born in full mature form at the bench and died in full stride. Here, retirement is metaphorical death. The life of a Justice is no longer the lifetime of the man or woman who became that Justice. All aspects—biographical and political—of *becoming* a Justice are symbolically suppressed. Those aspects are precisely the ones that would (though they cannot) resolve the indeterminacies linking the times of the individual, the law and the nation in relation to the power of the presidency and the Congress.

To continue the foregoing example, why did the Bashu resolve the problem of temporal indeterminacy with a sequential doubling (layman/chief), while American Justices are culturally denied not only their former social selves, but also their own public initiation? Perhaps one answer lies in a repetition of the question. The Bashu could construct a public ritual of becoming, while the Americans cannot. Why, then, was the transition to chiefship so explicit for the Bashu, and so tacit for the American Justices? I believe the answer has to do with their respective cultural conceptualizations and institutionalizations of politics and social order.

In the case of the Bashu, as already noted, the ultimate order of things moved through the chief, in his role as a central point of dispersal of local pollution. The installation ritual equated the chiefship with this role. Without the chief, there was no cosmic order, and when disorder accumulated, it was supposed to be a sign of the chief's suspended legitimacy. In the American case, Justices invoke a parallel image of serving as "an instrument" of the law[73] but with the difference that supposedly coordinate branches of government also create law on very different terms. The threat of disorder in the American judiciary is conceptualized as the overwhelming of the judicial by the political. If the American judiciary avoids articulating its own initiations, it is perhaps because to do so would be to offer too unambiguous a gesture toward the other branches. Those are the branches of events, *quid pro quos*, representation and fixed terms of office, that is, of linear time; the judiciary is the branch of all-times, demanding of Justices something between renunciation and charisma.[74]

Yet, part of the story of the world would be the story of rituals and meanings invented and lost. To turn to the example at hand, if there ever comes a day when new Supreme Court Justices are inaugurated in a public festival, or when Presidents are not, it will be a sign of a profound

72. *Id.* at 88.

73. This image was Chief Justice Marshall's. *See* J.B. White, When Words Lose Their Meaning 255 (1984).

74. *See* J.G.A. Pocock, *supra* note 1, at 243 (discussion of charisma and tradition as entailing different temporalities).

revolution in both the structure of American government and the belief of the people in the possibility of justice under anything like present terms.

CONCLUSION: CULTURE AND JUSTICE

In this Article, the central theme has been the connections—cultural connections—between Western conceptions of temporality and the ways in which the law (in the broad sense of the term) organizes and reproduces an essentially temporal myth. Linear time, which is the cultural preserve of national histories and the public institutions that comprise them, dominates those institutional settings only to the extent that the people who inhabit them (whether managers or employees, presidents or citizens) believe that linear time has a transcendent reality that allows it to absorb all the other temporal idioms that also suffuse daily life, and are potentially its rivals. The Western cultural capacity for that belief was established a thousand years ago, or longer, when institutional and social structural changes gave linear time a path from the sacred domain to the domain of the everyday. That capacity for belief is reproduced in the juxtaposition of institutional forms and temporalities which constitute everyday experience in the modern world. "The law" is cultural not only, or not first, in its patterned processes and outcomes, but in its constitution in multiple temporalities and their indeterminacies. Specifically, law—as an idea—carries cultural force because it engages these temporalities and their critical incongruities so directly.

By exploring contemporary cultural representations of the judiciary, one can find fresh traces of the journey that linear time makes from the sacred to the secular, and back again. In the ordered system of symbols that inhere in the Justices' idealized roles, the multiplicities of time and time's rival possibilities of order find renewed expression. It is beyond the scope of this Article to resolve the question of whether Supreme Court Justices live out the symbols that to some extent define them, or whether they should. Those are important questions, but of an entirely different character than the one this essay addresses. That question is about the means modern society has at its disposal for conceptualizing justice. If "justice" is constituted in a juxtaposition of temporalities—times and all-times—then "justice" implies both a progress for the world and a critique, that is, an imagined vantage point from which history itself might be judged. While legal actors' claims to legitimacy might be conventionally or historically cast in terms of the connection between reason and fixed (timeless) truths, the cultural interpretation developed in this essay has situated the cultural force of the law in its engagement and resolution of multiple, mutually contesting temporalities with the potential for posing rival claims on social actors. To say that the law is cultural does not by itself dismantle the force of the idea of justice, since just at the point where cultural and political inquiry would intersect, justice and Justices return to the separate temporal domains which, in cultural terms, give them life.

[14]

JOURNAL OF LAW AND SOCIETY
VOLUME 14, NUMBER 3, AUTUMN 1987
0263-323X $3.00

Law: A Map of Misreading. Toward a Postmodern Conception of Law

BOAVENTURA DE SOUSA SANTOS*

INTRODUCTION

In *Thus Spoke Zarathustra* Nietzsche announced that the spirit has undergone three metamorphoses.[1] In the first one the spirit becomes a camel; then the camel becomes a lion; and finally the lion becomes a child. While a camel, the spirit allows itself to be loaded with any values or beliefs humanity wants to load it with. But while speeding into the desert the spirit undergoes a second metamorphosis and the camel becomes a lion. The lion is the animal in revolt against the values and beliefs it was loaded with before. The lion is the spirit of negativity that substitutes 'I will' for 'thou shalt'. But because it merely acts against, the lion is a purely negative being, incapable of creating new values to replace the old ones. In order to take this further step the spirit must undergo a third metamorphosis through which the lion becomes a child. As a child the spirit is innocent and forgetting, it is a new beginning, the creation of new values. Only then will the spirit will its own will and conquer its own world.

I would like to suggest that law has also undergone three metamorphoses in the modern era. However, the sequence of the steps has been reversed. In the seventeenth and eighteenth centuries law started out as a child. The new theories of natural law and the liberal political philosophy were a magnificent new creation of values and beliefs that testified to the emergence and consolidation of bourgeois society. But as the nineteenth century wore on, the law became the lion of negativity. It was the time when law was resisting against the demands which the social question had given rise to and which were being pressed into the political agenda by emergent social and political forces. In the twentieth century, and particularly after the Second World War, the law underwent a third metamorphosis. It gave up resistance in docile submission to the whole range of values and beliefs – sometimes complementary, sometimes contradictory – that the different social and political

**Department of Sociology, School of Economics, University of Coimbra, 3000 Coimbra, Portugal.*

This paper is the Journal of Law and Society Annual Lecture, delivered at University College, Cardiff on 5 March 1987. I would like to thank those who in different ways helped me to draw this map of the law. Special thanks are due to Philip Thomas, António Gama, Maria Irene Ramalho, Maria Manuel Marques, Kristin Bumiller, Peter Fitzpatrick and Leonor Marinho Dias.

forces imposed upon it. In sum, law became a camel, and the welfare state is the most salient feature of this process of 'camelisation' of the law.

As we approach the end of the century and start thinking *fin de siècle*, many voices rise against the camelisation of the law. Habermas has spoken of the excessive colonisation of the life-world (*Lebenswelt*) by law.[2] Nonet and Selznick plead for a responsive law[3] and Teubner for a reflexive law.[4] In all these theories there is a call for a new metamorphosis of the law, one that will bring it back again to its proper and natural limits, whatever they may be.

In this paper I will not be interested in the nature or even the possibility of such a metamorphosis. If it can be said that numbers – like reason – play tricks on us, it may well be that the three metamorphoses having already taken place, the magical number three will not allow for a fourth metamorphosis. Or it may be, in Nietzschian terms, that such a metamorphosis will not engender a law with a new spirit but rather a law without a spirit, that is, the end of law, be it a rhetorical end, as in O'Hagan's *The End of Law?*,[5] or a literal end as in Foucault's denounced substitution of disciplinary power for juridical power.[6]

In this paper I am concerned rather with a preliminary task. My starting point is that the camelisation of law has brought with it the camelisation of the sociology of law and, accordingly, that before the 'decamelisation' of the law may be attempted, a full decamelisation of the sociology of law must be accomplished. What are the symptoms of the camelisation of the sociology of law? Probably better than anyone else, Richard Abel has denounced that:

> . . . social studies of law have reached a critical point in their development. The original paradigm is exhausted. Until new ones are constructed, scholarship will be condemned to spin its wheels, adding minor refinements to accepted truths, repeating conventional arguments in unresolvable debates.[7]

Two major factors are responsible for this impasse. The first one, identified by Abel, is that:

> . . . sociological studies have borrowed most of their research questions from the object of study – the legal system (whose problems are defined by legal officials) – and from those who studied it first – legal scholars (themselves lawyers).[8]

The second factor, recently emphasised by David Nelken, is that the law and society have been conceived in the conventional paradigm, as two separate and distinct realities or entities which are then juxtaposed in order to investigate the extent to which they correspond or do not correspond. The most important 'exemplars' of sociological research on law have been developed from this conception (the study of the relations between law in books and law in action and the study of the impact of society on law or, inversely, the study of the impact of law in society).[9]

In recent years there have been some attempts away from this theoretical gulag: I will mention three of them. The first one is the research on legal pluralism in contemporary society which challenges the conventional paradigm in two ways. On the one hand, while legal officials and legal scholars assume the state monopoly of legal production, research on legal pluralism maintains the existence and circulation in society of different legal systems, the state legal system being one of them, even if the most important one. On the other hand, such a broader conception of law indicates a more complex relation between law and society, since there is not one single law but a network of laws that must be matched with society.[10] The second new direction in socio-legal studies is the whole movement (and stasis) of critical legal studies in the United States of America and the United Kingdom as well as in France and Mexico or in Portugal and Italy. By transforming legal science and legal scholarship into an object of scientific research, critical legal studies carve out an autonomous field of enquiry and thus maintain "a critical distance from the self-conceptions of legal professionals", as Alan Hunt has put it.[11] The third attempt away from the conventional paradigm is the research on the obstacles or constraints limiting both the impact of law on society and the impact of society on law and, more generally, the research on the lack of correspondence between forms of law and social structures of which Stuart Henry's recent book on private justice is a good example.[12]

I am not going to dwell on any of these lines of research. I will only mention some of their shortcomings and the questions they leave unanswered. First, if we substitute the soft law of legal pluralism for the hard law of legal scholarship, where does pluralism end? What is law, and where is it? Secondly, in spite of their proclaimed distances in relation to conventional legal science, all these lines of research share its exclusive concern with the normative content of law. Normativity is surely the heavy reality of the law. But law is also imagination, representation, and description of reality. Where, then, is the non-normative dimension of the normative? How is it constructed? Thirdly, it is important to show that the correspondence between law and society is far more complex than previously admitted, or even that there is no correspondence. But these findings seem, then, to assume that the only possible relation between law and society is that of correspondence or lack of correspondence. This assumption leaves unanswered or even suppressed the question of whether law and society may relate other than through correspondence or lack of correspondence.

I have attempted to answer the first question elsewhere.[13] In this paper I will try to concentrate on the second and third questions. In order to do that, allow me to take you to some exotic places, both real and symbolic. The title of this paper is taken from the title of a book by Harold Bloom, one of the most creative literary critics of our time.[14] According to his theory of poetic creation, in order to be original each poem must misread the poetic tradition which comes down to it through the generations and generations of poems and poets that preceded it. Poets suffer from the anxiety of influence and poetry is always the result of the poet's attempt to deny it. Poets overcome the anxiety of influence by misreading (or distorting) poetic reality.

I chose this title for two reasons. Firstly, because I think that law, like poems, must misread or distort reality and for similar reasons. Poems misread in order to establish their originality, while laws misread in order to establish their exclusivity. Irrespective of the plurality of normative orders we detect in society, each of them, taken separately, aspires to be exclusive, to have the monopoly of the regulation and control of social action within its legal territory. This is most patently the case with state laws, be they labour laws, criminal laws, or administrative laws. In order to operate adequately, a given labour law, for instance, must not only negate the existence of other normative orders or informal laws (such as factory codes, production of customary laws, etc.) that might interfere in its realm of application, but also revoke all the state labour laws that have previously regulated the same labour relations. This is, as we well know, a double misreading of reality. On the one hand, as legal pluralist research tells us, other normative orders do operate and are effective in the same legal territory. On the other hand, since law and society are mutually constitutive, the previous labour laws, once revoked, nevertheless leave their imprint on the labour relations they used to regulate. Though revoked, they remain present in the memories of things and people. Legal revocation is not social eradication.

This misreading of reality is not chaotic. It occurs through determinate and determinable mechanisms. Moreover, the distortion of reality which it implies does not automatically mean a distortion of truth. We have assumed too lightly in the past that truth and reality are one and the same thing. Closer attention to the pragmatics of legality may force us to conclude that such an assumption is an illusion produced by the correspondence paradigm concerning the relations between law and society. Now, here lies the second reason for the title of my paper. In my view, the relations law entertains with social reality are much similar to those between maps and spatial reality. Indeed, laws are maps; written laws are cartographic maps; customary, informal laws are mental maps. This is a strong metaphor and as such it will be taken literally, hence the subtitle of this paper might very well be: "on taking metaphors literally". In the following section I will draw extensively on the work of cartographers and I will try to show how much sociology of law may learn from cartography. I will deal with the structural features of maps and map-making as well as with the phenomenology of using maps.

UNDERSTANDING MAPS

The main structural feature of maps is that in order to fulfill their function they inevitably distort reality. The great Argentinian writer Jorge Luis Borges has told us the story of the emperor who ordered the production of an exact map of his empire. He insisted that the map should be exact to the most minute detail. The best cartographers of the time were engaged in this important project. Eventually, they produced the map and, indeed, it could not possibly be more exact, as it coincided point by point with the empire. However, to their frustration, it was not a very practical map, since it was of the same size as the empire.[15]

To be practical a map cannot coincide point by point with reality. However, the distortion of reality thus produced will not automatically involve the distortion of truth, if the mechanisms by which the distortion of reality is accomplished are known and can be controlled. And, indeed, that is the case.

Maps distort reality through three specific mechanisms and since they are used systematically they become intrinsic or structural attributes of any map. Such mechanisms are: *scale*, *projection*, and *symbolisation*. They are autonomous mechanisms that involve different procedures and require separate decisions. But they are also interdependent. As the American cartographer Mark Monmonier put it:

> . . . all advantages and limitations of maps derive from the degree to which maps reduce and generalise reality, compress or expand shapes and distances and portray selected phenomena with signs that communicate without necessarily resembling visible or invisible characteristics of the landscapes. The three elements of a map are interdependent. Scale influences the amount of detail that can be shown and determines whether or not a particular kind of symbol will be visually effective.[16]

Maps should be convenient to use. There is thus a permanent tension in maps between representation and orientation. These are contradictory claims and maps are always unstable compromises between them. Too much representation may hinder orientation, as we saw in Borges's map. Inversely, a very accurate orientation may result from a rather poor and elementary representation of reality. When you are invited to a party in a house whose location you do not know, the host will probably draw a map which will be very effective in orienting you though very inaccurate in representing the features of the environment along the way to your destination. One more example: some of you may have seen medieval *portolans*, those maps of ports and coasts well-renowned in the Middle Ages which, though very poor as far as representation of the globe goes, were very effective in orienting navigators at sea.[17] There are maps that solve the tension between representation and orientation in favour of representation. These I would call, borrowing from French cartography, image maps. Other maps solve the tension in favour of orientation. These are instrumental maps.[18]

I would like to suggest that this dialectic of representation and orientation applies to law as much as it applies to maps. In the analysis of the relations between law and society we should substitute the complex paradigm of scale/projection/symbolisation for the simple paradigm of correspondence/non-correspondence. In the following I will linger on maps a little while to analyse in more detail each one of the procedures through which maps distort reality. In the process I hope to interest you in the fascinating world of maps. As Josef Konwitz has said, "It is a supreme irony that maps, though they are one of the most common cultural metaphors, are still far from occupying the place they deserve in the history of mentalities."[19]

The first major mechanism of representation/distortion of reality in maps is scale. Scale, as Monmonier has defined it, "is the ratio of distance on the map to the corresponding distance on the ground".[20] Scale involves, then, a decision on more or less detail. "Since large-scale maps represent less land on a given size sheet of paper than do small-scale maps, large-scale maps can present more detail."[21] Since maps are "a miniaturised version" of reality,[22] map-making involves the filtering of details, "the selection of both meaningful details and relevant features".[23] As Muehrcke put it, "what makes a map so useful is its genious of omission. It is reality uncluttered, pared down to its essence, stripped of all but the essentials."[24] One easily understands that the decision on scale conditions the decision on the use of the map, and vice-versa. "Small-scale maps are not intended to permit accurate measurements of the width of roads, streams, etc., but rather to show with reasonable accuracy the relative positions of these and other features."[25]

Geography, which shares with cartography the concern for spaces and spatial relations, has also contributed important insights on scales, both scales of analysis and scales of action. As to the former, there are phenomena that can only be represented on a small scale, such as climate, while others, like erosion, for instance, can only be represented on a large scale.[26] This means that the differences in scales are not simply quantitative but they are also qualitative differences. A given phenomenon can only be represented on a given scale. To change the scale implies change of the phenomenon. Each scale reveals a phenomenon and distorts or hides others. As in nuclear physics, the scale creates the phenomenon. Some of the fallacious correlations in geography derive from the superimposition of phenomena created and analysed on different scales. The scale is "a coherent forgetting" that must be carried out coherently.[27]

Mediating between intention and action, scale applies also to social action. Urban planners as well as military chiefs, administrators, business executives, legislators, judges, and lawyers define strategies on a small scale and decide day-to-day tactics on a large scale. Power represents social and physical reality on a scale chosen for its capacity to create those phenomena that maximise the conditions for the reproduction of power. The distortion and concealment of reality is thus a presupposition of the exercise of power.

The second mechanism of representation/distortion of reality is projection. To be useful maps must be easily carried about and stored. Flat maps can be rolled and folded. It is by means of projection that the curved surfaces of the earth are transformed into planes. The most convenient transformation cannot yield flat maps without distorting shapes and distance relationships. I am not going to bother you with the specifics of projections, the different types of projection and the distribution and degrees of distortion characteristic of each of them.[28] I will only make a few general remarks that are relevant to my argument. The first remark is that projections do not distort reality at random. Each type of projection creates a field of representation within which forms and degrees of distortion are unequally but determinably distributed. For instance, some projections distort the equatorial regions more than the polar regions, while others do the opposite. Moreover, the different projections distort the different features of the space differently. Some projections (called the conformal projections) preserve areas but distort angles and shapes and directions, while other projections (called equivalent projections) do the inverse. We cannot get the same degree of accuracy in the representation of all the different features and whatever we do to increase the accuracy in the representation of one given feature will increase the distortion in the representation of some other feature. It is very much like the uncertainty principle of Heisenberg in quantum physics, according to which we cannot measure the velocity and the position of the particles simultaneously and with the same degree of precision and whatever we do to increase accuracy in determining the position will distort the measurement of velocity.

Every map projection is thus a compromise. The decision on which kind of distortion to prefer is conditioned by precise technical factors but it is also based on the ideology of the cartographer and on the specific use intended for the map. For instance, during the cold war the western mass media used to show the Soviet Union on a world map designed according to the cylindrical projection of Mercator. Since this kind of projection exaggerates the areas in high and median latitudes in detriment of those in inter-tropical latitudes, such a map would inflate the size of the Soviet Union, thus dramatising the extent of the communist threat.[29]

The second remark on projection is that each map, each historical period or each cultural tradition of map-making has a centre, a fixed point, a physic or symbolic space in a privileged position around which the diversity, the direction, and the meaning of other spaces is organised. For instance, medieval maps used to put a religious site at the centre – Jerusalem in the European maps, Mecca in the Arab maps.[30] The same happens with mental maps, that is, with the cognitive visual images we have of the world around us. As Muehrcke said, "most of our mental maps would emphasise our own neighbourhood, with its environments assuming less significance."[31]

Symbolisation is the third mechanism of map representation/distortion of reality. It refers to the representation of selected features and details of reality in graphic symbols. Without signs the map will be as unusable as Borges's map. Such is the case of the Bellman's map in Lewis Carroll's *Hunting of the Snark*.[32] You may remember the verses:

> . . . One could see he was wise,
> the moment one looked in his face!
>
> He had brought a large map representing the sea,
> without the least vestige of land: And the crew were much pleased when they found it to be. A map they could all understand.
>
> "What's the good of Mercator's North Poles and Equators,
> Tropics, Zones and Meridian Lines?"
> So the Bellman would cry: and the crew would reply,
>
> "They are merely conventional signs!"
> "Other maps are such shapes, with their islands and capes!
>
> But we've got our brave Captain to thank"
> (So the crew would protest)
> "that he's brought *us* the best –
> A perfect and absolute blank!"[33]

Cartographic language is a fascinating theme and semiotics has provided its research with new analytical tools. The sign systems have evolved over time and still today different systems may be chosen according to the specific cultural context of the map-maker or according the purposes of the maps. In a recent book on this topic, J. S. Keates, drawing from semiotics, distinguishes between iconic signs and conventional signs.[34] Iconic signs are naturalistic signs that establish a relation of likeness with the reality represented (for instance, a bunch of trees to designate a forest) while conventional signs are far more arbitrary. "Convention holds that certain types of symbols are appropriate for certain types of phenomena" – for instance, linear symbols for roads and boundaries and graduated circles for cities and towns.[35] If we look at the historical record it will show that the sign systems used in maps were initially more naturalistic and gradually became more conventional.[36] But even today, according to many circumstances, maps may be more figurative or more abstract; they may rely on emotive/expressive signs or on referential/cognitive signs; they may be more readable or more visible.[37]

You may be surprised with this digression on maps. Clifford Geertz said that law was a way of imagining the real.[38] My argument is that there are many unresolved problems in the sociological study of the law that may be solved by comparing law with other ways of imagining the real. Maps are one such way. There are, in fact, striking similarities between laws and maps – both concerning their structural features and their use patterns. Obviously, laws are maps only in the metaphorical sense. But, as rhetoric also teaches us, the repeated use of a metaphor over a long period of time may gradually transform the metaphorical description into a literal description.[39] Today laws are maps in a metaphorical sense. Tomorrow they may be maps in a literal sense.

A SYMBOLIC CARTOGRAPHY OF LAW

I will now present the outline of what I would call a symbolic cartography of law. I will try to show that the national (and the international) territory consists of several social spaces which, though autonomous, interrelate in different ways. Within each social space and across spaces different kinds of juridical capital circulate: nationalised or state juridical capitals and private juridical capitals, sacred and profane juridical capitals, and so on. Each kind of juridical capital prompts a specific kind of actions and symbolic universes. In the modern era law has become the privileged way of imagining, representing, and distorting, that is to say, of mapping these social spaces and the capitals, the actions and symbolic universes that animate or activate them. In order to illustrate this point I will draw on theoretical sociology of law as well as on my own empirical research conducted in Portugal, in Brazil, and in the Cape Verde Islands. The research in Portugal deals with the contradictions between democratic legality and revolutionary legality during the revolutionary crisis of 1974-75, in the aftermath of the fall of the dictatorial regime that ruled the country for almost fifty years.[40] The research in Brazil, conducted in 1980 in the north-eastern city of Recife, deals with the social and legal battles of squatter settlers against the state and private landowners to obtain a legal title over the land they had invaded and upon which they had built their shacks and organised their urban lives.[41] The research in the Cape Verde Islands, conducted in 1984 and 1985, is concerned with the popular courts that have been created by the state since independence from Portuguese colonialism in 1975. These are non-professional courts organised on a residential basis and with jurisdiction over small civil disputes and petty crimes.[42]

1. *Law and Scale*

One of the main reasons for recommending the symbolic cartography of law is its ability to analyse the effect of scale on the structure and use of law. The modern state is based on the assumption that law operates on a single scale, the scale of the state. For a long time the sociology of law accepted this assumption uncritically. In recent times the research on legal pluralism has drawn our attention to forms of local legality in rural areas, in marginalised urban sectors, in churches, in sports, in the professions. These are forms of infra-state laws, most of them informal, unofficial, more or less customary. Most recently, the research on international economic exchanges has revealed the emergence of a new *lex mercatoria*, an international legal space in which different types of economic agents operate, whose behaviour is regulated by new international rules and contractual relations established by dominant multinational corporations, international banks or international associations dominated by both.[43] Transnational capital has thus created a transnational legal space, a supra-state legality, a world law. This legality is in general very informal. Based on dominant practices, that is, on the practices of dominant agents, it only makes sense to consider this world legality customary if we allow for the fact that new practices (for instance, a new type of contract invented by a multinational corporation) often create what we might call *instant customs*. Nor does it make much sense to consider it unofficial, since this world legality develops forms of immunity *vis-à-vis* both the national state law and the public international law.[44]

The legal developments reveal the existence of three different legal spaces and their correspondent forms of law: local, national and world legality. It is rather unsatisfactory to distinguish these legal orders by their respective objects of regulation because often they regulate or seem to regulate the same kind of social action. Local law is a *large-scale legality*. Nation state law is a *medium-scale legality*. World law is a *small-scale legality*. This concept has broad implications. First, it means that, since scale creates the phenomenon, the different forms of law create different legal objects upon eventually the same social objects. They use different criteria to determine the meaningful details and the relevant features of the activity to be regulated. They establish different networks of facts. In sum, they create different legal realities. Let us take the example of the labour conflict. The factory code, that is, the private justice of the workplace, as a form of local legality, regulates the relations in production in great detail in order to maintain workplace discipline, to prevent labour conflicts, to reduce their scope whenever they occur and eventually to settle them. The labour conflict is the nuclear object of the factory code because it confirms *a contrario* the continuity of the relations in production, which are the *raison d'être* of the factory code. In the wider context of the national state labour law, the labour conflict is only a dimension, however important, of industrial relations. It is part of a broader network of social, political and economic facts in which we easily identify, among others, political stability, inflation rate, income policy and relations of power among labour unions, business, and government. In the still wider context of the world legality of international franchising, or of international subcontracting, the labour conflict becomes a minute detail in international economic relations hardly worth mentioning.

Thus, the different legal orders operating on different scales translate the same social objects into different legal objects. However, in real socio-legal life the different legal scales do not exist in isolation but rather interact in different ways. Let us continue with our example and hypothesise that a labour conflict occurs in a Portuguese garment factory subcontracted by a multinational corporation.[45] In such a case the regulatory purposes of the three legal scales converge in the same social event. This creates the illusion that the three legal objects can be superimposed. In fact, they do not coincide; nor do their root images' of law and the social and legal struggles they legitimate coincide. Workers and sometimes the employer tend to have a large-scale view of the conflict, full of details and relevant features, a concept moulded by local legality. Union leaders and sometimes the employer tend to see the conflict as a crisis in a process of continuous industrial relations. Their view is predominantly moulded by national state legality and their actions in the conflict aim at a compromise between the medium-scale and the large-scale view of the conflict. For the multinational corporation, the labour conflict is a tiny accident which, if not promptly overcome, can be easily circumvented by moving the production to Taiwan or Malasia.

To analyse these discrepancies and unevennesses exclusively in terms of conflicting interests or degrees of class consciousness ignores the fact that law creates the reality that fits its application. Such creation is, among other things, a technique that operates according to certain rules, one of them being the rule of the scale. That is why we can only compare or contrast social interests and degrees of class consciousness within the same legal space. The difficulty lies in that socio-legal life is constituted by different legal spaces operating simultaneously on different scales and from different interpretive standpoints. So much is this so that in phenomenological terms and as a result of interaction and intersection among legal spaces one cannot properly speak of law and legality but rather of interlaw and interlegality. More important than the identification of the different legal orders is the tracing of the complex and changing relations among them. But if while doing this we forget the question of scale, we may find ourselves in the same distressing situation as a tourist who forgot to pack the voltage transformer that would enable him to use his electric razor in a foreign country.

While doing my research on popular justice in the Cape Verde Islands I was confronted with an intriguing fact. The philosophy underlying the organisation of popular justice consisted in integrating local customary laws as much as possible. This integration was facilitated by the fact that the judges were lay judges, that is to say, they were members of the local communities and the written laws governing the procedures and decisions of the courts were few and vague and were often unknown to or disregarded by the judges, without any reaction on the part of the Ministry of Justice. However, both the state and the party took great care in selecting the judges and tended to favour young or middle-aged males considered politically reliable, a fact that was sometimes a source of tension in the local communities for whom the exercise of justice was in general associated with old wise folks. It would seem that while the state felt unable to control the creation of law and sought to compensate for that by tightening the control of the application of law, the local communities paid no attention whatsoever to the creation of law and sought to keep control of its application (which for them, in fact, was nothing but its creation). On further reflection, this was a case of interlegality – a case of a complex relation between the customary law and the state law using different scales. For the local communities the customary law was the local law, a large-scale legality well adapted to prevent and settle local disputes. For the state the customary law was part of a broader network of social facts that included the consolidation of the state, the unity of the state legal order, political socialisation, and so on. On this smaller scale the customary law became part of state law and the latter became an instrument, though a specific one, of political action.[46]

The first implication of scale conception of law is that it draws our attention to the phenomenon of interlegality and to the complex mechanics of its operation. The second implication has to do with the regulation patterns and action packages that are associated with each scale of legality. I will start by illustrating different *regulation patterns*. I have already mentioned the dialectical tension between representation and orientation. Indeed, we have before us two antagonistic modes of imagining and constituting reality, one geared to identify position, the other geared to identify movement. The large-scale legality is rich in details and features; describes behaviour and attitudes vividly; contextualises them in their immediate surroundings; is sensitive to distinctions (and complex relations) between inside and outside, high and low, just and unjust. This applies to any social object of legal regulation, be it labour conflicts, family relations, contractual terms, crimes, or political rights. What I mean is that this form of legality favours a pattern of regulation based on (and geared to) representation and position. On the contrary, small-scale legality is poor in details and features, skeletonises behaviour and attitudes, reducing them to general types of action. But, on the other hand, it determines with accuracy the relativity of positions (the angles between people and between people and things), provides sense of direction and schemes for shortcuts and, finally, it is sensitive to distinctions (and complex relations) between part and whole, past and present, functional and non-functional. In sum, this form of legality favours a pattern of regulation based on (and geared to) orientation and movement.

When in 1970 I studied the informal law of the squatter settlements in Rio I had occasion to observe how adequately such local legality represented the socio-legal reality of urban marginality and how it contributed to maintain the status quo of their social positions as precarious inhabitants of shacks and houses built upon invaded land.[47] When ten years later I studied the legal battles of squatter settlers in Recife who aimed at securing land tenure or, at least, a legal lease, the form of law resorted to was the state law, a smaller-scale law, that represented the socio-legal position of the squatter settlers very roughly but, on the other hand, a law that very clearly defined the relativity of their positions, the angles of their relations *vis-à-vis* the landowners and the state, and, lastly, the shortest path to move from a precarious to a secure position under the social and political circumstances of the time.[48]

Besides inviting different regulation patterns, different scales of legality also condition different *action packages*. An action package is a connected sequence of actions structurally determined by predefined boundaries. I identify two kinds of boundaries: those defined by range and those defined by ethics. According to range, we can distinguish two ideal-types of action packages: *the tactical* and the *strategic action package*. According to ethics, we can also distinguish two ideal-types of action packages: the *edifying* and the *instrumental* action package. In the light of the previous examples I would suggest that large-scale legality invites tactical and edifying action packages, while the small-scale legality invites strategic and instrumental action packages. Social groups or classes that are predominantly socialised in one of these forms of legality tend to be specifically competent in the type of action package associated with it. In a situation of interlegality, that is, in a situation in which large-scale legality and small-scale legality intersect, the large-scale action package tends to be defensive and regulate normal, routine interaction or, at the most, molecular struggles, while the small-scale action package tends to be aggressive and to regulate critical, exceptional situations, triggered by molar struggles.[49] These tendencies hold true irrespective of the class nature of the social groups involved in the specific action package.

The third and last implication of the scale analysis of the law is the least developed but potentially very important. It refers to what I would call *regulation thresholds*. Irrespective of the social object it regulates and the purpose of regulation, each scale of legality has a specific regulation threshold which determines what belongs to the realm of the law and what does not. This threshold is the product of the combined operation of the three thresholds: the detection threshold, the discrimination threshold, and the evaluation threshold. The *detection threshold* refers to the smallest details of the social object that will be considered for regulation; it distinguishes between relevant and irrelevant issues. The *discrimination threshold* refers to the minimum detectable differences in the description of the social object that may justify qualitative differences in regulation; it distinguishes between the same – that which deserves equal treatment – and the different – that which deserves unequal treatment. Finally, the *evaluation threshold* refers to the minimum detectable differences in the ethical quality of the social object; it distinguishes between the legal and the illegal.

During the revolutionary crisis in Portugal in 1974-75, a rural worker was indicted for the murder of a big landowner. In his defence the worker invoked provocation and a long list of arbitrary and violent actions perpetrated by the *latifundiário* against the rural workers during the many years in which the Salazar dictatorship allowed him to rule the community despotically. For the state legality (called then the democratic legality) the two sets of action – that of the rural worker and that of the landowner – were very different, both in structural and ethical terms. For the revolutionary legality and from the point of view of their lower discrimination and evaluation thresholds, the two sets of actions were similar in that they were both illegal. The murder could not be considered a legitimate revolutionary act but, as a reaction against the landowner's past arbitrariness, it was understandable and could be pardoned.[50]

The three thresholds vary according to the scale of the legal form, but the same scale of law may allow for internal differences in its regulation threshold. It may, for instance, have a high detection threshold but a low evaluation threshold or vice versa, and the discrepancies may also occur across legal realms (for instance, labour law may have a higher regulation threshold than criminal or social welfare law). Moreover, the regulation threshold is not a fixed entity. It may move up and down within certain limits. But its movement is always the result of the combined movements of the different thresholds that constitute it. In the current social and political context calling for the deregulation of the economy and social interaction, the regulation threshold moves up as a result of higher detection and discrimination thresholds. But since, in practice, the socio-legal life always involves interlegality, the deregulation in one form of legality may be counteracted or compensated for by the increase of regulation in another form of legality.

2. *Law and Projection*

Legal orders can also be distinguished by the type of projection they use. Projection is the procedure by which the legal order defines the limits of its operation and organises the legal space inside them. Like scale and for the same reasons, projection is not a neutral procedure. Different types of projections create different legal objects upon the same social objects. Each legal object favours a specific formulation of interests and a specific concept of disputes and of modes of settling them.

Each legal order stands on a grounding fact, a *superfact* or a *supermetaphor*, as I would call it, which determines the specific interpretive standpoint or perspective that characterises the adopted type of projection. The private economic relations in the market are the superfact underlying modern bourgeois legality, while land and housing, as extra-economic, social, and political relations, are the superfact underlying the law of the squatter settlements in Rio.

According to the type of projection adopted, each legal order has a *centre* and a *periphery*. First, this means that, as is the case with money capital, the legal capital of a given legal order is not equally distributed across the latter's legal space. The central regions are those in which the legal capital is more concentrated and owns greater profits. Here the space is mapped in greater detail and absorbs greater inputs of institutional resources (legal professions, courts, etc.) and symbolic resources (legal science, legal ideology and culture, etc.). The second implication is that conceptualisations, interpretive styles and techniques as well as ideological configurations dominant at the centre tend to be taken out of their context in which they originate and exported to (and imposed upon) the periphery. They are then applied in the legal periphery with little attention to local regulatory needs, since such needs are always interpreted and satisfied from the point of view of the centre. It is very much a symbolic transfer of technology. Sticking to my examples, it is clear that the centre of the bourgeois state legality is occupied by the contracts, as witness the codification movement and, particularly, the Napoleonic code. Contracts – their types, concepts, theories, interpretations, general principles – have been the centre of modern legislation, of modern legal training, and of modern legal ideology. Moreover, the contractual perspective has been exported to other legal fields, be they the constitutional law, the administrative law, or even the criminal law. When we hear today about the end of the contract or, in Maine's case, the return from contract to status, we should not forget that in spite of important legal developments in recent times, contracts remain the privileged archeological site and, indeed, the ground metaphor of modern law and of modern society in general. The evidence is abundant, but I will only mention, for the most recent period, the theories of the new-contractualism in political philosophy and constitutional law.

Similarly, in the informal law of the squatter settlements, land and house transactions and the disputes they originate occupy the centre of the legal space. Whenever the residents' association, acting as an informal tribunal, ventures into criminal, public order or family matters, it always seeks a connection with land and housing matters and applies to the former the popular legal technology and legal competence gained in the latter.

The centre/periphery effect of projection shows that the legal mapping of social reality is not equally distortive. It seems to become more distortive as we move from the centre to the periphery. The periphery is also the legal region where the interpenetration between different legal orders is most frequent. It creates a twilight zone where the shadows of different legal orders converge.

The second effect of projection refers to the type of features of the social object that tend to be privileged no matter how central or how peripheral the social object. According to this effect, two general types of projection can be distinguished: the egocentric and the geocentric.[51] The egocentric projection favours the representation of personal and particularistic features, of voluntary or consensual social action. The geocentric projection favours the representation of objective and generalisable features, of patterned, bounded or conflictual social action. According to the dominant type of projection, two general forms of law can be distinguished: the *egocentric legality* and the *geocentric legality*. It is illuminating to analyse, in the light of these categories, some recent trends in legal change as well as some long-range developments in legal history as they have been described by Max Weber. While analysing in *Economy and Society* the forms of creation of rights, Weber drew our attention to the long and sinuous historical process by which what I call geocentric form of law gradually substituted for what I call egocentric form of law. In the past, Weber said, law arose as "volitive" and as "particularistic" law based on the agreed enactment of consensual status groups. There were different legal communities constituted in their membership by personal characteristics such as birth, political, ethnic or religious denomination, mode of life or occupation, and so on. Individuals or groups of individuals had their own personal legal quality and carried their law, their *professio juris*, with them wherever they went.[52]

The *ius civile* in Rome was the personal law of Roman citizens and the *ius gentium* was created to cover the legal needs of non-citizens. The idea of a law of the land developed only very gradually – the *lex terrae*, which was applicable to everyone independent of personal characteristics and imposed as a heteronomous law within the boundaries of a given territory. In the development of a geocentric form of law, the extension of the market economy and the bureaucratisation of consensual groups played a decisive role:

> The ever-increasing integration of all individual and all fact situations into one compulsory institution which today, at least, rests in principle on formal "legal equality" reached its climax in the French Revolution after which the state appears as the all-embracing coercive institution.[53]

Max Weber was aware that in modern society there are also volitive and particularistic laws but, unlike those in pre-modern times, they are based on economic or technical grounds, are never defined in terms of personal group membership, and are effective within the boundaries set by the national general law.[54]

In my view, this historical interplay between geocentric and egocentric legality cannot be definitely decided in favour of geocentric legality. Some recent trends in legal development seem to witness the emergence of new legal particularisms, that is to say, forms of egocentric legality that, by creating personal legal 'enclosures', empty or neutralise the conditions for the application of the law of the land. To illustrate this I return to the new type of world legality I identified above while discussing the scale of the law. The new international commercial contracts as well as the proliferation of charters, codes of ethics, codes of conduct or of fair practices covering the activities of multinational corporations and international economic and professional associations in fields so diverse as transfers of technology, stock markets, publicity, sales promotion, market studies, insurance, technical assistance, turn-key contracts, etc. – all these new forms of world legality create a transnational legal space which often conflicts with the national state legal space.[55] Such conflicts take several forms: the conception of liability in the new contracts is autonomous *vis-à-vis* national laws; the contracts introduce vague clauses on applicable law such as the general principles of law, the usages of commercial life, with the only purpose of eliminating or evading the application of the state law; the arbitration system is often resorted to with the same purpose; the commercial partners enter gentlemen's agreements or protocols that openly violate national laws (particularly those on fair competition); the national legislation enacted to police the contracts of transfer of technology has little efficacy; powerful multinational corporations impose their laws on the states. The violation of national state law is so widespread that the proposed code of ethics for multinational corporations includes the astonishing clause that "the multinational corporation will respect the laws of the state where it operates".[56]

All these latent or manifest conflicts are symptoms of a tension between the geocentric legality of the nation-state and the new egocentric legality of international private economic agents. Indeed, we are witnessing the emergence of a new particularism which echoes the personalistic laws of the ancient and medieval world described by Weber. Like the old status groups, each multinational corporation or international economic association has its own personal legal quality and carries its law wherever it goes. The new personalism derives also from the fact that this legality is closely tailored to the interests of the most powerful companies or banks. Goldman found that many 'standard contracts' were created by a single corporation powerful enough to impose them on its partners.[57] This explains why a new economic practice by a powerful corporation may become an instant custom. This new form of status privileges (corporate privileges) can also be found in the codes of international professional associations (for example, the International Franchising Association) because in general, as Farjat noted, there is a coincidence between the powerful economic agents and the professional authorities that write the codes.[58]

To conceive of the tension between the nation state law and the new transnational legality as deriving from two forms of law anchored in two different types of projection of social reality prevents us from falling into a reductionist view (be it economicist or otherwise) of the conflicts they express. Truly, there are conflicting interests and power relations, but they are played out through the intermediation of specific projective devices with their own hermeneutic logic. The legal forms thus ensuing have an autonomy of their own and an efficacy that extends beyond the stakes of the conflicting interests or power positions. For instance, the attention to types of projection shows the relativity of the distinction between law and fact. Clifford Geertz recently reminded us of such relativity when different legal cultures are compared.[59] But even within the same general culture the distinction between law and fact seems to be largely an effect of projection. Because of its emphasis on objective and generalisable features of reality, geocentric law tends to polarise law and fact and to be stronger on norms than on facts. Overridden by the fear of fact, it responds by sterilising or skeletonising fact. As Geertz has put it, facts became "close edited diagrams of reality".[60] It results in "a justice of law" in Pospisil's terms.[61] On the contrary, egocentric law tends to soften the distinction between law and fact and to be stronger on facts than on norms. It allows for the explosion of facts, as the case of instant customs mentioned above well documents. It results in a 'justice of fact'.

3. *Law and Symbolisation*

Symbolisation is the visible side of the representation of reality. It is the most complex procedure because it operates on the basis of and conditioned by scale and projection. Rhetoric as well as semiotics and cultural anthropology have contributed important insights into the complexities of the legal symbolisation of reality. From the synthetic perspective in which these contributions merge with that of literary criticism I shall distinguish two contrasting, ideal-typical modes of legal symbolisation: *the Homeric style of law* and *the biblical style of law*. These metaphorical designations refer to two polar, ideal-types, either of which legal orders existing in reality approximate in different degrees. The designations are borrowed from Erich Auerbach in his classical account of the different forms of representation of reality in western literature.[62] Auerbach has identified two basic types of literary representation of reality in European culture. He exemplifies the opposition between these two types by contrasting the Odyssey of Homer and the Bible. The Odyssey describes the tragic and sublime nature of heroic life: a fully externalised description, uniform illumination, uninterrupted connection, all events in the foreground, displaying unmistakable meanings, few elements of historical development and of psychological perspective. On the contrary, the Bible represents the sublime and the tragic in the context of commonplace and everyday life: a description attentive to the 'multilayeredness' of the human problem in which certain parts are brought into high relief, others left obscure, multiplicity of meanings and the need for interpretation, development of the concept of the historically becoming, and preoccupation with the problematic.

In my view this basic contrast in the literary representation of reality may also be found in the legal representation of reality. Accordingly, I identify two ideal-typical sign systems by means of which law symbolises reality. I shall speak of an Homeric style of law where the legal symbolisation of reality has the following characteristics: the conversion of the everyday continuous flux of reality into a succession of disparate solemn moments (contracts, legal disputes, etc.) described in abstract and formal terms through conventional cognitive and referential signs. This style of symbolisation presupposes a form of legality that I would call instrumental legality. In contrast, what I call the biblical style of law presupposes an image-based legality characterised by a preoccupation with inscribing the discontinuities of legal interaction into the multilayered contexts in which they occur, and with describing them in figurative and informal terms, and through iconic, emotive, and expressive signs. The biblical style of law is probably older than the Homeric, but in each historical period, no matter which one dominates, there is a tension between the two. For instance, modern state legal order is predominantly an Homeric style of law, but the biblical style of law shows its vitality in many ways. Returning to the example of the particularistic law created by the new transnational legal subjects, it is apparent that this emerging world legality tends to be formulated in a biblical style of law. Some specialists have called attention to the moralistic rhetoric in the use of non-cognitive, emotive and expressive signs in codes of ethics and standard contracts drawn by multinational corporations and the international associations co-opted by them, as illustrated in the recurrent use of expressions like concertation, common interest, reciprocal trust, trustworthiness, co-operation, assistance, and so on.[63]

But the contrast between the two types of legal symbolisation is most visible in those situations of legal pluralism in which social practice is a constant bridging between legal orders with different styles of symbolisation. Somehow all of my case studies mentioned above involve situations of this type. In the case of popular justice in the Cape Verde Islands there is an attempt at a fusion between local customary law and nation-state law. The tensions between the two contrasting sign systems manifest themselves in the way judges settle the disputes. While some – generally older – judges adopt a local, image-based view of law, describing law and fact without much distinction, in figurative and informal terms, resorting to verbal and gestual signs of the iconic, expressive, and emotive type, other – and generally younger – judges seek to impersonate the professional judge or even the political *cadre* and, consequently, adopt an instrumental view of law distinguishing law and fact, and describing both in abstract and formal terms by resorting to verbal and gestual signs of the conventional, cognitive, and referential type. But the same judge may in different situations adopt different styles of law. Nha Bia, for instance, a remarkable woman and judge presiding over the popular court of Lem Cachorro in the outskirts of the capital city of Praia (Santiago Island) adopts a biblical style of law in those cases she is most familiar with and when she feels more autonomous to deliver justice 'in her own way'. These are, for example, the water disputes involving women – disputes usually occurring in water lines over the order of the women in the line to fill the water cans at the public fountains or over the water supply to be used daily. Since the drought often lasts several years, this is a very common type of dispute. On the other hand, Nha Bia tends to adopt an Homeric style of law whenever the dispute is less common, or in cases in which her legal competence or jurisdiction may be challenged, such as those with political overtones or involving powerful members of the community.[64]

In the case of the social struggles in Recife, both the urban poor and the Catholic Church on their behalf seek a momentary and unstable complementarity between the unofficial law of the squatter settlements and the state official law. The construction or imagining of reality in the two legal orders follows different sign systems, the biblical and the Homeric style respectively. Community leaders and lawyers hired by the Church to represent the urban poor often find themselves in the position of having to translate one sign system into the other before the relevant audience of the moment – whether the audience is the people from the community, the state court, or the state administrative agency for housing matters. It may also occur that the two sign systems interpenetrate or superimpose, as when large groups of squatter settlers attending the trial of one of the land disputes in the state court start shouting slogans and singing religious songs.[65]

In the case of popular justice during the revolutionary crisis in Portugal there is neither an attempted complementarity nor fusion but rather an open contradiction between two forms of law – in this case between democratic legality and revolutionary legality. The democratic legality tries to insulate the legal representation of reality from the everyday experience of a revolutionary crisis and for that purpose it stresses the distinction between law and fact and resorts to a formal and abstract description of reality in which the sign system characteristic of an Homeric style of law dominates. On the contrary, the revolutionary legality tries to integrate and even dissolve the legal representation into the social and political context in which it occurs, and for that purpose it softens the distinction between law and fact, thus allowing for the explosion of facts as a mechanism of law creation, and privileges a figurative and informal description of reality.[66] In sum, it is a biblical style of law.

TOWARD A POSTMODERN CONCEPTION OF LAW

Chaim Perelman has written in his treatise on the new rhetoric that while classical thought favoured spatial metaphors, modern thought has favoured temporal ones.[67] It seems to me that postmodern thought will return to spatial metaphors, even though inspired by new spaces and spatialities. It is not surprising that postmodernism started as a debate within architecture, the art of space created by people.[68] The theory of a symbolic cartography of law sketched here may be considered a sociological attempt toward a postmodern conception of law.

Scale, projection and symbolisation are not neutral procedures. The choices made within each of them promote the expression of certain types of interests and disputes and suppress that of others. The autonomy of law as a specific way of representing, distorting, and imagining reality derives from the operation of these procedures. Since this symbolic cartography of law does not explain why the choices in the operation of these procedures are made, it may be viewed as relapsing into analytical formalism. However, our century has been too much overridden by the opposition between the formal and the informal, both concerning social action and scientific analysis.[69] Now, as we are approaching the end of the century, it is time to see the formal in the informal and the informal in the formal. At the level of the sociological analysis of law such a relational view is best obtained once we conceive of law in legal pluralistic terms.

Legal pluralism is the key concept in a postmodern view of law. Not the legal pluralism of traditional legal anthropology in which the different legal orders are conceived as separate entities coexisting in the same political space, but rather the conception of different legal spaces superimposed, interpenetrated, and mixed in our minds as much as in our actions, in occasions of qualitative leaps or sweeping crises in our life trajectories as well as in the dull routine of eventless everyday life. We live in a time of porous legality or of legal porosity, of multiple networks of legal orders forcing us to constant transitions and trespassings. Our legal life is constituted by an intersection of different legal orders, that is, by *interlegality*. Interlegality is the phenomenological counterpart of legal pluralism and that is why it is the second key concept of a postmodern conception of law.

Interlegality is a highly dynamic process because the different legal spaces are non-synchronic and thus result in uneven and unstable mixings of legal codes (codes in a semiotic sense). The mixing of codes is visible in all the case studies I mentioned. It is also visible in the ways in which the emerging world legal space appropriates local legal vernaculars. As I have demonstrated, the small-scale world legality mixes the telescopic view of reality with a moralistic rhetoric typical of large-scale legality. While broadening the legal space to a world or even planetarian scale it creates new particularisms and new personalisms, echoing the medieval privileges of the different *professiones juris*. The mixing of codes is still visible in the popular images of law. In a recent study Stewart Macaulay has shown how the mass media and particularly the television promote a fragmented and inconsistent view of law – a view of overlapping and contradictory legal messages, of rules and off-setting counterrules inciting both to obedience and to disobedience, to legal and illegal action.[70]

Such a conception of legal pluralism and interlegality calls for complex analytical tools. Those presented here aim to show that the fragmentation of legality is not chaotic. It is a social construction built according to the rules of scale, projection, and symbolisation. In a polycentric legal world the centrality of the state law, though increasingly shaken, is still a decisive political factor. But above all it is reproduced by multiple mechanisms of acculturation and socialisation. As there is a literary canon that establishes what is and what is not literature, there is also a legal canon that establishes what is and what is not law. Because people are permanently (even if inconsistently) socialised and acculturated in the types of scale, projection, and symbolisation that are characteristic of the national state legal order, they refuse to recognise as legal those normative orders that use different scales, projections, and symbolisations. They are beyond the minimum and the maximum threshold of legal cognition. Some (infra-state, local) legal orders are too close to everyday reality to be viewed as a fact of law (a *legal* fact). Other (supra-state, world) legal orders are too remote from everyday reality to be viewed as a law of fact (a legal *fact*). The symbolic cartography of law using as a metaphor such commonplace and vulgar objects as maps contributes to the creation of a *new legal common sense* which is the third key concept of a postmodern conception of law.[71] Modern scientific knowledge has been constructed in total insulation from common-sense knowledge and in opposition to it. A postmodern science is distant enough from common-sense knowledge to be able to refuse the existing common sense, but sufficiently close to conceive the creation of a new common sense as its sole objective.[72] As far as law is concerned, the new common sense will be a legal pluralistic common sense.

To achieve such a goal the sociology of law must change its priorities: instead of engaging exclusively in the critique of the existing state legality it must also uncover the latent or suppressed forms of legality in which more insidious and damaging forms of social and personal oppression frequently occur. Thus conceived, the sociology of law will become an edifying knowledge that, by enlarging and deepening our legal vistas, will contribute towards a radical democratisation of social and personal life.[73] Only then will law be an unqualified human good.[74]

To conclude, I shall go back to my starting point. This conception of law and of sociology of law shows that we are not yet definitely condemned to the 'camelisation' of law and that Nietzsche might graciously grant us a fourth metamorphosis. In such a case we may ask which animal will take the place of the camel that took the place of the lion that took the place of the child. In view of the emphasis put by the postmodern conception of law on legal pluralism, interlegality, mixing of codes, and non-synchronism, I dare to suggest that this animal will be the chameleon. By constantly changing its colours according to certain biological rules, the chameleon is truly not an animal but rather a network of animals – as much as law is a network of legal orders. Law as a chameleon may turn out to fit the postmodern conception of law.

NOTES AND REFERENCES

1 F. Nietzsche, "Thus Spoke Zarathustra" in *The Portable Nietzsche* (1982; ed. W. Kaufmann) p. 137.

2 J. Habermas, *Theorie des Kommunikativen Handelns* (2nd ed. 1982) Vol. 2, p.489.

3 P. Nonet and P. Selznick, *Law and Society in Transition: Toward Responsive Law* (1978).

4 G. Teubner, "Substantive and Reflexive Elements in Modern Law" (1983) 17 *Law and Society Rev.* p. 239.

5 T. O'Hagan, *The End of Law?* (1984).

6 M. Foucault, *La Volonté de Savoir* (1976); *Discipline and Punish* (1977); *Power and Knowledge* (1980).

7 R. Abel, "Redirecting Social Studies of Law" (1980) 14 *Law and Society Rev.* p. 826.

8 *Id.*

9 D. Nelken, "Beyond the Study of 'Law and Society'?: Henry's *Private Justice* and O'Hagan's *The End of Law?*" (1986) *American Bar Foundation Research J.*

10 See, J. Griffiths, "What is Legal Pluralism?" (1986) 24 *J. of Legal Pluralism* p. 1.

11 A. Hunt, "The Critique of Law: What is 'Critical' about Critical Legal Theory?" (1987) 14 *J. of Law and Society* p. 13.

12 S. Henry, *Private Justice* (1983).

13 B. Santos, "On Modes of Production of Social Power and Law" (1985) 13 *International J. of Sociology of Law* p. 299.

14 H. Bloom, *A Map of Misreading* (1975).

15 J. L. Borges, *Dreamtigers* (1970) p. 90.

16 M. Monmonier, *Maps, Distortion, and Meaning* (1981) p. 1.

17 See, A. G. Hodgkiss, *Understanding Maps. A Systematic History of their Use and Development* (1981) p. 103. In the sixteenth century Mercator, the famous Flemish geographer who developed the type of maps projections which now bears his name, wrote

the following instruction on his famous chart of 1569: "If you wish to sail from one port to another, here is a chart, and a straight line on it, and if you follow carefully this line you will certainly arrive at your port of destination. But the length of the line may not be correct. You may get there sooner or you may not get there as soon as you expected, but you will certainly get there." Quoted from W. W. Jervis, *The World in Maps. A Study of Map Evolution* (1936) p. 27.

18 F. Wahl, "Le Désir d'Espace" in *Cartes et Figures de la Terre* (1980; ed. Centre Georges Pompidou) p. 42.

19 Josef Konvitz, "Remplir la Carte" in *Cartes et Figures de la Terre*, *op. cit.*, n. 18, p. 314. On maps as *the* fundamental analogy, see A. Robinson and B. Petchnik, *The Nature of Maps: Essays Toward Understanding Maps and Mapping* (1976) p. 2.

20 Monmonier, *op. cit.*, n. 16, p. 4.

21 *Id.*

22 J. S. Keates, *Understanding Maps* (1982) p. 73.

23 M. Monmonier, *op. cit.*, n. 16, p. 4.

24 P. C. Muehrcke, *Map Use* (2nd ed. 1986) p. 10.

25 M. Monmonier, *op. cit.*, n. 16, p. 4.

26 See, Y. Lacoste, *La Géographie, ça sert, d'abord, à faire la guerre* (1976) p. 61; Y. Lacoste, "Les objets géographiques" in *Cartes et Figures de la Terre*, *op. cit.*, n. 18, p. 17.

27 See, J. B. Racine *et al.*, "Escala e acção, contribuições para uma interpretação do mecanismo de escala na prática da geografia" (1982) 45 *Revista Brasileira de Geografia* p. 126.

28 See, among others, M. Monmonier, *op. cit.*, n. 16, p. 15; J. S. Keates, *op. cit.*, n. 22, p. 72; P. C. Muehrcke, *op. cit.*, n. 24, p. 456; D. Muracciole, "Le rond et le plat" in *Cartes et Figures de la Terre*, *op. cit.*, n. 18, p. 235; A. G. Hodgkiss, *op. cit.*, n. 17, p. 32.

29 On the use of maps for propaganda purposes, see M. Monmonier, *op. cit.*, n. 16, p. 43; A. G. Hodgkiss, *op. cit.*, n. 17, p. 15; P. C. Muehrcke, *op. cit.*, n. 24, p. 395; J.-L. Rivière, "Cartes Polémiques" in *Cartes et Figures de la Terre*, *op. cit.*, n. 18, p. 351; H. Speier, "Magic Geography" (1941) 8 *Social Research* p. 310; L. Quam, "The Use of Maps in Propaganda" (1943) 42 *J. of Geography* p. 21; S. W. Boggs, "Cartohypnosis" (1947) 64 *Scientific Monthly* p. 469; M. Sharkey, "Cartography in Advertising" (1984) 22 *The Cartographical J.* p. 148.

30 See, A. Hodgkiss, *op. cit.*, n. 17, p. 29. For a slightly different view, showing the way the map centre changed as the Middle Ages developed, see D. Woodward, "Reality, Symbolism, Time, and Space in Medieval World Maps" (1985) 75 *Annals of the Association of American Geographers* p. 510. A. Henrikson, in "America's Changing Place in the World: from 'Periphery' to 'Centre'?" in *Centre and Periphery: Spatial Variation in Politics* (1980; ed. J. Gottmann) p. 73, shows how the progressive shift of the U.S.A. from the periphery to the centre of world affairs – a shift completed with the Second World War – resulted in changes in the types of map projections adopted or favoured: "The relationship of the United States to the major theatres of battle was such that a new picture of the world – a new global strategic map – was needed. Cylindrical maps projections, such as the conventional Equator-based Mercator, failed to show the continuity, unity, and organisation of the 'world wide arena' as Roosevelt called it. Hence, other map projections came into fashion, notably the North Pole-centred azimuthal projection. . . . The position of the United States on these polar maps was usually a central one." (p. 83). See also, A. Henrikson, "The Map as an 'Idea': The Role of Cartographic Imagery During the Second World War" (1975) 2 *The American Cartographer* p. 19.

31 P. Muehrcke, *op. cit.*, n. 24, p. 6.

32 L. Carroll, "The Hunting of the Snark" in *Complete Works* (1976) p. 757.

33 *Id.*, p. 760.

34 J. S. Keates, *op. cit.*, n. 22, p. 66.

35 M. Monmonier, *op. cit.*, n. 16, p. 6.

36 See, R. Caron, "Les Choix de Cartographe" in *Cartes et Figures de la Terre*, *op. cit.*, n. 18, p. 9.

37 See, J. S. Keates, *op. cit.*, n. 22, p. 69.

38 C. Geertz, *Local Knowledge* (1983) p. 232.

39 C. Perelman, *The New Rhetoric: A Treatise in Argumentation* (1971) p. 405.

40 B. Santos, "Law and Revolution in Portugal: the Experiences of Popular Justice after the 25th of April 1974" in *The Politics of Informal Justice* (1982; ed. R. Abel) Vol. 2, p. 251; B. Santos, "A Crise do Estado e a Aliança Povo/MFA em 1974-75" in *25 de Abril – 10 Anos Depois* (1985; ed. Associação 25 de Abril) p. 45; B. Santos, "Popular Justice, Dual Power and Socialist Strategy" in *Capitalism and the Rule of Law* (1979; ed. B. Fine *et al.*) p. 151.

41 B. Santos, "Law, State and Urban Struggles in Recife, Brazil" (1982) *University of Wisconsin-Madison Law School Working Paper*. See also, B. Santos, "Os conflitos Urbanos no Recife: o caso do 'Skylab' " (1983) 11 *Revista Crítica de Ciências Sociais* p. 9; B. Santos, "The Law of the Oppressed: The Construction and Reproduction of Legality in Pasargada Law" (1977) 12 *Law and Society Rev.* p. 5.

42 B. Santos, *A Justiça Popular em Cabo Verde. Estudo Sociológico* (1984; ed. Centro de Estudos Sociais, Faculdade de Economia da Universidade de Coimbra).

43 See, P. Kahn, "Droit International économique, droit du développement, *lex mercatoria*: concept unique ou pluralisme des ordres juridiques?" in *Le Droit des Relations Economiques Internationales* (1982; ed. P. Fouchard *et al.*) p. 97. See all the other articles in the same book. See also, C. D. Wallace, *Legal Control of the Multinational Enterprise* (1982).

44 See, G. Farjat, "Reflexions sur les codes de conduite privés" in *Droit des Relations Economiques Internationales*, *op. cit.*, n. 43, p. 47.

45 For an in-depth analysis of the economic and legal nature of subcontracting both in general and in the Portuguese context, see M. M. Marques, "Regulação das relações entre empresas: o caso da subcontratação" in *Estudos Económicos e Jurídicos* (1986; ed. Faculdade de Economia da Universidade de Coimbra) p. 247; M. M. Marques, "A empresa, o espaço e o direito" (1987) 22 *Revista Crítica de Ciências Sociais* p. 69.

46 See, B. Santos, *op. cit.*, n. 42, p. 33.

47 See, B. Santos, "The Law of the Oppressed", *op. cit.*, n. 41, p. 38.

48 See, B. Santos, "Law, State and Urban Struggles", *op. cit.*, n. 41 and "Os conflitos urbanos", *op. cit.*, n. 41.

49 For the distinction between molar and molecular struggles, see G. A. Miller *et al.*, "Plans" in *Culture and Cognition* (1972; ed. J. P. Spradley) p. 52 at p. 59.

50 See, B. Santos, "Law and Revolution", *op. cit.*, n. 40, p. 272.

51 This distinction is also used, in a slightly different sense, in the analysis of cognitive mapping (egocentric and geocentric mental maps). See, P. C. Muehrcke, *op. cit.*, n. 24, p. 4.

52 See, M. Weber, *Economy and Society* (1978) p. 695.

53 *Id.*, pp. 698 and 724.

54 *Id.*, p. 697.

55 On the new transnational legal space and its conflicts with the national legal space, see the authors cited in footnotes 43, 44 and 45.

56 See, Destanne de Bernis cited in G. Farjat, *op. cit.*, n. 44, p. 65.

57 See, B. Goldman, "Frontières du droit et *lex mercatoria*" (1964) IX *Archives de Philosophie du Droit* p. 180.

58 See, G. Farjat, *op. cit.*, n. 44, p. 57.

59 See, C. Geertz, *op. cit.*, n. 38, p. 167.

60 *Id.*, p. 173.

61 L. Pospisil, *Anthropology of Law: A Comparative Theory* (1971) p. 23.

62 E. Auerbach, *Mimesis. The Representation of Reality in Western Literature* (1968) p. 23.

63 See, for instance, G. Farjat, *op. cit.*, n. 44, p. 65.

64 See, B. Santos, *op. cit.*, n. 41, p. 105.

65 See, B. Santos, "Law, State and Urban Struggles", *op. cit.*, n. 41, p. 21.

66 See, B. Santos, "Law and Revolution, *op. cit.*, n. 40, p. 254.

67 C. Perelman, *op. cit.*, n. 39, p. 390.

68 See, among others, F. Jameson, "Postmodernism, or the Cultural Logic of Late Capitalism" (1984) 146 *New Left Rev.* p. 53.

69 See a fascinating analysis of law and informalism in P. Fitzpatrick, "The Rise and Rise of Informalism" in *Reconstructing Criminal Justice* (forthcoming; ed. R. Matthews). See also, U. Cerroni, "Formale e Informale" (1986) 23-24 *Scienzasocietá* p. 3.

70 S. Macaulay, "Images of Law in Everyday Life: The Lessons of School, Entertainment and Spectator Sports" (1987) 21 *Law and Society Rev*. p. 185.

71 On the vulgar and trivial nature of our daily encounters with maps, see A. G. Hodgkiss, *op. cit.*, n. 17, p. 11: "It is difficult to avoid being confronted by at least one or two maps during the daily routine. Perusing the morning paper in the commuter train we are likely to see small black-and-white maps serving to locate and explain some significant contemporary event. At home in the evening similar maps face us on the television screen, as a feature of the television news. The current state of the weather is indicated in the press and on television with the aid of satellite photographs and maps which have been specially designed so that their meaning should be clear to the untrained map user." The new legal common sense aims at trivialising our daily encounters with the laws so that their meaning becomes clear to the untrained law user.

72 See, B. Santos, *Um Discurso Sobre as Ciências* (1987).

73 On the possibility of an edifying knowledge, see R. Rorty, *Philosophy and the Mirror of Nature* (1980) p. 373.

74 And not before that, as E. P. Thompson claims. See, E. P. Thompson, *Whigs and Hunters* (1975) p. 258.

Part IV
Non-Western Perspectives

[15]

AFRICENTRIC SOCIAL SCIENCES FOR HUMAN LIBERATION

NA'IM AKBAR
Florida State University

Social science represents as much an expression of a people's ideology as it does a defense of that ideology (Asante, 1980). The extent to which that ideology contains elements of implicit oppression is the extent to which that particular social science is in fact an instrument of oppression. Nobles (1978a) discusses the fact that "Western Science, particularly social science, like the economic and political institutions has become an instrument designed to reflect the culture of the oppressor and to allow for the more efficient domination and oppression of African peoples." Consequently, the uncritical acceptance of the assumptions of Western science by African people is to participate in our own domination and oppression. Nobles, in the same discussion, goes on to justify the need for a social science system reflective of our cultural reality. Our objective in this discussion is to identify some characteristics of Western social science and to suggest some alternative assumptions for the establishment of an African social science.

African social scientists have failed to come to grips with the fact that the tools that they have acquired in the course of their training in the Western social science tradition have ill-equipped them to deal with the fundamental task of liberating

JOURNAL OF BLACK STUDIES, Vol. 14 No. 4, June 1984 395-414

African people—socially, politically, economically, and psychologically. The apparent paradox of increasing numbers of Africans being trained in the social sciences paralleling exponential increases in African social problems is resolved when we understand the implicit character of the training that the African social scientists have received. Again, Nobles (1978a), in his insightful discussion, characterizes the African social scientist operating from this alien framework as being "conceptually incarcerated." He astutely observes:

> The worldview, normative assumptions, and referential frame upon which the paradigm is based, must, like the science they serve, be consistent with the culture and cultural substance of the people. When the paradigm is inconsistent with the cultural definition of the phenomena, the people who use it to assess and/or evaluate that phenomena become essentially conceptually incarcerated.

Such an "incarceration" seriously handicaps the African social scientist in his or her objective of human liberation.

The "conceptually incarcerated" social scientist has bought the assertion made by Western social scientists that science is an objective and consequently superior form of inquiry. Jacob Carruthers (1972) argues against the valuelessness of science in his masterful discussion of "Science and Oppression." This writer has argued elsewhere (Akbar, 1980) that the "objective" approach does not preclude values because objectivity *is* a value. When an observer chooses to suspend from his or her observations certain levels of reaction, then this is a value judgment. This is a critical value because it often involves dismissing certain important sources of information that could critically alter what is perceived as real. Ornstein (1981) offers support for this point of view in his observation:

> Science as a mode of knowing involves a limitation of inquiry. The essence of a good experiment is successful *exclusion* [italics mine]. One factor may be manipulated while a very few other

> processes are measured. . . . the *method* of psychology has itself become the goal; this confusion has led, in the past sixty years, to a 'radical underestimation' of the possibilities.

If such a methodology has resulted in a "radical underestimation" of the possibilities for the Westerners for whom the method was intended to benefit, one cannot fathom the extent of underestimation it has incurred for the people intended to be oppressed by such a perspective.

CHARACTERISTICS OF EURO-AMERICAN SOCIAL SCIENCE

The model that characterizes Euro-American social science can most succinctly be seen in its model of normality. Normality is established on a model of the middle-class, Caucasian male of European descent. The more that one approximates this model in appearance, values, and behavior, the more "normal" one is considered to be. The inevitable conclusion from such assumptions of normality is a brand of deviance for anyone unlike this model. In fact, the more distant or distinct one is from this model the more pathological one is considered to be. The obvious advantage for Euro-Americans is that such norms confirm their reality as *the* reality and flaunts statements of their superiority as scientifically based "fact." The history of Western social science is replete with evidence of this ethnocentric assumption of normality. Sociology has identified the "middle class" as the normative group. Anthropology has identified all non-Western peoples variously as savage, primitive, or uncivilized. The volumes of psychological literature over the last 100 years has been based on observations primarily on Europeans, exclusively Caucasian, predominantly male, and as Robert Guthrie (1976) has noted, "even the rat was white." The formulations of most of the notable scholars who have shaped the thought of Euro-American psychology such as Freud, Jung, G. Stanley Hall, William McDougall, and B. F. Skinner have all directly or indirectly asserted the superiority of European races over non-European races.

Unaware of the ethnocentric assumptions of Western social science, many African scholars have become advocates of their own inferiority by utilizing these theories and their implicit norms. The research and scholarship of these African American social scientists have confirmed the negative assertions of their Euro-American counterparts. It has led to a preoccupation with deviance, deficiency, and an excessive involvement with "victim analysis." Native African scholars have often taken on the position of the neocolonialist scholar advocating the "improvement" of his or her people by the adoption of European personal traits and social patterns (see Fanon, 1967, 1968). African-American scholars have become the neo-slave master and neo-oppressor by advocating success by identification or integration with Euro-Americans as the only basis for success. Our position is not one of minimizing or denying the presence of rampant social and personal problems as a consequence of decades of colonialism and/or oppression and slavery. Such extreme human suffering is undeniable. The problem is that we are extremely limited in the capacity to alter any of these conditions because of the "conceptual incarceration" that Nobles has described and that we identify in this discussion as a kind of paradigmatic stagnation.

A similar difficulty is that of negative identification with the Euro-American social scientist. Such a perspective leads to rather extreme reactions against the Euro-American model. It advocates that whatever has been seen as positive in the European model must necessarily be viewed as negative in a Black model. Whatever has been viewed as negative about Blacks from the perspective of the White model is automatically assumed to be positive in the Black model. The point of this discussion, though it identifies real limitations with the Eurocentric approach, does not presume the Africentric approach to be the obverse. The Africentric model must be viewed as a perspective independent of the Eurocentric model; otherwise, it too will become merely reactive and therefore persistently dependent on the European model.

Models provide the definitions that give rise to methodologies. In fact, models or paradigms very clearly circumscribe not only the "askable" questions, but also the models of observation or methodologies. Ornstein (1981) observes:

> Any community of people holds in common certain assumptions about reality. Each scientific community of physicists, mathematicians, psychologists, or others, shares an additional set of implicit assumptions, called the paradigm. The paradigm is the shared conceptions of what is possible, the boundaries of acceptable inquiry, the limiting cases.

Methodologies make sense, then, only in the light of models that breed them. In fact, Curtis Banks (1980) argues that methodologies are merely ways to confirm preexisting models. Therefore, understanding of the Eurocentric paradigm is essential for understanding its methodology. In addition to the model being normatively based on the Caucasian, middle-class male of European descent, it also has other characteristics. Among these additional characteristics of the Eurocentric model are that it is individualistic, rationalistic, and materialistic. We shall demonstrate briefly how each of these characteristics, particularly to the exclusion of others, renders a Eurocentric psychology essentially useless as an instrument of human liberation.

The individualistic focus of the model operates with the assumption that the human identity is essentially in the individual. His corporate identity is of secondary significance in conceptualizing the person. As a consequence, much of Western psychology has focused on individual differences as its major consideration. Even sociology deals with society's impact on the individual and history with a series of individual heroes. So fundamental is the assumption that the subject for primary consideration is the individual that most thinkers have difficulty conceiving of an alternative approach without sacrificing or violating the supreme illusion of an autonomous human existence and the sacred freedom of the illusionary being called an "individual." There is, in fact, a growing controversy among Euro-American psychologists as to whether or not there has been an overassertion of the role of independence as a desirable attribute of human beings. Psychological concepts of external fate control, dependence, and submissiveness are all viewed as negative personality characteristics. Such a negation is only a camouflaged assertion for the desirability of the American ideal of the rugged individualistic European immigrant who "single-handedly conquered this wilderness and settled this great country." The idea of the primacy of the individual and his unique motivations, and the nuclear family and its exclusiveness are fundamental concepts in Euro-American social science.

Another characteristic of this model that extends the notion of individualism is the desirability of competition. The fundamental American economic theory is one that glorifies competition as essential for social progress. The most efficiently functioning individuals are those who are most assertive and competitive. The "achievement orientation" is lauded as the prize of Western progress. Human beings are assumed axiomatically to be in conflict and human accomplishment is realized by the triumph of the weak over the strong. The classic McClelland (1961) book, *The Achieving Society*, concluded that a people could be accorded the status of being civilized (that is, industrialized) only if their motivations were characterized by a high need for achievement. Predictably his data showed non-Caucasian, non-European, nonmale, non-middle-class people to be at the lower end of this fundamental individual characteristic.

Oppressed humanity has failed to realize that in the garb of "science" the Western world has utilized a social and psychological paradigm that functions to legitimize the assertion of their racial and national superiority. What has been assumed to be an apolitical, objective system is, in fact, the essence of Euro-American, Caucasian politics.

To assert that Euro-American social science is rationalistic is to imply that a science should be irrational. Certainly, this is not our intention. It is clear that science as conceived in the Western tradition has some frequently unacknowledged limitations. Ornstein (1981) observes: "Science as a mode of knowing involves a limitation on inquiry." Because of its limitations, critical aspects of the human social process are often excluded from consideration. Ornstein continues:

> It is incomplete to hold that knowledge is exclusively rational. Even scientific inquiry, that most rational and logical of our pursuits, could not proceed without the presence of another type of knowledge. . . . Scientific investigators act on personal knowledge, biases, hunches, intuition. It is the genius of the scientific method that the arational thought becomes translated into the rational mode and made explicit, so that others can follow it.

Ornstein's designation of the alternative to a rational system as "arational" rather than irrational seems appropriate.

One of the limitations of this rationalistic component of the Euro-American social science model is its exclusion of feeling or affect. Emotion is considered irrelevant at worst and disruptive at best in the scientific endeavor. Great energy is expended to maintain objectivity and to exclude any affective component of the inquiry. The consequence is that such a scientist develops a passive insensitivity that permits and even condones an American slavery system, an Auschwitz, or even a neutron bomb—calmly described as capable of destroying all people, but leaving buildings and physical structures standing. The economist need not address the elements of his or her theory that define excessive opulence for the few to be based on the privation of the many. The observer who gives any demonstration of affective or emotional involvement in his or her subject matter is viewed as inappropriate, distracted, or just irrational and therefore deserves being discounted. Ornstein (1981) makes an observation pertinent to this point:

> We deemphasize and even devalue the arational, nonverbal modes of consciousness. Education consists predominantly of "reading," "ritin" and "rithmetic," and we are taught precious little about our emotions, our bodies, our intuitive capabilities.

Because of our "uneducated" emotional selves we usually remain emotional idiots and fail to obtain the benefits of knowledge that comes from that modality.

The final characteristic of this model, at least for the purposes of this discussion, is its materialistic focus. It is assumed that outer characteristics are essential characteristics. Whether these characteristics are designated as "behavioral data," or "class data," the assumption is that what is directly observable is the "most real." Therefore, what is knowable and what is relevant is restricted to some aspect of the material. Ornstein (1981) again makes a relevant observation to this issue. He states:

> A strict emphasis on verbal intellectual knowledge has screened out much of what is or could be legitimate for study in contemporary psychology—"esoteric" systems of meditation are much misunderstood; the existence of "nonordinary realities" is not studied because they do not fit into the dominant paradigm, and neither, of course, do phenomena named "paranormal."

From the Western social science perspective, disparaging descriptions of non-Western peoples are made when inferences are made about the human being solely on the basis of material data. A dismissal of esoteric and nonmaterial information has resulted in the description of many intricate practices of non-Western people as "superstitious, pagan, or primitive." Such interpretations are a direct consequence of the Western social scientist's inability to grasp the esoteric. The tendency to fragment behavior from the broader context of the spiritual and esoteric dimensions of reality renders highly meaningful and significant human activities as meaningless and insignificant. It is not surprising that people with less opulent outer appearances are adjudged inferior, uncivilized, unintelligent, and barbaric, even when such people may far surpass the materially affluent in justice, charitableness, compassion, and peacefulness.

In summary, the Euro-American model or paradigm of social science views the characteristics of the Caucasian, middle-class male of European descent to be the paradigmatic norm for human beings. Individualism, rationalism, and materialism are other characteristics of this model that direct the perception and methodologies of Euro-American science. Although these components of any model of human functioning are critical, the limitation of the science ensues from the exclusive reliance on these modalities for observation. The premise of this discussion is that the exclusive reliance on these aspects of the model renders Western social science an effective instrument of human oppression and exploitation. The oppression is likely to be most evident among those least like the paradigmatic model that we have described above. The major objection is that all of these characteristics of Euro-American social science render it an ineffective instrument for human growth and liberation. It should not be surprising from this premise that Europe and America have the largest numbers of social scientists in the world and a greater number of social and human problems than any nation in the world. For example, child molestation, rape, bizarre sexual perversions, drug abuse, child abuse, and even racial conflict are virtually unknown occurrences in most parts of the world, but reach epidemic proportions as one approximates the characteristics of the Euro-American model. The importance of Euro-American social science in providing remedies to these problems is predictable as one evaluates this system as a model for human growth and liberation.

The methodologies emerging from this model are ones that reaffirm the basic assumptions of the model. The method is an "objective" one, the focus is on individual differences and the data is expressed through a count-and-measure system characteristic of material phenomena.

THE AFRICENTRIC MODEL OF SOCIAL SCIENCE

Our discussion of an Africentric model grows out of several assumptions. We do not argue that a model for human liberation should substitute the norm of a Black male of African descent for a Caucasian male of European descent. Such a concretization would merely substitute one limited model for another limited model. "Africentric" is utilized from the perspective that Africa constitutes the primordial context for human growth and liberation. African-Americans represent the most extreme examples of victims of human oppression and would be the most appropriate group on which to demonstrate a liberation psychology. Therefore, our focus is on the African ontological conception of man as a model of humanity in general since Africa represents probably the most "naturally human" concept. Though the model has specific relevance to the national liberation of all African people in the diaspora, it is more generally applicable to the transformation of human beings in whatever national context.

One of the difficulties entailed in describing this model in a comparative context with the Eurocentric model is the implication that the Africentric model represents a contrast or reaction to the former. As we have noted above, this is definitely not the case in that the Africentric model actually antedates the Eurocentric one that is actually a conceptual devolution from its predecessor. For the sake of cohesion and greater clarity, we will focus on some aspects of this Africentric model that demonstrate its relative strength to the characteristics of Western social science, which we have described above.

AFRICENTRIC NORM

The norm of the Africentric model is nature. The normative characteristics of this social science are based upon the exquisite order of human nature. Vague though this may seem and certainly "unscientific" in the Western tradition, it is considerably more consistent with the philosophical, religious, and symbolic tradition of the most enduring human societies. Though concretely undemonstrable, "human nature" ascribes an order that is both universal and absolute. It is, in fact, metaphysical. Human adaptation and aberration is not to be confused with human potential. Arguments to this effect have been advanced by such Western notables as Maslow, May, Rogers, and many others of the humanistic tradition. Though lacking in the precision of the intricately specific language of the Western social scientist, it is more consistent with the holistic, multidimensional polydeterminism of being human. The oversimplification of Western social science, though impressively more manageable, is disastrously myopic in its exclusion of blatantly causal realities. Logical positivism and reductionism have tried to make men and women thoroughly rational and minute enough to fit a micro model of a unidimensional view of humanity. The Africentric model is comfortable with global conceptions and metaphysical conceptions, and offers a macro model that actually exceeds the manipulation of the observing observer whose object of observation is ultimately himself or herself.

The example of a concept drawn from this naturalistic model is the concept of survival. A consistent characteristic of the natural order is its tendency to preserve itself. Self-preservation has been identified as the "first law of nature." This "law" is derived from folk knowledge and not scientific fact, though it is the type of adage, intuitive or folk wisdom that guides even the structuring of Western science. The Africentric theorist takes such an assumption as an element of his or her paradigm and seeks to observe the consistency with which phenomena obey this "law." It then identifies a norm that is all-inclusive and holistic, which says that normality is any process that operates in consistency with the tendency of nature's self-preservative character. Such a conclusion is not dissimilar to the eminently profound assertion of the "Law of relativity" which maintains that matter can be neither created nor destroyed, that is, it is self-preservative, observing the first law of nature.

Theorists in African philosophy and African psychology, specifically Mbiti (1970) and Nobles (1980), have identified a principle of African social science that they identify as the principle of collective survival or "survival of the tribe." Observations, then, of human behavior can be understood as normal or abnormal to the degree that it adheres to this principle. Behaviors that maintain, enhance, or secure the "survival of the tribe" are normal. Behaviors that threaten the survival of the tribe are abnormal. Again, as Nobles has illustrated, the "normal" family is neither nuclear (that is, the Eurocentric family models) nor extended, as some rejoinders to Eurocentric victim analysis have asserted. The normal family is in fact flexible or "elastic" (Nobles, 1978b), capable of maximizing the fundamental natural objective of its survival. Such a family can be as effectively nuclear as extended, depending upon what kinds of circumstances affected the survival of the family (tribe). The same point is true of functions within the family. According to Nobles (1978b):

> Functionally, or the performance of its (family) functions, would be fluid or elastic. That is, the performance of a particular function does or can "expand" into many other functions.

Such a characterization of family functioning begins to hint of pragmatism. It is functional, but the pragmatism is restricted within the guidelines of natural orderliness. Family survival does require security from harm; it does not require domination in order to secure itself. Though there are barbaric instances of predator orientations that exist in various arenas of nature, because of certain "moral" capabilities of human beings, such qualities cannot be justified as the basis for human oppression. This balancing "moral" component will be discussed at greater length below.

CHARACTERISTICS OF AFRICENTRIC MODEL

The Africentric approach to social science conceptualizes self as a collective phenomena. It does not deny "uniqueness," but it does deny the isolated notion of individualism, that is, that the person can be understood independent of other persons. The "other" is not just a mirror of the self in the Cooley sense but the "other" is an expression of self. The fundamental adage emerging from African philosophy that captures this collective experience of self is the proposition: "I am because we are and because we are, therefore I am." (Mbiti, 1970). This conception identifies the collective consciousness as the appropriate arena for human observation. Nobles (1980) refers to this as "experiential communality or the sharing of a particular experience by a group of people." The scientific question is not one of how do individuals differ, but in what ways are people fundamentally alike. Again, the holistic balance does not argue for a mass conforming national character, but a sharing of certain universal human values and goals and the degree to which a person's uniqueness facilitates those goals. For example, reproduction of effective human beings is a universal objective that is not violated by individual characteristics though individual freedom is circumscribed by the collective need to realize this objective. So, everyone does not have to reproduce, but everyone is accountable for the health of humanity's offspring.

Nobles (1980) maintains that the experiential communality is important in determining society's fundamental principles such as its belief about the nature of humanity and what kind of society humans should create for themselves. In other words, the work of the social scientist in describing, assessing, or even improving societies or human beings must be a collective rather than an individual phenomenon. African social theory ascribes preeminence to the group, unlike the Western ascription of this status to the individual.

Another characteristic of the Africentric paradigm is that it identifies the essence of the human being as spiritual. Certainly a holistic model must include the full dimensions of the human make-up: physical, mental, and metaphysical. In Western dualistic thought, not only is mind and body (reason and emotion) considered to be independent phenomena, but there is a trinitarian tendency that views spirit as independent of both mind and body. Usually, however, spirituality is completely discounted in Western social science. Increasingly, with the growing emphasis on behavior in the social sciences, even the mental dimension or consciousness has been discounted as irrelevant to understanding human functioning. Relative to the Eurocentric approach, the Africentric social scientists take a "quantum leap" when they identify spirituality as a relevant dimension of the human experience.

The concept of humanity's essential spirituality merely suggests that when men and women are reduced to their lowest terms they are invisible and of a universal substance. Such an assumption implies that, ultimately, people are harmoniously alike and not dissimilar to the essence of all that is in nature. Oneness with nature is a natural extension of this point of view that precludes assumptions of inevitable conflict among men and women and with nature. Material, by its very nature, is fragmented and in conflict, obeying principles of polarity and tension. To the extent that the material dimension of human beings is viewed as their essence is the extent to which conflict is viewed as axiomatic to human existence.

The Africentric approach, viewing humanity as ultimately reducible to a universal substance that is harmonious with the entire cosmos, implies the fundamental goodness of humans—goodness being the tendency of life to enhance life in a constructive direction. Human relationships are considered potentially as compatible as are the relationships among all of the mutually facilitating components of nature. Consequently, morality is endemic to this conception of man. The Africentric social scientist does not shy away from articulating that that which is normal is also good. Morality and spirituality are inseparate, which is why both dimensions have been relegated to the domain of the theologian in the Eurocentric approach. However, the values that are made explicit in the Africentric approach are implicitly present in the Eurocentric approach. As we have noted above, objectivity is as much an implicit value as that attributed to the explicit values in a subjective system. There is a widely accepted myth of objectivity among Eurocentric social scientists. Since spirituality implies order, harmony, interdependence, and perfectability then morality is a fundamental component of the human make-up. Morality, in the Africentric approach, is not in the form of the series of maxims found in the Eurocentric theological moral systems. Morality simply is an acknowledgement of a natural order and normality is man's harmony with that order.

Morality also constitutes a uniquely human trait. It represents the human being's capacity for self-mastery and self-direction. Unlike the lower animal species regulated by instinct, the human being has the unique capacity for self-regulation. This exonerates the human being from some of the more brutish components of the natural order. This moral form permits human beings to be in nature but not *of* nature in the sense of falling victim to some of its more destructive components. Morality becomes the instrumentation of balance and, in the Africentric model, it is an imperative of the human make-up and not an option.

However, the Africentric model does not deny the relevance of materiality. In fact, this model represents a balance between the extreme material and exoteric ontology represented in the

Eurocentric model and the extreme spiritual and esoteric ontology represented in the Eastern models. This model will permit cross validation between subjective and objective experience. An example of this model is perhaps seen in the African traditional healer. Such healers are simultaneously herbalists (users of objective power) and griots (reciters of "self" or conjurers of subjective power). The traditional healer recognized the interdependence of moral order and material order. A violation in either impacts on all dimensions of the human make-up. Such an approach does not demand a denial of material mastery or technological advancement, but it demands a balanced development of the inner and outer worlds. In such a world, one does not construct huge skyscrapers as a precipice from which the deranged may throw themselves. Instead, one's skill in scaling the heights of gravity is paralleled by exploring the depths of the human make-up.

The final characteristic of an Africentric social science is its epistemological assumptions. As we have observed above, the rationalism of Eurocentric social science precludes the arational, consequently excluding much of the human experience. The Africentric approach assumes a universal knowledge rooted in knowledge of the make-up of the human beings themselves. The most direct experience of the self is through emotion or affect. Vernon Dixon (1976) observes:

> Homeland and overseas African persons know reality predominantly through the interaction of affect and symbolic imagery, that is, the synthesis of these two factors produce knowledge. In the "pure" Africanized worldview of the unity of man and the phenomenal world, there is no empty perceptual space between the self and phenomena. Affect refers to the feeling self, the emotive self engaged in experiencing phenomena holistically.

This approach of Africentricity admits both symbols and affect as legitimate determiners of human activity. Emotional reactions as a means of knowing and as a balance for rationality is legitimate within this model. Similarly, the significance of symbols in the Jungian tradition as an expression of certain collective archetypes is also an approach of value. Cultural symbols and rituals (such as naming ceremonies and puberty rites in traditional societies) are considered as important causative dimensions in human experience. Such symbols in Western science would have little validity as either independent or dependent variables, but in the Africentric paradigm they could be either. Dixon (1976) further characterizes this affect/symbolic connection by observing:

> Affect, however, is not intuition, for the latter term means direct or immediate knowledge (instinctive knowledge) without recourse to inference from or reasoning about evidence. Affect does interact with evidence, evidence in the form of symbolic imagery.

Such holistic knowledge is critical in terms of both structuring the Africentric methodology as well as characterizing the appropriateness of certain observations. For example, rather than intelligence being defined as what is measured by an IQ test (that is, defining both a methodology and an arena of observation), intelligence would be defined by a person's adequacy in living and developing. Knowledge would be reflected in the degree to which a person is capable of maneuvering an environment offering obstacles to his or her development. So, intelligence would be reflected in the degree to which a person is capable of maneuvering an environment offering obstacles to his or her "collective self's" development. Consequently, intelligence would entail (1) knowledge of the collective reality of self, (2) knowledge of environmental obstacles to effective (collective) self-development, (3) actions initiated to remove or master such obstacles, and ultimately (4) knowledge of the Divine and universal laws that guide human development into knowledge of the Creator. An adequate assessment of intelligence would require effectively tapping the full range of a people's symbolic imagery (such as, words, gestures, tones, rhythms, rituals). One could not evaluate a person's "knowledge" without knowing how effectively that person conducts his or her full being. Therefore, the possibility of a man or woman being assessed a genius on the basis of his or her external knowledge yet proving to be morally inept would not be conceivable from the Africentric approach. Similarly, a society with opulent technology but social and moral decadence could not be viewed as an advanced or model civilization.

CONCLUSION

Africentricity is the form of a new paradigm for the social sciences. It grows out of the increasing inadequacy of the Eurocentric model to address the escalating social problems of Western society adequately. Most importantly, the model seeks to correct the indirect oppressive function played by traditional Western science. Although the model is based upon the tenets of traditional African philosophy, it does not exclude in its fundamental assumptions the possibility for normative activity on the parts of people of other ethnic origins. The new paradigm in fact formalizes and provides a context for many of the issues that are increasingly being raised by Western social scientists themselves. Theorists such as Abraham Maslow, Rollo May, Alan Watts, and many others out of the existential and humanistic schools have addressed many of the same issues that are raised within the Africentric context and are resolved within the Africentric model.

The most important element offered by the Africentric paradigm is the opportunity for genuine human liberation through the social science model. An objective of Africentric social science is human liberation. Since it deals specifically with the humanly oppressive conditions experienced by African people throughout the diaspora, it has an immediate objective of offering an instrument for the social, political, economic, and psychological liberation of our people. The holistic quality of the model offers direction not only for such social liberation but an avenue for human liberation in general.

The course of such liberation is through the vehicle of transformation. An individualistic, materialistic, and rationalistic model to the exclusion of other modalities seriously limits the possibility for human transformation. Human potential is limited according to this model and people can at best be modified, but not transformed. A collective, spiritual, and affect/symbolic system addresses a multidimensional being capable of vast potential and the capacity for transformation.

It is appropriate that this paradigm should be pioneered by African people. With our worldview completely denied in the Eurocentric paradigm, we became ready victims to the misrepresentation of their social science. It is within the humanistic tradition of Africans that we should evolve a system that not only retrieves our humanity but offers the opportunity of human advancement for all people.

REFERENCES

AKBAR, N. (1980) The evolution of human psychology for African-Americans. Published manuscript presented to SREB Student Conference, Atlanta.

ASANTE, Molefi K. (1980) Afrocentricity: The Theory of Social Change. Buffalo: Amulefi.

BANKS, C. (1980) Specifications for theories within Black Psychology. Presented at 13th National Convention of the Association of Black Psychologists, Cherry Hill, NJ.

CARRUTHERS, J. (1972) Science and Oppression. Chicago: Northeastern Illinois University Center for Inner City Studies.

DIXON, V. (1976) "Worldviews and research methodology," in L. King et al. (eds.) African Philosophy: Paradigms for Research on Black Persons. Los Angeles: Fanon Research and Development Center.

FANON, F. (1968) The Wretched of the Earth. New York: Grove Press.

———(1967) Black Skin, White Masks. New York: Grove Press.

GUTHRIE, R. (1976) Even the Rat was White: A Historical View of Psychology. New York: Harper & Row.

MBITI, J. (1970) African Religions and Philosophy. Garden City, NY: Anchor Books (Doubleday).

McCLELLAND, D. (1961) The Achieving Society. New York: Van Nostrand.

NOBLES, W. (1980) "African philosophy foundations for black psychology," in R. Jones (ed.) Black Psychology (2nd ed.). New York: Harper & Row.

———(1978a) African Consciousness and Liberation Struggles: Implications for the Development and Construction of Scientific Paradigms. Presented at Fanon Research and Development Conference, Port of Spain, Trinidad.

———(1978b) "The black family and its children: the survival of humaness." Black Books Bull. 6, 2: 6-14.

ORNSTEIN, R. (1981) The Psychology of Consciousness. New York: Penguin Books.

Na'im Akbar, Clinical Psychologist at Florida State University's Department of Psychology and Black Studies, is a recognized expert in the field of Black Psychology. In addition to his university position, he currently serves as the Southern Regional Representative to the National Association of Black Psychologists' Board of Directors and is Associate Editor of the Journal of Black Psychology. *While serving as the American Muslim Mission's Human Development Director (1975-1977), he represented the Mission throughout the Middle East, the Caribbean, and the United States. He has published three essay collections, entitled:* The Community of Self; Natural Psychology and Human Transformation; *and* From Miseducation to Education.

[16]

R. Panikkar

IS THE NOTION OF HUMAN RIGHTS A WESTERN CONCEPT?[1]

We should approach this topic with great fear and respect. It is not a merely "academic" issue. Human rights are trampled upon in the East as in the West, in the North as in the South of our planet. Granting the part of human greed and sheer evil in this universal transgression, could it not also be that Human Rights are not observed because in their present form they do not represent a universal symbol powerful enough to elicit understanding and agreement?

No culture, tradition, ideology or religion can today speak for the whole of humankind, let alone solve its problems. Dialogue and intercourse leading to a mutual fecundation are necessary. But sometimes the very conditions for dialogue are not given, because there are unspoken conditions which most partners cannot meet. It is a fact that the present-day formulation of Human Rights is the fruit of a very partial dialogue among

[1] This paper is an expanded and revised version of the presentation at the "Entretiens de Dakar," Senegal, to the annual session of the Institut International de Philosophie on *Philosophical Foundations of Human Rights*, a summary of which will appear in the Proceedings.

Is the Notion of Human Rights a Western Concept?

the cultures of the world. It is only recently that this question has been acutely felt.[2]

I shall not enter into the details of the history of Human Rights, nor into an analysis of their nature. I shall confine myself to the interrogation implied in the title: are Human Rights a universal invariant?

I. The Method of Inquiry

1. *Diatopical Hermeneutics*

It is claimed that Human Rights are universal. This alone entails a major philosophical query. Does it make sense to ask about conditions of universality when the very question about conditions of universality is far from universal? Philosophy can no longer ignore this inter-cultural problematic. Can we extrapolate the concept of Human Rights, from the context of the culture and history in which it was conceived, into a globally valid notion? Could it at least *become* a universal symbol? Or is it only one particular way of expressing—and saving—the *humanum?*

Although the question posed in the title is a legitimate one, there is something disturbing in this formulation as it was given to me. At least at first glance, it would seem to offer only one alternative: either the notion of Universal Human Rights is a Western notion, or it is not. If it is, besides being a tacit indictment against those who do not possess such a valuable concept, its introduction into other cultures, even if necessary, would appear as a plain imposition from outside. It would appear, once again, as a continuation of the colonial syndrome, namely the belief that the constructs of one particular culture (God,

[2] Cf. probably the first Symposium of its kind convened by UNESCO at Bangkok in December 1979, *Meeting of Experts on the Place of Human Rights in Cultural and Religious Traditions*, where nine major schools of religious thought discussed the issue and recognized "that many of them have not paid sufficient attention to human rights... (And that) it is a task of the different religions of the world to deepen and eventually to enlarge and/or reformulate the urgent and important issue of human rights." § 116 g of the Final Report SS-79/CONF. 607/10 of 6 February, 1980. The entire report is worth reading.

Church, Empire, Western civilization, science, modern technology, etc.) have, if not the monopoly, at least the privilege of possessing a universal value which entitles them to be spread over all the Earth. If not, that is, if the concept of Universal Human Rights is not exclusively a Western concept, it would be difficult to deny that many a culture has let it slumber, thus again giving rise to an impression of the indisputable superiority of Western culture. There is nothing wrong in admitting a hierarchy of cultures, but this hierarchical order cannot be assumed as the starting point, nor can one side alone lay down the criteria necessary for establishing such a hierarchy. There is then a prior question implied by asking whether the notion of Human Rights is a Western concept. It is the question regarding the very nature of Human Rights, and it directly submits this notion to cross-cultural scrutiny.

Our question is a case in point of *diatopical hermeneutics*: the problem is how, from the *topos* of one culture, to understand the constructs of another.[3] It is wrong-headed methodology to begin by asking: Does another culture also have the notion of Human Rights?—assuming that such a notion is absolutely indispensable to guarantee human dignity. No question is neutral, for every question conditions its possible answers.

2. *The homeomorphic equivalent*

I was once asked to give the Sanskrit equivalents of the twenty-five key Latin words supposed to be emblematic of Western culture. I declined, on the grounds that that which is the foundation of one culture need not be the foundation for another. Meanings are not transferable here. Translations are more delicate than heart transplants. So what must we do? We must dig down to where a homogeneous soil or a similar problematic appears: we must search out the *homeomorphic equivalent*—to

[3] By diatopical hermeneutics I understand a thematic reflection on the fact that the loci (*topoi*) of historically unrelated cultures make it problematic to understand one tradition with the tools of another, and the hermeneutical attempt to bridge such gulfs. Cf. R. Panikkar, *Myth, Faith and Hermeneutics*, New York, Paulist Press, 1979, pp. 8 sq.

the concept of Human Rights in this case. "Homeomorphism is not the same as analogy; it represents a peculiar functional equivalence discovered through a topological transformation." It is "a kind of existential functional analogy."[4]

Thus we are not seeking merely to transliterate Human Rights into other cultural languages, nor should we be looking for mere analogies; we try instead to find the homeomorphic equivalent. If, for instance, Human Rights are considered to be the basis for the exercise of and respect for human dignity, we should investigate how another culture satisfies the equivalent need—and this can be done only once a common ground (a mutually understandable language) has been worked out between the two cultures. Or perhaps we should ask how the idea of a just social and political order could be formulated within a certain culture, and investigate whether the concept of Human Rights is a particularly appropriate way of expressing this order. A traditional Confucian might see this problem of order and rights as a question of "good manners" or in terms of his profoundly ceremonial or ritual conception of human intercourse, in terms of *li*. A Hindu might see it another way, and so on.

* * *

In order to clarify the question of our title, I shall indicate some of the assumptions on which the notion of Human Rights is based and immediately insert some cross-cultural reflections which will lead us to the *locus*—the context—of the question and the justification for my answer, which I would like to anticipate by means of a simile: Human Rights are one window through which one particular culture envisages a just human order for its individuals. But those who live in that culture do not see the window. For this they need the help of another culture which sees through another window. Now I assume

[4] Cf. R. Panikkar, *The Intrareligious Dialogue*, New York, Paulist Press, 1978, p. xxii. The two words Brahman and God, for instance, are neither analogous nor merely equivocal (nor univocal, of course). They are not exactly equivalent either. They are homeomorphic. They perform a certain type of respectively corresponding function in the two different traditions where these words are alive.

that the human landscape as seen through the one window is both similar to and different from the vision of the other. If this is the case, should we smash the windows and make of the many portals a single gaping aperture—with the consequent danger of structural collapse—or should we enlarge the viewpoints as much as possible and, most of all, make people aware that there are—and have to be—a plurality of windows? This latter option would be the one in favor of a healthy pluralism. This is much more than a merely academic question. There can be no serious talk about cultural pluralism without a genuine socio-economic-political pluralism. This is, for example, what has led intellectual groups in India to ask whether "civil rights" are not incompatible with "economic rights." At any rate, to speak of cultural pluralism within what could be called a paneconomic ideology makes little sense and amounts to treating the other cultures of the world as mere folklore. The example of the notion of dharma from the Indian tradition will offer us a point of reference from which to formulate our conclusion.

II. Assumptions and Implications of the Western Concept

I take the expression "Human Rights" in the sense of the Universal Declaration of Human Rights adopted by the General Assembly of the United Nations in 1948.[5] The Western, mainly liberal protestant roots of the Human Rights Declaration are well known.[6] The Western world has known of the struggle for

[5] I shall capitalize Human Rights when these words have the particular meaning derived from this "Universal Declaration."

[6] The dates to recall are:

10 December 1948	— Proclamation in Paris of the Universal Declaration;
4 November 1950	— Adoption in Rome of the Convention safeguarding Human Rights and fundamental freedom, known as "The European Convention on Human Rights";
20 March 1952	— Adoption in Paris of the first additional Protocol to this Convention;
16 December 1966	— International Covenant on Economic, Social and Cultural Rights; International Covenant on Civil and Political Rights; Optional Protocol (to the latter—not passed unanimously).

Is the Notion of Human Rights a Western Concept?

citizens' rights since the Middle Ages.[7] This struggle for concrete rights, rooted in the practices and value system of a particular nation or country, is felt with greater urgency after the French Revolution.[8] Western Man passes from a corporate belonging in a community of blood, work and historical destiny, based on practically accepted custom and theoretically acknowledged authority, to a society based on impersonal law and ideally free contract, to the modern State, for which explicitly rational norms and duties are required. The problem becomes increasingly acute with the growth of individualism.

This paper assumes knowledge of the history of Human Rights, as well as of the fact that this transition from one form of collective life to another more modern form is said today to have acquired a worldwide character. We would like to concentrate on the more strictly philosophical *assumptions* which seem to be at the basis of the Declaration.

1. At the basis of the discourse on Human Rights there is the assumption of a *universal human nature* common to all peoples. Otherwise, a Universal Declaration could not logically have been

[7] For the astounding documents of the first nine Christian centuries, cf. the collection and translation with insightful introduction by H. Rahner, *Kirche und Staat*, Munich, Kösel, 1961. The first edition, published in 1943 during the Second World War with the title *Abendländische Kirchenfreiheit*, is in itself a document for Human Rights.

Because it is less known than the *Magna Carta* of King John of England in 1215, let us mention King Alfonso IX of León in 1188 with his rights to life, honor, home and property.

Interesting also is the statement and justification of Francisco de Vitoria in 1538: "Cuando los súbditos tengan conciencia de la injusticia de la guerra, no les es lícito ir a ella, *sea que se equivoquen o no*" (emphasis mine). *De los indios o del derecho de la guerra*, II, 23 (Ed. BAC, Madrid 1960, p. 831). ("When its subjects are aware of the injustice of a war, it is not lawful for them to go to it, *whether they are in error or not.*") And the reason he gives is to quote Rom. XIV, 23: "omne quod non est ex fide peccatum est," which he translates "todo lo que no es según *conciencia* es pecado" (*ibid*, emphasis added) The Pauline passage is usually rendered: "Whatever does not come from faith is sin." Vitoria's variation reads: "Whatever is not in accordance with one's *conscience* is a sin." Cf the Thomistic principle that the rational being that is Man has to follow his or her personal conscience in order to act morally.

[8] Just as a memorandum, we may recall:
1689 — Bill of Rights (England)
1776 — Virginia Bill of Rights
1789 (26 August) — Déclaration des droits de l'homme et du citoyen
1798 — American Bill of Rights

proclaimed. This idea in its turn is connected with the old notion of a Natural Law.

But the contemporary Declaration of Human Rights further *implies*:

a) that this human nature must be *knowable*. For it is one thing to accept human nature uncritically or mythically, and another to know it. Otherwise, the Declaration could not speak and legislate about Rights that are universal;

b) that this human nature is known by means of an equally universal organ of knowledge, generally called *reason*. Otherwise, if its knowledge should depend on a special intuition, revelation, faith, decree of a prophet or the like, Human Rights could not be taken as *natural* rights—inherent in Man. This must be a commonly-held knowledge. Otherwise, Human Rights could not be declared universal by an Assembly which does not claim to have a privileged epistemological status. This is made plain by the use of the word "Declaration," which stresses the fact that it is not an imposition from above but a public explication, a making clear of what is inherent in the very nature of Man;[9]

c) that this human nature is essentially *different* from the rest of reality. Other living beings inferior to Man obviously have no Human Rights, and creatures superior to Man are likely not to exist. Man is the master of himself and the universe. He is the supreme legislator on Earth—the question of whether a Supreme Being exists or not remains open, but ineffective.[10]

2. The second assumption is that of the *dignity of the individual*. Each individual is, in a certain sense, absolute, irreducible to another. This is probably the major thrust of the Modern question of Human Rights. Human Rights defend the dignity

[9] The Paris document is a *declaration*, a manifest statement making clear what is already there, an explication (*dēclārāre*, to make clear—from *de-clārāre*. Cf. *clārus*, clear, but also loud (*clamor*)). It is not a law, a superimposition, a human creation, but the recognition or discovery of something intrinsic to the nature of the thing; in this case "the inherent dignity and equal and inalienable rights of all the members of the human family," as the Preamble to the 1948 Declaration says.

[10] This practical a-theism and even practical ignorance of any ulterior philosophical issue or religious factor became patent in the presentation and discussion of the Bangkok Conference mentioned above, let alone in the more official meetings where Philosophy and Religion have hardly a voice.

of the individual *vis-à-vis* Society at large, and the State in particular.

But this in turn implies:

a) not only the distinction but also the *separation* between individual and society. In this view the human being is fundamentally the individual. Society is a kind of superstructure, which can easily become a menace and also an alienating factor for the individual. Human Rights are there primarily to protect the individual;

b) the *autonomy* of humankind *vis-à-vis* and often versus the Cosmos. This is clearly shown in the ironic ambivalence of the English expression, which means at the same time "*Menschenrechte*," "*droits de l'Homme*," and also "*menschliche Rechte*," "*droits humains*" (humane rights). The Cosmos is a kind of understructure. The individual stands in between Society and World. Human Rights defend the autonomy of the human individual;

c) resonances of the idea of Man as *microcosmos* and reverberations of the conviction that Man is *imago dei*, and at the same time the relative independence of this conviction from ontological and theological formulations. The individual has an inalienable dignity because he is an end in himself and a kind of absolute. You can cut off a finger for the sake of the entire body, but can you kill one person to save another?[11]

3. The third assumption is that of a *democratic social order*. Society is assumed to be not a hierarchical order founded on a divine will or law or mythical origin, but a sum of "free" individuals organized to achieve otherwise unreachable goals. Human Rights, once again, serve mainly to protect the individual. Society here is not seen as a family or a protection, but as something unavoidable which can easily abuse the power conferred on it (precisely by the assent of the sum of its individuals). This Society crystallizes in the State, which theoretically expresses the will of the people, or at least of the majority. The idea

[11] Cf. R. Panikkar, "Singularity and Individuality: The Double Principle of Individuation," *Revue internationale de philosophie* XIX, 1-2, No. 111-112 (1975) p. 141-166, where it is argued that the ontic status of human individuals is basically different from that of all other individual entities; in short, that we cannot treat human individuals as we could peanuts or cattle, by a merely numerical individuality.

of an Empire, or a People or a Nation with a transcendent destiny—whose duty it is to carry through the entrusted mission independent of the will of the members of that society—still exists today in some theocratic states, but even most of these try to palliate their messianic vocation by democratic endorsements.

This implies:

a) that each individual is seen as equally important and thus equally responsible for the welfare of society. Hence the individual has the right to stand by his or her convictions and propagate them or to resist impositions against his or her inherent freedom;

b) that Society is nothing but the sum total of the individuals whose wills are sovereign and ultimately decisive.[12] There is no instance superior to Society. Even if there were to exist a God or a superhuman Reality, this too would be filtered through human consciousness and human institutions;

c) that the rights and freedoms of the individual can be limited only when they impinge upon the rights and freedoms of other individuals, and in this way majority rule is rationally justified.[13] And when the rights of an individual are curtailed by "reasons of State," this is allegedly justified by the fact that the State is supposed to embody the will and the interests of the majority. It is interesting to note that the "Universal Declaration" speaks of "freedoms" in the plural and, even more intriguing, of "fundamental freedoms." The individualization does not stop at the individual, but divides this segregated entity even further into separated freedoms.

In enumerating these Assumptions and Implications I do not mean to say that they were actually in the minds of the framers of the Declaration. In fact, there is evidence to suggest that no unanimity could be found regarding the basis of the rights that were being declared. But the Declaration clearly was articulated

[12] "The will of the people shall be the basis of the authority of government;" —Art. 21,3 of the Declaration.

[13] "In the exercise of his rights and freedoms, everyone shall be subject only to such limitations as are determined by law *solely* for the purpose of securing due recognition and respect for the rights and freedoms of others and of meeting the *just* requirements of *morality, public order* and the general *welfare* in a *democratic* society." Art 29,2 (Emphasis of the problematic words added.)

along the lines of the historical trends of the Western world during the last three centuries, and in tune with a certain philosophical anthropology or individualistic humanism which helped justify them.

III. Cross-Cultural Reflections

1. *Is the Concept of Human Rights a Universal Concept?*

The answer is a plain *no*. Three reasons vouch for it.

a) No concept as such is universal. Each concept is valid primarily where it was conceived. If we want to extend its validity beyond its own context we shall have to justify the extrapolation. Even mathematical concepts imply the previous acknowledgment of a limited field defined by the axioms we postulate. Furthermore, every concept tends to be univocal. To accept the possibility of universal concepts would imply a strictly rationalistic conception of reality. But even if this were the theoretical truth it would not be the actual case, because *de facto* humankind presents a plurality of universes of discourse. To accept the fact that the concept of Human Rights *is* not universal does not yet mean that it *should* not *become* so. Now in order for a concept to become universally valid it should fulfill at least two conditions. It should, on the one hand; eliminate all the other contradictory concepts. This may seem improbable, but there is a logical necessity here and, theoretically, it would all be for the best. On the other hand, it should be the universal point of reference for any problematic regarding human dignity. In other words, it should displace all other homeomorphic equivalents and be the pivotal center of a just social order. To put it another way, the culture which has given birth to the concept of Human Rights should also be called upon to become a universal culture. This may well be one of the causes of a certain uneasiness one senses in non-Western thinkers who study the question of Human Rights. They fear for the identity of their own cultures.

b) Within the vast field of Western culture itself, the very assumptions which serve to situate our problematic are not universally recognized. The particular origin of the formulation of Human Rights is sufficiently well known. Probably the most important sources of dissent are three.[14]

i) *Theology*:

Human Rights need to be grounded, says the theological view, in a superior, transcendent and therefore unmanipulable value, whose traditional symbol is God as origin and guarantor of both human rights and duties. Otherwise, they are only a political device in the hands of the powerful. According to this view, the Declaration suffers from a naive optimism regarding the goodness and autonomy of human nature. Moreover, it implies a deficient anthropology, inasmuch as it seems to view the human person as merely a bundle of needs, material and psychological, of which it then proceeds to make an inventory.[15] And finally, in case of doubt or conflict, who is going to decide? Majority rule is only a euphemism for the law of the jungle: the power of the strongest.

ii) *Marxism*:

For the Marxist, so-called Human Rights are merely "*Klassenrechte*," class rights.[16] "There are no rights without duties and no duties without rights." They reflect the interests of a certain class and in many cases only its aspirations. There is no mention of the economic conditions for the effective realization of what are said to be universal human claims. Furthermore, there is something abstract and too general about most of these

[14] We do not include here a fourth source of dissent, namely the *political*, because the argument in such cases bears mainly on different interpretations of facts, emphases and factors other than those related to the nature of Human Rights. Cf. as a single example: *Colloques de Riyad, de Paris, du Vatican, de Genève et de Strasbourg sur le dogme musulman et les droits de l'homme en Islam*, Riyad, Ministère de la Justice; Beirut, Dar Al Kitab Allubhani, 1974; and D. Sidorsky (ed.) *Essays on Human Rights. Contemporary Issues and Jewish Perspectives*, Philadelphia, The Jewish Publication Society of America, 1979.

[15] "Human rights, in short, are statements of basic needs and interests." S.I. Benn, *The Encyclopaedia of Philosophy*, New York, Macmillan, 1967, *sub voce Rights*, speaking about the U.N. Declaration.

[16] Cf. K. Marx, *Zur Judenfrage* I, p. 352.

Is the Notion of Human Rights a Western Concept?

rights; they are not sufficiently grounded in the material and cultural reality of particular groups. Finally, their individualism is evident. The individual is conceived as being in confrontation with (rather than included in) society, although the latter is said to be the result of freely contracting individuals. Society is not merely the sum total of individuals and it has rights which the individual may not violate. History has transcendent power.

iii) *History*:

"Human Rights" appear to some students of recent history as another example of the more or less conscious domination exerted by the powerful nations to maintain their privileges and defend the *status quo*. Human rights continue to be a political weapon. Human rights were known long ago but only for the nobleman, or the free citizen, or for whites or christians or males, etc., and when they were hastily applied to "human beings" it was often defined just which groups belonging to the race could properly be styled "human." If not all humans had human rights, the claim of human rights on behalf of animals, plants and things would seem and still does seem bizarre, not to say ridiculous, in spite of occasional remonstrances delivered by Societies for the Protection of Animals. Animals and such may very well have rights, but not human ones. And, as we have seen, this particular notion of the "human" has not always been very humane. And who is to speak for the whole? History discloses that only the victors declare and promulgate "rights," which are simply what the powerful consider right at any given time.

c) From a cross-cultural stance the problem appears exclusively Western, i.e. the question itself is at stake. Most of the assumptions and implications enumerated earlier are simply not given in other cultures. Furthermore, from a non-Western point of view the problem itself is not seen as such, so that it is not merely a question of agreeing or disagreeing with the answer. If anything, the problem is that the issue is experienced in a radically different way. A *diatopical* hermeneutic does not deal

[17] "Keine Rechte ohne Pflichten, keine Pflichten ohne Rechte," Marx-Engels, *Werke* XVI, 521 *apud* G. Klaus, M. Buhr, *Philosophisches Wörterbuch*, Leipzig. VEB, 1976, *sub voce Menschenrechte*.

with just another point of view on the *same* problem. At issue here is not simply the answer, but the problem itself.

Now is it possible to have access to other *topoi* so that we may be able to understand other cultures from within, i.e. as they understand themselves? We may not be able to jump over our own categories of understanding, but it may not be impossible to have one foot in one culture and another in a second. Generally, we have only one culture as we have only one mother-tongue—but we may also have a father-tongue. We cannot *a priori* deny this possibility. I recall that, in certain parts of the East, to be illiterate means to know only a single language. It is in dialogue with others that we can encompass our common ground. We may not integrate more than one culture in ourselves but we may open the possibility of a wider and deeper integration by opening ourselves, in dialogue, to others.

The following parallelism may be instructive. To assume that without the explicit recognition of Human Rights life would be chaotic and have no meaning belongs to the same order of ideas as to think that without the belief in one God as understood in the Abrahamic tradition human life would dissolve itself in total anarchy. This line of thinking leads to the belief that Atheists, Buddhists and Animists, for instance, should be considered as human aberrations. In the same vein: either Human Rights, or chaos. This attitude does not belong exclusively to Western culture. To call the stranger a barbarian is all too common an attitude among the peoples of the world. And, as we shall mention later, there is a legitimate and inbuilt claim to universality in any affirmation of truth. The problem is that we tend to identify the limits of our own vision with the human horizon.

2. *Cross-Cultural Critique*

There are no trans-cultural values, for the simple reason that a value exists as such only in a given cultural context.[18] But there may be cross-cultural values, and a cross-cultural critique is

[18] Cf. R. Panikkar, "Aporias in the Comparative Philosophy of Religion," *Man in World*, XIII, 3-4 (1980), p. 357-383.

indeed possible. The latter does not consist in evaluating one cultural construct with the categories of another, but in trying to understand and criticize one particular human problem with the tools of understanding of the different cultures concerned, at the same time taking thematically into consideration that the very awareness and, much more, the formulation of the problem is already culturally bound. Our question is then to examine the possible cross-cultural value of the issue of Human Rights, an effort which begins by delimiting the cultural boundaries of the concept. The dangers of cultural westocentrism are only too patent today.

a) We have already mentioned the particular historical origins of the Declaration of Human Rights. To claim universal validity for Human Rights in the formulated sense implies the belief that most of the peoples of the world today are engaged in much the same way as the Western nations in a process of transition from more or less mythical *Gemeinschaften* (feudal principalities, self-governing cities, guilds, local communities, tribal institutions...) to a "rationally" and "contractually" organized "modernity" as known to the Western industrialized world. This is a questionable assumption. No one can predict the evolution (or eventual disintegration) of those traditional societies which have started from different material and cultural bases and whose reaction to modern Western civilization may therefore follow hitherto unknown lines.

Further, the very powerful Declaration of Human Rights also shows its weakness from another point of view. Something has been lost when it has to be explicitly declared. As the Chinese say: It is when *yi* (justice) declines that *li* (ritual) arises.[19] Or as the British and Spaniards repeat: There are things which you take for granted and about which you do not speak. And in some traditional societies, you cannot boast of being noble or a friend of the royal family because the very moment you do so, you lose your nobility and your friendship with the reigning house.[20] When Human Rights are declared, this is a sign that the

[19] *Tao Te Ching*, p. 18.

[20] The *Manavadharmaśastra* (2-4) puts the same idea in a more sophisticated way: To act from a desire for reward is reprehensible. Yet without that desire, no action is possible. Laws are needed to put order into those human actions.

very foundation on which they rest has already been weakened. The Declaration only postpones the collapse. In traditional words, when the tabu of the sacred disappears sacredness fades away. If you have to teach a mother to love her child, something is amiss with motherhood. Or, as some theoreticians of Human Rights have also recognized, the legislation on Human Rights is introduced in order to find a justification for contravening somebody else's freedom. Putting it positively, you need some justification to encroach on somebody's field of activity.

I am not saying this in order to revert to Utopian dreams of an earthly paradise, but just to sound another voice. You may promulgate laws, but you do not declare what is the case—unless it has ceased to be evident; you do not proclaim an "ought" if there are no transgressions at all.

b) We may now briefly reconsider the three assumptions mentioned above. They may pass muster, insofar as they express an authentically valid human issue from one particular context. But the very context may be susceptible to a legitimate critique from the perspective of other cultures. To do this systematically would require that we choose one culture after another and examine the assumptions of the Declaration in the light of each culture chosen. We shall limit ourselves here to token reflections under the very broad umbrella of a pre-Modern, non-Western state of mind.

i) There is certainly a *universal human nature* but, first of all, this nature does not need to be segregated and fundamentally distinct from the nature of all living beings and/or the entire reality. Thus exclusively *Human* Rights would be seen as a violation of "Cosmic Rights" and an example of selfdefeating anthropocentrism, a novel kind of apartheid. To retort that "Cosmic Rights" is a meaningless expression would only betray the underlying cosmology of the objection, for which the phrase makes no sense. But the existence of a different cosmology is precisely what is at stake here. We speak of the laws of nature; why not also of her rights?

Secondly, the interpretation of this "universal human nature," i.e. Man's self-understanding, belongs equally to this human nature. Thus to single out one particular interpretation of it may be valid, but it is not universal and may not apply to the entirety of human nature.

Thirdly, to proclaim the undoubtedly positive concept of Human Rights may turn out to be a Trojan horse, surreptitiously introduced into other civilizations which will then all but be obliged to accept those ways of living, thinking and feeling for which Human Rights is the proper solution in cases of conflict. It is a little like the way technology is often introduced in many parts of the world: it is imported to solve the problems that it has itself created. We have already made reference to this when criticizing the universalization of the concept of Human Rights.

ii) Nothing could be more important than to underscore and defend the *dignity of the human person*. But the person should be distinguished from the individual. The individual is just an abstraction, i.e. a selection of a few aspects of the person for practical purposes. My *person*, on the other hand, is also in "my" parents, children, friends, foes, ancestors and successors. "My" person is also in "my" ideas and feelings and in "my" belongings. If you hurt "me," you are equally damaging my whole clan, and possibly yourself as well. Rights cannot be individualized in this way. Is it the right of the mother, or of the child?—in the case of abortion. Or perhaps of the father and relatives as well? Rights cannot be abstracted from duties; the two are correlated. The dignity of the human person may equally be violated by your language, or by your desecrating a place I consider holy, even though it does not "belong" to me in the sense of individualized private property. You may have "bought" it for a sum of money, while it belongs to me by virtue of another order altogether. An individual is an isolated knot; a person is the entire fabric around that knot, woven from the total fabric of the real. The limits to a person are not fixed, they depend utterly on his or her personality. Certainly without the knots the net would collapse; but without the net, the knots would not even exist.

To aggressively defend my individual rights, for instance, may have negative, i.e. unjust, repercussions on others and perhaps even on myself. The need for consensus in many traditions—instead of majority opinion—is based precisely on the corporate nature of human rights.

A paragraph on language is required here. Each language has its own genius and its own particular way to see the world and even to be it and be in it. But from a cross-cultural perspective, each language has to show the flexibility necessary to incorporate other human experiences. I know that in current English "individual" is synonymous with "person," but this should not prevent me from using these two words in the sense I have suggested, and from recognizing a particular human trend which tends to identify the human being with the most salient features of a gross "individualized" body or at least to inscribe it within that framework. In drawing the distinction between individual and person I would put much more content in it than a French moral philosophy would do nowadays, for instance. I would like to adduce this case as a particular instance of two radically different anthropologies.

iii) *Democracy* is also a great value and infinitely better than any dictatorship. But it amounts to tyranny to put the peoples of the world under the alternative of choosing either democracy or dictatorship. Human Rights are tied to democracy. Individuals need to be protected when the structure which is above them (Society, the State or the Dictator—by whatever name) is not qualitatively superior to them, i.e. when it does not belong to a higher order. Human rights is a legal device for the protection of smaller numbers of people (the minority or the individual) faced with the power of greater numbers. This implies a quantitative reductionism; the person is reduced to the individual and the individual to the basis of society. I may put it more positively by saying that it is the way by which the individual as cornerstone of society is protected, and his or her dignity recognized. In a hierarchical conception of reality, the particular human being cannot defend his or her rights by demanding or exacting them independently of the whole. The wounded order has to be set straight again, or it has to change altogether. Other traditional societies have different means to more or less successfully restore the order. The rāja may fail in his duty to protect the people, but will a Declaration of Human Rights be a corrective unless it also has the power to constrain the rāja? Can a democracy be imposed and remain democratic?[21]

The policy of non-alignment subscribed to by many countries of Africa and Asia here strikes a much deeper chord than possible political opportunism, or just another way of being relevant in the contemporary political scene. It represents precisely this refusal to admit the vision of the world as a function of the just mentioned set of dilemmas represented by the so-called superpowers.

In short, the cross-cultural critique does not invalidate the Declaration of Human Rights, but offers new perspectives for an internal criticism and sets the limits of validity of Human Rights, offering at the same time both possibilities for enlarging its realm, if the context changes, and of a mutual fecundation with other conceptions of Man and Reality.

3. *Should the symbol of Human Rights be a universal symbol?*

It should be noted that I speak here of Human Rights as a symbol which, unlike a concept, is by its nature polyvalent and polysemic.

The answer is yes, and no.

a) *Yes.* When a culture as a whole discovers certain values as ultimate, these values must have a certain universal meaning. Only collective and culturally expressed universal values may be said to be human values. A mere private value cannot be called a *human* value. It is a humane value, but not necessarily a value for every human—as *Human* Rights claim to be. As a matter of fact, Human Rights come as a corrective to the former exclusive rights of the Whites, the Believers, the Rich, the Brahmans and others—without meaning to touch legitimate privileges in the traditional sense of the word. The Declaration of Human Rights must needs be considered, at least in its intention,

21 A recent example: A Catholic missionary, after over a year of really living together with an Asian tribe and sharing with the people their respective beliefs, thinks that the moment has come for some formal conversions, since they are already practically Christians. He talks matters over with the enthusiasts about Christianity: "Would you like to become officially and publicly Christians? You are already convinced..." *etcetera.* Answer: "No, because some other people in the tribe are not ready." "But it is your *right!*," says the missionary, "you have the *right* to decide by yourselves—all the more since you neither harm nor despise the others." The answer is cutting: "We only have the right to take this step if the whole tribe does it."

as a declaration with universal validity. To say that Human Rights are not universal would amount to saying that they are not human; they would cease to be *Human* Rights. The whole novelty of the Declaration lies precisely here, in the assertion that every human being, by the mere fact of being human, is endowed with inalienable rights that everybody should respect.

In that sense we may have here something rather unique and revolutionary in the Declaration of Human Rights. Here indeed we have the positive side of the individual *vis-à-vis* the person. Every single human being in its individuality, by the very fact of being born, has a dignity and rights equal to any other. It is not one's place in society, or degree of civilization, or intellectual, moral or religious endowments that counts. Certainly, limits will immediately appear: you may be subnormal or abnormal, and not only physically, but also morally—or, others would also add, intellectually or religiously. But the naked fact of being born is the universal symbol on which Human Rights is based. From this point of view, the claim to universality of Human Rights has found a solid basis.

Paradoxically enough, the Christian origin of this belief has been the cause of some of its degradation, i.e. when it became an ideology, a doctrine to serve the interests of one particular group. Everybody is born free and equal; all human beings are equal in the sight of God; every human person has the same rights as any other. Nonetheless, in order to justify the fact that the unbaptized, or the negro or slave or female or whoever, did not have the same rights, one was compelled to claim that they were not fully human beings, as history cruelly witnesses.

b) *No*. Because each culture expresses its experience of reality and of the *humanum* in concepts and symbols which are proper to that tradition and are as such not universal, and most likely not universalizable. This relationship between truth and the expression of truth in concepts and symbols is one of the most central philosophical problems. Truth has the inbuilt claim to be universally valid, here and there, yesterday and tomorrow, for you and for me. Yet my grasping and formulating it cannot sustain the same claim without charging all the others who do not agree with me with stupidity or wickedness. Hence the necessary *via media* between agnostic relativism and dogmatic absolutism. This is what can be called *relativity*.

Our particular case is a typical example of the *pars pro toto*: from the optic of the inside it looks like the whole; from the outside it looks like a part, a fragment. Similarly, Human Rights are universal from the vantage point of modern Western culture, and not universal from the outside looking in. Now, if we take from the inside the *pars pro toto*, are we able to take from the outside the *totum in parte*? Can another culture see in the Human Rights issue a universal language? Or should we say that it is only one way of looking at things, one way of speaking?

The answer which claims to discover the *totum in parte* is appealing, but not convincing. This is the temptation of the intellectual, who senses that any affirmation has the inbuilt tendency to be universally valid—or of the politician who, having neither the time nor the inclination to engage in such reflections, would like to see the *totum* in the *parte* of his party. But then we tend to become the self-appointed judges of all humankind. Now philosophy, being a situated reflection, makes us aware that nobody has direct access to the universal range of human experience. We can only indirectly and through a limited perspective come to know the totality. Even were we to know all the existing human opinions, ours would amount to just another opinion. One cannot view the *totum* except in and through one's own window. This is the case not only because the whole is more than the sum of its parts, but also because that *totum* does not exist independently from the *parte* through which it is seen. It is only seen in and through the respective *parte* and there is no stance from which one could proceed to the integration of all the parts. Co-existence is only possible on a common ground, a *co-esse* recognized by the different parties.

Here lies the crux. We cannot but aim at the *totum*, and yet we often forget that all we see is the *pars* which we then take *pro toto*. If a Christian, to put another example, were to say that Christ is not the universal savior, according to accepted custom he or she would cease to be a Christian. But a non-Christian cannot, and should not, agree with this. It is only in mutual dialogue that their respective views will change or evolve. Christ will be for the Christian the symbol of the totality; for the non-Christian, only the symbol of the Christians.

Myriad examples from the past, especially regarding the West, are all too striking for one not to be wary of the danger of repeating what was done in the name of the one God, the one Empire, the one Religion, and what is nowadays being done under the aegis of the one Science and the one Technology.

In brief, we need a new hermeneutic: the diatopical hermeneutic that can only be developed in a *dialogical* dialogue. This would show us that we must take neither the *pars pro toto*, nor believe that we see the *totum in parte*. We must accept what our partner tells us: simply that we take the *totum pro parte*, when we are aware of the *pars pro toto*; which is obviously what we will retort right back to him. This is the human condition and I would not consider it to be an imperfection. This, again, is the topic of pluralism.

Let us consider now an example of a different perspective without attempting to present any homeomorphic equivalent.

IV. An Indian Reflection

The word "Indian" here has no political connotations. It does not refer to the "nation" with the third largest Islamic population in the world, but to the traditional Hindu, Jain and Buddhist conceptions of reality.

Dharma (*dhamma*) is perhaps the most fundamental word in the Indian tradition which could lead us to the discovery of a possible homeomorphic symbol corresponding to the Western notion of "Human Rights." I am not advancing the idea that dharma is the homeomorphic equivalent of Human Rights. I am only indicating that a reflection at the level of dharma may help us find our footing on a common ground, so that we may know what we are looking for when we set out on our search for "Human Rights" in the classical Indian context.

As is well known, the meaning of the word dharma is multivocal: besides element, data, quality and origination, it means law, norm of conduct, character of things, right, truth, ritual, morality, justice, righteousness, religion, destiny, and many other things. It would not lead us anywhere to try to find an English common denominator for all these names, but perhaps etymology

Is the Notion of Human Rights a Western Concept?

can show us the root metaphor underlying the many meanings of the word.[22] Dharma is that which maintains, gives cohesion and thus strength to any given thing, to reality, and ultimately to the three worlds (*triloka*). Justice keeps human relations together; morality keeps oneself in harmony; law is the binding principle for human relations; religion is what maintains the universe in existence; destiny is that which links us with our future; truth is the internal cohesion of a thing; a quality is what pervades a thing with an homogeneous character; an element is the minimum consistent particle, spiritual or material; and the like.

Now a world in which the notion of dharma is central and nearly all pervasive is not concerned with finding the "right" of one individual against another or of the individual *vis-à-vis* society, but rather with assaying the *dharmic* (*right*, *true*, consistent...) or *adharmic* character of a thing or an action within the entire theanthropocosmic complex of reality.

Dharma is primordial. We cannot hope to understand it if we approach it with moral categories (cf. the case of the *Gītā*) or even epistemological ones. It embraces both the conflict and the resolution; both the ought and the ought not. There is no universal dharma above and independent of the *svadharma*, the dharma which is inherent in every being. And this *svadharma* is at the same time a result of and a reaction to the dharma of everyone else.

The starting point here is not the individual, but the whole complex concatenation of the Real. In order to protect the world, for the sake of the protection of this universe, says Manu, He, Svayambhū, the Self-existent, arranged the castes and their duties.[23] Dharma is the order of the entire reality, that which keeps the world together.[24] The individual's duty is to maintain his "rights;" it is to find one's place in relation to Society, to the Cosmos, and to the transcendent world.

[22] From the root *dhr*, to hold, to maintain, keep together. Cf. Latin *tenere* and English *tenet*.

[23] Manu, I, 31 and I, 87.

[24] Cf. the famous *lokasamgraha* of the *Gītā*, and the well known definition of the *Mahābhārata*: "that which maintains and sustains the peoples." (*Karnaparvam*, LXIX, 59).

It is obvious from these brief paragraphs that here the discourse on "Human Rights" would take on an altogether different character. It would distract us from the purpose of this article to look now for the homeomorphic equivalent of Human Rights in a culture pervaded with the conception of dharma. We adduce this Indian example only to be able to elaborate in a fuller way the question of our title.

Only one submission and one observation may be allowed here so as not to leave this thought incomplete. I submit that the homeomorphic equivalent is *svadharma*, and I make the observation that the homeomorphic equivalent does not mean the corresponding counterpart, as if all that is conveyed by Human Rights is also borne by *svadharma* or *vice versa*. Cultures are wholes, and do not fit into one-to-one correspondences. In order to have a just society, the modern West stresses the notion of Human Rights. In order to have a dharmic order, classical India stresses the notion of *svadharma*.

We shall now attempt to formulate without further development some reactions to the Western discourse on Human Rights from this Indian perspective. We should add immediately that this Indian critique does not imply that the Indian model is better, or that Indian culture has been faithful to its fundamental intuition—as the existence of the outcastes and the degeneration of the caste system sufficiently prove.

In confrontation and dialogue with the Western model, the Indian critique would stress fundamentally that Human Rights should not be absolutized. It would contest that one can speak of Human Rights as "objective" entities standing on their own in isolation from the rest of the Real. This is what seems to be implied in the very first article of the Declaration: "All human beings are born free and equal in dignity and rights. They are endowed with reason and conscience and should act towards one another in a spirit of brotherhood." Particular rights, privileges due to a special position in society, i.e. a relativization of rights does not seem to be compatible with this article.

Developing this point, the Indian vision would insist on the following points among others:

1. Human Rights are not individual Human Rights only. The

Is the Notion of Human Rights a Western Concept?

humanum is not incarnated in the individual *only*. The individual as such is an abstraction, and an abstraction as such cannot be an ultimate subject of rights. As we have already indicated, the individual is only the knot in and of the net of relationships which form the fabric of the Real. The knots may individually be all the same (either *jīva*, *ātman* or *anātman*), but it is mainly their position in the net which determines the set of "rights" an individual may have. Individuality is not a substantial category, but a functional one. The structure of the universe is hierarchical, but this does not imply that the higher echelons have the right to trample upon the rights of the lower ones—in spite of the dangers of this happening the moment the harmony of the whole is disturbed.

I am not entering into the merits or demerits of this world view. We should however bear in mind that this conception is intimately linked with the conception of karma, and thus should not be evaluated outside its proper context.

2. Human Rights are not Human only. They concern equally the entire cosmic display of the universe, from which even the Gods are not absent. The animals, all the sentient beings and the supposedly inanimate creatures, are also involved in the interaction concerning "human" rights. Man is a peculiar being, to be sure, but neither alone nor so essentially distinct. One could even ask whether there are specific human rights, or if this specificity is again only an abstraction for pragmatic reasons which defeats its own purpose the moment we forget its merely practical character.

Here again, another cosmology and another theology provide the justification for this conception. Whether modern India, accepting and adopting modern science as it is, will be able to maintain this conception for very long is another matter altogether. But we know also about the persistence of mythical patterns.

3. Human Rights are not Rights only. They are also duties and both are interdependent. Humankind has the "right" to survive only insofar as it performs the duty of maintaining the world (*lokasamgraha*). We have the "right" to eat only inasmuch as we

fulfill the duty of allowing ourselves to be eaten by a hierarchically higher agency. Our right is only a participation in the entire metabolic function of the universe.

We should have, if anything, a Declaration of Universal Rights and Duties in which the whole of Reality would be encompassed. Obviously, this demands not only a different anthropology but also a different cosmology and an altogether different theology—beginning with its name. That only human beings and not animals could make this Declaration would invalidate it only to the same extent that the Declaration of Human Rights could be contested because the Nagas and the Masai did not take part in the discussion and framing of the Declaration.

4. Human Rights are not mutually isolatable. They are related not only to the whole cosmos and all their corresponding duties; they form, among themselves as well, a harmonious whole. It is for this reason that a material list of definitive Human Rights is not theoretically feasible. It is the universal harmony that ultimately counts. This is not invalidated by the fact that India, as so many other countries, knows the codification of laws. India suffers, perhaps more than most countries, from legalistic *minutiae*, precisely because no juridical legislation will ever suffice.[25]

5. Human Rights are not absolute. They are intrinsically relative, they are relationships among entities. Moreover, these entities are determined by the relationships themselves. To say that my human value depends on my position in the universe would be a caricature of what has been said if we start by thinking of an individual in itself, whose dignity is then made to

[25] A recent example may illuminate the issue: In July 1981 the Indian nation is in an uproar because some 352 outcastes of the small village of Minakshipuram in Tamilnadu converted to Islam, probably in protest and reaction against their ostracism (to say the least) from the Hindu caste-communities. For our point it is interesting to remark that H.H. Sri Vishveshva Tirtha Swamiji of Pejavar Mutt along with many other Hindu religious leaders can now—for obviously political and opportunistic reasons—raise their voices against untouchability and discrimination without paying attention to the *Manavadharmaśastra* (III, 92, 150, 157; IV, 79, 213; IX, 238-239; etc.) and other sacred Laws sanctioning the system. Cf. the Indian press from May to August, 1981; e.g. *The Hindu* from Madras, May 26; July 15, 16, 18, 28, 29, 30; August 2; etc.

depend on whether he or she is rich or poor, of one caste or another, etc. The classical Indian vision would not subscribe to this—in spite of the failures of the system in the praxis and even the degeneration in time—but it would start from a wholistic conception and then define a portion of Reality by function of its situation in the totality. In a certain sense, the knot is nothing—because it is the whole net.

6. Both systems (the Western and the Hindu) make sense from and within a given and accepted myth. Both systems imply a certain kind of consensus. When that consensus is challenged, a new myth must be found. The broken myth is the situation in India today, as it is in the world at large. That the rights of individuals be conditioned only by their position in the net of Reality can no longer be admitted by the contemporary mentality. Nor does it seem to be admissible that the rights of individuals be so absolute as not to depend at all on the particular situation of the individual.

In short, there is at present no endogenous theory capable of unifying contemporary societies and no imposed or imported ideology can be simply substituted for it. A mutual fecundation of cultures is a human imperative of our times.

The Declaration defends the individual from the abuses of the State or Society. The Indian view would say that we are part of a harmonious whole on pilgrimage toward a non-historical goal. Interactions are the very warp and woof of the universe. Cultural and religious traditions offer a whole that cannot easily be dismembered without doing violence to their insights. Hindu karma outside its context may become fatalistic. Christian charity outside its system may turn oppressive. The universalization of Human Rights is a very delicate question indeed.

V. By Way of Conclusion

Is the concept of Human Rights a Western conception?

Yes.

Should the world then renounce declaring or enforcing Human Rights?

No.

Three qualifications, however, are necessary:

1. For an authentic human life to be possible within the *megamachine* of the modern technological world, Human Rights are imperative. This is because the development of the notion of Human Rights is bound up with and given its meaning by the slow development of that megamachine. How far individuals or groups or nations should collaborate with this present-day system is another question altogether. But in the contemporary political arena as defined by current socio-economic and ideological trends, the defense of Human Rights is a sacred duty. Yet it should be remembered that to introduce Human Rights (in the definite Western sense, of course) into other cultures before the introduction of *techniculture* would amount not only to putting the cart before the horse, but also to preparing the way for the technological invasion—as if by a Trojan horse, as we have already said. And yet a technological civilization without Human Rights amounts to the most inhuman situation imaginable. The dilemma is excruciating. This makes the two following points all the more important and urgent.

2. Room should be made for other traditions to develop and formulate their own homeomorphic views corresponding to or opposing Western "rights." Or rather, these other world traditions should make room for themselves, since no one else is likely to make it for them. This is an urgent task; otherwise it will be impossible for non-Western cultures to survive, let alone to offer viable alternatives or even a sensible complement. Here the role of a cross-cultural philosophical approach is paramount. The need for human pluralism is often recognized in principle, but not often practiced, not only because of the dynamism which drives the paneconomic ideology, linked with the megamachine, to expand all over the world, but also because viable alternatives are not yet theoretically worked out.

3. An intermediary space should be found for mutual criticism that strives for mutual fecundation and enrichment. Perhaps such an interchange may help bring forth a new myth and eventually a more humane civilization. The dialogical dialogue appears as the unavoidable method.

Is the Notion of Human Rights a Western Concept?

* * *

Perhaps a suggestion here may prove helpful. Playing on the metaphor of the knots (individuality) and the net (personhood) we could probably affirm that traditional cultures have stressed the net (kinship, hierarchical structure of society, the function to be performed, the role of each part in relation to the whole), so that often the knot has been suffocated and not allowed sufficient free space for its own self-identity. On the other hand, Modernity stresses the knots (individual free will to choose any option, the idiosyncracies of everyone, the atomization of society) so that often the knot has been lost in loneliness, alienated by its own social mobility, and wounded (or killed) in competition with other more powerful knots. Perhaps the notion of personhood as the interplay between the knots and the net, as well as the realization that freedom is not just the capacity to choose between given options but also the power to create options, could provide a starting point for the proposed mutual fecundation.

If many traditional cultures are centered on God, and some other cultures basically cosmocentric, the culture which has come up with the notion of Human Rights is decisively anthropocentric. Perhaps we may now be prepared for a cosmotheandric vision of reality in which the Divine, the Human and the Cosmic are integrated into a whole, more or less harmonious according to the performance of our truly human rights.

R. Panikkar
(*University of California, Santa Barbara*)

[17]

Chapter 12
*Three Dichotomies of Law in Pluralism**

1. Introduction

Legal culture, or legal pluralism, is growing to become one of the most frequently discussed problems in various fields of law. International associations in philosophy of law, anthropology of law, sociology of law, and comparative law[1], have begun to adopt topics related to this problem in their conferences, and many ad hoc international meetings treating related topics either were held or are under planning.[2] In virtue of these international activities, the problematic situation of contemporary legal culture or legal pluralism in the world has become more clearly known, though much of it is yet to be explored.

In contrast to the increasing awareness, the apparent lag is in elaborating methodology appropriate to such a new problem, as leading advocates for Third World jurisprudence complain:

> . . . a legal theory appropriate to western industrialized societies in the

*Originally, "Three Dichotomies of Law: An Analytical Scheme of Legal Culture," presented before a session of the ISA Research Committee on Sociology of Law, XI World Congress of Sociology, New Delhi, August 18-22, 1986; then published in *Tokai Law Review*, No. 1, 1987, pp. 1-11. Reprinted by allowance of the Dean, Faculty of Law, Tokai University.

[1] Besides established ones mentioned in the text, two new ones are remarkable: the Commission on Folk Law and Legal Pluralism, International Union of Anthropological and Ethnological Sciences (IUAES CFLLP), and the International Third World Legal Studies Association (INTWORLSA).

[2] Cf. Newsletters of IUAES CFLLP and INTWORLSA.

way it had evoled during the past two hundred years was inappropriate, in important aspects, to explain the functions and provide a philosophical basis for the legal systems of Third World countries (Marasinghe & Conklin, 1984: vi).

The methodological concern for devising a new conceptual scheme appropriate to the new demand has not been utterly neglected. M.B. Hooker, for instance, attempted to apply his dichotomic concepts — first 'dominant law vs. servient law' (1975) and then 'contract vs. status' (1978) — to the main components of legal pluralism; but he was unable to open new horizons because his concepts were adopted from among those originated in modern Western jurisprudence.[3] Some other scholars have proposed such concepts as 'law in small-scale societies' (Roberts, 1979) or 'people's law' (Baxi, 1982; Allott & Woodman, 1985) for law other than state law in non-Western societies, and 'indigenous law' for such law in American society (Galanter, 1981; cf. note 14, p.106). Also, 'folklaw' was suggested as a provisional label to embrace law other than state law in both non-Western and Western societies through three approaches with relation to its 'substantive law,' 'procedure' and 'interaction between a folklaw and the others or state law.'[4] On the whole, however, those efforts do not appear to have achieved any significant advancement beyond replacing old labels with new, or redefining known facts with new words.

I would like herein to attempt a new conceptual scheme by reformulating the schemes which I suggested in the past. Prior to methodological argument, however, it may be useful, or indeed necessary, to ascertain the objective to which the demanded methodology is to be applied. The objective is, whether expressed as legal culture or legal pluralism, the working whole structure of law of a people, constituted not of a single system of state law, but rather a complex of various systems of law called customary, religious, local, primitive, tribal or whatever,[5] on the one hand, and

[3]For my criticism as well as appreciation of Hooker's argument, see pp. 41-43, Ch. 3.

[4]From the "Term of Reference" of IUAES CFLLP.

[5][Postscript: Such concepts as *infra-droit*, *non-droit*, *polysystème*, and *système in-*

many ideational factors specifically relevant to the function of the law, such as ideas, values, beliefs, philosophies, attitudes and so forth, on the other. What is demanded, then, is a conceptual scheme capable of being utilized as an analytical tool to accurately observe and elucidate that working whole structure of law of a people, Western as well as non-Western.

2. Initial Scheme: Three-Level Structure of Law

My first conceptual scheme was devised as a working hypothesis to facilitate a joint research into Asian indigenous law which, starting in 1977, differentiated the whole structure of law into three levels (for detail, see Ch. 9). The first level, *official law*, was defined as "the legal system authorized by the legitimate authority of a country," typical of which was *state law* "directly sanctioned by the legitimate government of a state." Other types of law, such as religious law, family law, local law, ethnic law and so forth, may be classified also as official law insofar as they are officially authorized by state and functioning in consonance with state law. The second level was *unofficial law*, defined as the legal system which is "not officially authorized by the official authorities, but authorized in practice by the general consensus of a certain circle of people, whether of a country or within or beyond it," and limited to "one with some distinctive influences upon the effectiveness of the official law, supplementing, opposing, modifying or even undermining the official law." All types of law other than state law are classified as unofficial law insofar as they are not officially authorized by state law directly or indirectly. The third level was *basic law*, or "the system of values and ideals specifically relevant to both official and unofficial law in founding and orienting the latter," and constituted of established legal ideas, religious precepts and teachings, social and cultural postulates related to fundamental social structure, or political ideologies often closely connected with economic policies. As this level forms the idea-

formel de droit adopted in a dictionary are also to be counted here (cf. *Dictionnaire d'Eguilles*).]

tional foundation of the whole structure of law of a people, its variety of components must be capable of maintaining minimum integration in spite of some minor incongruities and conflicts among them. Later, in response to criticism that it was confusing to label the values and ideals of the third level as 'law' even limited to basic, I replaced the label 'basic law' first with 'jural postulate' in 1982 and again with 'legal postulate' since 1984, without substantial change in definition.

Called the three-level structure of law, this conceptual scheme was arrived at through theoretical examination of long-accumulated achievements in Western jurisprudence and recent findings in the socio-cultural study of non-Western law. It was thus a working hypothesis which required verification by empirical research. I accordingly organized two research projects to perform the task of verification.

One project, planned and organized in 1977, was in collaboration with five scholars from different countries which have cherished distinctive cultures originated in Asia; that is, Thailand with its Buddhism, India with its Hinduism, Egypt with its Sunni-Islam, Iran with its Shii-Islam, and multi-religious Sri Lanka.[6] I, of course, was charged with Japan characterized by its folk religion, Shintoism. Faced with various difficulties arising from both the geographical and cultural distance between the collaborators, this project finally reached completion in the form of Chiba, 1986a.

The other project was another joint research collaborated in by ten Japanese scholars from different fields of jurisprudence, anthropology and economic history. After two years of theoretical examination and practical preparation, the research group started an intensive field research in Sri Lanka in 1980 with the purpose of gathering reliable data from in Asia, in addition to attempting verification of the above-stated conceptual scheme. The result of

[6]While I was organizing this project, I wished to add at least two more countries noted for their traditional cultures: China and Indonesia. Unfortunately, it was only after the project had started with the positive collaboration of scholars from the five countries mentioned that I was able to reach capable scholars from those two countries. I regret this and hope that the idea may further be extended to other countries.

the research, carried out mainly in the summer of 1982 and supplemented by individual visits both before and after, was described in Chiba, 1984a, though in preliminary form. The final report of the project has recently been completed in Japanese (Chiba, 1988b, which will be summarized in English).

The results of these two projects are summarily described below insofar as related with verification of the conceptual scheme under consideration.

3. Verification of the Initial Scheme

The hypothetical conceptual scheme, the three-level structure of law with its component parts of official law, unofficial law and legal postulate, was found to be basically verified by the first joint project, both in its formulation and in the definition of its component concepts (Chiba, 1986a: 385-389). However, the empirical reviews of the six different countries presented various requirements to supplement and improve the basic scheme. As to official law, its sub-systems should be accurately classified and their mutual interrelation and interaction should be systematically arranged based on the data presented. Similar requirements seem to hold true for unofficial law; and it was also found that more data must be collected to supplement known data, after which an attempt must be made to redefine its concept and rearrange its nature in the overall scheme with relation to official law and legal postulate. A similar need was found to be true with regard to the concept of legal postulate, along with another requirement arising from its ideational nature, that is, the need to identify the whole mechanism of legal postulates, as well as to discern that basic component which distinctively contributes to the indispensable minimum integration of the whole mechanism.

In fact, an additional conceptual scheme had been prepared at the start of this first project, because law of non-Western peoples was the chosen objective of the joint project. This additional scheme dealt with the interaction between received law and indigenous law, with indigenous law defined as "law originated in the native culture of a people," and received law defined as "law which is received by a country from one or more foreign countries" (Chiba, 1986a: 7-8). In human society, at least in the contemporary world, it is next to impossible to find purely indigenous law because of the cultural diffusion among peoples; the dichotomy, indigenous law vs. received law, is therefore predestined to be of only relative validity. For instance, an old received law, after being assimilated into the culture of the receiving people, may be characterized as an indigenous law when encountered with a new received law. Another much more serious fact in the contemporary world is the conflict between the indigenous law of a non-Western people, which have existed since before their transplantation of modern Western law, and their transplanted law, whether that transplanted law was involuntarily imposed (cf. Burman & Harrell-Bond, 1979) or voluntarily received.[7]

This hypothetical conceptual scheme was also basically verified by the reported data in that they showed that the contemporary structures of law of the six countries are, respectively, the result of interaction between indigenous law and transplanted law. The data furthermore suggested that such interaction had taken place within certain limits which permitted preservation of the cultural identity of each people in law, leading us to assume that a basic legal postulate was functioning during the course of the interaction. This postulate has been labeled the *identity postulate of indigenous law* (for details, see Ch. 10).

The second project, that undertaken by Japanese scholars, began later than the first described above, and was therefore in a position to critically observe and improve on the original schemes. Accordingly, a remarkable advancement in reformulating those schemes was possible, as presented in the preliminary report on the project (Chiba, 1984: 17-21). That report, however, has not been publicly circulated; it was written in the nature of a special report to the Japanese government, which furnished grants to cover the expenses of the project. What I wish to do

[7]The term 'reception of law' is used in general and was used by myself for both voluntary and imposed cases. However, I limit its use here to voluntary cases, and use 'transplantation of law' for both cases and 'imposition of law' for imposed cases.

below is to go a step further and attempt a synthetic reformulation of the conceptual schemes to obtain a useful analytical tool for legal culture, or legal pluralism, in the contemporary world, both non-Western and Western.

4. Revised Scheme: Three Dichotomies of Law

The synthetic conceptual scheme described below may be called the *three dichotomies of law*, combining the schemes described above with the 'identity postulate of indigenous law' into a single set.

The first dichotomy comprises, in relation to the different modes of the authority of legal sanction, *official law* vs. *unofficial law*, terms which are defined respectively as the "legal system and its components authorized by the legitimate authority of a country," and "the legal system and its components not officially authorized by any legitimate authority, but authorized in practice by the general consensus of a certain circle of people, whether within or beyond the bounds of a country, when they cause distinct influences upon the effectivity of official law, supplementing, opposing, modifying or even undermining any of the official laws, especially state law." While state law, "the official law of a political body called state," is truly typical of official laws, it is not the only one as too often taken for granted. In addition to their state law, many capitalistic and some socialistic countries in the world are also officially regulated at least by religious law, whether Catholic, Protestant, Islamic, Judaic, Hindu, Buddhistic or others including supernatural and animistic. Still other types of law are found regulating certain groups of people with official authorization of the state government, thus forming official local law, family law, ethnic law and others often collectively called customary law. Such types of customary law are originally unofficial law, and remain unofficial when, as is usual in fact, not officially authorized. Different types of unofficial law in a country may function without systematic arrangement, indifferent to and even conflictingly with one another. In contrast, the different types of official law in a country are required to maintain a consonant system under a body of certain legal principles which is usually provided by the state law.[8] As a result, customary law as official law tends to develop differently from customary law as unofficial law.

The second dichotomy is the contrast of positive rules or legal rules, with postulative values or legal postulates. *Legal rules* are "the formalized verbal expressions of particular legal regulations to designate specified patterns of behavior," and *legal postulates* are "the particular values and ideas and their systems specifically connected with a particular law to ideationally found, justify and orient, or else supplement, criticize and revise the existing legal rules." While legal rules tend to be easily isolated from the rest of the cultural formalities, legal postulates are by and large difficult to isolate, with the exception of those specifically conceptualized, such as justice, equity, natural law in Western law, *Dharma* in Hindu law, and Heaven in traditional Chinese law.[9] Both the legal rules and legal postulates of a particular body of law coexist and co-function, as a rule, interactingly. However, in many cases they may fall into conflict, while in others either of them may cease to function or completely disappear. Such cases occur when either of them has lagged behind the other or the socio-cultural development of the society concerned. Among the various modes of relationship between the two, particularly to be noticed is the independent function of legal postulates when the supported legal rules have become outdated or disappear. In such a case, while they may be easily deserted from lack of a sound basis fortified by legal rules, legal postulates have the potential of reactivating outdated legal rules or even creating new legal rules to embody themselves.

The third dichotomy is especially serious to contemporary non-Western countries, though applicable to Western countries as well. It relates to the different origins of law in human society. The contrast here is *indigenous law*, broadly defined as "law origi-

[8]It is taken for granted by Western jurisprudence that such integrating principles are provided by state law, but I hesitate to conform to that view. For Muslims, *Shariah* may be the integrating principle; for socialists, socialism; for Hindus, *Dharma*; for traditional Chinese, Heaven; and so on.

[9]Of course these legal postulates are still of less rigid definition with greater flexibility than legal rules.

nated in the native culture of a people" and narrowly defined as "the law existing in the indigenous culture of a non-Western people prior to their transplantation of modern Western law," in contrast to *transplanted law*, broadly defined as "law transplanted by a people from a foreign culture" and narrowly defined as "the state law of a non-Western country transplanted from modern Western countries." It is noted that, as mentioned above, the contrast of indigenous law vs. transplanted law is a relative one to be exhibited differently with the degree of assimilation of foreign law, and that transplanted law may be typified by two types: that which is voluntarily received, and that which is involuntarily imposed. The alleged system of Western law is nothing but an integrated complex of indigenous laws and transplanted laws developed by Western genius before modern times (cf. Berman, 1983), while contemporary non-Western law is a working whole of indigenous laws and transplanted laws interacting in each country.

In sum, the law of an individual country may be accurately observed and analyzed in its working whole structure by the above analytical tool scheme of the three dichotomies of law. In other words, it may be elucidated as comprising different types of official law and unofficial law, each of which is constituted of legal rules and legal postulates as well as of indigenous law and transplanted law, received or imposed. The combination of the three dichotomies in reality vary country to country. Such variation will exhibit diverse examples of the proportion of two factors in each dichotomy, on the one hand, and transformation of those combination and proportion with time, on the other, which may result, in extreme cases, in the total replacement of a state's legal system. Still except in rare cases, peoples who have cherished their indigenous culture may preserve their legal culture[10] as well through transformation of the combination and proportion of the three dichoto-

[10]The term 'legal culture' is generally used for the characteristic values and attitudes related to law (see Section 2, Ch. 3). It may be useful to observe such a cultural feature of law, but it tends to overlook other features. I prefer to use the term here for the cultural configuration in law, in which configuration means "more or less consistent pattern of thought and action" as defined by Ruth Benedict (1934, 42-43, 225-227).

mies. In so far as a legal culture is preserved, a "basic legal postulate for the people's cultural identity in law," which I prefer to call the *identity postulate of a legal culture*,[11] must be presupposed as functioning. It guides a people in choosing how to reformulate the whole structure of their law, including, among others, the combination of indigenous law and transplanted law, in order to maintain their accommodation to changing circumstances.[12]

In conclusion, the three dichotomies of law, composed of official law vs. unofficial law, legal rules vs. legal postulates, and indigenous law vs. transplanted law, combined into a legal culture under the guidance of the identity postulate of a legal culture, is a useful analytical tool for accurate observation and analysis of the working whole structure of law of a people, individually or comparatively. It waits empirical verification and theoretical elaboration through cooperative work by scholars interested, both Western and non-Western.

[11]This postulate was first found related to indigenous law (Ch. 10). In consideration of its function to preserve indigenous law in interaction with transplanted official law, the concept was then found to cover the working whole structure of law and, extendedly, legal culture as stated in Ch. 11.

[12]I am convinced that I have identified the Japanese identity postulate of legal culture in what I have termed as the 'amoeba-like way of thinking' (1986a: 355-356; Chs. 6, 7), though in a provisional calling. Similar ones may be discovered working in the whole structure of law of other peoples through empirical research of related facts or theoretical reasoning based on them.

[18]

FOUR

LAW AND CUSTOM IN MELANESIA

Bernard Narokobi

LAW AND SOCIETY IN CLASSICAL MELANESIA

Custom has been most effective in criminal law, especially in mitigation of sentences for crime, and to a lesser extent in the development of defences for criminal offences. Custom remains prominent in the villages, in resolution of conflict over land, bride-prices, exchange ceremonies and in many other aspects of life. Village Courts, Local Land Courts and Local Government Councillors as well as village leaders continue to use custom to establish local control, and more recently, extend central authority over the people and introduce social change. Custom operates like a two-edged sword, continuing to be a control on what would otherwise be rapid change and at the same time, acting as a catalyst for change.

Melanesian Jurisprudence

Melanesia includes the whole island of New Guinea and its lesser islands, Solomon Islands, Vanuatu, New Caledonia and Fiji. Melanesians inhabit islands beyond in the islands of Torres Strait, Timor and Moluccas. All Melanesia was colonised by Europeans and the western end of New Guinea, in more recent times, by Asians of Indonesia.

Melanesian jurisprudence is the jurisprudence of the islands of Melanesia. Because of common historical influences, there are common trends in legal development. But, diversity in Melanesia allows for variety.

It is impossible to reconstruct the Melanesia of old. No systematic or coherent inquiry has ever been conducted of the customs or traditions or laws of the various peoples. In so far as it can be isolated as a science or discipline in modern nation states, law is not quantifiable as an autonomous institution, but is an aspect of the total way of life of the people.

A notion of classical Melanesian societies is introduced here to emphasise Melanesian societies before contact with the outside world. Melanesia since such contact and contemporary Melanesia will be referred to as such, or as Neo-Melanesian. Notions of law in Neo-Melanesian societies are greatly influenced by the notions of law of the colonising powers.

In the classical Melanesian context law was not an independent discipline, nor a specialised discipline restricted to an initiated few, but an integral part of the way in which people went about various tasks in the community. Many languages in Melanesia lack any concept of the 'rule of law'. In spite of the absence of such words, there was social order, discipline and control. Notions exist for codes of conduct, ethics and values.

In classical Melanesia, it is more accurate to refer to the phenomenon of law as the way of life or the fashion of the people. Different clans or tribes operate on different principles. If one mode of doing things causes conflict with persons or groups who prescribe a different mode of doing things, the emphasis centres not on the law or the rule or the norm, but on how to settle the conflict.

It is inherent in humans to copy from others or to impose on themselves or on others, one style of life in place of another. In colonisation, the latter is more apparent. It is a mark of social maturity to allow various modes of life to operate together. Humankind everywhere is endowed with reason to discern right from wrong, good from evil and an intellect to pursue the goals of one's choice in society. The fact that one society has a more developed mode of technology does not, by itself, make that society superior to others. Written laws, professional lawyers, judges and teachers of law do not, of themselves, make a society more just than one which is illiterate, less complex or less specialised.

One cannot logically conclude from the absence of a written theory of law in Melanesia that there was no law. By virtue of their humanity, Melanesians did have what in Western thought is equivalent to law or jurisprudence. On any theory or definition of law, Melanesian notions of social conduct would qualify as law.

The enforcement of English law through the imposed institutions such as the courts, the executive, the parliament, the economy, the religious and education systems, leaves no opportunity for the growth of any authentic theory of law from Melanesian social contexts. Even after constitutional independence, most Melanesian states adopted English changes significant enough to leave any observer with no doubt that the English concept of law dominates Melanesian legal systems.

The first Minister of Justice (Kaputin, 1975) condemned the law as 'a colonial fraud' and the first Prime Minister called for reform of the law; but as Tony Deklin observed in 1984. "There is very little evidence to suggest that they have changed the legal system, and by the end of 1974, the legal system still remained a 'colonial fraud' and... without reform, Papua New Guinea legal system will continue to reflect the values of other people whom Papua New Guineans cannot possibly resemble no matter how hard they may try."

Colonial View of Melanesian Law

Western observation of Melanesian societies produced universal assumptions, for example — that on the criminal side, there was no question of choice. According to Mr Justice Gore, an eminent Australian judge who worked for many years in Papua New Guinea, though the people had a sensible custom of land tenure and their marriage customs were sound 'in a primitive state', their criminal sanctions were so repugnant to a civilised conception of criminal justice that no regard could be given to them. Justice Gore epitomised the common view of the coloniser who held that there were no fundamental rules of conduct upon which to build a criminal system so there was no alternative but to apply the criminal system of the white settlers, which came to be the criminal code of Queensland.

The criminal code of Queensland was not a codification of English common law, but a statute 'imposing, mostly the common law of England' adapted to apply to both Melanesians and non-Melanesians. So positive law embodied the natural law perceptions of Englishmen, via Queensland, and imposed upon Melanesians in Papua New Guinea. In the Solomon Islands it was the British law, in New Caledonia French, and in Vanuatu a tragicomic amalgam of both.

In the Melanesian world-view, land is an integral part of the social order and human security. So long as a person is a member of a particular land-owning group, he or she is assured of rights to its use and enjoyment. Whether such a combination of large-scale proprietary rights and individual use rights is classified by such arbitrary terms as communal or individual, just or unjust, appears to me irrelevant.

By a combination of natural and positive law, the colonisers set themselves up as powerful instruments of imposition of what they perceived as the ideal or the just law. Colonisers used the law as a double-edged sword, as an instrument of colonial ideology to attack other possible or probable ideologies, and to defend themselves against the same enemy. It was not a challenge of a legal science, looking for universally applicable rules of 'acceptable' or 'decent' human conduct. The law of the colonisers was more of an imposition of the political will of the administrators.

The leading colonial judges failed to perceive that at one level natural law and positive law work as a unitary set of norms. They failed to recognise that the law, as an ideal, or as a regulatory force to achieve justice, was abstract and beyond the reach of humans. This was an inevitable by-product of the times when colonial officers had great admiration for their own social institutions including the law, and absolute scorn for anything that did not resemble their own. Had they realised the dualism of positive and natural law and recognised the limitations of their own civilisations, they might have developed Melanesian jurisprudence. In not recognising Melanesian institutions of social order, they unwittingly created the seeds for social disorder and the general 'breakdown in law and order' experienced today in Papua New Guinea.

For these reasons, I reject any suggestion that

Melanesian jurisprudence should be properly placed in the mould of natural law. In doing so, it might be suggested that we are pursuing a nationalistic or racial line of argument, concealed in the general notion of Melanesian jurisprudence. There is no place for law or philosophy based on race, but within the human race there are various social communities. An intelligent discussion of how one community conducts its affairs, without proclaiming its hegemony, is perfectly legitimate. If we sing our song without denigrating the right of others to sing theirs, we are in no way promoting one racial view against another. Indeed, humanity will be all the richer, if all communities espouse their ways of doing things. The only chance for human survival is not uniformity, but a recognition of diversity, and by free association, a working towards common values, brought about not by imposition of the will of a superior upon an inferior but necessitated by a common desire for survival. We do not want the dominance of European law in the 20th century replaced by dominance of East Asian law in the 21st century. We either co-operate and survive or we set ourselves up in conflict and perish.

The Hope of a Future Paradise

For most Melanesian communities, there is no law as an isolate. There is a way of life. The here and now is combined with the future. We have used the expression 'pasin' or 'fashion' — a 'way' or 'ways' of doing or not doing things. However, the law was more than just a set of rules or norms prescribing human conduct or its consequences.

In discussing law in classical Melanesia, we are concerned with the ways of the people in their total environment, both physical and metaphysical, tangible and intangible, concrete and abstract. If law is used to indicate an expected result or an outcome which would usually occur, but may not occur in a particular situation, then we would be prepared to accept the use of the term Law in Classical Melanesian societies.

But if the law is used as it is by Kelsen, to refer to "specific social techniques which consist of the bringing about the desired social conduct of man through the threat of a measure of coercion which is to be applied in case of contrary conduct" then, we would prefer not to use the term 'law' and instead use the English approximation of 'fashion' or the way of doing things to represent the law. We will adopt the former use of the word law.

Not every conduct or misconduct in Melanesia lends itself to inevitable reward or punishment. The absence of law may suggest a state of anarchy. To most modern minds, the equation of 'lawlessness' with anarchy conjures images of perpetual war, violence, disorder and chaos.

Nevertheless, just as there appears to the outsider a state of perpetual war, 'cold' though it may seem between the capitalist and communist blocs, there is nevertheless an ordered behaviour within both USSR and USA. Internal order and social controls depend on internal rules of behaviour. Whilst some rules of behaviour in the USSR may be unacceptable to the Americans, and vice versa, the emphasis must be on some rather than all. Similarly, in Melanesia, where tension exists between clans, tribes or villages, nevertheless, order exists within that tension.

Contemporary Melanesian Jurisprudence

Contemporary Melanesian jurisprudence is neither the 'pure' classical Melanesian jurisprudence, nor is it Anglo-Australian jurisprudence. It is a combination of the classical and the contemporary or the new ideas. whatever their sources or origins. Colonisers, whether in law or religion or politics, have been mainly concerned with satisfying particular interest groups. Classical Melanesian communities were concerned for the survival of their own communities as much as the modern ones. But, with the advent of Western and Eastern influences, Melanesian jurisprudence, if it is to survive, will have to innovate, and where appropriate, synthesise. Goals will need to be shared in order to establish mutual acceptance. Only through compromise and synthesis will one achieve jurisprudence of the new and old Melanesia.

Melanesian Social Order

Social 'order' is here represented with a singular, although Melanesia was constituted by various social and cultural units, or social 'orders'. By a social order is meant the existence among humans in a geographical entity (not necessarily continuous), giving rise to patterned social relations among humans, with nature and the supernatural. By virtue of this social existence, modes of acceptable behaviour and prohibited behaviour emerge. Melanesian law is to be found in that order. Each cultural unit was autonomous, possessed of its origins, and defined as to its territorial boundaries and legal postulates. Each was complete in itself, yet interdependent with others in some respects, as are nations today.

The following are ten basic characteristics of a Melanesian social order from which what is termed in the non-Melanesian world as 'the law' emerges or is a part.

1. A Community of People

The existence of a community is essential to the emergence of a social order. A locality may be believed to abound in gods, ancestor spirits, fairies or other supernatural beings. But alone they do not constitute a social order. If a human community exists next to the supernatural community, a dialogue and social relations would emerge. Such spiritual beings are identifiable by humans and are 'owned by' or have other relations with humans. But the human community is essential for a social order.

2. Living within a reasonably well-defined locality

The people were settled agriculturalists, hunters, fishermen and food-gatherers. However, this did not mean they always had the one fixed village or locality. They did move dwellings. A few communities were partly nomadic within a given territory, but with limited settled sites or fixed villages. Their movement was necessitated by a search for food.

The word 'living' is used to denote a sphere of influence, including hunting, fishing, food-gathering, gardening, sites for dwellings and canoes or other structures, for magical purposes or for leisure. In this sense, 'living' is broader than 'occupying' or 'owning', or dwelling or residing.

Territory is reasonably well defined, though the precise boundaries from a modern viewpoint could be vague. They were usually well delineated by ridges, streams, rocks, particular types of plants, whether planted or naturally growing.

A community's territory is large or small depending on its population, the quality of soil and other resources, the initial and contemporary history of conquest or other control, whether through warfare or settlement, or trade.

3. Having Social Relations among themselves

This is the key factor in any discussion of law, ethics, religion, culture, politics or any other sphere of human discourse. Whatever modern meaning might be given to social relations, here we refer to specific relations (1) among the people in and of a given territory and (2) with their natural environment and the spiritual realms.

Social relations are possible between people of a common social order — allowing room, of course, for intercourse with others, without subordination. This discussion is not concerned with discovering or describing a just order of human relationships. It is merely an exposition of social reality which will become important later for the interaction and relationship between these social orders and the nation state or its subordinate orders, such as Provincial or Local Governments and other state apparatus. It is a study of how men and women actually behave in a social context. Social relations are conducted on the needs of here and now. Within a village there exists a social order. A tribe is an amorphous political alliance for war and peace, feasting and debating. But the most significant social unit after the family is the village or 'haus lain'. My own village, Wautogig in the Sepik Province of Papua New Guinea, had a classical social and political structure which typified most coastal villages throughout Melanesia. Wautogig village is a member of a loosely knit political alliance known as the *chaumaun* — the shark totem — which extends over many villages on the coast and inland and covers both the Arapesh people and the Sausa people. The political alliance does not provide a common forum for a coherent social order. The most visible and effective social unit is the village.

Wantogig has a population of about 300, divided into seven 'auiros' or 'pisin', commonly understood in English as clans, each consisting of several families. A family consists of the father, mother/mothers (in case of polygamy) and children. The head clan traditionally provides the governing chief. Other clans have particular responsibilities or expertise relating to fighting, specific arts and so on. All activities in the community are conducted according to the social structure: marriage, exchange ceremonies, land ownership, social obligations, and duties, social rights and all aspects of life are conducted against the background of this clan (and sub-clan) structure

4. Recognising themselves as a social unit

A village recognises itself as an independent,

autonomous social unit and legal order. It exists by its own history, tradition and territory. Relations between people of a social unit which recognises itself as distinct are of a different order from those of other social units. Self recognition involves self-assertion of self-identity. The existence of such a unit is autochthonous and is self-executing (in that it does not depend on the state or any other higher authority).

Identity constitutes the unit as a 'corporation', an entity. The individual becomes a member of that unit by common identity criteria, including common socialisation and acculturation. One owes obligations to that community and looks expectantly for rights from it. By virtue of membership of that community one is bound by certain accepted norms, values and accepted or prohibited modes of behaviour. Obedience to internal orderings is a necessary precondition to recognition of one among all. If the community does not recognise itself as a separate unit, it either perishes or is incorporated into another order.

Any stranger coming into that community whether as a refugee, adoptee or spouse, must become a member of a given clan and must accept its obligations and responsibilities.

5. *Common Origin*

A Melanesian community usually comes into existence by a common origin, natural or metaphysical. In modern Melanesia common origin is not essential to create new social units. For example, in many squatter settlements in Melanesia, people come from different backgrounds. Nevertheless, they function as a new or modern village. Melanesian suburbs are as diverse in ethnicity as the countries concerned are diverse in nationality and linguistic communities.

Again, in the wake of new demands for cash cropping and education many independent villages relocated on new sites. Modern conglomerates of ancient, autonomous villages, function together, but each retains a unique historical identity and origin. These are not mere abstracts, but real social forces which give rise to varying social relations on a day-to-day basis. These notions of affinity continue to play a part in the discharge of national affairs in Melanesian states.

6. *Acknowledged Leadership*

However leaders are selected, authentic leadership provides the basis for the survival and continuity of the Melanesian social unit. Melanesian leadership is acquired in one or a combination of the following ways:

i. hereditary chieftainship and investiture
ii. through personal prowess, e.g. in war, in giving feasts, public debate etc, or by virtue of age and wisdom.
iii. through appointment by others (election or otherwise).

In any village with the kind of social structure outlined for Wautogig, each clan would have its own leader or 'big man'. But, usually, in a given village, there would be one overall head chief. In the context of the Arapesh, the head chief of each village would possess the *ginau* ('power', 'authority', 'rulership' or 'government'). Whilst the entire 'Abahinem' clan is the *ginau*, one person is singled out as the *mamokin ginau* or the 'mother' or ultimate power. He governs by wise counsel, generous giving, competency in public debate, skill in maintaining relations with other clan elders and proven ability in competition with his peers of other villages.

Where leadership is inherited, the priority goes to the first-born son. However, he does not inherit power unless he demonstrates the expected qualities at an early age. Even where power is conferred on him after proof of his abilities, he is liable to vacate his office if he is defeated in an important debate, or is unable to match others in giving feasts repeatedly.

Leaders in classical Melanesia do not make or give law. They give wise counsel of what ought to be, or be avoided. Through the institution of the meeting house — (separate and mutually exclusive houses for men and women in most Melanesian societies), masters in particular fields transmit their knowledge to their pupils. General knowledge and skills are open to everyone. Special knowledge and skills are secret and confined only to those entitled to receive them. Law does not exist as a phenomenon which controls society, but as a part of cognitive knowledge of a community. Leaders are bound to remind their folks of acceptable behaviour. Leaders who do not meet acceptable standards are tolerated for a while, but put away when the community learns of their unacceptable conduct.

7. *Sharing Common Social Values*

A value in this context is a desired objective. It is not ordained, but has positive effects on community continuity. I use social value to refer more to social well-being of the individual and the community. There is no known history of how a village acquires its social values. I assume they are acquired through the natural process of self-knowledge, through pain and suffering on the one hand and pleasure and enjoyment on the other.

This knowledge is acquired through trial and error, with no one person claiming the right or privilege of being the 'law giver'. Supernatural beings, even the One Supreme Being, where acknowledged, are not the source of good or bad conduct. The deities intervene in human affairs, but are not the original authors of social values.

Shared values do not suggest shapeless uniformity. For example, some members of a given community may, through their contact with other communities, acquire new values and seek to practice them. New values remain on the periphery until they are incorporated into the life of the people.

8. *Common Language*

Common language is not a determining factor in the establishment of common social orders. However, where different languages are spoken in one community, misunderstanding often arises. Where different languages are spoken, and especially among villages or communities along the borders of different languages, one often finds multi-linguists or bi-linguists.

In all my search among the Arapesh, I found no word for 'law', for 'customary', for 'jurisprudence' or for 'justice'. Nevertheless, trained as I am in Western jurisprudence, I use these words in English and have reasonable understanding of their meaning and scope. Thus, it would be intellectually dishonest either to coin a language word, less still apply alternative English words to denote those notions. Expressions like 'norms' or 'values' or principles are used sometimes, but they too do not have the necessary direct alternatives or translations. The absence of these expressions might mislead observers to conclude, as many may have done, that there was no law, no justice, no virtue, etc. in Melanesia.

In 'Melanesian jurisprudence', judgements are made on the basis of available knowledge to determine the quality of conduct, to be praiseworthy, reprehensible or indifferent. In making such judgements reference is made to previous knowledge of what constitutes acceptable, unacceptable or indifferent conduct. In all these, language plays an elementary role. But dreams, extra-sensory perceptions, sixth sense knowledge, blood flows, movement of limbs, even bird or animal communication are a part of the language of a community and all help to build its solidarity and unity.

9. *Recognised by others as different*

Recognition by others is the key principle in the establishment of new states in international law. It can be legal, factual or both. It is the necessary condition to acceptance into the community of nations. It appears to depend on the political view of those who control power in a given territory. It is not related to any 'moral' or value judgement of the methods or means used to establish an order, or to the conduct of humans subsequently. It does depend, however, on how those who take control are able to impose their will on the population generally.

Recognition in the Melanesian context was different. There was no community of nations to be recognised, and no requirement that the power wielders in a village or clan must be able to impose their will on the people effectively. Yet, recognition is important for the survival of a community. To survive, others must acknowledge its sovereignty and its entity, whether in the form of fear, trust or distrust, sharing of values or regular trade.

10. *Diplomatic Links*

The Arapesh term to denote this institution is *buainin* when it is internal, and *gabuk* when it links external communities. The literal English translation would be 'the road person' or the 'link person'. Trade and exchange across villages and tribes are conducted through these vital link persons. When the Arapesh link man travels officially, carrying the official mace — a black palm stick with cassowary feathers on top, or with leaves of a particular tree for peace, he cannot be harmed. He must complete his mission and return safely home.

Even among warring communities, when a 'road man' travels officially, he will be accorded protection, which is necessary for the mutual survival of the communities. The road man is not granted immunity, however. Thus, if he steals or assaults, he will be punished by those he harms.

However, within a community, the *buainin* is more a trade partner, someone you can give excess wealth to and receive excess wealth from. These links are developed to be of mutual benefit in competitions in feasting, gardening and debate. *Buainin* are never found within one clan. A person must find his trade partner in a different clan. Members of the same clan are brothers or sisters. As such, they can share, but they cannot compete or trade among themselves.

The growth of road, air and shipping transport, and development of new friendships through modern contacts, have diminished the role of this institution. But in rural Melanesia and to a limited extent in cities, these institutions continue.

BASIC COMMON FEATURES OF MELANESIA

Common characteristics throughout Melanesia until this century, which distinguished Melanesian communities from Asian or European communities and to some extent from Polynesian, and which were relevant to the context of Melanesian law, include:

1. Small self-contained communities.
2. Social structures based on common affinity.
3. Leadership seldom extended over large areas. (The technology did not exist to do it.)
4. Technology based on wood, stone and bone. The wheel and gun-powder were not known.
5. No written literature — oral traditions.
6. Basically non-expansionist.
7. Almost all production was direct from the land and/or sea.
8. Wealth consisted mostly of perishable items, with shells, feathers and other durable items as media of exchange.
9. Human communities were mostly settled, but often moved their hamlets within their territory.
10. They were agriculturalists with domestic pigs, dogs and fowls.
11. The spirituality of the people was characterised by a unity of man with nature, and the supernatural.
12. Language communities averaging under 3,000 persons (Some communities in Vanuatu have fewer than 300 persons per language).

Vanuatu, with a population of little over 130,000 claims 108 languages. Fiji is a partial exception. It is a cross-road between Melanesia and Polynesia. Chieftainship in Fiji tends to cover wider areas than in the rest of Melanesia and the now dominant Bauan dialect is widely used.

A significant recent characteristic of Melanesia is the fact that it has been colonised by Europeans, and has gone through a massive process of Christianisation and intense social change. With the exception of New Caledonia, all other Melanesian island states have become constitutionally independent. The western half of the great island of New Guinea has been absorbed into Indonesia. It is likely to suffer the greatest loss of cultural and ethnic identity in all of Melanesia.

In the independent Melanesian nations, political institutions are controlled by a majority of indigenous Melanesians. The economic infrastructure, however, and legal institutions tend to be controlled or greatly influenced by foreigners or non-indigenous nationals. All means of production, including non-native land, is under an English derived land tenure system. Constitutional efforts were made to 'de-colonise' Vanuatu land tenure by reverting to customary principles, but it remains to be seen whether this will work in reality.

Within this framework, I will discuss Melanesian jurisprudence. All state institutions are regulated by former colonisers' assumptions. The values that underpin the modern Melanesian legal system, economic and political as well as the 'institutionalised churches', breathe the life of colonial histories and practise the virtues and vices of those colonisers, though imperfectly.

Western and Eastern impact on Melanesia has been devastating and perhaps beyond restoration. No Melanesian community can ever hope to return to its classical state, nor would this be desirable in the contemporary context. In the case of Fiji, for example, the Indian population, brought by English sugar planters outnumbered indigenous Fijians in the 1980s (though since 1988 Fijians outnumber Indians). Any evolution of a Fijian jurisprudence will obviously wait until the May 1987 military coup's arrest of political power settles and a choice is made as to how much more emphasis will be given to Fijian custom.

New Caledonia (Kanaky) when it becomes independent, will not be able to ignore the Polynesian, Indonesian, French, and the Vietnamese interest groups. In the development of Kanaky jurisprudence, in an independent Kanaky, the legal system will have to consider the place of Kanak social and cultural values, or so much of those as can be recognised by the nation state to be. It is likely that Melanesians of New Caledonia will be a minority in that land that was once theirs — at least for a decade or two, as the Melanesian population is growing faster than the others. The real struggle will be whether minority Kanaks can make sufficient impact on the new state to reflect some vestiges of their ancient values.

Ni-Vanuatu face a different challenge. Although they are in the majority and in control of their legal canoe, the canoe itself is on one side derived from English law and on the other side from French. If the Vanuaaku Pati continues to dominate politics in Vanuatu and its leaders are committed to ni-Vanuatu values, they have a chance to evolve a jurisprudence based on those values. But the precedents and now established traditions of the former Anglo-French colonial condominium, and the continuing pressures from aid donors and trading nations, may continue to compromise Melanesian priorities.

The Solomon Islands and Papua New Guinea are similar in that they have diverse ethnic groups all within one racial classification of Melanesia, with distinct but tiny Polynesian communities. If their political, religious and intellectual leaders can transcend the constraints of colonialism and more recent foreign pressures, then like Vanuatu, they have the possibility to evolve a genuine Melanesian jurisprudence. What emerges as Melanesian jurisprudence will not be the same in all Melanesian states. However, provided what is developed in one state is available by way of reports, publications, theses or academic papers, there is a possibility of a sharing of experiences. These will consciously or unconsciously influence decisions within these countries. If, as has been suggested, a Centre for Melanesian Studies is established and makes available material in forms that can be used by jurisprudents, there is a possibility that Melanesiar jurisprudence will develop.

In any event, the struggle to evolve new values that either compromise the old and the new, or develop something quite new, is a long one. As society changes, so too will values change. New knowledge brings new hopes and new headaches. To the extent that the law attempts to forge a path of stability, certainty and cautious growth, law could be an important instrument of positive transformation. It will depend on the values which those who operate the instruments of power, espouse and wish to imprint on their societies.

Given the dynamic nature of Melanesia, it is reasonable to anticipate slow, but gradual movement away from the colonial institutions. However, the forces of multi-national interests may frustrate any hope for constructive reform, leaving room only for peripheral and marginal changes to cushion the rigours of Western and Eastern onslaught, as in Irian Jaya.

Where do we begin?

Now that we are in international contact with the rest of humankind, where do we go from here? What kind of people do we want to be? What kind of society do we want? These questions are often answered in ideological terms such as, do we want capitalism or socialism or a mixture of both; do we want Western, African, Eastern or other models. We must reject any one brand of 'ism'. All too often, leaders get caught in great 'isms' and deny or suppress the basic needs of their people.

An over-simplistic description of the predominant 'isms' in the world would be to place the concepts of 'individualism' and 'collectivism', at opposite ends of a continuum. The proponents of each considers theirs to be the more scientific, rational and 'freeing', and the other, more irrational, emotive and 'oppressive'. We are not alone in cautioning against blind adoption of one or the other.

Justice entails the giving of a full and proper place to the human experiences of our races and our peoples, giving full consideration to Melanesian norms, customs, sanctions, perceptions and methods of dispute settlement. This view is not to be understood from the Marxist view that societies pass through different stages of evolution from the 'gentile' to the 'slave' stage, the 'feudal' stage, the 'mercantilist', the 'capitalist', and the communist utopia. In my view Melanesian communities had no need to pass through any Marxist mill! The very nature of Melanesian communities afforded flexibility which is adequate to adjust the old orders to new institutional phenomena.

Marxists assume that through class struggle, there was an 'excluded majority', controlled and dominated by an all powerful minority. By revolution, law would be destroyed, and all superstructures would be controlled by a proletarian state under the guidance or dictatorship of the masses. Melanesian societies, on the whole, did not have an 'excluded majority', for even where there was a paramount chief, he rarely, if ever, issued orders without consultation with lesser chiefs or elders. Participation in the processes of decision making was high. Slavery was never practised and feudalism did not exist. An adaptation of a theory of 'dialectical materialism' could in our view run counter to Melanesian 'non-dialectical materialism'. Its inherent recognition of its shortcomings, has been its basic strength for innovation and adaptation.

Whilst no one Western idea or notion of law is practised throughout the West, nevertheless, there are common themes or features of the Western 'capitalist' law, which we can consider and accept, adapt or reject.

Whilst we reject the notion of dialectical materialism in Melanesian legal thought, we can still learn from Marxist analysis of social stratification and even heed Marxist warnings against National Executive Councils or even parliamentarians and public servants who manage the affairs of the 'governing class' who in reality are foreign states or multi-national corporations, using national fronts to achieve their own ends.

We have indicated our inherent suspicion of English and Australian law or justice in so far as we have experienced its application on our soil. In Blackstone's view the law meant the rules prescribed by the 'supreme power' in a state. Bentham and Austin rested the law on the theory of command wherein political superiors issue orders and the subjects 'obey' or face punishments. In our view this is the standard view of the law in England and Australia which has come to be imposed on Melanesian states. Courts are part of the sovereign machinery, authorised by the supreme power in the State, the Parliament, to enforce the law.

The pure theory of law, no less the analytical theory of law, recognises the state as the 'law' or the god of the law itself. Law is an order of human behaviour, where order is a system of rules or norms, through a specific technique of social organization — the state. No moral judgement of 'good' or 'bad' is implied.

The 'technique' by which the state and hence the law comes into being, from a human viewpoint leaves much room yet for any pure theory of law to have any practical application in Melanesia. The processes through which the 'governing party' or parties win elections, manipulate legislators, 'gag' debate and push through important legislation, lead any keen observer of the 'workings of the state' to doubt the ultimate efficacy of Efficacy!

Indeed, in Melanesian States today, there is a tendency even for foreign advisers, consultants, or experts to use instruments of the state, and manipulate power to achieve a 'sovereign' will, their will!

From an emergent nationalistic viewpoint, the pure theory of law offers both hope and despair. The hope is that, through the idea of the 'god of law' — the state — we can develop our ideas of law and justice — of what is an ideal society, being confident that the international community, through the pure theory of law, will recognise its efficacy. It offers despair in that, one of our two pre-independence 'gods of law' was a colonial imposition, based not on any scientific notion of law, but on colonial whims and social and moral values. Our other god was custom.

As a people, not from an objective viewpoint, nor from a cognitive stance, but from a purely emotive stance, we would be denying much of our past humanity if we ignored our pre-contact views of life. We cannot begin our history from the point of our contact with capitalists, communists, kings, autocrats or other legal systems. We must begin from as far back as our oral traditions can take us, and use what we can of that tradition, together with what we must of any other notion of law or justice, to create something new.

In our experience, an assumed 'scientific' view has often been a pretext, even a 'fraud' and a vehicle to plant colonial values in foreign soils. Even the notion of 'Divine Ordination' has been used as a 'social technique' to effect cultural genocide.

Justice has been heralded as the Supreme ideal of politics — freedom, equality, dignity, equal opportunity and so on. But political authority which creates the written law, is all too often dominated by powerful group interests whose primary motive is not equitable distribution or justice, but the maintenance of the status quo, or magnification of their interest.

Elimination of Law

From this scepticism of 'science', we return to our starting point. In Melanesia, there was no law, only diverse ways of life. Law as a distinct social phenomenon is very recent. Thus our observation of it through the Western lenses will be, as always, very poor, primarily because we do not know how to adjust the focus, and even when the lenses are correctly focused we tend to confuse the wood and the trees and consider shadows for the reality and vice versa.

Thus, it is counter-productive to postulate any particular definition of law which emerged among the greatest Western jurists, and to correlate our ways of life with it. We are not unmindful of the contributions of earlier thinkers which are a part of our modern heritage, but we will interpret them from our own perspectives.

Our task then is to link our Melanesian perspectives, using the English language as a convenient vehicle, with what has now come to be accepted universally as a social phenomenon — the law. I offer no definition of law because it did not exist as an independent institution. Law was the people's ways of life which we now call the 'Pasin'. In this context, we have the 'Old Pasin' and the 'New Pasin'. The Pasin can be divided into three historical periods — the old Pasin, the 'Colonial Pasin' (both of which have been discussed above) and the 'independent Pasin'.

The Independent Pasin

The modern independent pasin has its starting point at independence for Fiji in 1970, for Papua New Guinea 1975, for the Solomon Islands 1978, Vanuatu, 1980 (New Caledonia hopefully not too far in the future, but for West Papua unfortunately probably much longer). These were the dates Melanesian nations came into existence as sovereign nation states, with their own constitutions, said to be rooted in the will of the people through their elected representatives in Constituent Assemblies or other processes to enact the Constitution.

Each of the Melanesian constitutions follows the standard written constitutions of most modern states. In effect they entrench the contemporary political thoughts of 'liberal democracy', constitutional supremacy, parliamentary rule, judicial law enforcement and a limited parliamentary executive with collective and individual power to initiate policies, implement programmes and legislative imperatives. The principle of the rule of law (whatever that might mean) was also entrenched.

Political power was constitutionally entrenched in the one national political sovereign i.e. centralised. However, there is a substantial measure of decentralisation, perhaps more aptly described as devolution of power. The English Common law and equity as at the date of independence and the notion of Royal Prerogative were incorporated into most of these Constitutions as part of the underlying law of the new nations. The customs and usages of the Melanesian people were also declared to be a part of the underlying law of the State, though given varying degrees of importance.

A bill of fundamental rights and a series of qualified rights were also incorporated into Constitutions, along with a provision for the independence of various constitutional creatures in the discharge of their functions. The principal organs of the state apart from the Judiciary, the Executive and the Legislature, included the Police Force, the Defence Force (except in the Solomon Islands), the Public Accounts Committee, the Ombudsman Commission (in Fiji and Papua New Guinea), the Public Solicitor's Office and the Office of the Public Prosecutor.

An important foreign institution adopted into Melanesian soil was the acceptance of the Sovereign of Britain and Her Heirs and Successors as The Constitutional Head of the Independent States of Fiji, Papua New Guinea and the Solomon Islands. In Papua New Guinea, the Queen is to be represented by a citizen of Papua New Guinea, democratically elected by the Parliament, on the orthodox one-person, one-vote principle. In Fiji and the Solomon Islands the representative was selected on the recommendation of the Prime Minister. But Fiji became a Republic after the military coup of 1987 and the Solomon Islands is considering the possibility of doing so at some future date.

The chief national political personalities at the time of independence had no training in law, moral ethics or advanced political thought. Their education, from a formal standpoint in the Western sense, was limited to an equivalent of four years of post-primary education. The emergence of political parties primarily through Pangu Pati in PNG, Vanuaaku Pati in Vanuatu and the Alliance in Fiji, inevitably meant that English political thought would find its way into their Constitutions.

The challenge before us is to infuse appropriate degrees of Melanesian thought and practice into these systems, while being cognisant of the positive elements introduced from the West over the past century, and sensitive to the pressures from the Far East in the coming century.

[19]

THE PROCESS OF DECISION MAKING IN TRIBAL COURTS

Chief Justice Tom Tso*

In this Essay, I would like to discuss the process of decision making in tribal courts. I will speak about the Navajo Tribal Courts because that is what I know. It is difficult to discuss the process without first discussing the history and the background from which the Navajo courts developed.

HISTORICAL PERSPECTIVE

The history of the Navajo Nation and of the Navajo Tribal Courts is one of challenges. Today, we still face challenges to our sovereignty, our jurisdiction, and our right to exist as a people different from the dominant society. The ultimate challenge to the Navajo has always been survival. Those familiar with the history of the Navajo will recall that the Spanish and the United States Cavalry both attempted to exterminate us. In 1864, the United States Cavalry under Kit Carson succeeded in rounding up and driving thousands of Navajo several hundred miles from their traditional homes in Northern Arizona to Fort Sumner. The true objective of this mass removal, known as "The Long Walk," is unclear. What is known is that the cavalry engaged in the intentional, systematic destruction of Navajo villages and the herds and crops that supported the people. The starving Navajo were then forced to walk four hundred miles in inclement weather with inadequate food and clothing to their new "home"—a reservation surrounding Fort Sumner which was to be shared with the Mescalero Apache. Once located on the reservation, the Navajo, numbering between eight and ten thousand, were forced onto farming land poorly suited to agriculture. Failure of crops and the unwillingness of the government to provide the tools, clothing, and food necessary to permit the people to survive resulted in the government's abandonment of the Fort Sumner reservation. In effect, four years after the disastrous Long Walk, the government threw up its hands, telling us to take our sheep and go home. The return of the Navajo to their ancestral home marked the beginning of the end of federal governmental efforts to terminate our physical existence.

Since that time, the challenges have been to our cultural identity and existence. These challenges reflect the false assumption on which relations between Indians and the Anglo world have always been conducted. The

---

* Chief Justice, Supreme Court of the Navajo Nation.

false assumption is that the dominant society operates from the vantage point of intellectual, moral and spiritual superiority. The truth is that the dominant society became dominant because of military strength and power.

Examine this from the Navajo perspective. When people live in groups or communities they develop rules or guidelines by which the affairs of the group may proceed in an orderly fashion and the peace and harmony of the group may be maintained. This is true for the Navajos. As far back as our history can be verified and further back into the oral traditions of our origins, there is a record of some degree of formal organization and leadership among the Navajos. In the earliest world, the Black World, which was the first phase of our existence, it is said that the beings knew the value of making plans and operating with the consent of all. In a later world, Changing Woman appointed four chiefs and assigned one to each of the four directions. These chiefs convened a council, established clans, and organized the world. The chiefs and councils of Navajo oral history made decisions for the larger group and regulated the clans. The oral traditions indicate that there was a separation of functions between war leaders and peace leaders. One of the major responsibilities of the Navajo headmen was offering advice and guidance.

The people chose the headmen from among those who possessed the necessary qualities. The headmen needed to be eloquent and persuasive, since they exerted power by persuasion rather than coercion. Teaching ethics and encouraging the people to live in peace and harmony were emphasized.

One of the important functions of a headman was dispute resolution. When a dispute or conflict arose in the community, the people would go to the headman for advice. If the matter involved what we today would call a criminal offense, the headman would meet with the wrongdoer, his family, the victim, and the victim's family to discuss how to handle the matter. The discussion usually involved two issues: how to compensate the victim or his family for the wrong and how to deal with the wrongdoer. The discussion continued until everyone was in agreement as to what should be done.[1]

Prior to Kit Carson's arrival, we lived in communities. You might say we had a decentralized, grass roots government. We had our own mechanisms for resolving disputes. We had a profound respect for the separation of functions. Not only did we have various leaders for war and peace, we had our medicinemen, who occupied a very important role in the operation of our society. The training and the teachings of the medicinemen were respected, and no one interfered with their function. We had our own concepts of fairness in the way we handled disputes, seeking both to compensate the victim and to rehabilitate the wrongdoer.

After we returned to our land in 1868, the federal government began to tell us all the things we had to have. We had to have an organized government and a tribal council. We had to have courts. We had to have jails. We

1. This historical information previously appeared in Tso, *The Tribal Court Survives in America*, 25 JUDGES' J. 23 (1986).

had to have separation of powers.[2] These things and many more have been instituted. They work very well in the Navajo Nation. I believe the main reason the Navajos have, by Anglo standards, the most sophisticated and the most complex tribal court system is because we were able to build upon concepts which were already present in our culture. Navajos are also flexible and adaptable people. We find there are many things which we can incorporate into our lives that do not change our concept of ourselves as Navajo.

THE NAVAJO COURT SYSTEM

I regret that the outside world has never recognized that Navajos were functioning with sophisticated and workable legal and political concepts before the American Revolution. I regret even more that the ways in which we are different are neither known nor valued by the dominant society. Because we are viewed as having nothing to contribute, much time has been wasted. Let me be more specific. Anglo judicial systems now pay a great deal of attention to alternative forms of dispute resolution. Before 1868 the Navajos settled disputes by mediation. Today our Peacemaker Courts are studied by many people and governments.[3] Anglo justice systems are now interested in compensating victims of crime and searching for ways to deal with criminal offenders other than imprisonment. Before 1868 the Navajos did this. Now Anglo courts recognize the concept of joint custody of children and the role of the extended family in the rearing of children. Navajos have always understood these concepts. We could have taught the Anglos these things one hundred and fifty years ago.

Today the Navajo courts are structured very much like those in the state and federal courts. We have seven judicial districts. The district courts are courts of general civil jurisdiction and of limited criminal jurisdiction. Civil jurisdiction extends to all persons residing within the Navajo Nation or

2. Government regulation of Indian tribes has been anything but consistent. In the century since the Navajo return to the homeland, political philosophy and opinion have undergone dramatic changes, changes that resemble a pendulum swinging from one extreme to another. The overriding philosophy has been to assimilate Indians into the Anglo society and can be seen in most of the policy enactments. After assimilation as a stated policy failed, the new policy became allotment. After allotment, we saw the Indian Reorganization Act, which was followed by termination, which in turn was followed by self-determination.

It was, however, the Indian Reorganization Act that dictated the structural changes in Tribal organization referred to here. In so doing, the Act imposed the Anglo model of government on Indian Tribes and granted additional benefits and latitude in internal matters in return for compliance. *See generally* V. DELORIA & C. LYTLE, THE NATIONS WITHIN (1984); V. DELORIA & C. LYTLE, AMERICAN INDIANS, AMERICAN JUSTICE (1983); E. SPICER, CYCLES OF CONQUEST (1962).

3. In 1982, the judges of the Navajo courts implemented a new court system that was designed to integrate traditional Navajo dispute resolution methods with traditional Anglo-American judicial methods. Called the Peacemaker Court, it uses the traditional legal processes of mediation and arbitration to arrive at reasonable solutions to disputes while protecting the interests of the disputants.

The establishment of the Peacemaker Court represents a blending of the old with the new, with an eye towards accommodating needs that were simply not being met by the existing system. Recourse to the Peacemaker Court is voluntary; however, once the parties consent, the court has authority to enforce attendance through subpoena power. The court also has authority to compel the participation of any other person involved in the dispute. The activities of the Peacemaker Court are coordinated by and through the district courts. *See* Zion, *The Navajo Peacemaker Court: Deference to the Old and Accommodation of the New*, 11 AM. INDIAN L. REV. 89-109 (1983).

who cause an act to occur within the Nation.[4] The limitations on criminal jurisdiction are determined by the nature of the offense, the penalty to be imposed, where the crime occurred, and the status and residency of the individual charged with an offense.[5] Each district also has a children's court, which hears all matters concerning children except for custody, child support and visitation disputes arising from divorce proceedings, and probate matters.

The second tier of the Navajo court system is the Navajo Nation Supreme Court, composed of three justices. The Supreme Court hears appeals from final lower court decisions and from certain final administrative orders. The Supreme Court abolished trial de novo at the appellate level and now only hears issues of law raised in the lower court record. In addition, the Peacemaker Courts, established in each judicial district, use traditional mediation processes and are supported by the district courts' supervision and enforcement of the agreements reached through mediation.

The tribal government is rapidly developing an extensive network of administrative bodies with quasi-judicial functions. The final decisions of bodies such as the Tax Commission and Board of Election Supervisors are appealable directly to the Navajo Supreme Court. Recourse from the decisions of other administrative bodies is sought through an original action in the trial court.[6] All opinions of the Navajo Supreme Court, and some of the opinions of the district courts, are published in the *Navajo Reporter*. Additionally, the Navajo courts have established rules of procedure for criminal, civil, probate and appellate matters.

THE SELECTION OF JUDGES

Navajo judges and justices are chosen through a process designed to insulate them from politics. When a judge is to be selected, interested persons submit applications to the Judiciary Committee of the Navajo Tribal Council. The Judiciary Committee screens the applicants and draws up a list of the most highly qualified people according to the qualifications set forth in the Navajo Tribal Code.[7] This list is then sent to the Tribal Chairman who appoints a judge from the list for a two year probationary period. Each appointment must be confirmed by the Tribal Council. During the probationary period, the judge receives training from carefully selected judi-

---

4. NAVAJO TRIB. CODE tit. 7, § 253 (Cum. Supp. 1984-1985).

5. The most important criminal law statutes are the Indian Country Crimes Act (18 U.S.C. § 1152), extending federal enclave jurisdiction to interracial crimes which take place in Indian country; the Major Crimes Act (18 U.S.C. §§ 1153, 3242), punishing Indian offenders for commission of 17 articulated felonies in Indian country; and the Assimilative Crimes Act (18 U.S.C. § 13), permitting federal prosecutions for state law offenses.

For a discussion of criminal jurisdiction in Indian country, see Clinton, *Criminal Jurisdiction Over Indian Lands: A Journey Through a Jurisdictional Maze*, 18 ARIZ. L. REV. 503 (1976).

6. In a decision upholding the power of the Navajo Nation to tax mineral lessees on tribal lands, the United States Supreme Court said: "The Navajo Government has been called 'probably the most elaborate' among tribes. The legitimacy of the Navajo Tribal Council, the freely elected governing body of the Navajos, is beyond question." Kerr-McGee Corp. v. Navajo Tribe, 471 U.S. 195, 201 (1985) (citations omitted). Clearly, the thrust of this decision is to uphold the exercise of substantial autonomy in governing the internal affairs of the Navajo Nation.

7. NAVAJO TRIB. CODE tit. 7, § 354 (Cum. Supp. 1984-1985).

cial education establishments which offer a quality legal-judicial education. There are currently two such establishments: the National Judicial College in Reno, Nevada and the National Indian Justice Center in Petaluma, California. The Navajo Nation Bar Association, the Judiciary Committee and the Chief Justice all evaluate the probationary judge.

If the probationary judge receives an adequate performance evaluation and satisfactorily completes his or her course of training, the Chief Justice and the Judiciary Committee recommend the judge for permanent appointment. This permanent appointment must be confirmed by the Tribal Council. Thereafter, the judge remains in office until retirement or removal under procedures established in the Tribal Code.[8] Permanent judges continue to be evaluated each year and receive training in areas where the evaluations show that knowledge and skills are lacking. Through its careful selection process, its vigorous educational programs and its thorough evaluation procedures, the Navajo Nation maintains a high standard for its judiciary.

Substantive and Procedural Law in the Navajo Tribal Court System

Representation in Court

All parties may represent themselves in the courts. If a party chooses to be represented by counsel, a member of the Navajo Nation Bar Association must be chosen. Membership in the Navajo Nation Bar Association requires passing the Navajo bar examination, which is given twice a year. Both law school graduates and those who have not been to law school may practice in tribal courts. The practitioners who have not been to law school are called advocates and must complete either a certified Navajo Bar Training Course or serve an apprenticeship.

The contribution of the advocates to the Navajo court system is beyond measure. Both our language and our traditions make Anglo court systems strange to us. In traditional Navajo culture the concept of a disinterested, unbiased decisionmaker was unknown. Concepts of fairness and social harmony are basic to us; however, we achieve fairness and harmony in a manner different from the Anglo world. For the Navajo people, dispute settlement required the participation of the community elders and all those who either knew the parties or were familiar with the history of the problem. Everyone was permitted to speak. Private discussions with an elder who could resolve a problem was also acceptable. It was difficult for Navajos to participate in a system where fairness required the judge to have no prior knowledge of the case, and where who can speak and what they can say are closely regulated. The advocates helped the Navajos through this process, and the advocates continue to be an important link between the two cultures.

The Applicable Law

The law the Navajo courts must use consists of any applicable federal laws, tribal laws and customs. The structure of our courts is based upon the

8. *Id.* at §§ 352-353.

Anglo court system, but generally the law we apply is our own.[9] When the Navajo Tribal Courts were established in 1959, the Navajo Nation did not have extensive laws of its own, and there were no reported opinions to guide the judges in the decision-making process. In 1959, the Navajo Tribal Code required the courts to apply the applicable laws of the United States, authorized regulations of the Interior Department, and any ordinances or customs of the Tribe not prohibited by such federal laws. Any matters not covered by tribal or federal law had to be decided by the law of the state in which the case arose. As the Navajo Nation encompasses land in three states, this sometimes led to confusion and the application of different laws in different parts of the reservation.

In 1985, the Tribal Code sections regarding applicable law were amended. Now, the courts are required to apply the appropriate law of the United States and laws or customs of the Navajo Nation that are not prohibited by federal law.[10] If the matter is not covered by tribal or federal law, the courts may look to any state laws and decisions for guidance,[11] *or* Navajo courts may fashion their own remedies.[12] The Navajo Nation Supreme Court makes the ultimate decisions on these issues, thereby developing an internal body of law. As a result, many of the briefs filed in that court and many of the opinions issued by it cite only Navajo cases.

It is easy to understand that the Navajo Tribal Code contains the written law of the Navajo Nation, and that this law is available to anyone. When we speak of Navajo *customary* law, however, many people become uneasy and think it must be something strange. Customary law will sound less strange if I tell you it is also called "common law." Our common law is comprised of customs and long-used ways of doing things. It also includes court decisions recognizing and enforcing the customs or filling in the gaps in the written law. The common law of the Navajo Nation, then, consists of both customary law and court decisions. In a case decided in 1987, the Navajo Nation Supreme Court observed that:

> Because established Navajo customs and traditions have the force of law, this court agrees with the Window Rock District Court in announcing its preference for the term "Navajo Common Law" rather than "custom," as that term properly emphasizes the fact that Navajo custom and tradition *is* law, and more accurately reflects the similarity in the treatment of custom between Navajo and English common law.[13]

---

9. *See* Williams v. Lee, 358 U.S. 217 (1959).

> On June 1, 1868, a treaty was signed between General William T. Sherman, for the United States and numerous chiefs and headmen of the "Navajo nation or tribe of Indians." Implicit in . . . [the] treaty terms . . . was the understanding that the internal affairs of the Indians remained exclusively within the jurisdiction of whatever tribal government existed. . . . Today the Navajo Courts of Indian Offenses exercise broad criminal and civil jurisdiction which covers suits by outsiders against Indian defendants.

Id. at 221-22 (footnotes omitted).

10. Navajo Trib. Code tit. 7, § 204(a) (Cum. Supp. 1984-1985).

11. *Id.* at § 204(c).

12. *Id.* at § 204(b).

13. *In re* Estate of Belone, 5 Navajo Rptr. 161, 165 (1987).

The Navajo Nation Supreme Court through case decisions is developing rules for pleading and proving Navajo common law.

The Integrity and Independence of the Decisionmakers

Once a court makes a decision, that decision is subject to change only through judicial processes. No other part of the tribal government has the authority to overrule that decision. The basis of the concept of a separate and independent judiciary is found in both Navajo common law and in the Tribal Code. The Tribal Code establishes the Judicial Branch as a separate branch of government.[14] The integrity of court decisions, however, has its basis in the respect given to the peacemakers as leaders who helped settle community disputes. In a case decided in 1978, the Navajo Supreme Court ruled that the respect given the peacemakers extends to the courts because Navajos have

> a traditional abiding respect for the impartial adjudicatory process. When all have been heard and the decision is made, it is respected. This has been the Navajo way since before the time of the present judicial system. The Navajo People did not learn this principle from the white man. They have carried it . . . through history. . . . Those appointed by the People to resolve their disputes were and are unquestioned in their power to do so. Whereas once the clan was the primary forum (and still is a powerful and respected instrument of justice), now the People through their Council have delegated the ultimate responsibility for this to their courts.[15]

The Old and the New Way

A close look at the Navajo Tribal Government would reveal many characteristics that appear to be Anglo in nature. Actually, many concepts have their roots in our ancient heritage. Others are foreign to our culture but have been accommodated in such a way that they have become acceptable and useful to us. Ironically, the Navajo, whose governmental structure and operation are perhaps most like those of the Anglo world amongst United States Indian tribes, is the tribe that has no constitution. The Anglo world places much value on the written word and there is a tendency to believe that if things are not written down, they do not exist.

Navajos have survived since before the time of Columbus as a separate and distinct people. What holds us together is a strong set of values and customs, not words on paper. I am speaking of a sense of community so strong that, before the federal government imposed its system on us, we had no need to lock up wrongdoers. If a person injured another or disrupted the peace of the community, he was talked to, and often ceremonies were performed to restore him to harmony with his world. There were usually no repeat offenders. Only those who have been subjected to a Navajo "talking" session can understand why this worked.[16]

14. NAVAJO TRIB. CODE tit. 7, § 201 (Cum. Supp. 1984-1985).
15. Halona v. MacDonald, 1 Navajo Rptr. 189, 205-06 (1978).
16. See M. SHEPARDSON & B. HAMMOND, THE NAVAJO MOUNTAIN COMMUNITY 128-56

Today we have police, prosecutors, jails, and written laws and procedures. I am convinced that our Anglo-based system of law enforcement is no more effective than the ways we traditionally handled law enforcement problems. Our present system certainly requires more money, more facilities, more resources and more manpower. But we have this system now, and it works as well as those of our brother and sister jurisdictions. My point is that the Anglo world has said to tribes, "Be like us. Have the same laws and institutions we have. When you have these things perhaps we will leave you alone." Yet what the Anglo world has offered, at least as far as Navajos are concerned, is either something we already had or something that works no better than what we had.

The popular concept of tolerance in America is based upon its image as a melting pot, where everyone blends together to form an indistinguishable mixture. This is fine for people who come to this country and *want* to jump into the pot. The melting pot can, however, become a good place to hide people. When differences cause discomfort or problems, it can make everyone the same. The real measure of tolerance and respect for tribes may well be how successfully the outside world can coexist with tribes. We are part of the total environment of America and at least as important as the snail darter or the California condor. What a tragedy if fifty years from now a news commentator should report on how the government has set aside a preserve in the desert where nine Indians are being saved from extinction and how it is hoped they will reproduce in captivity.

As economic development plans progress, the Navajo Nation Courts are likely to face a wide range of issues. The jurisdiction statutes of the Navajo Nation provide that the tribal courts have jurisdiction over all civil causes of action where the defendant resides within the Navajo Indian Country or, regardless of residence, has caused an action to occur within the territorial jurisdiction of the Navajo Nation.[17] Future litigation involving the land and resources of the Navajo Nation will no doubt challenge tribal court jurisdiction. In light of the decisions in *National Farmers Union Insurance Co. v. Crow Tribe of Indians*[18] and in *Iowa Mutual Insurance Co. v.*

(1970) for a discussion of social control methods among the Navajo. For a description of traditional legal practices among other tribes, see K. LLEWELLEN & E. HOEBEL, THE CHEYENNE WAY (1941).

17. NAVAJO TRIB. CODE tit. 7, § 253 (Cum. Supp. 1984-1985). The definition of Navajo Indian Country is consistent with the federal definition:

> The Territorial jurisdiction of the Navajo Nation shall extend to Navajo Indian Country, defined as all land within the exterior boundaries of the Navajo Indian Reservation or of the Eastern Navajo Agency, all land within the limits of dependent Navajo Indian communities, all Navajo Indian allotments, and all other land held in trust for, owned in fee by, or leased by the United States to the Navajo Tribe or any Band of Navajo Indians.

Id. at § 254.

> Except as otherwise provided . . . the term "Indian country" . . . means (a) all land within the limits of any Indian reservation under the jurisdiction of the United States Government, notwithstanding the issuance of any patent, and, including rights-of-way running through the reservation, (b) all dependent Indian communities within the borders of the United States whether within the original or subsequently acquired territory thereof, and whether within or without the limits of a state, and (c) all Indian allotments, the Indian titles to which have not been extinguished, including rights-of-way running through the same.

18 U.S.C. § 1151 (1982).

18. 471 U.S. 845 (1985).

LaPlante,[19] however, these questions will be decided in the Navajo Nation Courts.

Beyond the jurisdictional issues, questions of what law will be applied in civil disputes are likely to arise. Whether federal law will attach in a specific case will depend on the facts. In cases where federal law does not apply, tribal common law and statutes will be used. The Navajo Uniform Commercial Code, Navajo Nation Corporation Code, Water Code, and Mining Code are examples of statutory provisions enacted to regulate on-reservation business ventures and the use of natural resources.

Non-Indians may have concerns about the impact of tradition and custom on case decisions. Navajo custom and tradition are unlikely to call for law entirely different from that expected in Anglo courts. They are more likely to supply additional factors to consider in an already familiar context. For example, the Anglo system is familiar with the concept of valuation and payment for the taking of land.[20] Compensation for the loss of use to the surface user of land is an accepted concept in both Anglo and Navajo law. The difference will be in the valuation. Land that may appear to have little value to a non-Indian may be very valuable to a Navajo. It may have spiritual or historical value that has little to do with the income it can produce. The difficulty will be in assigning a dollar figure to values that have no measure in the market. This is not an impossible task. It is done every day in tort cases where damages are assessed for intangible harms like pain and suffering, intentional infliction of emotional distress, and loss of companionship.

Navajo courts will differ in the emphasis we place on the traditional relationship between Navajos and nature. We refer to the earth and sky as Mother Earth and Father Sky. These are not catchy titles; they represent our understanding of our place. The earth and sky are our relatives. Nature communicates with us through the wind and the water and the whispering pines. Our traditional prayers include prayers for the plants, the animals, the water and the trees. A Navajo prayer is like a plant. The stem or the backbone of the prayer is always beauty. By this beauty we mean harmony. Beauty brings peace and understanding. It brings youngsters who are mentally and physically healthy and it brings long life. Beauty is people living peacefully with each other and with nature.

Just like our natural mother, our Mother Earth provides for us. It is not wrong to accept the things we need from the earth. It is wrong to treat

19. 480 U.S. 9 (1987). The Court held that exhaustion of tribal court remedies, required in determinations of federal question jurisdiction under *National Farmers Union*, is also required in determination of diversity of citizenship jurisdiction. Justice Marshall wrote:

> In diversity, as well as federal-question cases, unconditional access to the federal forum would place it in direct competition with the tribal courts, thereby impairing the latter's authority over reservation affairs. . . . The federal policy of promoting tribal self-government encompasses the development of the entire tribal court system, including appellate courts. At a minimum, exhaustion of tribal remedies means that tribal appellate courts must have the opportunity to review the determinations of the lower tribal courts.

Id. at 15-16 (citations omitted).

20. The fifth amendment of the United States Constitution provides that "no person shall be . . . deprived of life, liberty or property, without due process of law; nor shall private property be taken for public use, without just compensation." U.S. CONST. amend. V.

the earth with disrespect. It is wrong if we fail to protect and defend the earth. It would be wrong for us to rob our natural mother of her valuable jewelry and to go away and leave her to take care of herself. It is just as wrong for us to rob Mother Earth of what is valuable and leave her unprotected and defenseless. If people can understand that the Navajo regard nature and the things in nature as relatives, then they will easily see that nature and the Navajos depend upon each other. Understanding this relationship is essential to understanding traditional Navajo concepts which may be applied in cases concerning natural resources and the environment.

We Navajos find it difficult to separate our lives into fragments or parts. Our ceremonies are religious, medical, social, and psychological. The seasons tell us how to live and what ceremonies to have. The earth gives us our food, the dyes for our rugs and the necessities for our ceremonies. These may be seen as *everyday* things. Today, the earth gives us income and jobs from mining, from oil, and from the forests. Water and earth combine to give Navajo Agricultural Products, Inc. the ability to produce large amounts of food for the Navajo people. Snow and rain and proper runoff from the mountains give us lakes for fishing. These may be seen as *commercial* things.

We cannot separate our needs and our relationships in the same fashion. This is why our laws and judicial interpretations must accommodate *both* of these things. For example, our tribal law requires that persons who want to harvest or remove anything from the forests have a permit. An exception is made, however, for persons who need to gather plants and forest products for ceremonial purposes. In a recent Navajo Supreme Court probate case,[21] the court held that any further division of the land would defeat the agricultural purposes of the land. Under Navajo common law, the parcel went to the heir who was best able to use the land for agricultural purposes. The other heirs were given set-offs in other items of the decedent's property. This case illustrates the Navajo Tribal Court system's ability to accommodate traditional values.

Conclusion

I have tried to give you a brief overview of the judicial decision-making process in the Navajo tribal courts, and to indicate some of the ways we attempt to accommodate the best from two cultures so that the Navajo Nation may proceed to develop within a framework that is familiar to us. We, the people, are a natural resource. Our culture and our history are natural resources. We are so related to the earth and the sky that we cannot be separated without harm. The protection and defense of both must be preserved. On the other hand, the dominant society views things in terms of separateness, of compartmentalization. For this reason, the Navajo Nation is best able to make the laws and decisions regarding our own preservation and development.

I have spoken of the Navajo experience, but I believe that much of what

21. In re Estate of Wauneka, 13 Indian L. Rep. 6049 (1986).

I have said applies to all Indian tribes. Understanding the challenges facing tribes is the first step toward meeting them. The process of making judicial decisions in the Navajo Nation reflects our response to these challenges.

Part V
Courts, Custom and Anthropologists

[20]

SHORTER ARTICLES, COMMENTS AND NOTES

THE RECOGNITION OF ABORIGINAL CUSTOMARY LAW: PLURALISM BEYOND THE COLONIAL PARADIGM—A REVIEW ARTICLE

A. *Group Identity and State Law*

The position of the Aboriginal people in Australian society is, 200 years after European settlement, in the throes of a radical reassessment. This has been engendered by the increasing assertion of a separate identity and special rights by the Aboriginal people—an assertion to which the Australian State is recognising the need to respond. The State legal system has inevitably been at the centre of the debate. State law has been both a prime cause and a prime indicator of Aboriginal disadvantage, but it must also attempt to reflect any revised consensus reached between the Aboriginal people and the Australian government.

A recent, and significant, report in the reassessment of State law in relation to the Aboriginal people is the Australian Law Reform Commission's 1986 report, *The Recognition of Aboriginal Customary Laws* (the "1986 report").[1] This article assesses the approach taken in that report to the recognition of customary law in terms of its wider significance for the comparative law of legal pluralism.

The argument presented here is that the 1986 report has sown the seeds of a new approach generally to cultural pluralism in the law, of particular, but not exclusive, relevance for the group identity of an indigenous minority people. In short this new approach is quite simply that groups do matter in the formulation of State legal policy. While this observation might appear simple, to the point of being trite, it in fact strikes at quite fundamental notions commonly held about the role of law, which are reflected in the form of State legal systems. At the heart of these, and as much a part of international human rights law as of national legal systems, is the idea that society is nothing more than a collection of individuals—citizens in isolation—and that, while the law can, indeed must, address itself to the relationship between the State and the citizen, it need not be concerned with the separate identity of groups as such. Coupled with this is the principle of one law for all—that it is somehow discriminatory for the law to recognise the cultural differences between groups in society, that all must be treated identically. Thus, while pluralism may exist and may be encouraged to exist at other levels of civil society, it may not receive recognition in the critical core area of the law.

The 1986 report challenges these notions, and suggests instead that legal pluralism is an ongoing process of conflict and compromise, in this case between an indigenous minority people and the State, a dialectic in which State law must

1. Australian Law Reform Commission, Report No.31, *The Recognition of Aboriginal Customary Laws* (1986), 2 Vols. and Summary Report. Subsequent references to paragraphs are to paragraphs in this report unless otherwise stated. A summary of the position of the Aboriginal people in contemplation of Australian law is provided by G. Nettheim, "Australian Aborigines and the Law" (1987) 2 *Law and Anthropology: International Yearbook for Legal Anthropology* 371.

continuously re-evaluate its own limits in relation to the separate sphere of indigenous customary law.

The conception of the recognition of customary law developed by the Commission is a new departure from previous models of the plural legal system. It is argued here that it is the colonial approach to the recognition of customary law which has characterised, and therefore limited, most plural legal systems to date. The form of such systems was dictated by the exigencies of colonialism itself, and does not yield value-free and ahistorical methods for recognising customary law. Moreover, the colonial paradigm never assumed that which is the basis of the Commission's approach, namely, that legal pluralism would be an indefinitely continuing phenomenon.

In order to establish these propositions, this article takes the following form. First, something of the position of the Aboriginal people and the context for the 1986 report is outlined. Part B.2 then defines the Commission's approach. No attempt is made to present the detail of the Commission's final recommendations, which are extensive. Rather the 1986 report is examined for those elements of its approach which lend support to the claim made here that it represents a novel approach to legal pluralism. Part B.3 explores the relationship between the recognition of customary law, which is an aspect of the group identity of an indigenous people, and self-determination, which represents the political and constitutional working out of group identity. Part C tackles the colonial paradigm for the recognition of customary law through an exposition of the principal tenets of colonial law. This is contrasted with the anomalous treatment accorded to Aboriginal customary law in Australia in the colonial period. Finally, Part D draws together the distinctive contributions to an approach to legal pluralism beyond the colonial paradigm made by the Australian Law Reform Commission.

B. *The Australian Law Reform Commission Report*

1. *Context*

Aboriginal people had inhabited Australia for at least 40,000 years before white settlement. Their societies were very diverse, with possibly as many as 600 language groups spread out across the continent. The effect on these societies of European settlement, which commenced formally in 1788, was devastating. British colonial law did not recognise the Aboriginal people as possessing sovereignty over Australia, nor did it recognise Aboriginal customary law. The reality of settlement was that the Aboriginal people "have been the subject of unprovoked aggression, conquest, pillage, rape, brutalisation, attempted genocide and systematic and unsystematic destruction of their culture".[2] Population levels plummeted from 300,000 or more in 1788 to a mere 30,000 in the early 1930s. There are now about 167,600 Aboriginal people, 1.1 per cent of the Australian population. They live in a great variety of communities, from traditionally oriented Aborigines who have had only limited contact with white society; to fringe-dwellers, living on the edges of country towns and cities; to urbanised communities. While they are now only a small minority of the total Australian

2. *Commonwealth* v. *Tasmania* (1983) 46 A.L.R. 625, 737, HCA (*per* Murphy J).

population, the Aboriginal people figure much more highly in all the indicators of disadvantage, including the criminal justice system. They are far and away the most disadvantaged group in Australia.

The 1986 report finds its context in a movement in official policy away from assimilation, which had persisted until the 1960s, to "self-determination". This has been expressed by the Commonwealth government as "the fundamental right of Aboriginals to retain their racial identity and traditional lifestyle, or, where desired, to adopt wholly or partially a European lifestyle".[3] Milestones in this process have been: the 1967 referendum which empowered the Commonwealth to make special laws for Aborigines;[4] the enactment of legislation, especially since the Woodward Commission in 1973,[5] to recognise Aboriginal land rights;[6] the establishment of various Aboriginal representative bodies and the development of Aboriginal self-management;[7] and proposals, which have not so far come to fruition, for a *makarrata*, or treaty between the Aboriginal people and the Commonwealth.[8]

The terms of reference,[9] presented to the Commission in 1977, reflected

3. Hon. R. I. Viner MHR, Minister for Aboriginal Affairs, cited in the 1986 report, para. 26.

4. Section 51(26) of the Australian Constitution.

5. Aboriginal Land Rights Commission (J. Woodward, Commissioner), First Report 1973, Second Report 1974 (Canberra).

6. Especially Aboriginal Land Rights (Northern Territory) Act 1976; on which see K. Maddock, *Anthropology, Law and the Definition of Australian Aboriginal Rights to Land* (1980), and see generally N. Peterson (Ed.), *Aboriginal Land Rights: A Handbook* (1981), and Nettheim, *op. cit. supra* n.1.

7. Especially the land councils established in the Northern Territory; and in South Australia, under the Pitjantjatjara Land Rights Act 1981 and the Maralinga Tjarutja Land Rights Act 1984; councils established under the Aboriginal Councils and Associations Act 1971 (Cwlth); the Aboriginal Development Commission; and Aboriginal Legal Services.

8. See Senate Standing Committee on Constitutional and Legal Affairs, *Two Hundred Years Later . . . Report on the Feasibility of a Compact or "Makarrata" between the Commonwealth and Aboriginal People* (1983).

9. I, Robert James Ellicott, Attorney-General, HAVING REGARD TO—

(a) the function of the Law Reform Commission, in pursuance of references to the Commission made by the Attorney-General, of reviewing laws to which the Law Reform Commission Act 1973 applies, of considering proposals for the making of laws to which that Act applies and of considering proposals for uniformity between laws of the Territories and laws of the States;

(b) the special interest of the Commonwealth in the welfare of the Aboriginal people of Australia;

(c) the need to ensure that every Aborigine enjoys basic human rights;

(d) the right of Aborigines to retain their racial identity and traditional lifestyle or, where they so desire, to adopt partially or wholly a European lifestyle;

(e) the difficulties that have at times emerged in the application of the existing criminal justice system to members of the Aboriginal race; and

(f) the need to ensure equitable, humane and fair treatment under the criminal justice system to all members of the Australian community.

HEREBY REFER the following matter to the Law Reform Commission, as provided by the Law Reform Commission Act,

TO INQUIRE INTO AND REPORT UPON whether it would be desirable to apply either in whole or in part Aboriginal customary law to Aborigines, either generally or in particular areas or to those living in tribal conditions only and, in particular:

(a) whether, and in what manner, existing courts dealing with criminal charges against growing concern and controversy over inequities in the application of the criminal justice system to Aboriginals. A community court had been proposed by Aboriginals at Yirrkala in the Northern Territory.[10] The *Anunga*[11] rules for the police interrogation of Aboriginal suspects had been proposed for enactment in the Senate.[12] A number of highly publicised cases had been construed, or misconstrued, as judicial applications of customary law.[13]

Although customary law has of late received some recognition in the courts and in legislation, the reference was essentially a first for Australia. It involved the Law Reform Commission operating in new and different ways, and it did experience serious difficulties initially in establishing its methods and objectives.[14] Nevertheless, the completed report is the product of the Commission's most extensive inquiry ever, and is based on wide-ranging consultations, especially with Aboriginal people themselves.[15] The Commission travelled all over Australia conducting hearings and discussions with many different Aboriginal groups.[16] It conceives its report as premissed upon the need for substantial Aboriginal acceptance and endorsement, and for continuing review in consultation with the Aboriginal people. An imposed "solution" would be at best ineffective and at worst destructive.

In the event, the Commission has moved a long way beyond its initial terms of reference, in the subjects which are discussed, which are not restricted to the criminal law, and, more important, in its overall approach. The 1986 report's significance lies as much in the approach to the recognition of customary law articulated in the Commission's discussion of the issues as in its final recommendations and legislative proposals.

Aborigines should be empowered to apply Aboriginal customary law and practices in the trial and punishment of Aborigines;
(b) to what extent Aboriginal communities should have the power to apply their customary law and practices in the punishment and rehabilitation of Aborigines; and
(c) any other related matter.

IN MAKING ITS INQUIRY AND REPORT the Commission will give special regard to the need to ensure that no person should be subject to any treatment, conduct or punishment which is cruel or inhumane.

10. 1986 report, paras.4, 707–712, 820–832.

11. These rules were developed by Forster J in *R.* v. *Anunga* (1976) 11 A.L.R. 412.

12. The Aborigines and Torres Strait Islanders (Admissibility of Confessions) Bill introduced as a private member's Bill by Senator Bonner; see 1986 report, para.4.

13. Especially *R.* v. *Sydney Williams* (1976) 14 S.A.S.R. 1, discussed by the 1986 report, para.433.

14. See A.L.R.C. Discussion Paper No.17, *Aboriginal Customary Law—Recognition?* (November 1980), which discusses and reflects these initial difficulties. See also a paper by J. Kirby, first Commissioner-in-Charge, "Australian Aboriginal Customary Law Progress Report", in A. Allott and G. R. Woodman (Eds.), *People's Law and State Law: The Bellagio Papers* (1985), p.327, where he comments, p.329, that: "The Commission is not permitted to conclude that the problems are too hard. It must complete its inquiry, deliver its report, and draft any legislation it proposes."

15. Cf. the ground-breaking Berger inquiry in Canada.

16. Of particular significance is the procedure developed by the Commission to consult Aboriginal women, on which see D. Bell, "Aboriginal Women and the Recognition of Customary Law in Australia", in H. W. Finkler (Ed.), *Papers of the Symposia on Folk Law and Legal Pluralism, XIth International Congress of Anthropological and Ethnological Sciences, Vancouver, Canada, 1983*, p.401.

2. Approach

The Commission distinguished three types of approach by the Australian State to the Aboriginal people. The first involved the delivery of government services, such as education, health, housing and social security. The second concerned basic issues of autonomy and self-government. The third attempted to ensure justice for Aborigines in their relations with the general legal system. It was this third approach which had guided the Commission:[17]

> The Commission's proposals are presented not only, or even principally, as a concession to Aboriginal claims or demands. The recognition of Aboriginal customary laws is not part of a negotiated and independent settlement of claims, nor is it as such a matter of self-government or autonomy. The recommendations are primarily a response to the legal system's search for justice in dealing with the Aboriginal people of Australia, a people with distinctive traditions and ways of life. Seen in this perspective, the recognition of Aboriginal customary laws has the aspect of a principled response to legal and cultural diversity, and not just of another government "service".

The phrase "a principled response to legal and cultural diversity" sets the focus for the report as primarily about the State *recognition* of customary law. It is a report on the general legal system, on its proper role, function and limits in relation to the Aboriginal community. It is not an exposition of the content of Aboriginal customary law.

An attempt to state the content of Aboriginal customary laws would have been a misplaced enterprise. The sheer diversity of Aboriginal society, before European settlement and currently, is reflected in the diversity of the content and present application of customary laws. Moreover, the Aboriginal people did not perceive their customary law in isolation from its social and religious context. It has been, and continues to be, dynamic in character, changing to meet new circumstances and conditions. A particularly important attribute of Aboriginal customary law is the secrecy surrounding it.[18] Knowledge of many of its norms and procedures is restricted to particular people.

All these factors suggested that any form of recognition based on a restatement or codification would have been inappropriate.[19] Such an approach necessarily involves a loss of autonomy and flexibility, which were attributes of their customary law that Aboriginals strongly wished to preserve. Codification is at any rate beside the point. It fails to address the problems of *interaction* between customary laws and the general legal system. It was these problems which were the focus of the Commission's inquiry. Similar considerations also led the Commission to reject both the general incorporation[20] of customary law into the

17. 1986 report, para.1037.
18. *Idem*, paras.115–116, 649–656.
19. *Idem*, paras.202, 460–462, 623. For a critique of codification in the African context see W. Twining, *The Place of Customary Law in the National Legal Systems of East Africa* (1963), and T. W. Bennett and T. Vermeulen, "Codification of Customary Law" (1980) 24 J. African L. 206.
20. *Idem*, paras.201, 406–407.

State legal system and the general exclusion[21] of State law from Aboriginals. These were alternatives which had been tried or proposed elsewhere, but which were neither desired by Aboriginals nor especially useful in dealing with the interaction of the two laws.

The Commission thus developed a method of recognition which it described as "specific" or "functional" recognition, a detailed examination of specific areas of the general law with a view to the accommodation of elements of Aboriginal customary law.[22] The latter would continue to define and develop its own preserve. The Commission's task was to take account of this in the general legal system.

A good example of "functional" recognition is the Commission's approach to customary marriage.[23] The evidence disclosed that marriage outside the Marriage Act 1961 and according to customary forms is still very common amongst the Aboriginal people. In the Northern Territory alone, it has been estimated that there are 4,889 "tribal unions" but only 151 "legal marriages".[24] Aboriginal customary marriage diverges in many critical respects from marriage under the general law and from international human rights standards. It will not be registered; it may involve under-age partners; it may be polygamous; it may have been arranged by the spouses' families; and custom does not usually prescribe a formal wedding ceremony. Yet failure to recognise customary marriages means that in important respects Aboriginal spouses are denied the benefits and protections of the general law.

Therefore the Commission recommended that, rather than equating customary marriage with marriage under the Marriage Act, which would have a number of unintended and undesirable consequences for both laws, customary marriage should be recognised in a number of specific areas, where it was just to do so. These areas included the status of children, adoption and fostering, succession, accident compensation, superannuation, social security, spousal compellability in court and tax. Many of these recommendations attached consequences to a customary marriage which would never have existed in customary law, but which are necessary to ensure the just application of the general law to Aborigines.

Marriage provides a classic example of "functional" recognition, but inherent in this concept is the idea that what is involved in recognition can vary considerably with the context. Thus the proposals for the recognition of hunting, fishing and gathering rights[25] are as much about the preservation of these activities in the context of competing resource uses as they are about the recognition of customary laws regulating hunting, fishing and gathering. Similarly, the proposals

21. *Idem*, para.203. Exclusion is a method especially associated with the US Indian, on which see M. B. Hooker, *Legal Pluralism: An Introduction to Colonial and Neo-Colonial Laws* (1975), pp.312–330, W. C. Durham, "The Aboriginal and Comparative Law: A United States Perspective" (1986) 34 A.J.C.L. Supp.1, and P. G. McHugh, "Maori Fishing Rights and the North American Indian" (1985) 6 Otago L.R. 62.

22. 1986 report, para.209.

23. *Idem*, chaps.12–14.

24. *Idem*, para.233.

25. *Idem*, Part VII.

on child custody, which recommend an "Aboriginal child placement principle"[26] are primarily designed to preserve Aboriginal families and groups by keeping Aboriginal children within them. They are only incidentally a recognition of customary law on adoption or child care.

This flexible approach runs through the 1986 report. The Commission, for example, avoided any rigid definition of "Aborigine". It endorsed the High Court's broad threefold definition ("a person of Aboriginal descent, albeit mixed, who identifies himself as such and is recognised by the Aboriginal community as Aboriginal")[27] and stated:[28]

> The application of the Commission's recommendations in appropriate cases is to be achieved by the substantive requirements of the provision in question, and by related evidentiary requirements. Indeed, there may be cases where it is appropriate that provisions for the recognition of Aboriginal customary laws should apply to persons who are not Aborigines.

Because the application of customary laws will be a matter of factual proof in each case, the Commission's recommendations are not restricted to traditionally oriented tribal Aborigines, but may apply to Aborigines in a wide range of communities.

The Commission also sought to develop proposals which would be flexible enough to accommodate change in Aboriginal lifestyles and customary law. It was clear that customary law had undergone and would continue to undergo considerable change. That in itself did not preclude the need for the reference. The Commission's concern was to recognise existing realities and to allow for future development, and not to preserve some imagined pre-contact system. Some submissions had however gone further:

> True "tribal law" is probably dead everywhere.[29]

> I frankly do not know how you can implement customary law in a community which is undergoing very rapid change and, in some respects, disintegration.[30]

While many patterns of behaviour had altered, the Commission found no evidence of the disappearance of customary law. Rather, it found many signs of its continuing—even renewed—vitality. The "outstation" movement[31] and the grant of land rights had enhanced this. There would thus be no "sunset clause" in the Commission's recommendations. The recognition of customary law was not a temporary special measure, like positive discrimination,[32] but an enduring distinction based on legitimate cultural differences.

The Commission applied its flexible approach to functional recognition in five

26. *Idem*, chap.16; and see R. Chisholm, "Towards an Aboriginal Child Placement Principle: a View from New South Wales", in B. W. Morse and G. R. Woodman (Eds.), *Indigenous Law and the State* (forthcoming).

27. *Commonwealth* v. *Tasmania* (1983) 46 A.L.R. 625, 817 (*per* Deane J).

28. 1986 report, para.95.

29. T. G. H. Strethlow, Submission 33 (14 July 1977), cited in *idem*, para.119.

30. J. Wootten, Submission 9 (15 Mar. 1977), cited in *idem*, para.123.

31. A movement of a number of Aboriginal people back to a more traditional lifestyle in remote communities: see *idem*, para.34.

32. *Idem*, para.219. But cf. the approach taken by the High Court of Australia in *Gerhardy* v. *Brown* (1985) 57 A.L.R. 472, a case on the validity of land rights legislation, under the federal racial discrimination legislation.

areas: marriage, children and family property; the criminal law and sentencing; problems of evidence and procedure; local justice mechanisms for Aboriginal communities; and hunting, fishing and gathering rights. In selecting these topics for detailed examination, the Commission was guided by the views of the Aboriginal people and others as to the areas which gave rise to the most pressing problems as a result of the non-recognition of customary law.

It did not deal with the much wider range of problems concerning Aboriginals in the State legal system generally. The Commission found, for instance, that in most cases in which Aboriginals came into contact with the criminal justice system, customary law had no real part to play. Alcohol-related offences, petrol sniffing amongst Aboriginal young people and Aboriginal/police relations were all outside the Commission's brief, although they presented arguably more pressing problems.[33] The recognition of customary law should not be seen as a panacea, although it may indirectly reduce the incidence of conflict and crime by making the general legal system more comprehensible to Aboriginal people.

3. *Self-determination and customary law*

There were nevertheless three areas, where customary law does have an important role, which the Commission expressly excluded from its report: land,[34] the cultural heritage[35] and self-determination.[36] These are issues which have been at the forefront of Aboriginal concerns, and which are closely bound up with each other. The political principle of self-determination, which is seen as being intimately linked with land rights, is a principle of overriding importance to the Aboriginal people, and to indigenous minority peoples generally.[37] It is therefore of critical importance to examine the (complex and shifting) interface between State recognition of customary law and self-determination. The Commission's position on this is not as clear cut as it may at first seem.

The Commission distinguished its inquiry as "primarily a response to the legal system's search for justice in dealing with the Aboriginal people",[38] from questions of self-government or autonomy. It considered that the international law principle of self-determination imposed no obligations on the Australian government in relation to the Aboriginal people.[39] It omitted land and the cultural heritage on the grounds that these areas were already receiving consider-

33. *Idem*, paras.211–216, 1033.

34. *Idem*, paras.211–212; see references cited *supra* nn.1 and 6; and refer to the Aboriginal Land Rights (Northern Territory) Act 1976 (Cwlth), the Pitjantjatjara Land Rights Act 1981 and the Maralinga Tjarutja Land Rights Act 1984 (South Australia) and the Aboriginal Land Rights Act 1983 (NSW).

35. *Idem*, para.213; and refer to Aboriginal and Torres Strait Islanders Heritage (Interim Protection) Act 1984 and the Protection of Movable Cultural Heritage Act 1986 (Cwlth).

36. *Idem*, paras.1035–1037; and see Senate Standing Committee, *op. cit. supra* n.8 and B. Morse, *Aboriginal Self-Government in Australia and Canada* (1984).

37. See B. Kingsbury, *"Indigenous Peoples" and the International Community* (unpub. M.Phil. thesis, Oxford, 1984).

38. 1986 report, para.1037.

39. *Idem*, para.172. See J. Crawford, "Self-Determination Outside the Colonial Context" (Colloquium on Self-Expression and Self-Determination in the Commonwealth Context, Edinburgh, 1986).

able attention in other fora, and thus the Commission's work would only involve duplication of effort, although, in the event, less progress has been made on these subjects than the Commission might reasonably have expected.[40]

At least initially, the 1986 report asserts a clear distinction between self-determination and the recognition of customary law:[41]

> To treat the recognition of Aboriginal customary laws as the channel for Aboriginal self-determination is to distort the issues . . . But it is as necessary to keep in mind that some of the demands being voiced by Aboriginal people and their organisations are essentially demands for self-government or autonomy, at least in certain areas, and that such demands are not able to be satisfied simply through recognition of Aboriginal customary laws and traditions. But the issues dealt with in this Report are important in their own right, however much it is necessary to place them in their proper context as part, and only part, of a wider debate.

Nevertheless the report concludes by referring to the Canadian experience and suggesting that a different approach to the recognition of customary law, and one more in accord with the principle of self-determination, would have been to have incorporated the issue into a wider process of negotiation between the Aboriginal people and the Australian government:[42]

> To postulate, as the Terms of Reference do, that Aboriginal people have the right to maintain their cultural identity and to practise their customary laws is to assume that this right, and the limits on it, are externally determined, and is not a recognition so much of cultural autonomy as of cultural subordination. Perhaps elements of ethnocentricity could only be avoided if recognition of Aboriginal customary laws was part of wider negotiations for autonomy conducted between Aboriginal people and government.

In many particular respects, the Commission's recommendations are posited on the principle of self-determination, and may, in turn, contribute to it. Codification and general recognition through the medium of judicial exposition are both rejected on the grounds of loss of autonomy. So, too, is any generally imposed scheme of local courts or an official agency to oversee implementation of the 1986 report. Some of the recommendations are more directed towards enhancing Aboriginal autonomy than to recognising Aboriginal customary law. This is particularly the case with hunting and fishing rights and with the Aboriginal child placement principle. The report generally is presented on the basis that its implementation is subject to the assent of the Aboriginal people, and that it is in no sense the last word on Aboriginal/Australian relations. It may assist in the promotion of self-determination, by demonstrating to the rest of Australia the importance and vitality of the distinct Aboriginal culture. As Eggleston commented,[43] "The official recognition of tribal law . . . would not only solve some

40. On 18 Mar. 1986, the Hon. Clyde Holding announced that the government had abandoned its previously announced proposals for national land rights legislation.

41. 1986 report, para.5.

42. *Idem*, para.1035.

43. E. Eggleston, *Fear, Favour or Affection: Aborigines and the Criminal Law in Victoria, South Australia and Western Australia* (1976), p.305. Elizabeth Eggleston pioneered work on Aboriginals and the State legal system.

practical difficulties but would be tangible recognition by white society of the value of Aboriginal culture."

It is true in many other contexts as well as the Australian one that customary law plays an important political role in the assertion of self-determination by indigenous peoples. At the most basic level, customary law is a symbol of the "differentness" of an indigenous people from the ambient population. It also represents continuity with a pre-colonial past. These factors can have legal implications, providing a basis, for example, for land rights claims or for wider legal guarantees of autonomy. Customary law was thus thrown into sharp relief in the transition into independence of many colonial territories in Africa and the Pacific. It is also much relied upon in claims made by indigenous minority peoples.

Nevertheless, self-determination is not wholly, or even principally, about customary law. Indigenous self-government and the grant of land rights or even of a separate territory may make more room for the exercise of customary law, but they will not dissolve the issue of recognition. Indigenous governments may well adopt more of the forms of State law than of customary law and, as experience in the newly independent countries of Africa and the Pacific—as well as in countries where an indigenous minority people has achieved a significant measure of autonomy—indicates, self-determination does not solve the issue of what to do about the recognition of customary law.

Thus the Australian Law Reform Commission may, as it itself suggests, have been made to put the cart before the horse by considering the recognition of customary law before any negotiation between the Aboriginal people and the Australian government on self-determination, but that does not invalidate the exercise.

In many ways, the Commission had no choice but to distinguish, as far as possible, self-determination from its exercise. It would have been fundamentally inappropriate for the Commission, an Australian government instrumentality, acting within its particular mandate on the recognition of customary law, to have made recommendations on land and self-determination. They are multiple issues, which involve many factors of a political nature, with wide implications for the Australian nation as a whole, and which are not concerned solely with customary law. Moreover, self-determination by its nature involves a process of direct negotiation between the Aboriginal people and the Australian government. This is not a process which a law reform commission could initiate.

Nevertheless, if, as experience elsewhere suggests, the issue of the recognition of customary law is one of continuing relevance, whatever degree of self-determination is achieved, the Commission's treatment will be of enduring significance. In fact the strength of the Commission's approach is that it shows that customary law is not inextricably bound up with a fixed territory or with an independent government, but is an attribute of a people, of group identity, and thus, in fact and in law, must apply personally and not territorially.

C. *The Place of Customary Law under Colonialism*

Now that the approach of the Australian Law Reform Commission has been analysed, it is possible to examine the place of its report in the context of the comparative law of legal pluralism.[44] It has been suggested that the dominant approach—the paradigm—for legal pluralism has been that developed under colonialism. It is the purpose of this part to present a model of the colonial treatment of the recognition of customary law, and then to contrast that, first, with the fate of Australian Aboriginal customary law in the colonial period and, second, with the Commission's approach.

1. *Colonial law*

British imperial expansion, at least until the late nineteenth century, was posited upon a principle of indigenous sovereignty. This was not merely a moral concession to the many native peoples who became subject to colonial domination; it was a legal principle, which involved a number of legal consequences, not only for the assumption of British sovereignty but also for the continuing status of customary law.[45] With respect to the assumption of sovereignty, it dictated that, where there were indigenous inhabitants, sovereignty could only be obtained by cession or, exceptionally, by conquest. This pattern may be observed time and again in Africa,[46] in North America and in New Zealand.[47] To this rule, Australia is the salutary exception, where no attempt was made to treat with the Aborigines.

However, the mere assumption of sovereignty neither resolved the fate of indigenous law nor exhausted the implications of indigenous sovereignty. Colonial law still had to resolve the issues of what law was applicable to govern the colonists, and relations between the colonists and the indigenous peoples, and what law was to govern the relations between the indigenous peoples in their dealings *inter se*.[48] In particular, the mere assumption of sovereignty did not determine the title to land and the survival of the customary law of land ten-

44. The classic general works on legal pluralism and the recognition of customary law are M. B. Hooker, *op. cit. supra* n.21; A. Allott, *New Essays in African Law* (1970) and H. F. Morris and J. S. Read, *Indirect Rule and the Search for Justice* (1972). Space does not permit a full citation of the literature, but see the proceedings of the Commission on Folk Law and Legal Pluralism, Bellagio (1981), Vancouver (1983) and Sydney (1986), published as Allott and Woodman, *op. cit. supra* n. 14 and Morse and Woodman, *op. cit. supra*, n.26, as well as the *Journal of Legal Pluralism and Unofficial Law* and P. G. Sack and E. Minchin (Eds.), *Legal Pluralism: Proceedings of the Canberra Law Workshop VII*, (1986). The International Academy of Comparative Law devoted two sessions of its XIIth Congress (Sydney, 1986) to "The Aborigine in Comparative Law" and "Mixed Civil and Customary Jurisdictions in Developing Countries".

45. See P. G. McHugh, *The Aboriginal Rights of the New Zealand Maori at Common Law* (Ph.D. thesis, Cambridge, 1987), which very fully discusses the developing norms of international law governing imperial expansion, British imperial practice, and the common law recognition of customary law throughout the Empire (and in the United States).

46. See Morris and Read, *op. cit. supra* n.44, at chap.2 and, generally, K. Roberts-Wray, *Commonwealth and Colonial Law* (1966), chap.3, "Acquisition of Territory". The *locus classicus* is *Campbell* v. *Hall* (1774) 1 Cowp 204 (*per* Lord Mansfield).

47. Treaty of Waitangi 1840.

48. See B. W. Morse, "Indigenous Law and State Legal Systems: Conflict and Compatibility" in Finkler, *op. cit. supra* n.16, at p.381; also to be published in Morse and Woodman, *op. cit. supra* n.26.

ure.[49] When the British acquired sovereignty over what in the language of the Age of Expansion was known as "Christian territory", where a legal system readily cognisable to the colonists was in operation, that system continued to operate, governing colonisers and colonised alike. A similar principle was also on occasion applied to "non-Christian territories".[50] It was even argued in the case of Australia:[51]

> This country was not originally desert, or peopled from the mother country, having had a population far more numerous than those that have since arrived from the mother country. Neither can it be called a conquered country as Great Britain was never at war with the natives, not a ceded country either, it, in fact, comes within neither of these, but was a country having a population which had manners and customs of their own, and we have come to reside among them; *therefore in point of strictness and analogy to our law, we are bound to obey their laws, not they to obey ours* [emphasis added].

In point of fact such a suggestion proved unworkable both in exercising the exigencies of government which sovereignty entailed, and in governing the relations of the colonists *inter se*. From the demands of the latter, especially in the context of the settlers in the American colonies, arose the doctrine that the common law was the birthright of the Englishman, which could be carried with him into settlements established in non-Christian territories. Thus:[52]

> English persons inhabiting non-Christian territory held the birthright to English law in their relations *inter se* . . . This did not displace the common law presumption of the continuity of the pre-colonial law so much as limit its applicability to the indigenous population . . . The exemption of the non-indigenous population from the Aboriginal law (that is, the transformation of the customary code from a territorial to personal character) was, therefore, a qualification upon the common law presumption of the continuity of the pre-colonial law.

From this root-stock of common law principles in relation to colonisation, which were themselves in a state of continuous evolution, British colonial practice developed many forms of accommodation of the indigenous order. While sanctioned by doctrine, this was also in many cases a simple recognition of reality and of administrative convenience. Indigenous orders did not simply melt away upon the imposition of *Pax Britannica*. Moreover, the economic motivations of colonialism, and the need to preserve order often justified the preservation of customary law.[53] As Moore comments acutely:[54]

> In the colonies, the laws of indigenous population were of major importance to the administering powers. Order had to be maintained with a small staff, limited funds, and little equipment. Colonial administrators could not possibly hope to revamp completely the indigenous legal/political system, and for that matter, in many

49. See Roberts-Wray, *op. cit. supra* n.46, at chap.14, "Sovereignty and Title to Land", McHugh, *op. cit. supra* n.45, at Part III, and McHugh, "Aboriginal Title in New Zealand Courts" (1984) 2 Cant.L.R. 235.

50. See Morse, *op. cit. supra* n.48 in relation to Canada.

51. *R.* v. *Jack Congo Murrell* (1836) 1 Legge 72 (*per* Stephen *in arguendo*).

52. McHugh, *op. cit. supra* n.45, at p.157.

53. On this theme see J. S. Furnivall, *Colonial Policy and Practice* (1948) and P. Fitzpatrick, *Law and State in Papua New Guinea* (1980).

54. S. F. Moore, *Law as Process: An Anthropological Approach* (1978).

places, did not aspire to do so. Like it or not they had to acknowledge the local legal order.

The observation that most of the comparative experience of plural legal systems[55] and of the "recognition" of customary law is rooted in the colonial encounter may seem so obvious as to be unnecessary, were it not that the systems of formal accommodation which the law developed are commonly perceived, by lawyers at least, as value-free techniques.[56] Nothing could be further from the truth. The attitude of the colonisers to customary law was not conditioned simply by the exigencies of governance or by economic factors, although both of those were important. It was also conditioned by a set of ideas, both about the nature of customary society and about the effect of colonisation upon it. These ideas produced a system which bore only a limited relationship to reality and which itself modified and transformed what it sought to preserve.[57] It was, in any event, only one possible response to the existence of customary law, and one which was more a reflection of colonialism than of custom. Nevertheless, as a system, it has shown remarkable persistence in post-colonial States: "proving most one of the more enduring legacies of European expansion".[58]

What, then, were the assumptions upon which the colonial pluralist legal order was built, and what were the basic elements of that order? The colonisers began with their own image of customary society as, above all, unchanging and hierarchical. That it should be unchanging squared both with the notion of custom in English law as existing from time immemorial,[59] and with a prevailing ideology of legal evolution which placed customary law alongside ancient law in

55. One should be careful to distinguish the plural legal system or "formal" legal pluralism from a descriptive theory of legal pluralism which seeks to account for the operation of a number of normative systems with the same field, irrespective of whether the dominant system "recognises" the others: J. Griffiths, "What is Legal Pluralism?" [1986] Journal of Legal Pluralism 1. See also F. von Benda-Beckmann, "Why Law Does not Behave: Critical and Constructive Reflections on the Social Scientific Perception of the Social Significance of Law", in Finkler *op. cit. supra* n.16, at p.232; G. R. Woodman, "Unification or Continuing Pluralism in Family Law: Past Experience, Present Realities, and Future Possibilities in Anglophone Africa" (paper to International Society on Family Law, Regional Conference on Social Change and Legal Reform in East, Central and Southern Africa, University of Zimbabwe, 13–16 Jan. 1987); and Morse and Woodman, "Introductory Essay: The State's Options", in Morse and Woodman, *op. cit. supra* n.26.

56. The formalist literature is considerable and includes Hooker and Allott, *op. cit. supra* n.44, as well as D. Pearl, *Interpersonal Conflict of Laws in India, Pakistan and Bangladesh* (1981), T. W. Bennett, *Application of Customary Law in Southern Africa: The Conflict of Personal Laws* (1985), E. Vitta, "The Conflict of Personal Laws" (1970) 5 Israel L.R. 170, and K. Lipstein and I. Szaszy, "Interpersonal Conflict of Laws" (chap.10, Vol.III, "Private International Law", *International Encyclopedia of Comparative Law*).

57. See notably J. S. Read, "Customary Law under Colonial Rule", in Morris and Read, *op. cit. supra* n.44, at chap.6, T. Ranger, "The Invention of Tradition in Colonial Africa", in E. Hobsbawm and T. Ranger, *The Invention of Tradition* (1983), F. Snyder, *Capitalism and Legal Change* (1981), M. Chanock, *Law, Custom and Social Order* (1985), and P. Fitzpatrick, "Traditionalism and Traditional Law" (1984) 28 J. African L. 20. The arguments are summarised by Chanock in "Neither Customary nor Law: A Case of Mistaken Identity", paper to the 1987 Harare Family Law Conference, *supra* n.55.

58. Griffiths, *op. cit. supra* n.55, at p.6.

59. See C. K. Allen, *Law in the Making* (7th ed., 1964), pp.112–160, and "Custom and Usage", Vol.12, paras.401–443, *Halsbury's Laws of England* (4th ed.).

its emphasis on status.[60] It also drew upon the "noble savage" tradition[61] in finding customary societies expressive of some changeless balance within the community and between the community and the environment. The image of hierarchy not only squared with common conceptions about customary societies as bound by status and ruled by chiefs, it also suited administrative and economic convenience. The chief became a conduit between the colonisers and the colonised: he conducted trade, carried out orders, held courts and represented views. The idea of the chief became so important that, if there were none, they were invented, and their power and position were bolstered in a way which suited the patriarchal face of colonialism.

Upon this conservative basis was built the celebrated and widely practised administrative philosophy of "indirect rule". Indirect rule, or government through existing indigenous institutions, seemed morally just, as involving the least violence to existing social patterns; administratively convenient, as it saved on the scarce resources of central government; and far-sighted, as the natives could be gradually trained to assume the responsibilities of government from a standpoint they could comprehend. In its application to law, the philosophy of indirect rule involved two spheres of operation, one applying to the colonial officials and settlers, the other to the natives. Racial status thus became the prime connecting factor in the application of laws.[62] These spheres for the operation of laws were rigid in the sense that they depended upon criteria of descent which could not be modified by choice. The science of determining into which legal system a person fell became a very complex and technical branch of colonial law known as the interpersonal conflict of laws. This contained and separated people into classes in a way which was superficially perfect and coherent, but which had no necessary connection with reality, and which masked "the jungle of legal pluralism"[63] in the way in which the system actually operated on the ground. However the *personal* application of law, rather than its territorial application, was a key feature of the colonial paradigm.

Customary law operated at two levels within the colonial system dictated by indirect rule. At the grass-roots level, which most directly and frequently involved the indigenous populations, it was administered through customary courts, which were part of the administrative rather than the judicial hierarchy and which, though typically founded on existing customary fora, were transformed through the supervision and the jurisdictional constraints of the colonial system. Within the State courts, customary law assumed an even more artificial life in its subjection to the alien procedures and requirements of the English judicial system.[64] This process intensified with the movement towards the integration of the courts in the approach to independence.

Colonial law did not, however, give free reign to customary law within the

60. See H. Maine, *Ancient Law* (1861).

61. See Kingsbury, *op. cit. supra* n.37, "The Legacies of Past Ideas", at pp.37–47.

62. See Allott, *op. cit. supra* n.44, at chap.6, "Factors Affecting Choice of Law: I Ethnic Origin", pp.182–202; cf. also Indian status in Canada.

63. A term coined by Benda-Beckmann, *op. cit. supra* n.55.

64. See Twining, *op. cit. supra* n.19, and G. R. Woodman, "How State Courts Create Customary Law in Ghana and Nigeria", in Finkler, *op. cit. supra* n.16, at p.297 and also to be published in Morse and Woodman, *op. cit. supra* n.26.

sphere of operation allotted to it. The introduction of English law carried with it the power to define and confine the scope of customary law, which was most often limited to land and family law. The crucial area of the criminal law, so closely bound up with the sovereign's powers of governance, was exclusively the province of English law, and received only minimal modification to take account of customary patterns. Moreover, the criminal law was used for a much wider range of coercive and administrative functions in the colonies than English law would have countenanced at home.[65]

If, as asserted at the outset, the colonisers viewed pre-colonial customary law as unchanging, they equally viewed its fate upon the full impact of European contact as inevitably sealed. The transience of customary law, as they perceived it, meant also that the pluralist legal system was a temporary state of affairs, "the messy compromise which the ideology of legal centralism feels itself obliged to make with recalcitrant social reality".[66] Unification was viewed as an inevitability and as a goal, which could, if necessary, draw upon elements of customary law, but only as part of a process of building a national legal system which would apply equally and identically to everyone. This goal became just as important, if not more so, to the new leaders of the post-colonial States, than it had been to the colonial administrators, who tended to be timid in overtly tampering with the indigenous systems.

The colonial paradigm, the barest elements of which have been suggested above, is vital to an appreciation of the position of Aboriginal customary law in Australia in at least two respects. First, Australia is the striking exception to the developments which ensued to some extent or other everywhere else in the British Empire in recognition of the pre-colonial order. Second, this meant that the work of the Australian Law Reform Commission was essentially a new beginning for Australia, and thus allowed the development of a new approach to pluralism, not against the background of colonial fictions, but as a reflection of the present position of Aboriginal customary law in fact. These distinctions must be elaborated.

2. *The Australian exception*

British sovereignty over Australia was acquired without any recognition of prior Aboriginal sovereignty. In particular, no attempt was ever made to enter into treaty relations with the Aboriginal people, so as to obtain the colony by cession, a pattern of conduct so widespread elsewhere in the Empire and which, in relation to indigenous minority peoples in North America and New Zealand, is proving such a potent basis for current negotiations. Indeed the treaty basis of indigenous rights, particularly in Canada, has been a critical determining factor in justifying and enhancing the special position of the indigenous peoples there, and has given rise to suggestions for a "compact" or *makarrata* in Australia.[67]

Further, Australia has always been regarded as a "settled" colony, although the consequences of this classification may not be as decisive for the recognition

65. See R. B. Seidman, "The Reception of English Law in Colonial Africa Revisited" (1968–9) 1–2 Eastern Africa L.R. and Fitzpatrick, *op. cit. supra* n.53.

66. Griffiths, *op. cit. supra* n.55, at p.7, and cf. Woodman, *op. cit. supra* n.55.

67. Senate Standing Committee, *op. cit. supra* n.8.

of Aboriginal customary law as the prevailing orthodoxy would have it.[68] Lord Watson, building upon previous authority,[69] held, in *Cooper* v. *Stuart*:[70]

> The extent to which English law is introduced into a British colony, and the manner of its introduction, must necessarily vary according to circumstance. There is a great difference between the case of a colony acquired by conquest or cession, in which there is an established system of law, and that of a colony which consisted of a tract of territory practically unoccupied, without settled inhabitants or settled law, at the time when it was peacefully annexed to the British dominions. The colony of New South Wales belongs to the latter class.

Blackburn J, in *Milirrpum* v. *Nabalco*,[71] held himself bound by this classification, although the High Court of Australia was subsequently evenly divided over whether the issue could be reopened.[72]

Nevertheless, whatever the accuracy of the classification, of more significance in the present context is its effect on the recognition of customary law. As has been earlier suggested, the mere manner of assumption of sovereignty did not in itself determine the future of indigenous law, especially as it applied to the relations of the indigenous people *inter se*. In fact the common law recognised the continuity of the pre-colonial law, at least in its application to the indigenous inhabitants. This seems to have been the initial position in Australia, or it was at least entertained by some judges and officials.[73] However, typically, most colonies which were primarily for settlement, and where the settler population rapidly outnumbered the indigenous population, entertained less sympathetic views to the survival of customary law. As a matter of administration, there was less practical need to do so. Moreover, Aboriginal society had a number of characteristics which disturbed the pattern which English law held necessary for the recognition of customary law. It was relatively small in population, and thus, as a practical matter, did not directly challenge the authority of the settler State. It was dispersed throughout the vastness of the continent, and culturally very diverse. The economic basis of life was one of hunting and gathering and this, coupled with an identification with land which was primarily spiritual, constituted a vastly different attitude to land ownership from that prevailing in the common law. Aboriginal societies were not generally centralised, chief-based societies, and so they could not easily be co-opted into the State system. Their laws and institutions did not conform to English conceptions.

All these factors militated against recognition of customary law in the colonial period, and by the mid-nineteenth century the position was settled. The British House of Commons Committee on Aborigines in British Settlements reported in 1837 of the Australian Aboriginals:[74]

68. This issue is discussed by the 1986 report, chaps.4 and 5. See also McHugh, *op. cit. supra* n.45 and R. H. Bartlett, "Aboriginal Land Claims at Common Law" (1985) 15 U. Western Australia L.R. 293.
69. McHugh, *op. cit. supra* n.45, at p.138 for references.
70. (1889) 14 App.Cas. 286, 291.
71. (1970) 17 F.L.R. 141.
72. *Coe* v. *Commonwealth* (1979) 24 A.L.R. 118.
73. See the discussion and citation of authorities in the 1986 report, paras.39–48.
74. Great Britain. House of Commons, Commons Committee on Aborigines (British Settlements) Report, Parliamentary Papers (1837) 7, section 425.

> So destitute are they even of the rudest forms of civil polity, that their claims, whether as sovereigns or as proprietors of the soil, have been utterly disregarded. The land has been taken from them without the assertion of any other title than that of superior force, and by the commissions under which the Australian colonies are governed Her Majesty's sovereignty over the whole of New Holland is asserted without reserve.

Full jurisdiction of English law over Aboriginals, and a refusal to recognise Aboriginal customary law were upheld by the courts in criminal matters,[75] in marriage[76] and in title to land.[77] What recognition did occur in the colonial period was haphazard and largely a matter of administrative discretion.[78]

The whole question was fully re-argued in a case, which has probably come to receive disproportionate attention as a turning point in Aboriginal/Australian relations, although it did not itself challenge the prevailing orthodoxy, and has subsequently been heavily criticised. The case was *Milirrpum* v. *Nabalco*, a decision of Blackburn J in the Supreme Court of the Northern Territory. In an exhaustive written decision he found against the plaintiffs, who were asserting Aboriginal ownership of land over which the Commonwealth had granted mining rights, on the basis of the continuity of pre-colonial customary title to land. While Blackburn J accepted Aboriginal customary law as a legal system, he found that Australia's status as a settled colony precluded the survival of that law; that Aboriginal concepts of land title did not meet the common law requirements; and that the plaintiffs could not at any rate prove the requisite continuity of title from the pre-colonial owners.

Milirrpum has been the subject of considerable criticism, the Supreme Court of Canada describing it as "wholly wrong".[79] Much of the criticism centres on what is seen as an incorrect connection between the mode of acquisition of sovereignty over Australia and the survival of pre-colonial law.[80] The issues it raised are at the time of writing receiving the consideration of the High Court of Australia in *Mabo* v. *Queensland and the Commonwealth*.

The Australian Law Reform Commission, while it did discuss the sovereignty and common law recognition issues, did not consider it to be appropriate or useful to premiss its proposals for the recognition of Aboriginal customary laws on such a revision of history. Such an exercise is essentially beyond the province of a law reform commission, being rather the responsibility of the executive and, possibly, the judiciary. Further, it has numerous political and constitutional ramifications, which go well beyond the scope of the recognition of customary law. There is a close connection here with self-determination, discussed in Part B.3 above. However, perhaps the most significant reason for rejecting an approach based on sovereignty or the common law was the fact that such an approach would not in itself resolve any of the problems relating to the inter-

75. *R.* v. *Jack Congo Murrell* (1836) 1 Legge 72, despite the arguments of Stephen cited in the text at n.51 *supra*.

76. *R.* v. *Cobby* (1883) 4 L.R. (N.S.W.) 355 (*per* Martin CJ).

77. *Milirrpum* v. *Nabalco*, *supra* n.71, and the discussion therein on colonial land policy at 242–262.

78. 1986 report, paras.41–59.

79. *Calder* v. *Attorney-General of British Columbia* (1973) 34 D.L.R. (3d) 145, 217 (*per* Hall J (Laskin and Spence JJ concurring)).

80. For example McHugh, *op. cit. supra* n.45, at pp.156–157.

action of Aboriginal and Australian law, on which the Commission had been directed to report.

D. A New Vision for State Recognition of Customary Law

In the event, then, the Commission developed its highly specific approach of functional recognition. In what ways is this a new departure from the colonial paradigm? First, the Commission tailored its proposals to a concept of customary law which was not immutable and rooted in some immemorial pre-colonial past, but which aimed to respond to changing patterns of Aboriginal living. Second, the 1986 report respects the separate and independent sphere of Aboriginal customary law. It does not attempt to co-opt Aboriginal institutions in order to promote the interests of the State, in the way that was characteristic of the methods of indirect rule. Indeed, the 1986 report goes out of its way to reject codification and State administration of customary law. The Queensland Aboriginal courts are sharply criticised on the grounds that they are an exercise in State control,[81] and considerations of Aboriginal autonomy and self-management are major reasons for the Commission's recommendation not to develop a comprehensive hierarchy of official Aboriginal courts[82] or a supervising agency.[83] Third, the proposals do not envisage the rigid classification of Aboriginals and other Australians into two separate spheres each governed by a separate legal system. That would neither accord with the reality of Aboriginal lifestyles nor with Aboriginal wishes.[84] Aboriginal people live in a great variety of circumstances and degrees of contact with the rest of Australian society. The Commission's approach does not exclude any Aboriginal person from the benefit of its proposals *ab initio*. In this way it differs from the rigid categories of Indian band status developed, for instance, in Canada.[85] Fourth, the report does not predetermine the areas in which State law will allow customary law to survive, as was common in the colonial approach, but rather examines areas of State law where the non-recognition of customary law has created injustice. Thus many of the Commission's proposals relate to the criminal law, an area where there was typically limited recognition under colonialism. Finally, the report does not envisage an inevitable withering away of customary law and an assimilation of the Aboriginal people. Rather, it creates conditions for the indefinite continuity of a plural legal system in Australia.

All these aspects amount to a significant step beyond the colonial paradigm, relevant not only for Australia but also for other countries where legal pluralism exists in fact (even if not in law), and especially where the alternative system to State law is the customary law of an indigenous minority people. In such a situ-

81. 1986 report, paras.723–746. See also Australia, Human Rights Commission, *Aboriginal Reserves, By-laws and Human Rights*, Occasional Paper No.5 (1983).

82. 1986 report, para.805.

83. *Idem*, paras.838–843.

84. See the comments of A. E. Tay in "Law and 'Legal Culture' " (1985) 23 A.R.S.P. 165, 167.

85. See Morse, *op. cit. supra* n.36. For the problems caused by the band membership system see the Commission's discussion of the *Lovelace* case, 1986 report, paras.176, 191 and *Attorney-General of Canada* v. *Lavell* (1973) 38 D.L.R. (3d) 481, discussed by *idem*, para.140.

ation, where the State legal system cannot be modified by applying customary law generally to all persons within the territory, a system of recognition based on the *personal* application of laws to the members of the indigenous people concerned is the essential starting point. But the proper role of State law is not to appropriate or define customary law. It is rather to take account of its existence and adjust itself accordingly.

In recognising the autonomous sphere of Aboriginal customary law, in accepting that it is the Aboriginal people themselves who must determine membership of the group, and the content and continuing path of their customary law, the 1986 report is premissed upon a basis of self-determination in relation to customary law. In recognising the possibility of a continuing plurality in the Australian legal system, the Commission has developed a concept of legal pluralism which is neither seen as temporary nor imperfect. The recognition of Aboriginal customary law is to be an enduring reflection of legitimate cultural distinctions. As such it does not involve discrimination. This has been accepted by the Minister for Aboriginal Affairs, the Hon. Clyde Holding, in a letter to the *Aboriginal Law Bulletin* acknowledging and endorsing the report:[86]

> . . . if equality of all before the law is a fundamental principle of our legal system—and surely that should be beyond argument—is it a concomitant that all citizens, without exception, must conform to a single legal mould? If so, is that fair to those people who were here long before our British-based laws were imported, and who had developed their own highly structured methods for regulating their affairs? On the other hand how can two different laws be applied to deal with the same issue?
>
> The report which the Commission has produced achieves, in my view, a sensible and sensitive balance.

The 1986 report thus makes a positive contribution to equality, rather than being a derogation from it.[87]

Underpinning all this, and of considerable significance for a developing comparative approach to State recognition of customary law is the 1986 report's fundamental premise that the continuing separate identity of an indigenous people and of their law positively requires an acknowledgement by the State of the limits of State law and a respect by it of the alternative sphere of indigenous customary law.

CAMPBELL MCLACHLAN[88]

ABORIGINAL FISHING RIGHTS IN NEW ZEALAND

THE purpose of this article is to focus attention on a far-reaching development in the law pertaining to aboriginal (native) rights, arising from a recent decision in

86. (1986) 23 Aboriginal Law Bulletin 5.

87. Cf. the comments of Brennan J in *Gerhardy* v. *Brown* (1985) 57 A.L.R. 472, 621–622: "The difference between land rights and apartheid is the difference between a home and a prison. Land rights are capable of ensuring that a people exercise and enjoy equally with others their human rights and fundamental freedoms; apartheid destroys that possibility."

88. The writer gratefully acknowledges many helpful discussions with Professor James Crawford (Sydney), Commissioner-in-Charge of the Aboriginal Customary Law Reference and Benedict Kingsbury (Fellow, Balliol College, Oxford).

[21]

NATIVE CUSTOM AND OFFICIAL LAW IN HAWAII

Mari J. Matsuda

Introduction

Native Hawaiian customary law has received little recognition except in the area of land use and land tenure. A once thriving body of custom has given way, in a relatively short period, to near-complete hegemony of state-created law, both U.S. federal and State of Hawaii. The results of this transformation provide useful lessons for other mixed jurisdictions, and the persistent claims of advocates for custom may yet provide a counter-hegemonic force in late twentieth-century Hawaii. This paper discusses the limited role of custom in Hawaii, and will close with a discussion of the value of custom.

Nature and Scope of the Civil and Customary Systems in Hawaii

The nature and scope of the competing systems of law in Hawaii is best described historically. At the outset, it must be noted that custom is not a system of law at all, rather it is the body of traditional practices and beliefs that were part of the Hawaiian understanding of human life and social organization before Western contact and the imposition of state-created law.

Stanley Diamond[1] argues that, 'customary law' is a misleading term, because the very purpose of law is to replace and alter traditional practices. This report will use the terms 'custom' and 'folk law' in lieu of 'customary law'.

As Laveley[2] noted, in all pre-Western-capitalist societies, land was held in common. Hawaii was no exception. The chiefs presided over roughly pie-shaped segments, called *ahupua'a*, that extended from mountain to sea and beyond[3]. Residency within the *ahupua'a* carried with it the privilege of harvesting the wealth of land and sea within the *ahupua'a* to the extent of one's needs. Surpluses were given in tribute to the chiefs. Individual claims to exclusive possession of land, water, sea, mountain, flora, or fauna, would have seemed absurd to the Hawaiians. Linnekin records the persisting role of exchange - the giving of gifts to family and friends - in creating status in Hawaiian culture[4]. Using and giving, rather than possessing, characterized attitudes toward land and its commodities.

Hawaiian social life was governed by a highly developed system of custom. The Hawaiians had explanations for all natural phenomenon. They saw the universe as an inter-connected whole where everything had a place. Their religion celebrated nature and respected many gods, including personal ancestral gods for each family[5]. The Hawaiians knew that certain acts were prohibited, and that punishment would follow violation under the religious *kapu*[6]. The *kapu* had a religious basis, but they met practical needs[7]. The fishing season *kapu*, for

136 example, conserved a basic protein source[8]. Pulea records similar resource-preserving religious beliefs in other Pacific societies[9].

The arrival of the *haole*, or whites, in 1778, tested the existing modes of norm enforcement. *Haole* broke *kapu* openly, without apparent consequence. They introduced western goods, which they traded for food, water, and the attentions of Hawaiian women. This new economic pressure disrupted the native systems of distribution of labor and goods.

Hawaii's strategic location, and later the sandalwood and whaling trades, brought many foreign ships[10]. The need to control foreigners introduced Hawaii's *ali'i*, by now organized into a class headed by an established autocratic monarchy, to the concept of sovereignty. They learned that they could charge docking fees to foreign ships, and that attempts to punish foreigners for crimes might lead to military or diplomatic retaliation by other nations. The monarchs needed to show that Hawaii was an independent nation capable of enforcing its laws and they needed to do this in a way that would satisfy western standards[11].

Another impetus toward the development of the westernized law came from the breakdown of the old religious *kapu* and the arrival of the missionaries in 1820. These descendants of the puritans came from Massachusetts. They arrived just when the old religious order was breaking down. The Hawaiians were skeptical of the old *kapu*, but they were still accustomed to the idea of strict codes of behavior and belief in the supernatural. The protestant religion filled a gap left by the fading of ancient beliefs. The missionaries taught basic skills that were somewhat appealing to the Hawaiians: trades, farming, homemaking, and literacy[12]. Influential members of the *ali'i* became converts, and the first criminal laws of Hawaii were drawn from the ten commandments[13].

Codification of Anglo American Law

By 1850, a tiny number of lawyers had arrived in Hawaii, and the King was able to draw on one, William Lee of Massachusetts, for assistance in drafting a criminal code. Lee borrowed extensively from Massachusetts Code of 1844, and Livingston's French-influenced Code of Louisiana[14]. Other early code provisions covered business relations, civil disputes, and taxes[15].

Hawaii needed codes. It didn't have the time or the institutional capability to develop the law on an as-needed common law basis. The nation of Hawaii had moved from pre-contact, Polynesian hierarchy to the nineteenth century world of commerce and international power struggle in just outside of fifty years. The Hawaiian monarchy, in the face of imperialistic threats from stronger and more developed nations needed to act quickly and to borrow the highly developed law of other states. The concept of codification was ideally suited to Hawaii's needs, and large bodies of state-created law were introduced in the late 19th century.

Most significant was the imposition of an entirely foreign system of land tenure on the Hawaiian Islands in the Great *Mahele*[16]. Foreign advisors who were the proponents of the *Mahele* wrote of their dream of a Hawaii peopled by yeoman farmers, spurred to health, happiness, and productivity by the private ownership of land[17]. The *Mahele*, a plan to separate out the interests of the king and *ali'i* in land, and the *Kuleana* Act, which then allowed *ahupua'a* residents to register formal claims to the land they occupied, were promoted to the *ali'i* by their Western advisors as a modern plan to benefit native Hawaiians and to help Hawaii achieve the status of a developed nation.

Others have written of the effect of the *Mahele*. The ultimate effect of the *Mahele* was to create and introduce private ownership of land and commodification of labor in Hawaii, and to hasten dislocation of natives.

Hawaiians and their descendants became a largely landless people, due in part to their unfamiliarity with the Western rules of land tenure. Many claims were never registered, and those that were, were frequently lost to fraud, adverse possession, tax sales, and undervalued sales to speculators. Small plots of rural land were useless to Hawaiians who required wide-ranging gathering rights to maintain a traditional subsistence lifestyle.

This interpretation has been disputed by missionary descendants. The common assertion that 'the damned missionaries stole all the poor kanaka's land' was condemned as 'gross libel' by Lorrin Thurston, a third generation missionary descendant, in his memoirs. Thurston claimed that missionary descendants who became large landowners 'began as poor' and worked for their wealth, which was used to purchase land in legitimate transactions[18].

The Hawaiian government continued to adopt Western laws governing property, crime, and contracts, eventually adopting the entire body of Anglo-American common law by a reception statute enacted in 1892[19]. When the monarchy was overthrown by revolution in 1893, the newly installed American-backed government continued the process, rapidly increasing judicial application of Anglo-American common law. With eventual annexation as a territory of the United States, the process of hegemony became nearly complete. United States law then became the law of Hawaii, pre-empting folk local law and custom except in limited circumstances. Hawaii became a state in 1959, adding a State Constitution to the hierachy of state-created law[20].

Legal Status

The current status of the various systems might be diagrammed as follows:

> *Sources of Law in Hawaii, in Order of Primacy:*
>
> *U.S. Constitution and Statutes:* Primary in Hawaii to the extent they explicitly or implicitly pre-empt state law.
>
> *Hawaii Constitution:* Creates the three branch state governmental structure, including courts for all disputes, two-house legislature for passage of statutory law, and a Governor with executive power. Primary where U.S. law is silent, and where rights auxiliary to or greater than rights in the U.S. Constitution are provided. The Hawaii Constitution explicitly acknowledges custom.
>
> *Hawaii Revised Statutes:* Sets forth all criminal laws, and laws governing a wide variety of non-criminal subjects; and gives limited recognition to 'Hawaiian Usage.'
>
> *Decisions of the Hawaii Supreme Court and the Intermediate Court of Appeals:* These decisions are binding as precedent and constitute the common law of Hawaii. Decisions also interpret

138 **the Hawaii Constitution and Hawaii Revised Statutes, creating interpretative precedent.**

> ***Common Law Decisions of Other U.S. States and Other Common Law Countries:*** **These are considered persuasive, but not binding. 'The common law' applies in Hawaii to the extent not otherwise provided for in Hawaii statutes or judicial opinions, and where not in conflict with Hawaiian usage.**
>
> ***Custom:*** **Custom is largely extinct or dormant, depending on one's orientation, except in the areas of land use and land tenure, where limited customary rights are recognized by the courts. 'Hawaiian Usage' is recognized by statute, but has been defined narrowly by the courts.**

Custom as a source of law is dwarfed by the proliferation of state created law. The Hawaii Revised Statutes consists of nine volumes, and several hundred chapters dealing with a plethora of subjects[21]. Hawaii Supreme Court decisions go back to 1847, covering 68 volumes. The recent addition of an Intermediate Court of Appeals has added to the volume of precedent. United States federal decisions and statutes provide even a greater volume of material, which easily fills several floor-to-ceiling bookcases.

Custom, in contrast, is not codified in Hawaii. There is no recognized repository for custom, and no designated institution responsible for customary pronouncements. Custom exists in a few scattered places. The only state-recognized sources of custom are the decisions and statutes that explicitly recognize and define customary rights. These are few in number, and are discussed at section 'Legal Texts and Authorities' below. These cases sometimes rely on *kama'aina* testimony, or the memories of long-time residents, as to customary usages. Unofficial repositories include anthropological literature, continuing practice, and the unrecognized claims of squatters, of religious practitioners, and of native Hawaiian activists[22]. Unofficial sources sometimes become official by judicial recognition.

State sources explicitly recognizing custom include Article XII, Section 7, of The Hawaii Constitution, which states:

> The state reaffirms and shall protect all rights, customarily and traditionally exercised for subsistence, cultural and religious purposes and possessed by ahupua's tenants who are descendants of native Hawaiians who inhabited the Hawaiian Islands prior to 1778, subject to the right of the State to regulate such rights.

The reception statute that adopts the common law also explicitly recognizes 'Hawaiian usage':

> The common law of England, as ascertained by English and American decisions, is declared to be the common law of the State of Hawaii in all cases, except as otherwise expressly provided by the Constitution or laws of the United States, or by the laws of the State, or fixed by Hawaiian judicial precedent, *or established by Hawaiian usage*; provided, that no person shall be subject to criminal proceedings except as provided by the written laws of the United States or of the State. (emphasis added) Hawaii Rev. Stat. § 1-1

The statutes and decisions that make up the civil law of Hawaii are by their own force applicable to all individuals within the boundaries of the Hawaiian islands, with minor immunity for certain military and government establishments, and possible exceptions for native Hawaiians as indigenous peoples under emerging international human rights standards[23]. There is no state-recognized exemption from application of laws for native Hawaiians, nor special bodies of law triggered by Hawaiian ethnicity, with the exception of access to Hawaiian Home Lands, rights as trust beneficiaries for ceded lands, rights as beneficiaries of the native Hawaiian rehabilitation fund, and the right to vote in quasi-governmental elections for the Office of Hawaiian Affairs. All of these special privileges, discussed as follows, are tied to a claimant's quotient of Hawaiian ancestry, and are of limited political or economic consequence in present-day Hawaii.

The Hawaiian Homes Commission, Haw. Rev. Stat. § 202 et seq., created pursuant to a 1920 United States Congressional mandate, designates certain lands for lease to persons of at least one-half native Hawaiian ancestry. Home improvement loans and technical assistance are also available. The lands set aside are not adequate to accommodate all qualified applicants, with some 8.000 Hawaiians on waiting lists[24]. The Commission has attempted to accelerate the granting of leases, but is impeded by limited funding and political pressure. Commissioners are appointed by the Governor. Critics charge that significant Home Lands are presently leased to non-Hawaiian commercial and military interests, and that funds generated by such leases are not expended in the best interests of Hawaiians[25].

Article 7, Section 4 of the Hawaii State Constitution provides that lands ceded to the State of Hawaii by the federal government at the time of admission to the United States shall be 'held by the State as a public trust for native Hawaiians and the general public.' The public trust concept has not been delineated by the courts. The special designation of native Hawaiians as beneficiaries plausibly indicates that Hawaiians are entitled to benefits as Hawaiians over and above any benefit as state citizens, but court decisions have made it difficult for Hawaiians to pursue trust benefits[26].

Proposed legislation to allow Hawaiians the right to sue to enforce these native land rights has not yet been passed into law.

Article 7, Section 5 of the Hawaii State Constitution creates an Office of Hawaiian Affairs (OHA) that will receive and allocate any funds or lands that may be awarded to native Hawaiians as a class. Thus far no such funds have been allocated. Possible future sources include reparations from the United States Congress for the overthrow of the Hawaiian monarchy. Reparation bills pending in Congress have not met with much success. OHA trustees are elected by persons who affirm that they have some quantum of Hawaiian ancestry.

Land tenure and land use decisions recognizing customary claims have not tied property rights to ethnicity, making the exercise of customary rights available to all who otherwise fall within the requirements of the decisions regardless of ethnicity. The decision providing for limited access to private property for gathering of natural material used in traditional Hawaiian religious practices and crafts is, for example, available to all practitioner-residents of an *ahupua'a*, regardless of ethnicity. (*See Kalipi v. Hawaiian Trust*, 66 Hawaii 1982)

Sources of state law are cited above. Cases of particular interest as sources of custom are described as follows:

The Hawaiian practice of *hanae*, or adoption, is recognized in the law of inheritance and torts. The Hawaiian extended family, and the practice of giving children to special relatives and friends, has created customary recognition of a parent-child relationship apart from biological facts. Linnekin notes that the practice of *hanae*, or the giving of children to be raised by another, is an element of exchange that supports the cohesiveness and productivity of Hawaiian communities even in the present day[37]. The courts have recognized this practice, holding that a testator's silence on the matter indicates a presumed intent that *hanae* as well as natural grandchildren will inherit as the 'heirs of the body' of a child named in a will (*Estate of Cunha*, 49 Hawaii 273 (1966)). In the law of torts, the Hawaii Supreme Court has allowed the award of damages to a young boy who witnessed his step-grandmother killed by an automobile as he walked with her in a crosswalk. The lack of a blood relationship was not controlling, given the custom of extended families in Hawaii (*Leong v. Takasaki*, 55 Hawaii 398 (1974)).

By far the most significant judicial references to custom are in land tenure and land use decisions. Much confusion resulted from the transformation to a concept of private ownership of land in Hawaii. Natives had survived for hundreds of years by fishing, gathering, hunting and tilling freely from mountain to sea. Immediate denial of access to wide ranges of land would have destroyed native means of subsistence, and in fact, private ownership did not result in immediate fencing off and denial of access. Architects of the new system, including King Kamehameha III., intended that natives have continued access to water and other items needed for subsistence, and assumed that natives would register land claims.

The scope of native access rights was uncertain and ill-defined, and private development of land progressed largely unhindered as natives abandoned the subsistence lifestyle and became urban wage earners. Plantation era courts were not sympathetic to claims of public rights in land, and absolute, exclusive fee-simple ownership became the norm.

In recent years, however, Hawaii courts have increasingly recognized customary public rights. In *Kalipi v. Hawaiian Trust*, 66 Hawaii 1 (1982), the court held that residents of an *ahupua'a* may enter upon undeveloped private lands within the same *ahupua'a* to gather native materials. Gathering rights were recognized in Hawaii Revised Statutes § 7-1, an 1859 statute that stated:

> *Building materials, water, etc.; landlords' titles subject to tenants' use.* Where the landlords have obtained, or may hereafter obtain, allodial titles to their lands, the people on each of their lands shall not be deprived of the right to take firewood, house-timber, aho cord, thatch, or ki leaf, from the land on which they live, for their private use, but they shall not have a right to take such articles to sell for profit. The people shall also have a right to drinking water, and running water, and roads shall be free to all, on all lands granted in fee simple; provided, that this shall not be applicable to wells and water-courses, which individuals have made for their own use.

These gathering rights were heretofore uninterpreted and unreconciled with the concept of fee simple title. The court found that a balancing of traditional rights with modern realities required limited recognition of such rights. The gathered materials must be used for native customs, gathering must be exercised only on undeveloped land, and only within the *ahupua'a* within which the gatherer resides. Even with these balancing limitations, the court's incursion into the concept of absolute, individual ownership was remarkable given past denigration of custom. 141

Similarly remarkable were decisions defining the extent of public interest in beachfront land and in water. In an island state, the land along the ocean is particularly valuable for ingress and egress, and for recreational and aesthetic purposes. Private landowners' attempts to exclude the public from waterfront land have been rejected by the courts and the legislature.

In *In re Ashford*, 50 Hawaii 314 (1968), the court held that private ownership begins at the vegetation line at the upper wash of the waves, rather than at the mean high tide mark. Using the upper wash as the boundary resulted in diminution of the land area claimed by waterfront owners. The court interpreted a boundary listed as *'ma ke kai'*, or along the sea, using the testimony of *kama'aina* witnesses that the upper wash was the boundary, but a vigorous dissenting opinion noted long-standing surveying practice to the contrary.

In a biographer's interview, Chief Justice Richardson, the native Hawaiian justice who wrote the *Ashford* opinion, revealed his concern for preservation of the Hawaiian tradition of beach access for sorting seaweed, for landing canoes, and for recreation. He would have preferred an even higher boundary line:

> If I had my way, the public would have even greater access to water and shoreline property. Hawaiian kings, I'm sure, intended to give their subjects more public seashore lands than we now allow. No one but a fool would leave his canoe at the vegetation line and let the waves wash it out to sea! The kings really must have intended to extend public property to that area on the beach where canoes could be left without danger of being washed away.
> With a broad smile, Richardson would then say: 'But there's no point in drawing blood from my critics!'[28]

The Chief Justice carried out this philosophy of favoring public against private uses in related cases. In *County of Hawaii v. Sotomura*, 55 Hawaii 176 (1973), a landowner who claimed an underwater boundary when the beachfront eroded was told that the new boundary would be measured at the vegetation line, following the *Ashford* rule, resulting in a shrinking lot size for the owner. In *Hawaii v. Zimrig*, 58 Hawaii 106 (1977), the court found that new land created by lava flows into the ocean did not belong to the adjoining landowner, but rather to the state. The Zimrigs, whose land was extended by lava flow, submitted evidence, including *kama'aina* testimony, of customary recognition of adjoining owners' rights to newly created land. The court rejected this evidence, following instead a more general understanding of custom. The ancient monarchy respected public uses of land, and the original grant of title must be read in light of a long-standing recognition of public access and use.

This tradition was also a paramount consideration in *Robinson v. Ariyoshi*, 54 Hawaii 174 (1973), popularly known as the *McBryde* case or the *Hanapepe* water case. This fascinating legal conflict began over two decades ago as a water rights litigation amongst private owners - primarily sugar companies - who

142 claimed ownership of water diverted from a natural stream. Diversion by upland owners - typically sugar plantations - was diminishing stream flow to downland users - typically Hawaiian taro farmers. When this fight reached the Hawaii Supreme Court, the startled litigants were told that the excess waters belonged to no individual private owner, but rather were part of the public domain to be distributed fairly by the state. According to Hawaiian custom and usage, water was not subject to private ownership. The court used as its sources historical evidence, and ignored as an invalid reading of history judicial precedents cited by the sugar companies. Those precedents were from the territorial courts, representing a period of Hawaii's history when judges were appointed by the federal government, often with direct involvement of sugar interests in the appointment process[29]. Hawaii's citizens did not then vote in federal elections.

The *McBryde* decision represents a court's efforts to recognize customary rights and usages and traditional collectivist approaches to natural resources, in the face of private claims of ownership and conflicting precedent. This raises jurisprudential questions of the role of the courts and the nature of law that will continue to arise as competition for Hawaii's limited resources escalates.

Relationship between Legal Systems

The relationship between the system of custom and state-created law in Hawaii is one of conflict, accommodation, hegemony, and counter-hegemony over time. The proliferation of state-created law, introduced by the westerners who seized control of Hawaii's government and economy in the nineteenth century, nearly buried custom in Hawaii. Several social and economic changes have led to a gradual resuscitation of custom, at least in the area of land use and land tenure, and to a rising minority voice calling for greater pluralism in Hawaii's legal system. With the end of World War II and the coming of the so-called democratic revolution in Hawaii, governance of the state was opened up to a wider spectrum of participants. The sugar industry, with its obvious interest in maintaining laws favorable to large private landowners and commercial interests[30] found itself faced for the first time with competition from the labor movement, from non-white immigrants, and later in the twentieth century, from environmentalists and native Hawaiian activists. The election of large numbers of non-Caucasian democrats to legislative and executive offices, the appointment of non-Caucasian judges, and the significant appointment of the first native Hawaiian Chief Justice since the days of the monarchy, led to the small beginning of recognition of dormant customary rights and practices[31]. Significantly, these decisions based on Hawaiian custom have not benefitted Hawaiians per se, but rather the public at large. Thus, the people of Hawaii, including the various immigrant groups that now predominate, share in the benefit of Hawaiian customs in such areas as beach access and water use. From the Hawaiian perspective, this may represent yet another exploitation of things Hawaiian to benefit non-Hawaiians.

The battle between custom and law has been waged largely in the courts, although proposals for legislative recognition of customary claims exist. An interesting recent development is the use of the federal courts by opponents of custom who have lost in the Hawaii state courts. The sugar companies in the *McBryde* water case used the federal courts to declare that the Hawaii Supreme Court's recognition of customary practices was a 'taking' of sugar company water rights without due process of law. This constitutional claim was accepted by the Hawaii District Court[32] and the U.S. Court of Appeals for the Ninth Circuit[33], in an astounding decision that has drawn serious critical commentary for its denigration of both custom and state sovereignty within a federal system[34]. The U.S. federal courts are thus another battleground for the clash between custom and law, and custom is thus far faring less than well.

The near-complete domination by the civil system is attributable to several factors. First, nineteenth century imperialism destroyed the sovereignty of the Hawaiian nation, and installed a government favorable to western law. The causes of imperialism are, of course, beyond the scope of this paper, but students of other mixed jurisdictions in the Pacific are familiar with the combined forces of western expansionism, nationalism, economic incentives, and religious missions, that drew outsiders and their law, to the Pacific. The successful exploitation of Hawaii's agricultural wealth, the development of a plantation system, and the strategic military use of mid-Pacific islands, all required the stable, predictable regime of western civil law, particularly laws creating private ownership in land. The reasons for the rise of law along the American liberal model are thus in the broadest sense no different in Hawaii than for other emerging modern states.

Effect of the Mixed System on Thinking and Practice

The history of law defeating custom, with minor victories for custom, mirrors and shapes developments in political and social life in Hawaii. Loss of custom has paralleled the loss of culture, language, and national identity for the native Hawaiian people. A recognized body of custom-in-law could possibly have slowed this loss. Adoption of American law no doubt spurred in-migration, investment, and development. Proponents of development would point to the relatively high standard of living, provision of public services, solid infrastructure and other artifacts of the developed world that grace these islands. Opponents note that the benefits of economic growth have remained concentrated in a few hands, that the environment has suffered, that irreplaceable elements of Hawaiian language, culture, art and life are gone forever, and that the native Hawaiians as a group suffer from a truly horrifying list of deprivations including above-norm rates of imprisonment, alcoholism, suicide, infant mortality, unemployment, illiteracy, and disease[35].

While law is not the cause in any direct sense of such social ills, the suspicion remains that the replacement of custom - of the Hawaiian regime of organized social life - with western law, has borne ill for the Hawaiian people. Evidence exists that Hawaiians are healthiest and happiest in the communities that have maintained a social order of custom[36].

Given the Hawaiian experience, it is the opinion of this writer that the demise of folk law hastens the demise of culture[37]. The loss of a culture, particularly one as rich with grace as that of the Hawaiian people, is an irreparable harm. It is hoped that the emerging trend for explicit recognition of custom by the courts will continue, and that the legislature will join in this process. If law can destroy culture, it can also preserve it, and there is a growing minority of scholars and political actors in Hawaii who see the value in preservation. The memory remains of a time in Hawaii where the land and its abundant gifts allowed none to go without, and where citizens by custom opened their door to all.

144 Many hold this vision not only as memory, but as a dream for a Hawaii of the future. Law, perhaps, is part of the path toward that dream.

NOTES

This paper was delivered as the National Report on Hawaii at the 12th Congress/Int. Acad. Comp. Law 1986, Topic 'Mixed and Customary Jurisdictions in Developing Countries'. The author wishes to thank Maivan Lam and Haunani Kay Trask for their critiques of an earlier draft of this paper.

1 Diamond, IN SEARCH OF THE PRIMITIVE: A CRITIQUE OF CIVILIZATION (1974).

2 Laveley, PRIMITIVE PROPERTY (1878).

3 For descriptions of traditional Hawaiian land tenure and land use SEE Kelly, CHANGES IN LAND TENURE IN HAWAII 1778-1850 (1956); Sahlins, STRUCTURE IN THE EARLY HISTORY OF THE SANDWICH ISLANDS (1981).

4 Linnekin, CHILDREN OF THE LAND, EXCHANGE AND STATUS IN A HAWAIIAN COMMUNITY (1985). The word 'status' in anthropological usage is problematic for some scholars of Hawaiian culture. L. Kame'eleihiwa suggests 'self-worth' as more appropriate in explaining Hawaiian giving practices.

5 For a description of Hawaiian religion and gods, see Kuykendall, THE HAWAIIAN KINGDOM, Vol. I, at 7, and Malo, HAWAIIAN ANTIQUITIES, (Moolelo Hawaii) translated by N. Emerson, 1898. Personal ancestral gods, the 'aumakua', are discussed in Pukui et al., NANA I KE KUMU, Vol. II.

6 ID.

7 Handy, 'Government and Society', lecture transcribed in ANCIENT HAWAIIAN CIVILIZATION (Charles L. Tuttle & Co., pub., 1965).

8 Fishing kapu are described in Kuykendall, THE HAWAIIAN KINGDOM, Vol. I, at 4.

9 Pulea, CUSTOMARY LAW RELATING TO THE ENVIRONMENT, SOUTH PACIFIC REGION: AN OVERVIEW (Mere Pulea and Associates, Fiji 1985).

10 Foreign ships began arriving regularly in 1786. Kuykendall, THE HAWAIIAN KINGDOM, Vol. I, at 20.

11 During the monarchy Hawaii faced threats to its sovereignty from England, France, Spain, Russia, and the United States. Hawaii did not have the military power to defend itself from aggressors, and it had to use instead its natural claims to sovereignty, and the shaky but mutually advantageous agreement of other nations to respect Hawaiian sovereignty so as not to upset the global balance of power. In this precarious position, Hawaii developed as a nation. The monarchy instituted a constitution, and began sharing some power with a partially elected legislature. The courts handled disputes of native and foreigners, and the number of statutes on the books increased. The Hawaii experience shows that adoption of civil law by emerging nations is often a defensive response to advances by more powerful nations. Daws, SHOAL OF TIME, at 51 (Russia in 1815); 103 (France in 1839); Kuykendall and Day, HAWAII, A HISTORY, at 33; Kuykendall, THE HAWAIIAN KINGDOM, Vol. I, at 212-213 (France and England); and 21 (Spain in 1791). In 1826, Queen Kaahumanu wrote to the captain of an American man-of-war:

> 'that she had a right to control her own subjects in this matter; that in enforcing the tabu she had not sought for money; that in apprehending and punishing the offending subjects she had done no injustice to other nations, or the foreigners who belonged to other nations; and that while seeking specially to save the nation from vice and ruin, they had been lenient to strangers, though he very well knew that strangers, passing from one country to another, are bound, while they remain in a country, to conform its laws.' Bingham, MISSIONARIES VS. MAN-OF-WARSMEN, A RESIDENCE OF TWENTY-ONE YEARS IN THE SANDWICH ISLANDS, 1847.

12 Hawaiians came eagerly to mission schools to learn to read, and the missionary diaries report surprise and delight at the intelligence of the native Hawaiians. SEE E.G., Laura Fish Judd, SKETCHES OF THE LIFE, SOCIAL, POLITICAL, AND RELIGIOUS, IN THE HAWAIIAN ISLANDS FROM 1828 TO 1861, Honolulu 1880. Chancellor Keat was moved to remark upon the teachability of the Hawaiians. Kent's Commentaries, Vol. 2, p. 199.

13 The first written criminal law, which appeared in 1827, stated:

WORDS ABOUT THE LAW

We proclaim the words, hearken those of that land, and those of this land, those of this land shall also obey, and those of that land also shall obey, those that hear these words, shall obey; but if it is not obeyed he shall be guilty.

I

We forbid murder; those of that land must not commit murder here, those of this land must not commit murder here; the one who commits murder shall die, by being hung.

145

II

This is the second; we forbid theft; the one who steals shall be put in irons.

III

This is the third; we forbid illicit intercourse between a male and female; and the illicit intercourse between a female and male, the one who has illicit intercourse, shall be imprisoned in irons.

IV

This is the forth; we forbid the selling of rum here; the one who sells rum, shall be put in irons.

V

This is the fifth; we forbid prostitution; the one who is a prostitute, shall be fined in money.

VI

This is the sixth; we forbid gambling; the one who gambles shall be imprisoned in irons.

(Translated from Hawaiian)

This code was, like many early criminal codes, short. It had the characteristics of defined offenses and proscribed punishments. It did not define degrees, nor did it claim exclusivity. While it proscribed crimes against property, its tone was moral. It was not promulgated with direct economic, instrumental intent, but it did meet the instrumental need for order. The missionaries arrived with the ten commandments at the same time that pressure from foreign contact was moving the Hawaiian nation into the global community. Hawaii's monarchy felt the need for a fixed legal system and they asked their trusted missionary advisors for advice on the creation of a legal system from scratch.

14 Lee's preface to the Code of 1850.

15 SEE Laws of 1842.

16 For a general legal history of the Mahele, SEE Chinen, THE GREAT MAHELE: HAWAII'S LAND LAW OF 1848 (1957).

17 William Lee, in his 1st Annual Chief Justice's Report, noted the need to 'stop indolence' and 'promote industry by selling the people lands at low prices - by protecting them in their kuleanas' (Kuleanas were native land holdings).

18 Thurston, MEMOIRS OF THE HAWAIIAN REVOLUTION (1936). Thurston's outrage de-monstrates conflicting cultural attitudes toward the legitimacy of buying and selling land.

19 Hawaii Rev. Stat. § 1-1.

20 SEE Matsuda, 'Law and Culture in the District Court of Honolulu 1444-1845: A Case Study in the Rise of Legal Consciousness' AMERICAN JOURNAL OF LEGAL HISTORY 1988.

21 Hawaii Revised Statutes governs such subjects as elections (Title 1); local governments (Title 6); public safety (Title 10); agriculture and animals (Title 11); conservation (Title 12); taxes (Title 14); transportation (Title 15); motor vehicles (Title 17); education (Title 18); business, banks, trade corporations, and insurance (Titles 22-27); property, probate and family law (Titles 28-31); court proceedings and evidence (Titles 32-35); torts (Title 36) and crimes (Title 37).

22 Such claims are regularly mentioned in KaWaiOlaOHA, a native Hawaiian newspaper.

23 Native religious practitioners have challenged state employment of geothermal energy technology, alleging that tapping the energy of the volcanoes interferes with customary relations with the volcano goddess. This legal challenge rests in part on claims as indigenous peoples. SEE also Trask, HAWAIIANS, THE UNITED NATIONS, AND HUMAN RIGHTS, discussing rights of native Hawaiians under international law. Hawaiians have also made claims under international law in occupying and resisting military practice-bombing on Kaho'olawe, an island rich with archeological treasures and sacred sites.

24 'Aina Ho'opulapula, Department of Hawaiian Home Lands, 1983-84 ANNUAL REPORT.

25 Trask, NATIVE NATIONALISM: THE STRUGGLE FOR HAWAIIAN INDEPENDENCE, speech presented at the Korean Studies Center, University of Hawaii, April 26, 1985. Trask, a Hawaiian and Professor of American Studies, stated in part:

> According to the Federal-State Task Force report of 1983, 123.000 of the 200.000 acres (of Hawaiian Home Land) are not used for homesteading purposes. Within this trust, nearly 88.000 acres are leased to non-natives who in turn sub-lease these lands for millions of dollars in profit. In addition, thousands of acres have been taken by Governor's Executive Orders for forest reserves and military use. Meanwhile, since its inception 65 years ago, the Hawaiian Homes Commission has made a total of only 3.400 awards to Hawaiian families. More than 9.000 families remain on the waiting list. Some have been waiting literally for decades. The vast majority die long before their names are even close to being considered.

26 KEAUKAHA-PANAEWA COMMUNITY ASSOCIATION V. HAWAIIAN HOMES COMMISSION, 588 F.2d 1216 (9th Cir. 1978) (Denying a private right of action to enforce the homestead law).

27 Linnekin, CHILDREN OF THE LAND, EXCHANGE AND STATUS IN A HAWAIIAN COMMUNITY (1985).

28 Dodd, THE RICHARDSON YEARS, (1983).

29 Chang, 'Unravelling Robinson v. Ariyoshi: Can Courts Take Property?' 2 HAWAII LAW REVIEW 57 (1980), and n. 30, infra.

30 For a general history of economic control of Hawaii, SEE Kent, HAWAII, ISLANDS UNDER THE INFLUENCE, 1983; and Fuchs, HAWAII PONO, A SOCIAL HISTORY, 1961.

31 For a discussion of these changes SEE Fuchs, n. 30, supra. A biography of the first Hawaiian Chief Justice is cited at n. 28, supra.

32 ROBINSON V. ARIYOSHI, 441 F. Supp. 559 (D. Hawaii 1977).

33 ROBINSON V. ARIYOSHI, 753 F.2d 1468 (9th Cir. 1985).

34 SEE Chang, MISSING THE BOAT: THE NINTH CIRCUIT DECIDES A HAWAIIAN WATER CASE, Western Natural Resources Digest (1986).

35 SEE Trask, speech at the East West Center, Nov. 1986.

36 Linnekin, CHILDREN OF THE LAND, EXCHANGE AND STATUS IN A HAWAIIAN

146 COMMUNITY (1985).

37 For a discussion of the effect on culture of active Hawaiian use of the courts during monarchy period, SEE Matsuda, 'Law and Culture in the District Court of Honolulu, 1844-184 Case Study in the Rise of Legal Consciousness' AMERICAN JOURNAL OF LEGAL HISTO 1988.

[22]

The Ifoga: the Samoan Practice of Seeking Forgiveness for Criminal Behaviour.

La'auli A. Filoiali'i[1]

Lyle Knowles[2]

Introduction

Public law regulating the relationships between individuals and the government in Western societies has evolved largely from the Code of Hammarubi. This in part spelled out the extreme practice *lex talionis*, which literally meant 'an eye for an eye'. Technically, such a precept does not allow the guilty person the option of rendering an apology to the party harmed or his associates in lieu of prescribed punishment. Such an alternative may be taken in some instances, but most often victimized individuals, families, organizations or governments are rarely satisfied until the guilty party has been appropriately punished. The Samoans, however, have found it possible within a non-violent cultural framework to provide for an option of apology and forgiveness, leading to continued harmonious relationships between and among those concerned.

The Samoan people are traditionally non-violent and do not believe in rebellious behaviour. They simply want to live in peace and harmony, maintaining a cultural environment that is as free as possible from violence. But, as in other human societies, incidents occur that require the attention and action of leaders who are responsible for overseeing the conduct of group members and maintaining a system of regulatory judicial process and practice.

The current paper describes a facet of the traditional system of justice as practised in Samoa and in the urban setting of the United States. The central theme is the practice of *ifoga*,[3] which is defined as the traditional practice of seeking forgiveness and rendering a formal apology resulting from a hostile event involving physical injury and/or the verbal degrading of a family reputation.

The practice of *ifoga* can be performed by a family as a whole or by the village. The parties can be one individual versus another individual, one family versus another family, one village versus another village, the Village Council versus a family, and so forth. The *ifoga* is usually performed when the act is one of great bodily harm and death or near death. It is initiated by the guilty party or whichever of the guilty parties created the most damage resulting in the greatest degradation to the reputation of the family. The *ifoga* is also performed when a verbal attack or threat is made against the reputation of a family or village. *Ifoga* is an integral part of the *fa'a-Samoa* or Samoan way of life. Because of the non-violence that permeates the society, the *ifoga* is of relatively rare occurrence. The first of us observed only three during 20 years of residence.

[1] Graduate School of Behavioural Sciences, California State University, Dominguez Hills, California, U.S.A.

[2] Claremont Graduate School, Claremont, California, U.S.A.

[3] A term derived from the word *ifo*, which in liberal interpretation means 'to bow down in a respectful manner or with respectful conduct'. Within a religious context *ifo* means worshipping God with all human respect.

Lyle Knowles

Samoan Social Structure

Samoan society is based upon extended family (*aiga*), where uncles, aunts, cousins and in-laws may be included in the household group. Households average 8 to 12 members or more (Gilson 1970) and are headed by a *matai*, who is a father, grandfather, or other senior male member. He administers all household affairs, controls all activities such as the distribution of wealth and property within the unit, and ensures that it maintains a good reputation and image in the village. The close structure of the household means that unacceptable or hostile behaviour on the part of any of its members reflects upon the group as a whole and damages its prestige and reputation.

Individual members are expected to abide by the laws of the land and to behave within the boundaries of acceptable moral conduct. Deviant acts are dealt with by the *matai*, who is the mediator in resolving problems or conflicts. He ensures that the guilty party renders an apology to the injured or offended family member who, in turn, accepts and forgives.

The Village Council

As part of the *matai* system, each village is headed by a Village Council or *fono* comprised of *matai* with titles of High Chief (*Ali'i*), High Talking Chief (*To'o To'o*), and Common Talking Chief (*Tulafale*). This body makes up the executive, legislative, and judicial components of the village governmental and political system and is responsible for policies and decision-making. Untitled men (*taule'ale'a*) enforce village rules and regulations. The power of the Village Council is illustrated by the following case.

Soon after Christian missionaries arrived in 1830, King Tui Manu'a Tauveve instructed the people of Tau Island that the London Missionary Church would be the only one. For over 100 years they abided by this command. Because of American influences during this period, the kingdom was abolished as a ruling system, and the population was governed by Village Councils. In the 1940s one village *matai* allowed a missionary from a different faction of the Christian faith to which he was connected to introduce his version of worship and practice. The residents were furious and insisted that the sponsoring *matai* re-establish his membership in the Samoan Church. He refused. The situation came to the attention of the Village Council and was given due consideration. It decided to exile the *matai* from the village. He was placed in a canoe and allowed to drift out to the open ocean with orders never to return to the village.

Thus the Village Council penalizes people who violate the rules. Traditional Samoan Society had no appellate system of a Supreme Court or formal village court as such before Christian missionaries arrived in 1830. The respective *matai* resolved violations within families or between families at the appropriate level, resulting in commensurate punitive action or the performance of the *ifoga*. Samoan society is patriarchal, and men normally perform the ceremony.

Violation of Village Laws

When an act that creates a disturbance comes within the purview of the Village Council the members meet, examine the facts, and determine the punishment. The working out of the penalty comes under the jurisdiction of the family *matai*, who ensures that payment is made to the Village

Council in the form of foodstuffs or fine mats.[4] To satisfy the will of the village, a *matai* who refuses to pay must perform the *ifoga* before the Village Council enacts a more severe punishment. Persons who do not abide by the Council's decision may receive more severe forms of punishment, such as the destruction of property, including houses, animals, and plantations. Indeed, some families whose *matai* have created disturbances or violated the edicts and rules of the Council have had their titles taken away, an immense disgrace.

The Ifoga

In an effort to avoid the more extreme punishments the guilty *matai* and his family most often seek forgiveness from the Village Council through a formal apology. They cover their heads and bodies with mats and sit outside the main village house. The *ifoga* normally begins early in the morning.

As the guilty parties sit outside the Village Council building the Council deliberates and decides on a time to call the *ifoga* party to come inside for a hearing. Sometimes it lets the *ifoga* party sit in the hot sun all day. In extreme cases the members do not recognize the *ifoga* party at all during the first day, and the group must return the next morning and continue the vigil.

The *ifoga* party is ultimately asked to come in and appear before the Council, at which time a specified Council member brings forth the issue. The *matai* of the guilty family or the leader of the *ifoga* (who is sometimes a High Chief, High Talking Chief, or Common Talking Chief) must then apologize to the Village Council members, asking them to forgive the indiscretion. The family or *matai* performing the *ifoga* must also feed the Council by preparing delicacies such as taro, roast pig, fish, and so forth. When the guilty party is asked into the house and the *ifoga* is accepted, the result is always positive in that the act is forgiven and severe punishment not exacted.

Fine Mats as 'The Cover of Life'

The fine mats as a 'cover of life' find their roots in Samoan tradition. According to Samoan myth, in ancient times the King of Tonga Island suspected that his son had been killed by the daughter of King Tui Manu'a of Manu'a Island. In punishment the accused woman was sentenced by the Tongan King to be burned at the stake. As a final request, she asked that her woven mat that she had brought with her from Manu'a Island be brought to her. She wrapped herself in it.

This was the first time that the people of Tonga had seen such a mat, and they believed that she was attempting to bewitch the Tongan people. In addition, they recalled that her father, King Tui Manu'a Moa Atoa, had once caused a previous Tongan king to die (although he later came back to life) by drowning through the use of the *mana*[5] or magical power.

As a result of the recollection, the King of Tonga freed the daughter of King Tui Manu'a and allowed her to return to Samoa. She believed that her escape had something to do with the mat, and she named it *pulou ole ola* or the 'cover of life'. For this reason, Samoans use fine

[4] Fine mats are used as a medium of exchange in traditional Samoa and as a display of wealth, particularly for celebrations at weddings and funerals. Money has taken their place in modern financial dealings.

[5] Literally, 'supernatural powers' possessed only by a king or a god.

mats when seeking forgiveness. A major objective is to ensure that the *ifoga* party will not be attacked by the victims of the injured person and family members.

INTRA-FAMILY FEUDS

Feuds or difficulties between families usually occur over boundaries between neighbouring properties, where one family may falsify the line by moving some mark from its proper place. If a fight resulting in death were to break out, then revenge could be sought.

In order to avoid this, the accused family hurriedly gathers its members and plans the *ifoga*. When the time is right, the *matai* is responsible. The *ifoga* party must go to the residence of the dead victim, making sure that they are covered with fine mats. Members of the group sit outside the home of the offended family until its *matai* calls to them from within the house and invites them in to discuss the formal apology and the process of forgiveness. An instance of such a family dispute is described below.

During a beer drinking party in 1976 a fight occurred between two male participants. One struck the other, who died from the blow. In order to avoid violent repercussions from the family of the deceased, the family of the killer immediately organized an *ifoga* to be held the day following the funeral service. Two days were required before the mourners accepted, and during this time the party sat outside in the sun from sunrise to sunset. After the *ifoga* was accepted and forgiveness rendered, the two families were reconciliated and resumed social relations.

IFOGA OF MAJOR SIGNIFICANCE

The following recounts an unusual difficulty that occurred between two islands. It was resolved by the *ifoga*.

In 1978 the Principal of Manu'a High School on Tau Island was struck with a rock thrown by one of the islanders. The injury was serious and almost caused the man's death. Since he was from another island (Tutuila), the Tau residents organized the *ifoga*, headed by village High Talking Chiefs who covered their heads with fine mats in the traditional manner. This was immediately accepted, and relations between the two islands were resumed.

The *ifoga* described below involved an instance when the reputation of an entire village was threatened.

In 1965 in the village of Lumā on Tau Island the pastor who served two neighbouring villages visited Lumā on Christmas Eve and found some of the male residents celebrating with beer. At the next Sunday's church service he openly accused the Lumā *matai* of drinking on Christmas Day and asked the Lumā residents, including women and children, to leave the service. The following Sunday an assistant pastor, who was a *matai* in the village, held the service in his own home. The pastor subsequently found this out and discussed the situation with the assistant pastor who reminded him that he had asked everyone in the entire village to leave his church. The assistant pastor then reported back to his village, and the elders recommended an *ifoga*.

Several days later the oldest High Chief of the village covered himself with a fine mat and, accompanied by some 200 men, women, and children from the village, sat outside the pastor's house, performing the *ifoga*. He ignored them from 8 a.m. until noon, at which time they left to reconsider, but they returned again and sat from 2 p.m. to 4 p.m. During the interim the pasters from the other villages advised him to accept. He did so but resigned his post during the following Sunday church service and then left the village.

The Ifoga in Urban America

Crimes committed in the United States are, of course, under the jurisdiction of the laws of the land. However, the *ifoga* is still practised by Samoans as a process to resolve disputes of ill feelings between families in an effort to maintain a continued sense of harmony and well-being. But when the *ifoga* is performed within the urban setting the group is allowed to enter the house of the offended party so as not to disturb the neighbours or bring undue public attention to the situation. The application of the *ifoga* in an extreme case is given below.

A criminal incident occurred in 1978 in southern California when a Samoan discovered that his wife was having an affair. He killed her by striking her a number of times with an axe, and her family was angry with him as a result. The latter quickly organized the *ifoga* and went covered in fine mats to the woman's family. The apology was eventually accepted. The husband is currently serving a prison sentence for premeditated murder, but relations between the man and his family with his in-laws are comfortably reconciled.

References

Gilson, R. P. (1970). *Samoa 1830 to 1900.* Oxford University Press, London.

CULTURE AND CULPABILITY: A STUDY OF CONTRASTS

By Alison Dundes Renteln*

**Ms. Renteln is Assistant Professor of Political Science at the University of Southern California. Her undergraduate degree is from Radcliffe College; she studied at the London School of Economics, and received her M.A. and Ph.D. from the University of California at Berkeley in jurisprudence and social policy.*

In a pluralistic society it is common to encounter "culture conflict." When new citizens arrive, they bring with them legal standards which may differ significantly from those of their new homeland. The question which inevitably arises is whether or not the new citizens should be held criminally liable for conduct which violates American law. Is it justifiable to punish a person in the United States for engaging in activities which were customary in his or her country of origin? This kind of situation in which multiple legal systems are to be found is called legal pluralism. It is the conflict among the various systems that has given rise to a theory of criminal responsibility known as the cultural defense.

This article concentrates on some of the conceptual problems associated with the cultural defense. In particular I will take the view that: (1) the ideology of cultural pluralism does not require the adoption of the cultural defense, (2) mechanisms already exist within the American legal system which can take culture into account, and (3) the consequences of utilizing the cultural defense would be highly undesirable. The cultural defense will be discussed in the context of the United States and of other countries by examining selected cases. Some analysis of the problems in general will be made, paying attention to the distinction between immigrants and indigenous peoples. Although there are many types of crimes for which the cultural defense might be used, such as polygamy in nations that permit only monogamy, the analysis below will focus primarily on cases involving homicide. While cultural sensitivity is arguably an admirable posture, pluralism (actually relativism) does not require the rejection of one's own legal standards. Ultimately, it appears that the cultural defense is a dangerous and unnecessary doctrine.

United States Cases — Immigrants

Two factors appear to be primarily responsible for the recent (1980's) resurgence of interest in the cultural defense. The first is the unusually large influx of (mainly Southeast) Asians into the United States, especially Southern California. The second is the highly publicized case of *People v. Kimura*.[1] This case illustrates not only the context in which the cultural defense has been considered as a possible device for denying responsibility for criminal action but also the way in which American commentators have misinterpreted cultural differences.

Fumiko Kimura discovered that her husband had deceived her by keeping a mistress and had thus shamed the family. On January 29, 1985, she attempted to commit *oyako-shinju*, the Japanese custom of parent-child suicide. She took her two chil-

[1] *People v. Kimura*, No. A-091133 (Los Angeles Cty. Super. Ct., filed April 24, 1985).

dren, a daughter, Yuri, six months old, and her son, Kazutaka, four years old, on a bus ride from their Los Angeles home to the beach in Santa Monica. Then, carrying Yuri and leading Kazutaka by the hand, she walked into the ocean. This was a culturally accepted course of action in the Japanese tradition, not to leave the children behind to bear the shame alone. Although onlookers on the shore managed to rescue Kimura, her two children died.

The district attorney charged Kimura with first degree murder in their deaths. Four thousand members of the Los Angeles Japanese-American community signed a petition stating that her act would not be treated as murder in Japan and urging officials to apply modern Japanese law. This would mean charging her with involuntary manslaughter at most. The district attorney refused the request, however, and left a first degree murder charge in place which could have brought the death penalty. The district attorney rejected the use of Japanese law but indicated that Kimura's background could, in fact, be taken into account in determining her mental state at the time of the incident. The crime itself could not be mitigated by legal or cultural standands from another country.

The issue was whether or not a person from another culture should be judged according to standards other than those in force in the United States. Kimura's attorney evidently considered but chose not to use the cultural defense. Interestingly, he relied instead on testimony from six psychiatrists to show that Kimura was "ill" and "mentally deranged," and therefore lacked the intent necessary for first degree murder because the element of malice was absent. A plea bargain ultimately reduced the charge to voluntary manslaughter, and Kimura received five years probation, intensive psychiatric treatment and one year in the county jail (with credit for time already served). It is hard to say whether it was culture or (attributed) insanity which helped change her fate.

Several observations are in order. First, Kimura's act is not legally acceptable in Japan. It is simply more culturally acceptable. Even in Japan, ritual parent-child suicide is still a crime. The culture conflict here is not based on an act which is entirely legitimate in country A but illegal in country B. Rather, the conflict is over the proportionality, *i.e.*, what is the appropriate punishment which corresponds to the crime. Second, even though the defense attorney did not explicitly invoke the cultural defense, the fact that there was a plea bargain suggests that culture was taken into account to some extent. Third, the legal system, as exemplified in this case, treats the logic of another culture as analogous to insanity. Kimura was ordered to undergo intensive psychiatric counseling. In spite of the absence of a formal cultural defense, Kimura's cultural background was influential in determining the disposition of her case. She was treated with compassion though as if mentally disturbed. Finally, Kimura raises another issue worthy of consideration. For what period of time would a "new" citizen be permitted to avail herself of the cultural defense? Would it be necessary to establish a "presumption" of assimilation after a specified period of time elapsed? Kimura herself had lived in the United States for nine years but had not become fully "Americanized" because she had remained extremely isolated.

United States Cases — Refugees

Refugees arriving in the United States from other countries have had their share of legal problems. In some instances they commit acts that are not considered crimes in their native lands but which violate American law.

In the last several years almost thirty thousand Hmong, a people from Laos, have settled in the area of Fresno, California. Some of their traditions involve activities which are illegal here such as polygamy and the use of opium. The Hmong also have a habit of butchering pigs in their backyards in violation of local ordinances. It seems that, among other things, the pigs' squealing disturbs the neighbors.

A more serious matter concerns a practice called *zij poj niam* which, loosely translated, means marriage by capture.

People v. Moua[2] centered on the interpretation of the traditional courtship ritual among the Hmong. According to custom, there is an exchange of gifts between the man and the woman who are to be married. It is expected that the man will exercise his right to abduct his chosen bride and then consummate the marriage at his family's home. Custom requires that the woman display resistance by weeping and moaning and declaring that she is not ready. Otherwise, she will not appear virtuous enough. The man is supposed to show force or else he will not appear strong enough. After the event, the woman is viewed as "unmarriagable" by other Hmong men.

In this case Kong Moua followed custom but his "wife," Xeng Xiong, an "Americanized" nineteen-year-old, rejected tradition and called the police. Consequently, Moua was charged with kidnapping and rape but these charges were dropped when he agreed to plead guilty to a misdemeanor charge of false inprisonment. After hearing testimony about traditional Laotian marriage rituals and after reviewing a doctoral dissertation on the subject, the judge reduced the sentence for Moua from 180 days to 90 days.[3] Some have claimed that the judge implicitly recognized the cultural defense.[4]

Even though the cultural defense was not officially used, it appears that culture played a role in this case. The rule in American law is that if a reasonable, good faith belief in the woman's consent was evident, the act would not constitute rape. This means that although the conduct may not be excused because it is motivated by cultural tradition, it is possible that the motivation may be relevant in establishing the defendant's state of mind.[5] Culture served not to absolve Moua of responsibility altogether but to mitigate the sentence, as in *Kimura*.

We can see the undeniable influence of enculturation and the power of moral injunction in another case, also called *People v. Moua*.[6] In this case a Hmong man by the name of Tou Moua killed his wife when he learned that she planned to take a job working for another man. Evidently, this is an act tantamount to adultery in Hmong culture. Moua's defense attorney explained that in his culture a wife's adultery is punishable by death and that it was "culturally demanded that he [Moua] execute justice, even if it meant his own personal pain and personal loss to do so.[7] Moua's attorney argued for a mitigation of the sentence because of the cultural circumstances involved. The sentencing judge denied the request, however, and sentenced the defendant to eight years in prison.

Belief/Action Distinction

While the American ideology of cultural tolerance has instructed citizens to respect different ways of life, there is a longstanding commitment in the American legal system to a belief/action distinction. As early as 1879 in *Reynolds v. U.S.*[8] the Supreme Court refused to overturn a conviction for bigamy where this was mandated by the defendant's religious beliefs. The court held that to allow such an excuse of illegal conduct would be:

> . . . to make the professed doctrines of religious belief superior to the law of the land, and in effect to permit every citizen to become a law unto himself. Government could exist only in name under such circumstances.[9]

Not only have Mormons been denied the right to have polygamous marriages, but

---

[2]*People v. Moua* (Kong), No. 315972-0 (Fresno Cnty. Super. Ct., Feb. 7, 1985); Alan Dershowitz, 'Marriage by Capture' Runs into the Law of Rape, *Wall Street Journal*, June 14, 1985, at 5, col. 1.

[3]Julia B. Sams, The Availability of the "Cultural Defense" as an Excuse for Criminal Behavior, 16 *Georgia Journal of International and Comparative Law*, 335, 336-337 (1986).

[4]Mark R. Thompson, Immigrants Bring Cultural Defense into U.S. Courts, *Wall Street Journal*, June 6, 1985, p. 28; Mark R. Thompson, Cultural Defense, 14(1) *Student Lawyer* 24, 28 (1985).

[5]John C. Lyman, Cultural Defense: Viable Doctrine or Wishful Thinking, 9 *Criminal Law Review* 87, 94 (1986).

[6]*People v. Moua* (Tou, F-9083403 (Fresno Municipal Court 1985); 328-106-0 Fresno County 1985).

[7]Anon., Cultural Defense Fails to Mitigate Wife-Slayer's Sentence, *Los Angeles Daily Journal*, Nov. 29, 1985, col. 1, p. 15.

[8]*Reynolds v. United States*, 98 U.S. 145 (1879).

[9]*Id.*, at 167.

Jehovah's Witnesses have been compelled by the law to have blood transfusions.[10] In the case of *In re Application of Jamaica Hospital*[11] the court ordered a competent adult woman who was eighteen weeks pregnant and suffering from internal bleeding to accept blood transfusions for the sake of her fetus. Because she was a Jehovah's Witness, a religious group which believes that the Scriptures forbid "drinking blood" and that receiving a blood transfusion is the equivalent of "drinking blood," she refused on religious grounds. But the court held: "The state has a highly significant interest in protecting the life of a mid-term fetus, which outweighs the patient's right to refuse a blood transfusion on religious grounds."[12]

The law will reject or require actions based on beliefs if they lead to harming others. In the case just mentioned the court was willing to intervene when the one at risk was a previable fetus. In another case a court ordered a woman to undergo childbirth by Cesarean section when she refused on religious grounds.[13] The physician had predicted that a vaginal delivery would have a 99% risk of the infant dying and a 50% chance for the mother. After the court order was issued, she fled and gave birth to a healthy child a few days later, uneventfully without intervention.[14]

Snake-handling for religious purposes has also been denied by the courts.[15] In *Swann v. Pack,*[16] for example, the Supreme Court of Tennessee held that the handling of dangerous and poisonous snakes in a crowded church (with virtually no safeguards and with children roaming around unattended and with handlers in trances) meant that the Pastor had, in fact, committed a public nuisance. The Court remanded the case so that the trial court could enter an injunction perpetually enjoining and restraining all parties from handling snakes. Although the Court recognized that the decision would impose stringent limitations on a religious practice, it concluded that "paramount considerations of public policy" precluded less stringent solutions.[17]

The courts have been unwilling to allow drug use for religious rites.[18] The freedom to believe is virtually absolute whereas the freedom to act is not. This distinction is central to the analysis of the cultural defense. Cultural pluralism encourages us to recognize the existence of other value-systems but does not force us to relinquish our own standards for judging action. Even where an action is arguably an integral part of the belief system, the legal system has consistently acted to sustain its own legitimacy.

Ignorance of the Law Is No Excuse

Some of the opponents of the cultural defense base their argument on the traditional maxim — ignorance of the law — the mistaken belief that one's conduct is lawful — is no excuse for criminal behavior. They maintain that the court should not create an exception to this rule because of cultural differences. The notion that the cultural defense depends on ignorance suggests that there is a lack of understanding as to the basic premise of the defense. The cultural defense does not presuppose ignorance of the law. Even if the defendants are aware of American legal standards, their cultural conditioning is so powerful that they cannot discard their own standards in favor of American ones. Enculturation shapes their perceptions to such an extent that they cannot readily embrace those of another culture.

[10]Ford, Refusal of Blood Transfusions by Jehovah's Witnesses, 10 *Catholic Lawyer* 232 (1964); Cantor, A Patient's Decision to Decline Life-Saving Medical Treatment: Bodily Integrity Versus the Preservation of Law, 26 *Rutgers Law Review* 228 (1973).

[11]In re Application of Jamaica Hospital, 128 Misc. 2d 1006, 491 N.Y.S. 2d 898 (N.Y. Sup. Ct. 1985).

[12]*Id.*, at 1008; at 899.

[13]*Jefferson v. Griffin Spalding County Hospital Authority,* 247 S.E. 2d 457 (1981).

[14]Lawrence Nelson, Brian Buggy, and Carol Weil, Forced Medical Treatment of Pregnant Women: 'Compeling Each to Live as Seems Good to the Rest.' 86 *Hastings Law Journal* 703, 707 (1986); George J. Annas, Forced Cesareans: The Most Unkindest Cut of All, 23 (3) *Hastings Center Report* 16 (1982).

[15]*Lawson v. Commonwealth,* 164 S.W.2d 972 (Ky 1942).

[16]*Swann v. Pack,* 527 S.W.2d 114 (1975).

[17]*Id.*at 114.

[18]*U.S. v. Kuch,* 288 S.W.2d 972 (Ky 1942), *U.S. v. Leary,* 383 F.2d 851 (1967).

In the cases already discussed, it was apparent that the lawyers were not arguing on the basis of ignorance. The prosecutors and judges were not asked to excuse the defendants because they did not comprehend that their actions were considered criminal in the eyes of Americans. The point of the cultural defense is to recognize that the power of enculturation makes it exceedingly difficult for someone from another culture to make his conduct conform to standards of the dominant American culture. The underlying notion is that a person's criminal behavior should be judged according to the legal standards of his or her culture.

Governmental Responsibility

Since the government arranged to bring refugees to the United States, one could advance the argument that the government is responsible for ensuring that new citizens become familiar with particularly important American laws. When it becomes known that certain communities, *e.g.*, the Hmong engage in activities which are not compatible with American legal standards, then there is all the more reason to expect the government to establish some form of educational programs. Even though the cultural defense does not depend on ignorance, in some instances ignorance may be a factor. Moreover, even where refugees are cognizant of American crimes, they may not be as fully aware of the punishments which they face for violation. When the American government brings a large refugee population within its borders, it bears some measure of responsibility for providing information about American customs and laws.

In some cases the duty to inform may turn out to be problematic. There may not be any words or concepts in the language of the new group which can capture the idea of the American crime. And besides technical difficulties the government has to contend with the negative symbolic dimensions, specifically of having Americans trying to indoctrinate newly arrived citizens. Despite these problems, however, the government can obviate the need for the cultural defense to some extent by ensuring knowledge of both crimes and punishments.

United States Cases — Native Americans

Since immigrants and refugees make a conscious decision to move to a new country, one might argue that they should adhere to the legal standards of the new country. But even if one decides that these groups ought to be bound by American law, this does not necessarily mean that indigenous peoples who controlled the territory first should have to surrender to the colonial or dominant legal regime.

That there are major conceptual differences in traditional Native and modern American legal ideals is known.[19] In fact, Native Americans have experienced an unusual legal status, *i.e.*, semi-sovereign status. Federal law has allowed Native American societies some limited rights of self-government but has retained control insofar as violent crimes are concerned (18 U.S.C. 1153). For the most part state courts have jurisdiction unless a Native American commits a proscribed act on Native American land in which case the federal courts have jurisdiction.

There are numerous cases in which the conduct of Native Americans has been judicially evaluated, and in some of them courts have been willing to take culture into account. For example, the case of *United States v. Whaley*[20] in 1888 makes this clear. The defendants were all Native Americans charged with the murder of Juan Baptista, also a Native American. Baptista was a doctor but not a very good doctor. In fact, he was so unsuccessful that the members of the tribe were convinced that he had been systematically poisoning his patients. All of his patients, approximately twenty, had died.

Finally, Hunter Jim, who was extremely popular within the tribe, fell ill and had to be treated by the doctor. The members of the tribe decided to hold a council at which

[19]Sandra R. Weber, Native-Americans Before the Bench: The Nature of Contrast and Conflict in Native-American Law Ways and Western Legal Systems. 19 *Social Science Journal* 47 (1982); Laurence French (ed.) *Indians and Criminal Justice*. Totowa, New Jersey: Allanheld, Osmun (1982).

[20]*United States v. Whaley*, 37 F. 145 (1888).

time they informed the doctor that if Hunter Jim died, they would kill him. Hunter Jim died, and so the four defendants were appointed by the council to carry out its determination. They shot the doctor the following morning.

The court decided that the law did apply to Native Americans (which was somewhat in question) but felt that the defendants had not committed murder because malice was absent, an essential element for the crime of murder. Though the offense if committed by a "white man" would certainly have been murder, the court said that in view of the "Indian nature," customs, superstition, and ignorance, they had not committed murder. The prosecutor did not press for a murder charge but for manslaughter. The judge decided that justice should be tempered with mercy and imposed a sentence of five years of imprisonment for each as well as a one dollar fine.

A 1985 Oregon case raises a slightly different set of issues because the murder did not involve only Native Americans. In *State v. Butler*[21] three members of the Siletz tribe were accused of murdering a man who was caught desecrating Native American burial grounds. It was alleged that when they found him digging up Native American artifacts to sell in local antique shops, they smashed his fingers and cut his throat as punishment. The presumption seems to be that this was the culturally determined proportionality, but this is not made clear in what has been written about the case.

Defense counsel stated that he would not use the cultural defense because he did not think it would be fruitful. Instead he intended to show that they did not commit the act charged. But some of the Native Americans in the area felt that the acts committed against the grave-robber could be regarded as justifiable acts of war or self-defense. In the end it appeared that all three defendants were acquitted based on insufficient evidence, rather than cultural considerations. Although the judge did not want the case to center on the culture conflict, he did allow a member of the Siletz tribe to explain their religious convictions concerning burial traditions.[22]

A Principle

The central question is what principle should govern culture conflict. There are two choices: (1) Might makes right — meaning that the dominant legal system controls or (2) Who arrived first — meaning that the indigenous peoples ought, at the very least, to be permitted to retain control over their own matters. Since it is admittedly quite unrealistic to expect colonial regimes or their descendants to relinquish control because the second principle is determined to be correct, it is possible that the cultural defense ought to function for indigenous groups. Perhaps there should be some guarantee that culture will be considered to mitigate sentences. Since immigrants have come voluntarily to the United States, they should be educated about American law and expected to abide by it. Indigenous peoples, however, made no such choice and should, in theory, have the right to handle legal matters within their own system. When it is necessary for them to enter American courts, culture should probably be taken into account in mitigating sentences.

The Cultural Defense in Other Countries

Killings based on a belief in the supernatural are found across the globe and have been documented in such places as Colombia, Fiji, Papua New Guinea, South Africa as well as in various countries in Africa.[23] But where defenses are tried in such cases, they generally fail. For example, a number

[21]*State v. Butler*, No. 44496 (Lincoln Cty. Cir. Ct. filed Mar. 11, 1981).

[22]Tia Nichols, Belief in the Way: Native Americans in the Western Legal System, 1987, unpublished paper.

[23]Bernard M. Narokobi, Adaptation of Western Law in Papua New Guinea, 5 *Melanesian Law Journal* 52 (1977); Kharisu S. Chukkol, Supernatural Beliefs and Criminal Law in Nigeria, 25 *Journal of the Indian Law Institute* 444 (1983); L. O. Aremu, Criminal Responsibility for Homicide in Nigeria and Supernatural Beliefs, 29 *International and Comparative Law Quarterly* 112 (1980); David S. Clark, Witchcraft and Legal Pluralism: The Case of Celimo Miquirucama, 15 *Tulsa Law Journal* 679 (1980). For more general references on the cultural defense in other countries, see Sebastian Poulter, *English Law and Ethnic Minority Customs*. London: Butterworths,

(Footnote continued on next page)

of cases involving sorcery killings have arisen in Papua New Guinea and defenses of all kinds are rejected because the courts take an extremely inflexible view of such killings.[24] In Africa there are also many cases in which the courts rigidly apply common law doctrines in witchcraft, juju, and other supernatural cases despite widespread belief in these practices. One legal scholar attests to the depth of commitment to the beliefs, even among the educated and Westernized. Aremu found in one of his criminal law classes in Nigeria that more than 90% of the students (aged 20 and older) believed strongly in witchcraft. Nevertheless, the (formerly colonial) courts in their administration of criminal justice refuse to recognize the supernatural to the dismay of some African legal scholars:

> This attitude, apart from being patently unjust to the accused who had killed under the influence of such forces, also failed to take into consideration prevailing views on criminal law and culture conflicts . . .[25]

It seems that these scholars favor a cultural defense because it represents the only realistic possibility for invoking traditional norms. One wonders whether they would support the reinstitution of traditional courts.

The device which the courts have employed to avoid any consideration of culture is the so-called reasonable man standard. Because they rely on an "objective" version of it, they simply define the state of mind of the person (who killed to defend himself against witchcraft) as unreasonable. For instance, in the Nigerian case of *Gadam v. R.*[26] (1954) the Court held that "though prevalent, such a belief is unreasonable, being fraught as it is with such terrible results." In this case the defendant's wife had a miscarriage and became mortally ill. The man attributed this unhappy turn of events to two women. He struck one of them on the head with a hoe-handle in the belief that by so doing he would destroy the spell cast over his wife. The woman whom he hit died, and he was soon convicted of murder, which was affirmed on appeal. Because the belief was considered to be "unreasonable" by the court in its consequentialist reasoning, he was held responsible.

Although the courts will not entertain a cultural defense, they recognize how pervasive supernatural beliefs are. Oddly enough, this undermines attempts to use the insanity defense as can be seen in the Kenyan case of *Philip Muswi v. R.*[27] (1956). The defendant had been having trouble with his first wife after he took a second one. He believed that his first wife was practicing witchcraft against him. In fact, she was trying to alienate their children from him. When she took away their young son from his home, he became so furious that he killed her.

At the trial he testified that he did not know what he was doing and that it was not even until the next day that he remembered having killed his wife. The insanity defense was not persuasive because a belief in witchcraft does not prove insanity where it is so common:

> Even if the defendant believed he was justified in killing his wife because she was practicing witchcraft, there is again no evidence that such belief arose from any mental defect; it is a belief sometimes held

1986, Sebastian Poulter, Hyde v. Hyde — A Reappraisal. *International and Comparative Law Quarterly* 475 (1976); Sebastian Poulter, Foreign Customs and the English Criminal Law 24 *International and Comparative Law Quarterly* 136 (1975), Alec Samuels, Legal Recognition and Protection of Minority Customs in a Plural Society in England, 10 *Anglo-American Law Review* 241 (1981); Justin Lewis, The Outlook for a Devil in the Colonies. 1958 *Criminal Law Review* 661 (1958); A. Gledhill, The Reception of English Law in India, In William B. Hamilton (ed.), *The Transfer of Institutions* (pp. 165-191). Durham, N.C.: Duke University Press, 1964. David Weisbrot, Note: Law Reform Commission Working Paper No. 6- Criminal Responsibility: Taking Customs, Perceptions and Beliefs into Account. 5 *Melanesian Law Journal* 164 (1977); T. O. Elias, Customary Law: The Limits of Its Validity in Colonial Law, 13 *African Studies* 97 (1954).

[24]Narokobi, *Id.* at 60.

[25]Aremu, *supra* note 23, at 113.

[26]*Gadam v. R.*, 14 W.A.C.A. 442 (1954).

[27]*Philip Muswi s/o Musele v. R.*, 23, E.A.C.A. 622 (1956).

> by entirely sane Africans. The question whether the appellant's act was or was not contrary to tribal law is irrelevant.[28]

The defendant in such a court finds himself in a dilemma: there is no cultural defense because a belief in the supernatural is not reasonable; but it is not unreasonable enough to warrant the insanity defense.

In some places courts have been willing to mitigate sentences on the basis of culture in witchcraft cases. For instance, in March 1985 in Oakland, California, an Ethiopian man, Hagos Gebreamlak, was accused of attempting to kill a woman whom he claimed had placed a spell over him.[29] There were suggestions that the shooting had followed a lovers' quarrel. At the trial the public defender relied on the defense that beliefs concerning the bouda, voodoo and spells could arise from the man's background. Over strenuous objections from the prosecution, the judge allowed the defense to call an anthropologist as a witness to testify on Ethiopian customs. A psychologist also testified that the man was depressed and under considerable stress. The jury found the defendant not guilty of attempted murder but convicted him of a lesser charge, assault with a deadly weapon. It may be that the jury was more sympathetic to him because he did not actually kill the woman at whom he fired.

The degree to which cultural beliefs are accepted varies considerably. One way to anticipate whether or not culture will be considered is to ascertain what kind of reasonable man standard is used. Where the standard is an "objective" one, cultural beliefs are treated as irrelevant. But where it is "subjective," culture is taken into account. In the Enga Jury case in Papua New Guinea two village surgeons were charged with manslaughter after they operated on an ailing man with bamboo knives who then died. At first they were acquitted because no local Enga jury would have thought they had acted with reckless disregard for human life. But on appeal the court relied on an "objective" standard:

> It is sufficient, in my opinion, to state that the reasonable man is for the purposes of this case to be presumed to be one whose state of knowledge and prudence is such that appreciates the difference in training and skill between the qualified doctor and "the village surgeon" without any medical qualification.[30]

In the case of *R. v. Noboi-Bosai* (1971-1972)[31] a "subjective" reasonable man standard was used. Here the accused were charged with improperly or indecently interfering with a corpse. They cooked and ate parts of the body from another village. The judge explicitly applied a standard which was based on the "reasonable primitive Gabusi villager of Daldalibi and Yulabi in early 1971." He concluded that eating the body of the deceased villager was "neither improper nor indecent behavior on their part, being normal and reasonable behavior on their part." For the most part the "objective" standard convicts whereas the "subjective" one will acquit or at least mitigate the sentence.

Westerners in Asian Courts

Two Australians were convicted of drug trafficking in Malaysia. They received the death penalty and were executed.[32] Since the death penalty was approved in 1975 and made mandatory in 1983, 36 men and women have been hanged in Malaysia for the offense of drug trafficking. Although some foreigners were hanged, all were Asians. More than 70 others have been sentenced to death, some of whom are foreigners, including some Westerners.

Capital punishment remains the norm in Asia. Both Thailand and Singapore also provide for the death penalty for drug

---

[28] *Id.* at 625.

[29] Anon., Profile, *Los Angeles Daily Journal*, Oct. 25, 1985, pp. 1,17.

[30] Narokobi, *supra* note 23, at 60.

[31] *R. v. Noboi-Bosai* (1971-1972), P. & N.G.L.R., 271; see Narokobi, *supra* note 23 at 58; *see also*, Howard, What Colour is the "Reasonable Man"? 1961 *Criminal Law Review* 41.

[32] Nick B. Williams, Malaysia Standing Firm on Drug Laws, *Los Angeles Times*, July 5, 1986; anon., 2 Australians Hanged by Malaysia for Drug Crimes, *Los Angeles Times*, July 6, 1986, p. 4.

offenses. These countries are trying to cope with the severe drug problems they experience because they are geographically near the "Golden Triangle," famous for the growth of heroin. One estimate of the number of narcotics addicts in Malaysia was 500,000 of the total 15 million population. Should one expect Malaysian courts to use Australian or Western guidelines in sentencing?

Analysis

Most of the debate about the cultural defense takes place in the language of pluralism.[33] The language tends to obscure the real issues underlying culture conflict, issues which are most appropriately addressed in the framework of relativism. Pluralism simply means that a given society is composed of various groups with different mores. The concept of relativism, on the other hand, focuses less on the structural relationships and more on the psychological disposition of individuals within the group. Relativism holds that each person perceives reality in accordance with inculcated standards that have been uncritically accepted and may be unconscious. It is not simply the existence of different groups which gives rise to culture conflict. Rather, it is the power of enculturation which leads each group to perceive reality according to internal standards.

Many of those who see relativism as the issue fail to understand what acceptance of the theory does and does not require. In particular, many anthropologists, philosophers, and social scientists erroneously believe that relativism logically entails tolerance. They cast the theory of relativism as a value or prescriptive theory, which it is not. Unfortunately, this has caused great difficulty for the theory as a whole and for those who mistakenly believe that, by accepting the theory of relativism, they are automatically committed to endorsing the cultural defense.

Relativism is actually a descriptive theory and not connected to any particular value:

> . . . the two parts of the doctrine are not logically or necessarily interdependent. The first part says that people are brought up to see the value in things that their local experience has suggested. The second part says that we should respect all cultures. But there is no true "therefore" between these two parts. It cannot be proved from the proposition that all values are relative, that we ought to respect all systems of values. We might just as well hate them all.[34]

In essence, relativism asks us to acknowledge that there are different ways of looking at the world; but taking a relativist approach certainly does not require us to surrender our own standards. Because enculturation leads to ethnocentrism, if anything, relativism reinforces our commitment to our own standards. So, the argument advanced by some that pluralism (relativism) compels us to adopt the cultural defense is seen to be a misguided one. Cultural sensitivity does not involve abandoning one's own laws.

Secondly, the cultural defense is not needed because culture is already taken into account at the various stages of charging and sentencing. Prosecutors, for example, often will not press charges against Laotian defendants because members of the community are reluctant to testify against one another and prefer to settle disputes by traditional mechanisms. In a number of cases such as *Whaley, Kimura*, and *Moua* (Kong), the sentences were mitigated, most likely because of culture.

One advocate of the cultural defense argues that a formal cultural defense is preferable to the informal use of culture.[35] The allegation is that where discretion exists in the United States legal system, it

[33] Milton E. Gordon, Models of Pluralism: The New American Dilemma. 454 *Annals, American Academy of Political and Social Science* 178 (1981); Charles M. Lamb, Legal Foundations of Civil Rights and Pluralism in America, 454 *Annals, American Academy of Political and Social Science* 13 (1981).

[34] Robert Redfield, *The Primitive World and Its Transformations*. Ithaca, New York: Cornell University Press, 1962 at 146-147; see also Alison Dundes Renteln, Relativism and the Search for Human Rights, 90 *American Anthropologist* (1988).

[35] Anon., The Cultural Defense in the Criminal Law, 99 *Harvard Law Review* 1293 (1986).

works most often to the disadvantage of minorities. But the cases show this proposition to be false. Moreover, if there is a problem of having prejudiced judges within the system, that should be remedied. It does not necessarily justify having a cultural defense. Furthermore, if judges are unwilling to consider culture, it remains unclear how a formal cultural defense would force them to take culture into account. Judges need not, for instance, accept the insanity defense.

For immigrants there is no real justification for having a cultural defense. But where individualized justice merits it, judges can use culture to mitigate sentences. In the case of individuals upon whom a system of legal norms has been imposed, the cultural defense may not be feasible. This is because adherence to an "objective" reasonable man standard prevents the consideration of culture. For these societies two solutions are possible: (1) restore traditional courts which follow customary law (unless the traditional system is no longer desired), or (2) modify the Western judicial structure so that it incorporates traditional norms. For example, perhaps self defense ought to be allowed in witchcraft killings if the vast majority of citizens want it. Although some may be uncomfortable with the idea of sanctioning defenses for such crimes as witchcraft killings, using the law to force social change is equally troublesome.[36]

Finally, it is necessary to recognize the negative consequences that would follow the adoption of the cultural defense. Anarchy would reign if each person could claim a different cultural immunity from prosecution. One extreme reaction to the attempted use of the cultural defense in the *Moua* (Tou) case was a claim that acceptance of it would lead to a rash of wife killings. While this may seem far-fetched, it is possible that in the absence of any deterrent whatsoever, immigrants might be less circumspect when continuing their customary ways in the United States. Moreover, those who prefer not to follow the traditional way of life would fall prey to the cultural defense. If the perpetrator is not held responsible, women who seek their rights will have no recourse. Women's rights and children's rights will never be protected if their traditions follow them wherever they go.

Even if we assume for the sake of argument that the cultural defense is desirable because it reflects cultural sensitivity, we must acknowledge the overwhelming negative connotations it has. The cultural defense is often compared to the insanity defense. This seems to suggest that different cultural logics are viewed as being delusional.

The use of the cultural defense also presents dangers of distortion. If Americans mistakenly believe that Japanese women kill their children whenever their husbands take mistresses, this could trigger intensified racial prejudice. In fact, the inexcusable treatment of Japanese-Americans in the 1940's stemmed from racial stereotypes. Not only is there a possibility that the culture itself will be distorted, but the facts in a particular case may be molded to accommodate the cultural defense. Some argue that the trial of Hagos Gebreamlak illustrates this occurrence. It is possible that his beliefs in the bouda were not genuine, suggested by his failure to apply traditional remedies such as using garlic and wearing amulets to break the spell. The district attorney in that case maintained that the public defender had invented the bouda defense merely to absolve Gebreamlak of responsibility.[37] In the long term the cultural defense would probably have serious and detrimental effects, even upon the individuals it was designed to protect.

---

[36]Studies indicate that it can be disastrous to employ law as a vehicle for social change when the values in the society support the retention of traditional legal norms. See, for example, Gregory Massell, Revolutionary Change in Soviet Central Asia. In D. Black and M. Mileski (eds.), *The Social Organization of Law* (pp. 226-261). New York: Seminar Press, 1973; Haleh Afshar, The Legal, Social, and Political Position of Women in Iran, 13 *International Journal of the Sociology of Law* 47 (1985); F.J.M. Feldbrugge, The Role of Soviet Law in the Integration of Non-Slavic Peoples, 3 *Review of Socialist Law* 3 (1977).

Conclusion

Some contend that the cultural defense is necessary if we are a truly pluralistic society. This is erroneous. American law recognizes an important distinction between belief and action; the former is absolute, while the latter is not. A culturally sensitive outlook does not require that we relinquish our standards. Others argue that we must reject the cultural defense because we must force new citizens to become assimilated as soon as possible. This is an example of cultural arrogance because retaining our criminal laws does not mean that we should impose *all* of the beliefs in the dominant value-system upon new citizens! While it is true that punishment educates and socializes, there are certainly less repressive ways to achieve the same result.

We can be culturally sensitive and retain our standards. There is no need for a cultural defense because mechanisms already exist which can take culture into account. The negative consequences of the defense such as undercutting the legitimacy of government, undermining women's and children's rights, and treating the logic of other cultures as insane all represent good reasons for rejecting the cultural defense.

---

[37]*Lauren Arenson, Hagos Gebreamlak v. California*, 1987, unpublished paper.

[24]

The Anthropologist as Expert Witness

LAWRENCE ROSEN
Princeton University

Anthropologists representing each of the subfields of the discipline have appeared as expert witnesses in a wide range of legal cases. Their appearance raises a number of significant questions about the appropriateness of anthropological knowledge to adversary proceedings, and poses difficult ethical problems for the participant and the profession. The present article reviews a series of cases in which anthropologists have served as expert witnesses and proposes a set of recommended standards and reforms for this activity. [ethics, expert testimony, legal anthropology, American society, applied anthropology]

INTRODUCTION

AS SCHOLARS AND TEACHERS, governmental advisers, and agency bureaucrats, anthropologists play a number of different roles in American society. Each role entails certain intellectual and moral issues, but there are few roles that confront conscientious anthropologists with more serious scholarly and ethical problems than those posed by their appearance in legal proceedings as expert witnesses. Drawing on specialized knowledge and ostensibly attuned to a professional superego that demands an impartial analysis of the data, the expert witness is brought, usually by one of the adversary parties, into a proceeding whose form and goals often appear foreign, if not overtly antithetical, to scholarly capacities and purposes. Although his awareness of the experiences of other expert witnesses—particularly anthropological witnesses—may be limited and his vision of legal proceedings drawn more from popular stereotypes than detailed knowledge, the expert witness will doubtless be aware that American courts have made frequent reference to sociological data and that the expert's testimony may prove significant to the outcome of the case. Regardless of personal affinity to the position argued by the party calling him as a witness, the anthropologist may not understand how expert testimony fits together with judicial reasoning and legal precedent, and precisely how the court's investigation of the facts articulates with the form of knowledge he possesses.

The general use of experts in American courts is familiar to almost everyone. We have all seen enough Perry Mason shows to know that the prosecution or defense, or the parties to a civil proceeding, may call expert witnesses to the stand to testify on anything from the findings of a ballistics test or the nature of tire tracks to the medical condition of an accident victim or the blood type of an alleged father. The use of expert psychiatrists in cases involving the insanity defense or competence to stand trial is also widely known. Less familiar are the regulations affecting expert testimony and the historical context of their development.

The use of expert witnesses is nothing new in the Anglo-American system of adjudication. Their role is deeply intertwined with the development of the jury system, and many of the rules governing expert testimony, as well as many of the difficulties posed for it, are associated with the emergence of this distinctive institution of legal fact-finding.

The early English jury was a very different institution than its contemporary successor. In the 12th to 14th centuries, juries consisted of groups of neighbors who were already acquainted with the facts of a case or regarded as easily capable of discovering them. In a sense, jurors in this period were as much witnesses as judges of the facts. In some cases, particularly those involving disputes among tradesmen or other specialists, the jury was drawn from people with expertise in the matter. Occasionally, the court itself summoned an expert to supply information on a given topic. In these instances, the information was probably furnished directly to the court, rather than to the jury, and the judge was apparently left to decide whether and how the jurors should be informed of the testimony (Hand 1901:41-42; Rosenthal 1935:408). It was only in the 16th century, as the jury was transformed from a panel of co-residents or colleagues to a group of uninformed arbiters who, instead of bringing their own knowledge of the facts to bear on a case waited for evidence to be presented to them in court, that experts were brought in by the contending parties to give testimony.

Special rules have also developed concerning the presentation of expert testimony in court. Whereas ordinary witnesses were increasingly barred from expressing their own opinions on many issues, various jurisdictions created an exception for the expert witness. Although different courts follow significantly different rules, most contemporary American courts permit the judge to exercise substantial discretion in deciding the propriety and qualifications of proffered expert witnesses. None of the uniform rules proposed for the regulation of expert testimony has received widespread acceptance (Travis 1974). However, several jurisdictions, including the federal courts, have encouraged the use of court appointed experts in addition to those who may be presented by the parties.

Although the general use of expert witnesses is not new and the rules governing their appearance largely ignores special problems attendant on various types of expert testimony, the use of social science by the courts is both more recent and unfamiliar. Sociologists have been called as expert witnesses in cases involving the custody of children of mixed racial parentage (Rose 1956:210), the relationship between race and the application of the death penalty (Wolfgang 1974), and the impact on minorities of segregated schooling (Levin and Hawley 1975). Linguists have testified on the readability of a back-pay agreement in a dispute involving minority employees (United States District Court, Western District of Pennsylvania 1976). Sociologists and social psychologists have applied their studies of social indicators in trademark disputes (Barksdale 1957) and determinations of parental fitness. In addition to actual testimony, courts and attorneys have frequently cited the work of social scientists in their decisions and briefs (Rosen 1972).

Anthropologists, too, have appeared in an astonishingly wide range of cases. As we shall see, they have testified on everything from racial segregation, miscegenation laws, and child custody to the blood types of putative fathers, the nature of religious communities, and the cultural background of criminal defendants. Their predominant role has been in cases involving American Indians. In suits brought before the Indian Claims Commission, they have testified to the nature of aboriginal land titles, the identification of Indian social groupings, and the comprehension by Indians of treaties signed with the federal government. In nonclaims cases, they have testified as to the nature of Indian peyotism, the nature and consequences of acculturation, and the religious significance of Indian ritual artifacts. In all of these different kinds of cases certain general issues present themselves. These issues are shared by many other kinds of expert witnesses, and present questions the individual anthropologist and the profession as a whole cannot and should not avoid.

The first set of problems raised both for the anthropologist and the court concerns the adequacy, context, and form of presentation of anthropological evidence in an adversary proceeding. Does the mere fact that one holds a doctorate in anthropology qualify one as an expert in all aspects of the discipline or one of its subdivisions? In what sense is the anthropologist's testimony adequate to the interpretation of a highly specific issue that often turns on prospective consequences? Is it true for anthropologists—as most psychiatrists and some sociologists argue for their disciplines—that the kinds of questions which they are capable of addressing are not the same as those posed by a legal case, and that their evidence is therefore either inappropriate for or distorted by the context of a courtroom proceeding? What is the expert's relation to the attorney and how have anthropologists viewed the process of cross-examination and the introduction of a contending expert's testimony? In the courtroom setting, as well as in the presentation of depositions and supporting documents, what evidentiary standards do anthropologists appear to set for themselves, and how do the forms of argument used in these situations compare to those employed when writing for a scholarly or popular audience? Indeed, what relationships exist between the "facts" to which anthropologists testify and the theories that inform those facts, and how sensitive are the courts and lawyers to anthropologists' unstated theoretical biases?

A second set of questions revolves around the mutual effect that courts and anthropologists have had on one another. How have anthropologists' own concepts been affected by the experience of such litigation, and how has the experts' testimony shaped judicial thought? Having participated in such proceedings, will the anthropologist be so concerned with the possible legal significance of his work that his future scholarly investigations will be altered in some fashion?

Finally, serious questions are raised about anthropologists' conceptions of their role in such proceedings, and how the courts and the profession may contribute to appropriate reforms in the present system. Are anthropologists really the providers of crucial information from which judgments are actually derived, or are they merely important personages whose presence in court is simply useful for rationalizing judgments that are founded on other, perhaps judicially less palatable, bases? How, if at all, should anthropology as a profession approach the ethical implications of expert testimony? What reforms might appear most useful given the experience of anthropologists and others as participants in the judicial process?

In order to explore these questions within the context of the specific situations in which they arise, a series of cases will be analyzed in which anthropologists have been involved as expert witnesses. In each, the aim is to sharpen understanding of the issues presented and to show that while no incontrovertible answers exist for the questions posed, this fact alone justifies neither the self-serving relativism nor the moral self-righteousness to which both anthropologists and lawyers may fall prey.

ANTHROPOLOGICAL TESTIMONY AND RACIAL DISCRIMINATION

> *Justice Frankfurter*: . . . [W]e are here in a domain which I do not yet regard as science in the sense of mathematical certainty. This is all opinion evidence.
> *Mr. Greenberg:* That is true, Your Honor.
> *Justice Frankfurter*: I do not mean that I disrespect it. I simply know its character. It can be a very different thing from, as I say, things that are weighed and measured and are fungible. We are dealing here with very subtle things, very subtle testimony [Oral argument in Gebhart v. Belton, in Friedman 1969:172-173].

In the years leading up to the 1954 *Brown v. Board of Education* decision, in which the Supreme Court ruled that segregated education was inherently unequal, lawyers for the black litigants placed considerable stress on the writings and testimony of social scientists. As part of their strategy, lawyers for the National Association for the Advancement of Colored People (NAACP) sought to use social science testimony to strengthen their argument that discriminatory classifications are unconstitutional if, among other things, they are lacking in any rational justification (United States Supreme Court 1949:449). The NAACP was well aware of the implicit psychological and sociological ideas that suffused the "separate but equal" doctrine announced by the Court's 1896 decision in *Plessy v. Ferguson*. They knew, too, that at least since the introduction of the Brandeis Brief, with its frequent citation of social and economic indicators, the Court had become familiar with reliance on sociological data (Rosen 1972). It was not, however, until the desegregation cases that social science testimony took so central a place in constitutional litigation.

Four years before the *Brown* decision, the Supreme Court was called on to decide whether the education afforded whites at the University of Texas Law School and that afforded blacks at a separate state institution could be supported under the separate but equal doctrine. The case, *Sweatt v. Painter*, was unusual in that NAACP lawyers called as a witness one of the leading anthropologists of the day, Robert Redfield. Redfield was, in many respects, an ideal choice. Trained as a lawyer before coming into anthropology and possessing years of experience in integrated education as Dean of the Social Sciences at the University of Chicago, "Redfield proved a brilliant witness whose every word suggested a cool, considered judgment with great authority behind it" (Kluger 1976:264). The thrust of Redfield's testimony dealt less with specific anthropological studies of the composition and character of the races than with the social consequences of segregated education and the possible repercussions of court-ordered integration. His testimony was intended to support the argument that if legislators sought to give a rational, constitutional basis to racial discrimination they would find nothing in the experience of social science to support their position (cf. Redfield 1963:165-168).

The following excerpts from Redfield's testimony indicate something of the force and direction of the anthropologist's direct testimony, as conducted by the NAACP's Thurgood (now Mr. Justice) Marshall, and the cross-examination by counsel for the State of Texas, Price Daniel:

[*On direct examination by Mr. Thurgood Marshall:*]

Q: Dr. Redfield, are there any recognizable differences as between Negro and white students on the question of their intellectual capacity?

Mr. Daniel: Your Honor, we object to that. That would be a conclusion on the part of the witness. It covers all negro students and all white students. It isn't limited to any particular study or subject or even show what it is based on.

The Court: I suppose his qualifications he has testified to would qualify him to draw his conclusions.

. . . .

A: We got something of a lesson there. We who have been working in the field in which we began with a rather general presumption among our common educators that inherent differences in intellectual ability of capacity to learn existed between negroes and whites, and have slowly, but I think very convincingly, been compelled to come to the opposite conclusion, in the course of long history, special research in the field.

. . . .

Q: . . . [W]hat is your opinion as to the effect of segregated education . . . ?

A: . . . [I]t prevents the student from the full, effective and economical coming to understand[ing of] the nature and capacity of the group from which he is segregated. . . . It is my view that education goes forward more favorably if the community of student, scholar and teacher is fairly representative of the whole community. . . . [S]egregation . . . accentuates imagined differences between negroes and whites. These false assumptions . . . are given an appearance of reality by the formal act of physical separation.

[*Cross-examination by Mr. Price Daniel:*]

Q: Do you think the [segregation] laws should be changed tomorrow?

A: I think that segregation is a matter of legal regulation. Such a law can be changed quickly.

Q: Do you think it has anything to do with the social standing in the community?

A: Segregation itself is a matter of law, and that law can be changed at once . . .

. . . .

Q: . . . [D]o you recognize or agree with the school of thought, that regardless of the ultimate objective concerning segregation, that if it is to be changed in southern communities . . . it must be done over a long period of time. . . ?

A: That contention, I do not think, will be my opinion on the matter scientifically.

Q: Does that represent, scientifically, a school of thought on that, in your science, in the matter?

A: There are some that feel that way.

Q: Yes, sir. You are acquainted with the history of the carpetbagger days in the Civil War?

A: I feel better acquainted with it today, sir, than anybody.

Q: Dr. Redfield, let me get you clearly on that. You are not talking about your own trip down here, are you, to Texas? You say you are acquainted with it today?

A: It just drifted into my mind.

. . . .

Q: Doctor, are you acquainted with the Encyclopedia Britannica, the publication by that name?

A: I have a set. I don't look at it very often.

Q: You are from the University of Chicago?

A: Yes.

Q: Is that publication now published under the auspices of that University?

A: Yes, sir; and it badly needs rewriting.

Q: It is published under the auspices of your University?

A: Yes.

Q: Have you read the article therein on education, and segregation of the races in American Schools?

A: If I have I don't remember it.

Q: You don't remember it. Have you written any articles for the Encyclopedia Britannica?

A: No, we are just beginning a revision of anthropological articles, and it seems there has to be a very drastic change.

. . . .

Q: Could you give us some of the authorities that you think we would be justified in taking as authorities on the subject you have testified to us about? Have you written any books on the subject?

A: Not with respect to the American Negro. I have written on the general subject with respect to other racial groups. Franz Boes [*sic*], Ruth Benedict, Ashely [*sic*] Montague, Otto Klineberg. Is that enough?

Q: Give us one more.

A: I will make it a good one. Then, Dr. Leslie White.

Q: Do all of these scientists have the same, share your ideas as to segregation?

A: I don't know.

. . . .

Q: But on your conclusion as to education, you told me there were authorities in the field who disagreed with your conclusion?

A: I think not.

Q: Maybe I am speaking about the gradual change.

A: I don't know who I could cite for that.

Q: That is all.

[United States Supreme Court 1949:192-193, 194-195, 198, 203, 204-205].

Redfield's testimony was an early and important basis for the contention that no rational foundation for segregation could be found in the social science literature.[1] Ultimately, the Supreme Court avoided the implication of Redfield's argument—that separate education is inherently unequal—and simply found that the facilities provided by the segregated law schools of Texas were not, in fact, equivalent (United States Supreme Court 1950). But Redfield's testimony was also read into the record of *Briggs v. Elliott*, a South Carolina case which was joined before the Supreme Court with *Brown* and several other cases, and to which Marshall made frequent reference in his briefs and oral argument. By then, a considerable number of social scientists—most notably the psychologist Kenneth B. Clark—had testified in the various desegregation cases, and a number of scholars, Redfield among them, were signatories to the statement by social scientists that formed an Appendix to Appellant's Briefs (Chein et al. 1955).

When the desegregation cases came before the Supreme Court, the Justices, especially Mr. Justice Frankfurter, pressed counsel on the relevance and implications of the sociological data. Through his questioning, Frankfurter asserted the Court's right to read, as well as hear, what social scientists have to say (Friedman 1969:63), and responded to counsel's argument that there was no social science support for the segregationist argument by saying: "But the testimony of a witness is subject to intrinsic limitations and qualifications and illuminations. The mere fact that a man is not contradicted does not mean that what he says is so" (Friedman 1969:172). Expressing the common concern of the Court, Frankfurter probed for the perceived consequences of an order striking down the "separate but equal" doctrine, and responded favorably when the NAACP stuck to its constitutional argument that if the states could supply no scientific or other basis for their racial classifications blacks should not have to bear the demonstrated burdens of this discrimination (Friedman 1969:44-45). The Court also let pass the remarks of John W. Davis, arguing for the states, that "much of that which is handed around under the name of social science is an effort on the part of the scientist to rationalize his own preconceptions. They find usually, in my limited observation, what they go out to find" (Friedman 1969:59).

When the Court handed down its unanimous decision it adopted the finding that segregated education does indeed have "a detrimental effect upon the colored children," that "the policy of separating the races is usually interpreted as denoting the inferiority of the negro group," and that "a sense of inferiority affects the motivation of a child to learn"

(United States Supreme Court 1954:494). The Court then formally repudiated the implicit psychology of the "separate but equal" doctrine and supplied a footnote reference to the writings of Clark, Chein, Myrdal, and other social scientists to support their assertion that the harm of segregation "is amply supported by modern authority" (United States Supreme Court 1954:494).

The Court's decision, and particularly its footnote reference to social science, has sparked great controversy. Some Southern Congressmen labeled the social scientists as "Commies" and "foreigners" (Garfinkel 1959:37; Rosen 1972:173-175), and Senator Eastland sought to undercut the constitutional basis of the decision by introducing a Senate Resolution that began: "Whereas this decision was based solely and alone on psychological, sociological and anthropological considerations . . ." (Greenberg 1956:965). More responsible commentators were also concerned that the Court had indeed relied more on sociology than law in its decision and that the particular social science findings used were altogether inadequate (Berger 1957:475; Cahn 1955; Van den Haag 1960). The social scientists defended the relevance and quality of their findings (Clark 1953, 1959-60, 1969), and numerous commentors have attempted to assess the merits of each side's contentions (Garfinkel 1959; Kluger 1976:355-356; Rosen 1972:182-196).

Throughout this controversy, the precise importance of the social science testimony to the Court's decision has remained elusive. Chief Justice Warren said the Court cited the testimony simply to counter the argument in *Plessy* that the harm of discrimination was a figment of the Negro's imagination (Kluger 1976:706). Judge Wisdom has written (1975:142): "The social science evidence was the kind of support a court likes to find in a record to lend factual and scientific aura to a result sustainable by other, purely abstract and sometimes formalistically legal, considerations, but dictated by the moral necessity of changing social attitudes." And one of the NAACP lawyers has asserted that the testimony aided in the general awareness of the adverse effects of segregation, and that if the sociological data were inadequate the defendants had ample opportunity to demonstrate this during cross-examination (Greenberg 1956; see also Clark 1969:xxxvi). Whether, as the NAACP argued, the demonstration of segregation's effects was at "the heart of our case" (Friedman 1969:18) or was simply the only mechanism available for attacking directly the legal issues surrounding racial discrimination, a close reading of the history of the desegregation cases shows that the arguments of Redfield and others not only preempted the pseudo-scientific assertions of the segregationists but supported, and perhaps even compelled, acceptance of the argument that segregation was without constitutional justification.

The desegregation cases are not the only legal actions concerning race in which anthropological evidence has been employed. Physical anthropologists have appeared in cases involving mixed racial marriages (Maslow 1959-60:245), and numerous citations were made to anthropological works in *Loving v. Virginia*, a 1967 case in which the Supreme Court struck down antimiscegenation laws as unconstitutional (Kurland and Casper 1975a:784-785, 874-886, 942-943, 958, 987-991). Recently, an anthropologist testified about racial classifications in the case of an East Indian who claimed to have been dismissed from his job as a result of racial discrimination. In that case the court, obviously confused as to how anthropologists might once have classified some dark-skinned persons as Caucasian but now relied more on blood group data, simply told the jury to ignore the expert testimony and determine the "race" of the plaintiff on the basis of their own preceptions and common sense (Edward Jay, personal communication).

Each of these cases raises serious issues about the adequacy, impact, and appropriate presentation of social science findings. In the desegregation cases, such data and interpretations contributed to a result which is consonant with both the professional and personal positions adopted by virtually every anthropologist. However, agreement on interpretations and the suitability of anthropological knowledge are not invariably so clear. When such knowledge stems mainly from theoretical orientations and is directed toward prospective consequences, the difficulties inherent in expert testimony become more sharply posed.

THE COMMUNITY AND THE LAW

In 1972 the United States Supreme Court, in the case of *Wisconsin v. Yoder*, held that the state had violated the constitutional rights of the defendant Amish parents by requiring them to send their children to school beyond the eighth grade. Arguing that "only those interests of the highest order and those not otherwise served can overbalance legitimate claims to the free exercise of religion," (United States Supreme Court 1972:215), the Court found that the Amish religious faith and their mode of life were so inseparable and interdependent that the social repercussions of compulsory high school attendance would necessarily infringe on the well-being of the community as a religious entity. In reaching its decision, the Court made frequent reference to the testimony given at the trial court level by the anthropologist John A. Hostetler.

Hostetler testified that "as a part of their way of salvation [the Amish] require a church community that is separate from the world" (1970:49). "I think," he said, "that if the Amish youth are required to attend the value system of the high school as we know it today, the church-community cannot last long, it will be destroyed" (1970:51). In response to direct examination, he said that this is because "great psychological harm can be done to the children," and hence the community, as a result of the alienation that can arise from a clash of values (1970:52). In the Amish view, he testified, higher learning is regarded as "wisdom not responsible to the community" (1970:54A). The Amish, he asserted, train their children to be members of a self-sufficient community, and Amishmen never place a burden on American society as a result of delinquency or welfare requirements.

On cross-examination, the state's attorney tried to bring out that the Amish do not object to sending their children to public school through the eighth grade and that Amish children come into contact with outsiders on their occasional trips to town. Hostetler reasserted, in the following testimony, that the prosecutor's approach was not without its own bias:

Q. Are you saying in effect, Professor, that to minority groups, which includes the Amish, that they should govern themselves as far as education; should minority groups, be it Amish or otherwise, would you say be permitted to set up their own rules as to whether they shall or shall not be educated?

A. I think we need to know a great deal more about how to teach the culturally different child, know the poverty children, and I think it is dangerous to put all children through the same type of value orientation.

Q. Isn't that the reason then, Professor, in the institutions of higher learning, high school and up, you will have elective courses so the children won't all have to take the same.

A. The trouble is it is still the same environment, it doesn't matter what courses they take.

Q. The principal purpose to attend school is to get education, is it not, isn't that the primary purpose?

A. Yes, but I think there is a great deal of difference what education means, education for what.

Q. To put it bluntly, education so the child can make his or her place in the world?

A. It depends which world.

Q. This one, the one we live in?

A. I think education—this is one of the myths in American society—all education is good; education must be tied to a culture that emotionally guides the child in the direction he knows he is going to live when he is an adult.

Q. Well in other words, Professor, you are saying that education should be tied in the sense to culture, is that right?

A. Yes. Anthropologists would say there isn't education without culture climate at all.

Q. So if I am in one culture and you another the education we receive should be different?

A. I would say if there is this difference in Amish society we should have a parallel culture in the society to know each other as common Americans but a different heritage [Hostetler 1970:67-68].

Finally, the state raised the issue of the effect of insufficient education on those who later chose to leave the community:

Q. Is it fair to say, Professor, that an adult who in his childhood might well be an Amish and now decided not to stay with the Amish is at a handicap because he did not receive the education he might have received were he not an Amish?

A. The conclusion is that the skills required to become an adult are such that if one doesn't have an adult high school education, well, normally people are always looking for people to do manual work. I don't believe any segment is deprived by not having education.[2]

Q. Even those who later cease to become members of the Amish faith and find themselves having to compete in the worldly world?

A. No, I don't think they are deprived [Hostetler 1970:69].

In deciding in favor of the Amish the Supreme Court adopted the reasoning, and indeed many of the phrases, contained in Hostetler's testimony. The Court summarized its position in the following terms:

> It cannot be overemphasized that we are not dealing with a way of life and mode of education by a group claiming to have recently discovered some "progressive" or more enlightened process for rearing children for modern life. Aided by a history of three centuries as an identifiable religious sect and a long history as a successful and self-sufficient segment of American society, the Amish in this case have convincingly demonstrated the sincerity of their religious beliefs, the interrelationship of belief with their mode of life, the vital role that belief and daily conduct play in the continued survival of Old Order Amish communities and their religious organization, and the hazards presented by the State's enforcement of a statute generally valid to others. Beyond this, they have carried the even more difficult burden of demonstrating the adequacy of their alternative mode of continuing informal vocational education in terms of precisely those overall interests that the State advances in support of its program of compulsory high school education [United States Supreme Court 1972:235-236].

Only Mr. Justice Douglas dissented from the majority opinion. He pointed out that attrition from Amish communities is often quite high, and he argued that, although the case involved criminal charges against the parents for violation of compulsory school attendance laws, the interests of the children should have been represented in the case. He also objected to granting an exception only to groups whose values had a religious, rather than philosophical, basis (United States Supreme Court 1972:247-249).

Leaving aside the wisdom of the Supreme Court's unprecedented decison to grant the Amish, because of their religious beliefs, an exception from the requirements of a valid criminal statute, the case raises important issues concerning expert anthropological testimony. The Court was correct when it noted that the state had presented no expert to contradict Hostetler's assessment of Amish life. Nor did the state succeed in undermining the expert's contention that religious and social life are inseparable in Amish communities and that an attack on the one was necessarily an attack on the other. And yet, from the testimony alone, it might appear that Hostetler's interpretation of Amish culture rests on an unstated and unexamined theoretical assumption—namely, that Amish society is the sort of homeostatic, functionally integrated, organically constituted entity which can be analyzed in terms of structural-functional theory. Although this theoretical approach does not pervade his scholarly writings on the Amish, does not his statement that "When culturally different children attend a school that teaches an unattainable identity, an identity that would demand the rejection of the values of the home . . . what can be expected but alienation and rebellion?" (Hostetler 1972) ignore the possibilities of growth, development, evolution, or change? Another expert, or another lawyer, might have pointed, as Mr. Justice Douglas did, to Hostetler's own findings concerning drinking patterns and tension among the Amish (Hostetler 1968:281-283; United States Supreme Court 1972:246-247), and might have challenged the view that two years of additional education would have increased the attrition rate referred to only by Mr. Justice Douglas. If the courts are going to balance state and religious community interests, should anthropological witnesses be encouraged, by their profession if not by the law, to become, in effect, experts for the court, presenting a wide range of data and theoretical alternatives, or is cross-examination an adequate safeguard? Indeed, should prospective assessments of the likely impact of a given practice be stated solely in terms of personal opinion or should the expert explain and evaluate alternative interpretations before voicing his own opinion?

A second issue concerns the expert's own affinity to the cause of the side for whom he appears. Hostetler himself was raised as an Amishman and feels very close to the people. At one point in the testimony he even referred to "*our* Amish culture" (1970:71, emphasis added). The attorney for the Amish, on oral argument to the Supreme Court, effectively pointed to Hostetler as an example of someone who was indeed able to make his way in higher education after being raised in an Amish community (Kurland and Casper 1975b:816). This background was not raised at the trial level. John Hostetler is clearly the most conscientious and thorough of scholars, and his deep concern and commitment to the Amish represents the finest in humanistic anthropology. Of what relevance should it be, then, that he was raised an Amishman and what, if any, obligation for disclosure should be imposed as a general rule on all experts?

Finally, a close reading of the Supreme Court opinion clearly demonstrates that the anthropological testimony in this case may well have been indispensable to the Court's assertion that enforcement of the school attendance law would have had an unusually harsh effect on the entire community of Amish people. Moreover, to the extent that Hostetler's enlightened and responsible testimony raises general problems of the structure of expert testimony in American courts it demonstrates that one does not necessarily lose one's scientific distance by becoming a scholar allied with a cause.

THE BATTLE OF THE EXPERTS

In the desegregation and Amish cases anthropologists appeared on the side of only one of the parties in the case. Quite often anthropologists appear on opposite sides of a case, and one is confronted with what to some is the rather unseemly—and to others the thoroughly delightful—spectacle of two anthropologists, with varying degrees of experience in such proceedings, being delivered up to the tender mercies of the adversary system. In most instances legitimate differences of interpretation exist, and equally competent and honest experts bring their separate perspectives to bear on the legal questions posed. Cases of this type raise major ethical and scholarly issues for the anthropologists involved (Lurie 1956, Manners 1956). I know, because I have been peripherally involved in several such cases concerning American Indians.

During the summer following my second year in law school, while working with an American Indian litigation group, I was asked to prepare the cross-examination of expert anthropologists appearing as witnesses against our clients in several important cases. One of these was the case of *United States v. State of Washington*. The case was one of several suits brought over the past decade involving the fishing rights of Indians along the Northwest Coast. Basically, the State of Washington argued that the Indians are subject to all state conservation laws and fishing regulations when netting salmon off their reservations. The federal government, as trustee of the Indian's rights, argued that the treaty provisions permitting Indians to fish at all their "usual and accustomed" sites exempt the Indians from state control even when the fishing takes place at sites that are no longer part of reservation lands.

One of the arguments put forth in support of the state's case was that the Indians of northwestern Washington have become so acculturated to American life that their tribes have effectively ceased to exist. Since the original treaty rights were granted to the tribes as organized bodies and since the organization of these groups had been fundamentally altered by their contact with whites, the present litigants were not, the state argued, entitled to the rights accorded the pre-existing tribes.

In furtherance of this general line of argument, the state presented the testimony of an expert anthropologist. He noted that by the 1850s, when the treaties in question were signed, the Indians had been so decimated by disease that they could no longer be regarded as solidary units even if some of the groups ever possessed an overall political structure (United States District Court, Western District of Washington 1973:13, 30-31). On the question of Indian acculturation he testified as follows:

Q. What do you mean when you use the term "culture" or "native culture?"

A. Having an historical ethnological orientation, I tend to think in terms of culture rather than in terms of society. I will give a very simple definition of culture: That is totality of learned behavior, the kind of behavior that we learn rather than the behavior that is part of our biological heritage. A "native culture" is the learned behavior of a given group of people, especially that behavior that sets them off from other groups.

Q. Is there a native culture in Western Washington today?

A. At least among groups I have investigated, acculturation has proceeded pretty far. Western Washington Indians wear western clothes, use modern technology, speak English, share in Western religious traditions, are United States citizens, and, generally speaking, look at the world through Western-European eyes. The amount of "Indianness" varies from group to group and certainly between young and old. I wonder how many Western Washington Indians under 21 today really speak native languages [1973:22].

Clearly, this testimony presented substantial difficulties. To argue that the region was characterized by "village autonomy and . . . no tribal structure" seemed to ignore the whole concept of acephalous organization, the existence of intervillage ties, and the situational nature of group alliances and leadership in the region (Sahlins 1968:21). I was troubled by the expert's definition of culture as the "totality of learned behavior," and his consequent assertion that the Indians had taken on the culture of the whites and had come to see the world through their eyes. Wasn't this behavioristic theory of culture regarded as inadequate by most anthropologists (Singer 1968:540)? Didn't we know that different meanings might be attributed to similar symbolic forms and that students of the region had found that "in spite of an almost complete replacement of material goods and century-long conflict between white and native beliefs and practices, basic features of native social organization remain" (Suttles 1963:516)? Is it not possible for people to be bicultural, as well as bilingual, and is "acculturation" capable of scientific measurement?

As I prepared our attorney for his appearance in the case, my sense of indignation and my resolve in the wisdom of our own arguments grew. Yet at some point along the way I found myself asking how I, who had no field experience in the area, could be so sure that our own interpretations were correct. We had the detailed testimony of a highly qualified expert appearing for our side, and most of the anthropological arguments in the case could probably have been rendered secondary to purely legal issues. I knew that while some of the adverse expert's assertions were subject to attack, the federal court would not be unmindful of the fact that state courts in Washington had earlier relied on such testimony when they referred to Indians as similar to Irish- or Italian-Americans in their adoption of American culture. In fact, the state supreme court had even suggested that perhaps the special privileges accorded the Indians were so excessive as to violate the constitutional prohibition against granting any citizens titles of nobility! But even in the face of these absurdities, how could I be so sure that we were right? As I read through the ethnographic literature I could not get a simple yes or no answer as to whether the groups involved should somehow be characterized as "acculturated." I appreciated that for anthropologists, as for many other expert witnesses, the categories of law or judicial reasoning were not always very appropriate to scholarly inquiry. Categories that courts might regard as conclusory, social scientists might see as shorthand formulations, general glosses, or purposely ambiguous rubrics covering details that cannot be summed up as categorical responses to certain kinds of questions. As an anthropologist, I was less certain that I was right about many of the arguments I was, as a lawyer-to-be, encouraging our counsel to make. I could, of course, rationalize it all by saying that the final determination was for the court and that I was just helping to bring out additional facts, but I found this line of reasoning no more comforting in myself than in the system at large. To say that there are simply different interpretations of social life and history and that I was just engaging in their formulation was equally dissatisfying. This was no mere academic debate but a legal proceeding, and the Indians would have to live with the results for years to come. I was pleased that the court eventually found in favor of the Indians and declared that the anthropological testimony on our side was more credible (United States District Court, Western District of Washington 1974:350). Nevertheless, I began to look at other situations in which anthropological testimony had been used in courts, and wondered what effects such testimony might have not only on the courts but on subsequent scholarly work.

THE RECIPROCAL EFFECTS OF ANTHROPOLOGICAL TESTIMONY

The bulk of anthropological testimony has come in proceedings before the Indian Claims Commission. Established in 1946, the Commission was authorized to hear Indian claims against the government, including those based on treaties or on the harm done by less than "fair and honorable dealings" with the Indians.[3] Under the statute, only a "tribe, band, or identifiable group" was permitted to file suit (Indian Claims Commission 1963). Moreover, in most cases the plaintiffs have been unable to show that a group, as opposed to a collection of individuals, is involved, without demonstrating that the group exclusively occupied a definite territory for a long period of time. From the inception of the Commission, the testimony of anthropologists has been central to these determinations.

In many instances sharply differing interpretations have been given by the experts involved. Julian Steward related one such case:

> An important difference between witnesses concerning the nature of acculturation can be illustrated by the Northern Paiute case. Omer C. Stewart, witness for the Plaintiffs, assumed that territorial "bands" and "chiefs" mentioned by recent informants and by certain early observers were aboriginal features which continued to exist long after White occupation of the area. I, representing the Government, interpreted the same evidence as indicating that after horses were acquired predatory groups developed and lasted only during a brief phase of acculturation, when the native economy was changed by the presence of livestock and other foods that could be acquired through raiding. These bands had limited cohesion and transient membership, and they operated under "chiefs" whose function was to lead these forays. None of these functions had an aboriginal basis. The Northern Paiute case also illustrated the hopeless inadequacy of using "nation," "tribe," "band" and "chief" to convey any precise meaning [Steward 1955:298].

The legal meaning of such terms as "tribe" and "band" were so peculiar to many anthropologists that, as one writer put it: "When the ethnologist is asked whether a group in question is a fragment of a tribe he is not certain what is intended by these terms" (Lurie 1955:370). Yet the need to formulate more discriminating categories may have helped some scholars to rethink the categories they applied in their studies. Thus, Julian Steward implied that his own distinction between different kinds of bands—patrilineal hunting bands, composite hunting bands, and predatory bands—was further spurred by his involvement in Claims Commission proceedings (Steward 1955:295). Similarly, the question of Indian concepts and practices of property ownership sharpened Steward's conclusion that: "The plain fact is that anthropology has failed to come to grips with this crucially important problem of 'property' in detail and concreteness" (Steward 1955:293-294).

The experience of anthropologists testifying before the Indian Claims Commission marked the real beginning of anthropological expert testimony in this country, and the subsequent impact on the use of such testimony by the courts has been significant. Involvement in Claims Commission proceedings has not only served to educate many anthropologists in the nature of expert testimony but has served to educate courts and lawyers in the use and relevance of anthropological knowledge. Proceedings before the Commission provided support for a great deal of basic research in ethnography and ethnohistory, and provided scholars with "the opportunity and necessity for reappraisal of long accepted technical and methodological approaches and consequent reaffirmation or abandonment of each of these" (Ray 1955:287). Such proceedings have also placed the anthropologist in a curious role because, as Steward noted: "He himself becomes 'evidence' in that his testimony is based to an incalculable extent upon his theory (explicit or implicit), his experiences among the people, his travels over the territory . . ." (Steward 1955:300-301). Whatever their impact on developing judicial concepts and doctrine, and whatever the merits of alternative modes of presenting their data to a legal proceeding, it is clear that participation in legal cases has had a reciprocal effect on anthropological thinking. A series of unrelated cases in which anthropologists have sought to apply their concept of culture to various legal cases illustrates this point even more sharply.

THE CULTURAL ARGUMENT

Anthropologists are frequently called on to explain to a court of law certain aspects of the culture of those who have sought their help as expert witnesses. The cases, both civil and criminal, present problems of interpreting to the court the language and concepts of the party involved, and the relation between the legal issues posed and the relevance of anthropological findings. Working closely with counsel, anthropologists have also been instrumental in formulating highly creative arguments that may influence the course and result of a case.

Consider, for example, the case of *United States v. Diaz*. The defendant was charged with removing an Apache ceremonial mask from its resting place in a cave on the Indian reservation, in violation of a federal criminal statute forbidding interference with any "object of antiquity" situated on government controlled lands. Since the mask was only a few years old, the defendant argued that it was not protected by the statute. The government, however, brought to the stand an anthropologist, Keith Basso, who testified that the mask was simply the most recent material vehicle for the perpetuation of a traditional ceremony, and that the "object of antiquity" to be preserved was the ancient ritual of which the mask was an indispensable part. The trial court accepted the argument and decided in favor of the Indians. However, the appellate court reversed this decision, stating that if a recently made artifact could qualify as an "object of antiquity," a person would be unable to know in advance which of his actions might subject him to a criminal penalty. Accordingly, the court held, the statute itself was unconstitutionally vague (United States Court of Appeals, Ninth Circuit 1974).

Similar cultural arguments have been made by several anthropologists involved in litigation surrounding the use of peyote by American Indians. Anthropologists not only appeared in court to explain the relation between peyote and the beliefs of the members of the Native American Church; they also made their views known to legislators working on the problem (La Barre et al. 1951). In time, the courts found that Indian peyotism is immune from governmental interference (United States Court of Appeals, Tenth Circuit 1959; California Supreme Court 1964), and special statutes were passed to protect these religious practices. Anthropological data have played a similar role in cases involving snake-handling cults (Tennessee Supreme Court 1975).

A more difficult issue is raised by attempts to argue that the social and cultural backgrounds of defendants are relevant considerations in a criminal proceeding. Some American courts have recognized that cultural factors may affect the ability of a person to form the intent necessary for criminal culpability or to control and direct his actions in an acceptable fashion (United States Court of Appeals, District of Columbia Circuit 1967:453). Various arguments have been put forth for a social defense similar to the insanity defense. As one commentor has put it:

> [T]he person whose criminal behavior is primarily engendered by poverty or persecution may be motivated by forces which are just as powerful and unrelenting as those which motivate the emotionally disturbed offender [Halleck 1967:211].

Several scholars have argued for the introduction to the law of a concept of "social incapacitation" based on social background (Shuman 1973:853-855; Walker 1969:288-290); others recommend that if extraneous social conditions—ghetto upbringing, a history of discrimination, etc.—are the proximate cause of a defendant's violent acts the jury should be instructed that it could find the defendant guilty of a less serious offense than that charged (Rafalko 1967:96-97). Data on social background are often considered by courts in determining an appropriate sentence (Connecticut Superior Court 1964:38).

Whatever the merits of these approaches, the proffered testimony of anthropologists on the social background of criminal defendants has largely been denied by the courts. For example, in *People v. Poddar*, the court refused to allow an anthropologist to testify on the direct consequences of the cultural background of an ex-untouchable from India charged with the murder of a Berkeley co-ed who had rejected him. The court said that the anthropologist could testify on the cross-cultural aspects of the case but that the testimony could not be directed toward the issue of diminished capacity since only a psychiatrist would be competent on that point (California Court of Appeal, First District, Division Four 1972:88). A similar case arose in *Chase v. United States*, in which a group of antiwar protestors who destroyed draft files argued that, insofar as they could not conform their actions to accepted standards and could not distinguish right from wrong in the same way as others in American society, they should be able to avail themselves of a defense of "cultural insanity." The court refused to allow an anthropologist to testify about the cultural relativity of insanity. In the court's words: "Defendants' proffered definition of insanity, whatever its anthropological or sociological validity, is not determinative of the issue of criminal responsibility" (United States Court of Appeals, Seventh Circuit 1972:149). In some situations and other countries, however, anthropological data have had significant impact on the outcome of murder trials involving "arctic hysteria," witchcraft murders, and the defense of provocation (Goldstein et al. 1974:985-998; Milner 1966).

The range of cases in which anthropologists have testified, or been prepared to testify, is practically as broad as the discipline itself. They have involved the impact of public works projects on ethnic communities (Aswad 1974), the social repercussions of severe facial injuries (Macgregor 1973), and the effect of decisions made by the Department of Defense on the people of Enewetak Atoll (Kiste 1976). Anthropologists are also becoming involved in environmental disputes, especially in the formulation of environmental impact statements under a law which instructs federal agencies to "utilize a systematic, interdisciplinary approach which will insure the integrated use of the natural and social sciences and the environmental design arts in planning and in decision-making which may have an impact on man's environment" (National Environmental Policy Act 1970, Section 4332 (A); Catalano et al. 1975). In all of these cases, as well as those reviewed earlier, common problems of relevancy, form, and ethical implications arise. Let us, then, return to the questions raised at the outset of this discussion and review them in the light of some of the cases mentioned.

ANALYZING AND REFORMING EXPERT TESTIMONY

Like many other kinds of expert witnesses, social scientists who have appeared in legal proceedings have been deeply troubled by the ethical implications of their work and alienated by some aspects of American trial procedure and tactics (Rose 1956; Wolfgang 1974). Many judges, lawyers, and legal scholars have also been critical of existing relations between expert testimony and the adversary system, and numerous suggestions have been made to reform the rules of evidence and procedure. Different jurisdictions have the power to establish different rules, and attempts to adopt uniform rules of expert testimony have not succeeded (Travis 1974). Hence, it may be useful for the professions themselves to consider what standards of conduct they would regard as appropriate to expert testimony and to formulate approaches that judges, in their wide discretion on this matter, could adopt in their courtrooms. In time, these standards might also influence the development of formal legislation. The following discussion analyzes several aspects of the process of expert testimony as it applies to anthropologists and suggests certain reforms that could be made in the present system.

Adversary and Court-Appointed Experts

Perhaps the most troubling aspect of American legal procedures encountered by expert witnesses centers around the nature and rationale of the adversary system. Law, it has been said, is not history: one cannot hope to recapitulate on trial the precise occurrences on which a legal case is based. Therefore, the argument continues, one must rely on the parties who have a vested interest in the outcome to present a neutral court with evidence they consider necessary to their case, while the law must determine whether the relevant proofs offered achieve an appropriate level of persuasion. But as Judge Frankel has remarked, "we know that many of the rules and devices of adversary litigation as we conduct it are not geared for, but are often aptly suited to defeat, the development of the truth" (1975:1036). Despite their recognition of legitimate differences of interpretation, scholars appearing as expert witnesses often feel that courts should place less emphasis on trial gamesmanship and more on a sincere search for truth—even that truth which is not fully understood or unchanging.

A frequent suggestion made in this regard is that the law should rely mainly on court-appointed experts rather than experts presented by contending parties. This, it is argued, would have the advantage of decreasing the expert's tendency to be an advocate for one side and would increase the scientific stature of the expert's testimony. For some years, several New York courts have effectively utilized neutral medical experts chosen by local professional societies, and similar processes have been used in various European systems (Travis 1974; Anonymous 1961). Section 706 of the new Federal Rules of Evidence also permits court appointment of experts, a power courts have possessed though rarely exercised for many years (Sink 1956). Critics of the exclusive use of court-appointed experts point out that such a procedure would not lessen bias since the expert would represent only his own point of view or that of a single school of thought, and would be cloaked with a false air of neutrality (Diamond and Louisell 1965; Levy 1961). Similar failings have been noted by others studying the use of appointed experts in France, Germany, and Italy (Ploscowe 1935; Schroeder 1961).

Whether court-appointed experts would, as one lawyer contends (Griffin 1961), be less prone to mislead than adversary experts and whether they seldom represent schools of thought that are widely divergent are doubtful propositions in light of some of the cases reviewed. However, as will be discussed below, appropriate standards of professional conduct might alleviate these problems. For the moment, the question is not whether court-appointed experts should ever be used but under what circumstances and in what ways they might best be presented.

Many commentors have long been struck with the irony that, as Samuel Butler put it, "the public do not know enough to be experts, yet know enough to decide between them." Confronted with this seeming anomaly, Judge Learned Hand, at the turn of the century, said that what juries need is "a deliverance to them by some assisting judicial body of those general truths, applicable to the issue, which they may treat as final and decisive" (1901:55). Recalling early English practice, Hand suggested the use of a board of experts whose findings would be presented as evidence to a jury that could ignore it only at the risk of having the court dismiss their verdict as unsupported by the evidence (Hand 1901:56-57). Hand's proposal, which is of doubtful constitutional merit, never received support, but less categorical suggestions warrant closer attention. Court-appointed masters have long been used in complex commercial litigation. Where the evidence to be presented appears complicated, technical, or inadequate, the court may appoint a master to help with its finding of the facts. The use of masters has basically been limited to nonjury trials, but their use could be extended to any case involving social data. In such instances, they would primarily serve to simplify and hasten the trial by narrowing the issues involved, educating the court on extrinsic social facts, and investigating and reporting on matters to be considered on trial (Beuscher 1941; Anonymous 1948; Silberman 1975a, 1975b). This information could be used at the discretion of the courts, in addition to that supplied by adversary witnesses. Counsel on both sides would retain the right to cross-examine the court-appointed experts.[4]

Whenever one of the parties to a case indicates that social science data constitute an essential element of the evidence to be presented, and particularly when only one side intends to bring an expert anthropologist to the stand, the court should seriously consider the appointment of its own expert or master. It has been argued that the Federal Rules of Civil Procedure wisely leave disclosure of the expert's official status to the judge's discretion and refrain from requiring disclosure of his fee (Travis 1974:520). However, it might be more advisable for the court to indicate to the jury that the witness has been chosen, rather like a consulting physician, to give a second opinion on the issues, and that his status and payment in no way imply that he is more believable than experts presented by the adversary parties. Like all witnesses, the expert would be subject to full cross-examination by both sides after the presentation of his findings.

A final issue concerns the choice of court-appointed experts. The use of a standing panel of experts holds the risk of encouraging the development of an exclusive guild resistant to new approaches. This is particularly true if it is left to a professional association to choose the roster of experts (Wigmore 1914; Travis 1974). It would perhaps be wiser to encourage professional associations to prepare lists of all those persons—whether or not they belong to the association—who voluntarily ask to have their names placed on the roster of available expert witnesses. It would then remain the court's task to choose its own expert. The lists would aid courts and lawyers, who often do not know how to seek such expertise, in much the same way that lists of doctors and lawyers are made available to the residents of a community. No association should seek to certify or otherwise restrict access to the lists. They could, however, apprise those listed of the recommended standards of professional conduct adopted by their colleagues. These standards might include a recommendation that whenever an anthropologist consents to work on a case he or she should have an agreement with the attorneys that the court and opposing counsel will be apprised of the existence of such lists in the event that either chooses to seek additional expert witnesses.[5]

Pretrial Procedures

Once experts have been chosen, by the contending parties and/or the court, there are several pretrial procedures that could increase the quality and efficiency of the legal process. For example, it has been suggested that some form of pretrial conference be held in which all of the experts, representatives of the parties, and perhaps the presiding judge would be involved (Lurie 1955:360; Manners 1956; Ordover 1974b; Travis 1974; Wigmore 1974). The purpose would be to narrow factual issues, to allow the experts to confront one another directly and discuss the nature of their findings and opinions, and to permit the experts themselves to consider whether they wish to prepare a joint report to be filed with the court. Provided that counsel have agreed to such a conference, they should be barred from preventing the preparation of a joint statement of expert findings for presentation at the trial. The advantage to the lawyers of such a conference is that they would be able to prepare more fully for their respective cross-examinations. Moreover, counsel could be required to raise at that time all objections to the proferred testimony. These objections could be ruled on by the court prior to trial. This would not only speed the trial but lessen the interruptions and grandstanding by lawyers when the case comes to trial.

At the very least, there should be full discovery of all expert testimony well in advance of trial (cf. Friedenthal 1962). Following the lead of several jurisdictions, written reports, and even written depositions of pretrail direct testimony similar to that which will be repeated in court, should be made available to both sides and the court. Anthropologists should be encouraged by the recommended standards of professional conduct to insist that these reports or testimony include statements of experience, methods, data limitations, and theoretical foundations. A bibliography of works relied on should also be attached. Like the pretrial conference, this would afford anthropologists the opportunity to tell their full story, to consider each other's assertions, and to provide lawyers and judges with a better understanding of the nature of anthropological knowledge.

The Presentation of Expert Testimony

Usually, the testimony of an expert witness is conducted orally in open court, first through the direct examination of the attorney who has called the witness and then through the cross-examination of opposing counsel.[6] The judge may choose to ask questions of the witness but usually keeps them to a minimum. One of the problems with a question and answer format is that it may interfere with the expert's full explication of his findings and opinions, and may stifle the need to explain why qualified and limited assertions appropriate to much social scientific knowledge are nonetheless informative and important. It has been wisely suggested that experts be permitted to present their testimony in narrative form or to read from the stand all or part of the testimony entered in the record (Diamond and Louisell 1965:1345-1346; Ordover 1974a, 1974b; Wigmore 1914). If court procedures do not explicitly provide for such narrative testimony, the expert should, during preparation with counsel, require that ample opportunity be given on direct testimony to provide a full explanation of assertions before being turned over for cross-examination.

Moreover, the expert must utilize the opportunity to phrase testimony in terms that are no more definite than the data permit. As Marvin Wolfgang has said:

> Conditional clauses should be employed despite the fact that they are more vulnerable to cross-examination. Such words and phrases as "may," "probable," "other things being equal," "holding constant certain variables," and "associated" rather than "cause" are important verbal accouterments of the probabilistic language of science, and should not be neglected when presenting evidence in court [1974:245].

There should also be an understanding with counsel that witnesses will be able to explain in their own terms the research methods, forms of reasoning, data limitations, and contrary viewpoints surrounding their testimony.[7] As we have seen in several of the cases reviewed, neither opposing counsel nor the court can be relied on to be aware of these factors or to explore them adequately.

Finally, it is a common complaint of expert witnesses that they are asked questions that tend to distort or misconstrue the thrust of their testimony (Wolf 1976:112-113; Wolfgang 1974). Before leaving the stand, the court should ask the witness whether the points of his testimony have been adequately conveyed and whether he would like to make any final comments. This would afford the expert witness an opportunity to summarize his testimony without interfering with the right of counsel to present alternative conceptions of the testimony in their closing remarks. Wherever practicable, it might also be advantageous for the court to request that contending experts be brought to the stand soon after one another so that the judge or jury will have the earlier testimony fresh in mind.

The Role of Professional Associations

Early in this century, Lee M. Friedman, in a discussion of the reform of expert testimony, wrote: "The remedy is not in the enactment of any new statute. No act of the legislature will make witnesses learned or honest. The reform must come from the professions themselves . . ." (1910:252). Kenneth B. Clark, whose testimony played an important role in the desegregation cases, has also called for the establishment by professional societies of safeguards against the abuse of their position by social science expert witnesses (1953:9-10). And Judge Frankel has suggested that the ethical standards governing lawyers should not only command loyalty to and zeal for the client, but a positive obligation to aid in the search for truth (1975:1057-1059). Each of these assertions poses difficulties, while highlighting the roles that professional associations can take in restructuring expert testimony.

It is, I believe, valuable for anthropological associations to formulate standards that will help to guide those serving as expert witnesses. These standards should be posed as recommendations rather than as requirements, and should carry no sanctions of any sort. Some ethical issues confronting expert witnesses are already covered by existing ethical standards. Thus, the question of what should be done if one's pre-testimony research runs counter to the interests of those who have commissioned it is partially dealt with by the free publication standard of the American Anthropological Association's code of ethics.[8] More specific standards of good practice have been noted above. The point to be stressed here is simply this: As recommended and nonsanctioned standards develop, and as anthropologists begin to share with one another their experiences in courtroom situations, it is possible to have a substantial influence on changing legal procedures and on the ways in which social science will be used in legal proceedings. Without exaggerating their own importance to the final decisions, anthropologists, using their professional associations, can formulate guidelines that will aid their own constituents as well as the members of the legal profession.

CONCLUSION

The frequency with which anthropologists appear as expert witnesses is likely to increase in the coming years. Although the Indian Claims Commission will conclude its work in the foreseeable future, anthropologists will doubtless become more involved in environmental, familial, and race-related cases. All of the subfields of anthropology have been represented in such proceedings, but the lack of communication within and beyond anthropology has inhibited the recognition of common problems and the development of potential reforms. Whether anthropological testimony is central to a legal decision or serves to point out the inadequacy of causal assumptions underlying public policies, anthropology can both serve and benefit from appropriate involvement in the legal process.

Obviously, more is involved in such proceedings than the simple presentation of objective data. Difficult factual and ethical issues are also posed, and anthropologists who appear as expert witnesses may find in the courtroom, as they may earlier have found in the field, that their knowledge and commitments cannot be taken for granted. Carl Sandburg once remarked that "an expert is just a damned fool a long ways from home." Perhaps anthropologists in the courtroom can avoid this characterization by understanding the roles that their colleagues have played in similar proceedings and thinking carefully in advance about the nature and form of their contribution to the decision of legal cases.

NOTES

Acknowledgments. This paper has profited greatly from the comments and experiences related to me by David Aberle, James A. Boon, Tamie Bryant, Paul Edson, John A. Hostetler, Robert C. Kiste, Elizabeth Loftus, Nancy O. Lurie, Frances C. Macgregor, and A. Kenneth Pye. Support for part of the research came from the Duke University Research Council. The opinions and interpretations expressed in this paper are the sole responsibility of the author, and do not necessarily represent those of the individuals, academic institutions, or legal aid groups with whom the author has been associated.

[1] Redfield's actions off the witness stand also demonstrated his opposition to segregation in Texas. " 'The courtroom was integrated at the beginning," recalls Charles Thompson, who followed Redfield to the witness stand, "but then it began to get more crowded and the whites coming in later on couldn't find room. A big white policeman—this fellow must have been seven feet tall—came in and saw the whites standing against the wall and then started telling our people, 'Come on now, you know better than that.' It was a state court, remember, and so he began to segregate the audience to make room for the whites. But Dr. Redfield and the dean of Penn law school, they wouldn't move when the fellow told them to. They said they wanted to stay right where they were—with us" (Kluger 1976:266).

[2] The intended reference in this last statement is to *high school* education. Personal communication from John Hostetler.

[3] In fact, the Commission has tended to act more as a court than as a body which, because of its special status, could develop new principles that would be adopted by the apellate courts. Thus, anthropologists have not had an opportunity to help develop meaningful concepts of "fair and honorable dealings" with the Indians, although their testimony under other provisions of the Act has been more elaborate. (See Lurie 1957.)

[4] Another suggestion is that a public agency be created that would act as a depository for social and technological data. "Its mission would be to receive and catalogue social impact studies that qualify for judicial attention. The criteria for determining whether a study qualifies for approval would not be agreement or disagreement with its content or recommendations but only a finding that its design and methods fall within the range of accepted standards of scientific inquiry. These standards would be akin to 'standard accounting principles' in financial practice" (Rosenberg 1976:590; see also Anonymous 1948). The authors do not indicate how and by whom accepted standards of inquiry are to be applied in as interpretive a field as social science research.

[5] Another issue concerning the impartiality of adversary witnesses is raised by the use of experts' contingent fees. Until recently, bar association rules have generally not permitted lawyers to pay fees to experts contingent on the outcome of the case. However, a federal court in New York has recently invalidated a bar association disciplinary rule to this effect. Such a rule, said the court, means that less affluent or indigent litigants do not have an opportunity equal to that of wealthier litigants to have a full hearing of their case. One cannot automatically assume, the court continued, that experts will bias their testimony because they have been hired on a contingent fee basis; a blanket rule barring such fees is too irrational to withstand constitutional inspection (United States District Court, Eastern District of New York 1976). In the light of this ruling, expert witnesses may want to draw more fully on some of the recommended standards described in this paper when entering into an agreement with the client and his attorney. (See Addendum, page 578.)

[6] Expert witnesses have frequently cited, as one of the more annoying and demeaning aspects of their appearance in court, the challenge to their professional credentials by the cross-examining attorney. Cases could, however, be cited in which an ethnomusicologist testified in a child custody case, or a social scientist with a degree in "World Cultures" testified on the archaeological record of a California Indian tribe. Where a challenge to credentials is aimed at putting the witness in a defensive position or leading the witness to make more categorical assertions than might otherwise be made, it is incumbent on the court and the lawyers to gauge their response accordingly. It is, however, the primary responsibility of anthropologists to determine, when first approached, whether their knowledge is truly appropriate to the issue, and to refuse to participate whenever they feel that their studies and experience are not specifically applicable to the case. Beyond this, anthropologists must recognize that litigants have every right to question the basis of experts' assertions.

[7] On the expert's relation to the attorney, and general suggestions to lawyers and experts on the conduct of expert testimony, see Louisell (1955) and Rose (1956).

[8] "An anthropologist should undertake no secret research or any research whose results cannot be freely derived and publicly reported" (American Anthropological Association 1973, Section 3[a]). On the problem of reporting contrary findings, see Wolfgang (1974:243). A federal court has recently held that in certain circumstances the research findings of a scholar who is not a party to the case are entitled to confidential status, and a court may not require the scholar to testify or produce documents concerning his research interviews (United States District Court, Northern District of California 1976; Anonymous 1976; Nejelski 1976).

REFERENCES CITED

American Anthropological Association
1973 Professional Ethics: Statements and Procedures of the American Anthropological Association. Washington: American Anthropological Association.

Anonymous
1948 Social and Economic Facts—Appraisal of Suggested Techniques for Presenting Them to the Courts. Harvard Law Review 61:692-702.
1961 The Present Status of the Impartial Medical Expert in Civil Litigation. Temple Law Quarterly 34:476-486.
1976 U.S. Court Shields Data of Scholar. New York Times, p. 20, col. 8, 8 June.

Aswad, Barbara C.
1974 The Southeast Dearborn Arab Community Struggles for Survival Against Urban "Renewal." *In* Arabic Speaking Communities in American Cities. Barbara C. Aswad, ed. Pp. 53-83. New York: Center for Migration Studies of New York.

Barksdale, Hiram C.
1957 The Use of Survey Research Findings as Legal Evidence. Pleasantville, New York: Printers' Ink Books.

Berger, Morroe
1957 Desegregation, Law and Social Science. Commentary 23:471-477.

Beuscher, J. H.
1941 The Use of Experts by the Courts. Harvard Law Review 54:1105-1127.

Cahn, Edmond
1955 Jurisprudence. New York University Law Review 30:150-169.

California Court of Appeal, First District, Division Four
1972 People v. Poddar. California Reporter 103:84-93.

California Supreme Court
1964 People v. Woody. Pacific Reporter 394:813-822.

Catalano, Ralph, Steven J. Simmons, and Daniel Stokols
1975 Adding Social Science Knowledge to Environmental Decision Making. Natural Resources Lawyer 8:41-59.

Chein, Isador, et al.
1955 Appendix to Appellants' Briefs: Statements by Social Scientists. Social Problems 2:227-235.

Clark, Kenneth B.
1953 The Social Scientist as an Expert Witness in Civil Rights Litigation. Social Problems 1:5-10.
1959-60 The Desegregation Cases: Criticism of the Social Scientist's Role. Villanova Law Review 5:224-240.
1969 The Social Scientists, the Brown Decision, and Contemporary Confusion. *In* Argument: The Oral Argument before the Supreme Court in Brown v. Board of Education of Topeka, 1952-1955. Leon Friedman, ed. Pp. xxxi-l. New York: Chelsea House.

Connecticut Superior Court
1964 State v. Rodriguez. Atlantic Reporter 204:37-38.

Diamond, Bernard L., and David W. Louisell
1965 The Psychiatrist as an Expert Witness: Some Ruminations and Speculations. Michigan Law Review 63:1335-1354.

Federal Rules of Civil Procedure
1972 *In* United States Code Annotated, Title 28, Rule 26(b)(4). St. Paul: West.

Federal Rules of Evidence
1975 *In* United States Code Annotated, Title 28, St. Paul: West.

Frankel, Marvin E.
1975 The Search for Truth—An Umpireal View. University of Pennsylvania Law Review 123:1031-1059.

Friedenthal, Jack H.
1962 Discovery and Use of an Adverse Party's Expert Information. Stanford Law Review 14:455-488.

Friedman, Lee M.
1910 Expert Testimony, Its Abuses and Reformation. Yale Law Journal 19:247-257.

Friedman, Leon, ed.
1969 Argument: The Oral Argument before the Supreme Court in Brown v. Board of Education of Topeka, 1952-1955. New York: Chelsea House.

Garfinkel, Herbert
1959 Social Science Evidence and the School Segregation Cases. Journal of Politics 21:37-59.

Goldstein, Joseph, Alan M. Dershowitz, and Richard D. Schwartz
1974 Criminal Law: Theory and Practice. New York: Free Press.

Greenberg, Jack
1956 Social Scientists Take the Stand. Michigan Law Review 54:953-970.

Griffin, F. Hastings, Jr.
1961 Impartial Medical Testimony: A Trial Lawyer in Favor. Temple Law Quarterly 34:402-415.

Halleck, Seymour L.
1967 Psychiatry and the Dilemmas of Crime. New York: Harper and Row.

Hand, Learned
1901 Historical and Practical Considerations Regarding Expert Testimony. Harvard Law Review 15:40-58.

Hostetler, John A.
1968 Amish Society. Baltimore: Johns Hopkins Press.
1970 Transcript of Testimony in Wisconsin v. Yoder. Wisconsin Circuit Court, Green County, Wisconsin. Mimeograph.
1972 Dr. John A. Hostetler. Temple University News Release.

Indian Claims Commission
1963 *In* United States Code Annotated, Title 25, Section 70. St. Paul: West.

Kiste, Robert C.
1976 The People of Enewetak Atoll versus The U.S. Department of Defense, *In* Ethics and Anthropology: Dilemmas in Fieldwork. Michael A. Rynkiewich and James P. Spradley, eds. Pp. 61-80. New York: Wiley.

Kluger, Richard
1976 Simple Justice: The History of *Brown v. Board of Education* and Black America's Struggle for Equality. New York: Knopf.

Kurland, Philip B., and Gerhard Casper, eds.
1975a Landmark Briefs and Arguments of the Supreme Court of the United States: Constitutional Law. Vol. 64. Pp. 687-1007. Arlington, Virginia: University Publications of America.
1975b Landmark Briefs and Arguments of the Supreme Court of the United States: Constitutional Law. Vol. 71. Pp. 803-826. Arlington, Virginia: University Publications of America.

La Barre, Weston, et al.
1951 Statement on Peyote. Science 114:582-583.

Levin, Betsy, and Willis D. Hawley, eds.
1975 The Courts, Social Science, and School Desegregation. Law and Contemporary Problems 39:1-432.

Levy, Elwood S.
1961 Impartial Expert Testimony—Revisited. Temple Law Quarterly 34:416-451.

Louisell, David W.
1955 The Psychologist in Today's Legal World. Minnesota Law Review 39:235-272.

Lurie, Nancy Oestreich
1955 Problems, Opportunities, and Recommendations. Ethnohistory 2:357-375.
1956 A Reply to: "The Land Claims Cases: Anthropologists in Conflict." Ethnohistory 3:72-81.
1957 The Indian Claims Commission Act. The Annals of the American Academy of Political and Social Science 311:56-70.

Macgregor, Frances Cooke
1973 Traumatic Facial Injuries and the Law: Some Social, Psychological, and Economic Ramifications. Trial Lawyers Quarterly 9:50-53.

Manners, Robert A.
1956 The Land Claims Cases: Anthropologists in Conflict. Ethnohistory 3:72-81.

Maslow, Will
1959-60 How Social Scientists Can Shape Legal Processes. Villanova Law Review 5:241-246.

Milner, Alan
1966 M'Naghten and the Witch Doctor: Psychiatry and Crime in Africa. University of Pennsylvania Law Review 114:1134-1169.

National Environmental Policy Act
1970 *In* United States Code Annotated, Title 42, Sections 4331-4335. St. Paul: West.

Nejelski, Paul, ed.
1976 Social Research in Conflict with Law and Ethics. Cambridge, Massachusetts: Ballinger.

Ordover, Abraham P.
1974a Use of Written Direct Testimony in Jury Trials: A Proposal. Hofstra Law Review 2:67-95.
1974b Expert Testimony: A Proposed Code for New York. New York Law Forum 19:809-831.

Ploscowe, Morris
1935 The Expert Witness in Criminal Cases in France, Germany, and Italy. Law and Contemporary Problems 2:504-509.

Rafalko, Walter A.
1967 Sociological Evidence as a Criminal Defense. Criminal Law Quarterly 10:77-98.

Ray, Verne F.
1955 Anthropology and Indian Claims Litigation: Introduction. Ethnohistory 2:287-291.

Redfield, Robert
1963 The Social Uses of Social Science: The Papers of Robert Redfield, Vol. 2. Margaret Park Redfield, ed. Pp. 163-168. Chicago: University of Chicago Press.

Rose, Arnold M.
1956 The Social Scientist as an Expert Witness. Minnesota Law Review 40:205-218.

Rosen, Paul L.
1972 The Supreme Court and Social Science. Urbana: University of Illinois Press.

Rosenberg, Maurice
1976 Anything Legislatures Can Do, Courts Can Do Better? American Bar Association Journal 62:587-590.

Rosenthal, Lloyd L.
1935 The Development of the Use of Expert Testimony. Law and Contemporary Problems 2:403-418.

Sahlins, Marshall D.
1968 Tribesmen. Englewood Cliffs: Prentice-Hall.

Schroeder, Horst
1961 Problems Faced by the Impartial Expert Witness in Court: The Continental View. Temple Law Quarterly 34:378-385.

Shuman, S. I.
1973 The Placebo Cure for Criminality. Wayne Law Review 19:847-872.

Silberman, Linda J.
1975a Masters and Magistrates. Part 1: The English Model. New York University Law Review 50:1070-1118.
1975b Masters and Magistrates. Part 2: The American Analogue. New York University Law Review 50:1297-1392.

Singer, Milton
1968 The Concept of Culture. International Encyclopedia of the Social Sciences. Vol. 3, pp. 527-543. New York: Macmillan.

Sink, John M.
1956 The Unused Power of a Federal Judge to Call His Own Expert Witness. Southern California Law Review 29:195-214.

Steward, Julian H.
1955 Theory and Application in Social Science. Ethnohistory 2:292-302.

Suttles, Wayne
1963 The Persistence of Intervillage Ties among the Coast Salish. Ethnology 2:512-525.

Tennessee Supreme Court
1975 State ex rel. Swann v. Pack. South Western Reporter 527:99-114.

Travis, William J.
1974 Impartial Testimony under the Federal Rules of Evidence: A French Perspective. International Lawyer 8:492-522.

United States Court of Appeals, District of Columbia Circuit
1967 Washington v. United States. Federal Reporter, Second Series 390:444-462.

United States Court of Appeals, Ninth Circuit
1974 United States v. Diaz. Federal Reporter, Second Series 499:113-115.

United States Court of Appeals, Seventh Circuit
1972 Chase v. United States. Federal Reporter, Second Series 468:141-149.

United States Court of Appeals, Tenth Circuit
1959 Native American Church v. Navajo Tribal Council. Federal Reporter, Second Series 272:131-135.

United States District Court, Eastern District of New York
1976 Person v. Association of the Bar of the City of New York. Federal Supplement 414:139-144.

United States District Court, Northern District of California
1976 Richards of Rockford, Inc. v. Pacific Gas and Electric Co. Federal Rules Decisions 71:388-391.

United States District Court, Western District of Pennsylvania
1976 Rodgers v. United States Steel Corp. Federal Rules Decisions 70:639-648.

United States District Court, Western District of Washington
1973 United States v. State of Washington, Transcript of Testimony. Mimeographed.
1974 United States v. State of Washington. Federal Supplement 384:312-423.

United States Supreme Court
1949 Briefs and Records, Sweatt v. Painter. Pp. 189-208. Washington, D.C.: United States Supreme Court.
1950 Sweatt v. Painter. United States Reports 339:629-636.
1954 Brown v. Board of Education. United States Reports 347:483-496.
1972 Wisconsin v. Yoder. United States Reports 405:205-249.

Van den Haag, Ernest
1959-60 Social Science Testimony in Desegregation Cases—A Reply to Professor Kenneth Clark. Villanova Law Review 6:69-79.

Walker, Owen S.
1969 Why Should Irresponsible Offenders be Excused? Journal of Philosophy 66:279-290.

Wigmore, John Henry
1914 The Bill To Regulate Expert Testimony. Illinois Law Review 9:353-356.

Wisdom, John Minor
1975 Random Remarks on the Role of Social Sciences in the Judicial Decision-Making Process in School Desegregation Cases. Law and Contemporary Problems 39:135-149.

Wolf, Eleanor P.
1976 Social Science and the Courts: The Detroit Schools Case. The Public Interest 42:102-120.

Wolfgang, Marvin E.
1974 The Social Scientist in Court. Journal of Criminal Law and Criminology 65:239-247.

Submitted 1 September 1976
Accepted 14 December 1976
Final revisions received 1 March 1977

ADDENDUM

While this article was in press, the decision referred to in Note 5 was reversed by the appellate court, United States Court of Appeals, 2d Circuit, *Person v. Association of the Bar of the City of New York* (Federal Reporter, 2d Series 554:534-539, 1977). The decision, however, may be appealed to the U.S. Supreme Court.

Name Index

Abel, Richard 71, 72, 75, 136, 144, 290, 342
Adewoye, Omoniyi 142
Ah Tam 310
Allende 144
Alliot, Michel 39, 40
Allott, Anthony N. 13, 14, 43, 44
Anderson, J.N.D. 14, 43
Aristotle 8
Arjomand, Said 108
Armstrong, R.G. 20
Arnold, Thurmond 19
Arthurs, H.W. 147
Arusha 61
Aubert, Vilhelm 18, 19, 108, 288, 289
Auerbach, Erich 357
Auerbach, Jerold S. 143
Austin, John 59
Ayoub, V. 7, 11

Baariin 261, 263, 265–8, 278–81
Bachofen, J.J. 3, 9
Bacon, M.K. 12
Bailey, F.G. 20, 57, 69
Banaji 82
Banks, Curtis 371
Baptista, Juan 491
Barnes, J.A. 10, 13
Barry, H. 12
Barton, R.F. 3, 10, 13
Basso, Keith 512
Beals, A.R. 16, 20
Becker, Alton 178
Beidelman, T.O. 21
Benda-Beckmann, Franz von 142
Benda-Beckmann, Keebet von 144
Benedict, Ruth 161, 162
Bentham, Jeremy 289
Bentley, G. Carter 150
Berger, Peter 191, 192
Berndt 3
Berreman, G.D. 20
Beuchat, M.H. 9
Bittner 146
Black 285, 291, 295
Blackburn, Judge 464, 465
Blackstone, Sir William 6–7
Blaxter 83
Blok, Anton 108
Bloom, Harold 343
Bodin, Jean 41
Bohannan, P.J. 3, 6, 10, 11, 22, 55, 56, 58, 67, 72, 81
Boissevain, Jeremy 107
Boorstin, D.J. 6
Borges, Jorge Luis 344
Bourdieu, Pierre 105, 177, 178, 181, 183, 186, 187
Brandeis 15
Brigham, John 143
Brown, George 310
Burman 288
Burridge, K.O.L. 10
Busia, K.A. 10

Canter 80
Cappelletti 73
Carlin, J.E. 15, 16
Carroll, Lewis 346
Carruthers, Jacob 368
Carson, Kit 435, 436
Chabas, J. 39
Chanock, Martin 131
Chein 505
Chiba 419
Child, I.L. 12
Childe, V. Gordon 165
Chowning 295
Clark, Kenneth B. 504, 505, 516
Cochrane 55
Cohn, Bernard S. 13, 17, 19–20, 57, 109
Coke 56
Collier, George 107, 109
Collier, Jane F. 54, 55, 59, 69, 80, 105, 297
Colson, Elizabeth 12, 13, 16, 69, 105
Comaroff, Jean 153
Comaroff, John 78, 105, 153, 286, 296
Cook, Captain 188, 190
Cox, B. 3
Cozzens, James Gould 19

D'Andrade, R.G. 261, 262
Danet 72, 78
Danzig, Robert 74
David, Professor R. 38, 41

Davis, John W. 504
Deklin, Tony 426
Diamond, Stanley 58, 61, 137, 469
Dicks, Pater 309
Dixon, Vernon 382, 383
Douglas, Mr Justice 507, 508
Douglas, Mary 170
Dumont, Louis 169
Dupreel, E. 42
Durkheim, Emile 6, 8, 9, 68, 77, 161, 170, 171

Edgerton, R.B. 6
Edward III 327
Eggleston 457
Ehrlich, E. 13, 58, 59, 135
Engel, David 136
Engels 4, 165
Epstein, A.L. 12, 260, 287, 293
Errington, F.K. 310, 311
Evan, W.M. 15
Evans-Pritchard, E.E. 17, 294

Fallers, L.A. 13, 14, 58
Farjat, G. 356
Felstiner 70, 147
Fitzpatrick, Peter 80, 82, 83, 136, 145, 146, 150, 291–4
Forde, Daryll 43
Foucault, Michel 108, 145, 150, 186, 342
Frake, C.O. 21
Frank 14
Frankel, Judge 513, 516
Frankfurter, Justice 504
Freeman 147
Freud, S. 168, 169, 369
Fried, Morton 59
Friedman, Lee M. 516
Furnivall 79
Fustel de Coulanges 3, 9

Galanter, Marc 60, 74, 136, 138, 139, 140, 144
Gebreamlak, Hagos 494, 496
Geertz, Clifford 106, 132, 148, 149, 161–5, 177, 184, 185, 263, 285, 347, 356
Gibbs, J.L. 20, 54
Giddens, Anthony 105, 146, 178, 179, 183
Gilissen, J. 42
Ginsberg, M. 9, 105
Glasse, R.M. 21
Gluckman, Max 3, 7, 8, 10, 11, 12, 14, 16, 20, 22, 25, 43, 57, 67, 81, 163, 164, 212
Glueck, E. 23
Glueck, S. 23
Goldman 356
Gore 426
Gramsci, Antonio 60, 182, 185
Greenhouse, Carol 108
Griffiths, John 79, 80, 133, 136
Grotenberg, Hanneke 107
Gulliver, P.H. 3, 6, 13, 18, 55, 56, 67, 68, 69, 72, 77, 78, 107
Gurvitch, Georges 135
Guthrie, Robert 369
Gutmann, B. 3

Habermas, J. 342
Hall, G. Stanley 369
Hamnett 77, 289, 290, 301, 302
Hand, Judge Learned 514
Harper, E.B. 12
Harrell-Bond 288
Harris, G.G. 264
Harris, Marvin 159, 166, 171
Hart, H.L.A. 5, 58, 59, 121–3, 126–8
Hastings, Warren 109
Hayden, Robert 107
Hazard, J.N. 12
Henry, Stuart 146, 343
Hobbes 4, 121
Hobhouse, L.T. 9, 105
Hoebel, E.A. 3, 7, 8, 9, 10, 11, 13, 14, 18, 19, 22, 24, 54, 57, 58, 61, 66, 67, 79
Hogbin, H.I. 3, 7
Hohfield 7
Holding, Hon. Clyde 467
Holleman, J.F. 152
Holmes, Oliver Wendell 15
Homer 357
Hooker, M.B. 133
Hostetler, John A. 240, 506–8
Houphouet-Boigny, Dr 47
Howard 15, 16
Howell, P.P. 3, 13
Huckleberry 56
Hume 121
Humphreys, Sally 108
Hunt, Alan 80, 343
Hunter, Jim 489–90
Huxley, Julian 166

Jakubowska, Longina 105
James 264
Jayawardena, C. 16
Jones, Edgar H. 15
Jung 369

Kaberry, P.M. 10

Kafka 53
Kamehameha III, King 474
Kantorowicz, H. 4
Kaplan, I. 14
Keates, J.S. 347
Kéké, J. 38
Kelsen 427
Keuning, J. 13, 14
Khomeini, Ayatollah 108
Kidder, Robert L. 136, 138, 288
Kimura, Fumiko 487–8
Kleintitcschen, Pater 309
Kluckhohn, C. 22
Koch, K.F. 3, 59, 62, 72, 293, 295
Konwitz, Josef 345
Kotiik 261, 263, 265–7, 278, 280, 281
Kuper, Jessica 105

Labouret, Henri 39
Lafont 41
Laveley 469
Lawrence 293
Layish 59
Leach, Edmund R. 14, 175
Lee, William 470
Lengat 41
LeRoy 78, 83
Lévi-Strauss, Claude 163, 168–9, 170
Lévy-Bruhl, Henri 39, 48, 50, 68
Lévy-Bruhl, Lucien 68
Lewis, O. 16, 21
Livingston 470
Llewellyn, K.N. 3, 10, 11, 18, 24, 54, 66, 67, 79
Locke, John 4
Lowy 59
Lozi 8
Luckmann, Thomas 191, 192

Macaulay, Stewart 135, 139, 140, 360
Machiavelli 60
Maddox, Richard 105
Maine, Sir Henry S. 3, 7, 8, 9, 13, 25, 66, 105, 106, 320
Malengreau 41
Malinowski, B. 3, 4, 7, 8, 13, 17, 18, 58, 66, 68, 69, 105, 161
March, J.G. 7
Marshall, Alfred 171
Marshall, Mr Justice Thurgood 502, 504
Marx, K. 4, 9, 77, 82, 165, 168, 169, 171, 172, 180
Maslow, Abraham 377, 384
Massell, Gregory 142
Massignon 41
Mather 70
Maunier 39
Mauss, Marcel 9, 35, 68, 170
May, Rollo 377, 384
Mbiti, J. 378
McClelland, D. 372
McDougall, William 369
McLennan, J.F. 3, 9
Mead, M. 8, 161
Meggitt, J.M. 119, 299
Merry, Sally Engle 144
Merton 320
Metzger, D. 6. 8, 12, 18, 24
Miller, J.C. 12
Milliot 41
Modjeska 297
Monmonier, Mark 345
Montesquieu, C.L. 9, 66
Moore, Sally Falk 10, 55, 56, 57, 59, 78, 80, 106, 135, 136, 140, 142, 144, 291, 460
Morgan, Lewis Henry 3, 4, 165
Moscovici, S. 261
Moua, Kong 489
Moua, Tou 489
Muehrcke, P.C. 345, 346
Mukhopadhyay, T. 10, 12, 15
Murphy 332
Murray 81
Myrdal 505

Nadel, S.F. 4, 7, 10, 11, 12, 13
Nader, Laura 3, 6, 9, 12, 14, 18, 20, 21, 22, 24, 54, 56, 57, 59, 62, 68, 69, 71, 72, 74, 87, 107, 144
Napoleon I 35
Napoleon III 35
Nash 107
Needham, Rodney 170
Nelken, David 342
Nicholas, R.W. 10, 12, 15
Nietzsche, F. 342, 361
Nobles, W. 367, 368, 370, 378, 379
Nonet, P. 342

O'Connor, R.A. 150, 336
O'Gorman, H.J. 15
O'Hagen, T. 342
Ornstein, R. 368, 371, 373, 374

Paliwala 82
Pareto, Vilfredo 171
Parnell 80
Parsons, Talcott 161, 171, 183, 192

Perelman, Chaim 358
Peter 145
Pirenne, Count 41
Poirier, Jean 38, 44
Pool 142
Pospisil, Leopold 3, 6, 7, 14, 53, 54, 55, 57, 58, 67, 79, 105, 132, 135, 139, 150, 357
Possoz 41
Pound 13, 14, 15, 56
Provine, Marie Doris 147

Radcliffe-Brown, A.R. 4, 161
Ranger, Terence 138
Rappaport, Roy 166
Reay 294
Redfield, Robert 3, 8, 502–4
Rheinstein 14, 17
Richardson, Chief Justice 475
Richardson, Jane 3, 9, 10
Riesman, D. 3, 15, 18, 19
Roberts, J.M. 3, 12, 23, 61, 67, 72, 78, 80, 105, 286, 296
Rogers 377
Rosen, Lawrence 108
Rothenberger, J.E. 9
Rouhette, A. 41
Rousseau 190
Ruffini 80
Ryle 264

Sacco 19
Sahlins, Marshall 165, 166, 181, 188–90
Said, Edward 176
Sandburg, Carl 517
Santos, Boaventura de Sousa 75, 78, 136, 143, 149
Sarat, Austin 147
Sassway 210
Schapera, I. 3, 13, 14, 43, 55, 67
Schneider, David M. 6, 10, 12, 18, 163, 164, 169, 190
Schubert, G.A. 15
Schwartz, R.D. 12
Selassie, H.I.M. Haile 38
Selznick, P. 342
Senghor, L.S. 47
Service, Elman 165, 166
Siegel, B.J. 16
Silbey, Susan S. 146
Simmel, G. 16
Simonett, John 16
Skinner, B.F. 369
Skolnick, J.H. 15, 16
Smiegl, E.O. 15
Smith, Adam 180, 289
Smith, W. 3, 57, 61, 80
Snyder, Francis 107, 135, 136, 137–8
Sohier, A. 41
Sohier, J. 41
Sorokin 320
Spradley 60, 70
Stanley 216
Starr, June 69, 71, 80, 105, 106, 142, 145
Steward, Julian 161, 165, 510, 511
Stewart, Omer C. 511
Stirling, P. 13
Strathern, A. 297
Strodtbeck, F. 15
Sugarman, David 147

Tagogo 309
Tancredi, L.R. 260
Tappan, P.W. 16
Teubner, G. 342
Thompson, E.P. 178
To Kabinana 313
To Purgo 313
Todd 54, 144
Toratoro, Pius Pio 309
Tui Manu'a Moa Atoa 483
Tui Manu'a Tauveve, King 482
Turner, Victor W. 16, 69, 161, 162, 163, 164
Twining, William 105, 106
Tylor, E.B. 165

Uchendu, V.C. 8

Van Rouveroy 80
Van Velsen 55
Van Vollenhoven 68
Vanderlinden, J. 41
Vanzetti 19
Verdier, Raymond 40
Vincent, Joan 106
Vinogradoff 13

Warren, Chief Justice 505
Watson, Lord 464
Watts, Alan 384
Weber, Max 9, 58, 59, 77, 161, 171, 180, 355, 356
Werbner 80
West, James 19
Wheeler, G.C. 9, 105
White, Leslie 161, 165, 166
Whiting, Beatrice 22
Whiting, J.W.M. 12, 13
Williams, Raymond 178, 182

Winans, E.V. 6
Witty 80
Wolf, Eric 159
Wolfgang, Marvin 515

Xiong, Xeng 489

Yngvesson, Barbara 54, 56, 57, 71, 146

www.ingramcontent.com/pod-product-compliance
Lightning Source LLC
LaVergne TN
LVHW102106300926
849161LV00014B/3065
* 9 7 8 0 8 1 4 7 7 9 5 4 5 *